Lecture Notes in Artificial Intelligence 4248

Edited by J. G. Carbonell and J. Siekmann

Subseries of Lecture Notes in Computer Science

Steffen Staab   Vojtěch Svátek (Eds.)

Managing Knowledge in a World of Networks

15th International Conference, EKAW 2006
Poděbrady, Czech Republic, October 2-6, 2006
Proceedings

Series Editors

Jaime G. Carbonell, Carnegie Mellon University, Pittsburgh, PA, USA
Jörg Siekmann, University of Saarland, Saarbrücken, Germany

Volume Editors

Steffen Staab
University of Koblenz-Landau, Institute for Computer Science
56016 Koblenz, Germany
E-mail: staab@uni-koblenz.de

Vojtěch Svátek
University of Economics
Department of Information and Knowledge Engineering
13967 Prague 3, Czech Republic
E-mail: svatek@vse.cz

Library of Congress Control Number: 2006933225

CR Subject Classification (1998): I.2, H.4, J.1, C.2

LNCS Sublibrary: SL 7 – Artificial Intelligence

ISSN 0302-9743
ISBN-10 3-540-46363-1 Springer Berlin Heidelberg New York
ISBN-13 978-3-540-46363-4 Springer Berlin Heidelberg New York

Springer is a part of Springer Science+Business Media

springer.com

Printed in Germany

Typesetting: Camera-ready by author, data conversion by Scientific Publishing Services, Chennai, India
Printed on acid-free paper SPIN: 11891451 06/3142 5 4 3 2 1 0

Preface

The 15th International Conference on Knowledge Engineering and Knowledge Management (2006), held on October 6-10, 2006 in Poděbrady, Czech Republic, followed a long tradition of European Knowledge Acquisition Workshops (from 1987), which eventually acquired the format of conference (in 2000) while keeping their open-minded and interactive spirit.

During the nearly 20 year lifespan of the series, the discipline of knowledge engineering (KE) evolved greatly. While knowledge acquisition (KA) techniques dominated in the very first years, formal approaches to knowledge-based inference and various new streams such as knowledge discovery from data/texts later came into play. During the late 1990s and afterwards, EKAW became a founding community for ontology and Semantic Web Research, which was also reflected in the sub-titles of the 2002 and 2004 editions: "Ontologies and the Semantic Web" and "Engineering Knowledge in the Age of the Semantic Web," respectively. The 2006 edition, in turn, only slightly refocussed this trend. Its sub-title is "Managing Knowledge in a World of Networks," which reflects the fact that semantics typically arises not only as a result of explicit engineering activities (as in Semantic Web) but also emerges from interaction of a high number of interconnected documents, ontological concepts, software applications and — especially — human users. The importance given to the interconnection of human users in a sense loops back to the knowledge acquisition roots of EKAW and its 'holistic' view of knowledge engineering.

Another special flavor was given to the 2006 edition by the fact that it was for the first time that the EKAW series crossed the border from 'Western' to 'Eastern' Europe. This can be viewed as recognition that knowledge engineering research in the new EU member (and candidate) states in this region is becoming increasingly popular, with new groups sprouting all around.

EKAW-2006 attracted 119 paper submissions, which represents an almost 60% increase over the last (2004) edition; this reflects a stable and growing interest in EKAW key topics. The submissions came from 28 countries of 4 continents, Europe being, however, prevalent with 63%; the top three countries were the UK (18%), Korea (16%) and France (14%). Each paper was evaluated by at least three reviewers. Discussion then took place for all papers with uneven reviews. Eventually, 33 submissions were accepted, which yields an acceptance rate of 27.7%. Due to space limitations, accepted papers were further divided into long (16 pages) and short (8 pages) ones, following the ranking resulting from the review; there are 17 long and 16 short papers in the proceedings.

The invited talks were chosen so as to represent the current blend of EKAW's topics of interest. The talk by Alan Rector ("Whose Knowledge? Whose Questions? Whose Answers? Conflicting Preconceptions for Knowledge Intensive Systems") examined the roots of mainstream KE. The one by Pedro Domingos

("Learning, Logic, and Probability: A Unified View") attempted to build a common formal foundation for core, but so far separate, building blocks of knowledge engineering research and practice. Finally, the talk by Andrzej Nowak ("Information and Influence in Social Networks") underpinned the specific focus of this year's EKAW from the point of view of a social scientist.

Similarly, the topics of contributed papers reflect the usual as well as new foci of KE. The largest session was that of Knowledge Acquisition, with seven accepted papers. Other traditional sessions were those devoted to different aspects of the ontology lifecycle: Ontology Engineering, Ontology Learning and Ontology Mapping and Evolution. Somewhat more end-user-oriented research was reported in the sessions on Semantic Search and User Interfaces. In the Knowledge Discovery session, a specific mode of exploiting ontologies and other kinds of prior knowledge—for the discovery of new knowledge from data—was addressed. The session on Semantics from Networks and Crowds was devoted to KE aspects of (analysis of) large networks. Finally, there was a session dedicated to Applications developed for specific domains.

Additionally, the scientific programme of the conference featured two tutorials, a workshop, and a poster and demo session, each with their notes published separately. Most materials not present in this volume can be retrieved from the conference Web page http://ekaw.vse.cz.

We would like to express our cordial thanks to invited as well as contributing presenters for inspiring talks and papers, the PC members and additional reviewers for their careful work, and the Action M agency for handling most organizational issues. We also acknowledge the uneasy task of Heiner Stuckenschmidt as Workshop/Tutorial Chair, Helena Sofia Pinto as Poster Chair and Martin Labský as Demo Chair, and the effort of all tutorial presenters and workshop organizers. The efforts of Olaf Görlitz and Thomas Franz were invaluable as they tended to tedious administration issues of reviewing management and proceedings compilation. We thank Jan Nemrava and Marek Růžička, who took care of the conference Web site and the printable CFP.

Finally, special thanks go to the sponsors of this conference: the K-Space, NeOn and X-Media projects of the 6th EU Framework programme and our home institutions, the University of Economics, Prague, and University of Koblenz-Landau.

July 2006

Steffen Staab
Vojtěch Svátek

Organization

Conference Co-chairs: Steffen Staab, University of Koblenz-Landau, Germany
Vojtěch Svátek, University of Economics, Prague, Czech Republic

Workshop Chair: Heiner Stuckenschmidt, University of Mannheim, Germany

Tutorial Chair: Heiner Stuckenschmidt, University of Mannheim, Germany

Poster Chair: Helena Sofia Pinto, Technical University of Lisbon, Portugal

Demo Chair: Martin Labský, University of Economics, Prague, Czech Republic

Programme Committee

Karl Aberer, Epfl, Switzerland
Stuart Aitken, University of Edinburgh, UK
Hans Akkermans, Free University of Amsterdam, The Netherlands
Nathalie Aussenac-Gilles, IRIT- CNRS Toulouse, France
Richard Benjamins, iSOCO, Spain
Paulo Bouquet, University of Trento, Italy
Joost Breuker, University of Amsterdam, The Netherlands
Philipp Cimiano, University of Karlsruhe, Germany
Paul Compton, University of New South Wales, Australia
Olivier Corby, INRIA Sophia-Antipolis, France
Stefan Decker, DERI Ireland, Ireland
Rose Dieng, INRIA-Sophia-Antipolis, France
John Domingue, The Open University, UK
Martin Dzbor, The Open University, UK
Jerôme Euzenat, INRIA Rhône-Alpes, France
Dieter Fensel, University of Innsbruck, Austria
Aldo Gangemi, ISTC-CNR, Italy
Jennifer Golbeck, University of Maryland, USA
Asun Gomez-Perez, Universidad Politécnica de Madrid, Spain
Marko Grobelnik, JSI, Slovenia
Udo Hahn, Jena University, Germany
Michele Missikoff, CNR, Italy
Riichiro Mizoguchi, Osaka University, Japan
Enrico Motta, The Open University, UK
Mark Musen, Stanford University, USA

Enric Plaza I Cervera, Spanish Scientific Research Council, CSIC, Spain
Alun Preece, University of Aberdeen, UK
Alan Rector, University of Manchester, UK
Ulrich Reimer, University of Applied Sciences St. Gallen, Switzerland
Marie-Christine Rousset, University of Paris-Sud, France
Guus Schreiber, Free University of Amsterdam, The Netherlands
Nigel Shadbolt, University of Southampton, UK
Wolf Siberski, University of Hannover, Germany
Derek Sleeman, University of Aberdeen, UK
Pavel Smrž, Technical University of Brno, Czech Republic
Rudi Studer, University of Karlsruhe, Germany
Gerd Stumme, University of Kassel, Germany
York Sure, University of Karlsruhe, Germany
Annette ten Teije, Free University of Amsterdam, The Netherlands
Frank van Harmelen, Free University of Amsterdam, The Netherlands
Hannes Werthner, Vienna University of Technology, Austria
Mike Wooldridge, University of Liverpool, UK

Additional Reviewers

Sudhir Agarwal, AIFB Institute, Karlsruhe, Germany
Anupriya Ankolekar, AIFB Institute, Karlsruhe, Germany
Stephan Bloehdorn, AIFB Institute, Karlsruhe, Germany
Luka Bradesko, Jozef Stefan Institute, Slovenia
Janez Brank, Jozef Stefan Institute, Slovenia
Adriana Budura, EPFL, Switzerland
Vasilios Darlagiannis, EPFL, Switzerland
Rainer Endl, University of Applied Sciences St. Gallen, Switzerland
Blaz Fortuna, Jozef Stefan Institute, Slovenia
Rafael Gonzalez-Cabero, UPM, Spain
Elias Gyftodimos, University of Aberdeen, UK
Peter Haase, University of Karlsruhe, Germany
Robert Jäschke, University of Kassel, Germany
Martin Kejkula, University of Economics, Prague, Czech Republic
Fabius Klemm, EPFL, Switzerland
Markus Kroetsch, University of Karlsruhe, Germany
Steffen Lamparter, University of Karlsruhe, Germany
Holger Lewen, AIFB Institute, Karlsruhe, Germany
Edith Maier, University. of Applied Sciences St. Gallen, Switzerland
Ivana Podnar, EPFL, Switzerland
Quentin Reul, University of Aberdeen, UK
Christoph Ringelstein, University of Koblenz-Landau, Germany
Sebastian Rudolph, AIFB Institute, Karlsruhe, Germany
Jan Rupnik, Jozef Stefan Institute, Slovenia
Carsten Saathoff, University of Koblenz-Landau, Germany

Roman Schmidt, EPFL, Switzerland
Christoph Schmitz, University of Kassel, Germany
Christph Tempich, University of Karlsruhe, Germany
Edward Thomas, University of Aberdeen, UK
Johanna Völker, AIFB Institute, Karlsruhe, Germany
Denny Vrandecic, University of Karlsruhe, Germany
Le Hung Vu, EPFL, Switzerland
Yimin Wang, AIFB Institute, Karlsruhe, Germany

Poster Programme Committee

Stuart Aitken, Edinburgh University, UK
Harith Alani, University of Southampton, UK
Philipp Cimiano, University of Karlsruhe, Germany
Oscar Corcho, University of Manchester, UK
Mariano Fernandez Lopez, CEU, Spain
Marko Grobelnik, Jozef Stefan Institute, Slovenia
Siegfried Handschuh, DERI, Ireland
Andreas Hotho, Kassel University, Germany
Michel Klein, Vrije Universiteit Amsterdam, The Netherlands
Andreia Malucelli, Pontifical Catholic University of Paraná, Brazil
Peter Mika, Vrije Universiteit, The Netherlands
Alun Preece, University of Aberdeen, UK
Marta Sabou, The Open University, UK
Christoph Schmitz, Kassel University, Germany
Sergej Sizov, Koblenz-Landau University, Germany
York Sure, University of Karlsruhe, Germany
Maria Vargas-Vera, KMI, The Open University, UK

Sponsors

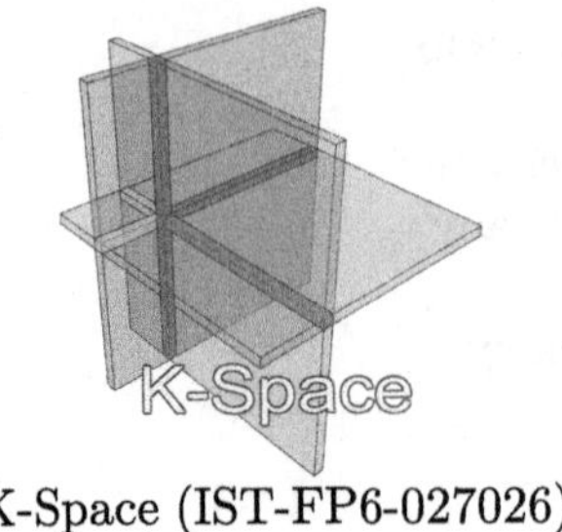

K-Space (IST-FP6-027026)

University of Economics, Prague

NeOn (IST-FP6-27595)

X-Media (IST-FP6-026978)

ISWeb, University of Koblenz-Landau

Table of Contents

Invited Talks

Knowledge Acquisition

Ontology Engineering

Ontology Learning

Ontology Mapping and Evolution

Semantic Search

User Interfaces

Knowledge Discovery

Semantics from Networks and Crowds

Applications

Information and Influence in Social Networks

Andrzej Nowak, Robin Vallacher, and Wiesław Bartkowski

Warsaw University, Poland

Abstract. Most research on social networks is concerned with information transmission per se Our aim here is to supplement the social network perspective by incorporating mechanisms that govern social influence Research in social psychology suggests that individuals interact, in large part, to construct a shared reality that consists not only of shared information but also of agreed upon opinions. In this process, they do not simply transmit information, but more importantly, they influence one another to arrive at a common interpretation of information. We will discuss similarities and differences in how networks structure shapes the spread of information and governs social influence. Both simulation and empirical data concerning these two processes show that they operate in a very different way. The spread of information, described as a contagion process describes how individuals learn about new facts. Social influence process describes how individuals evaluate and weight different items of information and how they change their opinions and attitudes. The results of numerous experiments have shown that three critical factors determine the impact of social influence: (1) the number of sources exerting the influence, (2) the immediacy of the source(s) to the target(s), and (3) the strength of the source(s). The process by which humans construct social reality may prove informative for designing rules of interaction among intelligent agents. The primary implication of the present model is that information is not merely acquired, but also evaluated and negotiated in a social context. The process by which humans evaluate information and construct social reality may prove informative for designing rules of interaction among intelligent agents. The primary implication of the present model is that information is not merely acquired, but also evaluated and negotiated in a social context.

S. Staab and V. Svatek (Eds.): EKAW 2006, LNAI 4248, p. 1, 2006.

Learning, Logic, and Probability: A Unified View

Pedro Domingos

University of Washington

Abstract. AI systems must be able to learn, reason logically, and handle uncertainty. While much research has focused on each of these goals individually, only recently have we begun to attempt to achieve all three at once. In this talk I will describe Markov logic, a representation that combines first-order logic and probabilistic graphical models, and algorithms for learning and inference in it. A knowledge base in Markov logic is a set of weighted first-order formulas, viewed as templates for features of Markov networks. The weights and probabilistic semantics make it easy to combine knowledge from a multitude of noisy, inconsistent sources, reason across imperfectly matched ontologies, etc. Inference in Markov logic is performed by weighted satisfiability testing, Markov chain Monte Carlo, and (where appropriate) specialized engines. Formulas can be refined using inductive logic programming techniques, and weights can be learned either generatively (using pseudo-likelihood) or discriminatively (using a voted perceptron). Markov logic has been successfully applied to problems in entity resolution, social network modeling, information extraction and others, and is the basis of the open-source Alchemy system.

(Joint work with Stanley Kok, Hoifung Poon, Matt Richardson and Parag Singla.)

S. Staab and V. Svatek (Eds.): EKAW 2006, LNAI 4248, p. 2, 2006.

KARaCAs: Knowledge Acquisition with Repertory Grids and Formal Concept Analysis for Dialog System Construction

Hilke Garbe[1], Claudia Janssen[2], Claus Möbus[1], Heiko Seebold[2], and Holger de Vries[2]

[1] University of Oldenburg, Germany
{garbe, moebus}@uni-oldenburg.de
[2] OFFIS Oldenburg, Germany

Abstract. We describe a new knowledge acquisition tool that enabled us to develop a dialog system recommending software design patterns by asking critical questions. This assistance system is based on interviews with experts. For the interviews we adopted the repertory grid method and integrated formal concept analysis. The repertory grid method stimulates the generation of common and differentiating attributes for a given set of objects. Using formal concept analysis we can control the repertory grid procedure, minimize the required expert judgements and build an abstraction based hierarchy of design patterns, even from the judgements of different experts. Based on the acquired knowledge we semi-automatically generate a Bayesian Belief Network (BBN), that is used to conduct dialogs with users to suggest a suitable design pattern for their individual problem situation. Integrating these different methods into our knowledge acquisition tool KARaCAs enables us to support the entire knowledge acquisition and engineering process. We used KARaCAs with three design pattern experts and derived approximately 130 attributes for 23 design patterns. Using formal concept analysis we merged the three lattices and condensed them to approximately 80 common attributes.

1 Introduction

Design patterns are an accepted method for improving the quality of software. The standard book about design patterns in object oriented software design is Gamma et al. [1], where a citation of Christopher Alexander is used to explain what patterns are: " Each pattern describes a problem which occurs over and over again in our environment, and then describes the core of the solution to that problem, in such a way that you can use the solution a million times over, without ever doing it the same way twice." [2]. Although Alexander was an architect his description is also suitable for patterns in the domain of object oriented software design. One purpose of design patterns is to capture design experience and make it available to other developers, so they can improve their designs. The standard elements of a pattern description are:

S. Staab and V. Svatek (Eds.): EKAW 2006, LNAI 4248, pp. 3–18, 2006.

Name. Every design pattern has a name.

Problem. This section describes the problem situation in which a pattern is applicable.

Solution. The solution describes how objects and classes can work together to solve the problem. The solution is a template that has to be instantiated for each specific situation.

Consequences. The consequences describe e.g. trade-offs that have to be considered if a design pattern should be applied.

Gamma et al. [1] describe 23 design patterns organized as a catalog. In addition there is an increasing amount of new patterns including for example architectural and J2EE patterns. Nevertheless, knowledge about design patterns is not very wide spread among software developers and the literature about patterns is often organized as catalogs; pattern by pattern. A software engineer has to read all (or at least many) pattern descriptions before he can decide which pattern is suitable for his problem situation. Tool support for selecting appropriate design patterns is rare. Meffert [3] supposes semantic source code annotations which can be analysed to capture the intent of a piece of software. These annotations can be compared to given pattern templates and if a match can be found, the source code elements can gradually be transfered to a pattern. Gomes [4] describes a case based reasoning approach for reusing software which uses Baysian Networks and WordNet as a common sense ontology. Both approaches work on source code or UML model artifacts. Our goal was to develop a dialog system that is able to approve possible design patterns [5] without analysing given source code or models. This dialog system can assist software developers in choosing a design pattern. Who, even if he has not read all the design pattern descriptions is able to benefit from the experiences of other software developers. Our dialog system questions him about his design problem and makes a suggestion which pattern might be applicable.

This article is organized as follows: Section 2 provides an overview of our proposed knowledge acquisition and engineering process. Section 3 describes our knowledge acquisition procedure containing repertory grids (3.1), formal concept analysis (3.2), and their integration in KARaCAs (3.3). The merging process for the results of different expert interviews is outlined in section 4. Our dialog system is based on BBNs (section 5) that are generated semi-automatically from the data we obtained in the expert interviews with KARaCAs. In section 6 we discuss conclusions and further work.

2 Requirements and Proposed Knowledge Acquisition Process

Our goal was to design an efficient dialog system that assists software developers to choose a design pattern for their specific problem situation. The intended dialog system should question the user about his specific problem situation. The user answers these questions with "yes", "no" or "I don't know". During this dialog the system successively reduces the set of applicable patterns until it proposes one.

This dialog system has to fulfill the following requirements:

1.1 **User input.** Requirements on how user input is processed:
  1.1.1 **Undo.** The user should have the possibility to reconsider a given answer and change it. The dialog has to adjust itself to the altered information.
  1.1.2 **Fault Tolerance.** The dialog has to be "fault tolerant". Even if a user gives a wrong answer about his problem situation he should have the possibility to continue the dialog and get a pattern suggestion.
  1.1.3 **No answer.** Additionally, he should be able to skip questions, since he might not be able to classify his problem situation completely and therefore might not be able to answer every question.

1.2 **Probabilities for suggestions.** The dialog system may not be able to comprehend the entire problem situation and context. This may be because the user has a diverging conception of his situation or the posed question and therefore enters misleading information in the dialog system. Another reason might be that there are institutional programming standards that are unknown for the dialog system. Because of this, a certain pattern can only be suggested with an approximated probability. The user should be informed about this probability. This information should be presented to him during the entire dialog.

As we were not able to extract the required knowledge from design pattern literature, we used a knowledge acquisition with design pattern experts. Deduced from the requirements for the dialog, we had the following requirements for the knowledge acquisition procedure:

2.1 **Free generation and naming of attributes.** The experts should not be restricted in generating and naming attributes for the problem situations a specific pattern can be applied to. We were interested in the terms experts use to describe problem situations for software engineers.
  2.1.1 **Shared attributes.** To set up an efficient dialog, attributes were required that are shared between two or more patterns. These attributes can be used to successively reduce the set of patterns that are relevant for the ongoing dialog. This is a very difficult task for design pattern experts. We made the experience that they first think of specific problem situations for every pattern, and finding shared attributes was a difficult task for them.
  2.1.2 **Differentiating attributes.** To identify a situation in which one specific design pattern can be suggested by the dialog system, every pattern should be identifiable by its attributes. Therefore the attribute sets of the patterns should be pairwise disjoint.

2.2 **Probabilities.** A design pattern is a template that can be adjusted to a given situation and the situations to which it can be applied can vary. Therefore the attributes of these situations can vary and so a specific attribute must not always be present. To capture this, we needed a method that can deal with probabilities.

2.3 **Visualization of results.** The results of the knowledge acquisition should be visualized in such a way, that the domain expert can understand them.

2.4 **Merging.** As we wanted to integrate the knowledge of different experts who can freely name attributes, the knowledge acquisition procedure should allow the possibility to merge different sets of attributes for the design patterns. This includes for example the assistance in identifying attributes that are used synonymously, as generalisation or specialisation of others. Because of the amount of attributes we have to deal with, this procedure has to be supported by the knowledge acquisition method.

To fulfill these requirements we propose a three stage knowledge acquisition process (Fig. 1). We first acquire knowledge from different experts. For these interviews we adapted the repertory grid technique and integrated Formal Concept analysis. The results of these interviews are merged with support of Formal Concept Analysis. From this aggregated information we semi-automatically generate a BBN for the dialog system. Using these different knowledge acquisition methods and engineering and integrating them into our tool KARaCAs we can support the whole process.

The three stages of the process will be described in sections 3 - 5.

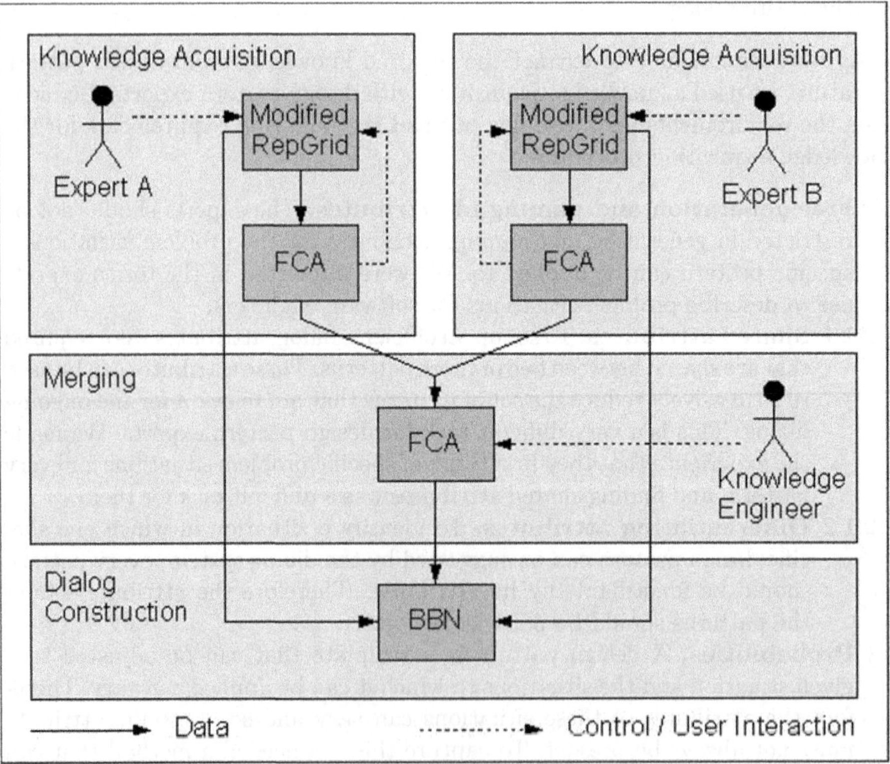

Fig. 1. Proposed Knowledge Acquisition Process

3 Knowledge Acquisition

For our knowledge acquisition process we used modified repertory grids and formal concept analysis. Both methods have distinct advantages but also some strong disadvantages in regard to our requirements. By combining the two the disadvantages for our application could be overcome.

3.1 Knowledge Acquisition with Repertory Grids

The Repertory Grid techniques was proposed by Kelly [6]. It was embedded in his Personal Construct Psychology. Delugach states: "In accordance with the theory, the repertory grid technique distinguishes the objects of a problem domain (called elements) through their attributes (called constructs)." [7]

The Repertory Grid technique has three steps.

1. The elements for the procedure are chosen. In Personal Construct Psychology the considered elements are usually persons or situations. Often elements are preselected instead of being acquired through an interview.
2. At the second step constructs are acquired by classification from three randomly chosen elements (triade) into two classes. The interviewed person has to explain in which way two elements of the triade are similar and how they differ from the remaining one. Elements and constructs are listed in a two-dimensional matrix called grid.
3. The last step is to rate all elements concerning the given constructs. This is normally done by rating each element on a given scale between the two poles.

Gaines and Shaw state: "The repertory grid was an instrument designed by Kelly to bypass cognitive defenses and give access to a persons underlying construction system by asking the person to compare and contrast relevant examples (significant people in the person's life in the original application)." [8]

Since 1955 several variations of the repertory grid technique have been developed, Castro-Schez et al. [9] give a short overview. Apart from the use in psychology (e.g. Spangenberg and Wolff [10]) Repertory Grids and its variations have often been used for knowledge acquisition in different domains (e.g. Gaines and Shaw [8], Richards [11] and Castro-Schez et al. [9]).

The repertory grid technique has a lot of advantages that makes it well suited for our knowledge acquisition process:

- It can be performed in natural spoken language without given items (requirement 2.1). Nevertheless we obtain formal and structured results which can be used as input in other procedures.
- The method supports the experts in generating shared (requirement 2.1.1) and differentiating (requirement 2.1.2) attributes for design patterns. By asking them to group two of three items they can concentrate on these. At each step only a small subset of the design patterns has to be considered. Therefore the expert is supported in generating these differentiating attributes.

- The two poles of every construct can be interpreted as attributes. By rating the attributes for the design patterns probabilities can be assigned to the relations (requirement 2.2).

There are some disadvantages:

- The triads are randomly chosen. In the worst case this leads to a very large amount of needed triads to get enough differentiating attributes. In addition, the repertory grid method can not assure that the sets of attributes for all design patterns are pairwise disjoint. (Requirement 2.1.1) If for example two very similar elements are presented in a triad, it can be expected that they are always grouped together (cp. Choisel and Wickelmaier [12]).
- The generated attributes depend on the presented triads, so possibly not every attribute the expert thinks to be important might be generated. If for example all elements have a very important attribute in common this would never be mentioned during the procedure. Considering the attributes that are generated during the repertory grid for a specific design pattern the expert might miss one or more attributes that are relevant for this pattern. The expert should have the possibility to complete the set of attributes to properly describe the design pattern.
- Bruder, Lengnink and Prediger [13] used repertory grids to ask mathematics students about their subjective theories about mathematical tasks. As a result of their studies they describe an additional problem: It was often very difficult for the students to find exact antipodes for attributes.

The result of the repertory grid method is a matrix with ratings for the elements concerning the constructs. This data has to be analysed and visualized properly to be understood and interpreted by the domain expert and the knowledge engineer. Several methods have been used for this and were implemented in tools (cp. Gaines and Shaw [8]). In our work we focus on Formal Concept Analysis for this purpose.

3.2 Ontology Engineering and Formal Concept Analysis

This section gives a short introduction to formal concept analysis. The combination of repertory grids and formal concept analysis is described in section 3.3. Formal Concept Analysis (FCA) is a method for qualitative analysis of data. Subject to FCA is a formal context. A formal context (G, M, I) is a subset of the Cartesian product $(I \subseteq G \times M)$ of a quantity of objects G (Gegenstände in German) and a quantity of attributes M (Merkmale in German). The term gIm means: object g owns attribute m [14]. FCA structures data into units, which are formal abstractions of concepts of mind. A formal concept comprises two parts, its extension and its intension. The extension enfolds all objects belonging to this concept. The intension covers all attributes shared by those objects. The extension of a concept determines the intension and the intension determines the extension [14]. This approach allows gathering all concepts of a context and introduces a subsumption hierarchy between them. The amount of all formalized concepts is called concept lattice of the formal context. This lattice can be visualized as a conceptual hierarchy (Hasse Diagram), which enables a different view on the structure of the data and supports its analysis. An area of application for FCA is Ontology Engineering by utilizing the ability to structure data by means of concept lattices. The generated hierarchies may be used as a starting point for the manual or semi-automatic creation of ontologies [15]. The concept lattice enables domain experts to identify incorrectness or missing coherence in the dataset (requirement 2.3). Gaps in the conceptual hierarchy indicate probable missing objects or attributes. With these hints the data ascertainment can be completed [16]. Because the concept lattices represent the data in a way domain experts intuitively understand [16,17].

3.3 Integrating the Methods - KARaCAs

A combination of repertory grids and FCA has already been used in different domains.

Spangenberg and Wolf used FCA [10] to reduce the amount of data acquired with repertory grids and discuss alternative approaches. They transform the repertory grid data into a multivalued context, which has to be reduced to an univalent context. Their repertory grid has a rating scale from 1 to 6. They interpret votes with values from 3 to 4 as indecisiveness and ignore those votes.

Bruder, Lengnink and Prediger [18] used line diagrams produced by FCA to visualize the structure of the repertory grid results. They asked mathematics students about their subjective theories about mathematical tasks and investigated the change over time. Based on their studies they describe two major problems [13]:

1. The set of objects (tasks) has a direct influence on the acquired attributes, therefore it must be possible for the students to add additional relevant attributes after the repertory grid procedure is performed.
2. Often it was very difficult for the students to find exact antipodes for attributes.

Delugach and Lampkin presented a method for knowledge acquisition using repertory grids, Formal Concept Analysis and Concept Graphs. They used: "repertory grids for acquisition, formal concept analysis for analysis, and conceptual graphs for representation." [7]

These groups mainly used FCA to analyse the results of repertory grids. They first questioned experts with repertory grids and analysed the data using formal concept analysis after the interviews. We integrated the two methods for a better use of the advantages and to overcome some of the disadvantages. We developed two versions of KARaCAs with an ascending level of integration.

We adapt the repertory grid method to allow attributes that are not exact opposite of each other (cp. Bruder et al. [13]). Steps 1 and 2 are performed the same way as describe in section 3.1. Step 3 is modified as follows:

3.1 First the expert is asked to assign one of the two attributes to each object (pattern in our case), if possible. This is done due to the fact that these two attributes are not necessarily the opposite of each other and neither may apply in some cases.

3.2 In the next step the expert has to quantify how certain a given attribute applies to a pattern. In contrast to Kelly's repertory grid method this evaluation is not done with the two attributes as boundary or poles.

Similar to the card sorting method Kelly proposed for the Grid we designed our graphical user interface using the card sorting metaphor (Fig. 2).

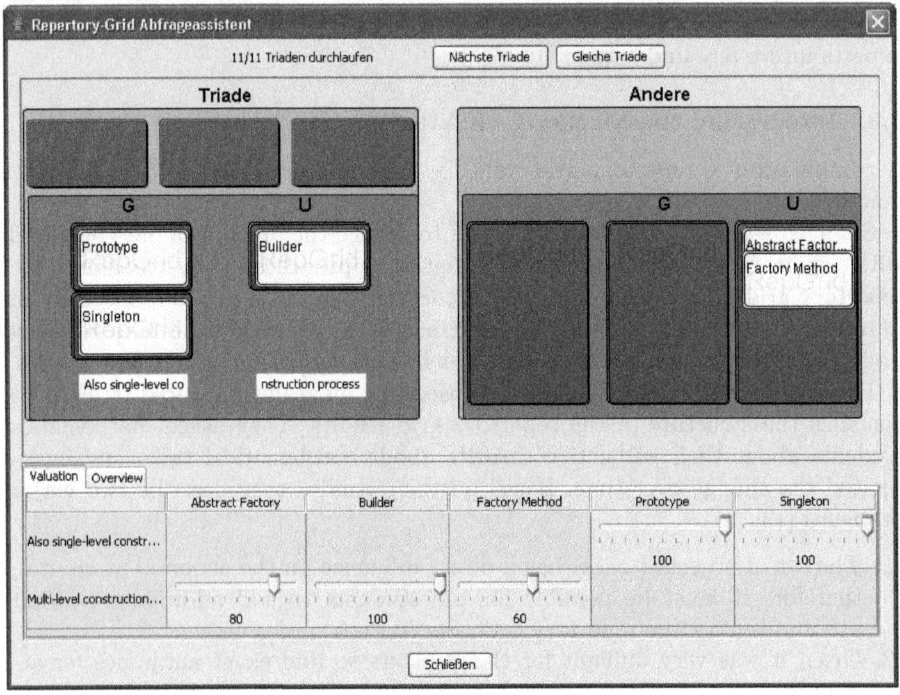

Fig. 2. KARaCAs: GUI for the adapted Repertory Grid

After each triad KARaCAs analyses the data with formal concept analysis. The elements and the associated attributes are transferred to a formal context. In the formal context each attribute is set in relation to an element it is assigned to. From this context a concept lattice is generated. The lattice in Fig. 3 shows a part of the generated attributes from an expert interview.

This new integration of FCA and Repertory Grid in one tool has two distinct advantages:

On the one hand performing the formal concept analysis after each triad gives the domain expert the possibility to inspect the results in form of a lattice (Fig. 3, Requirement 1.7) even during the interview with the repertory grid. By integrating both methods into one tool it is possible to switch between two different views of the acquired data, resulting in synergistic effects. The knowledge

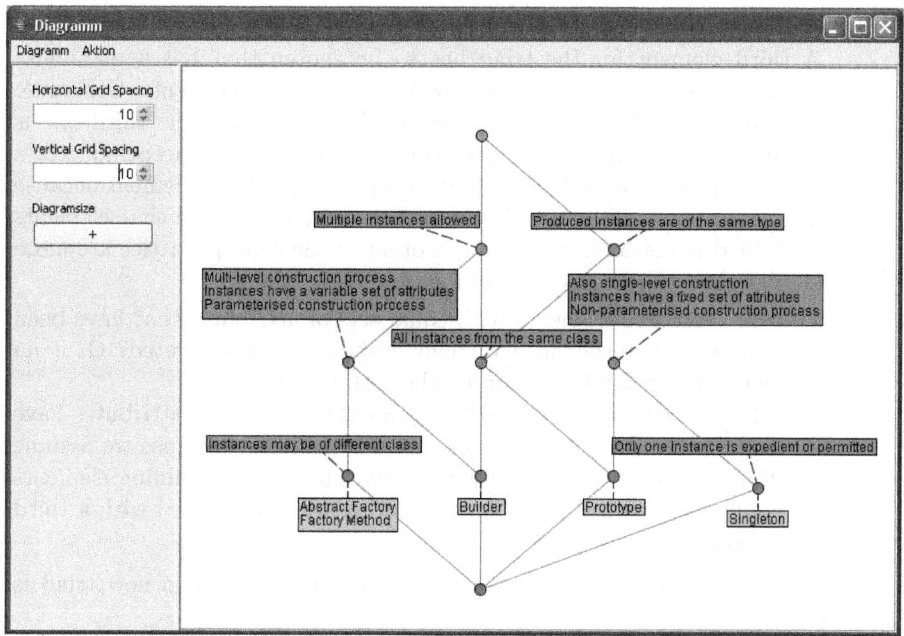

Fig. 3. KARaCAs: Corresponding Line Diagram for the context

engineer is able to present the lattice representing the so far obtained attributes to the expert during the acquisition and discuss it. The expert can see if a sufficient set of attributes was already acquired. The lattice in Fig. 3 e.g. shows that the design patterns Abstract Factory and Factory Method can not be distinguished by the attributes given so far. If the expert identifies such missing attributes while looking at the graph (compare Bruder, Lengnink and Prediger [13]) they can be directly added to the formal context and are also available after switching back to the repertory grid. The first version of KARaCAs contained this integration level of the two methods. It was used to acquire approximately 130 attributes from three different experts. Each of the interviews lasted about an hour which is a relatively short time span for the given task and shows the data acquisition efficiency of our method.

Furthermore, we can control the ongoing repertory grid. The second version of KARaCAs analyses the data with respect to the following questions:

1 Are there any two or more elements with attribute sets that are not pairwise disjoint?
  In this case, the next triad will be chosen so that the domain expert is forced to generate a differentiating attribute.
  1.1 Are there three or more elements with equal sets of attributes?
    The algorithm produces a triad containing three of these elements. Doing so, the expert is forced to distinguish one of these elements from the others and generate an appropriate attribute.

1.2 Are there two elements with equal sets of attributes?
A third element for the triad has to be chosen that has a maximum amount of attributes in common with the other two elements. Otherwise it is likely that the two remain grouped together and the third one is separated. We choose an element contained in a superconcept node or a subconcept node of a shared superconcept node as third element because they have the most attributes in common. It is assumed that elements contained in concepts near to each other in the concept lattice are more similar than object in concepts far from each other.

1.2.1 Are there two elements with equal sets of attributes that have been presented together in five triads without being separated? Or is no new triad possible containing these two elements?
The elements are presented as pairs and separating attributes have to be generated. At this point we use this limit because we assume that the two are very similar in relation to the remaining elements and would always be grouped together when presented with a third element.

2 If the attribute sets for all elements are pairwise disjoint no new triad is presented.

Using this algorithm we can ensure that the acquired attribute sets for all elements are pairwise disjoint at the end of the procedure. By choosing elements as similar as possible for triades we increase the efficiency of the repertory grid technique in regard to our requirements and minimize the required expert judgements.

4 Merging

Ontology merging is widely discussed and a lot of tools are developed to support this process (Stumme and Maedche [19] give a short overview). Ganter and Stumme describe the general task of ontology merging as follows: "Merging two ontologies means creating a new ontology in a semi-automatic manner by merging concepts of the source ontologies." [20] Stumme proposed the use of FCA for this purpose [19,21]. Our acquired source ontologies share the same objects: the given design patterns. Therefore, we only have to merge the acquired attributes for these objects. KARaCAs enables us to merge the results of different expert interviews (requirement 2.4) by aggregating the attribute sets in one large formal context. From this joint context a line diagram is generated, which helps the knowledge engineer to analyse the attributes.

We primarily investigated the lattices concerning the following two questions:

- Are different attributes used synonymously?
  If this is the case, one (or more) of them is redundant and is deleted from the merged context. In the corresponding lattice these attributes would be annotated to the same nodes (concepts).

– Do different experts assign very similar attributes A and B to different design pattern sets?

  This might occur if an attribute is only weakly connected to a specific design pattern. One expert might assign this attribute with a low probability to a specific design pattern and the other does not connect the two. Another possibility is that one expert forgot that an attribute is relevant for a design pattern. In this case, starting at the node that A is assigned to B would be annotated to a node on an upwards or downwards path.

Supported by this feature we condensed the approximately 130 acquired attributes to about 80 which form the basis for our dialog system.

5 Knowledge Representation with Bayesian Belief Networks

Bayesian Belief Networks ([22,23]) are the representation of choice for modeling uncertain knowledge (e.g.[24,25,26,27]). A BBN models this knowledge as a directed acyclic graph that represents a probability distribution. The nodes of the graph represent propositional variables and directed arcs represent probabilistic relationships between them. Probabilistic independence between variables is indicated by the types of path in the network and the lack of them. Furthermore, the relations are conditional probabilities (each variable conditioned on its parents in the network) that define a joint probability distribution of the variables.

We used BBN to express knowledge about the applicability of design patterns for a given problem situation. For this purpose the qualitative structure of the BBNs is grouped in two levels (see Fig. 4): the first level contains the actual design patterns while the second contains the attributes of a problem situation. Due to this template it is possible to create the qualitative and quantitative structure of the BBN automatically from the acquired data as presented in the following section.

5.1 Generating Bayesian Belief Networks

The generation of the BBN was performed in two steps: In the first step the qualitative structure of the network was created. The acquired attributes assigned to the corresponding design patterns and the necessary conditional probabilities were identified. For each attribute assigned to a design pattern in KARaCAs a relation between these two was created in the qualitative network. This step could be done automatically by KARaCAs. In the second step a quantitative structure of the networks was build. While acquiring the different attributes to the design patterns the experts were asked to judge the probability of the relation between design patterns and attribute. This probability statements were taken as simple conditional probabilities like $P(attribute\ A = yes|design\ pattern\ singleton = yes) = 0.9$, i.e. the expert judged that in 90% of the cases where a singleton is used the attribute A applies. However, to build the quantitative structure of the network more complex conditional statements which expressed the validity of an

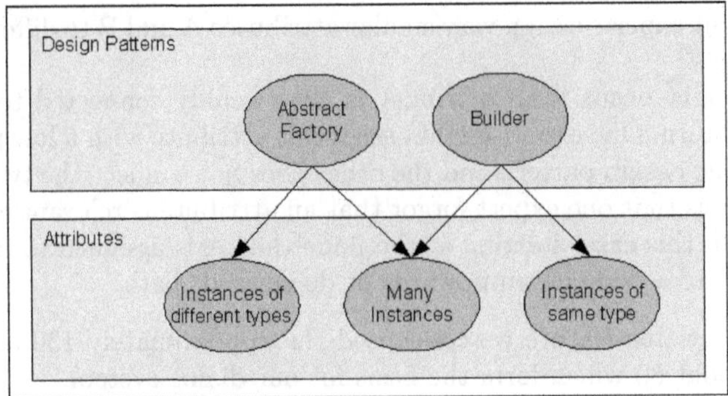

Fig. 4. Small Part of the generated Bayesian Belief Network

attribute under the influence of several design patterns were necessary. These probabilities could be calculated by using the "noisy-or" ([23]) by making some assumptions:

1. The chance that an attribute is valid without any of the regarding design patterns present is 0.05. This states how probable it is for an attribute to apply, if no design pattern is given. To get more accurate values for these probabilities it would be necessary to perform a more general statistical study about the frequency of occurrence of the attribute without a design pattern associated.
2. We assume that the factors inhibiting the influence of design patterns on an attribute are independent from each other.
3. In the early stage of the project the experts had to identify attributes for design patterns without stating the probability of the relation. Because in this stage the experts were asked to state only attributes which certainly apply, we assumed the probability of the relations to be 0.9.

Under these assumptions we were able to calculate the necessary conditional probabilities from the expert statements by using the "noisy-or" approach ([23]). Finally we had to obtain the a-priori-probability of the design patterns. Since we had no information if a design pattern is appropriate for a given problem, we assumed it has a 50% chance of being applicable at the beginning. To get a more accurate value for this probability a general statistical study about the frequency of application of the design patterns has to be performed. The calculation of the necessary probabilities is done automatically by KARaCAs.

5.2 A Dialog System Using Bayesian Belief Networks

The generated BBN is the basis for our dialog system. This system questions the user successively about his problem situation using the acquired design pattern attributes. The dialog is performed using the following algorithm:

1. Determine the design pattern node with the highest probability for the state "yes". If this probability is higher than 0.9 recommend the design pattern as applicable to the user. If the probability is lower proceed with the algorithm.

2. Determine the relevant attribute nodes for this design pattern node. This is done using Shachter's Bayes Ball algorithm [28].
3. Determine the node with the highest probability for "yes" from this set and question the user about the associated attribute of this node.
4. If the user answers "yes" or "no" enter this as evidence in the BBN and perform an inference on the net. If the user answer with "I don't know" mark the node as being asked already.
5. Restart with 1.

By always determining the design pattern that is applicable with the highest probability and asking about it's attributes we try to conduct the dialog according to the users expectations. We assume this dialog strategy minimizes questions that astonish the user because they are not related to his problem situation. Using BBN for the dialog we can fulfill the requirements listed in section 2. Each answer a user gives is entered as evidence in the BBN and the new probabilities for all design patterns and attributes are calculated. An undo (requirement 1.1.1) function for user inputs is easily implemented by deleting one piece of evidence and doing an inference on the BBN.

If probabilities of 0 or 1 are avoided in the specification of the attribute nodes the dialog can be made fault tolerant for unexpected user input (requirement 1.1.2). If a user answers for example "no" where the situation would imply a "yes" the applicable design pattern would get a very low possibility. But after the user answered the following questions (that try to establish an alternative design pattern) also with "no", the suitable pattern is assumed to get the pattern with the highest probability again. In this case the dialog will last longer than in the best case, but the user has the possibility to get a suggestion. If the user is not quite sure about how to answer a certain question he also has the possibility to say "I don't know" (requirement 1.1.3). The attribute node in the BBN is then marked and will not be answered again, but no evidence is entered into the BBN. Because new evidence is directly propagated through the network, it is possible to present a ranking list of the design patterns after each answer. The user always has an overview of the probabilities with which each pattern is suitable concerning his so far entered information.

Using Bayesian Belief Networks as knowledge representation for the dialog enabled us to fulfill the requirements from section 2. Alternative representations could have been for example the concept lattice produced by FCA or a decision tree. But both can't fulfill our requirements. Especially the representation of probabilities and the required opportunity to change any already given answer during the dialog is difficult to implement with these techniques.

6 Conclusion and Further Work

6.1 Conclusion

A knowledge acquisition method was presented that combines repertory grids and formal concept analysis on two ascending levels of integration. The first version of KARaCAs was used to acquire approximately 130 attributes from three design pattern experts. Each of the three interviews only lasted about one hour. During the interviews the visualization was used to analyse the data so far obtained. The concept lattice was easy to understand for the experts and helped them to reflect on their answers. Based on the experiences from these interviews we developed the second version of KARaCAs. The results of the three interviews were merged as described and condensed to about 80 attributes. These attributes are the basis for our dialog system. KARaCAs supports the entire knowledge acquisition process and automatically generates a BBN from the data that is used in the dialog system.

6.2 Further Work

The dialog system will be evaluated with computer science students at the University of Oldenburg. A special question for this evaluation is whether the attributes given by design pattern experts can be understood by beginners. Another one is the suitability of the dialog strategy which determines the questions that are presented to the user. To further support the experts in generating attributes we plan to do interviews with a dyad of experts. A small test with two experts showed that they discuss the grouping of design patterns and the naming of the attributes a lot. It seemed promising to do interviews with a peer group of experts to increase the quality of the acquired data. Furthermore we want to expand the dialog system. Our focus is on the domain dependent applicability of design patterns.

Acknowledgements

The development of KARaCAs and the dialog system was embedded in the multi-partner project InPULSE which was granted by the BMBF (German Federal Ministry of Education and Research). We thank Jan-Patrick Osterloh and Lars Weber for implementing our ideas and algorithms in KARaCAs and Steffen Kruse and Malte Zilinski for critical comments.

References

1. Gamma, E., Helm, R., Johnson, R., Vlissides, J.: Design Patterns: Elements of Reusable Object-Oriented Software. Addision-Wesley (1995)
2. Alexander, C., Ishikawa, S., Silverstein, M., Jacobson, M., Fiksdahl-King, I., Angel, S.: A Pattern Language. Oxford University Press, New York (1977)
3. Meffert, K.: Supporting design patterns with annotations. In: 13th Annual IEEE International Symposium and Workshop on Engineering of Computer Based Systems (ECBS'06). (2006) 437–445
4. Gomes, P.: Software design retrieval using bayesian networks and wordnet. In: Proceedings of the 7th European Conference on Case-Based Reasoning, ECCBR 2004. (2004) 184–197

5. Möbus, C., Seebold, H., Garbe, H.: A greedy knowledge acquisition method for the rapid prototyping of knowledge structures. In Clark, P., Schreiber, G., eds.: Proceedings of the 3rd International Conference on Knowledge Capture, 2005, New York, NY: ACM Press (2005) 211 – 212
6. Kelly, G.A.: Psychology of Personal Constructs. New York: W. W. Norton (1955)
7. Delugach, H., Lampkin, B.: Troika: Using grids, lattices and graphs in knowledge acquisition. In Stumme, G., ed.: Working with Conceptual Structures: Contributions to ICCS 2000, Aachen, Germany: Shaker Verlag (2000) 201–214
8. Gaines, B., Shaw, M.: Knowledge acquisition tools based on personal construct psychology. The Knowledge Engineering Review **8**(1) (1993) 49–85
9. Castro-Schez, J.J., Jennings, N.R., Luo, X., Shadbolt, N.: Acquiring domain knowledge for negotiating agents: a case study. International Journal of Human-Computer Studies **61**(1) (2004) 3–31,
10. Spangenberg, N., Wolff, K.: Datenreduktion durch die Formale Begriffsanalyse von Repertory Grids. In: Einführung in die Repertory Grid-Technik, Band 2, Klinische Forschung und Praxis. Bern, Göttingen, Toronto, Seattle: Verlag Hans Huber (1993) 38–54
11. Richards, D.: Ripple-down rules with formal concept analysis: A comparison to personal construct psychology. In Gaines, B., Musen, M., eds.: Proceedings of 11th Workshop on Knowledge Acquisition, Modeling and Management, Banff Canada, SRDG Publications, Calgary, Canada (1998)
12. Choisel, S., Wickelmaier, F.: Extraction of auditory features and elicitation of attributes for the assessment of multichannel reproduced sound. In: 118th Convention of the Audio Engineering Society, Barcelona, Spain (2005)
13. Bruder, R., Lengnink, K., Prediger, S.: Ein Instrumentarium zur Erfassung subjektiver Theorien über Mathematikaufgaben. Preprint Nr. 2265 des Fachbereichs Mathematik, TU Darmstadt (2003)
14. Ganter, B., Wille, R.: Formal Concept Analysis. Mathematical Foundations. Springer, Berlin, Heidelberg, NewYork (1999)
15. Cimiano, P., Hotho, A., Stumme, G., Tane, J.: Conceptual knowledge processing with formal concept analysis and ontologies. In: Proceedings of the Second International Conference on Formal Concept Analysis - ICFCA04. (2004) 189 – 207
16. Kollewe, W.: Begriffliche Wissensverarbeitung: Wie Begriffsstrukturen die Pflege und Recherche in Wissensdatenbanken unterstützen. In: Bitkom KnowTech. (2002)
17. Düwel, S.: BASE - ein begriffsbasiertes Analyseverfahren für die Software-Entwicklung. PhD thesis, Philipps-Universität Marburg (2000)
18. Lengnink, K., Prediger, S.: Development of the personal constructs about mathematical tasks - a qualitative study using repretory grid methodology. In: Proceedings of the 27th Annual Meeting of the International Group for the Psychology of Mathematics Education (PME), Hawaii (2003)
19. Stumme, G., Maedche, A.: FCA - MERGE: Bottom-up merging of ontologies. In: IJCAI. (2001) 225–234
20. Ganter, B., Stumme, G.: Creation and merging of ontology top-levels. In de Moor, A., Lex, W., Ganter, B., eds.: Conceptual Structures for Knowledge Creation and Communication, 11th International Conferebce on Conceptual Structures, ICCS 2003, Proceedings, Springer (2003) 131 – 145
21. Stumme, G.: Ontology merging with formal concept analysis. In Kalfoglou, Y., Schorlemmer, M., Sheth, A., Staab, S., Uschold, M., eds.: Semantic Interoperability and Integration. Number 04391 in Dagstuhl Seminar Proceedings, Internationales Begegnungs- und Forschungszentrum (IBFI), Schloss Dagstuhl, Germany (2005)

22. Pearl, J.: Probabilistic Reasoning in Intelligent Systems: Networks of Plausible Inference. Revised second printing edn. Morgan Kaufman Publishers, San Mateo, CA. (1998)
23. Jensen, F.: Bayesian Networks and Decision Graphs, Statistics for Engineering and Information Science. Berlin: Springer (2001)
24. Folckers, J., Möbus, C., Schröder, O., Thole, H.J.: An intelligent problem solving environment for designing explanation models and for diagnostic reasoning in probabilistic domains. In Frasson, C., Gauthier, G., Lesgold, A., eds.: Intelligent Tutoring Systems. LNCS (1086), ITS 96, Montreal, Canada, Berlin: Springer (1996) 353–362
25. Mislevy, R., Almond, R.G., Yan, D., Steinberg, L.: Bayes nets in educational assessment: Where do the numbers come from? CSE Technical Report 518, Center for the Study of Evaluation, University of California, Los Angeles (2000)
26. Bunt, A., Conati, C.: Assessing effective exploration in open learning environments using bayesian networks. In Cerri, S.A., Gouardres, G., Paraguacu, F., eds.: Intelligent Tutoring Systems, Berlin: Springer (2002) 698 – 707
27. Zapata-Rivera, J., Greer, J.: Student model accuracy using inspectable bayesian student models. In Hoppe, U., Verdejo, F., Kay, J., eds.: Artificial Intelligence in Education: Shaping the Future of Learning through Intelligent Technologies, Amsterdam: IOS Press (2003) 65 – 72
28. Schachter, R.D.: Bayes-ball: The rational pastime (for determining irrelevance and requisite information in belief networks and influence diagrams). In Cooper, G.F., Moral, S., eds.: Proceedings of the Fourteenth Conference on Uncertainty in Artificial Intelligence (UAI-98), Morgan Kaufmann (1998) 480487

Capturing Quantified Constraints in FOL, Through Interaction with a Relationship Graph

Peter M.D. Gray[1] and Graham J.L. Kemp[2]

[1] Department of Computing Science, University of Aberdeen, King's College, Aberdeen, AB24 3UE, UK
pmdgray@bcs.org.uk

[2] Department of Computing Science, Chalmers University of Technology, SE-412 96, Göteborg, Sweden
kemp@cs.chalmers.se

Abstract. As new semantic web standards evolve to allow quantified rules in FOL, we need new ways to capture them from end users in RDFS(XML). We show how to do this against a graphic view of Entities and their Relationships (associated or derived). This even allows inclusion of existential quantifiers in readable fashion. The captured constraint can be tested by generating queries to search for violations in stored data. The constraint can then be automatically revised to exclude specific cases picked out by the user, who is spared worries about proper syntax and boolean connectives.

1 Introduction

As new semantic web standards evolve to allow quantified rules in First Order Logic (FOL), we need new ways to capture them from end users, with names and terms taken from a specific ontology or data model. We concentrate on domain-specific constraints, such as the constraint that "the age of a pupil's teacher must exceed 21" expressed in FOL as:

$$(\forall p)\ pupil(p) \Rightarrow ((\forall a,t)\ teacherof(t,p) \wedge age(t,a) \Rightarrow a>21)$$

Extensions to an XML based syntax (FOL RuleML) to capture this, with explicit *forall* and *exists* quantifiers, are under discussion by W3C [1]. This format is, of course, intended for exchanging rules between computer systems, not for direct human readability. What we need is a way to generate them, by a sound theory, from a declarative and more readable expression of the constraints, e.g. for the above constraint:

```
constrain each p in pupil
    so that each t in teacherof(p) has age(t) > 21;
```

The functional form `teacherof(p)` would be written as `p.teacherof` in Java or SQL. However, such variations in syntax can easily be changed to suit end-user

[1] http://www.w3.org/Submission/2005/SUBM-FOL-RuleML-20050411/

S. Staab and V. Svatek (Eds.): EKAW 2006, LNAI 4248, pp. 19–26, 2006.

preference, since the captured version is in RDFS. For convenience, we modified a version of the constraint language CoLan which was used in the KRAFT project [4] to describe both design constraints and small-print constraints (extracted from product databases).

Note that we are not concerned just with simple constraints that can be captured easily by filling slots in forms, or columns in tables, since they usually refer just to the range bounds for a single attribute, e.g. "the age of a pupil must be between 12 and 17". Instead, we consider complex constraints, which may have several named attributes and variables with different quantifiers, for example: *each guidance teacher over 30 must be assigned at least one pupil.* This constraint uses entities of the types *teacher* and *pupil*, but uses an existential quantifier *exists at least one* for the *pupil* instead of the universal quantifier *for each* used with *teacher.* These differences are subtle, and require a background in predicate logic in order to spot them. Natural language programs are not yet good at recognising them and their many different equivalents.

Because of the key role of entity types (like *teacher*), which are connected to other entity types through *relationships* or associations (like *be assigned*), we needed to build an interactive graphical user interface to help an end user to visualise the entities and relationships involved. This *relationship graph* gave us something on which the user could point and click, and build up the constraint through well-formed intermediates, so that they could not possibly enter a constraint that used terms outside the ontology, or that would fail a syntax check or type check.

This overcomes a problem that often fatally discourages end-users of a formal language; they write something that looks plausible but the machine rejects it with a confusing comment. Instead, we generate only well-formed constraints, in stages. We even provide the means, described later, to test it against data. Some might argue that the real challenge for KA is to discover the constraint from data by Machine Learning. However, this is very hard for such complex constraints, and we need to bear in mind that scientists often have rich background knowledge about their data, and its experimental conditions, that may not be illustrated in the sample data. Thus it is worth providing a means to help them capture it in a form unfamiliar to them, which we require to be mathematically manipulable and web compatible.

We believe this use of a relationship graph is crucial to capturing complex FOL constraints. Its use in database schema design is of course well known, since over 30 years ago. More recently it is used in the well known UML Class Diagram, where it has been extended to include entity subclasses and cardinality information, just as we have it.

We had already pioneered using a relationship graph in a previous interactive query builder [3]. However, it was initially unclear how to present FOL visually to the user, and how to deal with the features of existential quantifiers. Further, for any captured constraint, we needed also to create a query that would compute the set of combinations of instances that violated it (hopefully empty). Here, as we show later, the use of well-formed set expressions and boolean connectives with quantifiers made this straightforward and sound. If we had used a language looking more like SQL we would have come up against many hard syntactic oddities and special cases, besides working at a low symbolic level instead of the higher (data format independent) knowledge level.

In addition to relationships that are stored in the database, the interface can also shows *derived relationships* on an entity-relationship diagram which enables the user to formulate constraints involving these. We demonstrate this with examples [6], based on the Biomolecular Interaction Network Database (BIND) [2]. This contains data about biomolecular interactions, complexes and pathways. Several key relationships between entity sets in the BIND database are not declared explicitly in the XML DTD file, but they can be defined in our algebraic language (currently by a database curator) for computation on demand. To illustrate this point, the DTD does not specify an explict relationship between *BIND_Pathway* and *BIND_Interaction*. However, the attribute *pathway* for the "epidermal growth factor" entity is {116, 118, 145, 148, 167, 1444, 1448, 1451} where these integers are the identifiers, i.e. the iids, of instances of *BIND_Interaction*. This attribute can be used to define a function relating pathway objects p to sets of interaction objects i:

```
define pathway_interactions(p in BIND_Pathway) ->> BIND_Interaction
  i in BIND_Interaction such that iid(i) in pathway(p);
```

This derived relationship is shown as the labelled arc *pathway_interactions* in the diagram in Figure 1. The end user needs some such arcs to navigate and capture constraints. Other examples in [2] illustrate the mathematical richness of the set operations used in defining these derived functions.

The design principles of our interactive graphical interface and its use in formulating universally quantified constraints are described in section 2. Its extension to support existential quantifiers is described in section 3. Related work involving visualisation and capture of integrity constraints is discussed in section 4 and the contributions of this paper are summarised in section 5.

2 Design Approach

2.1 Key Principles

The constraints are built incrementally using a major extension of a previous query builder [3] and continuing to use its two essential principles, which are widely applicable. The first was to have both a graphical depiction of the data model, in the style of an ER diagram or UML Class diagram, and an expanding textual description of the query, which was hyperlinked to the ER diagram, as shown in Figure 1. Thus the user can click on text which highlights the graphic object or vice versa. Note that the diagram is generated directly from textual schema declarations, and the user can drag the entities to get the diagram looking how they want.

[2] *http://www.csd.abdn.ac.uk/~pgray/ekaw2006extended.pdf*

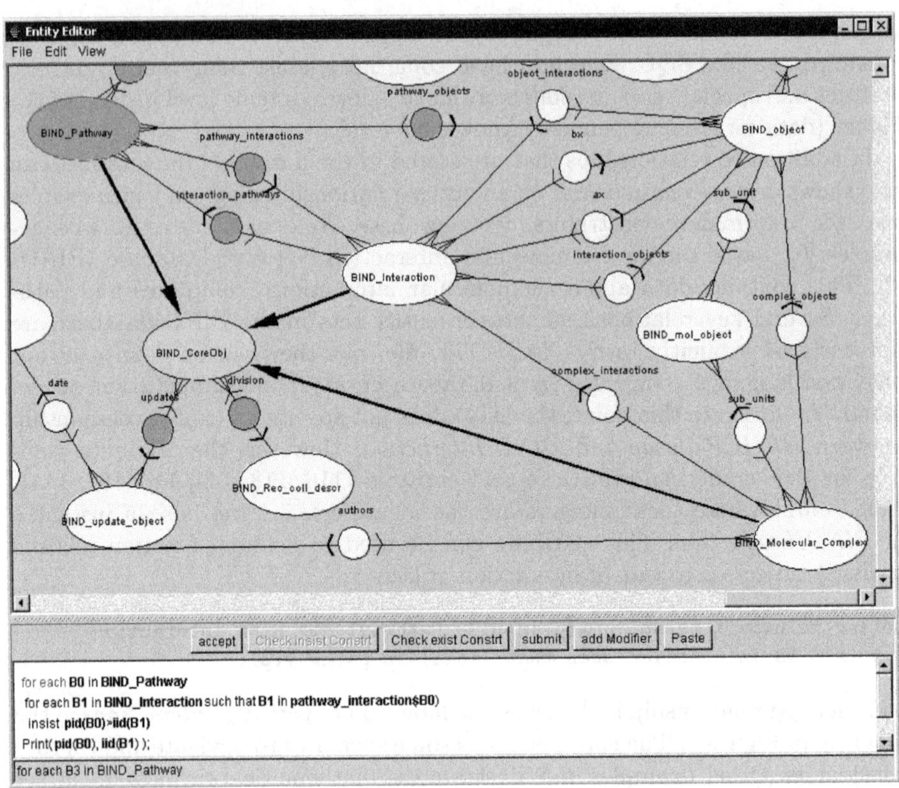

Fig. 1. Part of the BIND schema as an ER diagram. Thick arrows connect entity types to their subclasses. Labelled arcs show stored or derived relationships.

The second principle was to build the query incrementally, with opportunities to inspect intermediate results. Typically, a step involves adding a line to the query that brings in *another variable* ranging over a related entity type. This can only be done by clicking on a *relationship arc* starting from the current entity type in the ER diagram. This corresponds in SQL to adding an extra variable to the FROM clause. However, we make the user click on the relationship to help them see the data semantics, whereas frame-based systems such as Protégé) often do not distinguish relationships from other named attributes. In Figure 1 one can see examples of different relationships defined between the same pair of entity types. Also, observe relationship `division` on class BIND_CoreObj which is *inherited* by its subclasses (such as BIND_Interaction), so the GUI treats a click on the `division` relationship arc accordingly. As usual, any constraint captured on a superclass also applies to its subclasses.

The user may also extend the current query line with *restrictive filters*. These may involve comparisons with attribute values, computed expressions, subset-inclusion and set-membership tests. At any stage, one can undo a step or else choose to print extra attributes of any of the variables in the query so far. Thus, at every stage, the user is sure that the query or constraint they have so far generated is syntactically correct, and refers to items named in the ontology.

2.2 Adding an Insist Clause

In order to adapt the query generator to generate a constraint, (which is just a query delivering an invariant True value), we added an extra user action through the *Insist* button. This generates a line with the keyword **insist** followed by an empty box, which will specify the constrained expression to be held true. The keyword distinguishes it from a query and is easier for most users to understand than an implication in FOL, although it is isomorphic to it. It also allows them to think in terms of nested loops familiar to scientists and programmers.

The user then clicks on the empty box, to bring up an expression builder which helps them to fill in the box with known variables and ontology items. Thus, the constraint that the pid assigned to a BIND_Pathway must have a higher value than any of the iid values of the BIND_Interactions that make up that pathway would be as in Figure 1:

```
for each B0 in BIND_Pathway
  for each B1 in BIND_Interaction such that
    B1 in pathway_interactions(B0)
      insist pid(B0)>iid(B1)
        print(pid(B0),iid(B1));
```

The keyword `insist` captures the intention that, for the set of values of B0 and B1 selected by the enclosing loops, the boolean expression following insist has to be true. When the user is happy with the constraint, they can press the *Submit* button. This generates a query to find any *counterexamples* to the constraint, listing the values from the *print* statement in columns in a separate 'results' window. The constraint can then be revised using the built-in query editor facilities. Finally, when there are no counterexamples, a *Write Constraint* button is enabled which the user can press in order to capture and save the constraint in CoLan and XML form.

2.3 Using the Copy-and-Paste Facility

If one is searching a large amount of representative data, and a few counterexamples show up which are typical of a special case to be excluded, then the expert user may just click on these combinations, and ask for the correct boolean filter to be added to the constraint. Thus the following, apparently complex piece of FOL can be generated just by clicking on two data values:

```
for each B0 in BIND_Pathway
  for each B1 in BIND_object such that ...
    ... and not((pid(B0)=13042) and
                (short_label(B1)="GTP"))
```

This works for both *and* and *or* and for multiple values. Effectively they are controlling a rudimentary form of case-based adaptation, but are saved from struggling with boolean expression syntax.

3 Dealing with Existential Constraints

The next challenge is to include existential quantifiers such as:
Each Molecular Complex must be related through a BIND_object to interactions on its interaction list.

$(\forall B0)\ Molecular\_Complex(B0) \Rightarrow (\forall B1)\ complex\_objects(B0,B1) \Rightarrow ((\exists B2,I,L)\ object\_interactions(B1,B2) \wedge iid(B2,I) \wedge interaction\_list(B0,L) \wedge I\ in\ L)$

Following the approach of the insist construct, we define an *insist exist* construct which introduces an existentially quantified variable ranging over an entity type followed by *such that* specifying the relationship and (optionally) a boolean expression as used in the *insist* construct. We can then build the above constraint as:

```
for each BO in BIND_Molecular_Complex
 for each B1 in BIND_object such that B1 in complex_objects(BO)
   insist exist B2 in BIND_Interaction
    such that B2 in object_interactions(B1)
     and iid(B2) in interaction_list(BO);
```

We can easily extend this to several enclosing levels of *for each.* The *insist exist* construct introduces the last and innermost variable in the constraint (B2 in this case). This variable has to be connected by some relationship arc to one of the earlier variables (here B1 or B0). This differentiates it from the *insist* construct, where we do not introduce another variable.

Once again, we can algebraically manipulate the constraint to generate a query searching for counter examples:

```
for each ...
 for each e1 in entity such that ... and
  (no e in entity such that e in rel(e1) and (<predicate>) exists)
    print(...);
```

Because standard boolean algebra is being used, this still works correctly even when <predicate> includes several combinations of *and* and *or* inserted by copy and paste (as described above).

4 Discussion and Related Work

Although GUI builders for SQL are quite common, it is very unusual to see them related to an ER diagram. However, we believe relationships are crucial because they are the glue that links the different entity variables together. Thus, in order to introduce an extra variable quantified over an entity type, the user has to find an arc in the ER diagram relating that entity type to one already introduced.

One of our design aims, from early experience, was to eliminate the need for a user to key in brackets, partly because this might change expression meaning in subtle ways, and also because it might need extra levels of sub-expression builder which are confusing. Thus any existential quantifier must be on the right of the last implication. Likewise, any arithmetic expressions must have an unbracketed sequence of terms, but the constraint may include well formed bracketed terms generated by copy and paste. More complex formulae are rare, and can be pre-stored as a derived function.

Colan can express Cardinality Constraints by e.g. *constrain at most 2 x in D to ...* but we do not yet include such quantifiers in our GUI. [3]

Recently the developers of the Protégé-2000 system [8] have introduced a Protégé Axiom Language (PAL) also based on Predicate Logic, and using their frame-based data model. Recent papers show how it can be used to check consistency of the Gene Ontology [9]. It is with the arrival of such systems as Protégé and FOL RuleML that there will come a need to formulate and test increasingly complex constraints. Currently Protégé has neither a GUI builder for PAL, nor any means to query an instance of the knowledge base for counterexamples, such as we provide.

5 Conclusions

Recent developments, such as FOL RuleML and Protégé PAL, allow rules in FOL to be transformed and interchanged between different intelligent systems on the Semantic Web. We believe that capturing complex domain-specific constraints as rules requires the user to be able to relate them to a diagram showing *relationships* (derived or stored associations), to build them in stages (with the option to undo edits) and to be able to express *quantifiers* in a simple consistent fashion, as used in FOL. Thus we need graphic aids to help experts, particularly scientists; we cannot routinely learn such rules from often incomplete data.

We have shown a systematic and novel way to do this, by using an analogy with the familiar concept of nested loops, which makes a visual correspondence between quantifiers and relationships in the ER diagram. This has been implemented and tested and made available.[4] It includes the option at each stage to find counterexamples by runnning the embryo constraint against remote databases. Values from these can then be fed back by *copy-and-paste* to refine the constraint.

We have transformation programs [5,7] that can take the output and turn it into XML(RDFS) constructs which completely capture the ER diagram. The system is Data Independent, in that its abstract form applies across a wide range of data storage systems. Also it is independent of any program language; instead

[3] Full CoLan syntax at *http://www.csd.abdn.ac.uk/~pfdm/colan_syntax.html*

[4] software downloadable from *http://www.csd.abdn.ac.uk/~pgray/*

we give quantified formulae in FOL which can be mathematically transformed and combined with others across the web [4].

Acknowledgements

This work extends the GUI implemented by Ignacio Gil. The schema and data used in this work were derived from BIND DTD and XML files by Selpi. Related work [1,7] at Aberdeen is supported by EPSRC (GR/N15764) under the Advanced Knowledge Technologies (AKT) Collaboration.

References

1. S. Ajit, D. Sleeman, D.W. Fowler, and D. Knott. ConEditor: Tool to Input and Maintain Constraints. In E. Motta, N. Shadbolt, A. Stutt, and N. Gibbins, editors, *EKAW 2004, Proceedings*, volume 3257 of *LNCS*, pages 466–468. Springer, 2004.
2. G.D. Bader, D. Betel, and C.W.V. Hogue. BIND: the Biomolecular Interaction Network Database. *Nucleic Acids Research*, 31:248–250, 2003.
3. I. Gil, P.M.D. Gray, and G.J.L. Kemp. A Visual Interface and Navigator for the P/FDM Object Database. In N.W. Paton and T. Griffiths, editors, *Proceedings of User Interfaces to Data Intensive Systems (UIDIS'99)*, pages 54–63. IEEE Computer Society Press, 1999.
4. P.M.D. Gray, S.M. Embury, K.Y. Hui, and G.J.L. Kemp. The Evolving Role of Constraints in the Functional Data Model. *J. Intelligent Information Systems*, 12:113–137, 1999.
5. P.M.D. Gray, K. Hui, and A.D. Preece. An Expressive Constraint Language for Semantic Web Applications. In A. Preece and D. O'Leary, editors, *E-Business and the Intelligent Web: Papers from the IJCAI-01 Workshop*, pages 46–53. AAAI Press, 2001.
6. G.J.L. Kemp and Selpi. Pathway and Protein Interaction Data: from XML to FDM Database. In E. Rahm, editor, *Data Integration in the Life Sciences, First International Workshop, DILS 2004, Proceedings*, volume 2994 of *LNCS*, pages 212–219. Springer, 2004.
7. C. McKenzie, P.M.D. Gray, and A.D. Preece. Extending SWRL to Express Fully-Quantified Constraints. In G. Antoniou and H. Boley, editors, *Rules and Rule Markup Languages for the Semantic Web: Third International Workshop, RuleML 2004, Hiroshima, Japan, November 8, 2004. Proceedings*, volume 3323 of *LNCS*, pages 139–154. Springer, 2004.
8. N.F. Noy, R.W. Fergerson, and M.A. Musen. The Knowledge Model of Protégé-2000: Combining Interoperability and Flexibility. In R. Dieng and O. Corby, editors, *Knowledge Acquisition, Modeling and Management, EKAW 2000 Proceedings*, volume 1937 of *LNCS*, pages 17–32. Springer, 2000.
9. I. Yeh, P.D. Karp, N.F. Noy, and R.B. Altman. Knowledge acquisition, consistency checking and concurrency control for Gene Ontology (GO). *Bioinformatics*, 19(2):241–248, 2003.

Assisting Domain Experts to Formulate and Solve Constraint Satisfaction Problems

Derek Sleeman and Stuart Chalmers

Department of Computing Science, University of Aberdeen,
Aberdeen, AB24 3UE, Scotland, UK
{sleeman, schalmer}@csd.abdn.ac.uk

Abstract. Constraint satisfaction is a powerful approach to solving a wide class of problems. However, as many non-experts have difficulties formulating tasks as Constraint Satisfaction Problems (CSPs), we have built a number of interfaces for particular kinds of CSPs, including crypt-arithmetic problems, map-colouring problems, and scheduling tasks, which ask highly focused questions of the user, c.f., the earlier MOLE/MORE, and SALT knowledge acquisition systems. Information from each of these interfaces is then transformed initially into a structured format which is semantic web compliant and is secondly transformed into the format required by the generic constraint satisfaction problem solver. When this problem solver is run, the user is either provided with solution(s) or feedback that the problem is underspecified (when many solutions are feasible) or over-specified (when no solution is possible). The system has 3 distinct phases, namely; information capture, transformation of the information to that used by a standard problem solver, and thirdly the solving and user feedback phase.

1 Introduction

Constraint Satisfaction constitutes a powerful approach to problem solving, and over the last decade or so a range of tools have been implemented [4,7]. However, there are distinct skills involved in formulating tasks as CSP problems, the so called modelling problem. The format required by the solvers is deceptively simple: one has to specify a set of relevant variables, their domain values, and constraints between the variables. However the modelling process is still seen as challenging because the problem is often specified in a verbal form (eg as brain teasers), and it is the modeller's task to decide the relevant variables, the ranges associated with each variable, and most challengingly the constraints (relationships) which exist between the identified variables [8].

This paper addresses the modelling problem mentioned early by implementing a series of interfaces which ask for specific information about particular types of CSPs, e.g. map-colouring, cryptarithmetic problems and scheduling. This information is then transformed into representational schema currently used on the web, namely an OWL[1] ontology (for the domain knowledge) and CIF/SWRL [2] rules for the constraints. As we shall see this is further transformed into the representation required by a generic constraint satisfaction solver.

[1] www.w3.org/TR/owl-features/

[2] www.csd.abdn.ac.uk/research/akt/cif/

S. Staab and V. Svatek (Eds.): EKAW 2006, LNAI 4248, pp. 27–34, 2006.

One of the aims of this project is to produce a UI which corresponds to each of the types of CSPs (see section 4.2 for details). We then plan to produce a more generic UI which will handle a number of different CSP task types.

The overall architecture of the system implemented has 3 components. The role of the first is to CAPTURE information about a particular task, the second is to transform that information / knowledge into a form which a generic Constraint Problem Solver can use, and the third solves the task and reports the results to the user. We made a conscious decision to use OWL and SWRL as representational formalisms, as then it is, in principle, possible to augment the information created in the interfaces by other knowledge sources available on the web.

The rest of the paper is organized as follows: section 2 gives an introduction to CSPs; Section 3 gives a conceptual overview of the 3-staged system implemented; section 4 discusses a classification of CSPs and describes Knowledge Acquisition (KA) interfaces built for some of these types/classes; section 5 describes the implementation of a CSP solver; section 6 outlines future work and describes some related work.

2 Formulating Tasks as CSPs

CSPs have 3 aspects, namely (i) variables which are associated with (ii) domains (i.e. ranges of values) and (iii) the actual constraint expressions. Below we give examples of all 3 components:

$$\mathtt{a} \mapsto \mathtt{D_1\{0..5\}}, \mathtt{b} \mapsto \mathtt{D_2\{0..5\}}, \mathtt{c} \mapsto \mathtt{D_3\{0..5\}}$$

The above states that the variables a, b and c can be assigned any of the corresponding values given in the domains D_1, D_2, D_3 respectively. The following constraints, C1 and C2, restrict the possible assignments that the variables can take.

$$\mathtt{C1: a-b} > \mathtt{c}, \mathtt{C2: a*c} < \mathtt{b}$$

Given these constraints, the assignments of possible values are now restricted to:

$$\mathtt{a} \mapsto \mathtt{D_1\{2..5\}}, \mathtt{b} \mapsto \mathtt{D_2\{1..4\}}, \mathtt{c} \mapsto \mathtt{D_3\{0..1\}}$$

In general, a constraint satisfaction problem (CSP) is the process of satisfying a given set of statements by restricting the assignments of a given set of variables.

3 Main Aspects of the System: A Conceptual Architecture

Previous projects in constraint modelling (see section 6) have focused on creating new meta-languages for specifying problems [4] or have required the user to model the CSP task using an existing representation formalism e.g. UML and OCL [7]. Here we are focusing on classifying the types of CSP problems which exist, with a view to creating an interface for each type to enable the non-CSP specialist to communicate the essence of their task. For some CSP tasks it is clear the nature of the interface required, e.g. Map–colouring problems or Cryptarithmetic problems (of the form SEND + MORE = MONEY) whereas the differences between Scheduling / Configuration / Assignment /

Constraints / Positioning are in general much more subtle, and will need some further analysis before helpful distinctions can be made. (In fact, as noted in section 4.2, the Cryptarithmetic and Map–colouring tasks are both members of the Assignment class).

The general inspiration for this approach is the Knowledge Acquisition (KA) work done in the early 80's when several groups realised that KA could be made more focused if one acquires knowledge for a particular purpose. The MOLE [2] and MORE [5] systems, for instance, acquired knowledge which would support only classification/diagnosis and thus only needed to capture the several diagnostic classes and the corresponding diagnostic rules. Similarly, the SALT KA system [6] was designed to acquire knowledge to support the propose–and–revise algorithm and so elicited 3 types of knowledge/information from the domain expert namely:

- procedural knowledge to specify how an existing entity (such as a motor) could be enhanced/changed
- constraints to specify relationships which must or must not hold between variables
- fixes: what to do if a particular constraint is violated.

So the argument then is that a KA interface will be implemented for each of the classes of CSPs which will ask relevant focused questions. (We will address later the taxing question of how a non-CSP expert can choose the relevant KA interface for a particular problem they wish to solve.) In fact as figure 1 shows, we have conceptualised the task of formulating and solving CSP as three phases:

- CAPTURING the essence of the task (outlined above & discussed in section 4)
- TRANSFORMING the task from the information collected from each interface to a common formalism. In fact, we have chosen SWRL and OWL, emerging WWW standards, so that the information acquired can, in principle, be enhanced by other Web based Knowledge Sources.
- SOLVING & Providing User Feedback. The final phase attempts to solve the task and either provides the user with a result or information which indicates that the task is over- or under - specified.

4 Capturing Information: Creating KA Interfaces

4.1 Model Generation vs. Model Selection

Systems such as a CONJURE [4] provide the non-CSP expert with a high-level language in which to formulate the task s/he wishes to solve. This approach has the advantage of allowing a wide range of problems to be specified (in principle) but the disadvantage that it gives the user little guidance. We refer to this as the Model Generation approach. By contrast we refer to the approach being followed here as the model selection approach. Conceptually, at least we can think of this approach as providing the user with a series of templates (one corresponding to each of the CSP classes or perhaps subclasses). Each template has a number of slots which the user has to complete. If a user is able to provide a consistent set of responses to all the slots associated with a template, then we shall say that this task corresponds to that CSP class (e.g. Assignment). In practice we believe that this part of the system will be implemented as a

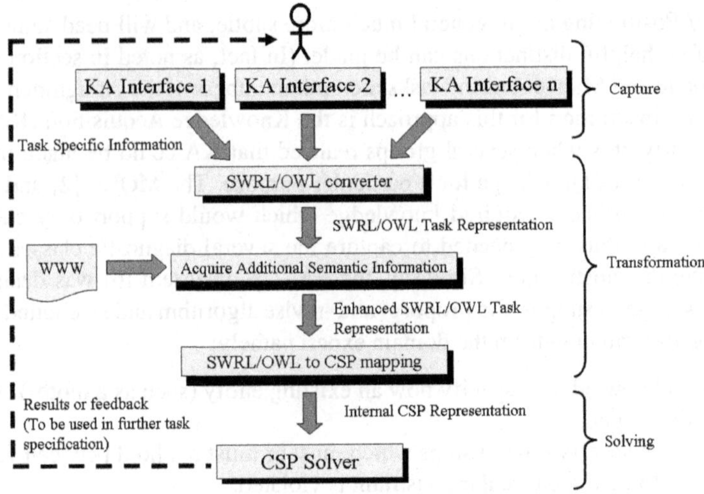

Fig. 1. Conceptual System Design showing 3 principal phases

series of "linked templates", so that at any stage of the specification of a task, it will be possible to specify:

- which classes have been ruled out (because certain information is *not* available)
- which classes are currently completely satisfied (could be null)
- which information is needed, to satisfy the remaining possible classes

4.2 Classes of CSP Tasks

As mentioned in section 3, we are interested in describing the number of CSPs in sufficient detail, so that we can identify distinctive classes and sub-classes. Miguel et. al[3], in their work with ESSENCE and CONJURE, have introduced a classification and suggest the following definitions:

- Scheduling - characterised by assigning start times to a series of tasks that have to be performed by some deadline with the possibility of precedence constraints between them (e.g. process A must be completed before process B can start).
- Configuration - where the problem involves assigning a unique value to a variable according to constraints between the values and their variables.
- Assignment - similar to configuration problems, but the assignment of values to variables is not a one-to-one relationship. Subsets of this class include permutation and partitioning problems.
- Construction - the object is to construct a set of variables according to a goal (such as maximising the values assigned to the set of variables). Constraints here can be on the membership of this set, and on the position of the variable in that set.

[3] http://www.cs.york.ac.uk/aig/constraints/AutoModel/Essence/Tree/

- Positioning - involve arranging objects according to spatial/geometric constraints. Typically all objects must lie within a boundary and objects are not permitted to overlap (where these restrictions are specified as a series of constraints).

Generally, we can classify each problem type by the relationship between the Variables (described as Objects by Miguel) and Assigned Domain Values (defined as Labels). For instance, in permutation problems each label is used only once (effectively saying that the values assigned to a set of variables must all be different), whereas with partitioning problems the actual assignment of the label value is unimportant, but what is important are the groups of variables which have the same values.

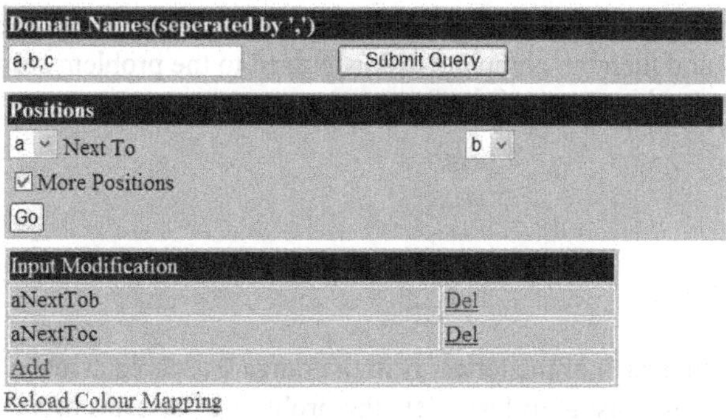

Fig. 2. The Map–colouring KA Interface

4.3 Implemented KA Interfaces

In the previous sub-section we discussed in some detail a classification for CSPs. Here we outline 2 User Interfaces which we have recently developed, namely:

- A Mapping task (this being a subset of the assignment class)
- A Cryptarithmetic Problem (which is a particular kind of assignment task)

A screen shot for the Mapping interface is given in Figure 2. The map colouring task specifies a number of physical areas (eg countries, counties, areas of a town) and specifies that adjacent areas should have **different** colours. So the task involves specifying the set of colours available, and the adjacency relationships between the several areas. A solution to the problem is one where all the adjacent areas have different colours. So for example if the objects to be assigned a colour are the 4 counties of the SouthWest of England, namely: Cornwall, Devon, Somerset & Dorset, and the relationships between the 4 objects are as given in the left hand diagram in figure 3, and the 3 colours to be assigned are white, grey & black, then the right hand figure would be an acceptable solution. The UI in figure 2 used to collect information about the task, initially asks the user to provide the names of the 4 objects (top left hand corner), then the user is asked to indicate the spatial relationships between the objects (this is done in the window called Positions), at which point the system allows the user to revise the relationships provided

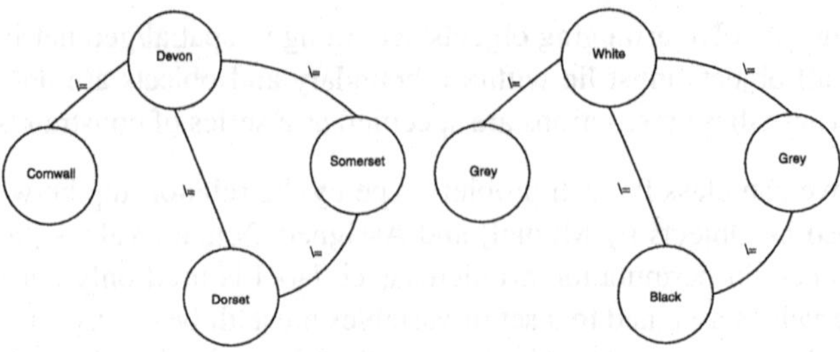

Fig. 3. An example Map Colouring Specification and solution

until they are happy with the resulting model. Finally, the system asks the user for the available colours, and then the complete task is passed to the problem solver.

Cryptarithmetic problems are of the form:

```
 CROSS +
 ROADS
 ------
DANGER
 ------
```

Where one is told that each of the letters is in the range `0..9`, each letter has a distinct value, and `D`$\neq$`0`. So it is usual to formulate the problem as a series of variables (in the case of this task: `C, R, O, S, A, D, N, G` & `E`). Note in this case the 2 entities are to be **added** to give the result DANGER. In formulating the main constraint for this problem we need to remember the significance/semantics of a column in an arithmetic task. The right hand column consists of units, the adjacent column represents units of 10s, and the next column represents 100s, etc. Bearing this in mind the main constraint can be expressed as[4]: 10000*C + 10000*R + 1000*R + 1000*O + 100*O + 100*A + 10*S + 10*D + S + S = 100000*D + 10000*A + 1000*N + 100*G + 10*E + R

The KA interface which we have implemented for this type of problem allows the user to input a wide range of cryptarithmetic problems; to date we have implemented both addition & subtraction tasks.

5 Solving: The CSP Implementation

A major design decision behind the implementation of this solver was to make the solving process freely available as a re-usable component. To this end, we have developed the CSP as a web service with an open queryable interface. We use AXIS[5] as the platform, with the interface defined using a combination of OWL–lite to represent the variables and their domains and CIF/SWRL to represent the actual constraints[6]. We also implement a number of parsing algorithms, to support the following information flow:

[4] There are 2 further constraints: `C`>`0`, `R`>`0`.

[5] http://ws.apache.org/axis/

[6] For a detailed description of the design and capabilities of the semantic interface implementation, see Aberdeen University Computing Science Technical Report AUCS/TR0604.

KA Interface $\mapsto$ CIF/SWRL + OWL $\mapsto$ CHOCO Solver data structures

For the principal classes of CSPs covered here, we have written a generalised finite domain constraint solver in CHOCO[7]. To formulate a problem in CHOCO we create a finite domain CSP instance. We then use mapping rules for each CIF/SWRL construct to transform the CIF/SWRL representation into CSP constraints.

6 Discussion and Future Work

A number of projects have looked at the problem of CSP modelling. An approach taken by [4] is to provide a high–level language, ESSENCE, for specifying CSP problems. This language is then translated into a CSP by a system, CONJURE, that refines the specification. Renker [7] uses UML and OCL to provide a modelling framework for constraints. Alternative approaches include Fish et. al [1] who look at diagrammatic modelling of constraints using "spider diagrams", a formalisation based on Venn diagrams.

We plan to evaluate the web-based KA interfaces for the cryptarithmetic and mapping problems. We will compare the numbers of tasks formulated and the average time taken by two groups namely one doing the task using pen-and-paper and the other using the CSP interfaces. We will also administer a questionnaire about how the interfaces could be enhanced. A further aim of our future work is to implement a KA interface for each of the CSP types identified in section 4.2, and then to link them so as to reduce the number of questions that a user needs to answer.

Another major issue we wish to explore is that of providing user feedback on problems to help with remodelling and repair. When a user specifies a set of constraints on a problem, there may be no solution returned for that set as the problem is over–constrained. In such circumstances, constraint relaxation [3] techniques aim to partially solve a given problem by maximizing the number of constraints applied. Alternatively, we may find a problem under-defined (i.e. there are a vast number of possible valid solutions) where we may wish to elicit more information from the user to constrain the problem further.

Our CSP implementation is based on a simple generalised finite domain solver, so we are not be able to solve the range of problems that a language such as ESSENCE can support. While it is not our intention to do this, we do wish to classify the subset of problems which can be solved as well as explore the representation of CSPs using existing semantic web technology. As discussed earlier in the paper, there were several motivations for using a semantic-web compliant representation for the CSP. The principal issues still to be investigated, is whether it is possible to exploit the fact that the intermediary representation of the CSPs is OWL and CIF/SWRL, by enhancing the initial user-provided information about a task with relevant information available from the semantic web [9].

In this paper, we have described a set of user interfaces to aid in the formulation of tasks as CSPs. We have described our representation of the CSPs using semantic web technology, namely OWL for variable and domain representation and CIF/SWRL for

[7] http://choco.sourceforge.net/

representing constraints. We have also described the flow of information, from the KA interfaces, to a semantic web representation and finally to the native constraint solving language.

Acknowledgments

This work is supported by the Advanced Knowledge Technologies (AKT)[8] Interdisciplinary Research Collaboration (IRC), which is sponsored by the UK Engineering and Physical Sciences Research Council (EPSRC). The AKT IRC comprises the Universities of Aberdeen, Edinburgh, Sheffeld, Southampton, and the Open University. The authors are also grateful to Lin Lin and Xuezhou Yuan, who provided the implementation of the web service gateway plus the CIF/SWRL transformation tools.

References

1. Fish A. and Flower J. Investigating reasoning with constraint diagrams. In *VLFM04, Visual Languages and Formal Methods*, volume 127, pages 53–69. Elsevier, Rome, April 2005.
2. L Eshelman. Mole: a knowledge-acquisition tool for cover-and-differentiate systems. In S. Marcus (Ed.), editor, *Automating Knowledge Acquisition for Expert Systems*, pages 37–80. Kluwer Academic, Norwood, Mass, 1988.
3. Eugene C. Freuder. Partial Constraint Satisfaction. In *Proceedings of the Eleventh International Joint Conference on Artificial Intelligence, IJCAI-89, Detroit, Michigan, USA*, pages 278–283, 1989.
4. A.M. Frisch, M. Grum, C. Jefferson, B. Martinez-Hernandez, and I. Miguel. The essence of essence: A constraint language for specifying combinatorial problems. In *Proceedings of the 4th International Workshop on Modelling and Reformulating Constraint Satisfaction Problems*, pages 73–88, 2005.
5. G Kahn. More: From observing knowledge engineers to automating knowledge acquisition. In S. Marcus, editor, *Automating Knowledge acquisition for Expert Systems*, pages 7–35. Kluwer Academic, 1988.
6. Sandra Marcus and John McDermott. Salt: a knowledge acquisition language for propose-and-revise systems. *Artif. Intell.*, 39(1):1–37, 1989.
7. Gerrit Renker. A modeling framework for constraints. In *8th International Conference on Constraint Programming*, pages 8–13, September 2002.
8. Barbara Smith. A tutorial on constraint programming. Technical Report 95.14, School of Computing Research Report, University of Leeds, April April 1995.
9. Yi Zhang, Wamberto Vasconcelos, and Derek Sleeman. Ontosearch: An ontology search engine. In *The Twenty-fourth SGAI International Conference on Innovative Techniques and Applications of Artificial Intelligence*, Cambridge, 2004.

[8] http://www.aktors.org

Knowledge Acquisition Evaluation Using Simulated Experts

Tri M. Cao and Paul Compton

School of Computer Science and Engineering
University of New South Wales
Sydney 2052 , Australia
{tmc, compton}@cse.unsw.edu.au

Abstract. Evaluation of knowledge acquisition (KA) is difficult in general because of the costs of using a human expert. In this paper, we use a general simulation framework to evaluate some aspects of KA. We focus on the importance of acquiring domain ontological structures and the use of stored or cornerstone cases to validate changes. We find that the for a higher level of expertise, an ontology is very useful, but cornerstone cases less so, but the weaker the level of expertise, the more valuable the cornerstone cases and the less helpful an ontology.

1 Introduction

Evaluation of KA tools and methodologies is difficult [7,9]. The essential problem is the cost of human expertise to build a KBS. A solution to this is the use of simulated experts in evaluation studies. A simulated expert is not as creative or wise as a human expert, but it readily allows for control experiments. We have previously described simulations using machine learning data sets [4], but the simulations then depend on the structure of domain. In the work here we use a more abstract simulation. The framework for this is described in [1]. In this section, we outline the main features of this framework.

We characterise an expert by two parameters: overspecialisation and overgeneralisation. Overspecialisation is the probability that a definition excludes data which it should cover. Overgeneralisation, on the other hand, is the probability that a definition includes data which it should not cover. This is depicted in Figure 1. In this figure, the human expert tries to capture a target concept by providing the system a rule or rules; however as the expert is not perfect, the defined concept deviates from target concept. The deviation can be quantified through two parameters: overspecialisation and overgeneralisation.

In classification based systems, errors of overspecialisation and overgeneralisation are often called false negative and false positive, respectively. These errors not only apply to individual classification rules, but to complex classifiers too. Moreover, they also apply to other aspects of knowledge based system. With a planning system, the KBS has error components that that cause an incorrect plan to be produced for the data provided. That is, the data was covered inappropriately; there was overgeneralisation. However, the system also failed to

S. Staab and V. Svatek (Eds.): EKAW 2006, LNAI 4248, pp. 35–42, 2006.

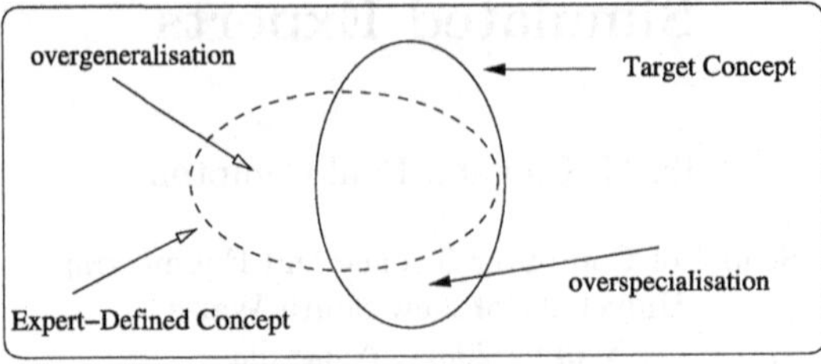

Fig. 1. Overspecialisation and overgeneralisation

cover the data correctly, and that was overspecialisation. In a similar manner, these errors also apply to ontology acquisition. The definitions of concepts, or the relations between them result in objects failing to be covered or being covered inappropriately. If an expert provides too many repeated low level definitions rather than developing abstractions, there is an overspecialisation error.

In this study, we simulate obtaining rules from the expert and so apply these errors at the rule level. A given rule may cover data for which the conclusion is not appropriate; that is, it is too general. Or the rule is too specific and so excludes some data that should be covered. The intuitive response to an overgeneralised rule is to remove conditions and for an overspecialised rule to add conditions. However, whether one does this or corrects the system in some other way depends on the KA tool or method being used.

These characterisations can be used to describe different levels of expertise (for example, experienced experts and trainees). These errors also increase with the difficulty of the domain. Trainees will be associated with higher overgeneralisation and/or overspecialisation errors than experienced experts in the domain. One major problem with previous work that used simulated experts is how to model levels of expertise. For example in [4], levels of expertise are represented by picking various subsets of the full condition. There is no such difficulty in our approach as we model the effects of different levels of expertise by using different combinations of overgeneralisation and overspecialisation.

As mentioned above, the simulation here is restricted to classification. Secondly the domain is assumed to be made up of non-overlapping regions. The minimum number of rules required is therefore the number of regions in the domain. This assumption is made for the sake of simplicity and can easily be relaxed to allow for more complex domains.

2 Knowledge Structure

We have used a very simple knowledge structures in these studies. Either simple rules where each rule make a conclusion, or rules which make an intermediate conclusion which is then refined to a final conclusion with a further rule. We assume that knowledge acquisition consist of adding rules and refining or narrowing rules. The details have been described previously in [1]. We assume that there is a stream of cases in random order and that experts add rules or correct rules to ensure the KBS provides the right classification for each case. This is motivated by our work on Ripple-Down Rules (RDR) [3,5]. Of course an expert may build a KBS off-line by imagining scenarios and creating and correcting rules, but when the KBS is put into use, correction of addition of rules will be because of the cases seen. In these simulations we simply construct the whole KB based on the cases seen. The simulation follows the same process. A case is presented to the KBS; if it is given a wrong conclusion or no conclusion a rule is added or corrected or both and the process repeated. Knowledge acquisition cost is measured simply as the number of cases for which the KBS needs to be changed. With RDR systems the time taken to correct a KBS for a case is a minute or two and does not increase or increases only slightly with KB size [5].

3 Cornerstone Cases

Cornerstone cases are data cases that trigger the creation of new rules. One of the hallmark features of RDR is the employment of cornerstone cases. They serve two purposes:

- as a means of maintaining past performance by imposing consistency
- as a guide to help the experts make up the new rules.

The cornerstone cases are used in the following manner: when a data case in misclassified by the system, an expert is consulted and asked to provide a new rule (or rules) to deal with this case. The new rule then is evaluated against all the cornerstone cases stored in the system. If any of the cornerstone cases is affected by the new rule, the expert is asked to refine it. Only when the system confirms that the new rule does not affect any of the cornerstone cases then it is added to the knowledge base, and the current data case becomes the new rule's cornerstone. In practice, the expert might decide to allow the rule to apply an existing cornerstone case, but this evaluation excludes this.

The first question for the evaluation is the importance of cornerstone cases. Or more generally, what is the importance of validating performance against test data after modifying a KBS.

3.1 Experimental Settings

The simulations here are restricted to two level of expertise:

- Good Expertise: the human expert is characterised by $(0.2, 0.2)$, i.e a rule made by this expert will include cases that it should not with probability 0.2 and exclude cases that it should cover also with probability 0.2.
- Average Expert: the human expert is characterised by $(0.3, 0.3)$.

Our naming of these levels of expertise is arbitrary; our intention is simply to distinguish higher and lower levels of expertise. With each level of expertise, we run the simulation with two options: with or without cornerstone cases. The simulation is run with 100000 data cases from a domain of 20 regions, and the number of required KA sessions is recorded.

3.2 Result and Discussion

The following figures show the number of KA acquisition sessions as a function of data cases presented to the system. As a KA is required each time a data case is misclassified, the slope of this graph can also be considered as the error rate for the acquired system.

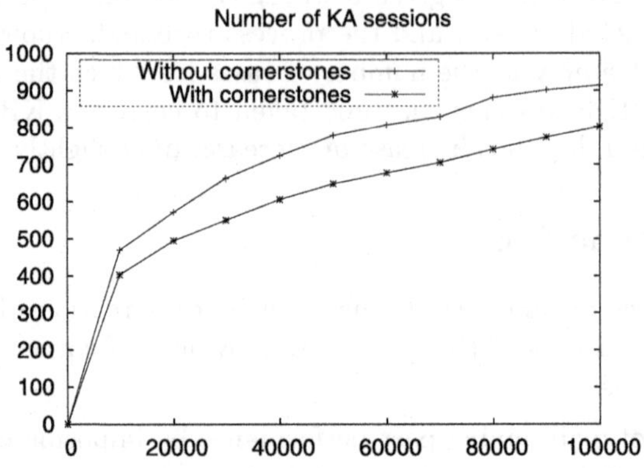

Fig. 2. Good expertise

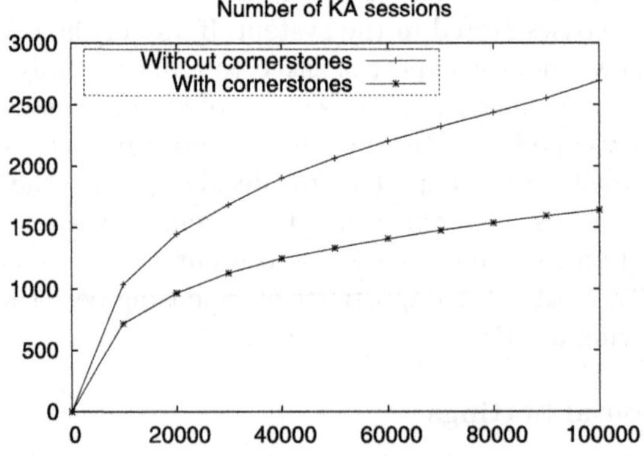

Fig. 3. Average Expertise

It can be seen from the graphs that when a good level of expertise is available, there is not much difference in the performance of the acquired knowledge base whether or not cornerstone cases are employed. However, when the available expertise is average, the system with cornerstone cases clearly outperforms the one without, in terms of the number of KA sessions (or error rate). In a KA session with the system that uses cornerstone cases, the expert is usually asked to create more primary rules. However, this is perfectly acceptable since the number of KA sessions is a better measure of human experts' time than the number of primary rules.

4 Domain Ontology Acquisition

In recent years, the use of explicit ontologies in knowledge based systems has been intensively investigated [11,6,8,10]. Heuristic classification was first introduced by [2] and remains a popular problem solving method (PSM). It can be understood as a PSM using a very simple ontological structure of intermediate conclusions. It is comprised of three main phases:

- abstraction from a concrete, particular problem description to a problem class definition that applies to
- heuristic match of a principal solution to the problem class
- refinement of the principal solution to a concrete solution for the concrete problem

This process can be seen in the following figure

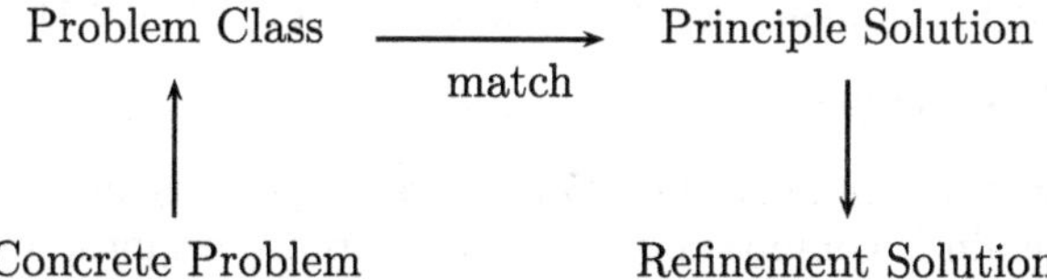

In practice, it is not always the case that all three phases of heuristic classification are employed. The example we look at in the next subsection will show how a simple taxonomy is used with classification systems.

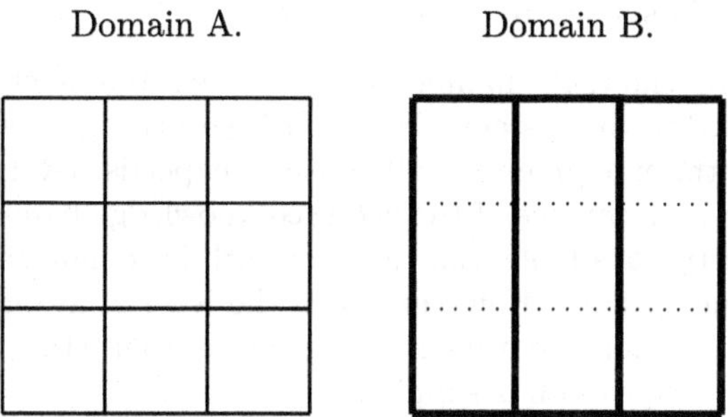

4.1 Example

We look at two domain structures as in the picture above. The task here is to acquire a classifier for this domain from human experts. There are nine elementary classifications as shown in case A. In case B, however, we assume that there is a known taxonomy of classifications: the domain is divided into three general classes and each general class contains three elementary classifications.

This taxonomy can be considered as a very simple ontology. We now describe how this explicit taxonomy of classification is used in a classification system and how we evaluate its usage.

In case A, the classifier produces one of the nine classifications. Revision of the knowledge base when a data case is misclassified is done similarly as in Section 3. On the other hand, in case B, classification is done in a two-step process. First, the classifier assigns a general class (from three classes in this particular example) to the input data. After that, the data is passed to a second sub-classifier which (based on the general class assigned) gives the sub-classification associated with this case. When there is a misclassification, the classifier (or classifiers) will be revised. As a consequence, one can argue that, revision in this case is likely to be more complex than that in case A. However, in our experiments, we still count each revision to deal with a case as a KA session.

4.2 Experiment Settings

The simulations here are restricted to two levels of expertise:

- Average Expertise: the human expert is characterised by $(0.3, 0.3)$,
- Bad Expert: the human expert is characterised by $(0.4, 0.4)$.

and two domain structures

- (A) the domain is composed of 25 non-overlapping regions
- (B) the domain is composed of 5 non-overlapping regions, and each region, in turn, is composed of 5 sub-regions.

Again, the naming of the levels of expertise is arbitrary. The simulation is run with 100000 data cases and the number of required KA sessions is recorded.

4.3 Result and Discussion

The following figures shows the number of KA sessions as a function of number of data cases presented to the system. The result is surprising because even with a fixed taxonomy in the experiments, a difference in expertise level can lead to such a difference in the performance of the acquired knowledge bases. While there is a reasonable expertise available, the classifier with a domain taxonomy clearly outperform the one without. However, when the level of available expertise is poor, performance is similar so it might be better not to use the domain ontology because knowledge acquisition is simpler.

5 Conclusion

In this paper, we use the simulation framework developed in [1] to investigate two interesting aspects of knowledge acquisition, namely, the usage of supporting data cases and explicit domain ontology. We do not claim that our model accurately reflects the real life situation, or our results quantitatively apply to the a real knowledge based system, the simulation still shows interesting observations.

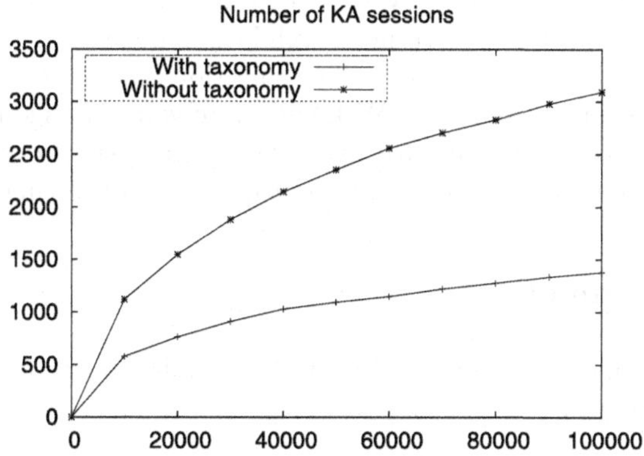

Fig. 4. Average Expertise

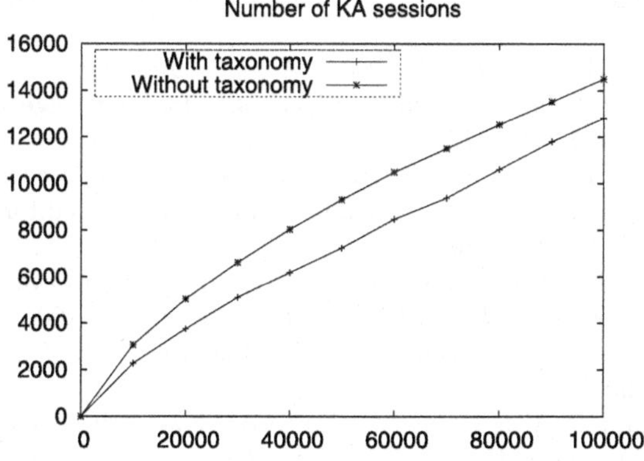

Fig. 5. Bad Expertise

We observe that the use of cornerstone cases in Ripple Down Rules system shows a real improvement of the knowledge base performance. While the expert has work a bit more at each knowledge acquisition session, the number of KA sessions will be less over time. In particular, when a high level of expertise is not available, the use of cornerstone cases significantly improves the experts' performance.

The second observation is that explicit domain ontology brings significant improvement in the resulting system's performance if high levels of expertise are available. However, explicit ontologies do not have as much positive effect when the domain is dynamic (due to its changing nature, or unestablished tacit knowledge).

Aspects of these conclusions are entirely obvious and would be accepted by all: that validation and ontologies are both useful. However, the methodology also raises the question that as we move into less well defined areas relating to personal and business preferences, validation becomes more critical while perhaps ontologies are less valuable. The question also arises that whether less certain ontologies in the Semantic Web will more value than simpler techniques.

In the future, we would like to investigate other aspects of evaluating KA: more complex domain structures or in multiple experts settings.

Acknowledgements

This work is supported by Co-operative Research Centre for Smart Internet Technologies, Australia.

References

1. T. Cao and P. Compton. A simulation framework for knowledge acquisition evaluation. In *Proceedings of 28th Australasian Computer Science Conference*, pages 353–361, 2005.
2. W. J. Clancey. Heuristic classification. *Artificial Intelligence*, 27:289–350, 1985.
3. P. Compton and R. Jansen. A philosophical basis for knowledge acquisition. *Knowledge Acquisition*, 2:241–257, 1990.
4. P. Compton, P. Preston, and B. Kang. The use of simulated experts in evaluating knowledge acquisition. In B. Gaines and M. Musen, editors, *9th Banff KAW Proceeding*, pages 1–12, 1995.
5. Paul Compton, Lindsay Peters, Glenn Edwards, and Tim Lavers. Experience with ripple-down rules. *Knowledge Based Systems*, to appear, 2006.
6. Asuncion Gomez-Perez. Evaluation of ontologies. *Int. J. Intelligent Systems*, 16:391–409, 2001.
7. T. Menzies and F. Van Hamelen. Editorial: Evaluating knowledge engineering techniques. *Journal of Human-Computer Studies*, 51(4):715–727, 1999.
8. Natalya Fridman Noy, Michael Sintek, Stefan Decker, Monica Crubézy, Ray W. Fergerson, and Mark A. Musen. Creating semantic web contents with protégé-2000. *IEEE Intelligent Systems*, 16(2):60–71, 2001.
9. N. Shadbolt and K. O'Hara. The experimental evaluation of knowledge acquisition techniques and methods: history, problem and new directions. *Journal of Human-Computer Studies*, 51(4):729–775, 1999.
10. York Sure, Asunción Gómez-Pérez, Walter Daelemans, Marie-Laure Reinberger, Nicola Guarino, and Natalya Fridman Noy. Why evaluate ontology technologies? because it works!. *IEEE Intelligent Systems*, 19(4):74–81, 2004.
11. G. van Heijst, A. Th. Schreiber, and B. J. Wielinga. Using explicit ontologies in kbs development. *Journal of Human-Computer Studies*, 45:183–292, 1997.

Stochastic Foundations for the Case-Driven Acquisition of Classification Rules

Megan Vazey[1]

[1] Department of Computing,
Division of Information and Communication Sciences,
Macquarie University,
Sydney NSW 2109
Australia
megan@excelan.com.au

Abstract. A predictive mathematical model is presented for the expected case-driven transfer of classification rules. Key insights are offered for Knowledge Acquisition in expert systems, machine learning, artificial intelligence, ontology, and folksomonies.

Keywords: Knowledge Acquisition, Group Decision Support Systems, Collaborative Tagging, Folksonomies, Knowledge Based Systems, Machine Learning, Knowledge Discovery in Databases, Case Based Reasoning, Ripple Down Rules, Expert Systems.

1 Introduction

In this paper, I examine the case-driven transfer of knowledge in which one or more parties transfers classification rules to another party as a result of a continuous and randomized stream of incoming cases, and I present a predictive stochastic model for the case-driven acquisition of classification rules. Importantly, my analysis does not assume any particular underlying Case-based Knowledge Acquisition (KA) technique. The resultant trajectories reflect the natural slowing of knowledge exchange in an environment where incoming repetitive and randomized cases are mapped to a bounded set of classes[1], and where the class mappings are defined by rules that examine the attributes of the incoming cases. The derived model provides very good insight to the rule acquisition data presented in previous machine-learnt and case-based KA simulations for Single Classification Ripple Down Rules (SCRDR) and Multiple Classification Ripple Down Rules (MCRDR) as discussed in [1] and [2], as well the tag acquisition data observed in folksomonies i.e. collaborative tagging forums as shown in [3, Fig. 3].

[1] Note that both over-specialisation and over-generalisation errors may result in more RuleNodes being acquired than is optimal. In the former scenario, multiple RuleNodes with different rules may refer to identical classifications. In the latter scenario, RuleNodes with different rules may be required to create exceptions to an invalid parent RuleNode.

S. Staab and V. Svatek (Eds.): EKAW 2006, LNAI 4248, pp. 43 – 50, 2006.

2 An Analysis of Case-Driven Knowledge Acquisition

The type of knowledge that this research concerns itself with is that which can be codified in the form of rules or RuleNodes that examine the properties (i.e. attributes) of incoming cases, and then map those cases to representative classes or classifications. Classification Knowledge can be acquired directly as top-down knowledge-based rules, or as bottom-up experience-based rules derived by examining specific cases. This paper focuses on the latter case-driven KA approach.

2.1 A Single Classification Case-Driven Equal Frequency KA Example

Say that the target knowledge domain will be comprised of m RuleNodes in a decision tree that maps incoming cases to their representative classes. In order to examine the case-driven KA process I randomly generated N = 1000 cases each comprising one of m = 100 different integers. The m different integers were represented with equal frequency in the example. In this experiment, a case with a novel integer was used to represent an exemplar case for a novel class or classification. For single classification case-driven KA, each novel exemplar case represents an opportunity for the KBS to acquire a new RuleNode in the decision tree.

Next, I took the sequential set of cases and cumulatively counted the number of times a case with a novel integer was seen. I then plotted the number of novel integers seen versus the number of cases seen. Fig. 1 shows the Actual trajectories for 5 independent case-driven KA scenarios, together with the Expected trajectory, and the Best Case straight-line trajectory for m = 100.

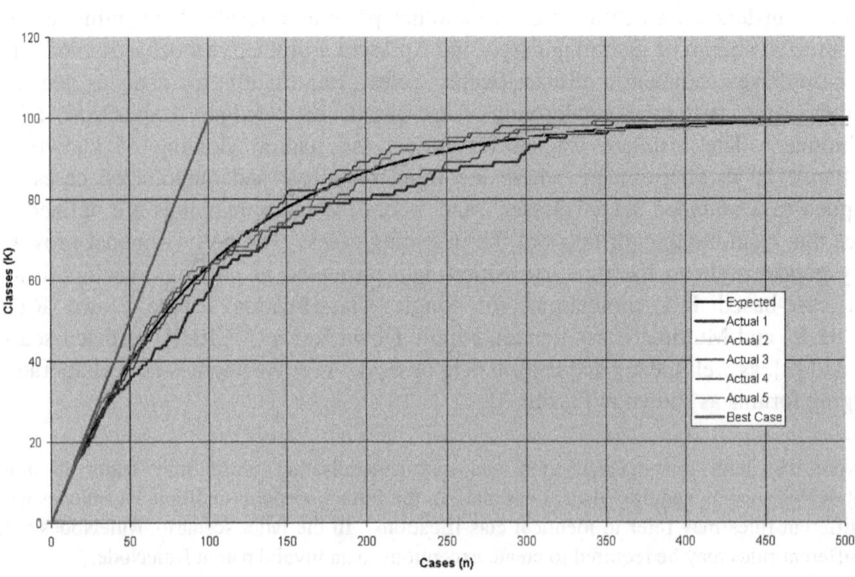

Fig. 1. Expected, Actual and Best-Case Single-Class Case-Driven KA trajectories

Every time newly generated random data is used a slightly different KA trajectory results with varying quantum KA steps. For instance on one draw, the system might fetch 50 consecutive cases all being exemplars for the same class, where-as on another draw the system might fetch 50 consecutive cases all being exemplars for novel classes. The varying trajectories represent the stochastic nature of the randomized incoming case data.

The formula for the Expected case-driven KA trajectory is provided in Theorem 1:

Theorem 1: The expected number of RuleNodes K_n that will be acquired after n cases by a single classification case-driven KBS is given by:

$$\mathbf{K_n = n - (1/m * \Sigma_{(i = 1\ to\ n)} K_{i-1})} \tag{T1}$$

where:

- n is the number of cases seen;
- K_n is the number of RuleNodes accumulated after n cases and $K_0 = 0$ and $K_1 = 1$; and
- m is the total number of classes or RuleNodes in the domain M′.

This theorem was used to construct the Expected KA trajectory that is the smooth monotonically increasing and rapidly slowing asymptotic curved line shown in Fig. 1. It provides a way of predicting how much knowledge K_n in the form of RuleNodes will be acquired after n cases have been seen by a case-based knowledge acquisition system. Unfortunately, proofs and some formulas have had to be omitted from this paper in order to comply with the EKAW short paper format. Please contact the author for proofs and additional formulas as required.

Let $K_{Error\ n}$ refer to the difference between the amount of knowledge K_n acquired after n cases, and the maximum amount of knowledge that could be acquired m. Hence the remaining error $K_{Error\ n}$ is as follows:

$$K_{Error\ n} = m - K_n \tag{1}$$

where K_n is given by Theorem 1.

A reciprocal formula for the Expected case-driven KA trajectory is provided in Theorem 2:

Theorem 2: The expected number of cases n_K needed to acquire K of m RuleNodes in a single classification case-driven KBS is given by:

$$\mathbf{n_K = \Sigma_{(i = 1\ to\ K)} [(m-(i-1))/m) * \Sigma_{(j = 1\ to\ \infty)} \{j * ((i-1)/m)\char`^(j-1)\}]} \tag{T2}$$

where:

- n is the number of cases required;
- K is the amount of RuleNodes to be accumulated; and
- m is the total number of classes or RuleNodes in the domain M′.

Theorem 2 provides a method for discovering how many cases would be required to acquire some number of the m RuleNodes in a domain M′. However its formula is computationally more expensive than the reciprocal formula in Theorem 1 since it involves a complex summation of an infinite number of terms. This reflects the asymptotic nature of the expected trajectory. Depending on the number of classes, and the required resolution of the solution, for $K < m$ it is possible to trade-off the accuracy of the solution with the number of terms used in Theorem 2.

In an optimal (manual or machine learning) KA scenario all of the knowledge would be acquired up front. In that way the knowledge base would be prepared for all future scenarios up front, and in the case of manual KA, experts wouldn't have to put up with the tedious review of repeat exemplar cases[2] while offering their knowledge for novel exemplar cases.

Hence optimally, each new case would represent a unique class and the best-case KA trajectory would be a straight line as shown in Fig. 1. The likelihood of achieving the best case (shortest path) KA using a case-driven KA method is given by:

$$P_{BestCase} = m! \,/\, m\hat{}m \tag{2}$$

Hence for case-driven KA with a significant number of classes m the best case KA outcome is extremely rare.

It is possible to construct a matrix that shows the probability of arriving at a given class after a given number of cases for an m class system. The matrix is constructed by recognizing that the probability P_{yx} of achieving y classes with x repeats is given by the probability of achieving $(y\text{-}1)$ classes with x repeats, followed by achieving the yth class; plus the probability of achieving y classes with $(x\text{-}1)$ repeats, followed by yet another repeat. This can be expressed as follows:

$$\begin{aligned} P_{yx} &= P_{(y-1)(x)} * P_{y0} + P_{y(x-1)} * P_{01} \\ P_{yx} &= P_{(y-1)(x)} * (m-(y-1))/m + P_{y(x-1)} * y/m \end{aligned} \tag{3}$$

The derived matrix offers an insight to the distribution one might expect to see of actual KA trajectories about the expected trajectory.

Table 1 shows an example matrix for a 10 class system for the situation where repeat exemplars are drawn up to 10 times between each class. In Table 1, we can see that for a 10 class system, the probability of achieving 7 classes with only 4 repeats is 0.39 which is the same as the probability of achieving 6 classes with only 4 repeats (0.35) multiplied by the probability of achieving the 7th class (10-7+1)/10 plus the probability of achieving 7 classes with only 3 repeats (0.36) multiplied by the probability of yet another repeat 7/10.

From Table 1 it becomes clear that the probability of repeats is relatively low and almost zero in the early stages of KA (only two decimal places are shown but the values are actually non-zero), but as more classes are achieved, the probability of repeats and the variance of the number of repeats becomes much higher. The probability of repeats decreases with the number of repeats seen for all but the final class acquisition. For the final class acquisition, the probability of repeats actually increases, and the variance is infinite reflecting the asymptotic nature of case-driven KA.

---

[2] Note that repeat exemplar cases can offer some useful auxiliary knowledge in that they allow statistics to be gathered as to the number of times a particular RuleNode has been applied. This can lend credibility to the validity of RuleNodes in the knowledge base.

Table 1. An example KA probability matrix for a 10 class system

repeats (x) \ classes (y)	1	2	3	4	5	6	7	8	9	10
0	1.00	0.90	0.72	0.50	0.30	0.15	0.06	0.02	0.00	0.00
1	0.10	0.27	0.43	0.50	0.45	0.32	0.17	0.07	0.02	0.00
2	0.01	0.06	0.18	0.33	0.42	0.40	0.28	0.14	0.04	0.01
3	0.00	0.01	0.06	0.18	0.32	0.40	0.36	0.22	0.08	0.01
4	0.00	0.00	0.02	0.09	0.21	0.35	**0.39**	0.29	0.13	0.03
5	0.00	0.00	0.01	0.04	0.13	0.27	0.38	0.34	0.19	0.05
6	0.00	0.00	0.00	0.02	0.07	0.20	0.35	0.38	0.24	0.07
7	0.00	0.00	0.00	0.01	0.04	0.14	0.30	0.39	0.30	0.10
8	0.00	0.00	0.00	0.00	0.02	0.10	0.25	0.39	0.35	0.13
9	0.00	0.00	0.00	0.00	0.01	0.06	0.20	0.37	0.39	0.17
10	0.00	0.00	0.00	0.00	0.01	0.04	0.16	0.34	0.42	0.21

Remark 1. Please note: This table has been truncated at 10 repetitions.

Another interesting property of the matrix is that the probabilities on the diagonals add to 1. For example if you have seen 3 cases, you've either seen 1 novel exemplar and 2 repeats, 2 novel exemplars and 1 repeat, or 3 novel exemplars.

2.2 Generalising to Multiple Classification KA systems

For case-driven KA where cases are mapped to more than one class it is possible that more that one RuleNode may be acquired for each case.

In order to examine the multiple-classification case-driven KA process I created 3 sets of data, each with $N = 1000$ randomly generated cases. Cases in the first set of data were each mapped to one classification represented by one of $m = 100$ different integers. Cases in the second set of data were each mapped to two classifications represented by two of $m = 100$ different integers. Cases in the third set of data were each mapped to three classifications represented by three of $m = 100$ different integers. The m different integers were randomly distributed and occurred with equal frequency in each example. Again, each novel integer represented a novel class or classification and hence an opportunity for the KBS to acquire a new RuleNode.

I cumulatively counted and plotted the number of novel integers seen versus the number of cases seen. Fig. 2 shows the expected and actual trajectories for a KA system with $m = 100$ classes and $N = 1000$ cases in which 1, 2, and 3 classes are mapped to each case. Since more than one classification may occur for each novel exemplar case in a multiple classification KA system, we can expect that its case-driven KA trajectory would rise faster than in an equivalent single classification KA system i.e. less cases need to be seen before the same level of knowledge is acquired. It turns out that this corresponds to a linear shrinking of the x-axis (see Theorem 2) in

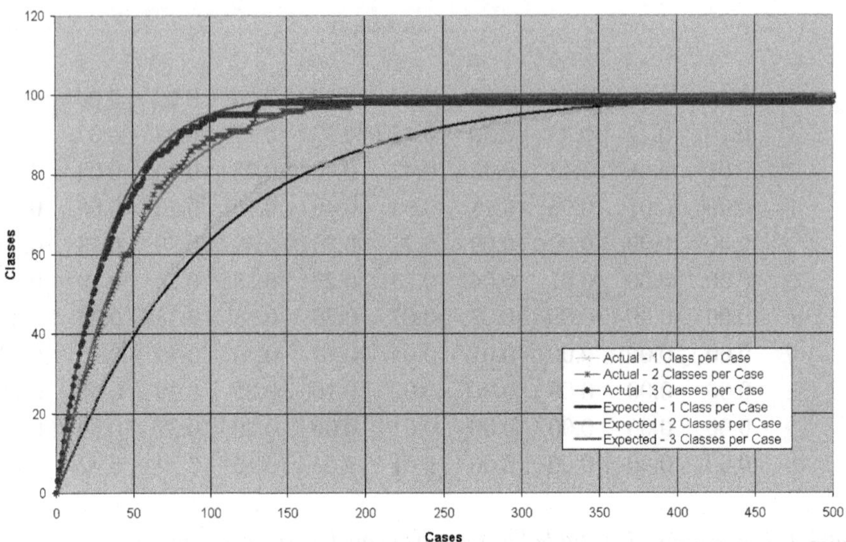

Fig. 2. Expected and Actual Multi-Class Case-Driven KA trajectories

proportion to the number of classes acquired per case. For example, in Fig. 2, 80% of the classes are achieved after 150 cases for a uni- classification system, after 75 cases for a bi- classification system, and after 50 cases for a tri-classification system. Please contact the author for the formulas for the expected trajectories as required.

Note that in a real-life multiple classification scenarios, certain combinations of classes may be more likely to co-occur than others. In the next section I discuss classes that occur with different frequencies for single classification systems.

2.3 Classes occurring with Different Frequencies

In many domains, the classes being acquired do not occur with equal frequency across the cases seen. To model this scenario I generated a Pareto distribution of classes and cases: I randomly generated $N = 1000$ cases each comprising one of $m = 100$ different integers. The first 20% of the m different integers = m_1 were represented in 80% of the cases = r_1. The last 80% of the m different integers = m_2 were represented in only 20% of the cases = r_2. I sorted the cases so that the order of classes represented by them was completely random. Again I took the sequential set of cases and cumulatively counted the number of times a case with a novel integer was seen. I then plotted the number of novel classes seen vs the number of cases seen.

Fig. 3 shows the Best Case, Actual and Expected trajectories of the randomly generated case data for $m = 100$ for the single classification equal frequency class example and for this unequal (Pareto) frequency class example. The component parts of the expected Pareto trajectory are also shown. From this figure we can see that the

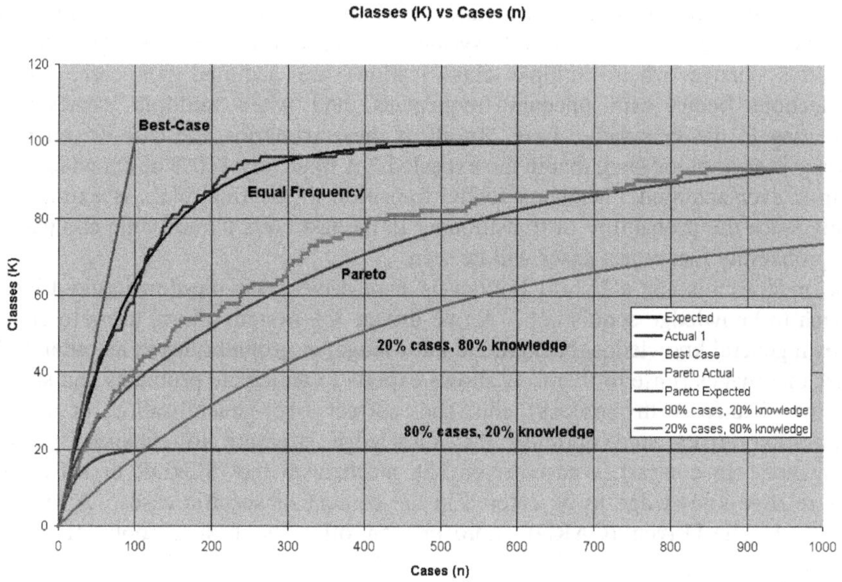

Fig. 3. KA for classes with both equal and different frequencies

total rate of knowledge acquisition for data with a Pareto style distribution is much slower than for data that represents a number of different classes with equal frequency. Please contact the author for the formulas for the expected Pareto trajectory as required.

What we can see from Fig. 3 is that although the total KA is much slower for a Pareto-style distribution, the most frequently demanded knowledge is generally acquired first, and the least frequently demanded knowledge is generally acquired last. Hence the variation of frequencies between the classes acquired is unlikely to reduce the effectiveness of case-driven KA as a KA mechanism. In fact, in many domains knowledge acquired for the highest volume problems has the best potential to save on labor costs and is therefore of top priority.

2.4 Multiple Parties Transferring Knowledge

If multiple parties are randomly transferring knowledge to the KBS we can model their contributi3on as a round-robin contribution on the basis of cases seen. In that case the knowledge acquired as a function of the cases seen by a particular user will be much more rapid since other users are contributing to the same KBS and the user will need to see fewer cases for the same amount of knowledge gain.

3 Conclusions

In this paper I have presented formulas and trajectories for the expected number of classes that will be acquired as a function of the number of cases seen, and the expected number of cases seen as a function of the number of classes acquired in case-driven single classification KA systems. I have also discussed how these trajectories change when multiple classifications are acquired per case, when classifications occur with unequal frequencies, and when multiple parties are contributing to the knowledge base. In all of these scenarios, the case-driven KA trajectory is asymptotic such that in the expected KA trajectory 100% of knowledge is seldom if ever acquired. Mathematically, transition to the final class is extremely unlikely since the probability of transitioning to the last class is miniscule compared to the probability that repeat cases will be seen.

The model calls for a hybrid bottom-up case-driven and top-down rule-driven approach to knowledge acquisition. A rule-driven KA system allows users to enter top-down general knowledge, background knowledge, or ground rules in an order and manner that makes sense to them. It allows experts to anticipate problems and share them in advance with novices; edit and correct over-generalisation or over-specialisation errors; and optimise the knowledge structure to enhance system performance. In contrast, a case-driven KA mechanism like SCRDR or MCRDR allows relative knowledge to be entered in the context of specific cases. A hybrid Case- And Rule-Driven (CARD) approach can offer the best of both of these approaches.

Acknowledgments. Many thanks to Terje Petersen for valuable insight and discussions leading to Theorem 1. Thanks also to Oden, Zac and Jasmin. Thanks to Debbie Richards and Lee Flax at Macquarie University. Finally, thanks to my industry sponsor for ongoing financial support.

References

1. Compton, P., Preston, P. and Kang, B. (1995). The Use of Simulated Experts in Evaluating Knowledge Acquisition in B Gaines & M Musen, Proceedings of the 9th AAAI-Sponsored Banff Knowledge Acquisition for Knowledge-Based Systems Workshop (Banff, Canada, University of Calgary), pp 12.1-12.18.
2. Kang, B. H., Lee, K., Kim, W., Preston, P., Compton, P. (1998). Evaluation of Multiple Classification Ripple Down Rules. Eleventh Workshop on Knowledge Acquisition, Modeling and Management (KAW 18-23 April) Banff, Alberta, Canada
3. Golder S. A., Huberman B. A. The Structure of Collaborative Tagging Systems. (2003). HP Labs.
4. Compton, P., Simulating Expertise in Compton, P., Hoffman, A., Motoda H., Yamaguchi T. (2000). Proceedings of the 6th Pacific Knowledge Acquisition Workshop, Sydney, p51-70.
5. Kang, B., Compton, P. and Preston, P. (1995). Multiple Classification Ripple Down Rules : Evaluation and Possibilities. Proceedings of the 9th AAAI-Sponsored Banff Knowledge Acquisition for Knowledge-Based Systems Workshop, Banff, Canada, University of Calgary.

From Natural Language to Formal Proof Goal*

Structured Goal Formalisation Applied to Medical Guidelines (Extended Abstract)

Ruud Stegers, Annette ten Teije, and Frank van Harmelen

Vrije Universiteit, Amsterdam

Abstract. The main problem encountered when starting verification of goals for some formal system, is the ambiguity of those goals when they are specified in natural language. To verify goals given in natural language, a translation of those goals to the formalism of the verification tool is required. The main concern is to assure equivalence of the final translation and the original. A structured method is required to assure equivalence in every case.

This article proposes a goal formalisation method in five steps, in which the domain expert is involved in such a way that the correctness of the result can be assured. The contribution of this article is a conceptual goal model, a formal expression language for this model, and a structured method which transforms any input goal to a fully formalised goal in the required target formalism. The proposed formalisation method guarantees essential properties like *correctness*, *traceability*, *reduced variability* and *reusability*.

1 Introduction

The main problem encountered when starting verification of goals for some formal system, is the ambiguity of those goals when they are specified in natural language. No matter what domain, or what source of the goals: there are always many implicit assumptions and interpretations that must be made explicit before they can be used for formal verification. An ad-hoc method, in which the expert on the formal system makes the translation by hand directly into the logic of the target system, may work sometimes, but is error prone due to the obvious domain specific choices and interpretations that have to be made.

Incorporating a domain expert in the formalisation process seems to be a necessity, however the gap between the natural language representation and the logic of the verification tool is far to big to close without help. This article proposes a structured method, understandable by the domain expert and yet with enough expressive power for the formal methods expert. This article will focus on suitable representations and required steps for the formalisation of natural language goals. The contribution of this article is a common frame of reference

* This work has been partially supported by the European Commission's IST program, under contract number IST-FP6-508794 Protocure-II.

S. Staab and V. Svatek (Eds.): EKAW 2006, LNAI 4248, pp. 51–58, 2006.

for all the experts involved (the goal model), a formal expression language for this model (*GDL*), and a five-step method which transforms any input goal to a fully formalised goal in the required target formalism. The proposed formalisation method may be applied to any domain and guarantees essential properties like *correctness*, *traceability*, *reduced variability* and *reusability*.

Although the proposed method is domain independent, its origins can be found in the medical domain. An example from this domain will be used to illustrate the individual steps throughout this article. The goal shown below is used to verify medical guidelines as used by care providers. Those guidelines provide directives and instructions for the diagnosis and treatment of selected deceases and injuries. By applying verification techniques to guidelines, these may be improved: the aim is both to increase the quality of the care, and to prevent unnecessary medical tests and treatment.

Original - Example

"The percentage of patients in the last year, with whom the possibility of breast reconstruction was discussed before mastectomy was performed."

The example goal is what is called an *indicator*: in hospitals indicators are used to measure the quality of the care on a periodic basis (typically each year). With help from a doctor and the proposed method, this indicator will be formalised so it becomes a suitable goal for formal verification.

The proposed formalisation method has been evaluated on several goals from the medical domain[1]. The four chosen goals apply to guidelines for treatment of diabetes, jaundice and breast-cancer. In the Protocure project[2,3], these guidelines have been formalised for that purpose using Asbru, a plan oriented modelling language. In the same project, these models were translated to the temporal logic of KIV, a tool that allows the guidelines to be verified using symbolic execution[4]. The example of this article is one of those four goals. The resulting formalised goal has successfully been proven for the breast-cancer guideline using KIV.

In the next section the goal model which provides the shared frame of reference for both experts (e.g. medical expert, formal methods expert) is explained. Subsequently, Sect. 3 defines five requirements for the formalisation process followed by a discussion of the method itself. Section 4 discusses related work, followed by the conclusion in Sect. 5.

2 The Goal Model

To provide a common frame of reference for both the domain expert, and the formal methods expert, a high level goal model is required. This model is depicted in Fig. 1.

A goal is expressed in terms of a *start event*, a *(pre) condition* for this event, an *end event*, and some *desired behaviour* in between. From the moment the start event

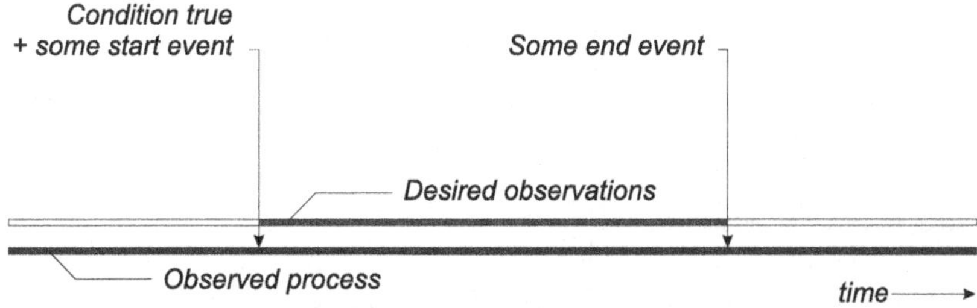

Fig. 1. Shared goal model

is seen while the condition is true, the process model (i.e. the guideline) should adhere to the prescribed behaviour for as long as the end event does not occur.

The simple nature of this shared goal model makes is easy to understand, however practical use has also shown that the model allows for sufficiently expressive goal descriptions. The next sections will show that the common goal model maps naturally to both natural language and to a formal representation (i.e. *GDL*).

3 The Formalisation Method

Having a shared frame of reference is only the start. The process itself of how to get from an arbitrary natural language goal to the target formalism via the goal model is equally important. The following requirements must be met by the formalisation process:

- **Ambiguities.** Identify and clarify all assumptions and ambiguities present in the original goal.
- **Correctness.** Ensure correctness of every change to the goal: the domain expert should be able to validate changes to ensure their validity.
- **Traceability.** Ensure traceability. The formalisation must be completely reproducible by means of the intermediate results and the documentation.
- **Reusability.** Enable reusability of work at different stages. Maintain generality for as long as possible.
- **Variability.** Reduce variability of the formalisation result.

The numbered steps depicted in Fig. 2 assure compliance with those requirements. The blocks on the left hand side represent the goal in natural language. On the right side the blocks represent the formal expression of the same goal. The individual steps will now be demonstrated for the example.

1. Reduction. Due to the variety of the source of goals, the first step is to make sure that the desired behaviour is explicitly described. This explicit description preserves the quality aspects of the goal, while getting rid of non-essential information. The domain expert is the one primarily performing the reduction. The main responsibility of the domain expert in this and subsequent steps, is that

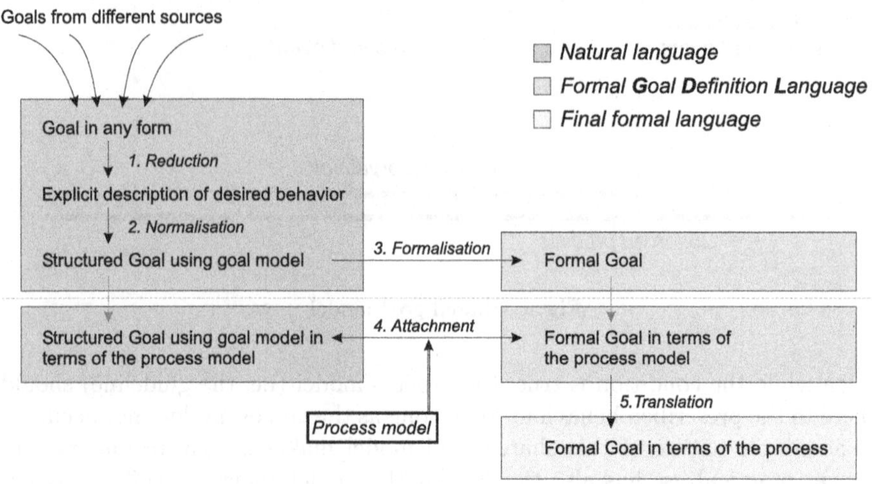

Fig. 2. Life-cycle of a goal

the essence of the goal is not altered, or if it is, that this happens deliberate and well documented.

> **Reduction** - Example
>
> "The possibility of breast reconstruction should be discussed with all patients prior to mastectomy."

For the example (refer to Sect. 1 on page 52), the knowledge of the medical expert is used to establish that the percentage mentioned in the original version should preferably be as high a possible. This allows removal of references to this percentage (*the percentage of patients* becomes *all patients*). Additionally, by realising that this indicator is repetitively applied every year, it is concluded that in this case the patient must always be informed about possibilities for breast reconstruction prior to mastectomy:

2. Normalisation. After the reduction, the next task is to rewrite the goal in terms of the goal model: some behaviour that should be adhered to between some start and some end event. Not only the terms, but also the structure of the goal model is imposed on the goal: the goal is transformed into a normal form.

The normal form consist of four elements in brackets (Condition, Start, End and the Behaviour), however, the whole sentence must be well-formed. During the normalisation ambiguities and implicit assumptions concerning temporal relations between events are almost automatically being taken care of: rewriting into this structure raises questions which, when answered by the domain expert, clarify the ambiguities of this kind. The reduction and normalisation are just another way of writing down the original goal. By not making adjustments specific to the object of verification (models), the normalised goal may be reused for verification of many models.

Normalization - Example

> ^{C}[For women with breast-cancer], ^{S}[after start of the medical care] but ^{E}[before commencing mastectomy], ^{B}[the possibility of breast reconstruction should have been discussed with the patient].

3. Formalisation. The next step is to transform the structured natural language version to a formalised version which can be used by the formal methods expert. The formal expression of the goal will be provided by *GDL*, the *Goal Definition Language*[1]. This newly developed language is specifically designed to reflect the structure of the goal model and will therefore also stay very close to the structured version. Due to this close relation, changes in one version are easily duplicated in the other version. This makes that the formal methods expert and the domain expert can discuss the same goal using their own representations.

The Goal definition Language, *GDL*, consists of two parts: A general part, *Generic GDL*, that represents the goal model itself, and a task specific extension to *GDL* that defines the exact conditions and events that can be used. The formalisation of the example is shown here in presentation syntax. Only *Generic GDL* is used at this stage for the formalisation:

Formalisation - Example

Goal Example
Precondition
For women with breast-cancer

Time-specification
From the start of the medical care
Until start of mastectomy

Observe-during-period ≥ 1
discuss possibility of breast reconstruction with the patient

The elements from the goal model are easily recognised (Condition, Start, End and the Behaviour). Although the overall structure is fixed, several elements may be replaced. The most important of those is the behaviour. The available choice of elements raises questions which clarify behaviour related ambiguities. (e.g. the difference between 'observe once' or 'observe at least once'.)

[1] A full language specification including formal semantics are available in [1].

4. The Attachment. Given the formalisation result so far, the only thing left is to formalise the natural language parts with according to concepts available in the process model (i.e. the guideline model). The task consists of finding an equivalent concept in the process model, for every concept in the goal. During the attachment the domain expert makes sure that the concepts which are 'attached' are indeed equivalent, and where necessary, adjustments may be made. To be able to evaluate every adjustment, both versions of the goal (*GDL* and structured natural language) are kept synchronised: changes made to one, should be reflected in the other. That way, both experts can evaluate the (intermediate) result using their own representation. Also here, documentation is essential in order to be able to verify the formalisation result. Notice the additional information about the model to which the goal has been attached to between brackets in the example.

Attachment - Example (BC Ch1 23.11.2005)

Goal Example
Precondition
always-true

Time-specification
From Transition ch1-treatment **enter** active
Until Transition mastectomy-proper **enter** active

Observe-during-period
Planstate patient-information-reconstruction = completed

Since the process model may be described by any formal language – each with specific elements and features – a specialised *GDL* extension is needed for the specific modelling language used. The model verified using the example goal is the Dutch guideline for treatment of breast cancer which has been formalised in Asbru. Therefore, an Asbru specific extension – ***GDL***-Asbru – was developed, which consists of Asbru specific conditions and events. Asbru is a plan-specification language defined as part of the Asgaard/Asbru project[5].

5. Translation. The translation of *GDL* to the logic of the verification tool should be a strictly mechanical step. This is essential since changes at this stage would be impossible to detect and validate by the domain expert. The mechanical nature of the translation makes it trivial from a process perspective. The only consideration that must be taken into account is that the translation must have the same semantics as *GDL*.

The guidelines under investigation are being verified in KIV, a tool which – amongst others – allows symbolic execution of parallel programs[4]. To this end, the Asbru models were translated to parallel programs in KIV. For the goals, an efficient modular translation of *Generic GDL* and ***GDL***-Asbru to KIV has been made. Using this translation, KIV was successfully used to close the proof on the example goal.

4 Related Work

In the software engineering area the same problem is investigated, namely the transition from natural language to a formal representation, for instance [6,7,8]. [6] presents the approach of lightweight formal methods which starts with natural language and ends up with a semi-formal representation. Our proposal goes further and continues to the end (i.e. to a full formal representation).

In contrast with [6], [7,8] mainly focus on the transition from the semi-formal to the formal representation. This means the first step from natural language to semi-formal is rather large. In our case this step is more fine grained. Furthermore in our case the both experts (domain, formal methods) have their own representation. Whereas in [7,8] one representation is used. The final result with [7,8] consists of the pseudo-code respectively the objects of the application. Our method aims to end up with the logic of the verification tool. Notice that in requirements engineering part of the effort goes into identifying the requirements of the user, whereas for the proposed method of this article, the requirements in natural language are considered given.

5 Conclusion

This article has proposed a method of formalising natural language goals in such a way that the domain expert is involved in every step that may change the meaning of the goal. The contribution of this article is a common vocabulary between the domain expert and the formal methods expert in the form of the goal model. The five step method adds a structured and controlled way of rewriting goals via this goal model to any target formalism. Five requirements have been formulated in section 3, which will be evaluated below.

- **Ambiguities.** During the formalisation process, each step targets different kinds of ambiguities. The biggest reduction of ambiguity is achieved during the normalisation. To rethink a goal in terms of the goal model automatically raises questions. During the formalisation details of the behaviour are made specific by forcing a choice for a specific kind of behaviour. During the attachment, conceptual ambiguities are resolved by connecting the concepts in the goal to available concepts in the model: by evaluating their equivalence the exact meaning needs to be established. By following the steps, ambiguities are naturally solved.
- **Correctness.** The main instrument to achieve correctness is the continuous involvement of the domain expert. An up-to-date natural language version of the goal is maintained throughout the process which allows the expert to focus on the meaning of the goal in a familiar form. The domain expert decides whether a proposed change is correct or not. By means of the formal *GDL* semantics the correctness of the translation step can be confirmed.

- **Traceability.** The main tool to achieve traceability is by adding documentation to the intermediate result after each step. Additionally, the subdivision in steps with specific tasks reduces the amount of required documentation: in the context of the task, many transformations are straight forward and don't need to be explained. In that respect, traceability follows from the method.
- **Reusability.** During the formalisation process, there are two distinct points where the intermediate result may be reused. First of all, the formalisation result may be reused for different process models. The attachment result may be translated to different tools. One example of reuse of an attached goal would be the translation both to KIV and to the SMV model checking environment.
- **Variability.** The task oriented subdivision of the formalisation process causes the first reduction in variability. The fixed order of steps works towards a uniform result. Additionally, the canonical forms force the result into the right direction. Finally, the vocabulary of the goal model in general, and of *GDL* specific, do not allow many different ways to express a single goal. Every step tries to achieve convergence to the unique *GDL* expression. The mechanical nature of the translation enforces invariance in the last step. The only real source of variance in the result are differences in interpretation by the domain expert of the original goal. However, this cannot be avoided.

References

1. Stegers, R.: From natural language to formal proof goal: Structured goal formalisation applied to medical guidelines. Master's thesis, Free University Amsterdam, department of artificial intelligence (2006) Available from: `http://www.stegers.info/Ruud/MastersThesis.pdf`.
2. ten Teije, A., et al.: Improving medical protocols by formal methods. Artificial Intelligence In Medicine **36**(3) (2006) 193–209
3. Deliverable D4.2: Specification of guideline properties & indicators, Protocure Project-II, IST-FP6-508794 (2006) `http://www.protocure.org/`.
4. Balser, M.: Verifying Concurrent Systems with Symbolic Execution. PhD thesis, University of Augsburg, Augsburg (2005)
5. Shahar, Y., Miksch, S., Johnson, P.: The asgaard project: A task-specific framework for the application and critiquing of time-oriented clinical guidelines. In: Artificial Intelligence in Medicine. Volume 14. (1998) 29–51
6. George, V., Vaughn, R.: Application of lightweight formal methods in requirement engineering. In: CrossTalk. The Journal of Defence Software Engineering. (2003)
7. Bryant, B.R.: Object-oriented natural language requirements specification, Canberra, Australia (2000)
8. Cooper, K., Ito, M.: Formalizing a structured natural language requirements specification notation. In: Twelfth Annual International Symposium of the International Council On Systems Engineering (INCOSE), Las Vegas, Nevada USA (2002)

Reuse: Revisiting Sisyphus-VT

Derek Sleeman, Trevor Runcie, and Peter Gray

Department of Computing Science, University of Aberdeen,
Aberdeen, AB24 3UE, Scotland, UK
{sleeman, truncie, pgray}@csd.abdn.ac.uk

Abstract. Reuse has long been a major goal of the Knowledge Engineering community. The focus of this paper is the reuse of domain knowledge acquired for an initial problem solver, with a further problem solver. For our analysis we chose a knowledge base system written in CLIPS based on the propose-and-revise (PnR) problem solver, and which had a lift/elevator knowledge base (KB). Given the nature of the problem solver, the KB contained 4 components, namely an ontology, procedural statements which specify how the artifact, the lift, could be enhanced/modified, a set of constraints to be satisfied, and a set of fixes to be applied when constraint violations occurred. These 4 components were first extracted manually, and were used with both an Excel spreadsheet and a constraint problem solver (ECLiPSe) to solve a range of tasks. The next phase was to implement ExtrAKTor which extracts the same 4 knowledge sources virtually automatically from the CLIPS knowledge base (held by Protégé), and transforms these so that they are usable with a number of problem solvers. To date Excel & ECLiPSe have been selected, and again we have demonstrated that the resulting systems are able to solve a variety of lift configuration tasks. This is in contrast to earlier work which produced abstract formulations of the problem but which were unable to perform reuse of actual knowledge bases.

1 Introduction

Reuse has long been a major goal of the Knowledge Engineering community. The vision being that if knowledge sources/bases about particular topics, and domain-independent problem solvers were available, then it should be possible to create a new Knowledge base System by selecting from these components and in some way linking them. This vision was partly materialised in the early days of Expert Systems, when a number of domain independent "Inference Engines" were implemented and used with a wide range of domains. For instance, the EMYCIN [2] shell was used with Knowledge Bases (KBs) for Infectious Diseases and Civil Engineering - to mention just 2 applications.

Subsequently, the Expert System community in the later 70's / early 80's described a range of Problem Solving methods which, they claimed, would cover the whole spectrum of problem solving, [5,15]. The important theme of articulating and defining PSMs was developed subsequently, for example, by the KADS project [12,3] (section 2); however, as we shall see, these activities produced a largely theoretical framework. Reuse was still seen as an issue in 2000 when the Advanced Knowledge Technologies (AKT) project included it as one of the challenges it intends to address in supporting

S. Staab and V. Svatek (Eds.): EKAW 2006, LNAI 4248, pp. 59–66, 2006.

the KB lifecycle, [16]. The other 5 challenges being: Knowledge Acquisition/Capture, Knowledge Modeling, Knowledge Retrieval, Knowledge Publishing and Knowledge Maintenance.

On the other hand, Reuse has become a reality for the software engineer, who regularly, once the specification of a system has been finalised, starts the implementation process by searching for suitable (Java) libraries. The vision of the Knowledge Engineer is that, having built at considerable cost (largely due to the cost associated with building the domain Knowledge Base) a KBS which is able to design, say a lift, it is highly desirable to reuse most/all of the domain knowledge, when developing a KBS to diagnose faults in the same domain. Further, the vision has also always been that this process should be relatively straightforward and could be handled by a domain expert rather than by a highly specialised Knowledge Engineer/ Researcher in Knowledge Representation. The following paragraphs give a scenario for a user-friendly Reuse system.

A technician has access to a domain ontology & related design information (such as procedural upgrades, constraints & fixes) necessary to complete a design task. The technician invokes a Problem Solving (PS) agent to provide a plausible configuration. The PS agent then selects an appropriate Problem Solver. Subsequently, the Problem Solver (or the agent) recognizes that certain initialization information is missing and prompts the technician for it. The PS Agent then ideally provides a design solution; or prompts the user for further information; or reports that there is no solution. The important aspects of this scenario are that the technician should:

- not require a high level of computing science expertise
- not require detailed experience of the Problem Solvers

1.1 Opportunities and Challenges for Knowledge Engineering in the Context of the Semantic Web

The opportunities which the world-wide-web provides for Knowledge Engineering is very considerable in principle as the types of components involved, once made available on the web, can then be reused by a sizeable number of users. Additionally, a further mode of operation is possible where domain-independent inference engines are made available as web services; then to use such a service it is only necessary to "send" the web service, Knowledge Source(s) in the required format and an answer would be returned. The great challenge of the Web, on the other hand, is being able to locate appropriate domain-independent problem solvers and domain-dependent Knowledge Sources. This requires, for instance, that the capabilities of the problem solvers are adequately described; various languages such as DAML-OIL & OWL-S, have been developed to allow services to be described, and these could be used again in this context. Such approaches require the developer of the service to describe its purpose, as well as the nature of the inputs required by the service and the nature of the output produced. Searching for an appropriate Knowledge Source is a related problem. However, some sophisticated search engines such as Swoogle [6,17] and OntoSearch [14,18] enable users to specify keywords to describe the sorts of content required of Knowledge Sources such as Ontologies; OntoSearch additionally allows users to specify other desirable properties which should hold in the retrieved Knowledge Sources such as structure between classes, properties of some key attributes, etc.

The structure of the rest of the paper is as follows: Section 2 describes the VT (Vertical Transport) design task, the Sisyphus-II challenge [24], outlines related work, and gives an overview of constraint satisfaction techniques; Section 3 reports the work done to manually extract domain knowledge from a CLIPS [19] Propose and Revise algorithm for the lift domain, and describes a system developed to (semi)-automatically extract the same domain knowledge; and Section 4 reviews the work and suggests possible future work.

2 The VT Problem, Sisyphus-II Challenge, and Related Work

2.1 VT Problem

The Vertical Transportation (VT) domain is a complex configuration task involving the interaction of all of the components required to design a lift (elevator) system. These components are shown in Figure 1. The parameters such as physical dimensions, weight and choice of components are regulated by physical constraints. The VT domain [7] was initially used to solve real-world lift design by Westinghouse Elevator Company. The original VT Domain included some potentially conflicting fixes. For example, if the "traction ratio" is exceeded then one fix is to increase the "car-supplement-weight", but if the "machine-groove-pressure" is exceeded, one fix is to decrease the "car-supplement-weight". The conflict occurs if both the "traction ratio" and the "machine-groove-pressure" are exceeded. Should the "car-supplement-weight" be increased or decreased? This original VT domain knowledge was simplified and the above conflicts removed to form the Knowledge Acquisition Sisyphus-II Challenge. The Sisyphus [24,11,21] version of the VT domain was created so that researchers would have a common KB for experimentation. It is the Protégé version of the VT system from Stanford University which has been used in this project, [20].

2.2 A Review of Problem-Solving Methods (PSMs)

Problem-solving methods (PSMs) describe the principal reasoning processes of knowledge based systems (KBs). Benjamins and Fensel [1] provides a summary of PSM related research up to 1998; examples of PSMs are "heuristic classification" [4] and "propose-and-revise" [8]. In the mid-80s, researchers realised that PSMs all have goals to be achieved, actions needed to achieve the goals, and knowledge required to perform the actions. For the next decade or so there was a detailed investigation of the nature and number of PSMs, before the field attempted to analyze in detail the subcomponents which make up the PSMs. It was appreciated that the benefits that accrue from such a PSM library could be significant, as new KBSs constructed using proven reusable components rather than building from scratch should reduce development time and improve reliability. This area of research has been most notably investigated through the KADS/CommonKADS Expertise Modeling Library, the Protégé PSM Library, and also the IBROW project. For details of these approaches see [10].

The biggest issue with these three approaches is that none support the execution of a KBS. Having stated that CommonKADS has hundreds of PSMs [5], the same Fensel and Motta paper states "None of these methods is implemented". A recent critique of

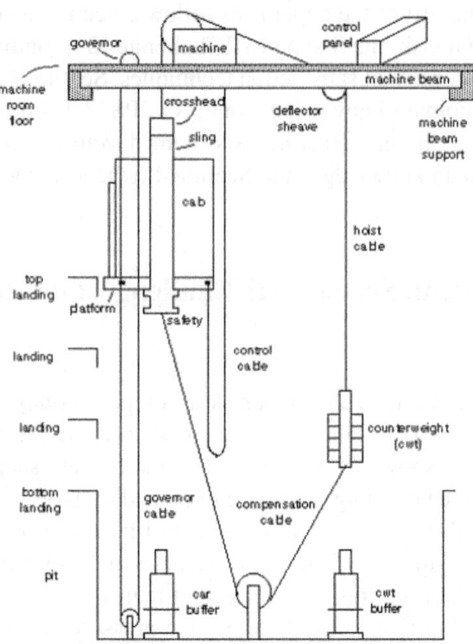

Fig. 1. VT System Components

CommonKADS [15] suggests that in addition to the three levels of knowledge description a fourth type of "operationalisation" or "code" should have been included since there is no executable PSM code. There is a similar issue with the Protégé-2000 PSM Library, as the PSM librarian webpage [22] states "the current version of the PSM Librarian tab does not support actual activation". Fensel and Motta [5] highlights a major issue with work in the PSM and PSM library field as "Configuring the optimal problem solver may have an order of magnitude higher complexity than the problem that should be solved by the problem solver." In our view Problem Solving Methods serve little purpose if they do not support the development of operational KBS [9].

2.3 An Overview of Constraint Satisfaction Techniques

Constraint Satisfaction [13] techniques attempt to find solutions to constrained combinatorial problems, and there are a number of efficient toolkits in a variety of programming languages. The definition of a constraint satisfaction problem (CSP) is:

- A set of variables X= X 1,..., X n,
- For each variable Xi, a finite set Di of possible values (its domain), and
- A set of constraints $C_{<j>} \subseteq D_{j1} \times D_{j2} \times \ldots \times D_{jt}$, restricting the values that subsets of the variables can take simultaneously.

A solution to a CSP is a set of assignments to each of the variables in such a way that all constraints are satisfied. The main CSP solution technique is consistency enforcement, in which infeasible values are removed from the problem by reasoning about the constraints. ECLiPSe [23] is a software system for the cost-effective development and execution of constraint programming applications.

3 Extraction of Components and Their Reuse

3.1 Introduction and Manual Reuse

The initial task undertaken here was to analyse the VT-Sisyphus code which consisted of 20,000 lines of CLIPS code that included domain knowledge and a version of the Propose and Revise (PnR) algorithm. This was done manually in order to reveal the underlying processes involved, which could then be automated. The manually extracted data was then reused in both an Excel "emulator" spreadsheet and ECLipSe constraint solver.

3.2 Semi-automatic Reuse

The next stage of the project was to create a tool that could semi-automate the extraction and transformation processes that had been demonstrated manually. The tool developed is known as ExtrAKTor and was designed to support the idealized design session defined in Section 1. The starting point for the process was the VT domain ontology represented in Protégé. This ontology was part of the Stanford solution to the VT-Sisyphus challenge [24]. The development tools used to implement ExtrAKTor were the Protégé PrologTab and GNU Prolog. PrologTab provides a tight coupling between the Protégé environment and GNU Prolog. A Prolog environment was selected because of the availability of PrologTab and its syntactical similarities to ECLiPSe. Conceptually there are three phases to the basic ExtrAKTor process, namely extraction of knowledge, creation of a new KBS, and KBS execution.

Extraction of Knowledge. Firstly the various knowledge components have to be extracted from the original KB. They are essentially: the ontology, the procedures to enhance/modify the artifact (in this case a lift), the domain constraints and the fixes. ExtrAKTor assumes that the constraints and fixes have been gathered together in a single class. This was the case for the Stanford Protégé based VT ontology. To initiate the analysis ExtrAKTor requires the analyst to provide slots names for the constraints and a parent class for components information. In VT, for constraints these slots are "constraint.condition", "constraint.variable", "constraint.expression"; for components the class is "elvis-models". Because different ontologies use different names for these entities it is at present necessary for the analyst to identify these variables. Alternatively, if these names were to be standardized then this stage could be done automatically. Clearly, the current situation where the analyst is required to have some knowledge of the implementation (the domain variables) is at odds with the vision outlined in Section 1. Further, it has been assumed that variable names in the formulae correspond to slot names in the ontology. PrologTab allows these slots to be accessed directly using "mapped" predicates. More details can be found in Runcie [9].

Creation of a New KBS (CSP). The next phase in the process was the creation of a new KB from the extracted knowledge for use with an appropriate domain-independent problem solver, in this case ECLiPSe. The processing of the component information is simply a case of taking as input the component data from the intermediate ASCII file which is formatted as a Prolog list structure and reformatting and outputting this in a Prolog database format. The constraint information requires a little more work since the expressions are stored in a CLIPS format and these need to be parsed and reformulated in a Prolog format (including variable names). Once all of this information has been stored to a file, the KB is ready for the execution phase.

Execution of the New KBS (CSP). In order to execute the ECLiPSe KB, a goal must be specified. The goal, entered as a variable name or a list of variable names, can be used to find the value for a single variable, or many variables. So the "'ALL"' option solves for all (unknown) variables; to solve for variables Counterweight_to_platform_rear, and Counterweight_space, the user must enter the goal vt(Counterweight_to_platform_rear, Counterweight_space). One of the main advantages of ECLiPSe for use with this class of design problem is that it supports real numbers. Additionally, if a number cannot be precisely determined, a range will be reported. e.g. 2.345...3.456. This is a major benefit, because it gives the user feedback as to the "'flexibility"' of the resultant designs and the user can then further refine the input. After refinement, the user can treat this as input for a new scenario (i.e. a sub-design) and can re-execute the solver again.

Similarly the information which has been extracted from the original CLIPS program could also be used with other problem solvers. The processes involved in producing KBs are captured in Figure 2.

An Extension to the ExtrAKTor System. In the simple process the desired goal is specified after the entire knowledge base has been extracted and the new KBS created. If the goal is specified earlier in the process, it is possible to generate a simplified and more focused KBS only containing the knowledge required to solve the desired problem. The size of the original KB is probably the deciding factor in determining the most efficient choice. For a large ontology or KB, creating a simplified and focused KBS is probably more appropriate. The disadvantage of this approach is that every goal specification requires a separate extraction process, and a separate KBS is produced for each.

4 Discussion and Future Work

The main focus of this paper is the extraction of components from the VT-Sisyphus domain so that they can be reformulated and re-used in conjunction with different problem solvers. There have already been some early successes in this project, as the automated extraction of an ontology, formulae, constraints, and fixes has demonstrated. Significantly, this extracted information has been used to solve real problems with different problem solvers. Further, as far as we have ascertained, no other research has used constraint solvers with the VT domain.

As noted earlier the KBS based on the ECLiPSe system executes the standard lift configuration task very rapidly (0.01 second). However, it is important to note that the

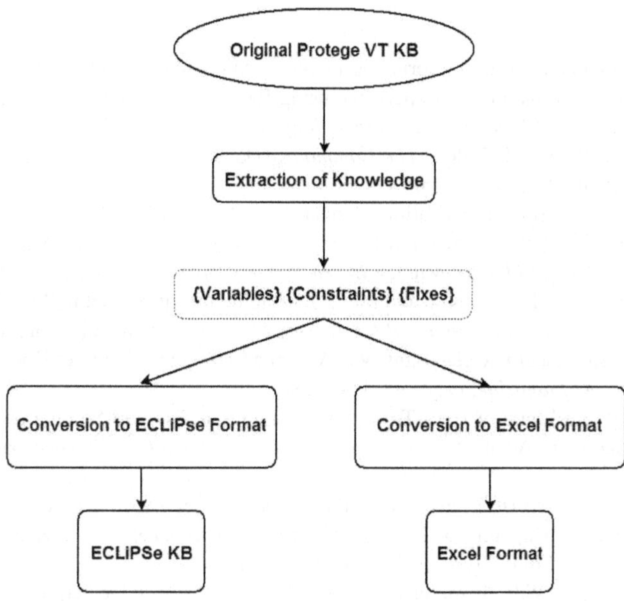

Fig. 2. Overview of ExtrAKTor and the stages needed to create both ECLiPSe and Excel KBs

equational nature of this problem may make it highly suited for solution by ECLiPSe and hence delivers the exceptional execution speed observed. Additionally, the VT problem may be under-constrained, or even deterministic, and this could also explain the exceptional performance.

Planned future work includes:

- Introducing fixes into the CSP formulation of a task
- Dealing with mutually inconsistent fixes; these fixes were removed in the Sisyphus-II simplification of the VT domain KB
- Using ExtrAKTor with additional KBs (it is planned to use the UHAUL task)
- Developing a Java based open source version of ExtrAKTor
- Making ExtrAKTor a web-service

Acknowledgments

This project has benefited from an association with the Advanced Knowledge Technologies (AKT) Interdisciplinary Research Collaboration (IRC) which is sponsored by the UK's Engineering and Physical Sciences Research Council (EPSRC) under grant GR/N15764/01. We acknowledge useful discussions of Research issues with Tomas Nordlander & David Corsar. Additionally, we also acknowledge discussions with various members of the Protégé team at Stanford University, including Mark Musen who also made available their version of the Sisyphus-VT code.

References

1. R. Benjamins and D. Fensel. Editorial: problem-solving methods. *IJHCS*, 49:305–313, 1998.
2. J. Bennett and R. Engelmore. Experience using EMYCIN in Rule-Based Expert Systems. *AISB Journal Special Issue on Agent Technology*, 1(1):314–328, 1984.
3. J. Breuker and W. Van de Velde. *The CommonKADS Library for Expertise Modeling*. IOS Press, Amsterdam, Holland, 1995.
4. W.J. Clancey. Heuristic Classification. *Artificial Intelligence*, 27:289–350, 1995.
5. D. Fensel and E. Motta. Structured Development of Problem Solving Methods. In *11th Knowledge Acquisition for Knowledge-Based Systems Workshop*, Banff, Canada, 1998.
6. et al Li Ding. Swoogle: A Search and Metadata Engine for the Semantic Web. In *Thirteenth ACM Conference on Information and Knowledge Management*, Washington DC, 2004.
7. S. Marcus, J. Stout, and J. McDermott. VT: An Expert Designer That Uses Knowledge-Based Backtracking. *AI Magazine*, pages 95–111, 1988.
8. J. McDermott. Preliminary Steps Toward a Taxonomy of Problem-Solving Methods. Automatic Knowledge for Acquisition for Expert Systems. *Artificial Intelligence*, pages 225–254, 1998.
9. T. Runcie. *PhD Thesis (in Preparation)*. PhD thesis, University of Aberdeen, August 2006.
10. T. Runcie, D. Sleeman, and P.M.D. Gray. Pragmatic Approaches to Knowledge ReUSe: the Sisyphus-VT Case Study. Technical report, May 2006.
11. A.T. Schreiber and W.P. Birmingham. The "Sisyphus" knowledge-acquisition benchmark experiments. *IJHCS*, 44(3/4):275–280, 1996.
12. et al. Schreiber, G. CML: the CommonKADS conceptual modeling language. In *EKAW94*, 1994.
13. Barbara Smith. A Tutorial on Constraint Programming. Technical Report 95.14, School of Computing Research Report, University of Leeds, April April 1995.
14. E. Thomas. OntoSearch: a Semantic Web Service to Support the Reuse of Ontologies. In *Artificial Intelligence*, 2004.
15. A. Valente, J. Breuker, and W. Van de Velde. The CommonKADS library in perspective. *IJHCS*, 49:391–416, 1998.
16. AKT. *http://www.aktors.org/publications/reuse*, August 2004.
17. Swoogle. *http://swoogle.umbc.edu*, March 2006.
18. OntoSearch. *http://www.onsosearch.org*, March 2006.
19. CLIPS. *http://www.ghg.net/clips/CLIPS.html*, December 2005.
20. Protege VT Sisyphus Ontology. *ftp://ftp-smi.stanford.edu/pub/protege/S2-WFW.ZIP*, August 2004.
21. Sisyphus II. *http://ksi.cpsc.ucalgary.ca/KAW/Sisyphus*, December 2005.
22. PSMTab. *http://protege.stanford.edu/plugins/psmtab/PSMTab.html*, December 2005.
23. ECLiPSe. *http://eclipse.crosscoreop.com/eclipse*, April 2006.
24. G. Yost. Sisyphus 1993 - Configuring Elevator Systems. Technical report, SMI, 1994.

Role Organization Model in Hozo

Eiichi Sunagawa, Kouji Kozaki, Yoshinobu Kitamura, and Riichiro Mizoguchi

The Institute of Scientific and Industrial Research, Osaka University
8-1 Mihogaoka, Ibaraki, Osaka, 567-0047 Japan
{sunagawa, kozaki, kita, miz}@ei.sanken.osaka-u.ac.jp

Abstract. The establishment of a computational framework of roles contributes effectively to the management of instance models because it provides us with a useful policy for treatment of views and contexts related to roles. In our research, we have developed an ontology building environment, which provides a framework for representation of roles and their characteristics. In this paper, as an extension of the framework, we present a framework for organizing roles according to their context dependencies. We especially focus on defining and organizing compound roles, which depend on several contexts.

Keywords: Role Modeling, Context Dependency, Ontology Development.

1 Introduction

Currently, Ontological Engineering attracts a lot of attention in many research areas and has been investigated from various view points; fundamental theory, development, application, and so on. One of the major roles of ontology is to properly represent the underlying conceptual structure of the messy world reflecting the reality as much as possible. All the existing ontology building tools are designed to help people develop such a good ontology. However, few ontology development tools have enough frameworks to provide an advanced framework for ontology description compliant with fundamental theories of ontology.

It is one of the important and essential topics for ontology development to discriminate *role concepts* from the others [1, 2, 3, 4]. By a role concept, we mean a concept of a role itself which an entity plays in a context. And, by a basic concept, we mean the other concept which can be defined without referring to other concepts. For example, role concepts include Lerner, Fuel and Food. Then, we strictly distinguish them from basic concepts such as Human, Gasoline and Yogurt.

However, it is difficult to represent roles in computer properly. For example, a parent is often represented by a *property* such as a *parent-of* property or a *parent* property in RDF(S) or OWL without fundamental discussion of their conceptualization. Furthermore, these representations are often confused with each other in spite of that they have to be differentiated from each other. The former is a relation which is conceptualized according to a parent-child relation and represented also as a binary relation like "*parent-of(A, B)*". On the other hand, the latter is conceptualized according to a parental characteristic and represented as a unary

S. Staab and V. Svatek (Eds.): EKAW 2006, LNAI 4248, pp. 67 – 81, 2006.

predicate like "*parent(A)*". Without recognition of such a difference, they are often represented as properties in the same manner.

Needless to say, parent is a role which is specified according to a manner of a person's participation in a relation between a parent and a child. This conceptualization of a Parent Role is based on a clear discrimination of a parent-child relation from a parental characteristic. However, it is not easy to represent this definition only in the framework which most of the ontology description languages provide, since we are often confused by the gap between our recognition of concepts and the conceptual framework of ontology languages.

In order to represent characteristics of roles and to ensure their semantic interoperability, developers need to specify conceptualization of roles based on a consistent policy for dealing with them. One of the approaches to this issue is to realize a framework which helps to make necessary and sufficient differentiation among concepts and represent them with a high fidelity to conceptualizations by developers. This is why intensive work has been done on OWL representation patterns of *part-of, has-part, attribute, etc.* in the best practice working group[1].

In this background, we have developed an ontology building environment, named Hozo, which provides a framework based on the theory of role concepts and their characteristics [4, 5]. Although Hozo allows users to represent roles better than other existing tools, its theoretical foundation is left unclear and it has some room for improvement concerning the generality of how to deal with roles. In the Hozo framework, role concepts are organized in a basic-concept-centered view and their definitions are scattered around in the respective related concepts which give the context of the roles. This is why Hozo users still have some amount of difficulty in representing relations among role concepts. In this paper, as an extension of the previous framework, we present a framework for organizing role concepts in a hierarchy in the role-centered view. After an overview of the idea of role concept in Hozo, we investigate how to organize role concepts according to their contextual dependencies. We especially focus on defining and organizing a role concept which depends on several contexts, that is, the case where a role plays a role by introducing the idea of role aggregation. And we design a system to realize organization of role concepts. We also discuss related work followed by concluding remarks.

2 Role Concepts

2.1 Needs of Differentiation of Role Concepts

Context-dependence is one of the important characteristics of roles and explains how and why an entity changes its roles to play according to the context it depends on. For example, John is regarded as a Teacher in his School and as a Husband in his Marital Relationship. While such roles can be modeled in connection with time passing, its context-dependence is also necessary semantics for properly capturing roles.

Improper modeling of roles will greatly influence the semantics of *is-a* hierarchy of concepts. We focus here on the semantics of *is-a* that an instance of a concept is always

[1] http://www.w3.org/2001/sw/BestPractices/

recognized also as an instance of its super-concept. For example, in WordNet[2], Dairy Product and Food are treated as hypernyms of Yogurt. If role concepts are not discriminated from the others and these lexical hyponymies among the words are regarded as *is-a* relations among concepts with no distinction, instances of Yogurt are always recognized as an instance of Dairy Product and also Food. In such a model, however, we may often have to struggle for faithful representation of events in the real world. To represent that some yogurt has been eaten, we delete the instance of Yogurt. And, it in turn means deleting instances of Dairy Product and Food, which is totally OK. However, in the case where a yogurt has rotted and become inedible, we need to manage instances more sophisticatedly. Because the instance of Yogurt has lost an identity as Food but keeps one as Dairy Product, we can delete only the instance of Food. These managements of an instance model might force us to make different semantics of is-a relation and to establish routines for ad-hoc management of instances. Such a strategy detracts from the value of an ontology, which ensures consistency of an instance model. Moreover, it is difficult in such a model to represent the instance of Yogurt changes its roles to play such as Load, Merchandise, Foodstuff, etc. according to the changes of its contexts or aspects. We believe it is advisable for a computer model and an ontology behind it to correspond to the real world as truly as possible.

On the other hand, based on fundamental theories of roles in an ontology [2, 5], we can clearly differentiate role concepts, e.g. *food*, from the others and can cope with the problems caused by adulterating role concepts and the others. For example, the hyponymy between *yogurt* and *food* is not regarded as an *is-a* relation. And, we acquire a consistent policy to manage instances of *yogurt* and *food* consistently. It is not easy but worth for ensuring quality of an ontology as a backbone of an instance model to differentiate role concepts from others and organize them.

2.2 Role Concepts in Hozo

2.2.1 Role Concepts and Basic Concepts

With citing work by Charles S. Peirce, Sowa introduced the *firstness*, the *secondness* and the *thirdness* of concepts [1, 6]. The *firstness* can be roughly defined as a concept which can be defined without mentioning other concepts. Examples include iron, a man, a tree, etc. In a similar way, the *secondness* can be defined as a concept which cannot be defined without referring to other concepts. Examples include a wife, a teacher, a child, etc. The *thirdness* links the *firstness* and the *secondness*. Examples include paternity, brotherhood, etc. Based on these theories, we call one kind of the *secondness* type a role in this paper.

Roughly speaking, by **role**, we mean what is recognized according to the way of participation of an entity in a context. Because, roles cannot be discussed without their context, we have been focusing on their context-dependencies as essential attributes rather than "player" link to date. The idea of dependency on the context corresponds roughly to "founded" of roles and "Role-of" [7, 8]. And, by basic concept, we mean a thing except roles in order to bring the contrast.

---

[2] http://wordnet.princeton.edu/

2.2.2 Role Concept, Potential Player and Role-Playing Thing

Here, we introduce important distinctions among Role Concept, Potential Player and Role-Playing Thing (Role-Holder). A ***role concept*** represents a role itself and is defined as a concept played by something. By a ***potential player***, we mean a thing which is able to play a role. It is called also a ***class constraint*** from the view point of that it constraints classes which can be a player of the role. And, while an entity is actually playing the role and behaving as its ***role-playing thing***, the entity becomes a ***role-holder***.

The fundamental scheme in which we capture roles is "In a *context*, a *player (class constraint)* can play a *role concept* and then becomes a *role-holder*." In the case of school teacher, for example, "in a *school*, a *person* plays a *teacher role*[3] and then, becomes a *teacher*." This means that roles are divided into two kinds: a role concept and a role-holder in our terminology. And, players are also divided into two kinds: a potential player and a role-playing thing (a role-holder). The latter is applied only to relations among individuals.

Fig. 1 shows the conceptual framework of role we have proposed. These are properties of teacher role, person and teacher role-holder. They are divided into three groups. Properties in group A are determined by the definition of a role concept itself independently of its player. The second group B is shared by both of the role concept and the player. And, the last group C is what the role concept does not care about. In the case of a Teacher, his/her Subject and Class can be determined only by its role independently on its player (a Person). On the other hand, a teacher's Name and the Age limit are defined in relation with properties of a Person. And, his/her Height and Weight does not matter for description of a Teacher Role.

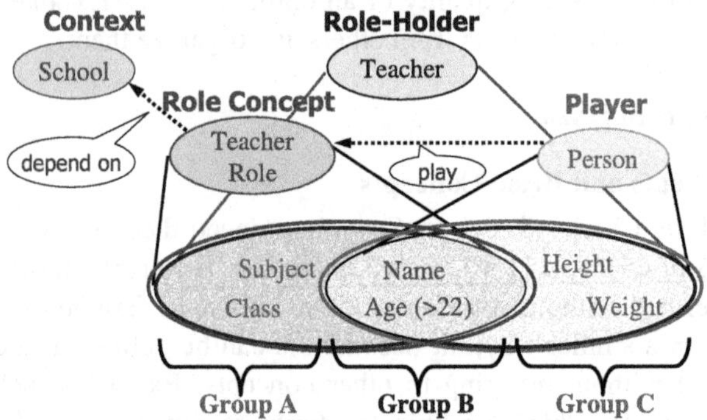

Fig. 1. Conceptual framework of role

In general, a role concept is defined by describing these properties in the context. Its player is defined by oneself. And, the role-holder is defined as a result and eventually includes all of these properties. Therefore, the individual corresponding to a teacher is the composite of these two individuals and totally dependent on them.

In these considerations of role concepts, we have developed an ontology building environment, which provides a framework for representation of role concepts and

[3] When we mention a particular role, we put "role" after the role name like "a teacher role".

their characteristics. The system is named Hozo[4] [4, 5] and composed of Ontology Editor, Onto-Studio, Ontology Server and Ontology Manager. Users of Hozo can browse and modify ontologies with its ontology editor (in Fig.2). In Hozo, two kinds of basic concepts: a whole concept and a relational concept are defined. And, a role concept is defined within the context specified by the basic concept. The system manages some basic concepts as contexts of role concepts and provides a framework to define a role concept. Fig.2-a) shows the form of presentation for definitions of concepts on a browsing panel of Ontology Editor. A role concept is represented as a node connected with the other node representing a concept as its context. The connection is shown as a link representing a *part-of* relation (denoted by "p/o") or a *participate-in* relation (by "p/i") according to the classification of its context. For example, Fig.2-b) represents that a **Person**, who is referred to as the class constraint, plays a **Teacher Role**, and then becomes a role holder a **Teacher**.

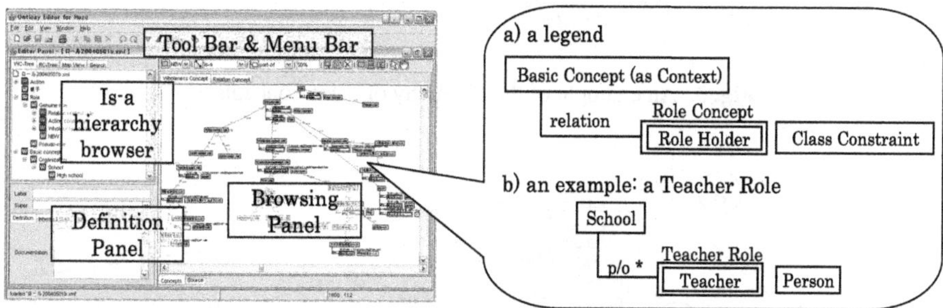

Fig. 2. Ontology Editor in Hozo and its form of presentation for definitions of role concepts

3 Organizing Roles

In this section, we present a framework for organizing roles in an ontology. By organizing roles, we mean mainly constructing a hierarchy of role concepts in order to explicitly grasp and represent relations among them and structures of their context dependences. In the following sections, we explain some considerations as guides to organizing roles through discussions on two hierarchies: hierarchies of basic concepts and role concepts constructed with using Hozo. The hierarchies are composed of some concepts in school[5] (in Fig.3 and Fig.4).

To begin with, a **Role** is defined at the top of the hierarchy of role concepts (in Fig.4-a) as a class which has three slots: *context*, *holder*, *role part*. The first is related by a *participate-in* relation and describes in what context the role concept is recognized. The second is also related by a *participate-in* relation and show a basic concept which can carry the role concept. The third is related by a *part-of* relation and associated with role aggregation (described in 3.2).

---

[4] http://www.hozo.jp

[5] This ontology is developed in order to discuss semantics of role concepts. So, it is incomplete and concepts are not defined in detail.

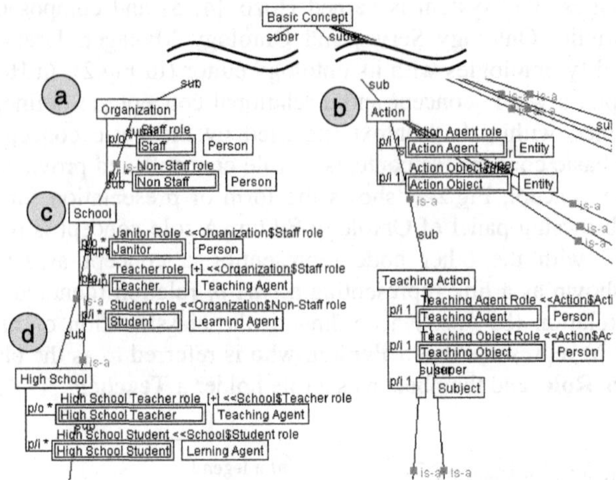

Fig. 3. An example of the hierarchy of basic concepts

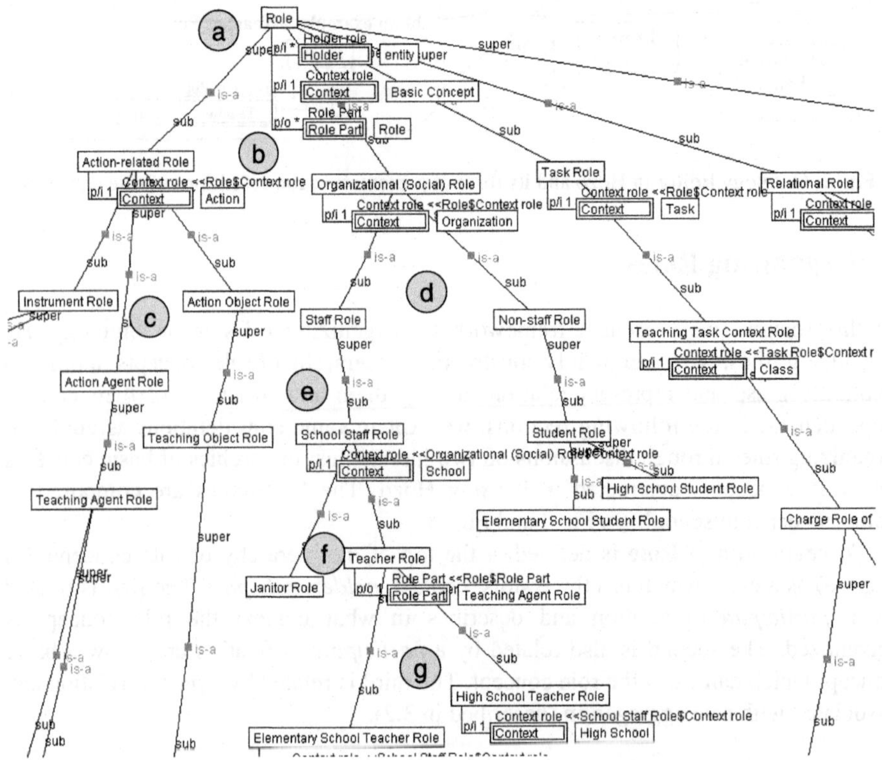

Fig. 4. An example of the hierarchy of basic concepts

3.1 Organizing Role Concepts According to Classification of Their Contexts

Roles are recognized in a context. So, in order to classify role concepts, we can utilize them as the foundation. For example, task knowledge for solving problem can be discriminated from domain knowledge of a target world. Then, we can identify task-specific roles such as symptom role in a fault diagnostic task and conclusion role in a reasoning task. And, in a functional context in the artifact world, a steering wheel role (played by a wheel) and a level control valve role (played by flow control valve) are classified into a functional role [9]. Note here that we do not claim artifact is role. We believe wheel is a wheel and flow control valve is a flow control valve in its nature. We are claiming that they can play another role according to functional contexts. Likewise, we can classify role concepts into an action-related role, a relational role and so on. Although the enumeration is not exhaustive, Fig. 5 shows typology of typical roles.

In Fig. 4, an **Action-related Role** and an **Organizational (Social) Role** are defined and classified into a **Role** as a top-level category of the hierarchy (Fig.4-b). The relations among these role concepts describe from the role-centered view that an **Action** and an **Organization** are categorized as contexts at the top-level of the hierarchy of basic concepts (Fig.3-a, b).

- Task Role
  - Symptom Role (Fault Diagnosis)
  - Conclusion Role (Reasoning)
- Functional role
  - Steering Wheel role (Steering Function)
  - Level control valve role: played by a flow control valve (Function)
- Action-related role
  - Actor role (Any action)
  - Teaching Agent role (Teaching Action)
  - Target object role (Action object)
- Process-related role
  - Product role (Final output)
  - Residue role (How it is processed)
- Relational role
  - Friend role (Friendship)
  - Parent role (Parent-Child Relation)

Fig. 5. Categories of role concepts

3.2 Aggregation of Role Concepts

Because some roles are conceptualized from several viewpoints and depend on several contexts, it is difficult to organize them simply according to their contexts. For example, a **Teacher** is recognized not only as a **Teaching Agent** but also as a **School Staff**. Such a role needs to be played together with other roles. In other words, some role will automatically become un-played if its player stops to play any one of the other roles. This kind of relation between roles cannot be explained only with a well-known characteristic of roles: an entity can play multiple roles simultaneously. Some other researchers discusses it as "requirement" [7] or "roles can play roles" ("role-holders can play roles" in our terminology) [3].

We differentiate role concepts into two kinds: a ***primitive role concept*** and a ***compound role concept*** which have single-context and multiple-context dependences, respectively. Primitive role concepts can be organized simply and easily according to the categories of their contexts as described in 3.1. In order to deal with compound role concepts, we devise the idea of ***Role Aggregation***. It is represented in both hierarchy of basic concepts and role concepts. And, the two representations have the same semantic information on role aggregation. Fig.6 shows hierarchies extracted from the hierarchies shown in Figs. 3-c and 4-f in order to focus on role aggregation.

Two central purposes of role aggregation are decomposition of a compound role concept and clear decision on its essential context[6]. To summarize an outline of role aggregation, we here organize an example of a compound role concept which depends on two contexts. At the start, the essential context is chosen among the two contexts after investigating and decomposing the context dependence of the role concept. Assume that a **Teacher Role** depends on two contexts: an **Organization** as its essential (primary) context and a **Teaching Action** as its secondary one. And then, two primitive role concepts are identified; a **Staff Role** and a **Teaching Agent**. They depend on each of those contexts respectively.

In our framework as described in 2.2, we can constrain on a class whose instances may play certain roles. In our previous work, a class constraint refers to only basic concepts. Here, we extend our framework and enable the class constraint to refer to also role holders. In this way, a role holder, which is playing some role(s) already, can play other role(s). It also means aggregating context dependences of these roles. This role aggregation is represented in the following manner (Fig.6-a); a **Teacher Role** is defined as a specialized concept of a **Staff Role** and a **Teaching Agent** (role holder) is referred to as a class constraint of a **Teacher Role**. Then, a **Teacher Role** is defined as a role concept which depends on both contexts of a **Staff Role** and a **Teaching Agent Role**.

Next, we explain role aggregation in a hierarchy of role concepts (Fig.6-b). A compound role concept is classified into a role concept which depends on an essential context of the compound role. Role aggregation is represented by using *is-a* relation and *part-of* relation[7] as the following manner; a **Teacher Role** is defined as a sub-concept of a **Staff Role** through *is-a* relation, and a **Teaching Agent Role** is defined as a part concept of a **Teacher Role** through *part-of* relation. By ***Role Part***, we mean a role concept defined as a part of a compound role concept.

---

[6] The decision on essential contexts of compound roles enables to organize them in an *is-a* hierarchy. We do not discuss and conclude what the essential context should be in general. Based on the relativity of essence, we think essences of concepts are decided by the developers intended as far as the decision is consistent in the while ontology.

[7] Here, we focus on a semantics of *is-a* relation that a sub-concept inherits properties of its super-concept and *part-of* relation that a whole concept possesses properties of its part concepts. Besides this, the *part-of* relation among roles here represents that a compound role concept (the whole one) can not exists without its role-part(s) (the part one(s)). As far as our discussion, that relation among roles has general common semantics of part-whole relation like transitivity, anti-symmetry and so on.

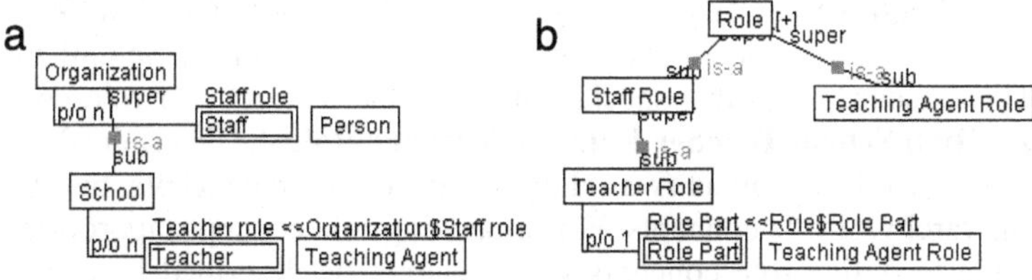

Fig. 6. An example of role aggregation

Our framework for ontology development is based on the consistent policy that an *is-a* hierarchy of concepts are formed according to their essential properties. The policy is indispensable for organizing roles, especially compound roles because, if their essential properties are not determined, they might be just listed in disorder. In this reason, we represent inheritance of dependence on an essential context between roles with an *is-a* relation and discriminate it clearly from the inheritance of other characteristics of the roles. Thus, we did not adopt other methods, say, multiple inheritance, to organize role concepts which might cause an unnecessary disorder to role aggregation.

3.3 Further Considerations for Organizing Roles

After classifications of role concepts according to categories of their contexts (described in 3.1), they are organized in detail. This kind of organizing role concepts is located in a middle layer of a hierarchy of role concepts between top categories of role concepts and aggregated role concepts from the bottom (described in 3.2). Here, we mention three significant points of organizing role concepts.

The first is to organize role concepts according to the aspects of entity playing the roles and manners of its participation into contexts. They are clarified in definitions of the contexts and their categories depend on the definitions. For example, we classified a **Weapon Role** and a **Learner Role** as an **Action-related Role**. And, with investigation of them in more detail, we conclude that the former participates in an action context as an instrument and the latter participates as an agent. Then, we can define an **Action Instrument Role** and an **Action Agent Role** and classify them as subclasses of an **Action-related Role**. In the example of the hierarchy of role concepts (in Fig.4-d), a **Staff Role** and a **Non-staff Role** are classified into **Organizational Role** depending on an **Organization** as its context. This classification represent that a **Staff Role** and a **Non-staff Role** are defined as parts of an **Organization** in the hierarchy of basic concepts (in Fig.3-a).

The second is to organize role concepts based on an *is-a* relation between basic concepts as contexts. In general, role concepts related to an *is-a* relation depends on the same category of context. Assume that there are a sub-concept and its super-concept in a hierarchy of basic concepts. A role concept depending on the sub-concept is recognized by specialization of the context of the role concept depending on the super-concept. Then, in a hierarchy of basic concepts, a relation between these role concepts is represented by using overriding. And, in a hierarchy of role concepts, it is represented as an *is-a* relation. In the example of the hierarchy of basic concepts (in Fig.3-d), a **High School Teacher Role** is defined as a part of a **High School** and is recognized by specialization of the context of **Teacher** from a **School** to a **High School**. Then, according to this specialization, in the hierarchy of role concepts (in Fig.4-f,g), **<High School Teacher Role** *is-a* **Teacher Role>** is determined.

The third is also based on an *is-a* relation between basic concepts, but it is shown only in a hierarchy of role concepts. For organizing role concepts appropriately, it is indispensable to define role concepts which cannot be described in a hierarchy of basic concepts. Such role concepts are defined for constraint of contexts as intermediate concepts among role concepts described in a hierarchy of basic concepts. They are used mainly for constraint of contexts and not instantiated directly. We call them ***Abstract Role Concepts*** like an abstract class in an object oriented programming. In the example of the hierarchy of basic concepts (in Fig.3-c), a **Teacher Role** and a **Janitor Role** as parts of a **School** is defined by specializing a **Staff Role** as a part of **Organization**. So, in the hierarchy of role concepts, **<Teacher Role** *is-a* **Staff Role>** and **<Janitor Role** *is-a* **Staff Role>** are held (in Fig.4-d,f). And then, according to **<School** *is-a* **Organization>**, **<School Staff Role** *is-a* **Staff Role>** is described (in Fig.4-d,e). In this case, according to their context dependences, a **School Staff Role** is classified into a **Staff Role** and defined as a super class of a **Teacher Role** and a **Janitor Role** in the hierarchy of role concepts (in Fig.4-e).

4 Instances of Roles

In this section, we discuss what characteristics of instances of role concepts should be represented in their instance model. Instance model provides us with semantics of classes and individuals by specifying their interdependencies concerning their appearance and extinction. It is indispensable for application of ontologies developed with Hozo and clarification of our strategy for treatment of roles to consider the characteristics of the instances of role concepts.

While we have investigated basic issues of role concepts in our previous work [4], it does not include consideration of compound role concepts. So, in this paper, we generalize the framework of role concepts. In the following, **R** denotes a compound role concept, $\mathbf{C_1 \ldots C_n}$ its depending contexts, $\mathbf{R_1 \ldots R_n}$ role concepts aggregated into **R** as its *role-parts* and **P** a concept referred to as the class constraint by **R**. An instance of **P** can play the role conceptualized as **R**. We explain the framework using an actual example of a **Teacher Role** described in section 3.

(A) States of an instance of a role concept

An instance of **R** has the following two states. (1) Only the role conceptualized as **R** is instantiated (realized). (2) An instance of **P** plays the **R**.

For example, an instance of a **Teacher Role** has two states. One is a teacher role just defined as a part of an instance of **School**. As a vacant position, it is undetermined about who will play it. The other is a role which some person is playing when he/she is recognized as a **Teacher** (role holder).

(B) Dependence of instances of role concepts on their context
An instance of **R** exists only if all instances of $\mathbf{C_1...C_n}$ are instantiated. When, at least, one of them is deleted, so does the instance of **R**.

For example, a **Teacher Role** is instantiated and a **Teacher** is recognized, on the assumption that a **School** and a **Teaching Action** are instantiated. When the school is closed down or when a teaching class is finished, an instance of a **Teacher Role** is deleted.

(C) Dependence of instances of role concepts on their players
In general, an instance of a role is dealt with as a incomplete instance until an entity plays the role because roles can not behave without its players. When instances of **R1...Rn** as constituents of **R** are played by the same instance of **P**, a role holder of **R** is recognized with being composed by an instance of **R**.

For example, when someone is employed as a staff by a school and he/she teaches, all values or ranges of properties of **Teacher** (role holder) are fixed. Then, a **Teacher Role** can be instantiated and he/she is recognized as a teacher.

(D) Extinction of a role holder
A role holder of **R** is recognized as the summation of both instances of **R** and **P**. Here, they are denoted **Ri** and **Pi**. Then, there are four cases in which the role holder is disappear: (1) **Pi** has been disappeared. (2) **Ri** has been disappeared. (3) **Pi** has stopped playing **Ri**. (4) At least, one of role holders of $\mathbf{R_1...R_n}$ is disappeared.

For example, there are three cases in which a person is not recognized as a Teacher. They are (1) when he/she has died, (2) when the post he/she filled has disappeared because of closing down his/her school, personnel reduction and so on, (3) when he/she has retired his/her job as a teacher and (4) when his/her teaching class has been finished.

5 Implementation

As an extension of the ontology editor in Hozo, we provide a pane for constructing a hierarchy of role concepts and function to support organizing role concepts.

We add a pane for building and editing a hierarchy of role concepts to the ontology editor in a line of panes for basic concepts provided previously (Fig.7). The pane provides almost the same functions as those of the panes for basic concepts. And, we improve the ontology editor to support organizing role concepts in the strategies described in section 3. Firstly, we extend the framework to define concepts for representation of role aggregation. Secondly, we add a function for keeping consistency between role concepts defined in the hierarchies of basic concepts and those defined in the one of role concepts. This function is based on the fact that some parts of the role concepts defined in both of the hierarchies share the common semantics. For example, if a developer aggregates role concepts in a hierarchy of role concepts, this aggregation is represented automatically also in a hierarchy of basic concepts. And, we provide some wizards for organizing role concepts. They support operation to deal with role concepts and guide ontology developers.

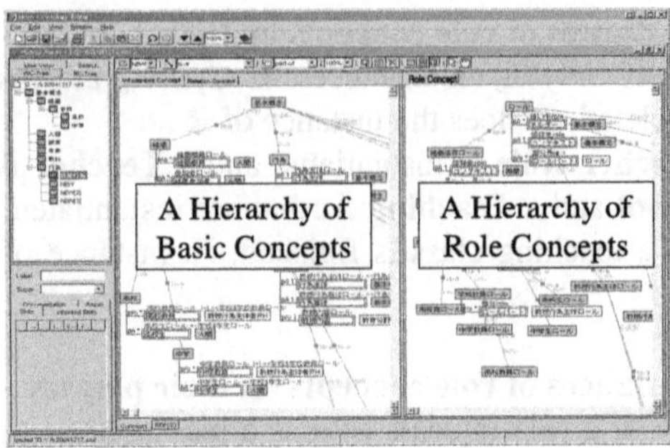

Fig. 7. Panes for building and editing hierarchies of basic concepts and role concepts in Ontology Editor

Besides this, we are investigating how to deal with characteristics of roles in OWL. See Fig.8 and Fig.9. We define *hozo:BasicConcept* class and *hozo:RoleConcept* class to expresses basic concepts and role concepts. And so, the domain of *hozo:dependOn* property is a *hozo:RoleConcept* Here, we emphasize that role concepts are dealt with not as an *owl:ObjectProperty* but as an *owl:Class*. A *hozo:playedBy* property represents a relation between classes of role concepts and classes of their potential players. Its domain is *hozo:RoleConcept,* and its range is *hozo:BasicConcept.* The definition of *hozo:RoleConcept* has a restriction on this property, and there the property indicates role-playable thing discussed in 2.2. And when a relation between an instance of a role concept and its player is represented as a *hozo:playedBy* property, the property means a *playing relation* between them. And a *hozo:RoleHolder* class represents a role-holder. It is composed of a role concept and a player, and *hozo:inheritFrom* property expresses its semantics that only definitions (properties) are inherited without identity. And, at the present, we are trying to clarify and regulate behaviors of roles with using SWRL (Semantic Web Rule Language) in more detail. The model presented here is utilized for extension of the function for exporting ontologies which are developed with Hozo in OWL.

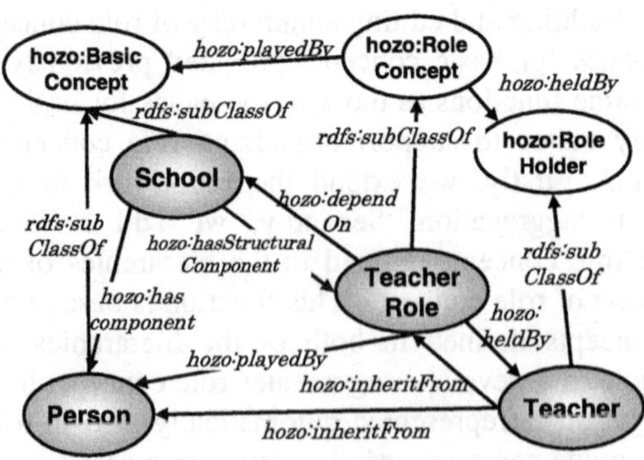

Fig. 8. Role representation in OWL

```
ObjectProperty(hozo:dependOn
    domain(hozo:RoleConcept))
ObjectProperty(hozo:playedBy
    domain(hozo:RoleConcept)
    range(hozo:BasicConcept))
ObjectProperty(hozo:inheritFrom
    domain(hozo:RoleHolder))
ObjectProperty(hozo:hasComponent
    range(hozo:BasicConcept))
ObjectProperty(hozo:hasStructuralComponent
    range(hozo:RoleConcept))
Class(hozo:BasicConcept partial
    DisjointClasses(hozo:RoleConcept hozo:RoleHolder))
Class(hozo:RoleConcept partial
    restriction(hozo:dependOn cardinarity(1))
    restriction(hozo:playedBy maxCardinarity(1)))
   restriction(hozo:heldBy maxCardinarity(1)))
Class(hozo:RoleHolder partial
    restriction(hozo:inheritFrom cardinarity(2))
    restriction(hozo:inheritFrom someValuesFrom(hozo:RoleConcept))
    restriction(hozo:inheritFrom someValuesFrom(hozo:BasicConcept)))
Class(TeacherRole partial hozo:RoleConcept
    restriction(hozo:dependOn allValuesFrom(School))
    restriction(hozo:playedBy allValuesFrom(person)))
Class(Teacher partial hozo:RoleHolder
    restriction(hozo:inheritFrom someValuesFrom(TeacherRole))
    restriction(hozo:inheritFrom someValuesFrom(Person)))
Class(School partial
    restriction(hozo:hasStructuralComponent
someValuesFrom(TeacherRole))
    restriction(hozo:hasComponent someValuesFrom(Person)))
```

Fig. 9. Role representation in OWL (Abstract Syntax)

6 Related Work

Guarino and his colleagues aim to establish a formal framework for dealing with roles [2, 7]. And Gangemi and Mika introduce an ontology for representing a context and states of affairs, called D&S, and its application to roles [10, 11]. Their research is concerned with formalities and axioms of an ontology. In contrast, we do not formalize role concepts because our goal is to develop a computer environment for building ontologies. Our notions of role concepts share a lot with their theory of roles; that is, context-dependence, specialization of roles, and so on. According to their theory, our framework can be reinforced in terms of axioms. They describe specialization and requirements as kind of sub-class relations between role concepts. The former corresponds to *is-a* and the latter to role aggregation in our framework. However, they do not describe clearly that *is-a* relations between role concepts are established only if the two concepts share the same category of context-dependency. While we have discussed how to define a role concept which has complicated context-dependences, they only point out a requirement relation. Our notions differ from their work on other two points; that is dynamics of a role and clear discrimination of a role from its player (role holder). Firstly, we focus on context-dependence of a role concept and its categories. So, time dependence of a role concept is treated implicitly in our framework because an entity changes its roles to play according to its aspect without time passing. As opposed to this, their framework deals with time-dependency explicitly. Secondly, we distinguish role concepts and role holders [4, 5]. On the basis of this distinction, we propose a tool for properties and relations on roles, such as an aggregation of role concepts.

Fan also recognizes the importance of constructing a hierarchy of role concepts based on differentiation of them from the others and shows an example in that a Thing is classified into an Entity and a Role in [12]. And, he gives an Agent and an Instrument as sub-concepts of a Role. However, he does not clarify a point of view for organizing them. To our knowledge, they are regarded as being organized according to their manner they participate in their contexts.

Breuker develops ontologies for legal domains based on epistemology and discusses characteristics of roles in [13]. He also mentions adulteration between a role itself and playing role and others between a role and its player. We share his notion in discriminations of these concepts and differentiate a role concept, a class constraint and a role holder from one another [4, 5]. He describes two kinds of roles; as a concept and as a relation. However, he does not organize them in more detail. And, in contrast of that he defines roles according to behavioral requirements and so on, we allow developers of an ontology to define role concepts just as the developers intended because it is outside the scope of our research to discuss how to conceptualize roles.

7 Conclusion

In this paper, we have discussed a framework for organizing role concepts in a hierarchy according to their context-dependences. Then, we investigated instances of role concepts to give semantics of role-related concepts. Although it was not discussed explicitly, our framework solves the so-called counting problem and universal/individual problem of roles. The definitions of role concepts can be translated into statements in OWL. In conclusion, our framework in Hozo provides a layer in which developers can construct ontologies with high quality description of role concepts and a mechanism for setting it in the current linguistic expression. As future work, we plan to implement the framework in Hozo and investigate a theory of organizing role concepts (e.g. semantics of *is-a* relation between role concepts).

References

1. Sowa, J. F.: Top-level ontological categories, International Journal of Human-Computer Studies, Vol.43, Issue 5-6, pp.669-685 (1995)
2. Guarino, N.: Some Ontological Principles for Designing Upper Level Lexical Resources. In Proceedings of the First International Conference on Language Resources and Evaluation, pp.527–534, Granada, Spain (1998)
3. Steimann, F.: On the Representation of Roles in Object-oriented and Conceptual Modeling, Data & Knowledge Engineering, Vol.35, Num.1, pp.83-106 (2000)
4. Kozaki, K., Kitamura, Y., Ikeda, M. and Mizoguchi, R.: Hozo: An Environment for Building/Using Ontologies Based on a Fundamental Consideration of Role" and "Relationship". In Proceedings of the 13th International Conference Knowledge Engineering and Knowledge Management (EKAW2002), pp.213-218, Sigüenza, Spain (2002)

5. Kozaki, K., Kitamura, Y., Ikeda, M. and Mizoguchi, R.: Development of an Environment for Building Ontologies which is based on a Fundamental Consideration of "Relationship" and "Role", In Proceedings of the 2000 Pacific Knowledge Acquisition Workshop (PKAW2000), pp.205-221, Sydney, Australia (2000)
6. Sowa, J. F.: Knowledge Representation: Logical, Philosophical, and Computational Foundations (2000)
7. Masolo, C., Vieu, L., Bottazzi, E., Catenacci, C., Ferrario, R., Gangemi, A. and Guarino, N.: Social Roles and their Descriptions. In Proceedings of the 9th International Conference on the Principles of Knowledge Representation and Reasoning (KR2004), pp.267–277, Whistler, Canada (2004)
8. Loebe, F.: Abstract vs. Social Roles - A Refined Top-Level Ontological Analysis. Papers from the AAAI Fall Symposium Technical Report FS-05-08, pp.93-100, Virginia, USA (2005)
9. Mizoguchi, R., Kozaki, K., Sano, T., and Kitamura, Y.: Construction and Deployment of a Plant Ontology. In Proceedings of 12th International Conference on KnowledgeEngineering and Knowledge Management, pp.113-128, Juan-les-Pins, France (2000)
10. Gangemi, A., Guarino, N., Masolo, C., Oltramari, A., Schneider, L.: Sweetening Ontologies with DOLCE, In Proceedings of the 13th International Conference Knowledge Engineering and Knowledge Management (EKAW2002), pp.166-181, Sigüenza, Spain (2002)
11. Gangemi, A., Mika, P.: Understanding the Semantic Web through Descriptions and Situations. International Conference on Ontologies, Databases and Applications of SEmantics (ODBASE 2003), Catania, Italy (2003)
12. Fan, J., Barker, K., Porter, B., and Clark, P.: Representing Roles and Purpose. In Proceedings of the International Conference on Knowledge Capture (K-Cap2001), pp.38–43, Victoria, B.C., Canada (2001)
13. Breuker, J. and Hoekstra, R.: Epistemology and ontology in core ontologies: FOLaw and LRI-Core, two core ontologies for law, In Proceedings of the EKAW04 Workshop on Core Ontologies in Ontology Engineering, pp.15-27, Northamptonshire, UK (2004)
14. Kozaki, K., Sunagawa, E., Kitamura, K. and Mizoguchi, M.: Fundamental Consideration of Role Concepts for Ontology Evaluation, In Proceedings of the 4th International EON (Evaluation of Ontologies for the Web) Workshop (to appear) (2006)

Verification and Refactoring of Ontologies with Rules

Joachim Baumeister and Dietmar Seipel

Institute for Computer Science
University of Würzburg, Germany
{baumeister,seipel}@informatik.uni-wuerzburg.de

Abstract. Currently, the introduction of an appropriate rule representation layer for the semantic web stack is discussed. However, with the inclusion of rule-based knowledge new verification issues for rule-augmented ontologies arise.

In this paper we investigate the detection of anomalies as an important subtask of verification. We extend and revise existing approaches for the syntactic verification of ontologies with respect to the existence of rules, and we introduce new anomalies considering the understandability and maintainability of such ontologies.

1 Introduction

The use of ontologies has shown its benefits in many applications of intelligent systems in the last years. Whereas, the implementation of lower parts of the semantic web stack has successfully led to standardizations, the upper parts, especially rules and the logic framework, are still heavily discussed in the research community, e.g., see Horrocks et al. [1].

It is well agreed that the combination of ontologies with rule-based knowledge is essential for many interesting semantic web tasks, e.g., the realization of semantic web agents and services. This insight has led to many proposals for rule languages compatible with the semantic web stack, e.g., the definition of SWRL (semantic web rule language) originating from RuleML and similar approaches [2]. [1] SWRL allows for the combination of a high-level abstract syntax for Horn-like rules with OWL [4], and a model theoretic semantics is given for the combination of OWL with SWRL rules. An XML syntax derived from RuleML allows for a syntactical compatibility with OWL. However, with the increased expressiveness of such ontologies new demands for the development and for maintenance guidelines arise. Thus, conventional approaches for *evaluating* and *maintaining* ontologies need to be extended and revised in the light of rules, and new measures need to be defined to cover the implied aspects of rules and their combination with conceptual knowledge in the ontology.

In this paper, we revisit known approaches for the syntactic verification of ontologies and extend existing definitions with respect to rules if needed. Furthermore, we define novel measures detecting parts of the ontology that may create problems for the maintainability of the overall ontology. Such knowledge fragments are usually not responsible for inconsistencies, but their elimination often can improve the understandability and compactness of the ontology.

[1] Currently, SWRL [3] has the status of a W3C member submission.

S. Staab and V. Svatek (Eds.): EKAW 2006, LNAI 4248, pp. 82–95, 2006.

We focus on the basic features of SWRL and OWL, e.g., we omit a discussion of SWRL built-ins. Due to the use of rules with OWL DL the detection of *all* anomalies is an undecidable task, cf. [2]. Here, we only consider a subset of OWL DL, i.e., the combined use of rules with subclass relations and some property characteristics like transitivity, complement, and disjointness. In addition, we do not consider the evaluation of an ontology with respect to the intended semantical meaning, which for example is implemented by the OntoClean methodology [5] for taxonomic decisions made in an ontology. We also do not consider common errors that can be implemented due to mistakes with the logical understanding of OWL descriptions, e.g., as described by Rector et al. [6].

Here, the term *verification* denotes the syntactic analysis of ontologies for *detecting anomalies*. On one hand, the discussed issues of the presented work originate from the evaluation of taxonomic structures in ontologies introduced by Gómez-Pérez [7]. On the other hand, in the context of rule ontologies classical work on the verification of rule-based knowledge has to be reconsidered as done, e.g., by Preece and Shinghal [8,9]. However, the combination of taxonomic and other ontological knowledge with a rule extension leads to new evaluation metrics that can cause redundant or even inconsistent behavior. Here the concept of dependency graphs/relations from deductive databases can be used [10]. For the sake of simplicity we will use the term *ontology* with the meaning of *ontology with rules* in this paper.

We distinguish the following categories of anomalies: 1) *Redundancy* due to duplicate or subsuming knowledge in the ontology. 2) *Circularity* in taxonomies or rule definitions. 3) *Inconsistency* because of contradicting definitions. 4) *Deficiency* as a category comprising subtle issues affecting parts of an ontology with questionable design. Anomalies can occur for many reasons. For example, the integration of ontologies can yield redundant knowledge, and the manual development and evolution of a (large) ontology may introduce inconsistent definitions. Obviously, anomalies make the understandability, extensibility and evolution of ontologies more difficult.

The elimination of anomalies is done by *refactoring*. This term originates from software engineering research [11,12], and it denotes the modification of source code without changing the external behavior of the program. The modification only focuses on the improvement of the code design rather than on its functionality. Analogously, the refactoring of ontologies should target the improvement of the design of the ontology, especially its understandability and maintainability.

The rest of the paper is organized as follows: Section 2 introduces the basic notions that are necessary for the analysis of ontologies with rules. In Section 3 we present measures to detect redundancy in ontologies, and in Section 4 variants of circularity are given. Section 5 describes the identification of syntactic inconsistency, and Section 6 introduces typical examples for deficient parts of the ontology and appropriate refactoring actions are sketched. Section 7 concludes the paper and gives directions for future work.

2 Basic Notions and Scope

For the analysis of ontologies with rules we restrict the range of considered constructs to a subset of OWL DL: we investigate the implications of rules that are mixed with *subClassOf* relations and/or the property characteristics *transitivity*, *complement*, and *disjointness*.

For the following it will be useful to extend the relations on classes and properties to relations on class and property atoms. Given two atoms A, A', we write $\circledast(A, A')$, if both atoms have the same argument tuple, and their predicate symbols are related by $\circledast$, i.e., if A and A' both are

- class atoms, such that $A = C(x)$, $A' = C'(x)$, and $\circledast(C, C')$, or
- property atoms, such that $A = P(x, y)$, $A' = P'(x, y)$, and $\circledast(P, P')$.

For example, the relation $\circledast$ can be *is-a*, *disjoint*, *complementOf*, etc. Note, that from a relationship $\circledast(A, A')$ it follows that A and A' are of the same type.

The detection of anomalies has been implemented in SWI–PROLOG. Due to their compactness and formal manner we give the corresponding PROLOG definitions for the discussed anomalies. Rules $\beta \Rightarrow A$ are represented as `A-Body`, where `Body` is the list of body atoms (representing the conjunction β) and `A` is the head atom. Since SWRL rules with conjunctive rule heads can be split into several rules, we can (without loss of generality) assume rule heads to be atomic.

2.1 Classes and Properties

Given a class C and a property P. When used in rules we call $C(x)$ a class atom and $P(x, y)$ a property atom. Variables such as X, X', or X_i can denote both classes and properties, and A, A', or A_i can denote both class atoms and property atoms.

```
element(A) :-
   ( class(A)
   ; property(A) ).
```

In PROLOG, disjunction (or) is denoted by ";". Classes and properties are taxonomically related by *is-a* relations. In OWL such *is-a* relations are defined by *subClassOf* constructs. We denote a relation A *is-a* A' by `isa(A, A')`, where A, A' are either classes or properties.

2.2 Complements and Disjointness of Classes

For classes there exists the construct *complementOf* to point to instances that do not belong to a specified class. The complement relation between a class $C1$ and a class $C2$ is denoted by `complementOf(C1,C2)` in PROLOG.

In OWL the disjointness between two classes is defined by the *disjointWith* constructor; with `disjoint(C1,C2)` we denote the disjointness between two classes `C1` and `C2`. A set C = {`C1`,...,`Cn`} of mutually disjoint classes defines a disjoint partition; in PROLOG we denote this by `disjointP([C1,...,Cn])`.

We call two classes $C1$ and $C2$ *incompatible*, if there exists a disjoint or (even) a complement relation between them.

```
incompatible(C1,C2) :-
   ( complementOf(C1,C2)
   ; disjoint(C1,C2) ).
```

2.3 Taxonomic Relations and Rules

Obviously, relations B *is-a* A – where A and B are both class atoms or both property atoms with the same arguments – are equivalent to rules of the form $B \Rightarrow A$ with a single atom B in the body, and we can combine the two into a single formalism $B \rightarrow A$. We denote the transitive closure of $\rightarrow$ by $\rightarrow^*$. In PROLOG, $B \rightarrow A$ can be described as follows:

```
derives(B, A) :-
    ( isa(B, A)
    ; rule(A-[B]) ).
```

In the following we will need implementations of the transitive closure of various predicates <P>, which all look like follows:

```
tc_<P>(A, C) :-
    ( <P>(A, C)
    ; <P>(A, B), tc_<P>(B, C) ).
```

I.e., for every predicate <P> for which we need the transitive closure we have a rule of the form above.[2] We will use the generic transitive closure for the predicate isa, where tc_isa(A, A) expresses that A is envolved in a cycle of the taxonomy (the *is-a* relation), and for the predicate derives.

3 Redundancy

Parts of the ontology are redundant due to duplicate definitions or subsuming definitions. Moreover, there could be redundant atoms in rule bodies, and the consequent of a rule could be unsatisfiable.

3.1 Identity

We call identical formal definitions of classes, properties or rules, that can be only discriminated by their different names, *identity errors*. They can occur if some implied knowledge is not explicitly stated in the ontology, thus uncovering an incompleteness error. For example, identically defined classes may be distinguished by the developer by the introduction of an additional property for one of the identical classes. Also identity of classes or rules can be created by the integration of overlapping ontologies that share (partially) identical concepts.

3.2 Redundancy by Subsumption Between Rules

The redundant definition of taxonomic knowledge of classes and properties was already described by Gómez-Pérez [7]. Let X, Y be either two classes or two properties, such

[2] Note that a generic implementation of the transitive closure as a predicate tc(<P>, A, C) would of course be possible, but it would be less efficient, since the atoms <P>(A, C) and <P>(A, B) would have to be built repeatedly at run time.

that X *is-a* Y is stated in the taxonomy. Then we distinguish *direct repetition*, where X *is-a* Y is stated more than once, and *indirect repetition*, where X *is-a* Y is stated and can at the same time also be derived by a chain X *is-a* X_1 *is-a* ... *is-a* X_n *is-a* Y with $n \geq 1$. Direct and indirect repetition corresponding to the instantiation of classes and properties can be also defined on *instance-of* instead of *is-a* .

The redundancy of rule-based knowledge (in extended Horn clause representation) was considered for example by Preece and Shinghal [8]. A rule r is redundant with respect to the rule base, if for every environment (set of base facts) the exclusion of r would derive the same conclusions. In the following we define rule subsumption in general as well as two typical special cases.

Rule Subsumption. A rule $r = \beta \Rightarrow A$ subsumes another rule $r' = \beta' \Rightarrow A'$, if β subsumes β' and A subsumes A'. Then r fires more often than r' and derives more general consequences. This happens, e.g., if $A = A'$ and β' is a specialization of β.

```
anomaly(rule_subsumption, A1-Body1, A2-Body2) :-
   subsumes(Body1, Body2),
   subsumes([A1], [A2]).
```

This rule tries to instantiate A1-Body1 and A2-Body2 to A1'-Body1' and A2'-Body2', respectively, such that A1' subsumes A2' and Body1' subsumes Body2'. The instantiations generated in the call `subsumes(Body1, Body2)` are used in the subsequent call `subsumes([A1], [A2])`. There are two alternative implementations for the predicate `subsumes/2` depending on whether the first rule subsumes an instance of the second rule (partial subsumption), or it totally subsumes the second rule.

- The call `subset_non_ground(As1, As2)` in the first variant tries to instantiate As1 and As2 to As1' and As2', respectively, such that As1' is a subset of As2'. In that case As1 partially subsumes As2.

```
subsumes(As1, As2) :-
   subset_non_ground(As1, As2).
```

- In the second variant, before the call `subset_non_ground(As1, As2)` a copy As of As2 is made, which is afterwards compared to the new value of As2. If both are variants of each other, then As1 totally subsumes As2.

```
subsumes(As1, As2) :-
   copy_term(As2, As),
   subset_non_ground(As1, As2),
   variant(As2, As).
```

Implication of Superclasses. If A, A_i are either class or property atoms, then a rule $A_1 \wedge \cdots \wedge A_n \Rightarrow A$, such that $A_i \rightarrow^* A$ for some A_i, is redundant.

```
anomaly(implication_of_superclasses, A-Body) :-
   member(Ai, Body), tc_derives(Ai, A).
```

Here classes are only subsuming under certain conditions that are given in the rule condition, i.e., an incorrect assignment of the subclass relation may exist.

If $A_i \equiv A$, then the equivalence may be incorrectly assigned, since the rule condition denotes a restriction on the implication.

This can be seen as a special case of rule subsumption, since the fact $A_i \rightarrow^* A$ can be seen as a rule $A_i \Rightarrow A$, which subsumes the first rule given above.

Redundant Implication of Transitivity. If P is a transitive property, then a rule $P(x, y) \wedge P(y, z) \wedge \beta \Rightarrow P(x, z)$ embodies a redundant definition of P, which can be already derived by the OWL reasoner from the fact that P is transitive. Often such a redundancy can be explained by an erroneous assumption of the transitivity during an ontology integration process, since the rule defines a more restrictive condition of transitivity, if the conjunction β is non-empty.

```
anomaly(redundant_transitivity, P_xz-Body) :-
   P_xz =.. [P, X, Z],
   P_xy =.. [P, X, Y], P_yz =.. [P, Y, Z],
   subset_non_ground([P_xy, P_yz], Body).
```

This is a also special case of rule subsumption, since the transitivity of a property P can be expressed as a rule $P(x, y) \wedge P(y, z) \Rightarrow P(x, z)$, which subsumes the first rule given above.

3.3 Redundancy in the Antecedent of a Rule

For a rule $A_1 \wedge \cdots \wedge A_n \Rightarrow A$ we have $A_i \rightarrow^* A_j$ for two atoms in its antecedent. In this case the atom A_j is redundant and can be removed from the rule antecedent.

```
anomaly(redundancy_in_antecedent, A-Body) :-
   tc_derives(Ai, Aj),
   member(Ai, Body), member(Aj, Body).
```

As a special case, this form of redundancy can occur if $A_i \equiv A_j$ in the ontology. This anomaly may alternatively point to an incorrect mapping between the elements A_i and A_j.

3.4 Unsatisfiable Rule Condition

A rule has an unsatisfiable condition, if at least one literal neither unifies with an input literal (e.g., a given instantiation of the ontological concepts) nor with the consequent of another rule.

```
anomaly(unsatisfiable_condition, _-Body) :-
   member(A, Body),
   \+ fact(A),
   \+ rule(A-_).
```

With the rich semantics of OWL an unsatisfiable condition can also occur due to the contradictory use of *complementOf* or *disjointWith* descriptions.

```
anomaly(unsatisfiable_condition, _-Body) :-
   member(A, Body), member(B, Body),
   incompatible(A, B).
```

4 Circularity

Circular definitions in the ontology have a severe impact on the reasoning capabilities of the underlying knowledge. Here we distinguish circular definitions in the taxonomic structure of the ontology as described by [7], circular dependencies in the rule base as considered, e.g., by [8], but also circular dependencies that can occur due to the intermixture between taxonomic and rule-based knowledge.

Circularity in Taxonomy. There is a cyclic chain X_1 *is-a* X_2 *is-a* ... *is-a* X_n, such that $X_1 = X_n$, where all X_i are classes or all X_i are properties.

```
anomaly(circularity_in_taxonomy, A) :-
   tc_isa(A, A).
```

Circularity Between Rules and Taxonomy. There exists a rule $A_1 \wedge \cdots \wedge A_n \Rightarrow A$, such that for some atom A_i from the antecedent it holds $A \rightarrow^* A_i$.

```
anomaly(circularity_in_rules_and_taxonomy, A-Body) :-
   member(Ai, Body), tc_derives(A, Ai).
```

The specified rule should be considered as a restricted *is-a* relation between A and A_i, which may result in the detection of a misapplied taxonomic definition between the two concepts. This error is similar to *implication of subclasses*, but with an inverse *is-a* relation.

5 Inconsistency

Ambivalent definitions of ontological knowledge often cause unintended reasoning behavior. Besides partition errors concerning the taxonomic structure of the ontology, cf. [7], also ambivalent definitions within the rule base may occur, cf. [8]. However, due to the mixture of basic ontological knowledge and rules other ambivalence can be identified.

Partition Error in Taxonomy. Consider a disjoint partition of a class C into subclasses $C_1, \ldots, C_n$. On the class level, there is a partition error, if a class C' is a subclass of (at least) two disjoint subclasses C_i, C_j of C. On the instance level, a partition error, where some element e is an instance of (at least) two disjoint subclasses C_i, C_j of C, would lead to an inconsistency. The following rule defines a partition error on the class level:

```
anomaly(partition_error, A-[B, C]) :-
   disjoint(B, C),
   isa(A, B), isa(A, C).
```

Self-contradicting Rule. For a rule $A_1 \wedge \cdots \wedge A_n \Rightarrow A$ there exists a *complementOf* or a *disjointWith* relationship between A and one of its body atoms A_i. Note that, according to our definitions in Section 2, this means that $A = C(x)$ and $A_i = C_i(x)$ are class atoms with the same argument x, and that C and C_i are disjoint or complements.

```
anomaly(contradicting_rule_consequent, A-Body) :-
   member(B, Body), incompatible(A, B).
```

If such a rule would fire, then the derived conclusion A of the rule would contradict the assumption A_i in its antecedent.

Contradicting Rules. We say that a rule $r = \beta \Rightarrow A$ contradicts another rule $r' = \beta' \Rightarrow$ A', if β subsumes β', but A and A' are contradicting. If r' would fire, then also the stronger r would fire and the derived conclusions A' and A would be contradicting. The subsumption β subsumes β' can be defined by *equivalentClass/Property* relations as well as *is-a* relations. The consequents $A = C(x)$ and $A' = C'(x')$ are contradicting, if the corresponding classes C and C' are disjoint or complements.

```
anomaly(ambivalent_rule_pair, A1-Body1, A2-Body2) :-
   incompatible(A1, A2),
   subsumes(Body1, Body2).
```

An even more general form of the anomaly is given, if there are two sets of rules (not necessarily disjoint) that are deriving two semantically contradicting conclusions.

6 Deficiency

Deficiency is a subtle category comprising anomalies in an ontology that neither can be identified as redundant nor define inconsistent knowledge. Such anomalies can originate from the manual development of (large) ontologies, the evolution of ontologies, or as a side-effect of the integration of ontologies. Deficiency is usually not responsible for reasoning errors but affects the completeness, understandability or maintainability of the underlying knowledge.

Originally, such *design anomalies* had been identified and investigated for relational databases. In the last years, software engineering research has coined the term *bad smells* for parts of the source code that do not produce false behavior but are badly designed and should be improved for better maintainability, cf. [11]. Recently, a first step was taken to transfer this idea to the conceptual properties of rule-based knowledge [13] and OWL ontologies [14], respectively.

The identification of a bad smell is the starting point of a *refactoring*. Refactoring methods describe precise procedures to eliminate the corresponding smell without changing the meaning of the remaining knowledge. The following measures can be only seen as indicators for the occurrence of an anomaly. In any case the user has to decide whether and how to remove the possible anomaly. Then, refactoring methods provide constructive procedures that restructure the ontology and rule base by eliminating the anomaly.

In the following we present heuristics for the identification of some design anomalies, and we sketch the use of appropriate refactoring methods.

6.1 Lazy Class/Property

An element (class or a property) in the ontology that is actually never used in the real-world application is called *lazy*. The following facts indicate that an element could be lazy:

- the element represents a leaf in the hierarchy,
- no rules use this element,
- there exist no instances of the element.

Laziness can occur due to many reasons: The merge or the integration of two ontologies may include terms that are not useful or relevant in the actual domain. In addition, an element can evolve to be lazy if it was specialized or generalized to elements more appropriate to the application domain; consequently, the element was kept in the ontology although it is not used anymore. In PROLOG, a possibly lazy element A can be detected as follows:

```
anomaly(lazy_element, A) :-
   element(A),
   \+ isa(_, A),
   \+ in_rule(A),
   \+ instance(_, A).

in_rule(A) :-
   rule(H-Body),
   ( A = H
   ; member(A, Body) ).
```

The constraints stated above can be relaxed by tolerating very few rules with the considered object in their head or body. Then, these rules have to be inspected by the user and marked as not usable any more. Removing the unused element with the refactoring *delete element* should be considered with reasonable care:

1. The hierarchy has to be reconnected, i.e., every child of the term has to be linked as a child to every parent of the element.
2. The attributions of the term have to be reattached to its children, e.g., transitivity for a lazy property.
3. The corresponding rules have to be edited, i.e., every rule that contains the element either in its antecedent or in its consequent has to be reconsidered: rules with the element in their consequent should be removed from the ontology. Rules with the element in their antecedent are either removed (default for rules with the element as the only literal in the antecedent) or changed (remove literal with the element from the antecedent). For the latter we have to consider the creation of anomalies, such as the creation of redundant or ambivalent rules. In any case, changed rules should be presented to the developer for a manual revision.

6.2 Chains of Inheritance

The backbone of an ontology is described by classes with corresponding taxonomic relations, i.e., classes are hierarchically connected by *is-a* relations. If ontologies are manually build in a distributed environment or are developed by the integration using parts of other ontologies, then the indented subclass structure can degenerate to *is-a* cascades in some areas of the taxonomy.

A taxonomic chain

$$C_1 \textit{ is-a } C_2 \textit{ is-a } \dots \textit{ is-a } C_n \,,$$

of classes C_i, such that all intermediate concepts $C_2, \dots, C_{n-1}$ are contained in no other *is-a* relations except the ones in the chain is called a *chain of inheritance*. The following observations for these intermediate classes C_i can be used as a heuristic to strengthen the suspicion that a chain is anomalous:

- there exist no or very few instances for the C_i,
- the C_i are not extensively used in rules or other ontological definitions, e.g., property restrictions

In any case the user has to decide if the chain should be eliminated by the refactoring *collapse hierarchy*. Then, the chain is reduced to

$$C_1 \textit{ is-a } C_n \,,$$

and the intermediate concepts C_i $(2 \leq i \leq n-1)$ are subsequently removed from the ontology as follows:

1. All *properties* where C_i occurs as the domain, as the range, or in a restriction have to be modified. In many cases the occurrence of C_i can be changed to the upper class C_1. But in some cases these properties may appear to be redundant or useless, then the property should be considered to be removed as well.
2. All *rules* containing C_i have to be modified. If there exist many rules containing C_i in the antecedent or consequent, then the refactoring may not be practical. However, a reasonable heuristic may be to change the occurrences of C_i to C_1, if $2 \leq i \leq n/2$, or to C_n, if $n/2 < i \leq n-1$, i.e., to change the class to the nearest remaining neighbor.
3. For all *instances* of C_i – similar to the handling of rules – the user has to decide if the existing instances should be translated to instances of C_1 or C_n.

Finally, a new subclass relation C_1 *is-a* C_n, which replaces chain, is created, and the classes $C_2, \dots, C_{n-1}$ are removed from the ontology.

6.3 Lonely Disjoint Class

The anomaly *lonely disjoint class* can occur as a result of an ontology integration task. A lonely disjoint class is a concept that is not disjoint with any of its siblings, but has disjoint relations to a collection of classes that are mutual siblings in another branch of the taxonomy.

```
anomaly(lonely_disjoint, C) :-
    siblings(Cs),
    disjointP([C|Cs]),
    \+ ( sibling(C, M), disjoint(C, M) ).
```

Besides an integration task such a lonely disjoint class can also occur due to the manual modification of the ontology, i.e., moving a class into another branch without the subsequent adaptation of the disjoint relations.

If the user has classified the disjoint relation as an actual error, then the elimination of this anomaly is quite simple: the disjoint property can be removed from the lonely disjoint class. However, its existence can cause unindented reasoning behavior.

6.4 Over-Specific Property Range

Developers tend to be very specific when manually defining value ranges for the particular properties. For example, the value range of a property *temperature* may be

$$R_{\mathit{temperature}} = \{\ \textit{very high, high, normal, low, very low}\ \}.$$

During the practical use of the ontology it might turn out that the values are too specific and that the coarser value range $R'_{\mathit{temperature}} = \{\ \textit{high, normal, low}\ \}$ would work much better. If rules are defined containing this property, then the anomaly can be identified by the existence of many analogous rules for the particular values. In our example, rules for the values *high* and *very high* could be present. In such cases, the refactoring *coarsen value range* forms groups of equivalent values, e.g., *high'* = { *high, very high* } and *low'* = { *low, very low* }.

The following rule determines pairs of rules having variants *has_value(P, Vi)*, i=1,2, of property values in their antecedent (after deleting these variant atoms their bodies are identical):

```
anomaly(over_specific,
      R1, R2, has_value(P, [V1, V2])) :-
   rule(R1), rule(R2),
   R1 = A1-Body1, R2 = A2-Body2, R1 \= R2,
   delete(has_value(P, V1), Body1, B1),
   delete(has_value(P, V2), Body2, B2),
   A1-B1 = A2-B2.
```

An analogous rule can be stated for rule consequents. The refactoring also replaces the original values with the aggregated ones in the corresponding rules, which is illustrated by the following example.

For the automatic *refactoring* of the corresponding rules the developer needs to define a mapping $M : R_{\mathit{temperature}} \mapsto R'_{\mathit{temperature}}$ from the original range to the coarsened range, e.g.:

v	very high	high	normal	low	very low
M(v)	high	high	normal	low	low

Every rule containing the property *temperature* is refactored by the application of the mapping function. Every atom in the head or body with *has_value(temperature, v)* is replaced by another atom *has_value(temperature, v')*, where *v'* = *M(v)*. Analogously, we have to replace all values in OWL constructs where values are explicitly used, e.g., in *hasValue* property restrictions.

With the application of the refactoring *coarsen range* redundant rules may be produced. In the case of a semantically inconsistent mapping function *map* even inconsistent rules can occur. In consequence, the existence of such anomalies has to be checked in a subsequent step.

6.5 Property Clump

The manual and distributed development of a larger ontology or the integration of existing ontologies can produce unintentionally repeated definitions in different classes of the ontology.

A *property clump* is a set $\mathcal{C}$ of classes having a relatively large set $\mathcal{P}$ of properties in common. These properties include the instantiation of DataType properties and Object properties.

For *refactoring*, the repeated use of the property clump $\mathcal{P}$ can be caught by a new class $C_{\mathcal{P}}$, which gets the properties in $\mathcal{P}$. The original classes $C \in \mathcal{C}$ are linked to $C_{\mathcal{P}}$ instead of linking them to the properties in $\mathcal{P}$. For ontologies with rules, we have to change all rules having property atoms $P(x, y)$ for $P \in \mathcal{P}$ in their antecedent or consequent.

The use of such an abstract property class $C_{\mathcal{P}}$ may increase the compactness and the maintainability (with respect to chances, extensions, fixes) of the ontology. A property clump in ontologies is comparable to the repeated use of code fragments in traditional software, so-called *clones*. The extraction of such repetitions into a single method or data structure is a common refactoring, which improves the compactness and maintainability of the code. The procedure of the corresponding refactoring *extract concept* is sketched for ontologies by the following example.

Example (Extract Concept for Property Clump)
The repeated definition of the *String* DataType properties

$$\mathcal{P} = \{\, \textit{hasAddress, hasPhone, hasEmail} \,\}$$

having the classes $\mathcal{C} = \{\textit{person, company}\}$ as domain can be aggregated to a new concept $C_{\mathcal{P}} = \textit{addressInfo}$. If the user decides that the aggregation of these properties is a meaningful self-contained concept, then the refactoring *extract concept* can automatically perform the following steps:

1. Create a new class $C_{\mathcal{P}} = \textit{addressInfo}$ and add the class *addressInfo* as a new possible domain for all identified properties in $\mathcal{P}$.
2. Create a new object property *hasAddressInfo* connecting the classes $C \in \mathcal{C}$ with the new class *addressInfo*, where $range(hasAddressInfo) = \{addressInfo\}$ and

$$domain(hasAddressInfo) = \bigcup_{P \in \mathcal{P}} domain(P).$$

3. Create and redirect instances: For each instance of a class in $\mathcal{C}$, create an appropriate instances of class *addressInfo* and property *hasAddressInfo* and redirect the original properties in $\mathcal{P}$ with respect to the newly created property *hasAddressInfo* and class *addressInfo*.
4. Change rules having properties $P \in \mathcal{P}$ in their antecedent. E.g., for the property *hasAddress(X,Y)* a new rule is created

$$hasAddressInfo(C, C') \wedge hasAddress(C', A) \Rightarrow hasReAddress(C, A) \qquad (1)$$

and every original rule, e.g.,

$$hasAddress(C, A) \wedge hasLoc(A, L) \Rightarrow hasAdrLoc(C, L) \quad (2)$$

is changed to

$$hasReAddress(C, A) \wedge hasLoc(A, L) \Rightarrow hasAdrLoc(C, L) \quad (3)$$

We see that for each property $P \in \mathcal{P}$ a new rule (1) is created, and the property P of the original rule (2) is replaced by the newly created property which was defined in rule (1), see adapted rule (3). This is reasonable if the property is used in many rules and these rules should be kept as compact as possible. Otherwise, we would encode the redirection in the original rules, i.e., instead of rule (1) and rule (3) we simple would modify rule (2) by exchanging the atom $hasAddress(C, A)$ in the antecedent by the conjunction

$$hasAddressInfo(C, C') \wedge hasAddress(C', A),$$

which enlarges the antecedent by one literal.

5. Change rules having properties $P \in \mathcal{P}$ in the consequent. For example, the rule

$$hasLoc(C, L) \wedge hasAdrLoc(L, A) \Rightarrow hasAddress(C, A) \quad (4)$$

with *hasAddress(C, A)* in the consequent is replaced by the rule

$$hasLoc(C, L) \wedge hasAdrLoc(L, A) \wedge hasAddressInfo(C, C') \Rightarrow hasAddress(C', A) \quad (5)$$

7 Conclusions and Future Work

The implementation of the semantic web stack currently focuses on the integration of rules into the web ontology language OWL. At the moment, SWRL, the semantic web rule language, is a proposal for such an integration, and it has the status of a W3C member submission. With the use of rule-based knowledge in combination with taxonomic definitions of the ontology, new evaluation questions arise. In consequence, evaluation measures have to be revisited and extended in order to include rules.

In this paper, we have presented a revised approach for the verification of rule augmented ontologies which also includes extended measures for the verification of ontologies with respect to more subtle anomalies concerning the understandability and maintainability. With the description of the anomalies we also sketched appropriate *refactoring methods* for eliminating the detected problems.

In general, the work is not limited to the expressiveness of the SWRL ontologies, but it can be also applied to similar rule extensions of ontologies. However, the presented approach is only a starting point for an extensive framework for the verification and refactoring of ontologies. Here, only parts of the expressiveness of OWL DL were considered; e.g., the implications of possibly existing property restrictions (universal and existential quantification, cardinalities) are not investigated in the presented work.

Besides the consideration of the full expressiveness of OWL DL and of SWRL and its extensions, e.g., to first-order logic by SWRL FOL [15], we also need to consider the availability of *non-monotonicity*, which is expected to play an important role in real life ontologies and knowledge bases. Here, some work has been done on the verification of non-monotonic rule bases [16], that should be also integrated in a more elaborated framework.

References

1. Horrocks, I., Parsia, B., Patel-Schneider, P., Hendler, J.: Semantic Web Architecture: Stack or Two Towers? In Fages, F., Soliman, S., eds.: Principles and Practice of Semantic Web Reasoning (PPSWR). Number 3703 in LNCS, SV (2005) 37–41
2. Horrocks, I., Patel-Schneider, P.F., Bechhofer, S., Tsarkov, D.: OWL Rules: A Proposal and Prototype Implementation. Journal of Web Semantics **3**(1) (2005) 23–40
3. Horrocks, I., Patel-Schneider, P.F., Boley, H., Tabet, S., Grosof, B., Dean, M.: SWRL: A Semantic Web Rule Language - Combining OWL and RuleML, W3C Member Submission . `http://www.w3.org/Submission/SWRL/` (May 2004)
4. Bechhofer, S., van Harmelen, F., Hendler, J., Horrocks, I., McGuinness, D.L., Patel-Schneider, P.F., Stein, L.A.: OWL Web Ontology Language Reference – W3C Recommendation. `http://www.w3.org/TR/owl-ref/` (Feb. 2004)
5. Guarino, N., Welty, C.: Evaluating Ontological Decisions with OntoClean. Communications of the ACM **45**(2) (2002)
6. Rector, A.L., Drummond, N., Horridge, M., Rogers, J., Knublauch, H., Stevens, R., Wang, H., Wroe, C.: OWL Pizzas: Practical Experience of Teaching OWL-DL: Common Errors & Common Patterns. In: Engineering Knowledge in the Age of the Semantic Web: 14th International Conference, EKAW, LNAI 3257, Springer (2004) 157–171
7. Gómez-Pérez, A.: Evaluation of Ontologies. International Journal of Intelligent Systems **16**(3) (2001) 391–409
8. Preece, A., Shinghal, R.: Foundation and Application of Knowledge Base Verification. International Journal of Intelligent Systems **9** (1994) 683–702
9. Preece, A., Shinghal, R., Batarekh, A.: Verifying Expert Systems. A Logical Framework and a Practical Tool. Expert Systems with Applications **5(3/4)** (1992) 421–436
10. Ceri, S., Gottlob, G., Tanca, L.: Logic Programming and Databases. Springer, Berlin (1990)
11. Fowler, M.: Refactoring. Improving the Design of Existing Code. Addison-Wesley (1999)
12. Opdyke, W.F.: Refactoring Object-Oriented Frameworks. PhD thesis, University of Illinois, Urbana-Champaign, IL, USA (1992)
13. Baumeister, J., Seipel, D., Puppe, F.: Refactoring Methods for Knowledge Bases. In: Engineering Knowledge in the Age of the Semantic Web: 14th International Conference, EKAW, LNAI 3257, Springer (2004) 157–171
14. Baumeister, J., Seipel, D.: Smelly Owls – Design Anomalies in Ontologies. In: Proc. of the 18th International Florida Artificial Intelligence Research Society Conference (FLAIRS), AAAI Press (2005) 215–220
15. Patel-Schneider, P.F.: A Proposal for a SWRL Extension to First-Order Logic. `http://www.daml.org/2004/11/fol/proposal` (Nov. 2004)
16. Zlatareva, N.: Testing the Integrity of Non-Monotonic Knowledge Bases Containing Semi-Normal Defaults. In: Proc. of the 17th International Florida Artificial Intelligence Research Society Conference (FLAIRS), AAAI Press (2004) 349–354

Ontology Selection for the Real Semantic Web: How to Cover the Queen's Birthday Dinner?

Marta Sabou, Vanessa Lopez, and Enrico Motta

Knowledge Media Institute (KMi) & Centre for Research in Computing,
The Open University, Milton Keynes
{r.m.sabou, v.lopez, e.motta}@open.ac.uk

Abstract. Robust mechanisms for ontology selection are crucial for the evolving Semantic Web characterized by rapidly increasing numbers of online ontologies and by applications that automatically use the associated metadata. However, existing selection techniques have primarily been designed in the context of human mediated tasks and fall short of supporting automatic knowledge reuse. We address this gap by proposing a selection algorithm that takes into account 1) the needs of two applications that explore large scale, distributed markup and 2) some properties of online ontology repositories. We conclude that the ambitious context of automatic knowledge reuse imposes several challenging requirements on selection.

1 Introduction

The effort of the Semantic Web community to migrate and apply its semantic techniques in open, distributed and heterogeneous Web environments has paid off: the Semantic Web is evolving towards a *real* Semantic Web. Not only has the number of ontologies dramatically increased, but also the way that ontologies are published and used has changed. Ontologies and semantic data are published on the open Web, crawled by semantic search engines (e.g., Swoogle [3]) and reused by third parties for other purposes than originally foreseen (e.g., Flink [9] derives social networks from automatically crawled FOAF profiles). Many ontology based tools are evolving from relying on a single, fixed ontology to harvesting the rich ontological knowledge available on the Web [6].

Robust mechanisms for selecting ontologies are crucial to support knowledge reuse in this large scale, open environment. The context of reuse has a major influence on the requirements for the selection algorithm and should be taken into account when developing such algorithms. We further discuss and contrast the requirements imposed by the contexts of human mediated and automatic reuse. As background for our discussion, consider the following news snippet[1]:

The Queen will be 80 on 21 April and she is celebrating her birthday with a family dinner hosted by Prince Charles at Windsor Castle.[2]

[1] Example inspired by Her Majesty's birthday coinciding with the submission deadline.

[2] http://news.billinge.com/1/hi/entertainment/4820796.stm

S. Staab and V. Svatek (Eds.): EKAW 2006, LNAI 4248, pp. 96–111, 2006.

Human mediated tasks. Imagine a person wishing to annotate this news snippet and in search of an ontology containing the *Queen, birthday* and *dinner* concepts. When queried for these terms, a selection mechanism is expected to return an ontology that best covers them. It is not a problem if the returned ontology contains only a subset of the terms (partial coverage) as the user can extend the ontology according to his needs. It is also admissible for the system to make mistakes when mapping between the query terms and ontology concepts as the user can filter out such errors (imprecise coverage). For example, ontologies containing the concept *Queen* as a subclass of *Bee* or *dinner_fork* as an approximation for *dinner* will be rejected as irrelevant for this user's context. Finally, users are willing to wait some minutes for reusable ontologies, since this time is negligible compared to that needed to build an ontology from scratch.

Automatic knowledge reuse. As opposed to the previous scenario, imagine that the output of the selection is automatically processed. For example, a semantic browser such as Magpie [4] which identifies and highlights entities of a certain type in Web pages needs to find an ontology according to which to describe the page above. The requirements are much stricter than before. First, a *complete coverage* of the query terms is needed to fully support the sense making activity offered by the browser. If no completely covering ontology is found, a set of ontologies that jointly cover the query could be returned. Or, alternatively, an ontology with more generic concepts such as *woman, event* and *meal* could be useful, provided that a machine interpretable explanation of the relation between the query terms and the returned concepts is available (e.g., a *dinner* is a kind of *meal*). Indeed, another requirement relates to the quality of mappings between terms and concepts. Errors such as those described in the context of human mediated tasks are not admissible. Finally, a quick response becomes more important when the selection is used at run time as in this case.

The four selection mechanisms that we are aware of (see [11] for a detailed description and comparison) have been developed in the context of human mediated tasks. OntoKhoj [10] and Swoogle [3] complement automatically populated ontology libraries and use a PageRank-like algorithm on semantic relations between ontologies (e.g., imports) to select the most popular ontology containing a certain term. OntoSelect [2], also part of an ontology library, combines measures about coverage, popularity and the richness of ontology structure. Finally, the ActiveRank [1] algorithm is independent of an ontology library and uses a set of ontology structure based metrics. These metrics were inspired by and reflect characteristics that human ontology builders find important, for example, coverage, compactness, density (richness of knowledge structure).

All these approaches function well in the context of human mediated tasks, but are insufficient when it comes to automatic knowledge reuse. Regarding the level of coverage, none of the existing approaches enforces complete coverage. Further, the quality of the mapping between query terms and concept labels is quite low, as all these approaches rely only on syntactic matches. For example, ActiveRank, currently the most advanced algorithm, uses a fuzzy match between terms and concept names (i.e., *project* is mapped to *projectile*) but makes no provision to filter out obviously irrelevant hits. The meaning of the concepts given by their position in the hierarchy is not considered by any of the approaches. Finally, our only indication about performance is that ActiveRank needs 2 minutes to evaluate each ontology - a baseline that needs improvement in the case of automated tasks.

We consider that, while ambitious, the context of automatic reuse complements that of human mediated reuse and raises novel challenges that can lead to further development of existing selection algorithms. In this paper we derive a set of requirements imposed by two applications that are extended to perform automatic knowledge reuse (Section 2) and we present an initial design of a selection algorithm that balances between obtaining a complete and precise coverage and offering a good performance (Section 4). We also consider characteristics of online ontologies explored through a set of indicative experiments (Section 3).

2 Requirements for Supporting Automatic Knowledge Reuse Scenarios

While current ontology selection tools primarily target human users, we are working on two Semantic Web tools (Sections 2.1 and 2.2) that are evolving from using a single, rich and manually crafted ontology to exploring and combining ontologies available on the Web. These tools rely on automatic ontology selection on which they pose a set of requirements (Section 2.3).

2.1 Ontology Based Question Answering

AquaLog [7] is an ontology based question answering system which relies on the knowledge encoded in an underlying ontology to disambiguate the meaning of questions asked using natural language and to provide answers. To shortly give an impression about how the system operates, consider that it is aware of an ontology about academic life[3] which has been populated to describe KMi related knowledge[4]. Also, suppose that the following question is asked[5]:

Which projects are related to researchers working with ontologies?

In a first stage the system interprets the natural language question and translates it to triple-like data structures. Then, these triples are compared to the underlying ontology centered knowledge base using a set of string comparison methods and WordNet. For example, the term *projects* is identified to refer to the ontology concept *Project* and *ontologies* is assumed equivalent to the *ontologies* instance of the *Research-Area* concept. After the modifier attachment is resolved by using domain knowledge, two triples are identified:

(projects, related to, researchers) and *(researchers, working, ontologies)*

[3] http://kmi.open.ac.uk/projects/akt/ref-onto/

[4] See the populated ontology at http://semanticweb.kmi.open.ac.uk

[5] See the AquaLog demo at http://kmi.open.ac.uk/technologies/aqualog/

The relations of the triples are also mapped to the ontology. For example, for the second triple, there is only one known relation in the ontology between a *Researcher* and a *Research-area*, namely *has-research-interest*. This relation is assumed to be the relevant one for the question. However, when disambiguating the relation that is referred to by *related to*, the system cannot find any syntactically similar relation between a *Project* and a *Researcher* (or between all more generic and more specific classes of the two concepts). Nevertheless, there are four, alternative relations between these two concepts: *has-contact-person, has-project-member, has-project-leader, uses-resource.* The user is asked to choose the relation that is closest to his interest. Once a choice is made, the question is entirely mapped to the underlying ontological structure and the corresponding instances can be retrieved as an answer.

While the current version of AquaLog is portable from one domain to another, the scope of the system is limited by the amount of knowledge encoded in the ontology used at that time. The new implementation of AquaLog, PowerAqua [6], overcomes this limitation by extending the system in the direction of open question answering, i.e., allowing it to benefit from and combine knowledge from the wide range of ontologies that exist on the Web. One of the challenges is the selection of the right ontology for a given query from the Web.

2.2 Semantic Browsing

The goal of semantic browsing is to exploit the richness of semantic information in order to facilitate Web browsing. The Magpie [4] Semantic Web browser provides new mechanisms for browsing and making sense of information on the Semantic Web. This tool makes use of the semantic annotation associated with a Web page to help the user get a quicker and better understanding of the information on that page. Magpie is portable from one domain to another as it allows the user to choose the appropriate ontology from a list of ontologies that are known to the tool. However, similarly to AquaLog, the current version relies on a single ontology being active at any moment in time. This limits the scope of the sense making support to the content of the current ontology.

Our current research focuses on extending Magpie towards open browsing. This means that the tool should be able to bring to the user the appropriate semantic information relevant for his browsing context from *any* ontology on the Web. This extension relies on a component that can select, at run time, the appropriate ontologies for the given browsing context.

In the case of Magpie, the query for the ontology selection is more complex than for AquaLog as it is defined by the current browsing context. This includes the content of the currently accessed Web pages and, optionally, the browsing history and the profile of the user. Web pages typically span several different topics. For example, the following short news story[6] is both about trips to exotic locations and talks. Therefore, the query sent to the selection mechanism is likely to contain terms drawn from different domains.

[6] `http://stadium.open.ac.uk/stadia/preview.php?s=29&whichevent=657`

"For April and May 2005, adventurer Lorenzo Gariano was part of a ten-man collaborative expedition between 7summits.com and the 7summits club from Russia, led by Alex Abramov and Harry Kikstra, to the North Face of Everest. This evening he will present a talk on his experiences, together with some of the fantastic photos he took."

2.3 Requirements for Ontology Selection

Hereby we formulate the requirements imposed by our applications on ontology selection and discuss to which extent they are addressed by current approaches. These requirements drove the design of our selection algorithm (Section 4).

1. **Complete coverage.** A complete coverage is probably the most important requirement for our applications (though it might not be so important for other tools). Because in these applications the retrieved knowledge is automatically processed, they require that all the needed knowledge should be retrieved. While existing approaches rank ontologies that cover most terms as best, they do not enforce a complete coverage.
2. **Precise coverage.** Automatic knowledge reuse requires a rigorous mapping between query terms and ontology concepts as well as a formal representation of the mapping relation (e.g., more generic). Assuming that a human user would filter out (and eventually enrich) the returned ontologies, current tools treat the comparison between query terms and ontology concepts rather superficially, relying only on (often approximate) lexical comparisons.
3. **Returning ontology combinations.** Our preliminary experiments indicate that the sparseness of knowledge on the Web often makes it impossible to find a single ontology that covers all terms (Section 3). However, it is more likely to find ontology combinations that *jointly cover* the query terms. Existing tools return lists of single ontologies rather than their collections.
4. **Performance.** Our applications rely on the results of selection at run time and therefore require a good performance. While simple selection tools perform rather well, the more complex ActiveRank needs 2 minutes per ontology to compute all its metrics. This is acceptable for supporting ontology building, but needs to be improved in an automatic scenario.
5. **Dealing with relations.** Our applications, especially PowerAqua, illustrate a need for considering relations and not just concepts when selecting an ontology. Currently, only OntoSelect considers relations.
6. **Dealing with instances.** Our applications help users in their information gathering activities. Most often, people are interested in finding out things about certain entities rather than generic concepts. This requires that selection should consider instances as well (i.e., match between instances in a query and those in online ontologies). Matching instances is a difficult problem in itself given the large number and high level of ambiguity when dealing with instances (e.g., many instances can share the same or similar names).

7. **Modularization.** Knowledge reuse is closely related to ontology modularization. Indeed, our tools would require selection mechanisms to return a relevant ontology module rather than a whole ontology. Note that the work in [1] has already considered this issue when introducing a metric to measure how close the hits in an ontology are (assuming that this indicates the existence of a module). As with instance mappings, ontology modularization is a difficult and as yet unsolved issue, though a large amount of work in this area [13] could be reused to some extent.

3 Preliminary Experiments

To better design our algorithm, we wanted to get an insight in the characteristics of the ontological data available online. Since the requirement of complete and precise coverage of the query terms was identified as the most important one in the context of automatic knowledge reuse, our experiments are centered towards 1) exploring the factors that hamper obtaining a complete coverage and 2) getting an insight in the nature of compound concept labels in preparation to provide a more precise mapping to query terms. We performed both experiments on top of Swoogle[7] because it is currently the largest ontology repository. It is important to note that our experiments have an exploratory role rather than trying to rigourously test our hypotheses.

3.1 Experiment 1 - Obtaining Complete Coverage

The goal of this experiment is to get an indication about how difficult it is to find a completely covering ontology when using Swoogle. One of the motivations for this experiment was that, while important, complete coverage has not been investigated in any previous work (although best covering ontologies are rated best). In fact, with the exception of OntoSelect, all selection algorithms are tested for the rather trivial case of one or two query terms. On the contrary, our tools require ontologies that cover at least three query terms (e.g., AquaLog translates each question in one or more triples).

Our intuition was that the *number, topic relatedness* and *type* of the query terms will influence the success of obtaining an all covering ontology. Namely, a single, all covering ontology is difficult to find if 1) there are many query terms, 2) if query terms are drawn from different topic domains or 3) relations are considered. According to these considerations, we devised four sets of queries. The first three queries represent an optimal scenario where few concepts are drawn from the same domain (we chose a well covered domain in terms of online ontologies, the academic domain). The second set of queries (4 - 6) have terms drawn from different (and less covered) topic domains. They were inspired by the actual text snippets in Section 1 and Section 2.2, therefore being representative for real life scenarios encountered with Magpie. The queries in set three (7 - 10) have terms drawn from the same domain but, unlike the first set, contain a

[7] We use Swoogle 2005 as our software was written before Swoogle 2006 was released.

relation as well (these are typical AquaLog queries). Our final queries (11 - 14) explore overcoming failure of finding a completely covering ontology by replacing query terms in queries 4, 6, 9 and 10 with their hypernyms.

The experimental software queries Swoogle for ontologies that contain concepts/properties that *exactly* match the query terms (variations in capitalization are allowed)[8]. For each query, the software outputs the number of ontologies that cover each term, their pairwise combinations and all terms.

Table 1. Number of ontologies retrieved for a set of queries. (X+ refines X.)

Query	(t_1, t_2, t_3)	(t_1)	(t_2)	(t_3)	(t_1, t_2)	(t_1, t_3)	(t_2, t_3)	(t_1, t_2, t_3)
1	(project, article, researcher)	84	90	24	19	13	9	8
2	(researcher, student, university)	24	101	64	16	15	38	13
3	(research, publication, author)	15	77	138	8	5	36	4
4	(adventurer, expedition, photo)	1	0	32	0	1	0	0
5	(mountain, team, talk)	12	25	9	2	1	1	1
6	(queen, birthday, dinner)	0	9	2	0	0	1	0
7	(project, relatedTo, researcher)	84	11	24	0	13	0	0
8	(researcher, worksWith, Ontology)	24	9	52	0	3	0	0
9	(academic, memberOf, project)	21	36	84	0	3	5	0
10	(article, hasAuthor, person)	90	14	371	8	32	2	0
11 (4+)	(person, trip, photo)	371	7	32	1	20	1	1
12 (6+)	(woman, birthday, dinner)	32	9	2	1	1	1	1
13 (9+)	(person, memberOf, project)	371	36	84	16	46	5	5
14 (10+)	(publication, hasAuthor, person)	77	14	371	2	52	2	2

The results are summarized in Table 1. Notice that as the number of terms increases less completely covering ontologies are found. The drop in the number of returned ontologies is significant when adding even one extra term. This phenomena is evident throughout the table even in our optimal scenario where terms were chosen from the same, well covered domain.

Our second set of queries containing terms drawn from different topic domains return less ontologies than previously (mostly zero). At a closer look, however, one might argue that the null results are caused by the fact that the domains from which the terms were drawn are weakly covered in Swoogle in the first place (indicated by the low number of ontologies returned for individual terms). While this observation does not necessarily undermine the intuition that topic heterogeneity has negative effects, it indicates that the knowledge currently available online is sparse, as many domains are weakly covered (or not at all). Therefore, null results can be expected even when query terms are topically related but refer to a weakly covered topic.

The third set of experiments indicates that the presence of relations seriously hampers retrieving an all covering ontology even when the query terms are chosen from the same, well represented domain.

[8] Exact matching is an extreme case (e.g., hasAuthor, authorOf, authored all mean the same thing) and as it will be evident from the results, it is too limiting.

In the last four queries, by refining query terms through hypernym replacement, better results were obtained. An obvious worry is that if the refinement uses too generic terms (e.g., Entity) the returned ontologies will be too generic to be of any use for the concrete knowledge reuse task at hand.

While only preliminary, our experiments do indicate that query size, topic heterogeneity and type might influence the chance to find an all covering ontology. They have also revealed the sparseness of the online knowledge. As a bottom line, independently of having verified our intuitions, we can observe that the chance to find an all covering ontology is rather low, especially in scenarios such as those provided by Magpie (many terms, drawn from different, possibly weakly represented domains) and AquaLog (properties as query terms).

3.2 Experiment 2 - Dealing with Compound Labels

Considering the results of the previous experiment, some mechanisms might be needed to expand the search for potentially relevant ontologies. Besides the synonym/hypernym extension, the more lexical oriented strategy of selecting concepts whose labels partially match the query terms can be explored. For example, Swoogle's fuzzy search functionality returns concept labels that contain the query term as a substring. This mechanism is rather brittle, and, while it returns several important hits (e.g., *GraduateStudent* when searching for *Student*), it also generates clearly invalid hits (e.g., *update* when searching for *date*).

To ensure our second requirement referring to precise coverage, all the compound labels returned by fuzzy search need to be interpreted in order to understand their relation with the query term. A special case of compound labels are those containing conjunctions (e.g., *BlackAndWhite*). Some researchers have proposed a set of rules to interpret such labels [8]. Naturally, reading, splitting and interpreting all these labels can seriously hamper the time performance, thus questioning the usefulness of performing a fuzzy search at all.

In this experiment we explore the feasibility of performing fuzzy search. We illustrate some cases when it pays off and some when it does not. We also evaluate how frequently conjunctions are used in compound labels.

To support our experiments we implemented a program (LabelSplitter) that splits compound labels according to the most common naming conventions and checks if a given term is a well formed part of that label (i.e., its base form is the same as the base form of one of the components of the label). For example, *TeachingCourse* is a relevant compound label (CL) for the term *teach*, but an irrelevant one for the term *tea*. In Table 2 we summarize the results obtained when querying some random terms and then some conjunctions showing the total number of hits returned by Swoogle, which is broken down into the number of exact matches, relevant and irrelevant CLs.

As expected, fuzzy search is a good mechanism to broaden the search space as it can return a lot of broader hits that contain the term. In general, in the case of longer words (less likely to be substrings of other words) more relevant than irrelevant compound labels are found. This is not true in the case of shorter words such as *tea* where an overwhelming number of irrelevant hits are returned.

Table 2. Analysis of the appearances of some conjunctions and other terms

Word	Total	Exact	Relevant CLs	Irrelevant CLs
project (clarifying example)	-	project	PastProject ProjectPartner	Projectile Projector
project	644	90	413	141
student	190	84	97	9
tea	492	3	23	466
mountain	36	12	21	4
university	86	64	22	0
and	2363	37	444	1882
or	18178	11	184	17983
of	6353	4	4743	1606
not	840	23	77	740
except	45	0	0	45
but not	0	0	0	0

Therefore, taking into account that fuzzy search is rather expensive, it should be used only when all other alternatives fail.

Regarding the frequency of conjunctions, in current online ontologies "or" appears the most frequently but in the large majority of cases as a substring and not a well formed part. While the "of" conjunction appears less often than "or" it is the most frequently used as a proper part of the compounds (mostly as part of property labels). "And" appears quite frequently as well in its role of well formed part (444). Surprisingly, negation and disjunction indicators appear infrequently or at all in the collection that we have queried. We conclude that interpretation rules for some conjunctions have to be written.

4 The Algorithm

In this section we present the design of an algorithm which aims to address some of the requirements stated in Section 2.3 and also draws on our conclusions regarding the nature of online ontologies detailed in the previous section. We first give an overview of the method in which we motivate our main design choices and then explore each major step of the algorithm in detail. The algorithm has been entirely specified and partially implemented (with the exception of the ideas reported in Sections 4.4 and 4.6) .

4.1 Overview

For our first implementation we wish to satisfy the first five requirements: we aim to identify ontologies (or combinations of ontologies - R3) that completely and precisely cover our query (R1 and R2). The query can contain both concepts and relations (R5). The performance of the algorithm should be such that it can be used by other applications at run time (R4). The final two requirements, related to instances and modularization, are not addressed yet.

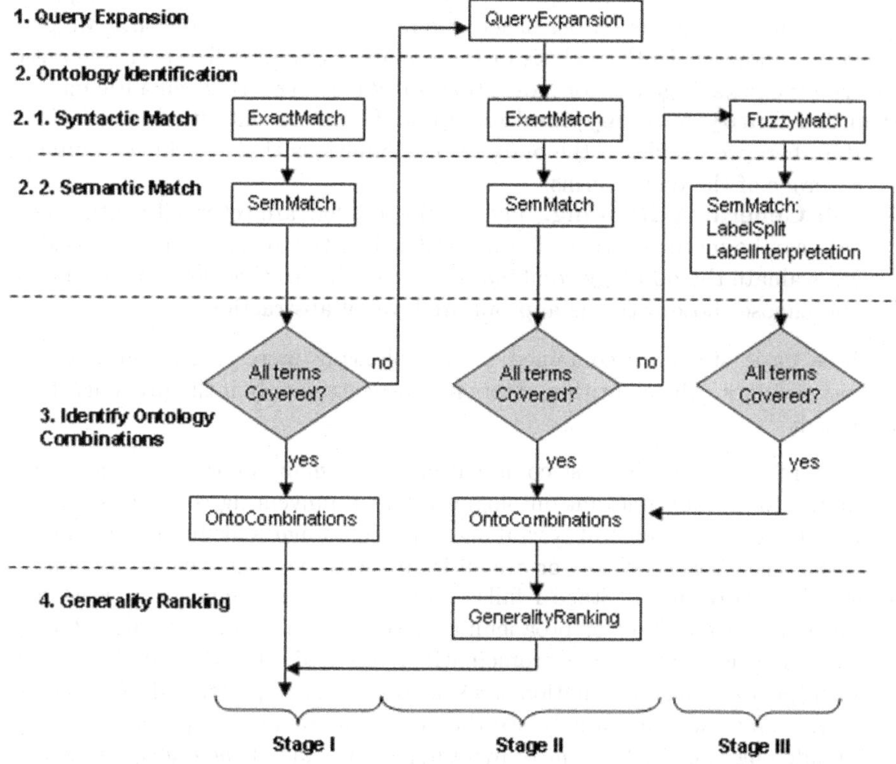

Fig. 1. The main tasks and stages of the selection algorithm

From our experiments we have learned that in cases when query terms are drawn from different domains or when they represent relations it is challenging to find ontologies that would cover all terms (therefore R1 is not so easy to fulfill). We have also seen that in such cases the search space can be expanded either 1) by query expansion with semantically related terms or 2) by searching for labels that incorporate the query term. However, our second experiment indicates that fuzzy search should be used only when absolutely needed.

Given these considerations, we have designed an algorithm that adapts itself to the particular context and can employ increasingly complex methods in order to achieve a complete coverage. The algorithm in Figure 1 executes increasingly complex combinations of a couple of main steps until complete coverage is achieved. We will first explain the role of each step and then describe how they are combined in increasingly complex stages.

Step 1: Query Expansion. This step supplements the query terms with their semantically related terms such as synonyms and hypernyms.

Step 2: Ontology identification. In this step we identify ontologies that cover to some extent the query terms. After an initial syntactic mapping between query terms (either exact or fuzzy) and ontology concepts, we perform a more in depth analysis of these mappings and define their semantic type (i.e., exact, generic or more specific). We call this task semantic match.

Step 3: Identify ontology combinations. Using the output of the previous step, here we decide on the ontology combinations that provide a complete coverage of the query terms.

Step 4: Generality Ranking. The ontologies that are returned contain hits that can be more generic or more specific than the query terms. In this step we evaluate the ontology combinations according to their level of generality and choose those with the appropriate level of abstraction.

These basic steps are combined in the following increasingly complex and expensive stages. The algorithm enters in a new stage only if the previous stage has failed:

Stage I relies on the simplest combination of the main steps. It uses an exact match to identify relevant ontologies thus circumventing complex semantic matching and the generality ranking step. This stage is likely to succeed only if the query terms are few or drawn from the same, well covered domain.

Stage II is used only if Stage I fails (no ontology was found for at least one term) and some kind of broadening of the search space is needed. Query expansion is used for the problematic terms and then the same ontology identification and combination steps as in stage I are performed. Notice that at this stage we can already use the generality ranking step because query broadening is likely to identify hypernyms for some of the query terms.

Stage III is the most complex one, as besides query expansion, it also relies on more flexible syntactic matching to identify even more concepts potentially related to the query terms. This fuzzy match complicates the semantic matching step as the retrieved compound labels need to be split and interpreted. After the semantic match has identified the semantic relations between query terms and ontology concepts we apply the ontology combination and generality ranking steps.

4.2 Step 1: Query Expansion

Query expansion is needed in order to broaden the search space for ontologies in cases when no or few ontologies are returned for a term. Our experiments indicate that such cases will be often encountered given the knowledge sparseness of online ontology collections. Term expansion allows searching not just for the term but for all its semantically related terms (e.g., synonyms, hypernyms). This can be allowed because we aim to perform a semantic rather than a syntactic selection and therefore synonyms that denote the same concept as the query term are relevant. Currently, we use WordNet to augment each query term with their synonyms and hypernyms The only system that uses a similar expansion approach is OntoKhoj [10].

4.3 Step 2: Ontology Identification

In this step we identify ontologies that contain the concepts specified in our query. This is in essence a mapping stage between the query terms and the concepts of the ontologies. We distinguish two substages:

Step 2.1. Syntactic Match. The syntactic match identifies lexically similar concept labels. It can be either *exact* (the query term is exactly the same as the concept label) or *fuzzy* (the query term is a substring of the concept label, e.g., the term *Student* is part of *GraduateStudent*). In the case when a fuzzy match is performed, this step is also responsible for splitting the compound labels and returning only the compound labels that are relevant for the given term (as done by the LabelSplitter module described in Section 3.2). Current ontology selection techniques only use syntactic matches when identifying relevant ontologies.

Step 2.2 Semantic Match. Semantic matching goes beyond the state of the art in ontology selection as it checks the soundness and the semantic nature of the previously identified syntactic mappings. Concretely, the input to this step is a term and a concept in an ontology that is lexically related to the term. The task is to find out the semantic relation between the term and the concept. This can be equivalence, more specific or more general.

An obviously relevant body of work is that on mapping techniques. However, according to a recent survey of mapping techniques [12] most matchers return a probability coefficient to describe the significance of a mapping rather than its semantic interpretation. A notable exception is the S-Match algorithm which returns the semantic category of each mapping in terms of (among others) the exact, more generic or more specific operators [5]. Following the general model of the S-Match algorithm, we distinguish two steps to obtain a semantic matching:

A. Acquiring the sense of the concept label also taking into account its position in the hierarchy (i.e., parent and children nodes).
B. Deriving the semantic relations between the term and the concept.

A. Acquiring the Sense of the Concept Label. We use information about the position of a concept in the ontology to determine its sense according to a method originally presented in [8]. In a nutshell, given a concept c and either one of its ancestors or descendants r all WordNet synsets for both labels are retrieved. Then, if any of the senses for c is related to any of the senses of r either by being a synonym, hypernym, holonym, hyponym or a meronym, then that sense of c is considered the right one. For example, if *Apple* (which can have two senses: tree and fruit) has *Food* as its ancestor, then there exists a hyponym relation between *apple#1* (fruit) and *food#1*, so we retain this sense and discard the one referring to apple being a tree.

B. Deriving Semantic Relations. After identifying the sense of the concept, we derive semantic relations between the terms and the concepts such as equivalence, more generic or more specific. We use a WordNet based comparison between the senses of the term and that of the concept label. Therefore, equivalence is established when two terms share a synset, and more general/more specific relations are indicated when hyponym/holonym (or even meronym/holonym) relations exist between their senses. In cases when none of these relations hold we investigate whether there is any similarity at all between the terms (and return a weaker "related" relationship). For this we investigate whether there exists an allowable "is-a" path in WordNet connecting their synsets by relying on the *depth* and *common parent index (C.P.I)* measures described in [7].

Matching relations. Our previous experience in AquaLog [7] was that mapping relations is more difficult than mapping concepts. One of the reasons is that many relations are vaguely defined (a classical example is *relatedTo* which can have a variety of meanings) and therefore can have a large number, hard to automatically predict lexical variations. Also, the meaning of a relation is given by the type of its domain and its range so the precondition of a mapping between two relations is that their domain and range classes match to some extent.

Inspired by our previous work [7], we treat relations as "second class citizens" and concentrate on finding matches for the classes that denote their domain and range first. Then, if only one relation exists between these classes we adopt it as such. If more relations exist we attempt a lexical based disambiguation of the one that is closest to the relation that we seek. An interesting case is when some relations are present in other ontologies as concepts (e.g., *hasAuthor* can be modeled as a concept *Author* in another ontology). This case is also explored.

4.4 Step3: Identifying Relevant Ontology Combinations

Ideally, one would expect that the selection mechanism finds a single ontology which contains all the query terms. However, in practice this is seldom the case. Most often query terms are spread over two or more ontologies. Unfortunately, previous approaches provide a set of ontologies ranked by the coverage of each *individual* ontology. Our task therefore is to identify the best combinations of ontologies that cover the query.

There are two criteria to rank ontology combinations. On one hand, the number of ontologies should be minimal. On the other hand, the number of terms that they cover should be maximal. The ultimate best is one ontology covering all terms, and the worst is a collection of ontologies each covering a single term. We are currently working on an optimal implementation of this multiple criteria optimization problem.

4.5 Step4: Generality Ranking

Due to our semantic matching, the returned concepts can be more generic or more specific than the query terms. In this step we identify the ontology combinations that are closest in terms of abstraction level to the query terms.

We are not aware of any work that directly addresses the issue of measuring the generality of an ontology or evaluating the generality of an ontology with respect to a set of terms. A recent publication investigates evaluating the generality of a document with respect to a query [14]. After concluding that most of the generality related work in the field of IR is based on statistical measures, they propose a method to compute the generality of a document with respect to a domain ontology (in that case, Mesh) by relying on the depth and proximity of the concepts in the domain ontology (i.e., the deeper and closer the concepts are in the ontology the more specific the document/query is). Generality is computed both for the query and the document and then the obtained scores are compared. The major drawbacks of this approach are that (1) it is time consuming because all terms need to be looked up in the oracle and their positions have to be computed and (2) it depends on the coverage of the used oracle.

We agree with [14] that generality computation should be based on the meaning of the terms rather than on statistical measures. Instead of computing generality both for the query and an ontology and then comparing them, we assume that the query provides the baseline and we only compute the generality deviation of the ontology from this baseline. Another optimization is that we circumvent the use of an external oracle by reusing the generality relation between terms and concepts as established by the semantic mapping step (we consider a function *genRel* between a term and its hit returning -1 if the concept is more specific, 0 if it is equivalent and 1 if it is more generic than the query term).

$$RD(T,O) = \frac{\sum_{i=1}^{n} |genRel(t_i,c_i)|}{n}; GS(T,O) = \sigma(\textstyle\sum_{i=1}^{n} genRel(t_i,c_i))$$

Given a set of n query terms ($t_{1,n}$) and their semantically related concepts ($c_{1,n}$) we compute the relative generality ($RD(T,O)$) of the ontology/ontologies containing these concepts with respect to the query as the mean of the absolute value of the *genRel* function. We also compute the sign of the generality deviation as the sign of the sum of all the values of the *genRel* function.

4.6 Extending Semantic Match to Deal with Compound Labels

Compound labels derived in Stage III complicate semantic matching. Hereby we describe some of the problems and the solutions that we are investigating.

A. Acquiring the sense of a ***compound*** *concept label.* Establishing the sense of compound labels by using WordNet is difficult as WordNet does not have an extensive coverage of compound words. We are currently investigating the strategy of interpreting the meaning of compound labels in terms of logical relations that hold between the senses of their constituents (similarly to work in [8] and [5]). According to this previous work, compound labels can be interpreted as the conjunction of their constituents and according to these rules:

Rule1. Commas and coordinate conjunctions are interpreted as a disjunction;
Rule2. Prepositions like *in* and *of* are interpreted as a conjunction;
Rule3. Exclusion expressions (e.g., *except*, *but not*) translate into negation.

However, we are not convinced that all these rules are useful in the context of online ontologies. For example, only five labels returned by Swoogle contain commas, so this is just an isolated case. Also, we found that no labels contain "except" and "but not", thus making the third rule redundant.

B. Deriving Semantic Relations between ***compound*** *terms.* The limited multi-word coverage of WordNet also prohibits using it to derive semantic relations between compound labels. We investigate a solution along the lines of that presented in [5] where compound labels, after being interpreted as logical formulas, are compared with the help of a reasoner.

5 Discussion and Future Work

Taking a step back from the details of the algorithm, the key contribution of this paper is that of exploring ontology selection in the context of automatic knowledge reuse. Indeed, as discussed in the introduction, this complements current selection techniques which have focused on human mediated tasks so far. While both contexts are equally important, we think that exploring the automatic context can lead to novel challenges and improvements of this technology.

We have analyzed the requirements of two Semantic Web tools, a question answering tool and a semantic browser, and concluded that current approaches only marginally address them. This is not a surprise in itself because these requirements raise hard to address research issues. In fact, our proposed algorithm limits itself to tackle only five of the seven requirements. These requirements indicate that selection will need to adapt techniques from currently developing research directions such as ontology evaluation, mapping and modularization.

Ontology mapping has been the focus of the proposed algorithm which balances between providing a complete, precise coverage and an acceptable performance. Our strategy is to use a self-adaptation metaphor, the algorithm adapts its complexity to the case of each query by invoking increasingly complex stages as necessary. As such, the simplest stage is just a bit more complicated than state of the art techniques, while the most complex stage raises yet unsolved research issues. The major difference from existing approaches is the emphasis on the correctness of the mapping between query terms and ontology concepts. We go beyond current techniques which exclusively rely on lexical matches by performing a semantic match. Naturally, establishing a semantic mapping at run-time without interpreting the entire ontology structure is a challenging issue by itself.

While, obviously, there are several complex issues to address, our immediate future work will concentrate on finalizing the implementation of a first prototype. In parallel, we will adapt our tools to use this selection algorithm. They will be used as a case study for evaluating selection in an automatic knowledge reuse scenario, thus paving the way towards a selection mechanism that fits the needs of the real Semantic Web.

Acknowledgements. We thank Yuangui Lei and Victoria Uren for their comments on this paper. This work was funded by the Advanced Knowledge Technologies (AKT) Interdisciplinary Research Collaboration (IRC), sponsored by the UK Engineering and Physical Sciences Research Council under grant number GR/N15764/01, and the Open Knowledge and NeOn projects sponsored by the European Commission as part of the Information Society Technologies (IST) programme under EC grant numbers IST-FF6-027253 and IST-FF6-027595.

References

1. H. Alani and C. Brewster. Ontology Ranking based on the Analysis of Concept Structures. In *Proceedings of the Third International Conference on Knowledge Capture(K-CAP 05)*, Banff, Canada, 2005. ACM.
2. P. Buitelaar, T. Eigner, and T. Declerck. OntoSelect: A Dynamic Ontology Library with Support for Ontology Selection. In *Proceedings of the Demo Session at the International Semantic Web Conference.* Hiroshima, Japan, 2004.
3. L. Ding, R. Pan, T. Finin, A. Joshi, Y. Peng, and P. Kolari. Finding and Ranking Knowledge on the Semantic Web. In Y. Gil, E. Motta, V.R. Benjamins, and M.A. Musen, editors, *Proceedings of the 4th International Semantic Web Conference*, volume 3729 of *LNCS*, pages 156 – 170. Springer-Verlag GmbH, 2005.
4. M. Dzbor, J. Domingue, and E. Motta. Magpie - towards a semantic web browser. In *Proceedings of the Second International Semantic Web Conference*, 2003.
5. F. Giunchiglia, P. Shvaiko, and M. Yatskevich. SMatch: An Algorithm and Implementation of Semantic Matching. In *The Semantic Web: Research and Applications. Proceedings of the First European Semantic Web Conference*, volume 3053 of *LNCS*, pages 61 – 75. Springer-Verlag, 2004.
6. V. Lopez, E. Motta, and V. Uren. PowerAqua: Fishing the Semantic Web. In *Proceedings of the Third European Semantic Web Conference*, 2006.
7. V. Lopez, M. Pasin, and E. Motta. AquaLog: An Ontology-portable Question Answering System for the Semantic Web. In *Proceedings of the European Semantic Web Conference*, 2005.
8. B. Magnini, L. Serafini, and M. Speranza. Making explicit the semantics hiden in schema models. In *Proceedings of the Human Language Technology for the Semantic Web workshop at ISWC'03*, 2003.
9. P. Mika. Flink: Semantic Web Technology for the Extraction and Analysis of Social Networks. *Journal of Web Semantics*, 3(2), 2005.
10. C. Patel, K. Supekar, Y. Lee, and E. K. Park. OntoKhoj: A Semantic Web Portal for Ontology Searching, Ranking and Classification. In *Proceeding of the Workshop On Web Information And Data Management.* ACM, 2003.
11. M. Sabou, V. Lopez, E. Motta, and V. Uren. Ontology Selection: Ontology Evaluation on the Real Semantic Web. In *Proceedings of the Evaluation of Ontologies on the Web Workshop, held in conjunction with WWW'2006*, 2006.
12. P. Shvaiko and J. Euzenat. A Survey of Schema-Based Matching Approaches. *Journal of Data Semantics*, IV:146 – 171, 2005.
13. S. Spaccapietra. Report on modularization of ontologies. Knowledge Web Deliverable D2.1.3.1, July 2005.
14. X. Yan, X. Li, and D. Song. Document Generality: Its Computation and Ranking. In *Proceedings of the Seventeenth Australasian Database Conference*, 2006.

Ontology Engineering, Scientific Method and the Research Agenda

Hans Akkermans[1,2] and Jaap Gordijn[1]

[1] Free University Amsterdam VUA
Business Informatics Department (FEW/BI)
Amsterdam, The Netherlands
gordijn@cs.vu.nl

[2] AKMC Knowledge Management BV
Koedijk, The Netherlands
Hans.Akkermans@akmc.nl

Abstract. The call for a "focus on content" in ontology research by Nicola Guarino and Mark Musen in their launching statement of the journal Applied Ontology has quite some implications and ramifications. We reflectively discuss ontology engineering as a scientific discipline, and we put this into the wider perspective of debates in other fields. We claim and argue that ontology is a new scientific method for theory formation. This positioning allows for stronger concepts and techniques for theoretical, empirical and practical validation that in our view are now needed in the field. A prerequisite for this is an emphasis on ontology as a (domain) content oriented concept, rather than as primarily a computer representation notion. We propose that taking domain theories and the associated substantive or content reference of ontologies really seriously as first-class citizens, will actually increase the contribution of ontology engineering to the development of scientific method in general. Next, ontologies should develop from the current static representations of relatively stable domain content into actionable theories-in-use, and a possible way forward is to build in capabilities for dynamic self-organization of ontologies as service-oriented knowledge utilities that can be delivered over the Web.

1 Introduction: Focus on Content?

Many believe that ontologies are first of all a computer science (CS) construct. There is some truth in this if one takes as a measure where the main locus and focus is in ontology engineering activities. On the other hand, in other scientific fields there is a significant interest in ontologies for (predominantly non-CS) reasons that relate to the development and growth of the respective domains. Many in computer science, and in knowledge engineering (KE) as well, have however a tendency to see this as 'just another application': something to be happy with because it proves the relevance of ontology engineering, but at the same time as something that is also of lesser (scientific) importance than the core CS issues in ontology such as computer-oriented representation, languages, reasoning techniques, systems development and tools.

In other sciences, we (amusingly?) see a mirror image with regard to CS. The preoccupation in CS with computing and systems-related issues is there often pejoratively

S. Staab and V. Svatek (Eds.): EKAW 2006, LNAI 4248, pp. 112–125, 2006.

viewed as 'just programming', in other words, as technical engineering that is important and useful to do — but it's not really (and at the very least, not necessarily) science. This view, commonly found among both natural and social scientists, also extends to ontology engineering.

In this reflective essay we argue that both views, the CS one as well as the non-CS one, are misguided. This has its roots in an inadequate positioning of what ontologies are and can do.

For the CS and KE side, the emphasis on representation and systems aspects is perhaps an understandable attitude, but it is also a self-limiting approach that in the end will not be able to exploit the full potential of the ontology idea. Outside 'application' domains are to be taken much more seriously, as *first-class citizens* in CS and KE. In their launching statement of the new journal Applied Ontology, Nicola Guarino and Mark Musen [1] call for a "focus on content" in ontology research. Offen [2] points out that "domain understanding is the key to successful system development". In this paper we explore some of the consequences for ontology research as a field of scientific endeavour.

For the non-CS side, we argue why and how ontology engineering is contributing to the further development of scientific method in general. The central contribution of this paper is our argument that *ontology is to be seen as a novel and distinct method for scientific theory formation and validation*. But to fully establish this, there are certain specific consequences to be drawn by CS and KE for the ontology research agenda.

2 Domain Understanding and the Dual Reference of Ontologies

Ontologies are generally defined as explicit and formal specifications of a shared conceptualization for some domain of interest [3]. The term *shared* refers to an agreement within a community of interest or practice over the description (i.e. conceptualization) of the domain, while *formal* indicates that the representation of this agreement is in some sort of computer-understandable format. Note the rather open notion of a domain conceptualization in the definition: ontology research makes no claim about the nature of the knowledge to be modelled [4].

Thus, as depicted in Figure 1, ontologies have a *dual* reference. They are not only 'CS' specs referencing a computational implementation (like conventional information systems (IS) or database models or schemas), but they have an explicit real-world *content or substantive reference* as well [5,6,1,7]. In current CS and KE research the computational reference seems to get more of the attention. However, we believe that the domain content reference is at least equally important, and not just because this is where future massive application of ontologies will be. Offen [2] makes the important general comment that "domain understanding is the key to successful system development". In our view, this is where the real value of ontologies lies.

We observe that developing this understanding — which is a key practical use of today's ontology building [4] — is in fact a (real-world domain) conceptualization and theory formation act. The content or substantive reference of ontologies means that ontologies function as ways to build and test what are in fact theories that purport to adequately model an, often empirical, domain or phenomenon. In other words, ontology

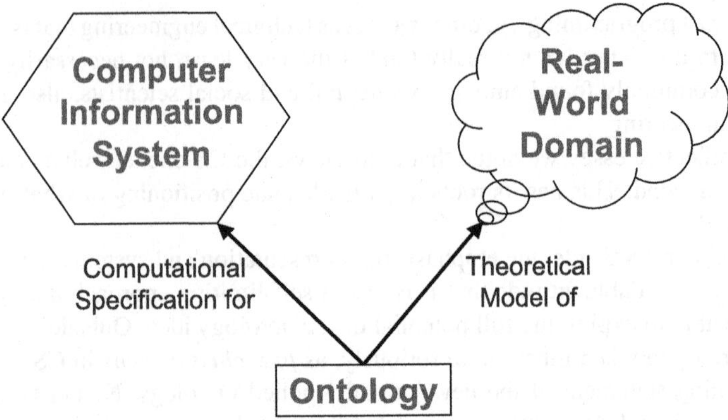

Fig. 1. The conceptualization triangle and the dual reference of ontologies

engineering can be viewed and employed as a method for theory formation. And it is one that appears to be useful for a wide variety of domains and disciplines.

3 The Conception of Theory in Other Sciences

Many works in the philosophy of science (e.g. [8,9,10,11]) and in scientific research methodology (e.g. [12,13,14,15,16]) emphasize the key importance, and difficulty, of conceptualization and theory formation in scientific research. We believe that the role of ontology as a rigorous instrument for conceptualization and theory formation in this sense is currently often overlooked, within CS and KE as well as outside.

Ontology engineering as a theory formation method is admittedly still at a relatively early stage. It potentially widens the scope and importance of ontology engineering as a scientific method of general interest, but it also comes with additional scientific issues and duties. And first of all, we have to ask the question *what actually counts as a theory* in scientific research.

Already a quick scan of the above-cited literature covering different disciplines, shows that there are very different notions in science what a theory is, ought to be, or looks like. There is sometimes the attitude among researchers that such 'philosophical' issues are external to the scientific debate in a research discipline. Nothing could be further from the truth. Perhaps this inside-the-box thinking is adequate for progress in mainstream normal puzzle-solving science (as Kuhn [8] calls it). In times of change it is different.

For example, in the constitutive era of classical mechanics, scientists such as Newton were not called physicists but (rightly) natural philosophers. Quantum mechanics as formulated by Bohr, Schrödinger, Heisenberg, and others was driven very much by a conceptual and philosophical discussion on foundations. The famous Einstein-Podolski-Rosen 'paradox' debated with Bohr in the 1930's in the Physical Review (not a philosophical journal, by the way) is a case in point [10]; there was not even any technical disagreement about the formalism or the equations or on how to compute things.

The birth of (symbolic) AI as a discipline in the 1950's is another good example (as are the debates concerning the pros and cons of symbolic vs. subsymbolic AI).

And closer to home, the history of Knowledge Engineering itself shows how strongly views concerning the broad conceptual and philosophical foundations of a field are influential in actually shaping it. There is a big difference between the mainstream view on KE during the heydays of expert systems (of, say, the late seventies to mid eighties) to the later conceptual model-based approach (see e.g. [17]) that is closely connected to today's ontology approaches. This becomes clear already by simply glancing over the (about twenty) years of the Proceedings of the present conference, EKAW (or its North-American counterpart KAW, now K-CAP).

Accordingly, different seemingly 'philosophical' views on the foundations of a field do have important practical consequences for research as it is actually organized, carried out, and reviewed (and so, accepted or rejected), cf. [18,19]. Elsewhere, we have discussed at some length various scientific disciplines and research approaches that turn out to have fundamentally different views on what a theory is and how it can or should be evaluated [20].

As pointed out there, theory in the natural sciences appears to be basically equated with formal math and its associated machinery. The logic-oriented research approaches in CS and KE are clearly heavily influenced by this image of science in what a theory is. However, another important element in natural science theorizing is the underlying assumption that the scientific method is first of all about uncovering the (abstract) fundamental 'first' principles as the (axiomatic) basis for universal theories and laws. This is not really the same as formal mathematical representation of theory (witness for example the mentioned Einstein-Bohr debate). It is first of all a matter of conceptualization that precedes the formal representation. Einstein is said to have the habit to start lectures with extensive fundamental conceptual discussions and only after some time to move to the formal equations: "Nun wollen wir *x*-en" — Now we will write down the *x*'s, the formal symbolism. An example of ontology research in this area attempting to combine formal math with conceptual modelling is the PHYSSYS ontology of [21] for physical systems modelling and simulation (Figure 2).

The social sciences provide yet other images of science that are relevant to ontology research (cf. Peter Mika's viewpoint article [22]). A major distinction here is that between the 'quantitative' and 'qualitative' schools of methodological thought (for extensive overviews, good sources are Robson [13] and Bryman [15]). Characteristic for the quantitative school is the reductionist approach from complex conceptual frameworks and concepts ('constructs') to *variables* as its theoretical languange and its preference for statistical methods for testing. Cohen's work on Empirical Methods for Artificial Intelligence [23] is in fact to a significant extent a translation of the school thought and empirical testing methodology of quantitative social research to AI and CS. Information Systems research as published in journals such as the MIS Quarterly, an important forum for much business school related research on IT, is also strongly influenced by this quantitative school. The prototypical form that theory assumes here is that of a small directed graph with variables as nodes; the edges represent the putative relationships between the variables and so supply the hypotheses to be tested.

Fig. 2. The PHYSSYS ontology has for example been used in the computer-aided design of this car. Constable Rob Piper shows the new electric patrol car of the Kidderminster police, England. Courtesy photograph: Associated Press Photo/David Jones.

The qualitative school in social research also has an empirical focus [24] but emphasizes that (unlike the natural sciences) it is not so much the outside and context-free view of the researcher/observer that is important in explaining the world, but the context-inclusive interpretation and meaning that people themselves attach to their social world. Works in KE close to the 'interpretive' or 'social constructivist' approach to science are for example the volumes Knowledge Acquisition as Modeling edited by Ken Ford and Jeffrey Bradshaw [25], and Expertise in Context edited by Feltovich et al. [26]. Characteristic for the qualitative and interpretive approach are methods such as interview, focus group, observation, ethnography, action research, case study — empirical research methods widely used in Information Systems research and practice (e.g. [27]) and, to a lesser extent, also employed in ontology research [6,5,28]. Theory in the qualitative school of thought is typically in the form of an extensive conceptual framework and argument put forward in an essay-like style, although there are attempts toward more formal approaches (cf. [24]; a specific example is grounded theory — which interestingly has similarities with good old bottom-up knowledge elicitation). In Knowledge Management theory, a good example is [29], but we also find it in AI (e.g. [30]; by the way, it also applies to the present paper). With respect to this style of theorizing, ontology methods and representations can add significant clarity and rigour, as we will argue below.

In sum, we believe it is important to investigate the underlying but often tacit assumptions made in researching, publishing and reviewing in the (theoretical as well as applied) ontology field. The content/substantive reference of ontologies implies that ontology engineering is an inherently multidisciplinary approach to theory formation. Therefore, it has to deal with very different conceptions and styles of scientific research and of what the form and nature of a scientifically acceptable theory is. This impacts for example the representation of ontologies: it is unlikely that with RDF and OWL as Web standards we have reached the end of representation (and even less so, of reasoning methodology), given the indicated highly diverse forms of scientific theorizing.

4 Ontology as Scientific Method for Theory Formation

The content reference of ontologies is the primary entry that makes ontologies interesting and useful for experts outside the CS domain. Ontologies as substantive theories offer ways to model phenomena of interest, and in particular model theories that are cast in the form of a conceptual framework (common in social sciences, as discussed above) in a much more rigorous fashion. In addition, and this is where the second, computational reference of ontologies comes in, they offer ways for testing such models by means of simulation, calculation, or other computational means. But even more importantly, ontology engineering — as an advanced branch of conceptual modelling — is providing richer and more flexible ways for conceptualization and theory formation than currently in use in many domains and scientific disciplines.

Scientific theory generally seems to assume two extreme forms: either formal-mathematical (as typically encountered in the 'exact' natural sciences), or informal in natural language and essayistic (common in social sciences and the humanities). In contrast, IS-style conceptual modelling and particularly ontology engineering have over the years developed novel methods for conceptualization that are more formal and rigorous than theories in natural language, thus allowing for stronger, computational and other forms of validation for example by CASE and simulation tools.

At the same time, the graphical and diagram representations developed and employed in conceptual modelling and ontology engineering make the associated theories much more understandable and accessible to experts and practitioners in other domains compared to formal math and logic. Conceptual and ontological analysis, graphical

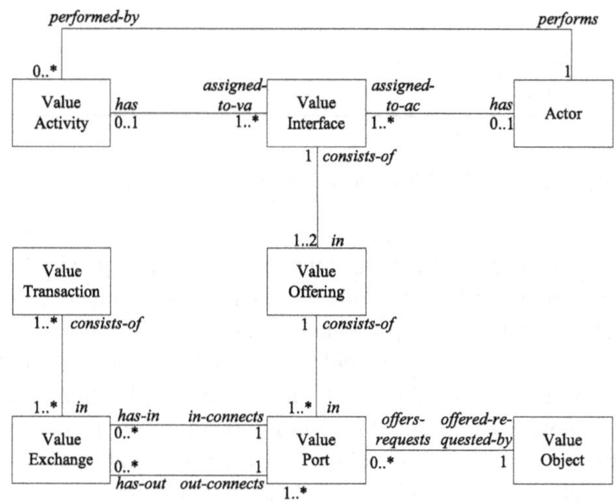

Fig. 3. The e^3*value* ontology for networked business models

diagramming methods, and their combination with formal computational reasoning techniques have over the years been elaborated into a fine art at a level of sophistication not found elsewhere.

A practical example that demonstrates several of the above points is the e^3*value* ontology for networked business modelling (Figure 3; [31,6,5,28]). As a theory, it effectively formalizes existing concepts from business research literature about which there is a good deal of consensus [31]. A formal ontology goes however much further: it includes rules and constraints (many of them present but rather implicit in the domain literature) which with it is possible to reason, and so to find out what the inferential consequences of a theory are. It is here that the computational paradigm shows its value with regard to other disciplines. In the present example, it makes it possible to design and reason about the potential of new business model ideas (including net present value and cashflow analyses in a business network). Given the complexity of such reasoning methods that surpasses the possibilities of manual analysis, computational tooling is necessary and important.

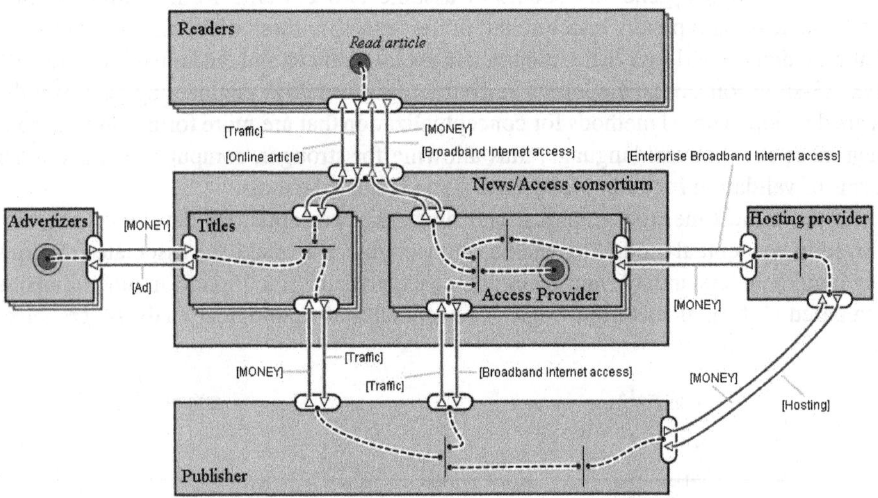

Fig. 4. Visual representation of an e^3*value* business model for a news media e-service

However, tooling should be ideally such that it hides the complexity 'under the hood' as far as possible, in order to facilitate work with users and practioners. Figure 4 shows an example of the graphical diagram representation of an ontology instance. The associated e^3*value* tool for networked business modelling (www.e3value.com) employs internally the formal ontology, but enables the user to develop the application ontology in an almost fully graphical way. The RDF(S) representation of the application ontology is not constructed by the user or ontology developer, but is automatically generated by the tool.

In summary, looking at ontologies from their content reference point of view suggests that ontology engineering can be usefully interpreted as a scientific method for conceptualization and theory formation, and one that brings several novel contributions.

5 Reuse: Ontologies as Middle-Range Theories

Conceiving the content/domain reference of ontologies as 'the application view' is quite natural for CS researchers, but overly limiting. Domain experts, on their turn, often see it equally simply the other way around: the CS work as the application side (or even worse: as 'just programming').

Ontologies as theories — that are to be sharable and reusable — go significantly beyond the application view. Already in ontology research quite long ago (e.g. [32,21]), distinctions have been made in different types of ontologies that have different levels of generality, and therefore of reusability. A simplified picture distinguishes three different levels of generality:

1. At the top level, with maximum genericity, we have the upper ontologies that formalize highly generic ('universal') concepts concerning, say, mereology, taxonomy, space, time, etc. (see for example IEEE Upper Ontology work at http://suo.ieee.org/SUO/SUMO/, or some ontology engineering patterns of the W3C Semantic Web Best Practices & Deployment Working Group, http://www.w3.org/2001/sw/BestPractices/Overview.html).
2. At the bottom level, we have the application ontologies that are key in driving specific applications and tasks, but in terms of their generality tend to trade reusability for practical usability.
3. In-between we have what we call middle-range ontologies: they concern a domain, are less universal than the top-level ontologies, but generic and reusable across many different applications. The *e*[3]*value* ontology is an example of an ontology as such a middle-range theory.

What in CS and KE are called application domains are in fact themselves broad areas where ontologies can be (made) sharable and reusable beyond a specific application context. Here, ontologies have the capability to express what in social science research are called "middle-range theories" (hence our terminology): theories that have a much wider applicability than the situations, contexts, or cases from which they actually originate.

For an interesting methodological discussion how to develop middle-range theories in scientific research, we refer to the book of one of the grand old men of sociology, Howard Becker [12]). One practical recommendation he gives to come to middle-range theories and hypotheses, is to describe case-study conclusions without being allowed to mention the specific case itself anywhere. This forces one to come up with and consider more generally valid formulations. It is also good advice for knowledge acquisition in ontology development.

6 Ontology Evaluation and Validation

Scientific theories are supposed to be empirically and/or pragmatically valid in their domain of reference. In terms of the dual reference of Figure 1, ontologies are to be both computationally and epistemologically adequate.

CS tends to focus on methods for the former, and indeed here it has a lot of added value for scientists and practitioners in other domains: it is usually impossible to foresee all consequences that a theory has manually, or to get a grip on all possible paths that motivating domain scenarios might follow. Computational implementation and test of ontologies is thus necessary and useful, but its strength is in forms of consistency and validity that are internal to the theory that is tested. It is restricted to what in philosophical terms is called a coherence conception of truth, and this is what logic-based and computational evaluation does for us.

If however we take the content reference aspect of ontologies seriously, a much stronger emphasis on empirical ontology validation is called for. Ontologies are good only insofar as they are empirically valid from the domain theory point of view. This requires more and different validation activities than just computer-oriented ones. This is a KE theme recurring in the work of Tim Menzies, e.g. [33], and it is also the thrust of Cohen's [23] call to AI. We believe that these authors make a point that is very valid in current ontology research. Richer and stronger notions of validation, in particular external validity, are in need of more emphasis in the ontology research field.

How can ontology evaluation and validation be practically done? In our view, there are several different approaches that may be employed in parallel. Not only there are, as discussed above, several different conceptions of theory, there are also multiple notions of validity that are applicable. In other sciences (notably social research), the various notions of validity have been discussed in quite some more depth than is the case in CS, and many corresponding suitable scientific methods for evaluation and validation have been developed. However, mainstream ontology research tends to employ an (overly) limited repertoire of available scientific methods for testing its claims.

As we have argued elsewhere [20], validation of claims to knowledge assumes in science the form of a *rational communicative argument* that must be defended and made credible. In scientific work, available empirical data and theory are systematically brought together such that knowledge claims follow in a step-by-step and transparent process of rational reasoning. Ontologies, as they represent knowledge structures that are reusable and community-sharable, should satisfy general criteria of validity concerning rational communicative argument.

The general structure and rules of argument have been investigated in past years in philosophy [34], communication theory [35], and critical thinking and informal logic [36]. A simple model of the general layout of arguments due to Toulmin [34] is depicted in Figure 5.

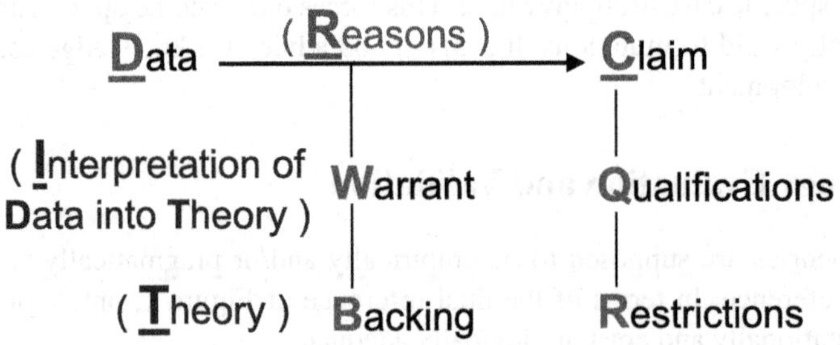

Fig. 5. The structure of argument

This model suggests a checklist of criteria and questions [20] that is also practically useful to review the adequacy of the computational and especially content references of ontologies:

1. *Descriptive validity* ***D***: do the supplied empirical (domain) data provide a truthful description of the situation or problem that is considered?
2. *Theoretical validity* ***T***: are the employed theories or conceptual frameworks explicated and shown to be appropriate for the (domain) purpose?
3. *Interpretive validity* ***I***: is the way in which all available data are mapped onto or interpreted in the employed theories or frameworks clear and adequate?
4. *Reasoning validity* ***R***: are all steps in the reasoning sound and, in addition, consistent and coherent with other knowledge that we possess?
5. *Internal validity* C_{int}: are the claims made acceptable 'beyond reasonable doubt' *within* the situation or context (or sample) considered in the study?
6. *External validity* C_{ext}: are any generalization claims that go *beyond* the studied situation sufficiently credible?

These different questions as to validity require different kinds of test methods [20,18,19]. In CS and KE, methods for logico-mathematical demonstration ('proof') are well developed: if a theory is sufficiently rigorously specified, certain desired properties may be strictly mathematically or logically derived. This is seen in formal ontology, from description logics to OntoClean.

A further step, one that is also well developed, is computational simulation and analysis: the computer has made it possible to run very high numbers of scenarios and explore a large parameter space. This approach to validation might be viewed as the computational extension of the thought experiment (a very ancient technique, famous as a result of the Einstein-Bohr debate on the interpretation of quantum mechanics — in today's terms very much a discussion on ontologies). In ontological analysis, the direct analogy with thought experiments are walkthrough methods that employ mental or paper simulations of simple application scenarios; they are in our experience a quite effective method at an early stage of development. A main caveat here is that in the end the motivating scenarios selected for computational evaluation should not be toy examples, but be sufficiently real-world like and cover a good part of the design space, in order to be convincing in terms of validation of claims. There is some room for improvement here in current CS and KE research.

These methods can establish the validity of the computational reference of ontologies. In terms of the above validity checklist, they establish reasoning validity and, but only partially, help answer other validity questions such as theoretical and internal validity. To validate the substantive content reference of ontologies, however, other notions of validity are more prominent, in particular descriptive and external validity, and they require other methods for their evaluation. It is here that CS and KE can learn quite a lot from other disciplines that have put major efforts into the development and refinement of experimental methods (in the lab, but for our purposes especially in the field) as well as of empirical methods for practice/experience-oriented field studies [13,15,14,16,24,37,12].

An essential issue for ontology evaluation and validation that needs to be more explicitly considered in research is the aspect of *context*. Ontologies are usable because they function successfully in specific domain, task, and/or application contexts that exist in the field. Ontologies are reusable only if we succeed in solving the (external validity) question to what extent they work satisfactorily across different contexts (compare also [22]). This issue is behind our above-discussed idea of ontologies as middle-range theories.

Our position here is that approaches to ontology evaluation and validation need to be (field) context inclusive, in ways that are in clear contrast with the orthodox context-free scientific ideals of empirical confirmationist/falsificationist research (often associated with writers such as Popper). These issues have been discussed extensively in social research, especially in the context of case study methodology [37] and action research [13,27], but they are too much ignored in CS and KE. Avoiding to deal with context is minimally a very (and in our view too) high price to pay for scientific research in ontologies, an important point that was already made in older KE work [25,26] but needs to be reiterated. Focus on content entails dealing with context.

7 No Ontology Without Methodology

The call for a "focus on content" in ontology research by Nicola Guarino and Mark Musen [1] in their launching statement of the journal Applied Ontology has quite some implications and ramifications. In particular, we have argued that:

- Ontology engineering offers a potential contribution to scientific method in general, as a fundamental approach to conceptualization and theory formation with new techniques valuable to many (non-CS) domains and disciplines.
- This however requires that the content or substantive reference of ontologies is taken to heart by ontology engineers in addition to the common CS issues.
- This goes against the not uncommon attitude that outside domains represent application research (that academically speaking has a lower rank than fundamental research).
- Especially, this requires that issues and methods of empirical and practical validation of theories — as much further developed in other scientific disciplines — become more prominent and adopted in ontology engineering.

Taking application domain theories and the associated content reference of ontologies really seriously as first-class citizens in our research will actually increase the contribution of ontology engineering to the development of scientific method in general.

A further step on the research agenda to be taken in our view is that ontologies should develop from the current static representations of relatively stable domain content into actionable theories-in-use (as opposed to 'espoused theories'; these are concepts stemming from organizational learning [38,39,40]). We believe it is a fair characterization of the state of the art to say that ontologies are still quite generally perceived as *static* representations and metadata annotations of knowledge.

However, ontologies have *to do* something for people: they are to provide actionable knowledge, and this involves system *dynamics*. Ontologies can therefore not (or no longer) be specified 'as such'. In addition, the specific forms and methods of reasoning they employ or presuppose is to become an inherent part of the specification.

An observation resulting from the mentioned context-relatedness of ontologies is that in practice there are many different methods that make them do useful work. This is already true if we limit ourselves to the formal logic-based approaches that go with different deduction engines. It is even more true if we consider reasoning machineries needed for Semantic Web Services. And the scope of dynamic methods is even broader if we consider ontologies as part of rational communicative argument (cf. Figure 5) constructed and shared within a community of practice, a perspective common in ontology-based Knowledge Management. In other words: no ontology without methodology.

Beyond this, a further way forward for the research agenda would be to start to employ the computational paradigm for the dynamic feedback loops in Knowledge Engineering and Knowledge Management themselves. Given the significant amounts of knowledge available on the Web, plus a broad repertory of dynamic reasoning methods available, it seems well possible to build in capabilities for *self-organization* of systems and services, in which ontologies act as service-oriented knowledge utilities that can be delivered over the Web. There are currently several useful hooks from ongoing research, although they are still in an early stage of technical development, content and detail. So that is a story to be told elsewhere, another time.

Acknowledgments. This work was partially supported by the European Network of Excellence KnowledgeWeb, the BSIK Freeband/FRUX project, and the VU* centre VUBIS for Business Information Sciences in Amsterdam. We are also grateful for the many interesting reactions by the Semantic Web and GREETING meeting participants in Amsterdam, where a first version of the present views was discussed by the first author.

References

1. Guarino, N., Musen, M.: Applied ontology: Focusing on content. Applied Ontology **1**(1) (2005) 1–5
2. Offen, R.: Domain understanding is the key to successful system development. Requirements Engineering **7** (2002) 172–175
3. Gruber, T.: A translation approach to portable ontology specifications. Knowledge Acquisition **5**(2) (1993) 199–220
4. Mika, P., Akkermans, J.: Towards a new synthesis of ontology technology and knowledge management. The Knowledge Engineering Review **19**(4) (2004) 317–345 DOI Online 11 November 2005.
5. Akkermans, J., Baida, Z., Gordijn, J., Peña, N., Altuna, A., Laresgoiti, I.: Value webs: Using ontologies to bundle real-world services. IEEE Intelligent Systems **19**(4) (2004) 57–66
6. Gordijn, J., Akkermans, J.: Value-based requirements engineering: Exploring innovative e-Commerce ideas. Requirements Engineering **8**(2) (2003) 114–134
7. Evermann, J., Wand, Y.: Ontology based object-oriented domain modelling: Fundamental concepts. Requirements Engineering **10** (2005) 146–160
8. Kuhn, T.: The Structure of Scientific Revolutions. The University of Chicago Press, Chicago (1970) Second Edition.
9. Lakatos, I., Musgrave, A., eds.: Criticism and the Growth of Knowledge. Cambridge University Press, Cambridge (1970)

10. Jammer, M.: The Philosophy of Quantum Mechanics. Wiley-Interscience, New York (1974)
11. Feyerabend, P.: Against Method. Verso, London (1993) Third Edition.
12. Becker, H.: Tricks of the Trade — How to Think About Your Research While You're Doing It. University of Chicago Press, Chicago (1998)
13. Robson, C.: Real World Research. Blackwell Publishers, Oxford, UK (2002) Second Edition.
14. Bowling, A.: Research Methods in Health: Investigating Health and Health Services. Open University Press, Maidenhead, Berkshire, UK (2002) Second Edition.
15. Bryman, A.: Research Methods and Organization Studies. Routledge, London, UK (1989)
16. Babbie, E.: The Practice of Social Research. Wadsworth Publishing Company, Belmont, CA (1998) Eighth Edition.
17. Schreiber, A., Akkermans, J., Anjewierden, A., de Hoog, R., Shadbolt, N., der Velde, W.V., Wielinga, B.: Knowledge Engineering And Management — The COMMONKADS Methodology. The MIT Press, Cambridge, MA (2000)
18. Wieringa, R., Maiden, N., Mead, N., Rolland, C.: Requirements engineering paper classification and evaluation criteria: A proposal and a discussion. Requirements Engineering **11**(1) (2006) 102–107
19. Hevner, A., March, S., Park, J., Ram, S.: Design science research in information systems. MIS Quarterly **28**(1) (2004) 75–105
20. Akkermans, J., Gordijn, J.: What is this science called requirements engineering? In Glinz, M., Lutz, R., eds.: Proceedings 14th IEEE International Conference on Requirements Engineering (RE06), Los Alamitos, CA, IEEE Computer Society (2006)
21. Borst, W., Akkermans, J., Top, J.: Engineering ontologies. International Journal of Human-Computer Studies **46** (1997) 365–406
22. Mika, P.: Social networks and the semantic web: The next challenge. IEEE Intelligent Systems **20**(1) (2005) 80–93
23. Cohen, P.: Empirical Methods for Artificial Intelligence. The MIT Press, Cambridge, MA (1995)
24. Miles, M., Huberman, A.: Qualitative Data Analysis. Sage Publications, Thousand Oaks, CA (1994) Second Edition.
25. Ford, K., Bradshaw, J., eds.: Knowledge Acquisition as Modeling. Wiley, New York, NY (1993)
26. Feltovich, P., Ford, K., Hoffman, R., eds.: Expertise in Context. AAAI Press / The MIT Press, Menlo Park, CA / Cambridge, MA (1997)
27. Checkland, P., Holwell, S.: Information, Systems and Information Systems — Making Sense of the Field. John Wiley & Sons Ltd, Chichester, UK (1998)
28. Gordijn, J., Yu, E., Van der Raadt, B.: e-Service design using i^* and e^3*value* modeling. IEEE Software **23**(3) (2006) 26–33
29. Nonaka, I., Takeuchi, H.: The Knowledge-Creating Company. Oxford University Press, Oxford, UK (1995)
30. Ford, K., Glymour, C., Hayes, P., eds.: Thinking About Android Epistemology. The MIT Press, Cambridge, MA (2006)
31. Gordijn, J., Akkermans, J., van Vliet, J.: What's in an electronic business model? In Dieng, R., Corby, O., eds.: Knowledge Engineering and Knowledge Management — Methods, Models, and Tools. Volume 1937 of LNAI., Berlin, D, Springer Verlag (2000) 257–273 (12th International Conference EKAW-2000).
32. Van Heijst, G., Schreiber, A., Wielinga, B.: Using explicit ontologies in KBS development. International Journal of Human-Computer Studies **45** (1997) 183–292
33. Menzies, T.: Model-based requirements engineering. Requirements Engineering **8** (2003) 193–194
34. Toulmin, S.: The Uses of Argument. Cambridge University Press, Cambridge, UK (1958) Updated Edition 2003.

35. van Eemeren, F., Grootendorst, R.: A Systematic Theory of Argumentation — The Pragma-Dialectical Approach. Cambridge University Press, Cambridge, UK (2004)
36. Fisher, A.: The Logic of Real Arguments. Cambridge University Press, Cambridge, UK (2004) Second Edition.
37. Yin, R.: Case Study Research — Design and Methods. SAGE Publications, Thousand Oaks, CA (2003) Third Edition.
38. Argyris, C.: On Organizational Learning. Blackwell Publishers, Cambridge, MA (1992)
39. Argyris, C.: Knowledge for Action. Jossey-Bass Publishers, San Francisco, CA (1993)
40. Argyris, C.: Reasons and Rationalizations — The Limits to Organizational Knowledge. Oxford University Press, Oxford, UK (2004) See especially Ch. 5: 'Features of Scholarly Inquiry that Inhibit Double-Loop Learning and Implementable Validity'.

Ontology Enrichment Through Automatic Semantic Annotation of On-Line Glossaries

Roberto Navigli and Paola Velardi

Dipartimento di Informatica
Università di Roma "La Sapienza"
00198 Roma Italy
{navigli, velardi}@di.uniroma1.it

Abstract. The contribution of this paper is to provide a methodology for automatic ontology enrichment and for document annotation with the concepts and properties of a domain core ontology. Natural language definitions of available glossaries in a given domain are parsed and converted into formal (OWL) definitions, compliant with the core ontology property specifications.

To evaluate the methodology, we annotated and formalized a relevant fragment of the AAT glossary of art and architecture, using a subset of 10 properties defined in the CRM CIDOC cultural heritage core ontology, a recent W3C standard.

Keywords: Ontology Learning, Core Ontology, Glossaries.

1 Introduction

Large-scale, automatic semantic annotation of web documents based on well established domain ontologies would allow various Semantic Web applications to emerge and gain acceptance. Wide coverage ontologies are indeed available for general-purpose domains (e.g. WordNet, CYC, SUMO[1]), however semantic annotation in unconstrained areas seems still out of reach for state of art systems. Domain-specific ontologies are preferable since they would limit the domain and make the applications feasible.

Recently, certain web communities began to believe in the benefits deriving from the application of Semantic Web techniques. Accordingly, they produced remarkable efforts to conceptualize their competence domain through the definition of a *core ontology*. Relevant examples are in the area of enterprise modeling (Fox et al. 1997; Uschold et al. 1998) and cultural heritage (Doerr, 2003).

Core ontologies are indeed a necessary starting point to model in a principled way the basic concepts, relations and axioms of a given domain. But in order for an ontology to be really usable in applications, it is necessary to enrich the core structure with the thousands of concepts and instances that "make" the domain.

---

[1] WordNet: http://wordnet.princeton.edu, CYC: http://www.opencyc.org, SUMO: http://www.ontologyportal.org

S. Staab and V. Svatek (Eds.): EKAW 2006, LNAI 4248, pp. 126 – 140, 2006.

In this paper we present a methodology to automatically annotate a glossary $\mathcal{G}$ with the semantic relations of an existing *core ontology* $\mathcal{O}$. The annotation of documents and glossary definitions is performed using regular expressions, a widely adopted text mining approach. However, while in the literature regular expressions seek mostly for patterns at the lexical and part of speech level, we defined expressions enriched with syntactic and semantic constraints. A word sense disambiguation algorithm, SSI (Velardi and Navigli, 2005), is used to automatically replace the high level semantic constraints specified in the core ontology with fine–grained sense restrictions, using the sense inventory of a general purpose lexicalized ontology, WordNet.

From each gloss *G* of a term *t* in the glossary $\mathcal{G}$, we extract one or more semantic relation *instances* $R(C_t,C_w)$, where R is a relation in $\mathcal{O}$, C_t and C_w are respectively the *domain* and *range* of R. The concept C_t corresponds to its lexical realization *t*, while C_w is the concept associated to a word *w* in G, captured by a regular expression.

The annotation process allows to automatically enrich $\mathcal{O}$ with an existing glossary in the same domain of $\mathcal{O}$, since each pair of term and gloss (t,G) in the glossary $\mathcal{G}$ is transformed into a formal definition, compliant with $\mathcal{O}$. Furthermore, the very same method can be used to automatically annotate free text with the concepts and relations of the enriched ontology $\mathcal{O}'$. We experimented our methodology in the cultural heritage domain, since for this domain several well-established resources are available, like the CIDOC-CRM core ontology, the AAT art and architecture thesaurus, and others.

The paper is organized as follows: in Section 2 we briefly present the CIDOC and the other resources used in this work. In Section 3 we describe in detail the ontology enrichment algorithm. Finally, in Section 4 we provide a performance evaluation on a subset of CIDOC properties and a sub-tree of the AAT thesaurus. Related literature is examined in Section 5.

2 Semantic and Lexical Resources in the Cultural Heritage Domain

In this section we briefly describe the resources that have been used in this work.

2.1 The CIDOC CRM

The core ontology $\mathcal{O}$ is the *CIDOC CRM* (Doerr, 2003), a formal core ontology whose purpose is to facilitate the integration and exchange of cultural heritage information between heterogeneous sources. It is currently being elaborated to become an ISO standard. In the current version (4.0) the CIDOC includes 84 taxonomically structured concepts (called *entities*) and a flat set of 141 semantic relations, called *properties*. Entities are defined in terms of their subclass and super-class relations in the CIDOC hierarchy, and a *scope note* is used to provide an informal description of the entity. Properties are defined in terms of *domain* (the class for which a property is formally defined) and *range* (the class that comprises all potential values of a property), e.g.:

P46 is composed of (forms part of)
Domain: E19 Physical Object
Range: E42 Object Identifier

The CIDOC is an "informal" resource. To make it usable by a computer program, we replaced specifications written in natural language with formal ones. For each property $\mathcal{R}$, we created a tuple $R(C_d, C_r)$ where C_d and C_r are the domain and range entities specified in the CIDOC reference manual.

2.2 The AAT Thesaurus

The domain glossary $\mathcal{G}$ is the Art and Architecture Thesaurus (AAT) a controlled vocabulary for use by indexers, catalogers, and other professionals concerned with information management in the fields of art and architecture. In its current version[2] it includes more than 133,000 terms, descriptions, bibliographic citations, and other information relating to fine art, architecture, decorative arts, archival materials, and material culture. An example is the following:

maestà
Note: Refers to a work of a specific iconographic type, depicting the Virgin Mary and Christ Child enthroned in the center with saints and angels in adoration to each side. The type developed in Italy in the 13th century and was based on earlier Greek types. Works of this type are typically two-dimensional, including painted panels (often altarpieces), manuscript illuminations, and low-relief carvings.
Hierarchical Position:
Objects Facet
.... Visual and Verbal Communication
.... Visual Works
.... <visual works>
.... <visual works by subject type>
.... maestà

We manually mapped the top CIDOC entities to AAT concepts, as shown in Table 1.

Table 1. Mapping between AAT and CIDOC

AAT topmost	CIDOC entities
Top concept of AAT	CRM Entity (E1), Persistent Item (E77)
Styles and Periods	Period (E4)
Events	Event (E5)
Activities Facet	Activity (E7)
Processes/Techniques	Beginning of Existence (E63)
Objects Facet	Physical Stuff (E18), Physical Object (E19)
Artifacts	Physical Man-Made Stuff (E24)
Materials Facet	Material (E57)
Agents Facet	Actor (E39)
Time	Time-Span (E52)
Place	Place (E53)

[2] http://www.getty.edu/research/conducting_research/ vocabularies/aat/

2.3 Additional Resources

To apply semantic constraints on the words of a definition (as clarified in the next Section), we need additional resources. WordNet (Miller, 1995) is used to verify that certain words in a gloss-string *f* satisfy the range constraints $R(C_d,C_r)$ in the CIDOC. In order to do so, we manually linked the WordNet topmost concepts to the CIDOC entities. For example, the concept E19 (Physical Object) is mapped to the WordNet synset "*object, physical object*". Furthermore, we created a gazetteer $\mathcal{I}$ of named entities extracting names from the Dmoz[3], a large human-edited directory of the web, the Union List of Artist Names (ULAN) and the Getty Thesaurus of Geographic Names (GTG) provided by the Getty institute, along with the AAT.

3 Enriching the CIDOC CRM with the AAT Thesaurus

In this Section we describe in detail the method for automatic semantic annotation and ontology enrichment in the cultural heritage domain. Let $\mathcal{G}$ be a glossary, *t* a term in $\mathcal{G}$ and *G* the corresponding natural language definition (gloss). The main steps of the algorithm are the following:

1. Part-of-speech analysis. Each input gloss is processed with a part-of-speech tagger, TreeTagger[4]. As a result, for each gloss $G = w_1\ w_2\ \dots\ w_n$, a string of part-of-speech tags $p_1\, p_2\ \dots\ p_n$ is produced, where $p_i \in \mathcal{P}$ is the part-of-speech tag chosen by TreeTagger for word w_i, and $\mathcal{P} = \{ N, A, V, J, R, C, P, S, W \}$ is a simplified set of syntactic categories (respectively, nouns, articles, verbs, adjectives, adverbs, conjunctions, prepositions, symbols, wh-words).

2. Named Entity recognition. We augmented TreeTagger with the ability to capture named entities of locations, organizations, persons, numbers and time expressions. In order to do so, we use regular expressions (Friedl, 1997) in a rather standard way, therefore we omit details. When a named entity string $w_i\ w_{i+1}\ \dots\ w_{i+j}$ is recognized, it is transformed into a single term and a specific part of speech denoting the kind of entity is assigned to it (*L* for cities (e.g. Venice), countries and continents, *T* for time and historical periods (e.g. Middle Ages), *O* for organizations and persons (e.g. Leonardo Da Vinci), B for numbers).

3. Annotation of sentence segments with CIDOC properties. We developed an algorithm for the annotation of gloss segments with properties grounded on the CIDOC-CRM relation model. Given a gloss *G* and a property[5] *R*, we define a *relation checker* c_R taking in input *G* and producing in output a set F_R of fragments of *G* annotated with the property *R*: <*R*>*f*</*R*>. The selection of a fragment *f* to be included in the set F_R is based on different kinds of constraints:

---

[3] http://dmoz.org/about.html

[4] TreeTagger is available at: http://www.ims.uni-stuttgart.de/projekte/corplex/TreeTagger.

[5] In what follows, we adopt the CIDOC terminology for relations and concepts, i.e. properties and entities.

- a **part-of-speech constraint** *p(f, pos-string)* matches the part-of-speech (*pos*) string associated with the fragment *f* against a regular expression (*pos-string*), specifying the required syntactic structure.
- a **lexical constraint** *l(f, k, lexical-constraint)* matches the lemma of the word in *k-th* position of *f* against a regular expression (*lexical-constraint*), constraining the lexical conformation of words occurring within the fragment *f*.
- **semantic constraints on domain and range** $s_D(f,$ *semantic-domain*) and *s(f, k, semantic-range)* are valid, respectively, if the term *t* and the word in the *k-th* position of *f* match the semantic constraints on domain and range imposed by the CIDOC, i.e. if there exists at least one sense of *t* C_t and one sense of *w* C_w such that: $R_{kind\text{-}of}^*(C_d, C_t)$ and $R_{kind\text{-}of}^*(C_r, C_w)$[6].

More formally, the annotation process is defined as follows: a *relation checker* c_R for a property *R* is a logical expression composed with constraint predicates and logical connectives, using the following production rules:

$c_R \rightarrow s_D(f,$ *semantic-domain*) $\wedge\ c_R'$
$c_R' \rightarrow \neg c_R' \mid (c_R' \vee c_R') \mid (c_R' \wedge c_R')$
$c_R' \rightarrow$ *p(f, pos-string)* | *l(f, k, lexical-constraint)* | *s(f, k, semantic-range)*

where *f* is a variable representing a sentence fragment. Notice that a relation checker must always specify a semantic constraint s_D on the *domain* of the relation *R* being checked on fragment *f*. Optionally, it must also satisfy a semantic constraint *s* on the k-th element of *f*, the range of *R*.

For example, the following excerpt of the checker for the *is-composed-of* relation (*P46*):

(1) $c_{is\text{-}composed\text{-}of}(f) = s_D(f,$ *physical object#1*) $\wedge$ *p(f,* "(V)$_1$(P)$_2$R?A?[CRJVN]*(N)$_3$")
$\wedge$ *l(f,* 1, "^(consisting|composed|comprised|constructed)$")
$\wedge$ *l(f,* 2, "of") $\wedge$ s(*f*, 3, *physical_object#1*)

reads as follows: "the fragment *f* is valid if it consists of a verb in the set { *consisting, composed, comprised, constructed* }, followed by a preposition "of", a possibly empty number of adverbs, adjectives, verbs and nouns, and terminated by a noun interpretable as a *physical object* in the WordNet concept inventory". The first predicate, s_D, requires that also the term *t* whose gloss contains *f* (i.e., its domain) be interpretable as a *physical object*.

Notice that some letter in the regular expression specified for the part-of-speech constraint is enclosed in parentheses. This allows it to identify the relative positions of words to be matched against lexical and semantic constraints, as shown graphically in Figure 1.

Checker (1) recognizes, among others, the following fragments (the words whose part-of-speech tags are enclosed in parentheses are indicated in bold):
(consisting)$_1$ **(of)**$_2$ semi-precious **(stones)**$_3$ (matching part-of-speech string: **(V)**$_1$**(P)**$_2$ J**(N)**$_3$)
(composed)$_1$ **(of)**$_2$ **(knots)**$_3$ (matching part-of-speech string: **(V)**$_1$**(P)**$_2$**(N)**$_3$)

---

[6] $R_{kind\text{-}of}^*$ denotes zero, one, or more applications of $R_{kind\text{-}of}$.

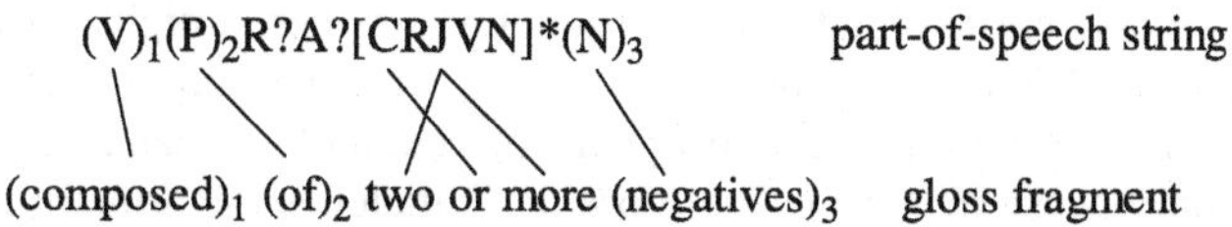

Fig. 1. Correspondence between parenthesized part-of-speech tags and words in a gloss fragment

As a second example, an excerpt of the checker for the *consists-of* (*P45*) relation is the following:

$$\begin{aligned} (2)\ & c_{consists\text{-}of}(f) = s_D(f, physical\ object\#1) \wedge p(f, \text{“(V)}_1\text{(P)}_2\text{A?[JN,VC]*(N)}_3\text{”}) \\ & \wedge\ l(f, 1, \text{“\^{}(make|do|produce|decorated)\$”}) \wedge l(f, 2, \text{“\^{}(of|by|with)\$”}) \\ & \wedge\ \neg s(f, 3, color\#1) \wedge \neg s(f, 3, activity\#1) \\ & \wedge\ (s(f, 3, material\#1) \wedge s(f, 3, solid\#1) \wedge s(f, 3, liquid\#1)) \end{aligned}$$

recognizing, among others, the following phrases:

- **$(made)_1$ $(with)_2$** the red earth pigment **$(sinopia)_3$** (matching part-of-speech string: **$(V)_1(P)_2$AJNN$(N)_3$)**
- **$(decorated)_1$ $(with)_2$** red, black, and white **$(paint)_3$** (matching part-of-speech string: **$(V)_1(P)_2$JJCJ$(N)_3$)**

Notice that in both checkers (1) and (2) semantic constraints are specified in terms of WordNet sense numbers (*material#1*, *solid#1* and *liquid#1*), and can also be negative ($\neg$*color#1* and $\neg$*activity#1*). The motivation is that CIDOC constraints are coarse-grained due to the small number of available core concepts: for example, the property *P45 consists of* simply requires that the range belongs to the class *Material* (*E57*). Using WordNet for semantic constraints has two advantages: first, it is possible to write more fine-grained (and hence more reliable) constraints, second, regular expressions can be re-used, at least in part, for other domains and ontologies. In fact, several CIDOC properties are rather general-purpose.

4. Formalisation of glosses. The annotations generated in the previous step are the basis for extracting *property instances* to enrich the CIDOC CRM with a conceptualization of the AAT terms. In general, for each gloss G defining a concept C_t, and for each fragment $f \in F_R$ of G annotated with the property R: <*R*>*f*</*R*>, it is possible to extract one or more property instances in the form of a triple $R(C_t, C_w)$, where C_w is the *concept* associated with a term or multi-word expression w occurring in f (i.e. its language realization) and C_t is the *concept* associated to the defined term t in AAT. For example, from the definition of *tatting* (a kind of lace) the algorithm automatically annotates the phrase *composed of knots*, suggesting that this phrase specifies the *range* of the *is-composed-of* property for the term *tatting*:

$$R_{is\text{-}composed\text{-}of}(C_{tatting}, C_{knot})$$

In this property instance, $C_{tatting}$ is the *domain* of the property (a term in the AAT glossary) and C_{knot} is the *range* (a specific term in the definition G of *tatting*).

Selecting the concept associated to the domain is rather straightforward: glossary terms are in general not ambiguous, and, if they are, we simply use a numbering policy to identify the appropriate concept. In the example at hand, $C_{tatting}$=*tatting#1* (the first and only sense in AAT). Therefore, if C_t matches the domain restrictions in the regular expression for R, then the domain of the relation is considered to be C_t. Selecting the range of a relation is instead more complicated. The first problem is to select the correct words in a fragment *f*. Only certain words of an annotated gloss fragment can be exploited to extract the range of a property instance. For example, in the phrase "depiction of fruit, flowers, and other objects" (from the definition of *still life*), only *fruit, flowers, objects* represent the range of the property instances of kind *depicts* (*P62*).

When writing relation checkers, as described in the previous paragraph of this Section, we can add *markers of ontological relevance* by specifying a predicate *r*(*f*, *k*) for each relevant position *k* in a fragment *f*. The purpose of these markers is precisely to identify words in *f* whose corresponding concepts are in the range of a property. For instance, the checker (1) $c_{is\text{-}composed\text{-}of}$ from the previous paragraph is augmented with the conjunction: $\wedge$ ***r*(*f*, 3)**. We added the predicate *r*(*f*, 3) because the third parenthesis in the part-of-speech string refers to an ontologically relevant element (i.e. the candidate *range* of the *is-composed-of* property).

The second problem is that words that are candidate ranges can be ambiguous, and they often are, especially if they do not belong to the domain glossary $\mathcal{G}$. Considering the previous example of the property *depicts*, the word *fruit* is not a term of the AAT glossary, and it has 3 senses in WordNet (the fruit of a plant, the consequence of some action, an amount of product). The property *depicts*, as defined in the CIDOC, simply requires that the range be of type *Entity* (E1). Therefore, all the three senses of *fruit* in WordNet satisfy this constraint. Whenever the range constraints in a relation checker do not allow a full disambiguation, we apply the SSI algorithm (Navigli and Velardi, 2005), a semantic disambiguation algorithm based on structural pattern recognition, available on-line[7]. The algorithm is applied to the words belonging to the segment fragment *f* and is based on the detection of relevant semantic interconnection patterns between the appropriate senses. These patterns are extracted from a lexical knowledge base that merges WordNet with other resources, like word collocations, on-line dictionaries, etc.

For example, in the fragment "depictions of fruit, flowers, and other objects" the following properties are created for the concept *still_ life#1*:

$$R_{depicts}(still\_\ life\#1, fruit\#1)$$
$$R_{depicts}(still\_\ life\#1, flower\#2)$$
$$R_{depicts}(still\_\ life\#1, object\#1)$$

Some of the semantic patterns supporting this sense selection are shown in Figure 2.

A further possibility is that the range of a relation *R* is a concept *instance*. We create concept instances if the word *w* extracted from the fragment *f* is a named entity. For example, the definition of *Venetian lace* is annotated as "Refers to needle lace

[7] SSI is an on-line knowledge-based WSD algorithm accessible from http://lcl.di.uniroma1. it/ssi. The on-line version also outputs the detected semantic connections (as those in Figure 2).

created **<current-or-former-location>** in Venice**</current-or-former-location>** [...]". As a result, the following triple is produced:

$$R_{has\text{-}current\text{-}or\text{-}former\text{-}location}(Venetian\_lace\#1,\ Venice{:}city\#1)$$

where *Venetian_ lace#1* is the concept label generated for the term *Venetian lace* in the AAT and *Venice* is an instance of the concept *city#1* (*city, metropolis, urban center*) in WordNet.

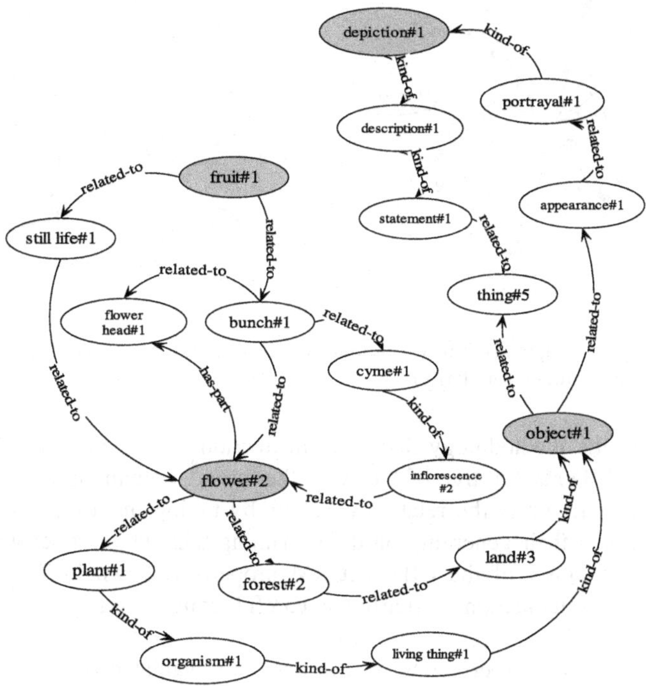

Fig. 2. Semantic Interconnections selected by the SSI algorithm when given the word list: "depiction, fruit, flower, object"

4 Evaluation

Since the CIDOC-CRM model formalizes a large number of fine-grained properties (precisely, 141), we selected a subset of properties for our experiments (reported in Table 2). We wrote a relation checker for each property in the Table. By applying the checkers in cascade to a gloss G, a set of annotations is produced. The following is an example of an annotated gloss for the term "vedute":

Refers to detailed, largely factual topographical views, especially **<has-time-span>**18th-century**</has-time-span>** Italian paintings, drawings, or prints of cities. The first vedute probably were **<carried-out-by>**painted by northern European artists**</carried-out-by>** who worked **<has former-or-current-location>**in Italy**</has former-or-current-location><has-**

time-span>in the 16th century**</has-time-span>**. The term refers more generally to any painting, drawing or print **<depicts>**representing a landscape or town view**</depicts>** that is largely topographical in conception.

Figure 3 shows a more comprehensive graph representation of the outcome for the concepts *vedute*#1 and *maestà*#1 (see the gloss in Section 2.2).

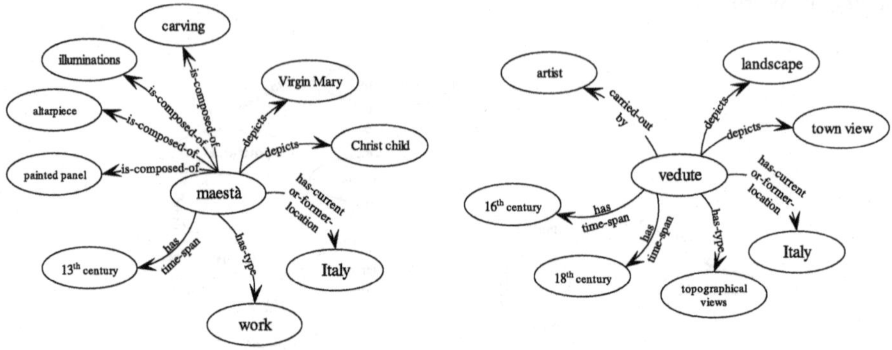

Fig. 3. Extracted conceptualisation (in graphical form) of the terms maestà#1 and vedute#1 (sense numbers are omitted for clarity)

To evaluate the methodology described in Section 3 we considered 814 glosses from the *Visual Works* sub-tree of the AAT thesaurus[8], containing a total of 27,925 words. The authors wrote the relation checkers by tuning them on a subset of 122 glosses, and tested their generality on the remaining 692. The test set was manually tagged with the subset of the CIDOC-CRM properties shown in Table 2 by two annotators with adjudication (requiring a careful comparison of the two sets of annotations).

We performed two experiments: in the first, we evaluated the *gloss annotation task*, in the second the *property instance extraction task*, i.e. the ability to identify the appropriate domain and range of a property instance. In the case of the gloss annotation task, for evaluating each piece of information we adopted the measures of "*labeled*" *precision* and *recall*. These measures are commonly used to evaluate parse trees obtained by a parser (Charniak, 1997) and allow the rewarding of good partial results. Given a property *R*, labeled *precision* is the number of *words* annotated correctly with *R* over the number of words annotated automatically with *R*, while labeled *recall* is the number of words annotated correctly with *R* over the total number of words manually annotated with *R*.

Table 3 shows the results obtained by applying the checkers to tag the test set (containing a total number of 1,328 distinct annotations and 5,965 annotated words). Note that here we are evaluating the ability of the system to assign the correct tag to *every word* in a gloss fragment *f*, according to the appropriate relation checker. We choose to evaluate the tag assigned to single words rather than to a whole phrase,

[8] The resulting OWL ontology is available at http://lcl.di.uniroma1.it/tav

because each misalignment would count as a mistake even if the most part of a phrase was tagged correctly by the automatic annotator.

The second experiment consisted in the evaluation of the property instances extracted. Starting from 1,328 manually annotated fragments of 692 glosses, the checkers extracted an overall number of 1,101 property instances. We randomly selected a subset of 160 glosses for evaluation, from which we manually extracted 344 property instances.

Table 2. A subset of the relations from the CIDOC-CRM model

Code	Name	Domain	Range	Example
P26	moved to	Move	Place	P26(installation of public sculpture, public place)
P27	moved from	Move	Place	P27(removal of cornice pictures, wall)
P53	has former or current location	Physical Stuff	Place	P53(fancy pictures, London)
P55	has current location	Physical Object	Place	P55(macrame, Genoa)
P46	is composed of (is part of)	Physical Stuff	Physical Stuff	P46(lace, knot)
P62	depicts	Physical Man-Made Stuff	Entity	P62(still life, fruit)
P4	has time span	Temporal Entity	Time Span	P4(pattern drawings, Renaissance)
P14	carried out by (performed)	Activity	Actor	P14(blotted line drawings, Andy Warhol)
P92	brought into existence by	Persistent Item	Beginning of Existence	P92(aquatints, aquatint process)
P45	consists of (incorporated in)	Physical Stuff	Material	P45(sculpture, stone)

Table 3. Precision and Recall of the gloss annotation task

Property	Precision		Recall	
P26 – moved to	84.95%	(79/93)	64.23%	(79/123)
P27 – moved from	81.25%	(39/48)	78.00%	(39/50)
P53 – has former or current location	78.09%	(916/1173)	67.80%	(916/1351)
P55 – has current location	100.00%	(8/8)	100.00%	(8/8)
P46 – composed of	87.49%	(944/1079)	70.76%	(944/1334)
P62 – depicts	94.15%	(370/393)	65.26%	(370/567)
P4 – has time span	91.93%	(547/595)	76.40%	(547/716)
P14 – carried out by	91.71%	(343/374)	71.91%	(343/477)
P92 – brought into existence	89.54%	(471/526)	62.72%	(471/751)
P45 – consists of	74.67%	(398/533)	57.60%	(398/691)
Average performance	**85.34%**	**(4115/4822)**	**67.81%**	**(4115/6068)**

Two aspects of the property instance extraction task had to be assessed:

- the extraction of the appropriate *range words* in a gloss, for a given property instance
- the precision and recall in the extraction of the appropriate *concepts* for both *domain* and *range* of the property instance.

An overall number of 233 property instances were automatically collected by the checkers, out of which 203 were correct with respect to the first assessment (87.12% precision (203/233), 59.01% recall (203/344)).

In the second evaluation, for each property instance $R(C_t, C_w)$ we assessed the semantic correctness of both the concepts C_t and C_w. The appropriateness of the concept C_t chosen for the domain must be evaluated, since, even if a term t satisfies the semantic constraints of the domain for a property R, it still can be the case that a fragment f in G does not refer to t, like in the following example:

pastels (visual works) -- *Works of art*, typically on a paper or vellum support, to which designs are applied using crayons **made of ground pigment** held together with a binder, typically oil or water and gum.

In this example, *ground pigment* refers to *crayons* (not to *pastels*).

The evaluation of the semantic correctness of the domain and range of the property instances extracted led to the final figures of 81.11% (189/233) precision and 54.94% (189/344) recall, due to 9 errors in the choice of C_t as a domain for an instance $R(C_t, C_w)$ and 5 errors in the semantic disambiguation of range words w not appearing in AAT, but encoded in WordNet (as described in the last part of Section 3). A final experiment was performed to evaluate the generality of the approach presented in this paper.

As already remarked, the same procedure used for annotating the glosses of a thesaurus can be used to annotate web documents. Our objective in this third experiment was to:

- Evaluate the ability of the system to annotate fragments of web documents with CIDOC relations
- Evaluate the domain dependency of the relation checkers, by letting the system annotate documents not in the cultural heritage domain.

We then selected 5 documents at random from an historical archive and an artist's biographies archive[9] including about 6,000 words in total, about 5,000 of which in the historical domain. We then ran the automatic annotation procedure on these documents and we evaluated the result, using the same criteria as in Table 3.

Table 4 presents the results of the experiment. Only 5 out of 10 properties had at least one instance in the analysed documents. It is remarkable that, especially for the less domain-dependent properties, the precision and recall of the algorithm is still high, thus showing the generality of the method. Notice that the historical documents

[9] http://historicaltextarchive.com and http://www.artnet.com/library

influenced the result much more than the artist biographies, because of their dimension.

In Table 4 the recall of P14 (*carried out by*) is omitted. This is motivated by the fact that this property, in a generic domain, corresponds to the *agent* relation ("an active animate entity that voluntarily initiates an action"[10]), while in the cultural heritage domain it has a more narrow interpretation (an example of this relation in the CIDOC handbook is: "the painting of the Sistine Chapel (E7) was *carried out by* Michelangelo Buonarroti (E21) *in the role of* master craftsman (E55)"). However, the domain and range restrictions for P14 correspond to an agent relation, therefore, in a generic domain, one should annotate as "carried out by" almost any verb phrase with the subject (including pronouns and anaphoric references) in the class Human.

Table 4. Precision and Recall of a web document annotation task

Property	Precision		Recall	
P53 – has former or current location	79.84%	(198/248)	77.95%	(198/254)
P46 – composed of	83.58%	(112/134)	96.55%	(112/116)
P4 – has time span	78.32%	(112/143)	50.68%	(112/221)
P14 – carried out by	60.61%	(40/66)	-	-
P45 – consists of	85.71%	(6/7)	37.50%	(6/16)
Average performance	**78.26%**	**(468/598)**	**77.10%**	**(468/607)**

5 Related Work and Conclusions

This paper presented a method, based on the use of regular expressions, to automatically annotate the glosses of a thesaurus, the AAT, with the properties (conceptual relations) of a core ontology, the CIDOC-CRM. The annotated glosses are converted into OWL concept descriptions and used to enrich the CIDOC.

Several methods for ontology population and semantic annotation described in literature (e.g. (Thelen and Riloff, 2002; Califf and Mooney, 2004; Cimiano et al. 2005; Valarakos et al. 2004)) use regular expressions to identify named entities, i.e. concept *instances.* Other methods extract hypernym relations using syntactic and lexical patterns (Snow et al. 2005; Morin and Jaquemin 2004) or supervised clustering techniques (Kashyap et al. 2003). Evaluation of hypernymy learning methods is usually performed by a restricted team of experts, on a limited set of terms, with hardly comparable results, usually well over 40% error rate (Caraballo, 1999; Maedche et al, 2002). When the evaluation is an attempt to replicate the structure of an already existing taxonomy, the error rate is over 50-60% (Widdows, 2003).

As far as the adopted ontology learning technique is concerned, in our work we automatically learn *formal concepts* (not simply instances or taxonomies, as in the literature) compliant with the semantics of a well-established core ontology, the CIDOC. In AAT the hypernym relation is already available, since AAT is a thesaurus, not a glossary. However we developed regular expressions also for hypernym

[10] http://www.jfsowa.com/ontology/thematic.htm

extraction from definitions[11] (Velardi et al. 2006). When applying these patterns to the AAT (for sake of space this is not discussed in this paper) we found that in 34% of the cases the automatically extracted hypernym is the same as in AAT, and in 26% of the cases, either the extracted hypernym is more general than the one defined in AAT, or the contrary, wrt the AAT hierarchy. This result quite favorably compares with available results in the literature.

Semantic annotation with relations other than hypernymy are surveyed in (Reeve and Han, 2005), and again, regular expressions are a commonly used technique. Reeve and Han's survey presents a table to compare system's performance, but in absence of well-established data sets of annotated documents, a fair comparison among the various techniques is not possible. Similarly, comparing the performance of our system with those surveyed in (Reeve and Han, 2005) is not particularly meaningful.

The method presented in this paper is unsupervised, in the sense that it does not need manual annotation of a significant fragment of text. However, it relies on a set of manually written regular expressions, based on lexical, part-of-speech, and semantic constraints. The structure of regular expressions is rather more complex than in similar works using regular expressions, especially for the use of automatically verified semantic constraints. The issue is however how much these expressions generalize to other domains:

- A first problem is the availability of lexical and semantic resources used by the algorithm. The most critical requirement of the method is the availability of sound *core ontologies*, which hopefully will be produced by other web communities stimulated by the recent success of CIDOC CRM. On the other side, *in absence of an agreed conceptual reference model, no large scale annotation is possible at all.* As for the other resources used by our algorithm, glossaries, thesaura and gazetteers are widely available in "mature" domains. If not, we developed a methodology, described in (Navigli and Velardi, 2005b), to automatically create a glossary in novel domains (e.g. enterprise interoperability), extracting definition sentences from domain-relevant documents and authoritative web sites.
- The second problem is about the generality of regular expressions. Clearly, the relation checkers that we defined are tuned on the CIDOC properties, however many of these properties are rather general (especially locative and temporal relations) and could easily apply to other domains, as demonstrated by the experiment on automatic annotation of historical archives in Table 4. Furthermore, the method used to verify semantic constraints is fully general, since it is based on WordNet and a general-purpose, untrained semantic disambiguation algorithm, SSI.

Finally, the authors believe with some degree of convincement that automatic pattern-learning methods often require non-trivial human effort just like manual methods[12]

---

[11] In the referenced paper we apply hypernymy-seeking patterns to automatically learn a taxonomy from an (automatically extracted) glossary of terms in the field of enterprise interoperability. The results have been evaluated in the large by the members of the INTEROP EC network of excellence (http://www.interop-noe.org).

[12] A similar concern is expressed also in the concluding remarks of the already mentioned survey by Reeve and Han: "all SAPs [semantic annotation platforms] require some type of lexicon and resource. Rule-based systems require rules, pattern discovery systems require an intial set of seeds, machine learning system require a training corpus.".

(because of the need of annotated data, careful parameter setting, etc.), and furthermore they are unable to combine in a non-trivial way different types of features (e.g. lexical, syntactic, semantic). A practical example is the full list of automatically learned hypernymy-seeker patterns provided in (Morin and Jacquemin, 2004). The complexity of these patterns is certainly lower than the regular expression structures used in this work, and many of them are rather intuitive, they could have easily written by hand.

However, we believe that our method can be automated to some limited degree (for example, semantic constraints can be learned automatically), a research line we are currently exploring.

References

S. A. Caraballo "Automatic construction of a hypernym-labeled noun hierarchy from text" In 37th Annual Meeting of the Association for Computational Linguistics: Proceedings of the Conference, pages 120-126,1999

M. E. Califf and R.J. Mooney, "Bottom-up relational learning of pattern matching rules for information extraction" Machine Learning research, 4 (2)177-210, 2004

E. Charniak, "Statistical Techniques for Natural Language Parsing", AI Magazine 18(4), 33-44, 1997

P. Cimiano, G. Ladwig and S. Staab, "Gimme the context: context-driven automatic semantic annotation with C-PANKOW" In: Proceedings of the 14th International WWW Conference, Chiba, Japan, May, 2005. ACM Press.

M. Doerr, "The CIDOC Conceptual Reference Module: An Ontological Approach to Semantic Interoperability of Metadata". AI Magazine, Volume 24, Number 3, Fall 2003.

M. S. Fox, M. Barbuceanu, M. Gruninger, and J. Lin, "An Organisation Ontology for Enterprise Modeling", In Simulating Organizations: Computational Models of Institutions and Groups, M. Prietula, K. Carley & L. Gasser (Eds), Menlo Park CA: AAAI/MIT Press, pp. 131-152. 1997

J.E. F. Friedl "Mastering Regular Expressions" O'Reilly eds., ISBN: 1-56592-257-3, First edition January 1997.

V. Kashyap, C. Ramakrishnan, T. Rindflesch. "Toward (Semi)-Automatic Generation of Biomedical Ontologies", Proceedings of American Medical Informatics Association, 2003

A. Maedche V. Pekar and S. Staab , "Ontology learning part One: On Discovering Taxonomic Relations from the Web" in In Web Intelligence. Springer, Chapter 1, 2002.

G. A. Miller, ``WordNet: a lexical database for English." In: Communications of the ACM 38 (11), November 1995, pp. 39 - 41.

E. Morin and C. Jacquemin "Automatic acquisition and expansion of hypernym links" Computer and the Humanities, 38: 363-396, 2004

R. Navigli and P. Velardi, "Structural Semantic Interconnections: a knowledge-based approach to word sense disambiguation", Special Issue-Syntactic and Structural Pattern Recognition, IEEE TPAMI, Volume: 27, Issue: 7, 2005.

R. Navigli, P. Velardi. Automatic Acquisition of a Thesaurus of Interoperability Terms, Proc. of 16th IFAC World Congress, Praha, Czech Republic, July 4-8th, 2005b.

Reeve, L., & Han, H. (2005). Survey of Semantic Annotation Platforms. Proceedings of the 20th Annual ACM Symposium on Applied Computing, Web Technologies

R. Snow, D. Jurafsky, A. Y. Ng, "Learning syntactic patters for automatic hypernym discovery", NIPS 17, 2005.

M. Thelen, E. Riloff, "A Bootstrapping Method for Learning Semantic Lexicons using Extraction Pattern Contexts", Proceedings of the Conference on Empirical Methods in Natural Language Processing, 2002.

M. Uschold, M. King, S. Moralee and Y. Zorgios, "The Enterprise Ontology", The Knowledge Engineering Review , Vol. 13, Special Issue on Putting Ontologies to Use (eds. Uschold. M. and Tate. A.), 1998.

Valarakos, G. Paliouras, V. Karkaletsis, G. Vouros, "Enhancing Ontological Knowledge through Ontology Population and Enrichment" in Proceedings of the 14th EKAW conf., LNAI, Vol. 3257, pp. 144-156, Springer Verlag, 2004.

Paola Velardi, Alessandro Cucchiarelli and Michaël Pétit "Supporting Scientific Collaboration in a network of Ecellence through a semantically indexed knowledge map" I-ESA 2006, Bordeaux, France, March 2006

D. Widdows "Unsupervised methods for developing taxonomies by combining syntactic and statistical information" HLT-NAACL 2003, Edmonton, May-June 2003

Discovering Semantic Sibling Groups from Web Documents with XTREEM-SG

Marko Brunzel and Myra Spiliopoulou

Otto-von-Guericke-University Magdeburg
{forename.name}@iti.cs.uni-magdeburg.de

Abstract. The acquisition of explicit semantics is still a research challenge. Approaches for the extraction of semantics focus mostly on learning hierarchical hypernym-hyponym relations. The extraction of co-hyponym and co-meronym sibling semantics is performed to a much lesser extent, though they are not less important in ontology engineering.

In this paper we will describe and evaluate the XTREEM-SG (Xhtml TREE Mining - for Sibling Groups) approach on finding sibling semantics from semi-structured Web documents. XTREEM takes advantage of the added value of mark-up, available in web content, for grouping text siblings. We will show that this grouping is semantically meaningful. The XTREEM-SG approach has the advantage that it is domain and language independent; it does not rely on background knowledge, NLP software or training.

In this paper we apply the XTREEM-SG approach and evaluate against the reference semantics from two golden standard ontologies. We investigate how variations on input, parameters and reference influence the obtained results on structuring a closed vocabulary on sibling relations. Earlier methods that evaluate sibling relations against a golden standard report a 14.18% F-measure value. Our method improves this number into 21.47%.

1 Introduction

The discovery of semantic relations among terms is a crucial task in many applications on the understanding of text and of semantics: ontologies, the backbone of the Semantic Web, rely on making semantic relations explicit. There are many methods for the discovery of vertical, hypernym-hyponym relations. There is less work on the discovery of concepts that stand in a horizontal relation to each other and are the children of a common, not a priori known (and possibly not interesting) parent concept. This horizontal relation can be referred to as co-hyponymy and co-meronymy.

In the field of ontology engineering, there are different approaches for the discovery of semantic relations. There are many approaches which use unstructured plain text (also semi-structured content is converted to plain text) as input [FN99, MS00, and BCM05]. On the other hand, there are approaches using existing structures such as dictionaries, glossaries or database schemas as input [K99, SSV02]. But these

S. Staab and V. Svatek (Eds.): EKAW 2006, LNAI 4248, pp. 141 – 157, 2006.

approaches are practically limited to the rare case that such resources are available. Out method uses semi-structured content as input.

In [BS06], we have presented the first version of XTREEM. In this publication we extend the workshop publication with an improved description of the process, including formalization and evaluation. We will show that the XTREEM-SG method helps to discover groups of terms that indeed stand in sibling relation with higher accuracy than earlier methods. The main contribution of XTREEM-SG is the identification of siblings in a data driven way without any a priory restrictions: No linguistic resources are needed, beyond the input vocabulary.

The paper is organized as follows: In the next section, we discuss related work. In section 3, we present XTREEM-SG. Section 4 and 5 are devoted to evaluation using two golden standard ontologies from the domain of tourism.

2 Related Work

The broad domain of research is *ontology learning*: A comprehensive overview on this subject has appeared recently in [BCM05]. Those approaches are focusing on ontology learning from text. There are also approaches performing *Ontology Learning from structure* [K99, SSV02]: However, these methods use existing database schemas or other conceptualizations as input and are therefore limited to cases where such schemas are available, which is usually not the case. Closer related are studies also discovering semantics on the Web.

Hearst patterns [H92] are used to find relations among terms in text collections. Also co-hyponym relations can be found with this approach. But the disadvantage is that such patterns are rare, the coverage is low, even on big document collections. Cimiano et al also discover (co-)hyponymy relations by finding examples of Hearst patterns via the Google API and then analyzing retrieved content [CS04]. In [P05] instances of WordNet concepts are found within big Web document collections with a rule base mechanism ignoring the mark-up. The document structure is also taken into account for the establishment of a knowledge base of extracted entities from the WWW in [E04]. There are also approaches from the field of ontology learning and ontology enhancement using the WWW [FS02, AHM00].

Kruschwitz [K01a, K01b] uses *mark-up* sections of Web documents to learn a *domain model*. Similarly to our approach, Kruschwitz exploits the mark-up for the representation of similar concepts inside Web documents. However, as opposed to our approach, the tree structure of (X)HTML documents is not incorporated. [ST04] uses also different tags of HTML documents for acquiring hyponymy relations. They only use list *itemizations*. There is no mentioning of using the tree structure of (X)HTML documents in general, where contributions also from other tags than item elements can be expected.

The idea of using structural similarities [ZLC03, B04], including path structures, of XHTML/XML documents is used for several goals, such as clustering documents on structural similarities [DCWS04, TG06, and CMK06]. In contrast we use the path information to infer siblings. The constitution of the paths is not used itself; no comparison with paths from other documents is performed with XTREEM-SP.

3 Finding Sibling Groups with XTREEM-SG

We present the XTREEM-SG method for the extraction of semantic relations through the exploitation of Web document Structure (Xhtml TREE Mining - for Sibling Groups). XTREEM-SG is based on mark-up conventions that are present in almost all Web documents in the (X)HTML format. Authors use different nested tags to structure pieces of information in Web documents, as shown in Fig. 1. We find terms that adhere to the same syntactic structure within an XHTML document and apply data mining to reduce the potential large amounts of candidate sets to find semantically related sibling terms. These desired semantically related “pieces of text” are not necessarily physically "co-located" i.e. appearing in the same narrow context window as can be seen in the headings example of Table 1. Both text-spans {WordNet, Germanet} share a common syntactic structure, the series of HTML tags they are placed in. We aim to use such syntactic structures to infer semantic relatedness.

Table 1. Semantically related terms, located in different paragraphs or separated by other terms

Headings, located in different paragraphs	Highlighted keywords, separated by normal text
... <h2>WordNet</h2> <p>Was developed ...</p> <h2>Germanet</h2> <p>Analogous ...</p> ...	... <p> ... there are different important standards for building the <strong>Semantic Web</strong>. ... is <strong>RDF</strong>. ... <strong>RDFS </strong> adds ... whereas <strong>OWL </strong> is ... </p> ...

The XTREEM-SG procedure, which aims to organize a given vocabulary of terms into co-hyponym groups, entails pre-processing (the innovative core of the XTREEM-SG approach), processing (clustering) and post-processing (cluster labelling), which are shown in the following data–flow diagram and described in the following sections.

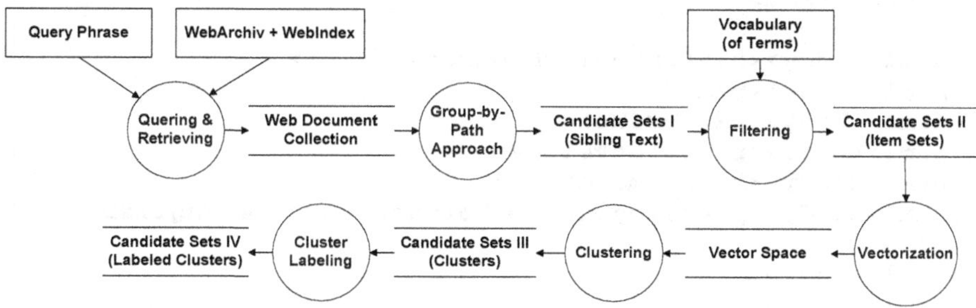

Fig. 1. Data-Flow Diagram of the XTREEM-SG procedure

3.1 The Group-by-Path Operation on Web Documents

First we will describe the operation which represents the core of the overall XTREEM-SG method. We consider Web documents to find sibling relations among terms. Specifically we use the following definitions.

Definition 1: A *Web document* (web page) D is a semi-structured document following the W3C XHTML standard. *D is a tree structure.*

XHTML is a XML dialect, wherein the former HTML standard has been adopted to meet the XML requirements. Traditional legacy HTML documents are converted to XHTML documents, as it is performed by all popular web browsers too. Hence, an XHTML document can be seen as a tree, text is represented by leaf nodes and the intermediate nodes are mark-up elements. We use the term text-span to denote the textual contents, the character data sequences of XML elements. The XML elements formed by the tags we will denote as mark-up elements or tags.

Definition 2: Let M be the set of tags supported in the XHTML format and let d be a Web document in XHTML format. A "tag path" p in d is a sequence of tags leading from the root tag element of d to a text-span appearing in d, i.e. p has the form $p=\langle m_1,m_2,\ldots,m_v\rangle$, where $m_i \in M$ $i=1,\ldots,v$. We use the notation (p,e) to indicate that e is the text-span to which p leads.

By this definition, p is a branch of an XHTML tree; for each m_i, m_{i+1} $(i=1,\ldots,v-1)$ it holds that m_i is the tag surrounding m_{i+1}. A Tag Path is therefore a special kind of Xpath expression. Moreover, a document *D is a collection of pairs* of the form (p,e), where p is a Tag Path and e is the text-span to which p leads.

For example, consider the example document of Fig.2: In line 8, we see the Tag Path "<html><body><h2>" leading to the text-span "Wordnet".

Let $B=\{e_1,\ldots,e_r\}$ be a set of text-spans. For one document several B can be found by the following Group-By-Path algorithm (Algorithm 1). This is different to traditional "text treatment", where for one text unit (e.g. document, paragraph or

```
<html>
<html><head>
<html><head>...
<html></head>
<html><body>
<html><body><h1>Lexical Resources ...</h1>
<html><body><p>...</p>
<html><body><h2>WordNet</h2>
<html><body><p>Was developed ...</p>
<html><body><h2>Germanet</h2>
<html><body><p>Analogous to WordNet for the English
...</p>
<html><body>...
<html></body>
</html>
```

Fig. 2. A XHTML Document viewed as a collection of Tag Path - Text-Span Pairs

sentence) a corresponding "Bag of Words" is obtained. Here a b is obtained for each distinct path p of a document d.

Let $A=\{B_1,\ldots,B_t\}$ be the collection which contains the sets of text-spans. The following Algorithm reflects the way A is obtained from D. This grouping operation is the core of the XTREEM-SG procedure.

Algorithm 1: The Group-By-Path algorithm on a XHTML document
Input: Web document D
Output: Collection A of sets of text spans B_i, i=1,...,t

```
extract from D the set Y=Y(D) of (p,e) - pairs, where p is a tag path
according to Def. 2 and e is its target text-span
A= ø
let Z be the set of tag paths in Y
for all p in Z
        set B={e | (p,e) in Y}
        insert B to A
end for
return A
```

We group text-spans that have the same tag path as its predecessor. E.g. in our example (Fig. 2), WordNet and Germanet both have `<html><body><h2>` as document path, and, thus become members of the same set of terms {WordNet, Germanet}. Usually, authors use different tags and therefore things separate according to different tags, resulting in different documents paths, therefore several text-span sets stemming from one document are possible. Here precision is preferred over recall, since only "valuable" sets of terms will frequently re-occur in a bigger Web document collection. D is now represented as a *collection of text-span sets.*

Summary: The Group-By-Path approach performs a transition of a Web document from a tree, to a collection of tag-path/text-span pairs to a collection of text-span sets.

3.2 The XTREEM-SG Procedure

We now introduce our algorithm XTREEM-SG that takes as input a collection of documents, observing each document as collection of text-span sets. A following clustering is used to perform a "compression"; groups of related terms are the result, such that the terms in each group stand in sibling relationship to each other.

Step 1 – Querying & Retrieving: The XTREEM procedure operates on a *Web Document Collection.* Such a Web document collection is obtained by querying a *Archive+Index Facility* on a *Query Q* with a Web document collection $W=\{D_1,\ldots,D_s\}$ as result, for which Q is satisfied. Q constitutes the domain of interest whereupon semantics should be discovered. It should therefore encircle the documents which are supposed to entail domain relevant content, e.g. "touris*".

The Web document collection should be big enough to contain manifold occurrences of the desired concepts. The Web document collection is not supposed to be a small manually handcrafted document collection; bigger amounts of web content which have an appropriate coverage of the domain are more desirable. Here, recall is more important than precision. To obtain such a comprehensive Web document collection, alternatively a focused web crawl can be performed; when a vocabulary is given, this vocabulary can also be used to obtain Web document references via the web services of internet search engines.

Step 2 - Group-By-Path: For each $D_i \in W$ with i=1,...,s the Group-By-Path algorithm (Algorithm 1, described in section 3.1.) is applied. As result we obtain the collection of text-span sets $H'=\{B_1,\ldots,B_u\}$.

Step 3 - Filtering: The aim of the procedure described in this publication is to group a given Vocabulary into semantically motivated sibling groups. Let $V=\{v_1,\ldots,v_p\}$ be the vocabulary of terms given as input. For the following steps we only consider all text-spans $e \in B$ which are contained in V. $H''=\{B_1,\ldots,B_u\}$ so that for all $e \in B$ it is also true $e \in V$.

In the following we will eliminate all sets b with cardinality of less than two, since only sets containing at least two elements are able to reflect a sibling relation among their elements. $H'''=\{B_1,\ldots,B_n\}$, $H'''=\subseteq H''$ where $B_i \in H'''$ if the cardinality of $B_i \in H''>1$ for i=1,...,u.

Step 4 - Vectorization: Let $F=(f_1,\ldots f_p)$ be the Feature Space of Vectorization X. F corresponds to the vocabulary V. X is obtained by creating vectors for each term set $B \in H'''$. TF-IDF [SB88] weighting is applied. X is a 2-dimensinal matrix given by values x_{ij} per term set $1 \leq i \leq n$ and feature $1 \leq j \leq p$. Thus each set of sibling terms is represented by a vector $x_i=(x_{i1},\ldots,x_{ip})$ over the feature space.

Step 5 - K-Means Clustering: The vectorization obtained in the prior step has a bias towards sibling related features. Clustering is a method to reduce the potentially large number of instances to a presentable limited number of patterns. Association Rules Mining would be an alternative method. For clustering a K-Means algorithm with cosine distance function was applied. The amount of clusters to be generated can be set on the algorithm. A cluster $C \subseteq X$ is a set of vectors. The clustering consist of k clusters $C=\{c_1,\ldots,c_k\}$. A cluster can be empty (cardinality=0).

Step 6 - Cluster Labelling: The clustering algorithm creates clusters of instances, which are not useful on our objectives themselves. The desired result (related terms) has to be obtained by the following post processing step.

A cluster label is a set L of frequent features f of a cluster c. A frequent feature is a feature which has an in-cluster-support over a threshold τ.

Definition 3: (in cluster support): Let $C \subseteq X$ be a cluster, where X is the vector space over the instances H''' for the feature space F. Let $f \in F$ denote a feature. The in-cluster-support of a feature f in C is the count of vectors $x \in X$ that contain feature f (i.e. $x_k \neq 0$) divided by the cardinality of C.

Let $L_k=\{f_1,\ldots f_v\}$ denote the set of features which have a in-cluster-support $> \tau$ within C_k. According to our hypothesis, the elements of L are siblings to each other.

Let $M=\{l_1,\ldots,l_w\}$ be the overall set of generated sibling groups. The cardinality of M may be less than K, since some clusters can be empty and some clusters may not have at least two features with an in-cluster-support $> \tau$.

Summary: XTREEM-SG performs a transition from potentially big numbers of syntactic siblings, obtained from Web documents, to a reduced number of semantic motivated sibling sets, to be presented to an ontology engineer.

4 Evaluation Methodology

There is an ongoing discussion on how evaluation of ontology learning can be performed. Despite that golden standard evaluation can be criticized; we will compare the automatic obtained results against reference semantics. The measured quality is not easily comparable (over different references), but it can help to show tendencies.

Our evaluation objective is: "How good does the method perform on structuring a given vocabulary into co-hyponym groups". We evaluate against golden standards, i.e. ontologies that deliver both the vocabulary (the terms) and the co-hyponymy relations among them. Our goal is to find those relations. The evaluation of sibling relations is performed in [CS05] with the *average sibling overlap* measure. We will compare our results on this measure.

First we investigated how much sibling characteristics are present in the instances obtained by the traditional Bag-of-Words vector space model. Further we used mark-up of the Web documents, without the path grouping. This approach [K01a] is also based on text-spans created by Tag boundaries.

There are different influences on the results which can be produced with XTREEM-Group-By-Path. First, we vary the documents used as input. We also vary the number of clusters, the cluster labelling thresholds and the required support of the features. The evaluation is performed against two reference ontologies.

It is stressed here that the objective of the evaluation is not the reconstruction of the complete hierarchy, i.e. the naming of the hypernym for each co-hyponymy set. In fact, XTREEM-SG is meant to discover co-hyponym sets, for which the hypernym may or may not be a priori known.

4.1 Description of Experimental Influences

Evaluation Reference: The Evaluation is performed on two golden standard ontologies (GSO), from the tourism domain. The concepts of these ontologies are also terms, thus in the following the expressions "concepts" and "terms" are used interchangeably. The "*Tourism GSO*"[1] contains 293 concepts grouped into 45 sibling sets; the "*Getess annotation GSO*"[2] contains 693 concepts grouped into 90 sibling sets.

There are three Inputs to the XTREEM-SG procedure described in the following:

Input(1): Archive+Index Facility: We have performed a topic focused web crawl on the "tourism" related documents. The overall size of the document collection is about 9.5 million Web documents. The Web documents have been converted to XHTML. With an n-gram based language recognizer non-English documents have been

[1] http://www.aifb.uni-karlsruhe.de/WBS/pci/TourismGoldStandard.isa

[2] http://www.aifb.uni-karlsruhe.de/WBS/pci/getess_tourism_annotation.daml

filtered out. The documents are indexed, so that for a given query a Web document collection can be retrieved.
Input(2): Queries: For our experiments we consider three document collections which result from querying the Archive+Index Facility. The constitution is given by all those documents adhering to Query1 - "touris*", Query2 - "accommodation" and by the whole topic focused Web document collection reflected by Query3 – "*".
Input(3): Vocabulary: The GSO's described before, are lexical ontologies. Each concept is represented by a term. These terms constitute the vocabulary and the feature space.

The overall XTREEM procedure is constituted of pre-processing, processing and post- processing:

Procedure(1): Pre-Processing method: For the evaluation of the Group-By-Path sub procedure we will contrast our Group-By-Path (GBP) method with the traditional Bag-Of-Words (BOW) vector space model and against the solely usage of mark-up (MU) [K01a]. The BOW is the widespread established method on processing of textual data, while MU is a rather new approach which also incorporates the mark-up of Web documents. The variation of these influences is object of our Experiment 1 and Experiment 2.
Procedure(2): Processing – Cluster Number: Each data set (vectorization) is processed by a K-Means clustering with different numbers of clusters to be generated, ranging from rather small to rather big numbers of clusters. For K we used values of 50, 100, 150, 200, 250, 500, 750 and 1000. These numbers encircle the range of numbers of clusters which are appropriate to be shown to a human ontology engineer. This variation is undertaken on all Experiments with exception of Experiment 1.
Procedure(3): Post-Processing – Cluster Labeling Support Threshold: The generated clusters are afterwards post-processed by applying the support threshold cluster labelling strategy. The support threshold is varied from 0.1 to 0.9 in steps of 0.1.

In our experiments we found that some of the terms of the vocabulary are never or very rarely found on rather big Web document collections. E.g. one reference contains the errors "Kindergarden" instead of the correct English "Kindergarten". To eliminate the influence of errors in the reference, we also vary the **Required minimum feature support**. The support is given by the frequency of the features (terms) in the overall text of the Web document collection. We used minimum support thresholds from 0 (all features are used, nothing is pruned) to 100000 (0, 1, 10, 100, 1000, 10000, 100000). When the support is varied, only those features of the vectorization and of the reference fulfilling these criteria are incorporated into the evaluation.

4.2 Evaluation Criteria

Each of the golden standard ontologies delivers a number of reference sets of terms in co-hyponymy relation. Each run of XTREEM-SG delivers a number of term clusters that are suggested as potential co-hyponyms. Intuitively, one would compare each of the suggested clusters against each of the reference sets, select the best match and then count the number of matches; clusters without match and reference sets for which no match was found would be observed as false positives or false negatives. However, the identification of a "best match" is not straightforward, nor is the selection of a "single" best match the most appropriate evaluation strategy.

To highlight this, consider an extreme but not unrealistic example: All towns of the world are co-hyponyms. Within this enormous reference set, there are many subsets of co-hyponyms in different contexts: all towns of the same country, all towns across the same river, all towns close to the same airport, all towns where the same language is spoken etc. Discovering that two towns are co-hyponyms in some of these contexts is more likely than assessing co-hyponymy for 3, 4 ..., n towns. Finding all co-hyponyms of some reference set is more challenging and finding the complete set of co-hyponym towns (all tourist towns of the world) from text analysis is quite improbable. At the same time, finding out that London and Tokyo are co-hyponyms according to several reference sets (capital cities, cities with airport, cities in island countries, very large cities) is information of interest for each of those reference sets. Therefore, we need for our evaluation a measure on the contribution of each cluster of terms to the reference sets of co-hyponyms. To this purpose, we use the "average sibling overlap" measure proposed by Cimiano and Staab in [CS05].

The average sibling overlap $SO_{average}$ is used in [CS05] to compare sets of siblings generated by an automated approach to reference sets of siblings, as delivered by an ontology. This measure is then used to compute F-measure values.

Definition of Average Sibling Overlap (according to [CS05]): Let A and B be two sets of co-hyponymy relations where a co-hyponymy relation is a set of sibling terms. Typically one of e.g. A comes from a reference while the other e.g. B is produced by a semi-automated approach. The average Sibling overlap $SO_{average}$(A,B) between a set G_A (e.g. co-hyponym groups) of sets H_A (e.g. concepts/terms) from source A to another set G_B of sets H_B from source B, is calculated as follows: For each H_A the relative overlap with each H_B is calculated. This relative overlap is the number of terms present in both sets, divided by the number of unique terms from both sets together. For each H_A, the H_B with the maximal relative overlap value is identified. Over all those maximal values the mean is calculated, representing the average Sibling overlap $SO_{average}$(A,B). $SO_{average}$(B,A) is calculated accordingly. The F-Measure on average sibling overlap (FMASO) combines both values:

$$\text{FMASO} = \frac{2 \cdot SO_{\text{average}}(A,B) \cdot SO_{\text{average}}(B,A)}{SO_{\text{average}}(A,B) + SO_{\text{average}}(B,A)}$$

5 Experiments

In the following we will show the results obtained from the experiments. Table 2 shows the number of documents which adhere to a certain Query. This corresponds to the size of the Web document collection which is processed by the subsequent following processing steps.

Table 2. Number of Web documents returned by the Web Archiv+Index Facility for the Queries used in the evaluation experiments

Query Name	Query Phrase	Number of Documents
Query1	"touris*"	1,468,279
Query2	"accommodation"	1,612,108
Query3	"*"	9,437,703

5.1 Experiment 1: The Sibling Semantics of the Group-by-Path Method

In our first experiment we want to investigate how much sibling semantics are captured by the Group-By-Path (GBP) method in contrast to the traditional Bag-Of-Words (BOW) vector space model and against the solely usage of mark-up (MU) [K01a]. To do so, the GBP step of the XTEEM-SG procedure was changed to BOW and MU.

We evaluated the collections of sibling sets for the following constellations of Query (Query1, Query2, and Query3); Pre-Processing Method (BOW, GBP and MU) against the reference sibling sets (GSO1 and GSO2) of two golden standard ontologies. Since the two ontologies have different numbers of terms, each constellation of Web document collection results in a different number of vectors after the Vectorization.

Table 6. Results of FMASO for different constellations of queries, pre-processing methods and references; column 2 (cardinality=0) and column 3 (cardinality=1) show the number of candidate sets which are filtered out because they are not true sets

Constellation (Query,Method,Reference)	Number of Sibling Sets (separated according to the cardinality of the set)			FMASO
	Card.=0[3]	Card.=1[4]	Card.>1	
Query1-BOW-GSO1	18,012	29,104	**1,421,163**	**0.206**
Query1-GBP-GSO1	12,589,016	817,289	**222,037**	**0.247**
Query1-MU-GSO1	794,325	343,891	**323,428**	**0.235**
Query2-GBP–GSO1	12,712,295	1,034,741	**293,225**	**0.252**
Query3-GBP-GSO1	63,049,135	3,485,782	**924,045**	**0.256**
Query1-BOW-GSO2	19,399	18,494	**1,430,386**	**0.160**
Query1-GBP-GSO2	12,478,364	831,969	**318,009**	**0.208**
Query1-MU-GSO2	753,657	332,973	**375,014**	**0.199**
Query2-GBP–GSO2	12,677,515	988,944	**373,802**	**0.196**
Query3-GBP-GSO2	62,572,763	3,559,356	**1,326,843**	**0.229**

From these results can be seen that for GSO1 the FMASO is higher for all constellations where the GBP method was involved (0.247, 0.252, and 0.256) compared to the alternative methods (0.235, 0.206). Though it was never claimed that the traditional BOW method is strong on capturing sibling semantics it resulted in the weakest results on capturing sibling semantics. For GSO2 the result of Query1 and MU is slightly better than the result of Query2 and GBP, though for the same Query, GBP performs again best. BOW performs gain worst.

---

[3] No match with given vocabulary.
[4] Single match with given vocabulary, no true sets, will not be processed.

Conclusion: The candidate sets (text-span siblings) generated by the Group-By-Path pre-processing reveal a stronger sibling characteristic than the traditional BOW vector space model. Though it was never claimed that BOW has significant sibling characteristics, it can be concluded that the GBP method does not capture sibling semantics by chance; the path information of Web document structure can be used to infer semantics.

5.2 Experiment 2: Sibling Semantics Obtained from Labelled Clusters

Additionally to the intermediate sibling sets evaluated in Experiment 1 also a K-Means clustering was performed for Query1 and the pre-processing methods (BOW, MU, and GBP). The cluster labelling threshold was set to τ=0.2.

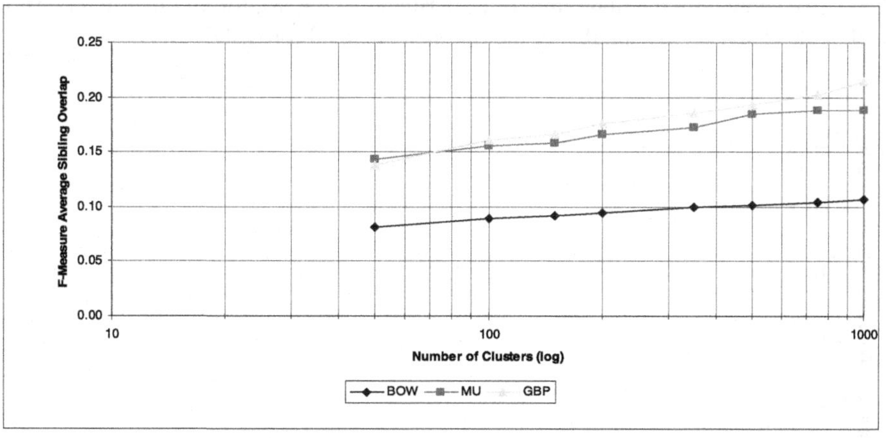

Fig. 3. FMASO on different K for different Pre-Processing methods (Query1, τ=0.2, GSO1)

Fig. 3 shows that the Group-By-Path approach performs also better when the sibling sets are clustered. There is a general trend to better results when higher number of clusters are generated, which is objetive of experiment 4. The analogous diagram for GSO2 (which is not shown) reveals the same finding but with lower values for all three approaches.

The difference between MU and GBP seems to be marginally. A possible explanation for this circumstance is, that when instances are created with MU, those instances have a big overlap with the instances created by GBP since they stem from the same Web mark-up created text-spans, caused by the rather small vocabularies used, which only allow for a fraction of the terms occurring in the Web document collections. Here, also the insensitivity of the FMASO may be responsible for the low measured difference: Whereas siblings not stated by the reference are regarded as false to the same extent as truly not sibling related nominations. This could only be solved by a human expert evaluation. On experiments judged by a human expert one can say that the strong sibling character caused by GBP is recognizable compared to MU.

Conclusion: These results are compatible with the Conclusions of Experiment 1 and verify our hypothesis that GBP performs well on capturing sibling semantics.

5.3 Experiment 3: Varying the Cluster Labelling Threshold

For Query1 in combination with GBP we varied the cluster labeling support threshold from τ=0.1 to τ=0.9 in steps of 0.1 resulting in the following chart of Figure 4. The best results have been obtained on the biggest used number of clusters (K=1000) in combination with a cluster labeling strategy using a support threshold of τ=0.2, resulting in an FMASO of 21.47% (Fig. 6). The results on GSO2 are (again) worse than the results for GSO1. The best FMASO of 15.88% for GSO2 is obtained on K=1000 and τ=0.3. The second reference ontology is more than twice as big as the first one, so structuring the vocabulary into sibling sets may be more difficult. We suspect that this has to do large size of the ontology. There are many terms, but not all sibling relations which can be found in the world, are explicit in the reference. For GSO2 we show only the diagramm of Experiment 5 (Fig. 8), for all other diagrams of GSO2 the charts are compatible to the findings obtained for GSO2.

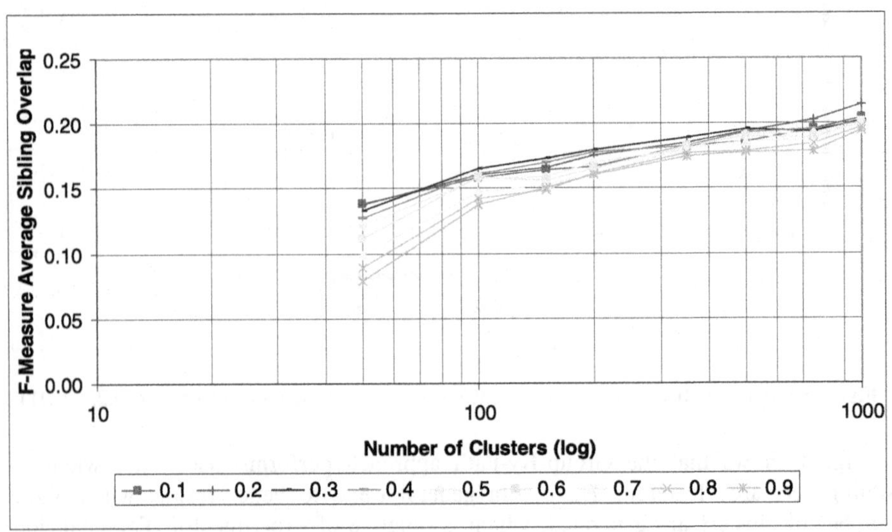

Fig. 4. FMASO on different K for different τ (Query1, GSO1)

5.4 Experiment 4: Observing the Number of Clusters

As already shown in Experiment 2 and Experiment 3, with an increasing number of clusters generated, the F-Measure on average sibling overlap increases too, but with saturation (the number of clusters is logarithmic scaled).

The increasing number of clusters has the drawback that the amount of information, which is compared against the reference, increases too. For automatic evaluation this is not a problem, but if a human would inspect the generated data, this is relevant. We additionally count the number of features appearing in the cluster labels for all clusters of a clustering. This sum of terms/features in the cluster labels over all clusters of a clustering we will refer to as "Sum of Features in Cluster Labels" (SOFICL). The number of distinct features/terms used for cluster labeling we will refer to as "Number of distinct Features in Cluster Labels" (NODFICL).

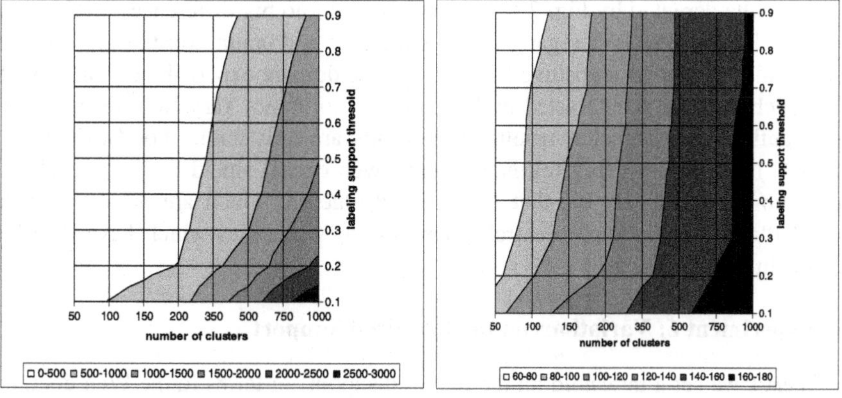

Fig. 5 (SOFICL) and **Fig. 6.** (NODFICL) for different K and τ (Query1, GSO1)

As Fig. 5 and Fig. 6 show, the values of SOFICL and NODFICL are correlated, with an increasing K (and decreasing τ) more terms are used for labeling in the sum (SOFICL) but also more distinct terms (NOFICL) are incorporated into the labeling. An increasing NOFICL means that a bigger share of the vocabulary is indeed incoprorated in the results. The lower right corner of Fig. 6 shows that for high numbers of clusters 160-180 out of 293 of the features are used for cluster labeling. The circumstance that on lower numbers of cluster many terms/features are not used for labeling may be caused by the different support the features have within the vectorization. The low frequent features may have never the chance to be frequent enough for cluster labelling. But this is rather a problem for automatic evaluation. In semi-automatic settings, one can present a ranked list of features for a cluster to the user, who is free to choose also lower frequent features.

5.5 Experiment 5: Variations on the Web Document Collection

Now we will investigate the influence of the processed Web document collection. Since the Web document collection is given by a Query, we will apply the XTREEM-SG procedure for Query1 ("touris*"), Query2 ("accommodation") and Query3 ("*"; whole topic focused web crawl).

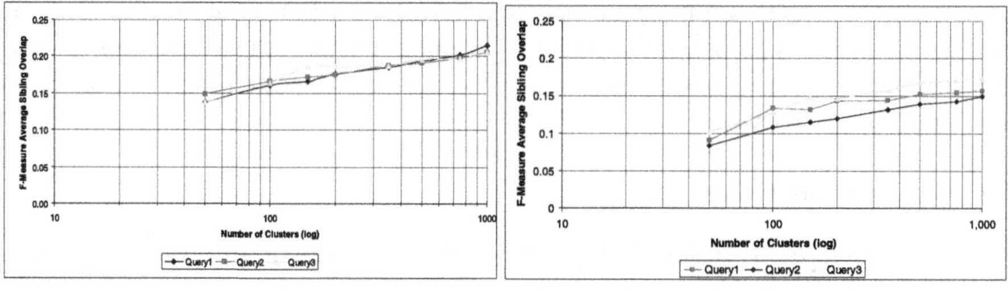

Fig. 7 and **Fig. 8.** FMASO on different K for different Queries (τ=0.2) for GSO1 and GSO2

The results depicted by Fig. 7 show, that there are no big differences on the results measured by the FMASO regarding the choice of a domain constituting query for GSO1. This is in so far a positive finding, that the domain expert should only roughly state which topic he is interested in. While doing so, minor varyations do not lead to significantly worse or better results. The results are quit stable. For GSO2 Query1 ("touris*") and Query3 (big tourism focused web crawl) shield the best results. An explanation for this may be, that Query1 and Query3, which are more broad than Query2 ("accommodation"), encircle more sibling semantics which have also been encoded in the GSO2.

5.6 Experiment 6: Variations on the Required Support

For Query1 we set a threshold on the required support of terms in the Web document collection. This means, terms/features which are rather weakly support are more and more ignored; both for cluster labeling as well as in the reference sets.

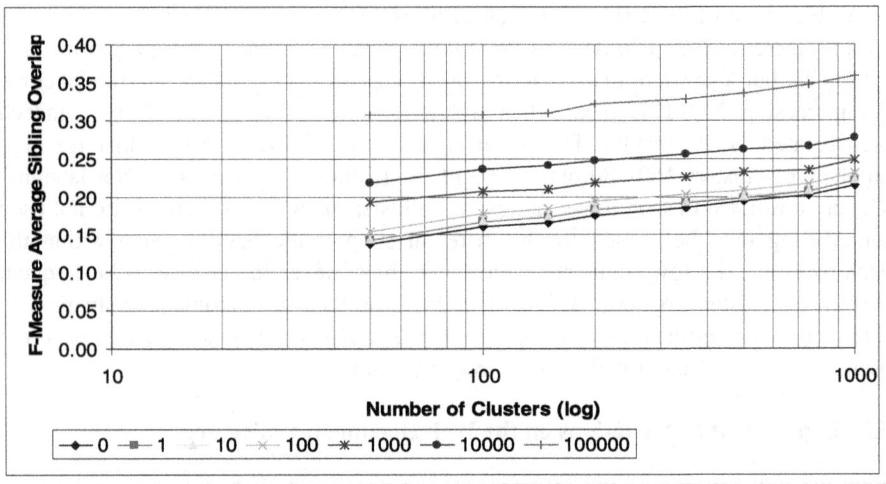

Fig. 9. FMASO for different frequency support levels (Query1, τ=0.2, GSO1)

Fig. 9 shows that while only observing frequent terms, better results on FMASO are shown. With a required minimum support also errors in the reference are smoothed. This is relevant in so far that the relatively low F-Measure values given by our and by other approaches on ontology learning are also caused by "not perfect golden standards", the parts of the reference which are supported by real world data are found reasonably well.

5.7 Conclusion of Evaluation

The application of a Group-By-Path pre-processing with a following K-Means-clustering processing enable to reduce the initial candidate sets significantly by retaining most of the quality measured by the F-Measure on average sibling overlap.

In [CS05] is described, that Cimiano and Staab have obtained average sibling overlap F-Measures from 12.40% to 14.18% on the tourism GSO. With these results, they realized a significant improvement in contrast to Caraballo's method [C99], which gave a sibling overlap F-Measures of 8.96%. We can get good results on this evaluation measure. Our best result gives an F-Measure of 21.47% using a K-Means clustering with 1000 clusters and labeling the clusters by using all features which have a support within the cluster of 20%. This is a significant improvement and confirms that the XTREEM approach delivers good results for mining co-hyponym semantics.

The amount of clusters influences the abstraction forced on the constitution of the resulting sibling groups. For real world settings the expert may decide to handle the tradeoff between reachable quality and the amount of generated information according to his objectives of how detailed the semantics should be. This golden standard evaluation does not capture this aspect, but this can be seen by manually inspecting the results. Cimiano and Staab reported that the results of their approach get better quality valuation by a human expert inspection; the same holds true for the results obtained with XTREEM-SG. The found sibling groups are surprisingly meaningful. On the other side this is not astonishing, the results are based on many thousands, often hand crafted, manifestations on the WWW.

6 Conclusions and Future Work

We have presented XTREEM-SG, a method for the discovery of semantic sibling relations among terms on the basis of structural conventions in Web documents. XTREEM-SG processes Web documents collected from the WWW and thus eliminates the need for a well-prepared document corpus. Furthermore, it does not rely on linguistic pre-processing or NLP resources. So, XTREEM-SG is much less demanding of human resources.

We investigated how variations on input, parameters and reference influence the obtained results on structuring a vocabulary on sibling relations. The reported results from the literature of an F-measure on average sibling overlap regarding a golden standard evaluation of 14.18% are improved by our approach to 21.47%.

Our method is only a first step on the exploitation of the structural conventions in Web documents for the discovery of semantic relations. In our future work we want to investigate the impact of individual mark-up element tags like <p>, <li>, and <dt> on the results. Discovering the corresponding hypernym for the co-hyponyms is a further desireable extension. We are also interested in minimizing the number of clusters which have to be inspected to find co-hyponym relations.

References

[AHM00] E. Agirre, O. Ansa, E. Hovy, and D. Martinez. Enriching very large ontologies using the WWW, *In Proc. of the Workshop on Ontology Construction ECAI-2000*

[B04] D. Buttler. A short survey of document structure similarity algorithms. *In Proc. of the International Conference on Internet Computing*, June 2004.

[BCM05] P. Buitelaar, P. Cimiano, Bernardo Magnini, Ontology Learning from Text: Methods, Evaluation and Applications, Frontiers in Artificial Intelligence and Applications Series Volume 123, IOS Press, Amsterdam, 2005

[BS06] M. Brunzel, M. Spiliopoulou. Discovering Multi Terms and Co-Hyponymy from XHTML Documents with XTREEM. *In Proc. of PAKDD Workshop on Knowledge Discovery from XML Documents (KDXD 2006)*, LNCS 3915, Singapore, April 2006

[C99] S. Caraballo, Automatic construction of a hypernym-labeled noun hierarchy from text. In *Proc. of the 37th Annual Meeting of The Association for Computational Linguistics ACL*

[CMK06] I. Choi, B. Moon, H-J- Kim. A Clustering Method based on Path Similarities of XML Data. *Data & Knowledge Engineering*, Feb. 2006

[CS04] P. Cimiano and S. Staab. Learning by googling. *SIGKDD Explorations,* 6(2):24-34, December 2004.

[CS05] P. Cimiano, S. Staab. Learning concept hierarchies from text with a guided hierarchical clustering algorithm. *Workshop on Learning and Extending Lexical Ontologies at ICML-2005*, Bonn 2005.

[DCWS04] T. Dalamagas, T. Cheng, K. J. Winkel, T. Sellis, Clustering XML documents using structural summaries, *In Proc. of the EDBT Workshop on Clustering Information over the Web (ClustWeb04)*, Heraklion, Greece, 2004

[E04] O. Etzioni, M. Cafarella, D. Downey, S. Kok, A.-M. Popescu, T. Shaked, S. Soderland, D. S. Weld, A. Yates. Web-Scale Information Extraction in KnowItAll. *In Proc of the 13th International WWW Conference*, New York, 2004.

[FN99] D. Faure, C. Nedellec. Knowledge acquisition of predicate argument structures from technical texts using machine learning: the system ASIUM. EKAW 99, LNCS 1621

[FS02] A. Faatz, R. Steinmetz, Ontology Enrichment with Texts from the WWW, *In Proc. of the First International Workshop on Semantic Web Mining, European Conference on Machine Learning 2002*, Helsinki 2002

[H92] M. Hearst, Automatic acquisition of hyponyms from large text corpora. *In Proceedings of the 14th International Conference on Computational Linguistics*, pp. 539–545, (1992).

[K01a] Kruschwitz, U. "A Rapidly Acquired Domain Model Derived from Mark-Up Structure". *In Proc. of the ESSLLI'01 Workshop on Semantic Knowledge Acquisition and Categorization*, Helsinki, 2001.

[K01b] U. Kruschwitz. Exploiting Structure for Intelligent Web Search. *In Proc of the 34th Hawaii International Conference on System Sciences (HICSS)*, Maui Hawaii 2001, IEEE

[K99] V. Kashyap. Design and creation of ontologies for environmental information retrieval. *In Proc. of the 12th Workshop on Knowledge Acquisition, Modeling and Management.* Alberta, Canada. 1999.

[MS00] A. Maedche and S. Staab. Discovering conceptual relations from text. *In Proc. of ECAI 2000*, pp. 321-325.

[P05] M. Pasca. Finding Instance Names and Alternative Glosses on the Web: WordNet Reloaded. *In Proc CICLing-2005*, Springer LNCS 3406, 2005.

[SB88] Gerard Salton and Chris Buckley. Term weighting approaches in automatic text retrieval. Information Processing & Management, 24(5):513-523, 1988.

[SSV02] L. Stojanovic, N. Stojanovic, R.Volz. Migrating data-intensive Web Sites into the Semantic Web. *In Proc. of the 17th ACM symposium on applied computing*. ACM press, 2002. 1100-1107.

[ST04] K. Shinzato and K. Torisawa. Acquiring hyponymy relations from Web Documents. In Proceedings of the *2004 Human Language Technology Conference (HLT-NAACL-04)*, pages 73--80, Boston, Massachusetts, 2004.

[TG06] A. Tagarelli, S. Greco. Toward Semantic XML Clustering. *6th SIAM International Conference on Data Mining (SDM '06)*. Bethesda, Maryland, USA, April 20-22, 2006

[ZLC03] Z. Zhang, R. Li, S. Cao, and Y. Zhu. Similarity metric for XML documents. In Proc. of the Workshop on Knowledge and Experience Management, October 2003.

Designing and Evaluating Patterns for Ontology Enrichment from Texts

Nathalie Aussenac-Gilles[1] and Marie-Paule Jacques[2]

[1] Institut de Recherche en Informatique de Toulouse (IRIT) - CNRS,
UPS, 118, route de Narbonne, 31062 Toulouse Cedex, France
aussenac@irit.fr
http://www.irit.fr/~Nathalie.Aussenac

[2] Équipe de Recherche en Syntaxe et Sémantique (ERSS) - CNRS,
Maison de la Recherche, UTM, 5, allées Antonio Machado, 31048 Toulouse Cedex, France
marie-paule.jacques@univ-tlse2.fr
http://www.univ-tlse2.fr:8880/erss/index.jsp?perso=mpjacques

Abstract. Pattern-based approaches for knowledge identification in texts assume that linguistic regularities always characterise the same kind of knowledge, such as semantic relations. We report the experimental evaluation of a large set of patterns using an ontology enrichment tool: CAMÉLÉON. Results underline the strong corpus influence on the patterns efficiency and on their meaning. This influence confirms two of the hypotheses that motivated to define CAMÉLÉON as a support used in a supervised process: (1) patterns and relations must be adapted to each project; (2) human interpretation is required to decide how to report in the ontology the pieces of knowledge identified with patterns.

1 Introduction

Relation extraction from texts can be an efficient means to rapidly structure a conceptual model and identify significant domain concepts. Possible approaches to identify relations from corpora include: using existing relations in lexical resources like WordNet [16] [5]; matching lexico-syntactic patterns [9] [10] [16]; learning dependencies between phrases through term distribution analysis [3]. Pattern-based approaches for knowledge identification in texts assume that linguistic regularities always characterise the same kind of knowledge, such as semantic relations. We defined CAMÉLÉON, a method and a supervised tool that supports a knowledge engineer to identify relations and concepts for ontology engineering [15]. CAMÉLÉON provides a set of generic patterns and relations to be adapted and applied on tagged corpora [2].

This paper reports how we built and evaluated a set of 70 generic patterns for the French language. After a presentation of the CAMÉLÉON process (§ 2), we describe how the tool supports pattern definition and evaluation (§ 3). Then we detail the corpora and method used for this experiment (§4), we report its results and discuss them (§5). We conclude by underlying the role of human interpretation to adapt patterns, to evaluate their instances, and later to enrich a conceptual model. This experiment also proves that, rather than generic, patterns should be adaptable and reusable.

S. Staab and V. Svatek (Eds.): EKAW 2006, LNAI 4248, pp. 158 – 165, 2006.

2 Semantic Relation Identification with CAMÉLÉON

CAMÉLÉON is a method and tool to extend an existing network of concepts with new terms, concepts and semantic relations by applying a pattern-based approach [15]. A conceptual model built up with CAMÉLÉON is a semantic network where concepts are associated with a set of terms (synonym terms). This model may be the starting point to design an ontology or it may be considered as a result by itself. Knowledge engineers and linguists are the intended users of the CAMÉLÉON[1] tool. This tool can be one of the components of a natural language processing and modelling chain from texts to ontologies, such as the one proposed in KAON [16], TERMINAE [1] or [7].

2.1 Pattern-Based Knowledge Identification

Patterns are lexical, semantic and/or syntactic characterizations of linguistic contexts in which one expects to find some specific piece of information. Hearst was the first one to experiment a pattern-based approach for the identification of lexical relation and semantic classes [9]. Hearst tested some general patterns mainly expressing definitions or hyperonymy. She noticed that linguistic regularities had to be tuned for each corpus and domain. Over the last ten years, patterns were widely used with success for information extraction or relation extraction like in [13]. To gain efficiency, research has investigated two mains tracks. Firstly, to reduce the cost of pattern definition and tuning, patterns may be learned from manually tagged corpora [5] [6][16]; they may refer to named entities and known semantic classes [8]. Secondly, to reduce the time required to select valid pattern instances and the noise of the overall process, various statistical text analyses have been experimented. Like [8], we consider that an alternative contribution would be to capitalize robust patterns and know-how about their use, together with information about their semantics, their precision and recall in various types of domains and documents.

2.2 Overview of the Approach

For a given project and corpus, CAMÉLÉON suggests a two-steps supervised process.

1) **Defining project-specific patterns:** The user is expected to define a specific set of domain relations and valid patterns for his project and corpus. They may be obtained first by adapting some generic patterns already available in CAMÉLÉON, second by manually defining new patterns for known domain relations, third by defining new relations and patterns after observing the contexts in which pairs of related terms occur (according to Riloff's suggestion [14]). Fixing patterns also includes evaluating the sentences obtained after pattern-matching. The pattern will be modified in order to reduce its noise and increase its precision.

2) **Extending the conceptual model:** The knowledge engineer checks one by one the sentences identified by matching patterns in the corpus. Validated sentences may suggest new concepts and relations. To save time, a default validation is possible. Then, suggestions of relations are presented in CAMÉLÉON ontology browser, when

[1] http://developer.berlios.de/projects/cameleonirit/

editing one of the concepts. The knowledge engineer must decide whether to define a new relation or not, and whether the concepts to be connected and the semantics of the relation are those suggested or other ones.

2.3 Building the Base of Generic Patterns

One of the strengths of CAMÉLÉON is to provide a set of robust and valid generic patterns as a bootstrap. This paper reports how this set was defined and evaluated. By doing so, we used and tested the available functions in the CAMÉLÉON software. It contributes to CAMÉLÉON global evaluation, which would be far more complex. A full evaluation should include the design of a real ontology for a well-determined application. Nevertheless, our experiment contributed to validate two foundational hypotheses (the need for pattern adaptation and human interpretation).

3 How the Tool Supports Relation Extraction

The CAMÉLÉON tool contains a project management interface and two main modules: one supports pattern definition, matching and evaluation; the other one helps to interpret the sentences that contain the patterns and to enrich the conceptual model. The first module includes a concordancer, KESKYA, which matches patterns on texts tagged with a Part Of Speech (POS) tagger. We used Tree-Tagger, but any tagger would do. The second module includes an ontology editor.

A CAMÉLÉON project entails a set of tagged texts - the corpus -, a set of specific patterns and relation types, and a conceptual model. To promote reusability and to avoid starting from scratch, the tool database stores several corpora and a set of generic patterns and relations. A project corpus may include reused corpora and/or tagged new texts. Project patterns are adapted from generic patterns or user-defined.

3.1 Pattern Design, Adaptation and Evaluation

The internal representation of patterns is the one required by the KESKYA concordancer. Patterns are supposed to be included in a single sentence. They are expressed mainly with lemmas and user defined semantic classes combined with POS tags, and a set of operators like *or* (| symbol), negation or iterations (*joker*). The interface makes it easier to define (or modify) each pattern, chunk after chunk. The user selects one of the listed options and adds it to the pattern (Fig. 1). Patterns characterize linguistic contexts where semantic relations between concepts may appear in texts. So the knowledge engineer must specify which parts of the pattern will refer to the related concepts (*X* and *Y*). Each of these chunks is turned into a particular colour that will be used later on to colour the words that may correspond to the related concepts.

Evaluating a pattern means checking some of the sentences where the pattern appears in each of the corpora (Fig. 2). The goal is to decide whether the pattern is to be rejected, modified or retained as a relevant pattern for this project.

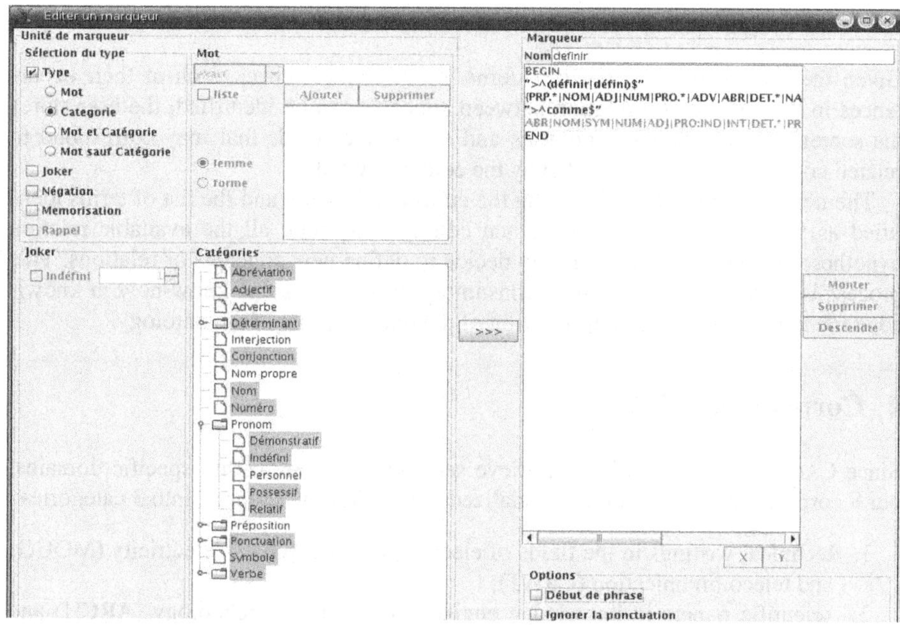

Fig. 1. CAMÉLÉON Pattern Editor. The edited pattern (*définir*) searches for forms like "X is defined as Y". The user preferred not to specify where X exactly could appear in a sentence (*BEGIN* is in the *X* colour), but the list above END constrains how Y could be formulated.

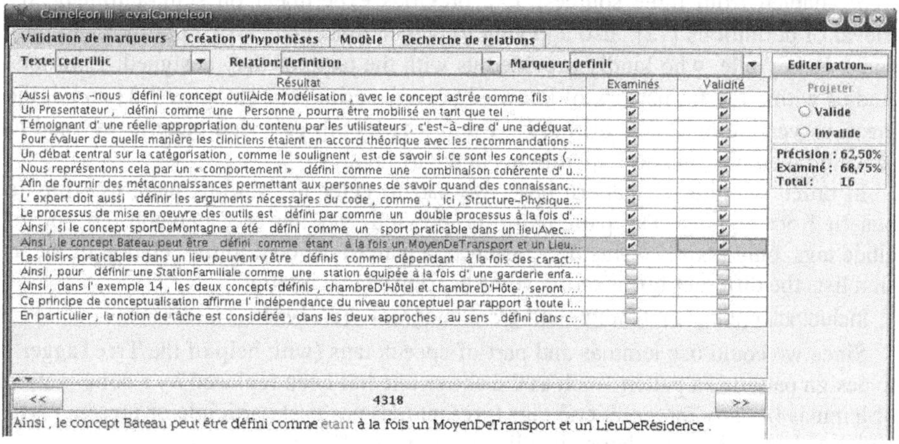

Cameleon III - evalCameleon

Validation de marqueurs | Création d'hypothèses | Modèle | Recherche de relations

Texte: cederilllc | Relation: definition | Marqueur: definir | Editer patron...

Résultat	Examinés	Validité
Aussi avons -nous défini le concept outilAide Modélisation , avec le concept astrée comme fils	✓	✓
Un Presentateur , défini comme une Personne , pourra être mobilisé en tant que tel .	✓	✓
Témoignant d' une réelle appropriation du contenu par les utilisateurs , c'est-à-dire d' une adéquat...	✓	✓
Pour évaluer de quelle manière les cliniciens étaient en accord théorique avec les recommandations ...	✓	✓
Un débat central sur la catégorisation , comme le soulignent , est de savoir si ce sont les concepts (...	✓	✓
Nous représentons cela par un « comportement » défini comme une combinaison cohérente d' u...	✓	✓
Afin de fournir des métaconnaissances permettant aux personnes de savoir quand des connaissanc...	✓	✓
L' expert doit aussi définir les arguments nécessaires du code , comme , ici , Structure-Physique...	✓	
Le processus de mise en oeuvre des outils est défini par comme un double processus à la fois d'...	✓	
Ainsi , si le concept sportDeMontagne a été défini comme un sport praticable dans un lieuAvec...	✓	✓
Ainsi , le concept Bateau peut être défini comme étant à la fois un MoyenDeTransport et un Lieu...	✓	✓
Les loisirs praticables dans un lieu peuvent y être définis comme dépendant à la fois des caract...		
Ainsi , pour définir une StationFamiliale comme une station équipée à la fois d' une garderie enfa...		
Ainsi , dans l' exemple 14 , les deux concepts définis , chambreD'Hôtel et chambreD'Hôte , seront ...		
Ce principe de conceptualisation affirme l' indépendance du niveau conceptuel par rapport à toute l...		
En particulier , la notion de tâche est considérée , dans les deux approches , au sens défini dans c...		

Projeter
Valide
Invalide
Précision : 62,50%
Examiné : 68,75%
Total : 16

<< 4318 >>

Ainsi , le concept Bateau peut être défini comme étant à la fois un MoyenDeTransport et un LieuDeRésidence .

Fig. 2. CAMÉLÉON Pattern Evaluation Screen. Given a text (*texte*), a relation type (*relation*) and a pattern, the pattern is matched in the text (*projeter*). Results are sentences listed for checking. When selecting a sentence, its full content is displayed in the editor on the bottom. Coloured words correspond to possible related concepts (X and Y). The pattern may be modified (*Editer patron*), rejected or validated (*invalide* or *valide* radio-button). The precision score (on the right) may guide this decision.

3.2 Text Fragment Selection and Model Enrichment

Given the set of project-specific patterns, the user must check each of their occurrences in the corpus. If a relation between concepts can be identified, the user stores the sentence as a relation hypothesis and selects the words that may correspond to related concepts (X and Y), guided by the coloured words.

The next step consists in browsing the conceptual model and the list of terms identified as possible concept labels. When editing a concept, all the available relation hypotheses are shown. The user may decide to define new concepts or relations. This process is quite complex and time-consuming. It requires some know-how in knowledge modelling and a good appreciation of the intended role of the ontology.

4 Corpora and Method

Since CAMÉLÉON is intended to retrieve semantic relations within specific domains, our 8 corpora are all made up of specialized texts. They are grouped into 3 categories:

1. technical writings in the fields of electric networks (GDP), electricity (MOUG) and telecommunication (CRAT);
2. scientific papers in knowledge engineering [4] (IC), archeology (ARCH) and geomorphology (ENC);
3. handbooks of geomorphology (GEO) and of paragliding (PAR).

The patterns which fill in the generic base were not designed from scratch, they were adapted from three sources: 1. a previous experiment on semi-automatic retrieval of definitions [12], also applying to tagged texts and carried out by L. Tanguy and J. Rebeyrolle, who kindly provided us with the patterns they designed; 2. various studies within the framework of knowledge engineering and ontology [11] and 3. the previous version of CAMÉLÉON [15]. The last two both provided patterns devoted to semantic relations such as hyperonymy and part-hood.

In order to build the pattern base, we had to enter the various patterns so as to benefit from tagging. The patterns in the previous version of Cameleon did not include tags, only lexical forms. For instance, a pattern devoted to the relation of inclusion lists the different forms of the verbs bearing such a relation:

inclut|incluent|incluant|intègre|intègrent|integrant (the symbol | means *or*)

Since we could use lemmas and part-of-speech tags (with help of the TreeTagger[2]) to design patterns, a pattern such as the above one has been replaced by a combination of lemmas (*inclure|intégrer*) and tags (present tense or past participle or present participle) which are easy to choose in a list, as shown in Fig. 1.

Each pattern has been sought, if necessary after having been refined, and the contexts have been evaluated. Note that this evaluation has been carried out by only one of the authors. After this, we obtained for each corpus a measure of the precision of each pattern, which was supposed to help us decide which patterns have to be retained to fill in the generic-pattern base.

[2] www.ims.unistuttgart.de/projekte/corplex/TreeTagger/

5 Results and Discussion

5.1 Results

We entered 71 patterns: 19 for definitions, 35 for hyperonymy, 14 for meronymy, 1 for reformulation, 2 'varia'. Due to lack of room, Table 1 below gives only a sample of the precision rates we obtained for the 8 corpora.

Table 1. Sample of the evaluation results (N= Number of contexts; P= Precision percentages)

	GDP		IC		GEO		MOU	
	N	P	N	P	N	P	N	P
définir	3	*100*	43	*98*	0		2	*100*
être-un	258	*17*	489	*18*	641	*23*	120	*8*
et Adv	10	*10*	15	*7*	56	*30*	6	*17*
sorte de	0		7	*57*	3	*67*	0	
inclure	75	*51*	32	*41*	16	*50*	18	*61*
partie de	0		0		7	*0*	0	
situé dans	40	*53*	63	*38*	38	*24*	4	*50*
c-à-dire	6	*67*	37	*54*	40	*80*	3	*100*
	ENC		PAR		ARCH		CRAT	
	N	P	N	P	N	P	N	P
définir	2	*100*	1	*0*	-		-	
être-un	375	*15*	62	*40*	181	*29*	-	
et Adv	66	*5*	2	*0*	13	*38*	19	*58*
sorte de	1	*100*	0		0		4	*100*
inclure	29	*62*	2	*100*	27	*19*	267	*48*
partie de	1	*100*	1	*0*	1	*0*	11	*18*
situé dans	55	*24*	4	*75*	36	*56*	291	*59*
c-à-dire	14	*29*	2	*100*	8	*63*	11	*64*

To give an example of pattern, 'définir' is 'lemma of verb *définir* (to define) followed by a joker followed by lemma of *comme* (as)': <définir> 1 <comme>. It yields a context[3] such as:

Un Projet Logiciel peut **se définir comme** un Processus de Développement.
A software project may be defined as a development process.

The major comment on Table 1 is that patterns differ considerably from each other regarding numbers of contexts and precision. Furthermore, the results of a one pattern may vary to a great extent as far as the corpus is concerned. To give but one example, the *inclure (include)* pattern ranges from 2 to 267 contexts yielded and from 19% to 100% in terms of precision.

Our experiment gives rise to two major issues: issues related to the elaboration of patterns itself and issues related to the results.

[3] Original sentences are in French, and we give a translation below. Bolded parts of the sentence are those that match the pattern.

5.2 Pattern Elaboration

In our experiment, the point of departure was a set of already-existing patterns which had to be adapted by replacing lexical forms with lemmas combined with tags. We could then see that a tagset offers a convenient method for designing patterns in that it facilitates the expression of abstract features while avoiding tedious entries of lists of forms. However, the accuracy of the tagset must represent a trade-off between the need for precision and manageability: the more accurate the tagset, the more difficult it is to understand the tags, especially when the user is not attuned to dealing with morpho-syntactic categories, and the more difficult the handling of the tagset.

Another point is the adaptation of the patterns to the different corpora. A given pattern is seldom convenient for each corpus; it is therefore necessary to modify it, generally to reduce irrelevant contexts. For example, the pattern NP1 <être> 1 DEF_ART NP2 DEF_ART (plus|moins) captures the following context:

La méthode KOD en **est** l'exemple **le plus** frappant

The KOD method is the most striking example of this

which does not express hyperonymy. To avoid it, we needed to specify that NP2 must not have *exemple, cas* or *résultat* as its head, which is an *ad-hoc* constraint.

Generally, it must be kept in mind that the so-called 'generic' patterns capture the most frequent or the most widespread constructions for a given relation. To a certain extent, it would be unrealistic to hope to take such a pattern and use it without modification. In this sense, one may wonder whether some patterns are really generic.

5.3 What Is a "Generic Pattern"?

The results presented in section 5.1, together with the above observations, challenge the notion of "generic pattern". If a generic pattern is the lexico-syntactic formulation of a semantic relation, which is said to invariably retrieve the same number of relevant contexts, whatever the corpus is, then we can conclude from our experiment that a generic pattern does not exist. Even the *is-a* pattern shows a huge difference between corpora, although it is acknowledged to be as generic as possible, in the sense that it "occurs frequently and in many text genres" [9: 540]. If one tests this pattern only on the PAR corpus, one will conclude this pattern is worth retaining since it has a 40% precision rate; while if the same pattern is tested only on the MOUG corpus, it is likely to be rejected, for the precision rate is 8%. If one wants to enhance the results for each corpus, one will have to introduce new constraints and to "fine-tune" the patterns, which is the contrary of what would be expected for a "generic" pattern.

6 Conclusion

We have presented a tool and an approach for supervised relation and concept identification. Our experiment shows that the performance of the semantic patterns used to retrieve conceptual relations within texts is highly corpus-dependent and that human supervision is therefore needed at various stages: pattern definition, sentence evaluation and model enrichment. Hence, the generic pattern base that comes with the CAMÉLÉON tool is thought of as a 'bootstrap' for elaborating and adapting convenient patterns and is not intended to be used "as is". Therefore, future work must be devoted to facilitating pattern elaboration and to browsing the resulting contexts. Firstly, we must ensure that "human-made" patterns actually surpass machine-learning approaches, which we would expect because of the complexity of their lexico-syntactic structures. Secondly, we must reduce the number of contexts the user has to check by filtering them via statistical methods. Thirdly, we must test how easy users find the overall pattern creation or adaptation task with CAMÉLÉON and improve on it.

References

1. Aussenac-Gilles N., Biébow B., Szulman S.: Revisiting Ontology Design: a method based on corpus analysis. Knowledge engineering and knowledge management: methods, models and tools. R Dieng and O. Corby (Eds). LNAI 1937. Berlin: Springer Verlag. (2000) 172-188
2. Aussenac-Gilles, N.: Supervised Text Analysis for Ontology and Terminology Engineering. Proc. of the Dagstuhl Seminar 05071 on "Machine Learning for the Semantic Web" (2005)
3. Bourigault, D.: Upery : un outil d'analyse distributionnelle étendue pour la construction d'ontologies à partir de corpus, Actes de Traitement Automatique des Langues Naturelles, Nancy (France) (2002) 75-84
4. Charlet, J., Zacklad, M., Kassel, G., Bourigault, D. (Eds): Ingénierie des connaissances Evolutions récentes et nouveaux défis. Paris : Eyrolles (2000).
5. Cimiano, P., Pivk, A., Schmidt-Thieme, L., Staab, S., Learning Taxonomic Relations from Heterogeneous Evidence. ECAI-2004 WS on Ontology Learning and Population, Valencia (Spain) (2004) 59-73
6. Faure, D., Poibeau, T.: First experiments of using semantic knowledge learned by ASIUM for information extraction task using INTEX. ECAI-2000 WS on Ontology Learning, Berlin (Germany) (2000) 7-12
7. Gillam, L., Tariq, M., Ahmad, K.: Terminology and the construction of ontology. Terminology, Volume 11, Number 1, (2005) 55-81
8. Girju, R., Moldovan, D.: Text Mining for Causal Relations. AAAI Conference (2002)
9. Hearst, M. Automatic Acquisition of Hyponyms from Large Text Corpora. In Proc. of the 15th Inter. Conf. on Computational Linguistics (COLING-92), Nantes (F) (1992) 539-545
10. Kavanagh, J.: The Text Analyzer: a Tool for Extracting Knowledge from Text. Master's of computer science Thesis, Univ. of Ottawa Canada (1996)
11. Marshman, E., Morgan T., Meyer I.: French patterns for expressing concept relations. Terminology, 8 (1) (2002) 1-30
12. Rebeyrolle, J., Tanguy, L.: Repérage automatique de structures linguistiques en corpus : le cas des énoncés définitoires. Cahiers de grammaire, 25 (2000) 153-174
13. Reinberger, M.-L., Spyns, P.: Discovering Knowledge in Texts for the learning of DOGMA-inspired ontologies. ECAI-2004 WS on Ontology Learning and Population, Valencia (Spain) (2004) 19-24
14. Riloff, E.: Automatically Generating Extraction Patterns from Untagged Text. Proc. of the 13th National Conference on Artificial Intelligence (AAAI-96). Portland (1996) 1044-1049
15. Séguéla, P.: Construction de modèles de connaissances par analyse linguistique de relations lexicales dans les documents techniques. Mémoire de thèse en Informatique, Université Toulouse 3, France (2001)
16. Staab, S., Maedche, A.: Ontology Learning for the Semantic Web, IEEE Intelligent Systems, Special Issue on the Semantic Web, 16(2) (2001) 72-79

Semantic Metrics

Bo Hu, Yannis Kalfoglou, Harith Alani,
David Dupplaw, Paul Lewis, and Nigel Shadbolt

IAM Group, ECS, University of Southampton, SO17 1BJ, UK
{bh, y.kalfoglou, ha, dpd, phl, nrs}@ecs.soton.ac.uk

Abstract. In the context of the Semantic Web, many ontology-related operations, e.g. ontology ranking, segmentation, alignment, articulation, reuse, evaluation, can reduced to one fundamental operation: computing the similarity and/or dissimilarity among ontological entities, and in some cases among ontologies themselves. In this paper, we review standard metrics for computing distance measures and we propose a series of semantic metrics. We give a formal account of semantic metrics drawn from a variety of research disciplines, and enrich them with semantics based on standard Description Logic constructs. We argue that concept-based metrics can be aggregated to produce numeric distances at ontology-level and we speculate on the usability of our ideas in potential areas.

1 Introduction

We are currently witnessing a shift of participation in ontology authoring from knowledge engineers to interested practitioners. This change is fueled, partly, by ever growing interest in the Semantic Web and in semantic technologies in general. It is causing an unprecedented influx of ontologies in the public domain. For instance, as of March 2006 we encountered at least 100 Wine related ontologies in various formats (e.g. OWL, RDF(S), DAML, etc.) and some 200 ontologies with definitions of the omnipresent concept *person*. This emerging "grass roots" approach to ontology engineering has put the onus on ontology management and calls for a variety of new tasks, such as ontology ranking, segmentation and evaluation, to name but a few. A common ingredient to accomplish these tasks is the assessment of similarity/dissimilarity between concepts within ontologies or between entire ontologies themselves.

We see several areas as relevant: knowledge representation, statistical clustering, data mining, information retrieval, all of which have contributed to the problem of computing similarity/dissimilarity between concepts. The very fact that there are so many options indicates that reaching a consensus on how to capture semantics embedded in ontologies is hard to achieve in the first place. We are particularly interested in building upon all the work from different disciplines and focusing on metrics leveraging the semantics of concepts.

In this paper we narrow our focus to the description logic (DL) based OWL language. We investigate a series of distance measures that our semantic metrics

S. Staab and V. Svatek (Eds.): EKAW 2006, LNAI 4248, pp. 166–181, 2006.

draw upon. These are discussed in Section 2. We then explore how different metrics can be semantically enriched and applied to the computation of distances between concepts in Section 3, and how can they be extended to ontologies themselves (Section 4). Finally, in Section 5, we present three major applications in which our metrics can be used as a complementary means of working with and enhancing existing technology and we conclude the paper with several issues that need further investigation.

2 Background

In this section, we review the meanings of distances in different disciplines from which our semantic metrics are drawn. We restrict our focus on ontology languages whose underlying logic satisfies the *Beth property*, e.g. OWL-DL.

2.1 Distance Measures

In mathematics, the concrete idea of *distance* between two spatial points has been abstracted as a metric or distance function over a set $\mathfrak{S}$ so that $\Delta : \mathfrak{S} \times \mathfrak{S} \rightarrow \mathfrak{R}$ where $\mathfrak{R}$, the set of real numbers, is the numeric representation of *distance*. Stemming from the spatial distance between two points, the term *distance* has been used in various domains and situations ranging from geometry and physics to information theory. An orthodox distance function must be **non-negative** and **symmetric** and satisfy the **triangle inequality**.

In two dimensional euclidean space, the distance between points, $\{p_1, p_2\}$ and $\{q_1, q_2\}$, can be computed as the *City Block (Manhattan) Distance*, the *Euclidean Distance*, or the *Chebyshev Distance*. Analogous to the two dimensional space distance, the *Euclidean Distance* is generalised in an m dimensional space to *Minkowski Distance*, $\Delta_{\mathrm{Min}}(p, q) = (\sum_i \mid p_i - q_i \mid^m)^{1/m}$.

The idea of distance, in the broader sense of measuring how far apart two objects are, has been applied to the computation of the discrepancy between documents in Information Retrieval (IR), disagreement between words in a lexical taxonomy in Knowledge Representation, and dissimilarity between strings in Information Theory. The semantic metrics that we propose in this paper stem from the general distance measures that are discussed as follows.

The vector space model (VSM) [19] has been widely used in traditional IR to compute the similarity of documents. VSM creates a space in which both the candidate documents and the queries are represented as vectors. Normally, VSM proceeds in three steps: 1) document indexing: by extracting content bearing terms from the document text, a document can be reduced to a vector of indexing *key-words*; 2) index weighting: the *key-words* are weighted to enhance the relevance between documents and the query; and 3) document ranking: the numeric similarity values between vectors of *key-words* are obtained (see Equation 1, [19]) based on which, the documents can be sorted.

$$\Delta_{VSM}(p,q) = -\log \mathtt{sim}_{VSM}(p,q) = -\log \frac{\sum_i p_i \times q_i}{\sqrt{\sum_i p_i^2}\sqrt{\sum_i q_i^2}}. \quad (1)$$

In information theory, *entropy* (denoted as $H(X)$) is borrowed from thermodynamics to measure the information content of a message or uncertainty of a message from the receiver's perspective [21]. A full account of Shannon's view of the mathematical theory of information, however, is beyond the scope of this paper. We restrict our focus to information gain with respect to one variable based on the observation of another and use such a measure as distance between arbitrary objects. This is captured by *conditional entropy* which measures how much uncertainty a variable Y has, if the knowledge regarding another variable X is completely known. Representing *conditional entropy* as $H(Y \mid X)$, it may be defined as

$$H(Y \mid X) = -\sum_{x,y} p(x,y) \log \frac{p(x)}{p(x,y)} \quad (2)$$

In practice *conditional entropy* can be regarded as a divergence measure between two variables, where $H(X \mid X) = 0$. The larger the conditional entropy, the less information one gains from X with regard to Y and the further apart X and Y are.

Meanwhile, in a discrete domain, the Kullback-Leibler divergence measures the disagreement of two distributions. Let p and q be discrete distributions of a variable, the "distance" between p and q is computed as

$$\Delta_{KL}(p,q) = \sum_i p_i \log \left(\frac{p_i}{q_i} \right)$$

Note that the Kullback-Leibler divergence is not symmetric and is positive definite [5]. It has several symmetrised variants that fit better as distance metrics.

2.2 Ontology and Ontology Languages

"What counts as an ontology?" is still a highly debated question with answers ranging from simple taxonomies to logically sound and coherent constructs whose underlying model supports logic inferences [2]. In order to discuss distances with regard to ontological entities and with regard to ontologies themselves, we need first to clarify our intuitions about ontologies. Instead of giving a full philosophical reflection on the term *ontology*, we take the Artificial Intelligence (AI) approach and restrict an ontology to be "a specification of a conceptualisation" [8]. Although the fact that many models, e.g. database schemata, UML models, and Semantic Network models [22], can be considered ontologies in a broader sense, we normally confine our view of *conceptualisation* to the following formalisation:

an ontology is a four-tuple $\langle \mathcal{C}, \mathcal{R}, \tau_c, \tau_p \rangle$, *where* $\mathcal{C}$ *is a set of unary predicates called concepts,* $\mathcal{R} \subseteq \mathcal{C} \times \mathcal{C}$ *a set of binary relations called properties and* τ_c *and* τ_p *introduction axioms of concepts and properties respectively.*

Description Logics (DLs) are a family of knowledge representation and reasoning formalisms that have attracted substantial research recently, especially after the endorsement of DL-based ontology modelling languages (e.g. OWL [14]) by the Semantic Web initiative [3]. Among the three "sub-species" of OWL, OWL-Lite is based on $\mathcal{SHIF}$ DL and OWL-DL is based on $\mathcal{SHOIN}$ DL [9]. DLs are based on the notions of concepts (i.e. unary predicates) and properties (i.e. binary relations). Using different constructs, complex concepts can be built up from primitive ones. Let CN denote a concept name, C and D be arbitrary concepts, R be a property, n be a non-negative integer, o_i $(1 \leq i \leq n)$ be an instance and $\top$, $\bot$ denote the top and the bottom. A $\mathcal{SHOIN}$ concept is:

$$CN \mid \mathsf{C} \sqcap \mathsf{D} \mid \mathsf{C} \sqcup \mathsf{D} \mid \neg \mathsf{C} \mid \exists \mathsf{R.C} \mid \forall \mathsf{R.C} \mid \geq_n \mathsf{R}.\top \mid \leq_n \mathsf{R}.\top \mid \{o_1, \ldots, o_n\}$$

Meanwhile, $\mathcal{SHOIQ}$ extends $\mathcal{SHOIN}$ with qualified number restrictions, $\geq_n$ $\mathsf{R.C}$ and $\leq_n$ $\mathsf{R.C}$.

An interpretation $\mathcal{I}$ is a couple $(\mathfrak{D}^{\mathcal{I}}, \cdot^{\mathcal{I}})$ where the nonempty set $\mathfrak{D}^{\mathcal{I}}$ is the domain of $\mathcal{I}$ and the $\cdot^{\mathcal{I}}$ function maps each concept to a subset of $\mathfrak{D}^{\mathcal{I}}$ while mapping each property (role) to a subset of $\mathfrak{D}^{\mathcal{I}} \times \mathfrak{D}^{\mathcal{I}}$. The uniform syntax and unambiguous semantics of DLs lend themselves to powerful reasoning algorithms that can automatically classify the domain knowledge in hierarchical structures.

Thus far, many ontology languages have been proposed and standardised, e.g. RDF(S) [12], OWL [14], etc. Despite the apparent differences, many of the current ontology languages aiming at facilitating semantic web applications can be regarded as tractable and decidable subsets of description logics.

3 Semantic Metric of Concepts

Distance between concepts is by no means a new idea. It can be approached from two directions, extensional and intensional. Extensional approaches normally assume an unbiased population of instance data from which a numeric similarity/dissimilarity can be obtained by applying probability distributions, concept co-occurrences and cosine measures of vectors, e.g. in [6] and [23]. Intensional approaches exploit features defined directly over the concepts and apply measures such as Tversky's model (e.g. in [4]) and graph-based ones (e.g. in [15]). More specifically, graph-based methods represent ontologies as directed acyclic graphs and count the total number of weighted edges, where the edges could be inheritance relationships and/or properties. Feature-based methods characterise concepts with discrete semantics bearing components, e.g. concept names, property names, domains, etc. and take a weighted average of the similarity/dissimilarity between each pair of components [13]. Both extensional and intensional methods have advantages and disadvantages. On one hand, it may be argued that instance data can best capture the semantics and there are plenty of well studied techniques that can be leveraged. In reality, however, an unbiased population is not always available, especially for ontologies published on the loosely regulated Web. The applicability of such approaches, therefore, is highly suspect. On the other hand, the intensional approaches would probably not win the battle due to: 1) the ambiguity of converting semantic distinctions—e.g. *equivalent*, *more general than*, etc.—into numeric values, 2) the computational complexity demonstrated by both graph-matching and SAT problems, and 3) their reliance on good modelling habits of those people constructing the ontologies. Intensional ones might also require more involvement from human observers, e.g. weighting different types of edges in graph-based algorithms. In this paper, we adopt an eclectic approach: we produce signatures characterising the logical restrictions of concepts and the distances of concepts are reduced to the distances between different vectors of such semantics bearing signatures.

In this section and throughout the rest of the paper, two ontologies are used as examples and test-beds for the proposed metrics. They are bibliography ontologies revised and simplified from publicly available ones and are denoted as $\mathcal{O}_m$[1] and $\mathcal{O}_p$[2] respectively.

3.1 Concept as a Set of Signatures

Each concept in an ontology encapsulates a subset of instance data from the domain of discourse. In a broader sense, concepts are effectively constraint systems against which instance data are evaluated. For instance, concept Book (defined as in Figure 1 using DL-based constructs) specifies that a book is a Document that has at least one title, at least one publisher, etc.

$$\begin{aligned}\mathsf{Book} \doteq\ & \mathsf{Document} \sqcap \geq_1 \mathsf{hasTitle} \sqcap \geq_1 \mathsf{hasYear} \\ & \sqcap \geq_1 \mathsf{hasPublisher} \sqcap \geq_1 \mathsf{humanCreator.Author} \\ \mathsf{Author} \doteq\ & \mathsf{Human} \sqcap \geq_2 \mathsf{hasPublication.Document} \\ & \mathsf{Document} \sqsubseteq \top \quad \mathsf{Human} \sqsubseteq \top\end{aligned}$$

Fig. 1. Book in $\mathcal{O}_p$ and related concepts

Unfolding concepts. Semantics of concepts are embedded in DL-based constructs which need to be explicated before computing the distance. Concepts are recursively unfolded till only primitive ones (i.e. concepts that are only defined by names) appear on the righthand side of the concept introduction axioms. If cyclic definitions are not allowed, i.e. such that no primitive concepts appear on both sides of a concept introduction axiom, it is possible to unfold the righthand side of all concept introduction axioms and guarantee the termination of such an unfolding process. For instance, let $\mathrm{CN} \doteq \mathsf{C}' \in \mathcal{O}$, CN_i and RN_j be concept and property names appearing in C' respectively, and $(\mathrm{CN}_i \doteq \mathsf{C}_i) \in \mathcal{O}$ and $(\mathrm{RN}_j = \mathsf{R}_j) \in \mathcal{O}$. It is possible to thoroughly expand C' by recursively replac-

[1] http://visus.mit.edu/bibtex/0.01/bibtex.owl.

[2] http://www.aktors.org/ontology/portal.

ing defined concept names appearing on the righthand side of CN $\doteq$ C′ with the concept definitions in $\mathcal{O}$, i.e. C [CN_i/C_i, RN_j/R_j] where $[x/y]$ defines the process of replacing all occurrences of x with y. Such a process terminates due to the acyclic nature of $\mathcal{O}$ and results in a finite set of logic formulae. Subsequently, semantic signatures are extracted from the unfolded concepts.

$\mathcal{S}$: a non-empty set of instances; $\mathcal{L}$: associating each $a \in \mathcal{S}$ with a set of concepts; $\mathcal{R}$: mapping each property to a subset of $\mathcal{S} \times \mathcal{S}$. For all a, $b \in \mathcal{S}$, if C, C_1, C_2 are concepts and R is property:

$\text{r}_\sqcap$: $C_1 \sqcap C_2 \in \mathcal{L}(a)$, then $C_1 \in \mathcal{L}(a)$ and $C_2 \in \mathcal{L}(a)$.
$\text{r}_\sqcup$: $C_1 \sqcup C_2 \in \mathcal{L}(a)$, then $C_1 \in \mathcal{L}(a)$ or $C_2 \in \mathcal{L}(a)$.
$\text{r}_\forall$: $\forall R.C \in \mathcal{L}(a)$ and $\langle a, b\rangle \in \mathcal{R}(R)$, then $C \in \mathcal{L}(a)$.
$\text{r}_\exists$: $\exists R.C \in \mathcal{L}(a)$, then $\exists b.b \neq a$ and $\langle a, b\rangle \in \mathcal{R}(R)$ and $C \in \mathcal{L}(b)$.
$\text{r}_\geq$: $\geq_n R.C \in \mathcal{L}(a)$, then $\exists b_1, \ldots b_k.b_i \neq b_j$ and $\langle a, b_i\rangle \in \mathcal{R}(R)$ and $C \in \mathcal{L}(b_i)$ and $k \geq n$.
$\text{r}_\leq$: $\leq_n R.C \in \mathcal{L}(a)$, then $\exists b_1, \ldots b_k.b_i \neq b_j$ and $\langle a, b_i\rangle \in \mathcal{R}(R)$ and $C \in \mathcal{L}(b_i)$ and $k \leq n$.

Fig. 2. Transformation rules of some DL constructs [2]

We adopted the tableau construction rules used in many DL-based inferential systems to facilitate the concept unfolding and the signature extraction process. In Figure 3, we present an example of how Book (defined in Figure 1) is unfolded by repetitively applying the transformation rules defined for each and every DL construct (see Figure 2 for the rules of some DL constructs)—a detailed description of such rules can be found in [2]. The unfolding process for Book stops when only primitive concepts and properties, namely Document and Human, remain. $\top$ is included for completeness.

As illustrated in Figure 3, concept Book is associated with one set of semantics-bearing signatures that fully capture the meaning of Book by means of primitive concepts and properties. There are two points to be addressed further. Firstly, there might be cases where concepts are defined as the union of other concepts that are either fully defined elsewhere in the same ontology or introduced as anonymous ones. Applying indeterminate $\sqcup$ unfolding rules (see Figure 2) results in alternative sets of formulae, each of which captures part of the intended meaning of the original concept. For instance, if we have "Human $\doteq$ Man$\sqcup$Woman" and Man and Woman as "…$\sqcap\forall$hasGenderMale$\sqcap$…" and "…$\sqcap\forall$hasGenderFemale$\sqcap$…" respectively. After unfolding, we have two separate sets of signatures.

$$^{i}\mathfrak{C}_1^{\mathsf{Human}} = \{\ldots,\ x : \forall \mathsf{hasGender.Male},\ \ldots\} \text{ or}$$
$$^{i}\mathfrak{C}_2^{\mathsf{Human}} = \{\ldots,\ x : \forall \mathsf{hasGender.Female},\ \ldots\}$$

Secondly, property universal quantifications can only be further expanded when there are instances defined over the property, i.e. y : Male is included, in the above

$$^{0}\mathfrak{C}_1^{\mathsf{Book}} = \left\{ \begin{array}{l} x : \mathsf{Document} \sqcap \geq_1 \mathsf{hasTitle} \sqcap \geq_1 \mathsf{hasYear} \sqcap \\ \quad \geq_1 \mathsf{hasPublisher} \sqcap \geq_1 \mathsf{humanCreator.Author} \end{array} \right\}$$

$$^{1}\mathfrak{C}_1^{\mathsf{Book}} = \left\{ \begin{array}{l} x : \mathsf{Document} \sqcap \geq_1 \mathsf{hasTitle} \sqcap \geq_1 \mathsf{hasYear} \sqcap \\ \quad \geq_1 \mathsf{hasPublisher} \sqcap \\ \quad \geq_1 \mathsf{humanCreator.(Human} \sqcap \geq_2 \mathsf{hasPublication.Document)} \end{array} \right\}$$

$$^{2}\mathfrak{C}_1^{\mathsf{Book}} = \left\{ \begin{array}{l} x : \mathsf{Document},\ x : \geq_1 \mathsf{hasTitle},\ x : \geq_1 \mathsf{hasYear}, \\ x : \geq_1 \mathsf{hasPublisher}, \\ x : \geq_1 \mathsf{humanCreator.(Human} \sqcap \geq_2 \mathsf{hasPublication.Document)} \end{array} \right\}$$

$$^{3}\mathfrak{C}_1^{\mathsf{Book}} = \left\{ \begin{array}{l} x : \mathsf{Document},\ \langle x, y_0 \rangle : \mathsf{hasTitle},\ \langle x, y_1 \rangle : \mathsf{hasYear}, \\ \langle x, y_2 \rangle : \mathsf{hasPublisher},\ \langle x, y_4 \rangle : \mathsf{humanCreator}, \\ y_4 : \mathsf{Human} \sqcap \geq_2 \mathsf{hasPublication.Document} \end{array} \right\}$$

$$^{4}\mathfrak{C}_1^{\mathsf{Book}} = \left\{ \begin{array}{l} x : \mathsf{Document},\ \langle x, y_0 \rangle : \mathsf{hasTitle},\ \langle x, y_1 \rangle : \mathsf{hasYear}, \\ \langle x, y_2 \rangle : \mathsf{hasPublisher},\ \langle x, y_4 \rangle : \mathsf{humanCreator}, \\ y_4 : \mathsf{Human},\ \langle y_4, z_0 \rangle : \mathsf{hasPublication.Document} \\ \langle y_4, z_1 \rangle : \mathsf{hasPublication.Document} \end{array} \right\}$$

$$^{5}\mathfrak{C}_1^{\mathsf{Book}} = \left\{ \begin{array}{l} x : \mathsf{Document},\ \langle x, y_0 \rangle : \mathsf{hasTitle},\ \langle x, y_1 \rangle : \mathsf{hasYear}, \\ \langle x, y_2 \rangle : \mathsf{hasPublisher},\ \langle x, y_4 \rangle : \mathsf{humanCreator}, \\ y_4 : \mathsf{Human},\ \langle y_4, z_0 \rangle : \mathsf{hasPublication},\ z_0 : \mathsf{Document} \\ \langle y_4, z_1 \rangle : \mathsf{hasPublication},\ z_1 : \mathsf{Document},\ x : \top \end{array} \right\}$$

Fig. 3. Unfolding concept Book in $\mathcal{O}_m$

example, if and only if there are $x : \forall\mathsf{hasGender.Male}$ and $\langle x, y \rangle : \mathsf{hasGender}$. They are left unexpanded otherwise.

The unfolding process stops when a fixed point is reached, i.e. $^{n}\mathfrak{C} = {}^{(n-1)}\mathfrak{C}$. As demonstrated in [9], by carefully selecting a subset of admitted conceptual constructs, e.g. the underlying logic models of OWL-Lite and OWL-DL [14], a termination is guaranteed with respect to acyclic ontologies.

Weighting signatures. Unfolding concepts can be seen as a process that gradually makes the semantics (the intended meaning of concepts) explicit. As a result, each concept is associated with finite sets of signatures in terms of the primitive concepts and properties. Effectively, concepts are deemed to hold parts of the information of the domain of discourse and thus, in spite of the apparent difference between ontologies and documents in the general sense, techniques for extracting and weighting document surrogates in IR can be applied analogically to concepts.

A straightforward approach to evaluate the influence of semantic signatures is to count the number of their occurrences in each $\mathfrak{C}_i$ of C. A signature is composed by the head (e.g. x and $\langle x, y_0 \rangle$ in Figure 3) and the tail (e.g. Document and hasTitle in Figure 3) separated by a colon. When counting, the heads of the signatures are ignored. The negative construct, $\neg$, states that the target concept is explicitly excluded and thus value -1 is given to emphasise the restriction. Unexpanded universal quantification, e.g. ∀R.B, is treated as an atomic signature, as the presence of B is uncertain in the absence of property R. In many ontologies, for many fully defined concepts, the number of primitive concepts and properties is small. Hence, we do not expect to encounter sparse vectors very often. For example, Phdthesis and Mastersthesis (see Figure 4(a)) from $\mathcal{O}_m$ are unfolded as illustrated in Figure 4(b). Their signature vectors and that of concept Book are presented in Table 1, where equal weights are assigned to every signature.

$$\begin{aligned}\mathsf{Phdthesis} &\doteq \mathsf{Document} \sqcap \geq_1 \mathsf{hasAuthor} \sqcap \geq_1 \mathsf{hasTitle} \sqcap \\ &\geq_1 \mathsf{hasSchool} \sqcap \geq_1 \mathsf{hasYear} \\ \mathsf{Mastersthesis} &\doteq \mathsf{Document} \sqcap \geq_1 \mathsf{hasAuthor} \sqcap \geq_1 \mathsf{hasTitle} \sqcap \\ &\geq_1 \mathsf{hasSchool} \sqcap \geq_1 \mathsf{hasYear}\end{aligned}$$

(a) Definition of thesis concepts

$${}^{n}\mathfrak{C}_1^{\mathsf{Phdthesis}} = \begin{aligned} &x : \mathsf{Document},\ \langle x, y_0\rangle : \mathsf{hasAuthor},\ \langle x, y_1\rangle : \mathsf{hasTitle}, \\ &\langle x, y_2\rangle : \mathsf{hasSchool},\ \langle x, y_3\rangle : \mathsf{hasYear},\ x : \top \end{aligned}$$

$${}^{n}\mathfrak{C}_1^{\mathsf{Mastersthesis}} = \begin{aligned} &x : \mathsf{Document},\ \langle x, y_0\rangle : \mathsf{hasAuthor},\ \langle x, y_1\rangle : \mathsf{hasTitle}, \\ &\langle x, y_2\rangle : \mathsf{hasSchool},\ \langle x, y_3\rangle : \mathsf{hasYear},\ x : \top \end{aligned}$$

(b) Unfolded thesis concepts

Fig. 4. Thesis concepts in $\mathcal{O}_m$

Table 1. Signature vector space of Book, Phdthesis, and Mastersthesis

	$\mathfrak{C}_1^{\mathsf{Book}}$	$\mathfrak{C}_1^{\mathsf{Phdthesis}}$	$\mathfrak{C}_1^{\mathsf{Mastersthesis}}$
⊤ (top)	1	1	1
Document	3	1	1
Human	1	0	0
hasAuthor	0	1	1
hasPublisher	1	0	0
hasPublication	2	0	0
hasTitle	1	1	1
humanCreator	1	0	0
hasSchool	0	1	1
hasYear	1	1	1

Weights of signatures are fine-tuned 1) using the *inverse document frequency weight* (*idf*) [11] scheme from IR with the assumption that signatures appearing in a small number of concepts are more significant for the purpose of discriminating between concepts than those that are frequently referred to by many concepts and 2) by reducing the weights of signatures referred to indirectly through properties. Let N be the number of concepts in an arbitrary ontology $\mathcal{O}$, n_{f_k} the number of concepts that refer to signature k, f_k, and $\mathrm{f}_{f_k,\mathsf{C}_i}$ the frequency of f_k in concept C_i, the *tf-idf* weight, w_{f_k,C_i}, of f_k in concept C_i is computed as

$$w_{f_k,\mathsf{C}_i} = \mathrm{f}_{f_k,\mathsf{C}_i} \times (\log_2 N/n_{f_k} + 1)\,, \text{ where } n_{f_k} \neq 0.$$

In $\mathcal{O}_m$, signatures such as Document, hasTitle, and hasYear appear in most of the concepts and thus are assigned low weights, whereas humanCreator appears in only one concept and thus is regarded as more important than others. Weights of indirect signatures are adjusted based on the weights of their related properties. For instance, z_0 : Document in Figure 3 is introduced because of humanCreator ∘ hasPublication and thus has less influence than x : Document. We decrease the weight of z_0 : Document to $w_{\mathsf{Document}} \cdot w_{\mathsf{humanCreator}} \cdot w_{\mathsf{hasPublication}}$.

Computing distances. By representing concepts as signature vectors, distances between concepts will then equal the distances between vectors in a high dimensional space. When there are more than one resultant $\mathfrak{C}_i$ due to disjunctive constructs (see Section 3.1), the shortest distance is computed.

$$\Delta(\mathsf{C},\mathsf{D}) = \min_{(\mathfrak{C}_i \text{ of } \mathsf{C}, \mathfrak{C}'_j \text{ of } \mathsf{D})} \tau(\mathtt{sim}(\mathfrak{C}_i, \mathfrak{C}'_j)) \tag{3}$$

$$\tau(\mathtt{sim}(\mathfrak{C}_i, \mathfrak{C}'_j)) = \begin{cases} -\log\left(\mathtt{sim}(\mathfrak{C}_i, \mathfrak{C}'_j)\right) & \text{if } \mathtt{sim}(\mathfrak{C}_i, \mathfrak{C}'_j) > 0 \\ +\infty & \text{if } \mathtt{sim}(\mathfrak{C}_i, \mathfrak{C}'_j) \leq 0 \end{cases} \tag{4}$$

$$\mathtt{sim}(\mathfrak{C}, \mathfrak{C}') = \frac{\sum_{w_i \in \mathfrak{C},\, w'_i \in \mathfrak{C}'} w_i \times w'_i}{\sqrt{\sum_{w_i \in \mathfrak{C}} w_i^2}\sqrt{\sum_{w'_i \in \mathfrak{C}'} w_i'^2}} \tag{5}$$

$$\mathtt{sim}(\mathsf{C},\mathsf{D}) = \max_{(\mathfrak{C}_i \text{ of } \mathsf{C}, \mathfrak{C}'_j \text{ of } \mathsf{D})} \mathtt{sim}(\mathfrak{C}_i, \mathfrak{C}'_j) \tag{6}$$

Due to the introduction of negative numbers for capturing the semantics of $\neg$, there are possibilities for non-positive similarities based on Equation 5. A value of $+\infty$, therefore, represents a pair of totally divergent disjoint concepts.

After taking into account the weighting factors, signature vectors in Table 1 can be refined, and we can approximate the distances among concepts as:

$$\Delta(\mathsf{Book}, \mathsf{Phdthesis}) = -\log(\mathtt{sim}(\mathsf{Book}, \mathsf{Phdthesis})) \approx 2.101$$
$$\Delta(\mathsf{Book}, \mathsf{Mastersthesis}) = -\log(\mathtt{sim}(\mathsf{Book}, \mathsf{Mastersthesis})) \approx 2.101$$
$$\Delta(\mathsf{Phdthesis}, \mathsf{Mastersthesis}) = -\log(\mathtt{sim}(\mathsf{Phdthesis}, \mathsf{Mastersthesis})) \approx 0$$

It demonstrates that the distance between the two types of theses is shorter than that between theses and book. Such a conclusion is evident if we consider properties as restrictions defined over concepts that screen out unqualified instances from the domain of discourse. Book requires at least two hasPublication. Intuitively, it presents a stronger constraint than those that do not have cardinality restrictions on the hasPublication property and thus there might be fewer instances satisfying all its restrictions. The zero distance between two types of theses also suggests that these two concepts might not be properly defined in that they are identical from the given signatures.

Discussion. We see that our distance metrics have the following advantages. Anonymous concepts, also known as restrictions, have always been the trouble maker in graph-based and feature-based approaches. When unfolding concepts, we expand restrictions together with other defined concepts, e.g. $x : \exists \mathsf{R}.\mathsf{C}$ is replaced by $\langle x, y \rangle : \mathsf{R}$ and $y : \mathsf{C}$. Anonymous concepts are, therefore, replaced by semantics bearing signatures that explicitly state the constraints imposed on the instances. We further collapse identical signatures so as to reduce the space complexity. Moreover, despite the apparent similarity, transforming ontologies into graphs cannot preserve the semantics *acoup sur*. Even with labelled edges, graph-based methods always have difficulty in justifying the semantic significance of transitive properties. For instance, it takes the distance between A and C in $A \rightarrow B \rightarrow C$ to be greater than that in $A \rightarrow C$ due to the fact that the introduction of the interim node B increases the length between A and C. This is intuitively incorrect and can be avoided if we fully unfold the interim concept B to the most basic signatures as well. Furthermore, many feature-based approaches adopt a weighting scheme to distinguish the contributions from different features, weights of which are normally set up manually by domain experts. We do not intend to undermine the importance of the role of human experts in understanding semantics. We, nevertheless, would like to introduce an automatic weighting mechanism to be complementary to their efforts. The *tf-idf* scheme borrowed from IR proposes a weight for each semantics-bearing (intensional) signature based on the significance of such a signature in introducing semantic discrepancies and thus is inline with the distance metrics. Finally, we consider our metrics as an improvement on techniques from feature-based families. This is evident partially from the fact that when constructing overall similarity/dissimilarity as a weighted average, feature-based approaches assume the semantic homogeneity of different features, which is not necessarily true.

4 Extending Semantic Metrics of Concepts

In this section, we demonstrate how to generalise the semantic metric discussed in previous sections to other ontology related measurements. Our work is based on the argument that the distances between concepts offer a fertile ground from which other metrics—that are effectively aggregations of concept-based distances—can be introduced.

4.1 Distance Between Concepts from Different Ontologies

Computation of $\Delta(\mathsf{C}, \mathsf{C}')$, where C and C' belong to different ontologies, needs to be bootstrapped by the similarity between primitive concepts and properties from respective ontologies. Ontology Mapping/Alignment techniques have been extensively studied recently and many tools have been developed to automatically or semi-automatically map ontological entities [7,10]. When bootstrapping $\Delta(\mathsf{C}, \mathsf{C}')$, we require only the similarities between primitive concepts and properties and thus simple string distance algorithms and/or those enhanced by external general-purpose lexicons, e.g. WordNet [16], are sufficient.

The similarity function (Equation 5) is adjusted to reflect the similarities computed by ontology mapping algorithms. Let w_i and w_i' be the weights of signatures f_i and f_i' from $\mathcal{O}$ and $\mathcal{O}'$ respectively, C and C' be the concepts from $\mathcal{O}$ and $\mathcal{O}'$ with $\mathfrak{C}$ and $\mathfrak{C}'$ respectively and f_i' be the most similar signature of f_i with $\delta_i = \mathtt{sim}(f_i, f_i')$,

$$\mathtt{sim}(\mathfrak{C}, \mathfrak{C}') = \frac{\sum\limits_{w_i \in \mathfrak{C},\ w_i' \in \mathfrak{C}'} \delta_i w_i \times \delta_i w_i'}{\sqrt{\sum\limits_{w_i \in \mathfrak{C}} (\delta_i w_i)^2} \sqrt{\sum\limits_{w_i' \in \mathfrak{C}'} (\delta_i w_i')^2}} \tag{7}$$

Once obtained, the adjusted similarity between signatures can be used in Equation 4 and 3 to compute the similarity between concepts from different ontologies.

$$\begin{aligned}
\mathsf{Book} &\doteq \mathsf{Publication} \sqcap \forall \mathsf{published\text{-}by.Organization} \\
\mathsf{Publication} &\doteq \mathsf{Reference} \sqcap \forall \mathsf{has\text{-}author.Person} \sqcap \forall \mathsf{has\text{-}date.Calendar\text{-}Date} \sqcap \\
&\quad\ \forall \mathsf{has\text{-}place\text{-}of\text{-}pub.Location} \\
\mathsf{Reference} &\sqsubseteq \top \quad \mathsf{Location} \sqsubseteq \top \quad \mathsf{Calendar\text{-}Date} \sqsubseteq \top \\
&\quad\ \mathsf{Organization} \sqsubseteq \top
\end{aligned}$$

(a) Definition of Book and related concepts

$$^{n}\mathfrak{C}_1^{\mathsf{Book}} = \begin{array}{l} x : \mathsf{Reference},\ x : \forall \mathsf{has\text{-}author.Person},\ x : \forall \mathsf{has\text{-}date.Calendar\text{-}Date}, \\ x : \forall \mathsf{has\text{-}place\text{-}of\text{-}pub.Location},\ x : \forall \mathsf{published\text{-}by.Organization},\ x : \top \end{array}$$

(b) Unfolded concept Book

Fig. 5. Book and related concepts in $\mathcal{O}_p$

We use the Book concept from $\mathcal{O}_p$ to explain how distance between concepts from different ontologies can be computed. Book (see Figure 5(a)) from $\mathcal{O}_p$ is unfolded as illustrated in Figure 5(b). With the initial correspondences between primitive concepts (e.g. Reference versus Document) and properties (e.g. hasPublisher versus published-by) from respective ontologies, which might be provided by an automatic mapping system or hand-crafted by human experts, we computed the distance between the two book concepts to be approximately similarly conceptualised. Apparently close concepts Book $\in \mathcal{O}_m$ (denoted as Book_m)

and $\mathsf{Book} \in \mathcal{O}_p$ (denoted as Book_p) are effectively semantically different. The absolute positive distance value between these two concepts indicates a semantic divergence which is evident from the fact that Book_m requires all books to have a title, a published year, a publisher, etc. while these are not mandatory for Book_p—an instance does not need to have a title, author, date, etc. to be qualified as a Book in ontology $\mathcal{O}_p$.

4.2 Distance Between a Concept and a Set of Concepts

There are occasions where the closeness is sought between a concept on the one hand and a set of interrelated concepts as a group on the other hand. For instance, one might need a measurement to represent how dense an ontology is with regard to an arbitrary concept. Let $\mathsf{C} \in \mathcal{O}$ be the target concept, $\mathsf{D} \in \mathcal{O}$ a concept from $\mathcal{O}$ that does not equal to C, Equation 2 can be rewritten as

$$\Delta(\mathsf{C}, \mathcal{O}) = - \sum_{\mathsf{D} \in \mathcal{O},\ \mathsf{D} \neq \mathsf{C}} p(\mathsf{D} \mid \mathsf{C}) \log p(\mathsf{D} \mid \mathsf{C}) \tag{8}$$

If we emulate $p(\mathsf{D} \mid \mathsf{C})$ as $\mathtt{sim}(\mathsf{C}, \mathsf{D})$ obtained using Equation 6, we can then approximate the closeness of the ontology $\mathcal{O}$ around C by aggregating the distances between C and every other concept in $\mathcal{O}$. Note that $\mathtt{sim}()$ is symmetric while $p(\mathsf{D} \mid \mathsf{C})$ does not equal $p(\mathsf{C} \mid \mathsf{D})$.

4.3 Distance Between Ontologies

As laid down in Section 2, we view ontologies as organisations of concepts and thus the distance between ontologies is computed out of those between concepts from the respective ontologies. In this paper, several methods are considered in order to aggregate individual distances.

Summation of feature distances. The *city block distance*—the sum of the distances between individual signatures—is the simplest aggregation function. Based on Equations 3 and 7, we define

$$\Delta(\mathcal{O}, \mathcal{O}') = \left(\sum_{\mathsf{C}_i \in \mathcal{O}} (\min_{\mathsf{C}'_j \in \mathcal{O}'} \Delta(\mathsf{C}_i, \mathsf{C}'_j))^{\lambda} \right)^{1/\lambda} \tag{9}$$

where λ might take the value of the number of concepts in $\mathcal{O}$ in which case the distance measure is not symmetric.

The disadvantage of a Minkowski style distance function is that if the distance between an arbitrary pair of signatures is significantly larger or smaller than that of others, the aggregated result might be falsely amplified or diminished.

Kullback-Leibler (KL) model. Also known as *relative entropy*, KL divergence is a natural quasi-distance measure of the extent to which one distribution agrees with another. In order to overcome the asymmetry of KL divergence, Jeffrey-divergence is proposed. Let $\mathsf{C}_i \in \mathcal{O}$ and $\mathsf{C}'_i \in \mathcal{O}'$ be two concepts from respective ontologies, then the distance between ontologies is computed as:

$$\Delta_J(\mathcal{O}, \mathcal{O}') = \sum_i p(\mathsf{C}_i) \log \frac{p(\mathsf{C}_i)}{p(\mathsf{C}'_i)} + \sum_i p(\mathsf{C}'_i) \log \frac{p(\mathsf{C}'_i)}{p(\mathsf{C}_i)}$$

An ontology is effectively a constraint system specifying how instances should be distributed among different concepts. In an arbitrary domain of discourse, the more rigorous the restrictions are, the fewer instances are qualified to instantiate a particular concept. We define an imaginary "perfect" concept, C_0, as one imposed with no restrictions except the domain top, e.g. ⟨`owl:Thing`⟩. Assume, the rigorousness of C_0 is 0. We can then compute the distance from an arbitrary "imperfect" concept C_k to C_0 as $\Delta(\mathsf{C}_k)$. The probability distribution of C_k can, therefore, be approximated as

$$p(\mathsf{C}_k) = \frac{\Delta(\mathsf{C}_k)}{\sum_{j=0}^{n} \Delta(\mathsf{C}_j)} \tag{10}$$

Asymmetric distance measure. Variants of KL divergency are established on the assumption that the ontologies are defined over largely overlapping domains and thus distances can be estimated by examining the distributions of "imaginary" instances. When such a prerequisite cannot be assumed, i.e. one does not have *a priori* knowledge of the interpretation domains of ontologies, distance ought to be obtained from mappings between fundamental semantics bearing signatures and is deemed an aggregation of those computed using Equation 8:

$$\Delta_A(\mathcal{O}, \mathcal{O}') = -\sum_{\mathsf{C} \in \mathcal{O}} p(\mathsf{C}) \sum_{\mathsf{D} \in \mathcal{O}'} p(\mathsf{C} \mid \mathsf{D}) \log p(\mathsf{C} \mid \mathsf{D})$$

where $p(\mathsf{C} \mid \mathsf{D})$ is the similarity based on Equation 6 and Equation 7 and $p(\mathsf{C})$ as in Equation 10. Note that Δ_A is asymmetric, i.e. $\Delta_A(\mathcal{O}, \mathcal{O}') \neq \Delta_A(\mathcal{O}', \mathcal{O})$.

5 Discussion and Conclusions

The increasing interest in employing rigorous logics to underpin ontology modelling languages has presented itself as a challenge to several ontology management tasks. In such circumstances, as meaning is emphasised, it is not straightforward to identify the similarity/dissimilarity between concepts, which should be a function of both syntactic and semantic divergences. In this paper, we have demonstrated how concepts can be decomposed into semantics-bearing signatures and how such signatures can yield distance measures among concepts, between a single concept and a group of concepts, and how they may be generalised to compute the distance between ontologies. The proposed semantic measures/metrics can be complementary to other metrics. Compared to traditional approaches, however, a DL-based one is capable of conveying not only the syntactic but also semantic information.

We envisage several applications of our distance measures/metrics in the context of semantically-enriched applications:

Ontology segmentation: An obvious application of the distance measures is ontology segmentation. With the growing interest in tackling interoperability issues, ontologies have quickly become a convenient vehicle for domain knowledge. Extensive efforts from different communities have resulted in many enormous knowledge corpora, especially in medicine, e.g. FMA [18] and GALEN [17]. The sheer size of such ontologies has put a tremendous burden on ontology management tools and have thus become a major obstacle to people who seek only a small part of the knowledge encapsulated in such ontologies. Ontology segmentation is envisaged as a neat solution to cope with the size issue. In a recent paper [20], the authors extracted a semantically complete part of an ontology by traversing upwards and downwards along *links*—concept inheritance relationships and properties—with the guidance of heuristic rules. Other approaches include graph-based clustering, query-based partitioning, etc. It is our contention that fragmenting an ontology is tantamount to computing semantic distance between concepts. The success of a segmentation strategy, therefore, depends directly on a good metric. As a complementary method to the existing segmentation techniques, our distance measures detect the semantic disagreement of different concepts and thus present criteria against which concepts can be filtered in/out. For instance, if one would like to extract a set of concepts around C, the segmentation can be formalised as $\texttt{segmentation}(\mathcal{O}, \mathsf{C}, d) = \{\mathsf{D} \mid \forall \mathsf{D} \in \mathcal{O}.\Delta(\mathsf{C}, \mathsf{D}) \leq d\}$ where d is an arbitrary real number.

Ontology ranking: Building an ontology is a time-consuming, error-prone process that requires trained eyes and minds. The Web has made such a task easier by offering search-and-access functionality to various on-line ontology repositories [1]. A search engine normally returns a list of candidates ranked according to a predefined ordering schema. Ranking resultant ontologies of a search query is effectively finding the closeness of a group of concepts w.r.t. those specified in the query. From discussions in Section 4.3, we have

$$\Delta(Q, \mathcal{O}) = -\sum_{\mathsf{C} \in Q} \left(p(\mathsf{C}) \sum_{\mathsf{D} \in \mathcal{O}} \texttt{sim}(\mathsf{D}, \mathsf{C}) \log(\texttt{sim}(\mathsf{D}, \mathsf{C})) \right)$$

Note that queries might be fragments of ontologies and thus cannot be fully unfolded. $\Delta(Q, \mathcal{O})$, therefore, might vary depending on the semantic completeness of queries and the initial similarities of respective semantics bearing signatures. $p(\mathsf{C})$ can be assigned manually by people submitting queries. As a default behaviour of querying, we assume people have some knowledge of the queries that they are formulating, are able to justify the relative significance of different parts of the queries, and can express the relative significance using numeric values. Having obtained the distances between Q and $\mathcal{O}_i$ from the candidate list, $\mathcal{O}_1, \ldots, \mathcal{O}_n$, one can then rank the resultant ontologies by comparing their numeric distance values, e.g. ranking ontologies with smaller $\Delta(Q, \mathcal{O})$ closer to the top of the list.

Ontology mapping: Ontology mapping is a complex and necessary task for most Semantic Web applications. The prospective users of such technology are faced with a number of challenges including ambiguity of the meaning of mappings, difficulties in capturing semantics, verification and validation of results and operationalisation in beneficiary Semantic Web application. The approach proposed in Section 4.1 provides a clear and straightforward metric for measuring the semantic discrepancy between concepts from different ontologies. An intuitive method is to nominate for a concept C from $\mathcal{O}_1$ a concept D_i from $\mathcal{O}_2$ that minimises the distance $\Delta(\mathsf{C}, \mathsf{D}_i)$.

Semantic metrics can be further improved. Firstly, universal quantification, thus far, is regarded as an atomic signature. Although it is semantically coherent, this approach might increase the size of signature corpus in practice. A possible solution could be to consider $\forall \mathsf{R}.\mathsf{C}$ as a complex signature whose weight is the product of w_{R} and w_{C}. The appropriateness of such a weighting scheme, nevertheless, needs further evaluation. Secondly, the complement (negation) construct results in a -1 count of the corresponding signature to differentiate it from missing signatures. It increases the possibility of similarities with negative numeric values. Currently, we equally assume that a pair of concepts having negative similarity do not overlap and thus are far apart from each other. We, however, do not distinguish cases with smaller negative similarity values from those with larger ones. The subtle differences between negative similarities might be necessary to answer such questions as "*are the distance of* $\mathsf{C} \sqcap \mathsf{D}$ *and* $\mathsf{C} \sqcap \neg\mathsf{D}$ *and the distance between* $\mathsf{C} \sqcap \mathsf{D} \sqcap \mathsf{E}$ *and* $\mathsf{C} \sqcap \neg\mathsf{D} \sqcap \neg\mathsf{E}$ *the same?*" Although an answer can be found indirectly by comparing similarities, a more elegant treatment is preferred. Finally, the use of two bibliography ontologies is only to demonstrate the applicability of semantic metrics. More empirical evaluation and a comprehensive comparative study against other approaches will further reveal the strengths and weaknesses of our approach.

Acknowledgements

This work is supported under the OpenKnowledge and HealthAgents STREP projects funded by EU Framework 6 under Grant numbers IST-FP6-027253 and IST-FP6-027213, and the Advanced Knowledge Technologies (AKT) IRC funded by UK's EPSRC under Grant number GR/N15764/01. The authors are grateful for the input of Srinandan Dasmahapatra in the preparation of this paper.

References

1. H. Alani and C. Brewster. Ontology ranking based on the analysis of concept structures. In *K-CAP '05: Proceedings of the 3rd international conference on Knowledge capture*, pages 51–58. ACM Press, 2005.
2. F. Baader, D. Calvanese, D. McGuinness, D. Nardi, and P. Patel-Schneider, editors. *The Description Logic Handbook: Theory, Implementation and Applications.* Cambridge University Press, 2003.

3. T. Berners-Lee, J. Hendler, and O. Lassila. The Semantic Web. *Scientific American*, pages 28–37, 2001.
4. A. Borgida, T. Walsh, and H. Hirsh. Towards measuring similarity in description logics. In *Proceedings of the Description Logics Workshop*, 2005.
5. T.M. Cover and J.A. Thomas. *Elements of Information Theory*. Series in Telecommunications. Wiley, 1991.
6. A.H. Doan, P. Domingos, and A.Y. Halevy. Reconciling schemas of disparate data sources: A machine-learning approach. In *SIGMOD Conference*, 2001.
7. M. Ehrig, J. de Bruijn, D. Manov, and F. Martin-Recuerda. State-of-the-art survey on Ontology Merging and Aligning V1. Technical Report Deliverable 4.2.1, Institut AIFB, Universität Karlsruhe, July 2004.
8. T. Gruber. A translation Approach to Portable Ontology Specification. *Knowledge Acquisition*, 5(2):199–221, 1993.
9. I. Horrocks and U. Sattler. A tableaux decision procedure for $\mathcal{SHOIQ}$. In *Proc. of the 19th Int. Joint Conf. on Artificial Intelligence (IJCAI 2005)*, 2005.
10. Y. Kalfoglou, B. Hu, D. Reynolds, and N. Shadbolt. Semantic integration technologies. 6th month deliverable, University of Southampton and HP Labs, 2005.
11. R. Korfhage. *Information storage and retrieval.* Wiley Computer Publishing, 1997.
12. O. Lassila and R.R. Swick. *Resource Description Framework (RDF) Model and Syntax Specification.* W3C, 1999.
13. A. Maedche and S. Staab. Measuring similarity between ontologies. In *Proceedings of the 13th International Conference on Knowledge Engineering and Knowledge Management.*, pages 251–263. Springer-Verlag, 2002.
14. D. L. McGuinness and F. van Harmelen. *OWL Web Ontology Language Overview.* W3C, 2003.
15. S. Melnik, H. Garcia-Molina, and E. Rahm. Similarity Flooding: A Versatile Graph Matching Algorithm and its Application to Schema Matching. In *Porceedings of the 18th International Conference on Data Engineering (ICDE)*, pages 117–128, 2002.
16. G. A. Miller. WordNet; a Lexical Database for English. *Communications of the ACM*, 38(11):39–41, 1995.
17. A. Rector and J. Rogers. Ontological Issues in using a Description Logic to Represent Medical Concepts: Experience from GALEN. In *Proceedings of IMIA WG6 Workshop*, 1999.
18. C. Rosse and José L. V.. Jr. Mejino. A reference ontology for biomedical informatics: the foundational model of anatomy. *J. of Biomedical Informatics*, 36(6):478–500, 2003.
19. G. Salton. *Dynamic information and library processing.* Prentice-Hall, Inc., NJ, USA, 1975.
20. J. Seidenberg and A. Rector. Web ontology segmentation: Analysis, classification and use. In *Proceedings of WWW2006*, 2006. to appear.
21. C.E. Shannon. A mathematical theory of communication. *SIGMOBILE Mob. Comput. Commun. Rev.*, 5(1):3–55, 2001.
22. J.F. Sowa. *Knowledge Representation: Logical, Philosophical, and Computational Foundations.* Brooks/Cole, Thomson Learning, 2000. ISBN 0-534-94965-7.
23. F. Wiesman and N. Roos. Domain independent learning of ontology mappings. In *AAMAS*, pages 846–853, 2004.

Matching Unstructured Vocabularies Using a Background Ontology

Zharko Aleksovski[1,2], Michel Klein[2], Warner ten Kate[1], and Frank van Harmelen[2]

[1] Philips Research, Eindhoven
[2] Vrije Universiteit, Amsterdam

Abstract. Existing ontology matching algorithms use a combination of lexical and structural correspondence between source and target ontologies. We present a realistic case-study where both types of overlap are low: matching two unstructured lists of vocabulary used to describe patients at Intensive Care Units in two different hospitals. We show that indeed existing matchers fail on our data. We then discuss the use of background knowledge in ontology matching problems. In particular, we discuss the case where the source and the target ontology are of poor semantics, such as flat lists, and where the background knowledge is of rich semantics, providing extensive descriptions of the properties of the concepts involved. We evaluate our results against a Gold Standard set of matches that we obtained from human experts.

1 Introduction

Semantic integration of heterogeneous datasources is widely regarded as technologically one of the most urgent and scientifically one of the most challenging problems [1–8]. Consequently, much recent work has appeared in this area. In the fields of AI, Knowledge Engineering and Semantic Web research, this problem goes by the name of *ontology matching* (see [1, 6, 7] for a number of recent surveys of this very active field).

According to [6], the methods to solve the problem of ontology matching can be divided into: *terminological* methods which try to identify lexical correspondences between the labels of concepts in the source and target ontologies, *instance-based* methods which use instance data in both source and target ontologies to discover matches [9], *structural* methods which use the structure of the ontologies, and *semantic* methods which use additional logical methods to induce the matches [5].

The majority of the approaches use a combination of terminological and structural methods, where the lexical overlap is used to produce an initial mapping, which is subsequently improved by using the structure of source and target. Hence, this majority of approaches crucially relies on two assumptions:

- sufficient lexical overlap exists between the source and target ontology
- source and target ontology have sufficient structure

In this paper, we will present a case-study where neither of these assumptions hold. In this case study, not only there is insufficient lexical overlap between source and target, but more crucially, the structures to be matched contain *no structure at all*: they

S. Staab and V. Svatek (Eds.): EKAW 2006, LNAI 4248, pp. 182–197, 2006.

are simply lists of terms, instead of richly structured ontologies. Consequently, current state-of-the-art matchers are expected to fail.

We believe that our case-study is representative of many realistic cases. Experience with Semantic Web applications shows that many of them rely on rather lightweight semantic structures, providing at most a hierarchy of terms, where often this hierarchy is only a 2-3 levels deep [10]. Hence, the reliance of existing ontology matchers on such structure is indeed an important limiting factor.

After showing indeed the failure of a number of state-of-the-art matchers in our case-study, we present a novel method for ontology matching that uses an additional source of *background knowledge* to compensate for the lack of structure to be found in source and target vocabularies as well as the freedom in choice of terminology.

The basic idea of our approach is to first align the concepts from the source and target ontologies with the background knowledge, then use the structure of this background knowledge to derive semantic relationships between the source and target concepts, and finally use these relationships to induce a mapping between them.

We built a system that implements this approach and tested it with the data from our case-study. We then score the performance of our system against a human-created Gold Standard, and show that on such poorly structured data, our system performs significantly better than existing state-of-the-art matchers.

In the following sections we first describe the details of our case (section 2), and we show the low success rate of some existing state-of-the-art matchers on these data (section 3). We then proceed to explain our own matching process, based on the use of background knowledge (section 4 and 5), and show in section 6) that we achieve considerably higher success rates than the existing matchers. The final section 7) concludes.

2 The Data in Our Case Study

In this section we describe the data involved in our case study. The challenge was to match two vocabularies that were taken from the medical domain. The vocabularies are lists of reasons for admission in the Intensive Care Unit (ICU) of two Amsterdam hospitals. A reason for admission describes a problem, why a patient was brought into the ICU. Each patient arriving at the ICU in either hospital is classified using one or multiple terms from the corresponding list. These classifications are used for monitoring patient progress, for planning of required ICU resources, and for off-line nationwide quality comparison of different ICU's.

Source vocabulary: As source vocabulary for our mapping case-study, we use a set of reasons for admission from the OLVG hospital in Amsterdam. It is a flat list of terms with no structure. The list is partly based on the ICD-9-cm[1] vocabulary, and on the Dutch "Classificatie van Medisch Specialistische Verrichtingen" (CMSV)[2], a classification of medical procedures. During its use in the past three years, the OLVG list has been extended with additional descriptions of medical conditions of patients

[1] http://www.cdc.gov/nchs/about/otheract/icd9/abticd9.htm

[2] http://www.nictiz.nl/kr_nictiz/2527

at the ICU. The resulting list is a mixture of problem descriptions at several levels of abstraction with minor redundancy. It does not only contain reasons for admission to the ICU, but also other medical conditions that are relevant during the stay of patients at the ICU. We limited our experiments to the list-elements actually used at admission, identified as those terms that are used for describing patients during the first 24 hour of their stay. The resulting list contains 1399 problem descriptions consisting of maximal 7 words each. 95% of these descriptions consist of no more than three words. The list is mainly in Dutch but also contains English terms.

Target vocabulary: As target vocabulary, we use a second set of reasons for admission, used at the AMC hospital in Amsterdam. The AMC vocabulary consists of a flat list of 1460 reasons for admission at the intensive care unit of the AMC hospital. This list was used as the target vocabulary in our experiments.

Background ontology: As outlined above, the essential idea of our aproach is to first align the unstructured source and target vocabularies with a given background ontology, and then to use the structure of the background ontology to derive matching relationships between the source and target vocabularies. In our case study, we use the DICE ontology as background knowledge. DICE has been developed by the Medical Informatics group at the AMC hospital. It is a medical terminology, formalized in OWL DL[3], of some 2300 concepts, described by some 5000 lexical terms. These concepts are related to each other with some 4300 relational links of 50 different relation types. DICE mainly aims to cover concepts in the Intensive Care domain, and is structured in five different hierarchies (called "aspects" in DICE): abnormalities (255 concepts), medical procedures (55 concepts), anatomical locations (1512 concepts), body subsystem (13 concepts), and causes (85 concepts). Together, these five vocabularies are the main organisational structure of DICE. Each aspect has a domain of possible values, organized in a tree structured taxonomy. The concepts in the aspect taxonomies are labeled with a language attribute, in the current version either Dutch or English. If a concept is named with multiple terms, one of the terms functions as 'preferred' term - label, and the others as synonyms.

3 Performance of State-of-the-Art Tools on Our Case Study

3.1 Ontology Alignment Tools

There are several other approaches for ontology matching. An overview can be found in [6, 1, 7]. In this section, we summarize three of the most prominent approaches.

- FOAM is an ontology alignment framework to fully or semi-automatically align two or more OWL ontologies, developed by the university of Karlsruhe [11]. It is based on heuristics (similarity) of the individual entities (concepts, relations, and instances). As result, it returns pairs of aligned entities. It can handle ontologies within the DLP-fragment of OWL. Part of FOAM is a machine learning component that optionally takes user feedback into account.

[3] `http://www.w3.org/TR/owl-guide/`

- Falcon-AO [12] is an automatic ontology matching tool, developed by the South East University of China. It outperformed all other ontology matchers in the 2005 ontology alignment initiative [13].Falcon-AO regards ontologies as graph-like structures, and then produces mappings between elements in the two graphs that correspond semantically to each other. Both of linguistic similarity and structural similarity are taken into account. There are two matchers integrated in Falcon-AO: LMO for syntactic comparison based on edit distance, and GMO for graph-based comparison.
- S-Match is a algorithm and tool developed by the University of Trento [14], based on CTXmatch[5]. S-Match takes two trees, and for any pair of nodes from the two trees, it computes the strongest semantic relation holding between the concepts of the two nodes. For this, it uses lexical techniques, background knowledge in the form of relations between synsets in WordNet, and the structure of the tree. S-Match is restricted to tree-like structures used for classification purposes.

As is already illustrated in the descriptions above, most alignment tools exploits a combination of syntactical comparison techniques and structural comparison techniques. This mixed approach can work well in practice, as the results in the ontology alignment initiative show. However, when one of the sources to be matched merely is a unstructured list, the mixed approaches reduce to lexical comparison of labels.

Only one of the tools, i.e. S-Match, exploits background knowledge to do the mapping. However, in the current version S-Match can only use a predefined set of background knowledge sources, such as Wordnet and UMLS. Moreover, it only uses the class hierarchy of background ontologies.

3.2 Performance of Other Tools

We have applied two of the ontology matching tools described above to the data that is described in our case study. We loaded an OWL representation of both the OLVG list and the AMC list plus the DICE background knowledge into the tools. In this section we only describe the amount of matches that we found, in section 6.1 we give an analysis of the correctness of these matches.

When using FOAM to align the two lists, we initially got 326 matches, but those included symmetric matches. Effectively FOAM found 159 matches. An analysis revealed that many obvious matches were missing because synonym labels were ignored. To solve this, we have regenerated the AMC list with separate concept definitions for each known synonym. This resulted in 696 effective matches.

We also used Falcon-AO.[4] Initially, the files were too large to run in one step. After splitting the AMC-ontology in several files, we were able to run the tool, and extrapolated that we would end up with less than 100 matches. However, because all matches were necessary based based on lexical measures only, we tried to use the lexical matcher component (LMO) in a stand-alone configuration. This has two advantages. First, the stand-alone LMO matcher is much more efficient, so that matching can run on the complete AMC ontology. Second, it returns a a ranking of all matches found, and not

[4] Experiments performed in collaboration with Dr. Wei Hu, South East University of China.

just the ones that are above the threshold. As a result, we get much more matches, but many of them with a low confidence level. When using the stand-alone LMO matcher, 683 matches were returned.

Unfortunately, because S-Match isn't freely available, we haven't yet been able to use S-Match on our dataset with a medical thesaurus as background knowledge.

4 Semantic Matching of Concepts from Unstructured Vocabularies

The scheme of our matching approach is depicted in Figure 1. The task is to match the source vocabulary to the target vocabulary, where both vocabularies are unstructured (flat) lists. Our approach consists of finding semantic matches by using a (richly structured) ontology that holds background knowledge about the domain. First, the source and target vocabulary are each matched with the background knowledge ontology producing so-called *anchoring matches*. Anchoring matches connect a source or target concept to one or more concepts in the background knowledge ontology, which we call anchors. Then, based on the relationships among the anchors entailed by the background knowledge, we induce in a second step how the concepts from the source are matched to the concepts in the target vocabulary, yielding the *semantic match* we are looking for. A concept can match to several anchors, in which case the collection of anchors is combined according to the semantics of the background knowledge.

In the following, we will describe the anchoring process (subsection 4.1) and the process of inducing the source-to-target semantic match (subsection 4.2) in more detail.

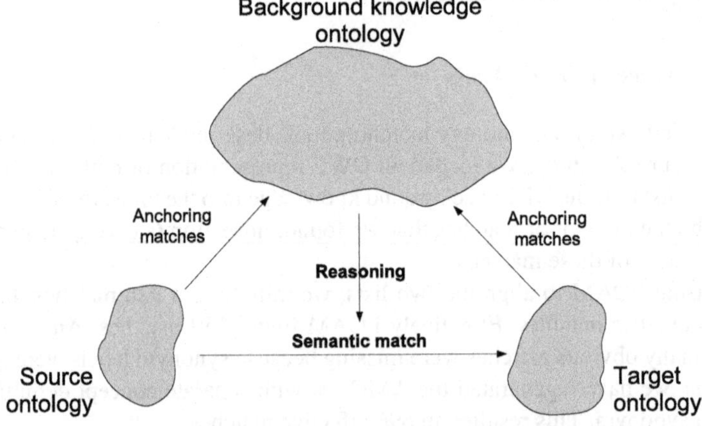

Fig. 1. Our general approach: Matching a source vocabulary to a target vocabulary using an ontology describing background knowledge.

4.1 Anchoring Vocabulary Concepts with the Background knowledge

As explained, the source and target vocabularies are anchored to concepts in the background ontology. The anchoring matches can be established manually by a domain expert, or automatically using existing concept matching techniques.

The automatic anchoring in our approach, is performed by a simple lexical heuristic that discovers partial matches between two strings. It makes use of the concept's labels and synonyms only. A concept's label is the string name assigned to the concept. Quite often, these labels come with a list of synonyms for the concept. We used both the labels and the synonyms in our comparison. Our heuristic is based on comparing the number of matching words: If all the words in a label or synonym of a concept A are found in a label or synonym of concept B, it concludes that A is an anchor of B. We also used some simple Dutch morphological rules to deal with the common Germanic construction of compound words that do not have a delimiting space between the words. For example, *"hersentumor"* (brain tumor) is a special case of *"tumor"*.

Figure 2 depicts an example of discovering an anchoring match.

Clearly, these heuristics are very simple, and it is not difficult to think of cases where they fail: In Figure 2, for example, *"long brain tumour"* would also end up being a special case of *"brain"*.

It would seem that such a simplistic lexical mapping would not suffice, and it would seem that we are replacing one ontology matching problem (source to target) by two ontology matching problems (anchoring source and target to the background knowledge). Why then, would this make our problem any easier? The surprising thing is, as revealed in our experiments, that this is indeed the case. After presenting our experimental data in the next section, we will discuss why the use of such simple lexical heuristics is sufficient for the anchoring process, while it is *not* sufficient for the direct source-to-target matching.

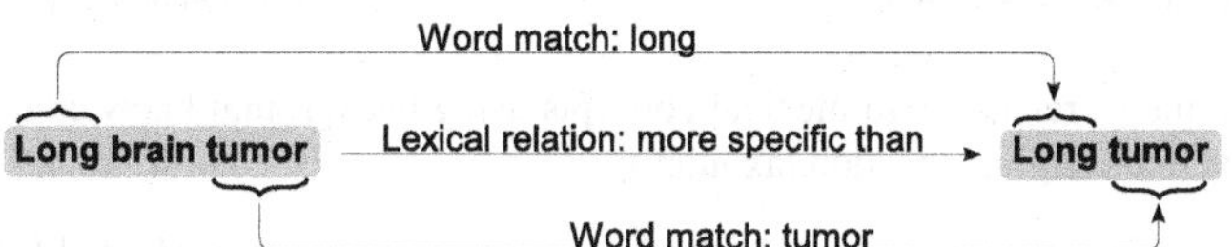

Fig. 2. An example of lexical anchoring by comparing two labels: *"Long brain tumor"* and *"Long tumor"*. The first consists of a superset of the words from the second label, so the second can be considered a property value filler of the first.

The anchoring process implicitly adds structure to the unstructured source and target vocabularies, and has established relations between source and target concepts through the relations between their anchors in the background ontology. We exploit this structure in the next step, to discover semantic matches between the source and target vocabulary concepts.

4.2 Semantic Matching - The Use of Background Knowledge

As said, we make use of the background knowledge ontology to perform the discoveries of semantic matches. When comparing two concepts A and B having anchors A' and B' respectively, we compare A' and B', and, if they are related, infer that A and B are related as well.

An example is given in Figure 3: the concept *"Dissection of artery"* is found to have location *"Artery"*, and the concept *"Aorta thoracalis dissection"* is found to have location *"Aorta thoracalis"*. A relation is inferred between these two medical concepts, since they describe related anatomical locations: according to the background ontology *"Aorta thoracalis"* is a kind of *"Artery"*. Hence, the source concept can be inferred to have a more specific location than the target concept. Notice that with pure lexical methods, no meaningful match between these two concepts could have been derived. The use of background knowledge was essential to derive this match.

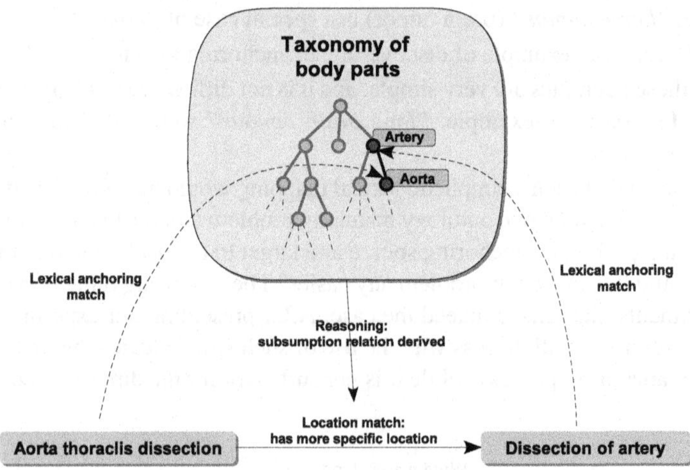

Fig. 3. An example of relating two medical concepts using background knowledge. A semantic match is discovered using the location taxonomy.

In general, either the source concept A or the target concept B could be anchored to multiple anchors and the background knowledge could reveal relationships on anchors that represent different properties. On the one hand, this makes the comparison more complex. On the other hand, if multiple anchors are related in similar ways, they reinforce that the main concepts A and B are related in the same way. In case the multiple anchors are related in incompatible ways (e.g. anchor A'_1 subsumes anchor B'_1, but anchor A'_2 is subsumed by anchor B'_2), a subsumption relation between the concepts cannot be inferred. However, they do reveal the source and target concepts have some relationship and are within some semantic distance.

This is illustrated in the example depicted in Figure 4, where we try to match the concepts *"Heroin intoxicatie"* and *"Drugs overdosis"*. According to the background knowledge, *"Heroin"* is a kind of *"Drugs"*, while *"Overdosis"* is a kind of *"Intoxicatie"*, i.e. the two aspects have a subsumption relationship to each other, however, in reverse direction between the concepts. Hence, the concepts are neither equivalent nor one subsuming the other. However, in the everyday understanding the two concepts do have a big semantic overlap. Again, note that these concepts do not have any lexical similarity - their describing labels consist of entirely disjoint sets of words. It was only possible to discover this match by using the background knowledge.

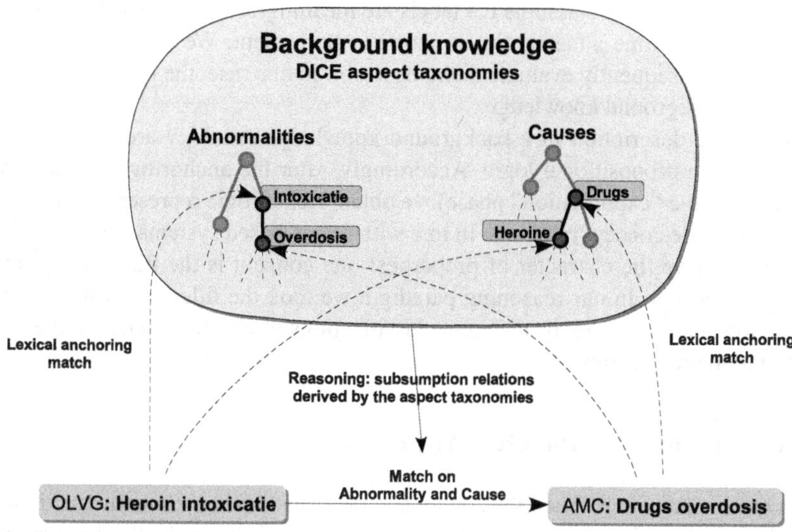

Fig. 4. An example of matching two concepts using background knowledge. The concepts are not equivalent but do have a big semantic overlap.

The successful application of the method depends on the richness of the background knowledge. As discussed later in Section 6, with increasing richness, the more likely it becomes that anchoring matches can be established in the first place, but, more importantly, the more likely it becomes a relation between the anchors can be found.

Experience in practice has shown that concepts from two matching ontologies are rarely precisely equivalent, but rather have some (otherwise unspecified) semantic overlap. Consequently, finding such semantic relationships seems more useful for integration purposes, than finding precise equivalences.

4.3 Comparison with Other Approaches

Our approach can be compared with the semantic coordination approach proposed by Bouquet et al. [5]. That approach assumes the source and target vocabularies do have some structure and each concept does have a label that is meaningful in natural language. It proceeds in two phases. In the first phase, called explicitation, the concepts from source and target ontology are transformed into propositional expressions, using the labels and surrounding structure such as ancestor and sibling labels. The words in the label are considered as propositional atoms. An additional source, such as WordNet[5], may be used to enrich the explicitation, by taking the senses returned by WordNet on each word in the label as the propositional atoms. In the second phase, the obtained propositional expressions are tested whether one implies the other, for example, in a SAT solver. Since the propositional expressions capture the semantics of the original concepts, valid implications indicate a semantic subsumption relation between the concepts.

[5] `http://wordnet.princeton.edu/`

In our scheme, we also assume the labels are meaningful in natural language. However, we do not assume a (semantic) structure to be present. We also create logic expressions and subsequently evaluate them, however, in our case, the logic framework is given by the background knowledge.

Usually, the description in a background knowledge ontology are expressed in a logic richer than propositional logic. Accordingly, after the anchoring (which may be compared with the "explicitation" phase) we obtain richer logic representations. In particular, we include concept relations. In line with frame-based systems, quite often concept relations have the character of properties: one concept is the filler of a property of the other concept. In our reasoning paradigm we took the fillers apart in a separate classification and combined the different classifications of all fillers to derive the match between the main concepts.

5 Experiments to Test Our Approach

In our experiments we matched the source and target lists (i.e. the unstructured OLVG and AMC vocabularies) both lexically, i.e. directly, and semantically, i.e. using the DICE ontology as background knowledge.

Experiment 1: Lexical matching. In the lexical match, we directly matched pairs of terms from the two vocabularies, using the lexical matching method described in Section 4.1. In testing for equality of terms, we allowed for edit-distance of two characters using Levenshtein string distance [15], to compensate for the typing mistakes in the lists. The result is a list of pairs of terms, that were either equivalent or related in a more-general-than relation.

Hypothesis: We expect that the results of this lexical matching step are comparable to the performance of existing tools on this data, such as discussed in Section 3, since on these data the existing tools are also reduced to performing lexical matching only.

Experiment 2: Semantic matching. When matching the vocabularies semantically, we followed the general scheme of our approach, depicted in Figure 1, using the five aspect taxonomies in DICE as the background knowledge. First, in the anchoring step, we lexically matched the terms from the OLVG and AMC source and target vocabularies to each of the five DICE aspects taxonomies, producing anchors in the background ontology for the terms from the vocabularies. For the AMC-DICE anchoring, besides anchoring through the lexical matching procedure, we also used a given anchoring schema that was created manually by experts from the AMC hospital. Important to notice is that our lexical matching is not crucial in this step, instead any matcher can be used to establish the anchoring matches. We used such simple lexical technique because our manual analysis indicated that using other more advanced techniques will only marginally change the result. After obtaining the anchors we used the relationships specfied between the anchors in the DICE taxonomies to infer a semantic match between the source and target concepts. Figure 5 depicts the scheme (which is essentially the general scheme from Figure 1 instantiated for our experiment). Note that each term from source and target ontology is matched multiple times to the background ontology, viz. once per aspect taxonomy.

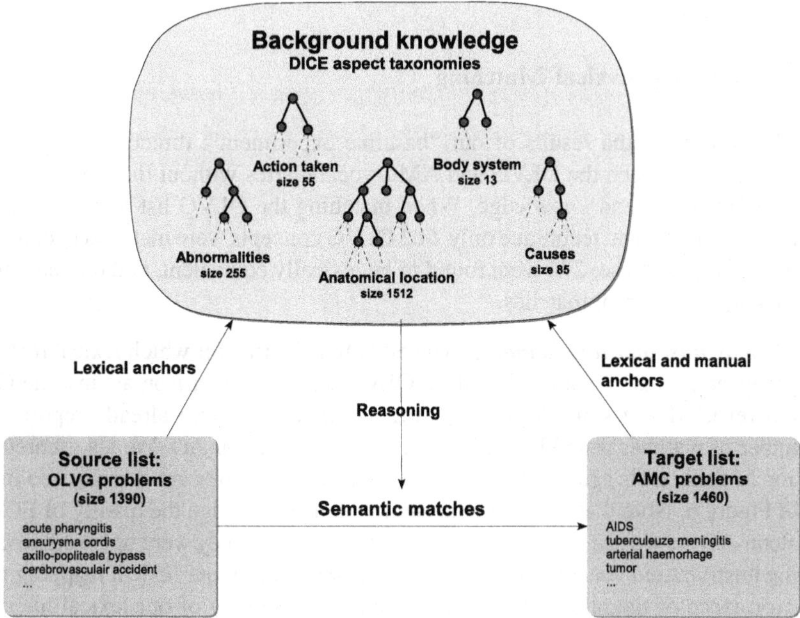

Fig. 5. Matching the OLVG and AMC vocabularies using the aspect taxonomies of DICE as background knowledge ontology (this is Figure 1 instantiated for our experiments.)

Hypothesis: We expect the results of semantic matching to be better than the results of direct lexical matching between the two vocabularies.

Evaluation: For measuring the performance of the various methods and tools, we created a Gold Standard solution for this problem. A medical expert was invited to create manually mappings between the OLVG and AMC vocabularies. Because the intended use case of the mapping is to classify patients that have been registered with OLVG terms in the AMC taxonomy, the expert was asked to specify for each OLVG term the AMC term that he would use to describe the medical problem.

The expert was given a random sample set of 200 concepts from the OLVG list, for which he was asked to find the matching concepts in the AMC list. This set was created as follows: 30 terms were selected for which we knew that good anchorings in DICE would be available, together with the top 15 most frequently used terms from the OLVG vocabulary, supplemented with randomly drawn terms to a total of 200 terms. For these 200 terms, the expert created matches for 125 concepts, leaving the other 75 "unknown". For each of the matched OLVG concepts he proposed one AMC concept as the most appropriate match. No statements about alternates were made. This yields a Gold Standard on the order of about 10% of the entire vocabulary, which is sufficient for reliable performance measurements.

6 Results

6.1 Experiment 1: Lexical Matching

We will first present the results of our "baseline experiment": directly trying to find lexical matches between the OLVG and AMC vocabularies without the mediating role of the DICE background knowledge. When matching the OLVG list to the AMC list directly, using the lexical technique only, 582 OLVG concepts were matched to concepts in the AMC list. Of these, 274 were found to be lexically equivalent, and the remaining 308 concepts were partial matches.

Evaluation against the Gold Standard The 582 OLVG terms for which lexical matches were produced represent some 42% of all OLVG terms. Comparison against the Gold Standard revealed that some 32% were correct. In section 3 we already reported on the number of matches found by tools like FOAM and Falcon-AO. We also scored the precision of these tools against the Gold Standard. These figures are summarised in the table in Figure 6. Note that these figures cannot be used to judge the quality of FOAM and Falcon-AO, as we use them here in a scenario for which they were not designed, i.e. mapping unstructured vocabularies. We compare the result of our lexical mapping with the performance of the other tools to show that the simplicity of our lexical mapping technique in the first experiment is not the explanation for the improvement that we hope to find in the second experiment.

	total matches found on corpus (n=1399)	correct matches found[6] on Gold Standard (n=200)
lexical matching	582	65 (=32%)
FOAM	696	41 (=20%)
Falcon-AO	683	28 (=14%)

Fig. 6. Results of the lexical matching experiment

A manual analysis revealed that around 260 concepts in the OLVG list (i.e. 19% of the corpus) have a large lexical overlap with concepts in the AMC list. The figures in the table show that both FOAM and our lexical matching method finds a comparable percentage of correct matches. A possible explanation for the fact that our method scores a higher percentage of correctness (32%) than the estimated lexical overlap (19%) is that the Gold Standard is slightly biased towards frequently occurring problems (see the description of the creation of the Gold Standard in the previous section), for which the lexical overlap can be higher.

The LMO module of Falcon-AO retrieves much fewer of correct matches. The most likely explanation of this effect is that Falcon-AO limits itself to 1-1 matches, preventing

[6] These figures are the numbers of correct matches on those matches for which the Gold Standard contained an answer.

many plausible partial matches. This is illustrated by the following example matches produced by Falcon-AO on our case-study data:

```
OLVG#Oesofagus_perforatie ↦ AMC#Oesofagus ruptuur
OLVG#Oesophagus_resectie  ↦ AMC#Oesofagus perforatie
```

although both by themselves reasonable, together these matches prevent the obvious match

```
OLVG#Oesofagus_perforatie ↦ AMC#Oesofagus perforatie
```

because Falcon limits itself to 1-1 matches: both of these terms are already part of another match. The obvious solution would be to allow terms to participate in multiple matches, producing an n-m matching as done by our lexical method.

6.2 Experiment 2: Semantic Matching

In the first step of semantic matching OLVG and AMC concepts are anchored into the DICE background ontology.

Experiment 2: Semantic matching, anchoring step. When anchoring the OLVG vocabularies to DICE, we used the lexical technique described earlier, and we found in total 549 of OLVG concepts anchored to DICE concepts, via 1298 anchors.

For anchoring the AMC vocabulary to DICE we used a combined expert- and automatic approach. An expert manually established 4568 DICE-anchors for the AMC vocabulary. We enhanced these anchor matches using the lexical matching technique and found a further 1248 new anchors, which increased the amount of anchors to a total of 5816, anchoring a total of 1404 concepts.

Notice that the anchorings are many-to-many relations: a single term from source or target vocabulary can have multiple anchor terms in DICE, either in a single or in different aspect taxonomies. Table 7 shows how many terms were anchored, and how often our lexical heuristics were able to establish anchorings to multiple DICE aspect taxonomies. Such anchoring in multiple aspects is important, because it will enable the inference step to use multiple DICE taxonomies to infer potential semantic matchings.

	OLVG	AMC
anchored on 5 DICE aspects	0	2
anchored on 4 DICE aspects	0	198
anchored on 3 DICE aspects	4	711
anchored on 2 DICE aspects	144	285
anchored on 1 DICE aspect	401	208
total nr. of anchored terms	549 (=39%)	1404 (=96%)
total nr. of anchoring relations	1298	5816[7]

Fig. 7. Results of the anchoring step in our experiment

[7] = 4568 manually + 1248 by lexical matching.

Table 7 shows that our simple lexical heuristics succeeded in constructing anchors for 39% of the OLVG vocabulary. This indicates that indeed our weak lexical heuristics are able to establish anchorings, to be used in the second step of our approach. The high percentage of anchoring for the AMC vocabulary is due to the contribution of the manually constructed anchors.

Figure 8 details how the anchors are distributed over the five DICE aspects (separate taxonomies). It shows that the anchors are very unevenly distributed over the various aspects (with only three anchors established from the OLVG vocabulary to aspect hierarchy on body-systems), and a similarly uneven relative contribution between expert-created and lexically found anchors across the different aspects (with again the body-systems aspect producing very few lexical anchors for the AMC vocabulary).

	AMC list			OLVG list
Aspect	Expert-manual	Additional lexical	Total	Lexical
Abnormality	1168	271	1439	354
Action taken	292	122	414	109
Body system	1217	2	1219	3
Location	1336	721	2057	255
Cause	555	132	687	60
	4568	1248	5816	781

Fig. 8. Distribution of anchors over the different DICE aspect taxonomies

Experiment 2: Semantic matching, inference step. In the second step, relationships between anchors in DICE are used to infer matches between source and target terms. As a result of this matching, a matching AMC term was derived for 538 OLVG terms. Of these, 413 matches were based on inference in a single DICE aspect, while 135 matches were supported by inference in two aspects (i.e. the inference in two DICE taxonomies produced support for the same match).

Evaluation against the Gold Standard The evaluation of semantic matches against the Gold Standard is made more complicated by the fact that the n-m anchors can also produce n-m matches between source and target vocabularies. When a single OLVG concept matches with multiple concepts in the AMC vocabulary, we ranked the matchings as follows:

1. If the match corresponds to a direct, lexical equivalence, it is ranked highest in the result set.
2. The remaining matches, were ranked according to the number of DICE aspect taxonomies that supported the match
3. Matches based on the same number of DICE aspects, were ranked according to the number of equivalence matches on DICE properties (ie preferring equivalences over part-of, contained-in, type-of, etc).

We assess the performance of our method on the Gold Standard containing human created matches for a random set of 200 OLVG concepts. For 69 concepts, our method produced the same results as the expert, proposing the matched AMC concept as a single best candidate. For 4 concepts, our method found the expert match in the first five suggested matches. For 43 concepts, neither our method, nor the expert produced any matching. For 50 concepts matched by the expert our method did not produce any, or produced matches of low confidence. For the remaining 34 concepts, the matches produced by our method were different from those by the expert. Manual inspection revealed that our method produced either new matches for which the expert did not produce any, but that did seem plausible, or other matches that seem a refinement of the proposed expert matches.

These figures are summarised in the table in Figure 9, including the results for the lexical approach reported already in Figure 6 above. This summary shows that on such semantically impoverished vocabularies as in our case-study, the use of semantic background knowledge as part of the matching can substantially improve both the number of matches found and the quality of these matches, as compared to either a purely lexical technique, or as compared to existing tools that, in the absence of any structure in the source and target vocabulary, default to lexical matching only.

7 Conclusion

We explored the use of a semantically rich background knowledge in semantic matching of semantically poor concept lists. We provided empirical evidence that background knowledge can improve the matching process considerably. The use of a background knowledge source is the only way to discover matches, when there is no terminological, instance or structural match between the matching ontologies.

Work by [5] has already shown the usefulness of simple background knowledge in the form of the WordNet hierarchy. We extended the method of [5] by using a much

	Semantic matching	Own Lexical matching	FOAM	Falcon-AO
agreement on single best match	69 (=35%)	65	35	22
agreement among top 5 matches	4 (= 2%)			
agreement on no match possible	43 (=22%)	43	26	32
improvement over expert match	34 (=19%)	8	6	6
TOTAL POSITIVE:	**150(=75%)**	**116 (=58%)**	**67 (=33%)**	**60 (=30%)**
wrong match found		5	47	78
incorrectly found no match	50(=25%)	79	86	62
TOTAL NEGATIVE:	**50(=25%)**	**84 (=42%)**	**133 (=67%)**	**140 (=70%)**

Fig. 9. Summary of evaluation on Gold Standard (n=200)

richer source of background knowledge. This enabled us to reason across multiple hierarchies in the background knowledge, and made it possible to discover relations between concepts which were not directly related in a subsumption relation.

8 Future Work

In future work we will focus upon testing with ontologies of larger size. Such tests can provide for stronger evidence whether this method can be successfully applied to the ontology integration problem. We are currently setting up experiments on mapping the anatomical subhierarchies of CRISP and MeSH, while using FMA as the background knowledge source, and using parts of the UMLS metathesaurus as the Gold Standard. To test for applicability in other domains, we are setting up similar experiments in the music domain. The goal in this case will be matching classes of music entities such as genres, while using rich background knowledge ontology extracted from Wikipedia[8] .

An interesting further question is how the number and quality of matches found increases with a growth in background knowledge. We are currently performing experiments on the same case-study from this paper (mapping the OLVG and AMC unstructured vocabularies), but while using increasingly more background knowledge. We are currently redoing the experiments from this paper, but by adding such sources as ICD10 and MeSH as background knowledge besides DICE.

Acknowledgements

This research was partly supported by the Netherlands Organisation for Scientific Research (NWO) under project number 634.000.020. We wish to thank to the expert for providing the reference matches and the OLVG and AMC hospitals for providing us with the lists.

References

1. Rahm, E., Bernstein, P.A.: A Survey of Approaches to Automatic Schema Matching. VLDB Journal **10**(4) (2001)
2. Doan, A., Madhavan, J., Domingos, P., Halevy, A.: Learning to Map Between Ontologies on the Semantic Web. In: WWW '02: Proceedings of the Eleventh International Conference on World Wide Web, ACM Press (2002) 662–673
3. Noy, N.F., Musen, M.A.: PROMPT: Algorithm and Tool for Automated Ontology Merging and Alignment. In: Proceedings of the Seventeenth National Conference on Artificial Intelligence (AAAI-2000), Austin, TX, AAAI/MIT Press (2000)
4. McGuinness, D.L., Fikes, R., Rice, J., Wilder, S.: The Chimaera Ontology Environment. In: Proceedings of the Seventeenth National Conference on Artificial Intelligence and Twelfth Conference on Innovative Applications of Artificial Intelligence, AAAI Press / The MIT Press (2000) 1123–1124
5. Bouquet, P., Serafini, L., Zanobini, S.: Semantic coordination: A new approach and an application. Technical report, University of Trento (2003)
6. Euzenat, J., Bach, T.L., Barrasa, J., Bouquet, P., Bo, J.D., Dieng, R., Ehrig, M., Hauswirth, M., Jarrar, M., Lara, R., Maynard, D., Napoli, A., Stamou, G., Stuckenschmidt, H., Shvaiko, P., Tessaris, S., Acker, S.V., Zaihrayeu, I.: Survey of scalability techniques for reasoning with ontologies. KnowledgeWeb Project deliverable D2.1.1 (2004)

[8] http://wikipedia.org/

7. de Bruijn, J., Martin-Recuerda, F., Manov, D., Ehrig, M.: D4.2.1 state-of-the-art-survey on ontology merging and aligning v1. SEKT Project deliverable D4.2.1 (2004)
8. Guarino, N., Masolo, C., Vetere, G.: Ontoseek: Content-based access to the web. IEEE Intelligent Systems 1094-7167/99 (1999)
9. Ichise, R., Takeda, H., Honiden, S.: Integrating multiple internet directories by instance-based learning. In: Proceedings of the eighteenth International Joint Conference on Artificial Intelligence. (2003)
10. Schlobach, S.: Semantic clarification by pinpointing. In: Proceedings of the second European Semantic Web conference, LNCS. Springer Verlag (2004)
11. Ehrig, M., Sure, Y.: Foam - framework for ontology alignment and mapping; results of the ontology alignment initiative. In Ashpole, B., Ehrig, M., Euzenat, J., Stuckenschmidt, H., eds.: Proceedings of the Workshop on Integrating Ontologies. Volume 156., CEUR-WS.org (2005) 72–76
12. Jian, N., Hu, W., Cheng, G., Qu, Y.: Falcon-ao: Aligning ontologies with falcon. In: K-Cap 2005 Workshop on Integrating Ontologies. (2005)
13. Euzenat, J., Stuckenschmidt, H., Yatskevich, M.: Introduction to the ontology alignment evaluation 2005. Technical report (2005)
14. Giunchiglia, F., Shvaiko, P., Yatskevich, M.: S-match: an algorithm and an implementation of semantic matching. In: Proceedings of the European Semantic Web Symposium (ESWC). (2004) 61–75
15. Gusfield, D.: Algorithms on Strings, Trees, and Sequences: Computer Science and Computational Biology. Cambridge University Press; 1st edition (1997)

Distributed Multi-contextual Ontology Evolution – A Step Towards Semantic Autonomy

Maciej Zurawski

CISA, School of Informatics, The University of Edinburgh,
Room 4.12, Appleton Tower, 11 Crichton Street
EH8 9LE, Edinburgh, United Kingdom
m.zurawski@sms.ed.ac.uk

Abstract. In today's world there is a need for knowledge infrastructures that can support several autonomous knowledge bases all using different ontologies and constantly adapting these to their changing local needs. Moreover, these different knowledge bases are expressing their unique points of view and constitute different local contexts. At the same time interoperability is needed in order to connect these semantically dispersed knowledge bases, and we formalized this as a type of consistency. Both these aspects are included in our definition of semantic autonomy. We present a layered framework that shows how to design a scalable system having this property. In our approach both ontology and mapping evolution take place, at the same time as the whole system is kept coherent using lightweight methods for maintaining global consistency. However, in order to achieve this several restrictions are necessary and the logical language used by the individual ontologies is kept simple. Finally, we present some experimental results that demonstrate the scalability of our approach.

1 Introduction and Motivation

Knowledge infrastructures represent codified knowledge of some domain, and if that domain is decentralized and there is no central authority governing over it, then the functionality of the knowledge infrastructure must work in a corresponding way. It will consist of several autonomous knowledge-bases that can initiate changes in their individual semantic models, i.e. ontologies.

This functionality is included in our definition of semantic autonomy (see Table 1 for a general specification – the technical solution itself is described in this paper). Some researchers [1] have argued why semantic autonomy is important, but without formalizing it to a bigger extent. We [2] have described how important this property is for an organizational distributed knowledge management system (DKMS). It has also been argued that one should model the social *process* of creating meaning in a distributed scenario [3], and we fully agree. In general, the framework that is presented here is useful in scenarios when there is a confined environment (e.g. an

S. Staab and V. Svatek (Eds.): EKAW 2006, LNAI 4248, pp. 198 – 213, 2006.

organizational knowledge infrastructure) and it consists of several autonomous units (e.g. organizational divisions). It is currently not applicable to the whole web (nor semantic web) as such, but only to confined parts of it, e.g. intranets or extranets where the semantics are formally defined, and where the amount of autonomous parts is limited to a small number.

Many approaches assume that several knowledge bases must use the same ontology, or re-use certain ontological fragments. These approaches are therefore more semantically centralized. However, the other extreme view - to gather several knowledge bases and to simply allow full inconsistency or to leave the connections between knowledge bases completely undefined, is neither satisfactory because the semantics are too detached from each other and it becomes difficult to talk about *one* infrastructure.

This paper gives a brief overview of a framework that balances these requirements and makes semantic autonomy (as defined here) possible, and we also present initial experimental results. The described framework can be seen as a *specification* of a knowledge infrastructure.

1.1 Novel Contribution

We are describing an ontology-based framework that specifies a knowledge infrastructure and formalizes semantic autonomy (as defined in Table 1) using these four aspects:

1. Distributed multi-contextual state-based semantics (i.e. a particular logic).
2. Distributed ontology evolution (i.e. an explicit *change process*).
3. Distributed mapping evolution (i.e. an explicit *change process*).
4. The distributed explicit *process of initiating* change.

in **one** framework. The reason for this is that we believe that all these four aspects are essential when defining and implementing semantic autonomy (although alternative approaches might be developed in the future for other scenarios). There is for example related work in the field of multi-agent systems that of course focuses on aspect 4, but perhaps not on aspects 1-3 at the same time. There is work in logic that is related to aspect 1 but doesn't include aspects 2-4 (see the section about related research). We have to stress at the same time that we have done

Table 1. The basic definition of semantic autonomy

The basic definition of *Semantic autonomy* requires these properties to hold:
1. The local contexts have the freedom to propose a change in their local ontology (i.e. the ontology of the local context).
2. The system does "in some way" maintain global ontological consistency.
3. The ontological language is dynamic and open-ended (i.e. not confined by a pre-defined set) but there is a knowledge source that can provide knowledge about this language.

simplifications and adopted some restrictions in order to make this integration possible, and we expect more elaborate integrated solutions to appear in the future.

2 Introduction to the Framework

Before we describe the framework and its layers in detail, we will clarify the basic terminology and show a motivating example. The framework describes that a certain local context can make a proposal to change its ontology or its ontology mappings to the ontologies of other local contexts. This theoretical framework could for example specify the distributed knowledge infrastructure of an organization, and every division in the organization would then correspond to a local context. Every local context has its own *ontology*. The ontologies that the current system supports are actually simple and can be visualized as *graphs* where very every node corresponds to a logical *concept* and every edge to an *ontological relation* (currently we define four different ones)[1]. Every *ontology mapping* between two ontologies (currently we define five different ones) can be visualized as an edge that connects the nodes of two different graphs. Another interesting property is that adding a certain ontology mapping to the whole system could introduce a logical contradiction, and in that case we could mark a subgraph within the network of the whole system that localizes the contradicted area.

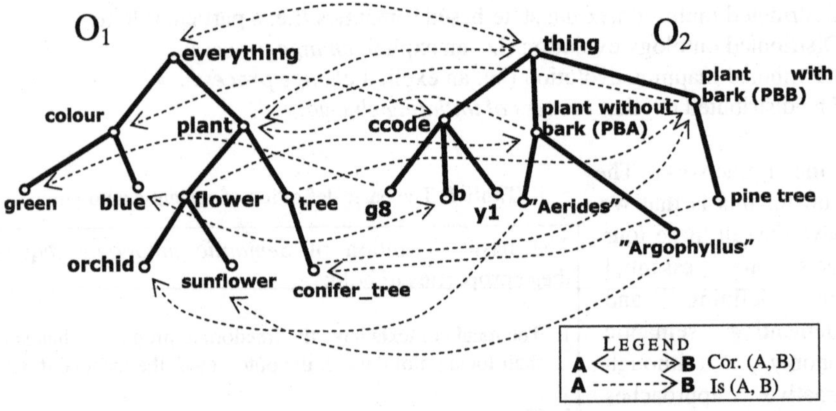

Fig. 1. The ontologies of two local contexts and some mappings between them

Figure 1 above shows an example of two local contexts and their ontologies. The dark edges within the ontologies are subsumption relations, whereas the dotted lines visualize the ontology mappings (two ontology mapping types are shown here: correspondence and the IS-mapping). Let us now conceive that the first local context

[1] This is just slightly more complex than taxonomies, that would just contain one relation type, namely submsupmtion.

initiates the proposal to add a new concept, e.g. **yellow** that actually is a type of **colour**. The framework mechanism should then consider this proposal and *formally investigate* its consequences. As the next step, the framework accepts these changes and then the first local context initiates a proposal to add an ontology mapping between **yellow** and e.g. **ccode** in the other ontology. Then both the framework mechanism has to formally investigate the consequences and the *opinions* of both local contexts have to be taken into account, before a potential change is made. Let us now look at the framework in general.

3 The Framework and Its Layers

Our framework consists of five layers (see fig. 2). The two bottom layers represent the assumptions whereas the three top layers constitute the executable system itself (they are the main focus of this paper). We will now describe the whole framework going from the top down (the reader that instead first would like to see the formal logical assumptions at the bottom should first read section 3.4).We will use a notation that allows these three types of statements:

- *entity*: *Predicate* (*parameters*) where (1)

entity=c_i | F (c_i is local context *i* and F the framework mechanism)

- *Predicate* (*parameters*) (2)
  (this has one of the two following values: {true, false})
- *statement1* ⇒ *statement2* (this is the definition of *rule*) where (3)

statement1= *entity*: *Predicate* (*parameters*) |

CNF$_j$(*entity*$_j$: *Predicate* (*parameters*$_j$)) ∧ *Predicate*(*parameters*)

statement2= *rule*$_1$ | *rule*$_1$ or *rule*$_2$ | *rule*$_1$ or *rule*$_2$ or rule$_3$ | *statement*$_1$

We will call the three types of statement type 1, 2 and 3 respectively. The first type of statement means that *entity* makes *Predicate* (*parameters*) true (we will specify if this in response to something, or if it by its own decision). The second statement type means that *Predicate*(*parameters*) returns its global truth value. The third type of statement is a rule where if *statement1* has been made true, then *statement2* by necessity automatically made true. If *entity* has made *statement1* false, then *statement2* is not made true. **CNF**$_j$(exp$_j$) means conjunctive normal form that can contain exp$_1$, exp$_2$, ... etc. If *statement2* is a disjunction of several rules, then they are investigated sequentially until one of them can be activated.

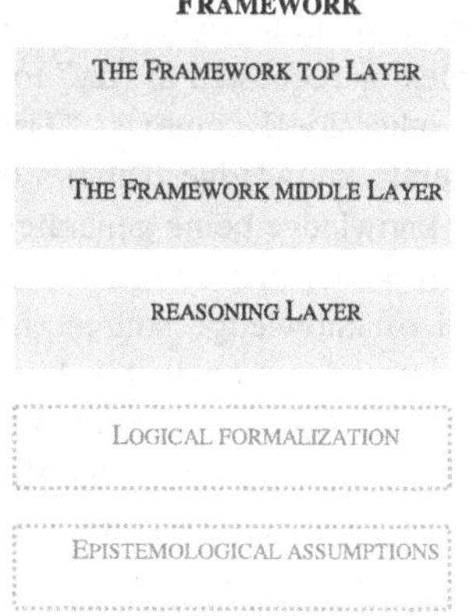

Fig. 2. Our framework

Some elements of this formalism have been inspired by [4], that however has much more expressive semantics. One short-coming of our formalism is that that message passing between entities is implicit.

3.1 The Framework Top Layer

The framework top layer describes the policy of how the system is to be used, and it describes constraints on which sequences of middle layer operations that are possible or obligatory. The whole system S consists of n different local contexts, their ontologies and the mappings between them. Firstly, any local context can *initiate* the synchronization processes of the whole framework by the following type 1 statement, assuming that the framework mechanism is in "waiting mode":

c_i: PROPOSE (ont_op), where $i \in \{1,..,n\}$

This statement means that c_i proposes to perform operation *ont_op*. So this is the formal sense in which the local contexts can exercise their semantic autonomy.

After this statement is invoked, the framework mechanism invokes the corresponding the procedural rules of the Middle Layer and that layer (as will be described later) in turn invokes the logical calculations of the Reasoning Layer. During this execution the framework mechanism is in "busy mode", and when it has finished and applied all the invoked rules of the lower layers, it goes back to "waiting mode". Consequently, the system can process one proposal a time. The top layer has these type 2 and type 1 statements:

NEWCONCEPT(d_j) that is true iff d_j was created in the previous state
F: REQUEST(c_i : PROPOSE (ont_op))

And this vocabulary is utilized in this conditional rule:

F: DO $(add\_ontorel(m, c_j, d_j))$ $\wedge$ NEWCONCEPT(d_j) $\Rightarrow$
F: REQUEST(c_j : PROPOSE(add_mapping(m, d_j, c_k))
where $k \in \{1,..,n\} \wedge k \neq j$

This means that if an ontology relation m has actually been created within the local context j and it connects a new concept d_j (to an existing concept c_j) then that local context is requested to "try" to generate proposals that would map this new concept to the other local contexts. "Try" means that it has to ask the knowledge source to generate knowledge that fits that pattern, and sometimes that will actually result in this knowledge being generated.

Proposals that describe relationships between two local contexts come from this kind of knowledge source (i.e. some kind of momentary shared understanding of these two local contexts). In reality a human is often this source of knowledge. An important question is if this knowledge source has to be a perfect oracle. The answer is no. We only assume that this knowledge source most often is able to codify some aspects of the domain, and that it *sometimes* commits errors. Because our framework allows for both creating and deleting ontology mappings and relations, it is well-suited for this situation, because the errors can be repaired. Also, proposals of change only within one local context, can be said to only require a local "knowledge source" (i.e. no shared understanding).

3.2 The Framework Middle Layer

Let us now look at the formalization of the middle layer. There is a set of local contexts c_i (i=1…n), and the set of ontology operations is the same as defined within the reasoning layer. This vocabulary will be used for defining this layer (and also some of the functionality of the reasoning layer):

c_i : CONFIRM (*ont_op*)
c_i : REFUSE (*ont_op*)
F: DO (*ont_op*)
F: COMM(*message*, *recipient*)
F: MCHOICE($\{c_j, c_k, \ldots\}$, ont_op_1, ont_op_2)

The CONFIRM() and REFUSE() commands are used together with some ontology operations, only when the framework mechanism is *asking* the local contexts about their opinions as regards certain changes and the local contexts *respond* (this is formalized within the MCHOICE command below).

The second set of statements can only be initiated by the framework mechanism itself. DO() is the statement executed by the framework mechanism when it actually performs an ontology operation. **It is actually the DO() statement that moves the whole system S to the next state** – simple because it changes S. COMM() is used when the framework mechanism sends a *message* to a *recipient* that must be a local context c_i. MCHOICE() is a choice between two mutually exclusive statements (e.g. *do* an ontology operation) that is done involving a set of local contexts (at least two) and sent back to the framework mechanism. The formalization below says that if all involved local contexts choose one of the ontology operations, then that becomes their joint choice, and if there is some disagreement then the joint choice is "nothing" (i.e. no change is done).

$$\text{F: MCHOICE}(\{c_j, c_k, \ldots), stat_1, stat_2) \Rightarrow$$
$$\left(\left(\bigwedge_{n=\{j,k,\ldots\}} c_n\text{: CONFIRM}(stat_i)\right) \wedge i \in \{1,2\} \Rightarrow stat_i\right) or$$
$$\left(i \in \{1,2\} \wedge \bigvee_{n=\{j,k,\ldots\}} c_n\text{: REFUSE}(stat_i) \wedge \bigvee_{n=\{j,k,\ldots\}} c_n\text{: CONFIRM}(stat_i) \Rightarrow DO(\varepsilon)\right)$$

We will now investigate in detail the special case when a local context initiates a proposal to add a mapping to another local context.

Case 1
This statement in the beginning of the rule means: a local context c_j is proposing to add a mapping from its ontology to another local context c_k. The reasoning layer decides which of the three rules that are actually activated.

$$c_j: \text{PROPOSE(add\_mapping}(m, c_j, c_k)) \Rightarrow$$

$$\left(\begin{array}{l} \text{F: C\_CONTRA(S, add\_mapping}(m, c_j, c_k)) \Rightarrow \\ \text{F: COMM("contradicted:"+F: CREASON(S, add\_mapping}(m, c_j, c_k)), c_j) \wedge \\ \text{F: MCHOICE}(\{c_j, c_k, \ldots\}, DO(\varepsilon), \\ \quad DO(\text{RC(S,CREASON(S, add\_mapping}(m, c_j, c_k))))) \end{array}\right) or$$

$$\left(\begin{array}{l} \text{F: IS\_INFERABLE(S, add\_mapping}(m, c_j, c_k)) \Rightarrow \\ \text{F: COMM("already\_known"}, c_j) \wedge \\ \text{F: MCHOICE}(\{c_j, c_k, \ldots\}, DO(\varepsilon), DO(\text{add\_mapping}(m, c_j, c_k))) \end{array}\right) or$$

$$\left(\begin{array}{l} \text{F: IS\_NEW(S, add\_mapping}(m, c_j, c_k)) \Rightarrow \\ \text{F: COMM("new"}, c_j) \wedge \\ \text{F: MCHOICE}(\{c_j, c_k, \ldots\}, DO(\varepsilon), DO(\text{add\_mapping}(m, c_j, c_k))) \end{array}\right)$$

Intuitively, this formalization says that if the proposed change would introduce a contradiction, then either nothing is done or one of the reasons for the contradiction is removed (but without adding the proposed mapping within the same step). Notice that all local contexts that have ontologies where one of the contradictions resides, have to participate in making this decision (this situation is referred to as "All involved" below). In the case that the mapping can already be inferred or is new, the change is allowed but the two local contexts involved have to decide if they actually want to have it performed (this situation is referred to as "Pair" below).

Table 2. A classification that summarizes how proposals to perform any of the four ontology operations are dealt with, i.e. c_j: PROPOSE(*ont_op*)

ont_op=	**C_CONTRA() is true**	**IS_INFERABLE() is true**	**IS_NEW() is true**
add_mapping(m, c_j, c_k)	All involved	Pair	Pair
delete_mapping(m, c_j, c_k)	N/A	Pair	N/A
add_ontorel(m, c_j, c_j)	All involved	Individual	Individual
delete_ontorel(m, cj, cj)	N/A	Individual	N/A

Now we have investigated the case when the proposal is to add a mapping between two ontologies, and the formalization showed what happens in the three cases.

Table 2 above summarizes how this formalization would look like to for the cases when the proposal is to delete an ontology mapping, or add or delete an ontology relation.

The term "individual" in the table means that the local context that created the proposal, can decide itself if it wants the logically allowed change to *actually* be performed. "N/A" in the table means that within our framework that situation cannot happen. More precisely, if the proposal is to delete a mapping or delete a relation within an ontology this always logically allowed, so the individual local context or the pair of contexts decide about if to actually perform this act. Note however that this policy is allowing for individual ontologies that are not always singly connected. The Framework Middle layer is dependent on the functionality of the reasoning layer.

3.3 The Reasoning Layer

The reasoning layer performs logical calculations and it is used for analyzing what hypothetical changes to ontologies or mappings would have resulted in. We will fully describe its *functionality*, but only briefly mention the reasoning algorithms themselves – they are not the focus of this paper (instead, see [6]). The operations at this level are for example necessary in order to verify if certain ontological changes will maintain the consistency of the system or break it. Other operations are used to calculate if certain changes would add redundant knowledge to the system. This layer should have good algorithmic complexity, i.e. be scalable. Experimental verification (see section 4) shows that our implementation is scalable (given certain assumptions).

The reasoning layer contains the ability to calculate the truth value of certain predicates, and all of them return some kind of answer. The framework mechanism is responsible for making these three type 1 statements true or false and one statement that is actually a function (and not defined in our current grammar):

F: C_CONTRA(*S*, *ont_op*) - One of these values is returned: {true, false}
F: IS_INFERABLE(*S*, *ont_op*) - One of these values is returned: {true, false}
F: IS_NEW(*S*, *ont_op*) - One of these values is returned: {true, false}
F: CREASON(*S*, *ont_op*) - A subset of *S* is returned

Their meaning is the following. C_CONTRA(*S*, *ont_op*) returns true if the *ont_op* ontology operation (these are defined below) would have introduced a contradiction (in the system S) if it would have been performed. Otherwise it returns false. IS_INFERABLE(*S*, *ont_op*) returns true if the *ont_op* ontology operation would have introduced an entity (mapping between ontologies or relation within an ontology) that already can be inferred from the existing structure S. This means that a redundancy would have been introduced. Otherwise it returns false.

In the case when C_CONTRA(*S*, *ont_op*) is true, CREASON(*S*, *ont_op*) returns one of the contradiction reason, i.e. one of the minimal subsets in the whole system S that show that S with the *ont_op* performed creates a contradiction. These subsets can be seen as "minimal proofs" and there must be at least one of them for a contradiction to be detected. The *ont_op* together with one of these minimal subsets is similar to what [5] call "Minimal inconsistent subontology" in the case of a singular ontology.

The meaning of IS_NEW() is the following (using standard logical notation):

IS_NEW(*S*, *ont_op*) $\leftrightarrow \neg$ C_CONTRA(*S*, *ont_op*) $\wedge \neg$ IS_INFERABLE(*S*, *ont_op*)
The current list of operations that evolve ontologies or mappings between them is the following (and the second mentions a special ontology operation):

ont_op = add_mapping(m, c_j, c_k) | add_ontorel(m, c_j, d_j) |
delete_mapping(m, c_j, c_k) | delete_ontorel(m, c_j, d_j) | ε
spec_ont_op= RC(*S*, *P*) [where $P \subseteq S$]

RC() is the whole system S that remains after one of the inconsistent subsets P (that can include concepts from ontologies of several local contexts) has been removed. Note, that if there are several alternative such inconsistent subsets, several of them might have to be removed in order to make the whole system S consistent.

Because of limited space we will not investigate the reasoning algorithms in detail in this paper. Instead, we have chosen to do a balanced overview of the whole framework. However, we have adopted the approach from [6] in order to do efficient and complete reasoning using this inexpressive language. We will now only mention a short summary. The logical meaning of every ontology mapping actually uses first-order logic and that defines relationships between concepts in different local context and how this relationship will persist in future states. However, that representation is transformed to one only using propositions, and C_CONTRA () and IS_INFERABLE() are implemented building refutation proof trees that use caching, loop-prevention and metareasoning.

3.4 The Logical Formalization

We will now briefly say something about the formalization of the ontology mappings and ontology relations. Because we model different cognitive perspectives that are expressed by different ontologies, and define ontology mappings between them, we have been informally inspired by the five ontology mappings proposed by [7] in the context-sensitive version of OWL, namely C-OWL. However, the *actual* semantics are different and are defined in this section ([6] gives more details about their practical usage). One important thing to notice is that there are several domain models ($D_{i,m}$), and they have two indexes: one for describing the state and the other the local context. Our earlier notion of *concept* in an ontology *j* is now actually formalised as a predicate $P_j()$. The formalization below allows the use of instances, but for reasons of simplification these are not yet modelled in the presented framework.

Defining the formal semantics

A proposition $P_i(a_i, b_i, \ldots)$ is a formula in local context c_i (in a state s_m).

A model **M** for a set of languages $L_{i,m}$ (m=0, 1, … and this corresponds to the states s_0, s_1, …, and i=0, 1, … and this corresponds to local contexts c_0, c_1, …) consists of a set of domains $D_{i,m}$ (that are non-empty sets, and m=0, 1, … and i=0, 1, …) and a set of interpretation functions $I_{i,m}$ (m=0, 1, … and i=0, 1, …) which are defined on the set of instances and predicate names in the vocabulary of $L_{i,m}$ and adhere to the following rules:

If b_i is an constant in $L_{i,m}$ then $I_{i,m}(b_i) \in D_{i,m}$
If P_i is an n-ary predicate name in $L_{i,m}$, then $I_{i,m}(P_i) \in D_{i,m}{}^n$.

The truth value of any possible formula is defined in this way (we implicitly assume that the truth valuation function $V_{i,m}$ uses the model **M**):

If $P_i(a_i, b_i, \ldots)$ is an atomic sentence in $L_{i,m}$ (i.e. the language of local context c_i in state s_m), then $V_{i,m}[P_i(a_i, b_i, \ldots)] = 1$ if and only if $\langle I_{i,m}(a_i), I_{i,m}(b_i), \ldots \rangle \in I_{i,m}(P_i)$ and $V_{i,m}[P_i(a_i, b_i, \ldots)] = 0$ if and only if $\langle I_{i,m}(a_i), I_{i,m}(b_i), \ldots \rangle \notin I_{i,m}(P_i)$.
Given a formula having the form $R_i \wedge Q_i$ in the state s_m, its truth value $V_{i,m}[R_i \wedge Q_i] = 1$ iff $V_{i,m}[R_i] = 1$ and $V_{i,m}[Q_i] = 1$ $V_{i,m}[R_i \wedge Q_i] = 0$ otherwise
Given a formula having the form $R_i \vee Q_i$ in the state s_m, its truth value $V_{i,m}[R_i \vee Q_i] = 1$ iff $V_{i,m}[R_i] = 1$ or $V_{i,m}[Q_i] = 1$ $V_{i,m}[R_i \vee Q_i] = 0$ otherwise
The truth value of $V_{j,m}[P_i(a_{in_1}, a_{in_2}, \ldots)]$ is undefined iff j≠i.

In order to simplify the formalism, we will use first-order logic when defining the ontology mappings and those definitions will internally utilise the valuation-functions above. This means that the mappings as such have a logical objective existence, although they map between different local (subjective) models. It would have been possible to investigate if the mappings as well should only have local existence, e.g. only exist within the local contexts (see for example [9]), but this would have made the formalism more complex. Instead, in this paper we want to focus on the dynamic aspects of the system and it is therefore more important that a certain local context is *responsible* for having proposed that a certain mapping is created (and this is not visible in the formal semantics as such).

Therefore, we will now use first-order logic and assume (for reasons of simplicity) that there is a domain D that contains all the local domains $D_{i,m}$ (*i* traverses all local contexts, and *m* traverses all existing states). There is a set of states T, and a relationship $L(s_x, s_y)$ that means that a state s_y succeeds a state s_x (L() is transitive, antisymmetric and irreflexive).

We then introduce the Rel() operator. Assuming we choose a fixed state s, then the domains $D_{1,s}$, $D_{2,s}$, …, actually overlap sometimes, and this is therefore the definition of Rel():

[in state *s*] $\mathrm{Rel}(b_i, d_j)=1$ iff $I_{i,s}(b_i)=e_1$ and $I_{j,s}(d_j)=e_2$ and $e_1=e_2$

Also, because the domains $D_{1,s}$, $D_{2,s}$, …, actually overlap, we can view them as subsets as of a domain D_s – i.e. what is true in a given state *s* independently of what the local contexts can see is true. However, we never use the domain D_s to create a centralised knowledge representation as such (these epistemological assumptions are briefly discussed in section 3.5).

We now introduce some symbols and they are used as quantifiers over many states, when expressing ontology mappings (i.e. they are a type of practical abbreviations).

$G_r(exp)$ iff $\forall(s'\in S)(L(r,s')\rightarrow exp|_{z=s'})$

$F_r(exp)$ iff $\exists(s'\in S)(L(r,s')\wedge exp|_{z=s'})$

$N_r(exp)$ iff $exp|_{z=r}$

We use the notation $exp|_{z=s'}$ to mean that in the expression *exp* we have substituted all occurrences of *z* with *s'*.

Let us now look at the ontology mappings. From a formal point of view, these mappings have an objective existence (given the domain D) and they can be seen as constraints on the model **M**.

These are the five potential ontology mappings between a concept A in ontology *i* and a concept B in ontology *j*:

COR(A_i, B_j)
IS (A_i, B_j)
IS2 (A_i, B_j)
DISJOINT (A_i, B_j)
COMPATIBLE (A_i, B_j)

COR(A_i, B_j) that is created in the state *r* is defined as:

$$N_r(\forall x_i, y_j(\mathrm{Rel}(x_i, y_j)\rightarrow V_{i,z}(A_i(x_i))=V_{j,z}(B_j(y_j))))\wedge$$
$$G_r(\forall x_i, y_j(\mathrm{Rel}(x_i, y_j)\rightarrow V_{i,z}(A_i(x_i))=V_{j,z}(B_j(y_j))))$$

IS (A_i, B_j) that is created in the state *r* is defined as:

$$N_r(\forall x_i, y_j(\mathrm{Rel}(x_i, y_j)\rightarrow (V_{i,z}(A_i(x_i))=0\vee V_{j,z}(B_j(y_j))=1)))\wedge$$
$$G_r(\forall x_i, y_j(\mathrm{Rel}(x_i, y_j)\rightarrow (V_{i,z}(A_i(x_i))=0\vee V_{j,z}(B_j(y_j))=1)))$$

IS2 (A_i, B_j)= IS (B_j, A_i)

COMPATIBLE (A_i, B_j) that is created in the state r is defined as:
$$\boldsymbol{F_r}(\exists x_i, y_j(\text{Rel}(x_i, y_j) \wedge V_{i,z}(A_i(x_i)) = 1 \wedge V_{j,z}(B_j(y_j)) = 1))$$

DISJOINT (A_i, B_j) that is created in the state r is defined as:
$$\boldsymbol{N_r}(\forall x_i, y_j(\text{Rel}(x_i, y_j) \rightarrow \neg(V_{i,z}(A_i(x_i)) = 1 \wedge V_{j,z}(B_j(y_j)) = 1))) \wedge$$
$$\boldsymbol{G_r}(\forall x_i, y_j(\text{Rel}(x_i, y_j) \rightarrow \neg(V_{i,z}(A_i(x_i)) = 1 \wedge V_{j,z}(B_j(y_j)) = 1)))$$

For example COR() describes that in all future states two concepts from two different ontologies will have the same meaning, whereas IS() expresses subsumption across ontologies (that will persist in future states). COMPATIBLE() is a logically "weak" relation between two concepts.

Secondly, we will now mention the language for expressing the ontologies themselves (without showing a too detailed formalization). Yes, it shows big similarity with the language for ontology mappings (both types have semantics that use states), but this time they describe relationships between concepts *within* one ontology *j*.

OWL Axiom	Our notation
$[Cn_1] \doteq [Cn_2]$	COR(C_{1j}, C_{2j})
$[Cn]_1 \subseteq [Cn]_2$	IS (C_{1j}, C_{2j})
$[Cn]_1 \supseteq [Cn]_2$	IS2 (C_{1j}, C_{2j})
$[Cn]_1 \subseteq \neg[Cn]_2$	DISJOINT (C_{1j}, C_{2j})

The first of these relationships is equivalency between two concepts, the second means "is subsumed by", the next "subsumes" and the last one expresses disjointness.

If we assume that a certain relationship was created in a certain state *n*, then we can translate axioms written in OWL to our own notation, using the table above. [Cn] denotes a *concept name* in OWL.

3.5 The Epistemological Assumptions

The epistemological assumptions are that

- There is an objective notion of what is true (but it is not expressible directly).
- There are several points of view that only express fragments of the objective notion, and using their own language.
- Both the notion of what is true (in a given state in the domain model that is independent of the points of view but inexpressible directly) and what the points of view can see can *change*.

The first assumption implies that the logical domains of all local contexts (in a given state) are subsets of one bigger domain. However, the vocabulary is never allowed to utilize that big domain directly. Instead the vocabulary is only connected to the localized domains (this is the second assumption). The third assumption explains why in the logical formalization there is a domain model that has two indexes (for expressing both point of view and state).

4 Experiments Performed Using a Scenario

Until now we have used the generic notion of local contexts that express their particular points of view. When now looking at an experimental scenario we will imagine that these local contexts express the local views of *divisions* within an *organization.* In this experimental scenario we conceive an organization that has two divisions. Both of them invent concepts that are added to their own ontologies (because they have their "local" reasons for doing so) and then propose mappings between these new concepts and a concept in the other divisions' ontology (because they want to maintain organizational unity). Instead of doing a case-study and evaluating if our system is *usable* in particular real-world scenario, we have instead automatically generated several different cases randomly that have properties we expect are similar to real scenarios, and we have measured the average *scalability* of the system (i.e. performance when the problem size grows).

The concepts of an organization will be represented by two divisions (d_1 and d_2) that have ontologies consisting of subsumption trees where every node has at most three children. Both ontologies have the same size n – that is the number of ontological relations (in this example subsumption relations). We begin with n=1. Then we choose one division i ($i,k \in \{1,2\}$ $i \neq k$) that invokes the framework middle layer by initiating the statements

c_i : PROPOSE (Is ($C_{new,j}$, $C_{old,j}$)) - a proposal to change the ontology j
c_i : PROPOSE (add_mapping(m, c_i, c_k)) - a proposal to add a mapping from ontology j to k

where the following random choice is made (by our scenario generation mechanism):

m= COR(C_{1i}, C_{2k}) | IS (C_{1i}, C_{2k}) | IS2 (C_{1j}, C_{2k})
| DISJOINT (C_{1i}, C_{2k}) | COMPATIBLE (C_{1i}, C_{2k})

and the mechanism of the framework is invoked (with some modifications described below). We alternate this process by choosing i=1 and i=2 (i.e. one local context is making the proposals – the second being a proposal to the other local context - and then they change roles). Also, we measure the time it takes for the reasoning mechanism to respond to the invocation. We observe that after each accepted proposal an entity has been added to a division or to their mappings, so $n \leftarrow n+1$ happens then. We use the same framework mechanism as described in Case 1 (see page 6) in the section about the The Framework Middle Layer and its definitions of IS_INFERABLE() and IS_NEW(), with the only difference being this definition:

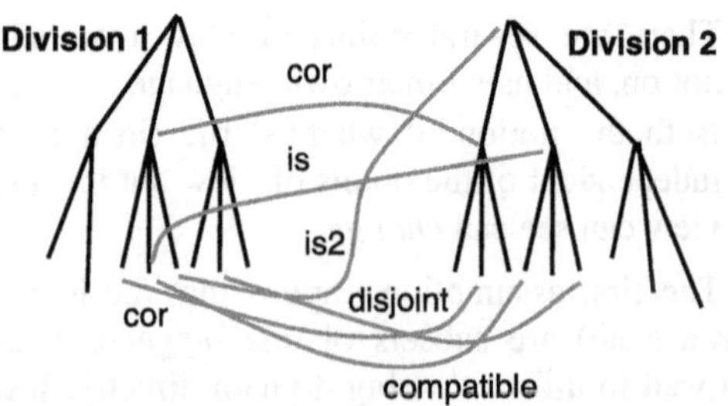

Fig. 3. A graphical example visualization of two ontologies in the experimental scenario, and mappings that connect them

F: C_CONTRA(S, add_mapping(m, c_j, c_k)) $\Rightarrow$ DO(ε)

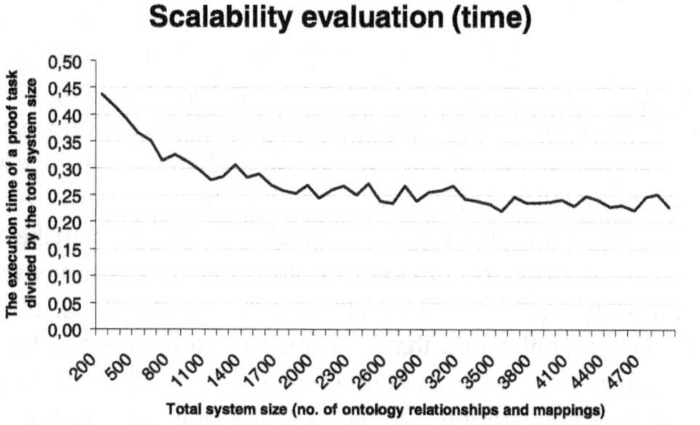

where the CONFIRM() that is used within MCHOICE({c_j, c_k} returns a random answer depending on the logical status of a proposal. If a certain proposal has been verified as being already known, then the divisions are individually 50% likely to confirm the proposal, whereas if the proposal was calculated to be logically new they are individually 70% likely to confirm it. To demonstrate scalability we have continued the described process until the size of the total system is 5000 (see Fig. 4). The execution time has already been divided by the problem size. In the experiments, every data point in the diagram is the average of 10 different randomized runs and 100 consecutive y-values (according to x). This means that the algorithmic time-complexity is linear (as a function of the total system size). In the figure, the y-axis unit is [milliseconds/"system entity"] (i.e. mapping or ontology relationship). We have measured the algorithmic complexity of the memory usage and that is linear as well. Therefore, assuming a setting like this, maintaining consistency between two local contexts that exercise their semantic autonomy is computationally feasible.

Fig. 4. This diagram shows how the average time of calculating a proof task, dived by the system size, varies when the total system size is increasing

5 Related Research

An organizational motivation describing why semantic autonomy is needed is given by [1] and it is described as the possibility of choosing the most appropriate conceptualization of what is locally known. However, they don't present any logical formalization of this notion. Another organizational motivation of semantic autonomy is given by [2] and we mention an initial definition that incorporates the evolution and consistency of both ontologies and instances. A motivation of why formalizing the social process of creating meaning is important is given by [3]. A pioneering proposal of how to handle changing ontologies in an open environment is given by [8]. It has some similarities to our work, but one difference is that we to a greater extent formalise how change is initiated and managed and how conflicts are resolved. Also, they don't explicitly investigate the question of scalability of their approach. Different approaches to the problem of how to deal with consistency in a singular evolving ontology are summarized in [5]. These are: consistent ontology evolution, repairing inconsistencies, reasoning with inconsistent ontologies and multi-version reasoning. Our approach is most similar to the first approach, but we evolve several ontologies and the mappings between them. The *logical* problem of reasoning with multiple ontologies connected by semantic mappings is formally investigated by [9]. Some similar work in logic is done by [10]. Their notions of compatibility and locality have *informally* inspired us. However, none of these two papers explicitly model the process of change nor evolution of ontologies or mappings. Nor do they model the distributed process of initiating change (see discussion in section 1.1).

An application-oriented presentation directed towards knowledge management is done by [11] and they present a system having a lot of functionality. However, their presentation doesn't provide enough formalism to make it transparent, and certain issues, e.g. how to combine the updating of semantics in several ontologies at the same time, are not problematized although that is an open research issue. Another interesting application that is using an ontology-based layered approach is given by [12]. However, their system is designed for the particular purpose of automating system administration and not for the general purpose of maintaining distributed semantics. The interaction process used when creating consensus about changes in a knowledge-base is described by [13], without formalizing the knowledge-level. The five types of ontology mappings in C-OWL are formalized by [7] but that is an *informal* source of inspiration because we have instead adopted [6].

6 Conclusions and Discussion

Some knowledge infrastructures are proposed where their different knowledge bases are governed by independent processes, but still have to use the same ontology. An alternative proposal is to gather several knowledge bases and allow full inconsistency or not care about how distributed meaning is inter-related. There are situations where the first approach is semantically too centralized and the other creates a system semantically too disconnected. In a knowledge infrastructure that has semantic autonomy, the individual knowledge bases are allowed to evolve, at the same time as consistency is preserved between them – that is a kind of glue that keeps the various cognitive points of view together and makes communication between them possible. We have presented a transparent and lightweight framework that shows that it is possible to implement such a system in a scalable way. However, in order to achieve this several restrictions are necessary, and both the logical language of the individual ontologies and the complexity of the ontology evolution operations are kept simple. We have mentioned that currently the framework doesn't model the evolution of instances – but we have defined their semantics. However, it has to be said that it still remains to evaluate the part of the framework that deals with actually removing discovered contradictions – so that is future research that has to be done. The question of how the issues of autonomy and meaning interact is not yet fully understood. Finally, we believe that automated reasoning should be utilized by ontology evolution, but that ontology evolution is not an end in itself. Instead, it should be seen as a component in a framework and as a step towards semantic autonomy – the ability to support decentralized semantics that can evolve according to their own local needs at the same time as a type of coherence keeps them together.

Acknowledgements

This research was funded by the Marcus Wallenberg Foundation for Education in International Industrial Enterprise and by The Foundation BLANCEFLOR Boncompagni-Ludovisi, née Bildt. The author would like to thank Dave Robertson and Alan Smaill at CISA for all their valuable comments and feedback.

References

1. Bonifacio, M., Cuel, R., Mameli, G., Nori, M., "A Peer-to-Peer Architecture for Distributed Knowledge Management", In: *Proceedings of the 3rd International Symposium on Multi-Agent Systems, Large Complex Systems, and E-Businesses (MALCEB'2002)*, 2002.
2. Zurawski, M., "Towards a context-sensitive distributed knowledge management system for the knowledge organization", *Workshop on Knowledge Management and the Semantic Web*, 14th International Conference on Knowledge Engineering and Knowledge Management (EKAW 2004), UK, 2004.
3. Froehner, T., Nickles, M. & Weiß, G., "Towards modeling the social layer of emergent knowledge using open ontologies". In: *ECAI Workshop on Agent-Mediated Knowledge Management (AMKM, Workshop Notes pp. 10-19).* 2004.
4. Robertson, D., "Multi-agent Coordination as Distributed Logic Programming", In: *Lecture Notes in Computer Science*, Volume 3132, Pages 416 – 430, 2004.
5. Haase, P., van Harmelen, F., Huang, Z., Stuckenschmidt, H., Sure, Y., "A Framework for Handling Inconsistency in Changing Ontologies", In: *Proceedings of the Fourth International Semantic Web Conference (ISWC2005)* (Eds. Y. Gil, E. Motta, V. R. Benjamins, M. A. Musen), volume 3729 of LNCS, pp. 353-367. Springer, November 2005.
6. Zurawski, M. "Reasoning about multi-contextual ontology evolution", *The First International Workshop on Context and Ontologies: Theories, Practice and Applications,* The Twentieth National Conference on Artificial Intelligence (AAAI-05), July 9-13, Pittsburgh, PA, USA, 2005.
7. Bouquet, P., Giunchiglia, F., van Harmelen, F.,Serafini, L., Stuckenschmidt, H. "C-OWL: Contextualizing Ontologies", Proceedings of the Second International Semantic Web Conference, K. Sekara and J. Mylopoulis (Ed.), pages 164-179, ", Lecture Notes in Computer Science. Springer Verlag. 2003.
8. Heflin, J., Hendler, J., "Dynamic Ontologies on the Web", In: *Proceedings of the Seventeenth National Conference on Artificial Intelligence (AAAI-2000).* AAAI/MIT Press, Menlo Park, CA, 2000.
9. Serafini, L., Tamilin, A., "DRAGO: Distributed Reasoning Architecture for the Semantic Web". In: *Proc. of the Second European Semantic Web Conference (ESWC'05)*, 2005.
10. Ghidini, C., Giunchiglia F., "Local Model Semantics, or Contextual Reasoning = Locality + Compatibility", In: *Artificial Intelligence*, 127(2), pages 221-259, 2001.
11. Maedche, A., Motik, B., Stojanovic, L., Studer, R., and Volz, R., "Ontologies for Enterprise Knowledge Management", In: *IEEE Intelligent Systems*, Volume 18, Number 2, pages 26-33, March/April 2003.
12. Stojanovic, L. Schneider, J., Maedche, A., Libischer, S., Studer, R., Lumpp, Th., Abecker, A., Breiter, G., Dinger, J., "The role of ontologies in autonomic computing systems", In: *IBM Systems Journal,* v.43 n.3, pages 598-616, July 2004.
13. Euzenat, J., "Corporate Memory through Cooperative Creation of Knowledge Base Systems and Hyper-Documents". In: *Proc. of Knowledge Acquisition Workshop (KAW'96),* Banff, Canada, 1996.

An Evaluation Method for Ontology Complexity Analysis in Ontology Evolution*

Dalu Zhang[1], Chuan Ye[2], and Zhe Yang[3]

Department of Computer Science and Technology, Tongji University, Shanghai 200092, China
daluz@ieee.org, shtjjsjyjx@126.com, hatasen@163.com

Abstract. Ontology evolution becomes extremely important with the tremendous application of ontology. Ontology's size and complexity change a lot during its evolution. Thus it's important for ontology developers to analyze and try to control ontology's complexity to ensure the ontology is useable. In this paper, an evaluation method for analyzing ontology complexity is suggested. First, we sort all the concepts of an ontology according to their *importance degree* (a definition we will give below), then by using a well-defined metrics suite which mainly examines the concepts and their hierarchy and the quantity, ratio of concepts and relationships, we analyze the evolution and distribution of ontology complexity. In the study, we analyzed different versions of GO ontology by using our evaluation method and found it works well. The results indicate that the majority of GO's complexity is distributed on the minority of GO's concepts, which we call "important concepts" and the time when GO's complexity changed greatly is also the time when its "important concepts" changed greatly.

1 Introduction

Ontology construction and development are necessarily an iterative, dynamic and parallel process [1]. The change of domain, the adaptation for different application background, the re-realization of the domain and the change of the conceptual world, all these would influence the ontology construction and evolution [2]. During ontology evolution, the size and complexity of ontology change a lot, which bring difficulties to the management and maintenance of ontology. Actually, it is for the reason of complexity, formal ontologies which are focused on in the field of ontology research have in pratice, yielded little value in real-world application [3].

Though ontology complexity analysis is important in ontology development and evolution, we find few effective methods or metrics related with ontology complexity. In this paper, we suggest an evaluation method for ontology complexity analysis. First, we make a definition of "importance degree", then we present a well-defined complexity metrics suite, which mainly examine the quantity, ratio and correlativity of concepts and relations. After that we sort all the concepts of GO[4] according to their importance degree and by using the formerly defined metrics suite we analyze the trend of GO's complexity evolution and distribution. The reason we choose GO as

* Supported by National Natural Science Foundation of China under Grant No. 90204010.

S. Staab and V. Svatek (Eds.): EKAW 2006, LNAI 4248, pp. 214–221, 2006.

our experimental object is: GO is an ontology that has tremendous application in the domain of gene and it has a full collection of varied versions since 2002.

The rest of this paper is structured as follows: section 2 presents related works about ontology evaluation metrics. In section 3 we suggest our evaluation method. Section 4 presents the complexity analysis results of GO. Section 5 presents the conclusion and outlook for future works.

2 Related Works

As far as now, most existing ontology evaluation metrics are used to analyze the description ability of ontology, few of them are focused on complexity issue.

In literature [5], authors present a structure complexity measure for the UML class diagram based on entropy distance. It considers complexity of both classes and relations between classes and presents rules for transforming complexity value of classes and different kinds of relations into a weighted class dependence graph. This method can measure the structure complexity of class diagrams objectively. Idris studied two conceptual integrity metrics based on graph theory in his PhD thesis [6], which are conceptual coherence and conceptual complexity, but these metrics are all characteristics of single concept. Chris Mungall researched the increased complexity of Gene Ontology [7]. He measured the average number of paths-to-top of a term and used the path-to-term ratio to measure the complexity in an ontology. This metric is simple and only shows the evolution of ontology complexity. Though evaluation methods in [5], [6] and [7] are for ontology complexity analysis, the correctness and soundness of their methods are not well verified.

In our evaluation method we analyze both ontology's complexity evolution trend and distribution trend. Before analysis, we sort all the concepts in ontology according to their importance degree, it is our consideration that different concepts have different contribution to the complexity of the whole ontology, concepts which have more relations with others may be more "important", thus have a higher contribution.

Literature [8] and [9] research methods of excavating important concepts in an ontology. Idris, author of literature [8] suggests several metrics that measure the core degree of concepts based on graph theory and according to the experimental result the author suggests that "betweenness centrality" is comparatively reasonable. But his experimental ontology is small, further more, according to the definition of "betweenness centrality", the core degree of all the leaf concepts is 0, this is not reasonable. The method in [9] is mainly used in extracting ontology from text and not appropriate for constructed ontology. Thus, we gave our definition of importance degree, which is the basis of our evaluation method for ontology complexity analysis.

3 Proposed Evaluation Method

3.1 Measurement of Concept's Importance Degree

The following are some definitions related to concept's importance degree:

$C = \{c_1, c_2, \ldots, c_m\}$: the set of m concepts defined explicitly in an ontology.

$R = \{r_1, r_2, \ldots, r_m\}$: the set of number of relations each concept has, equals to the outdegree of a concept. Here we only consider those inherited relations that reflect the hierarchy of concepts, such as "is a", "part of", etc.

In an ontology, concepts hierarchy is typically expressed in DAG(directed acyclic graph) showed in Fig 1. Each node represents a concept and each directed arc represents a subtype relation to present the hierarchical structure between concepts in ontologies.

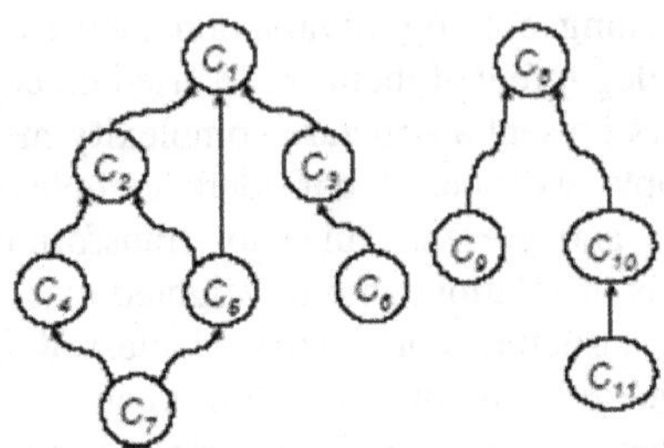

Fig. 1. Ontology in DAG

Path *:* A distinct trace in DAG from a specific particular concept to the most general concept in the ontology, which is the concept without any parent or superclass(e.g. $c_7-c_5-c_2-c_1$ in Fig 1). In Fig 1, there are 11 concepts(m=11), and c_1, c_8 are the two most general concepts.

$N = \{n_1, n_2, \ldots n_m\}$: the set of number of Paths each concept in an ontology has.

$P_i = \{p_{i,1}, p_{i,2}, \ldots p_{i,ni}\}$: the set of Paths a particular concept c_i has.

$PL_i = \{pl_{i,1}, pl_{i,2}, \ldots, pl_{i,ni}\}$: the set of path length of a particular concept c_i, length of a particular path is the number of edges that appear in the path.

$AvgPl_i = \sum_{j=1}^{ni} pl_{i,j} / n_i$: the average path length of a particular concept c_i.

$P = \{\{p_{1,1}, p_{1,2}, \ldots p_{1,n1}\}, \ldots \{p_{m,1}, p_{m,2}, \ldots p_{m,nm}\}\}$:the set of the set of paths of each concept in an ontology.

$IsIn(c_i, p_{j,k}) = 0$ (if c_i doesn't appear in $p_{j,k}$) or 1 (if c_i appears in $p_{j,k}$) .

IDC_i(Importance Degree of Concept) = $\sum_{p_{j,k}}^{P} IsIn(c_i, p_{j,k})$:a particular concept c_i's importance degree IDC_i is the number of times c_i appears in all the paths of all the concepts in an ontology.

After calculating all the concepts' IDC, we can sort the concepts according to their IDC by an descending order, concepts with the same IDC should be sorted according to their AvgPl by an ascending order.

See Fig 2, by using the sorting method above we have the result as table 1.

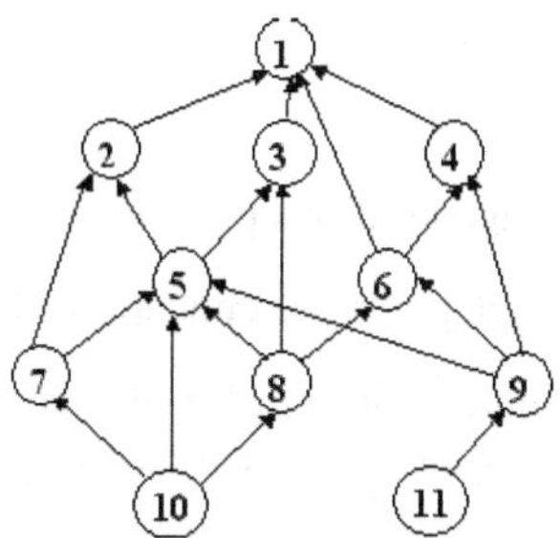

Fig. 2. An Example

Table 1. Sorting Result

id	1	5	2	3	6	8	9	10	4	7	11
IDC	35	16	11	11	10	10	10	10	8	6	5

From this example we can see: concept with id=1 is the most important, because it is the most general concept and appears in all the paths of all the concepts; concept with both higher outdegree and indegree may be more important because it has a higher chance to appear in other concepts' path set(see concept with id=5); concept that locates at a higher hierarchy may be more important, because it has a higher chance to appear in other concepts' path set, but this is not absolutely right (see the concept with id=4); leaf node concept that locates at the lowest hierarchy may be less important, because it can't appear in other concepts' path set, but this is not absolutely right (see the concept with id=10, its IDC is not the lowest because it has an outdegree of 3).

Compared with the betweenness centrality metric introduced in literature [8], which set all the leaf node concepts' betweenness centrality as 0, this importance degree measurement method is more reasonable.

3.2 Ontology Complexity Metrics

On the basis of 3.1, we present the definitions of our ontology complexity metrics.

TNOC(Total Number Of Concepts) =|C|=m: the number of concepts in the set C.

TNOR(Total Number Of Relations)= $\sum_{i=1}^{m} r_i$: the sum of the number of relations of each concept in an ontology.

TNOP(Total Number Of Paths)= $\sum_{i=1}^{m} n_i$: is the sum of paths of each concept.

As ontology consists of concepts and relations, TNOC and TNOR are the two basic attributes of ontology, we can see the change of basic size of an ontology by analyzing these two attributes. As path consists of relations and can reflect the inner structure and hierarchy of ontology, TNOP represents an ontology's hierarchical complexity and its value is proportionate to difficulties in navigating and visualizing the ontology[7].

μ =TNOR/TNOC: the average relations per concept in an ontology.

ρ =TNOP/TNOC: the average paths per concept in an ontology.

μ indicates the average connectivity degree of a concept. ρ must be equal to or greater than 1(each concept must have a parent except for the most general concept). If ρ =1, then the ontology is a tree, multi-relation concepts(higher μ ratio) result in higher ρ ratio for an ontology.

The analysis object of the metrics defined above is the whole ontology, the following are definitions of complexity metrics that are used for single concept in ontology.

d_i: the degree of a particular concept c_i(equals to the sum of c_i's indegree and outdegree). It represents the connectivity degree of a particular concept c_i.

n_i: the number of paths of a particular concept ci. It represents a particular concept ci's hierarchical complexity and its value is proportionate to the difficulty in visualizing the concept and its relations with other concepts in an ontology.

3.3 Our Evaluation Method

The main steps of our method are as follows:

1.Get all the evolution versions of an ontology, transform all of them into DAG (Each node represents a concept and each directed arc represents a subtype relation to present the hierarchical structure between concepts in an ontology.)

2. Sort the concepts of every single ontology by our sorting method. Calculate the d_i and n_i value of every concept c_i.

3. For all the evolution versions of the ontology, calculate their *TNOC*, *TNOR*, *TNOP*, μ and ρ value.

4. By using the result of step 2 we can analyze the complexity distribution of a single ontology, by using the result of step 3 we can analyze the complexity evolution of varied versions of ontology, and by analyzing both the results of step 2 and step 3 contrastively we can research deep into the internal cause of ontology complexity evolution and find the relations between complexity evolution and distribution.

4 Experimental Results and Conclusions

We measured and analyzed the growing complexity of different versions of GO [7] from Dec. 2002 to Sep. 2005, in which the obsolete terms are eliminated from our statistics.

4.1 GO's Complexity Evolution Statistics and Analysis

As GO evolves, its TNOC, TNOR and TNOP increases. Fig 3 is the quantity evolution of TNOC, TNOR and TNOP. The left Y-axis shows the increase of

TNOP. The right Y-axis shows the increase of TNOC and TNOR. The lines of TNOC and TNOR indicate they increase at a steady but slow rate. The line of TNOP indicates that it has a steady but rapid growth. Some enormous ladderlike increases take place at the time of Mar. 2003, Dec. 2004, Jan. 2005 and Apr. 2005, which shows that at these times GO went through some larger changes and became more complex.

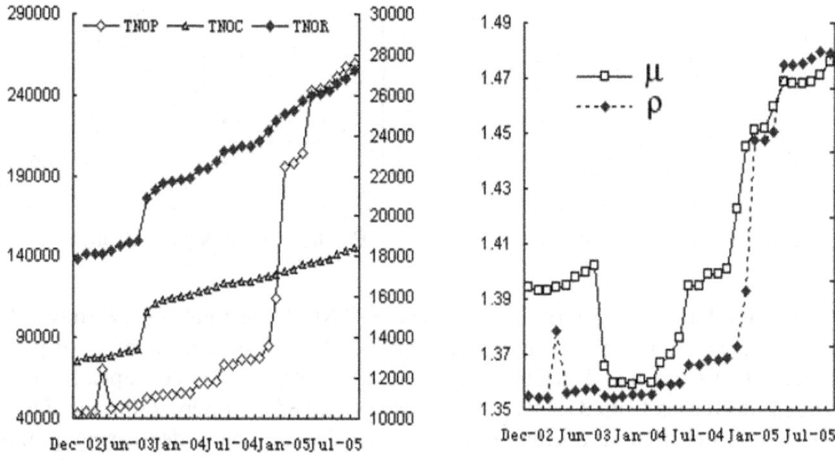

Fig. 3. Concept&Relation&Path

Fig. 4. μ & ρ

Fig 4 shows the changes of GO's μ and ρ from Dec. 2002 to Sep 2005. The left Y-axis shows the change of μ and the right Y-axis shows the change of ρ. In Fig 4, the line of μ indicates that μ has a relatively small change, basically between 1.35 and 1.50. The line of ρ indicates that ρ increases at a steady and rapid rate. Some enormous ladderlike increases occur at the time of Mar. 2003, Dec. 2004, Jan.2005 and April 2005. If we compare the two lines of TNOP in Fig 3 and ρ in Fig 4, we can find that they look almost the same and their enormous ladderlike increases occur at the same time. This is mainly because that *TNOP* is the result of $\rho \times$*TNOC*, while TNOC increases at a steady and a slow rate.

From the above analysis we conclude that the size of GO grew at a slow and steady rate, its complexity grew at a slow and fast rate with some sharp increasing points.

4.2 GO's Complexity Distribution Statistics and Analysis

We sort all the concepts according to their importance degree in all the GO versions from Dec. 2002 to Sep. 2005 and calculated their 70% number of paths distribution. Fig 5 is the result.

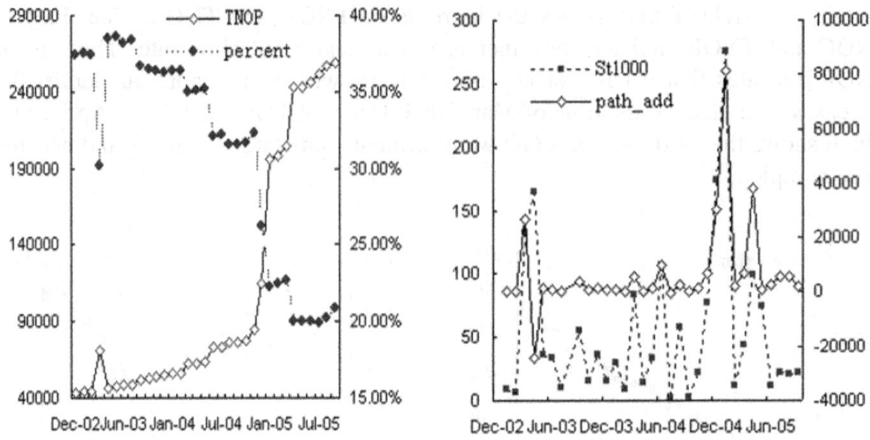

Fig. 5. Path distribution statistics

Fig. 6. Concepts&Paths Change

In Fig 5, the left Y-axis shows the increase of TNOP, the right Y-axis shows the change of "percent". The meaning of "percent" is: 70% of the total number of paths of a specific GO version is distributed on the first "percent" sorted concepts. It shows that percent decreases from 37.44% in Dec. 2002 to 20.85% in Sep. 2005, the line of "percent" indicates that it decreases steadily with some sharp decreasing points. Examine the two lines of TNOP and "percent", we see that they changed synchronously and the sharp increasing time of TNOP is also the sharp decreasing time of percent. The time points are: Mar. 2003, on which TNOP suddenly increased from 43776 to 70582 while percent suddenly decreased from 37.46% to 30.17%, Apr. 2003, Dec. 2004 and Jan. 2005. In some relatively smaller changes of TNOP and percent the time is also the same. The above analysis shows that every sharp increase of GO's TNOP leads to further concentration of GO's paths on important concepts.

We conclude that the majority of GO's complexity is distributed on the minority of its concepts which we call "important concepts" and as GO evolves, this trend becomes more and more evident.

In Fig 3, increasing forms of TNOC and TNOR can't explain increasing form of TNOP, so we have Fig 6. In Fig 6, the left Y-axis shows the change of St1000, the right Y-axis shows the change of path_add. We examine the first 1000 concepts of all the sorted GO versions, and St1000 represents the number of concepts that appear in a specific version of GO but not appear in the GO version that is one month before, path_add represents the change of TNOP of a specific GO version comparing with the GO version that is one month before, path_add below 0 indicates that there is a decrease of TNOP. From Fig 6 we can see that when the absolute value of path_add is small, St1000 is small too, and the time when path_add changes greatly is also the time when St1000 changes greatly. Some relatively sharp points of path_add occur at Mar. 2003(path_add=26806), Apr. 2003(path_add=-24637), Jun. 2004(path_add= 10122), Dec.2004(path_add=30065),Jan. 2005(path_add=81441),Apr. 2005(path_add =38317), and the corresponding values of St1000 are relatively large too, they are 132, 165, 107, 174, 276, 99(values of other times are much smaller, mostly no more than 50). There is only one exception, in May 2005, path_add is small(616), but St1000 is large(75).

From the analysis we have the conclusion that the time when GO's complexity changed greatly is also the time when its "important concepts" changed greatly. The great change of GO's complexity may be caused by the appearance of new important concepts, another possibility is that because of the re-realization of domain, the whole ontology structure changes, so the order of important concepts changes greatly. In the process of ontology engineering, we shall consider more on those important concepts, which is a major cause of the great change of ontology complexity.

5 Summary and Future Works

With the tremendous use of ontology, its size and complexity change a lot during its evolution. So it becomes very necessary to set up a suite of metrics for developers to understand the complexity evolution and distribution of ontologies in order to improve the quality, estimate cost and reduce future maintenance. In this study, an evaluation method for analyzing ontology's complexity is presented. By using this method, we had a detailed statistics and analysis of GO's complexity evolution and distribution. In the future, we will continue to work on the ontology complexity metrics and other ontology metrics and the improvement of measuring concept's important degree (e.g. consider more on ontology's hierarchy).

References

1. A.Das, W. Wu, D.McGuinness. Industrial Strength Ontology Management. The Emerging Semantic Web, IOS Press, 2002.
2. E Daniel,O Leary. Impediments in the use of explicit ontologies for KBS development. International Journal of Human-Computer Studies,1997,46(2-3):327-337.
3. Amit Sheth and Cartic Ramakrishnan. Semantic (Web) Technology In Action:Ontology Driven Information Systems for Search, Integration and Analysis. IEEE Data Engineering Bulletin, Special issue on Making the Semantic Web Real, December 2003, pp. 40-48.
4. The Gene Ontology Homepage, http://www.geneontology.org/
5. Dazhou Kang, Baowen Xu, Jianjiang Lu,William C.Chu. A Complexity Measure for Ontology Based on UML. 10th IEEE International Workshop on Future Trends of Distributed Computing Systems (FTDCS'04)pp.222-228
6. IdrisHis. Analyzing the Conceptual Coherence of Computing Applications Through Ontological Excavation. PhD Thesis Proposal, May 13, 2004.
7. Chris Mungall, BDGP / GO Consortium, Increased complexity in GO. http://www. fruitfly.org/~cjm/obol/doc/go- complexity.html
8. Idris His, Colin Potts, Melody Moore. Ontological Excavation: Unearthing the core concepts of the application. Proceedings of WCRE2003, November 13-16,2003,pp. 345-352.
9. Mustapha Baziz,Mohand Boughanem,Nathalie Aussenac-Gilles,Claude Chrisment. Semantic Cores for Representing Documents in IR. SAC'2005- 20th ACM Symposium on Applied Computing, Santa Fe, New Mexico, 13-17 mars 2005. p. 1020-1026, ACM Press ISBN: 1-58113-964-0, USA

Semantic Search Components: A Blueprint for Effective Query Language Interfaces

Victoria Uren and Enrico Motta

Knowledge Media Institute, The Open University, Milton Keynes, MK7 8QP, UK
{v.s.uren, e.motta}@open.ac.uk

Abstract. Formulating complex queries is hard, especially when users cannot understand all the data structures of multiple complex knowledge bases. We see a gap between simplistic but user friendly tools and formal query languages. Building on an example comparison search, we propose an approach in which reusable search components take an intermediary role between the user interface and formal query languages.

1 Introduction

The purpose of the *semantic web* [1] is to make the meaning of content explicit through semantic mark-up, thereby facilitating more intelligent services for users. In the case of search, it should produce more precise results because searching knowledge structured according to ontologies[2], which define the meaning in a domain, should reduce the ambiguity of query terms. Semantic (web) searching is at an early stage of development but different approaches are already emerging. We have identified two, which sit at opposite ends of a spectrum that balances usability against reasoning power. The first approach provides relatively simple search facilities, which exploit RDF triple structures. These systems give users routes into exploring semantic web data without having to be expert in specialist query languages or being required to know the structure of particular ontologies. The systems of the second approach use formal, structured query languages. These allow users to precisely define the knowledge they wish to retrieve but require them to be fluent in a query syntax, and to know the structure of the ontology, in order to formulate a search. While an expert user might learn a syntax, it is unlikely, in a semantic web scenario, where a user may need to interact with thousands of knowledge bases structured according to hundreds of ontologies, that they should know the structure of all the sources.

An excellent example of a system which provides a simple user interface and search services which are portable to a wide range of RDF based resources is Search on TAP [3]. This has three search components: a lightweight query interface called GetData that sends a SOAP message to a URL and returns the values of one or more properties of that resource, a search interface that identifies resources based on a query string, and a reflection component which explores the immediate vicinity of a node. The robust simplicity of the basic search is supplemented by a process that

S. Staab and V. Svatek (Eds.): EKAW 2006, LNAI 4248, pp. 222 – 237, 2006.

Guha & McCool call "semantic negotiation" which establishes semantic mappings between equivalent objects with different URLs [4]. Semantic negotiation plays a crucial role by allowing TAP to deal with the heterogeneity of the web by bootstrapping from what it already knows about semantic entities.

Our own question answering system, AquaLog [5] reformulates natural language queries into triples which can be searched against a knowledge base. The power of the AquaLog approach lies in the automatic reformulation process, which first uses domain independent methods based on a subset of natural (English) language to, for example, recognize the type of the question, as a "who" question which needs to be answered with one or more people's names, and produces an initial linguistic triple. Then this linguistic triple is mapped onto the domain using the Relation and Class Similarity Services (RSS and CSS), which try to match elements of the query against the knowledge base. By taking on the formalization of the query, AquaLog allows users to pose queries in natural language without having to remember a specific terminology for the domain. Currently its key limitations are that it can only search one knowledge base at once (we are addressing this in a new version called PowerAqua [6]), and that it can only answer a question that can be reformulated as no more than two triples that form a path.

At the opposite end of the spectrum, a number of query languages have been proposed for searching semantic web resources. These may be divided into those based on database query languages (e.g., RQL, SeRQL, SPARQL), and those which are related more closely to rule languages or logics (e.g. DQL, or the KAON2 reasoner). Query languages for the semantic web are reviewed in [7] and [8]. Haase et al. [7] set out the requirements for an RDF query as a set of use cases such as graph matching, relational models, aggregation, recursion etc. and benchmarks a number of query languages against them. These requirements are a good indicator of the direction of research in this area. The focus is on developing a language that has all the technical features required to get correct answers for the widest possible range of searches and support the needs of semantic web developers. It is not intended that these methods should be placed in the hands of the average user any more than one would expect the average user to access a database using SQL statements.

These two extremes by no means account for all the work on supporting search on the semantic web. For example, there is important work on developing methods for computing relevance metrics and ranking semantic results [9], [10], [11, 12]. There is also highly pertinent work on building effective user front ends for semantic resources, e.g. [13, 14]. However, these efforts were directed at single domains, allowing tailor-made solutions. We are aiming at a more widely applicable solution.

Identifying the usability vs reasoning power trade off led us to conclude that, while developers have access to powerful search systems, end users have much more limited means of finding semantic information. Specifically, they are not currently supported in formulating searches with multiple parameters, such as the example we will explore in this paper. In this paper we explore a novel approach that will overcome the current gap between the two major approaches to search. In particular, our hypothesis is that complex query formulation could be eased by a system which would rely on a set of components, each implementing a well-defined search task. By defining some abstract search tasks that are domain independent, we ensure their applicability over a wide range of ontologies. Therefore, a system built up by our generic components would be usable in the challenging scenario anticipated for the semantic web. The closest works we know of to the proposed approach are the OntoIQ interface [15] and VQL [16] each of which use query patterns as a basis for constructing more complex queries. The OntoIQ interface requires the user to read RQL, though not to write it; we believe that the user should not be exposed to formal syntax. VQL is a well developed language based on the principle "ask less, get more", to we we also subscribe. It does not currently include focusing operations which exploit ontology structures but does allow queries for a good range of query types and considers the issue of mapping queries onto semantic resources.

As part of specifying requirements for a semantic search engine based on search components we are exploring various search scenarios. In the example presented in this paper, we chose to work on a comparison query because comparison is a relatively common task with multiple parameters. The structure of the paper is as follows. First, we consider some heuristics for comparison. Next we work through an example comparing the fuel efficiency of a fictional 4-wheel drive vehicle, which we call "Behemoth", to other similar vehicles. We demonstrate that this comparison search is sufficiently complex that users of the semantic search engines will require support to formulate similar comparison queries. Finally, we sketch out a blue-print for a component based approach to supporting complex semantic queries.

2 Comparison Queries: Heuristics and an Example

Comparison is a very common activity on the internet and in general. Some special resources exist for making comparisons such as the Kelkoo eShopping site (http://www.kelkoo.co.uk/) and the British Government school league tables (http://www.dfes.gov.uk/performancetables/). The organization of these gives us some commonsense guidance to the nature of comparison problems from which we can derive some heuristics.

The first step of comparison defines a class of objects to compare. Both the Kelkoo and the DfES site start by dividing their worlds into types of thing. Kelkoo groups consumer goods under headings such as "Books", "Cars and Accessories", "Computers" and so on. The school league tables site divides schools into categories like "Primary School (Key Stage 2)" and "Secondary School (GCSE and equivalent)". From this we derive our first heuristic:

Only similar things should be compared (H1)

This forces us to ask what we mean by "similar". This is a loaded question and one which has received considerable attention from researchers. However, similarity is not the main focus of our discussion in this paper. Therefore, since we are interested in search in ontology based knowledge resources, we propose to use the following two heuristics, which draw on fundamental ontological concepts, as our starting point for thinking about similarity:

Similar things have a common parent. (H2)
Similar things share properties (slots). (H3)

Intuitively, this fits the examples from the comparison sites. For example, both the "Laptops" and "Desktops" section of the Kelkoo site are sub-divisions of the parent "Computers" and both share properties such as "brand" and "processor".

Our second heuristic draws on the observation that both our typical comparison sites focus on *properties* that are shared by all, or many, of the things in a given class. In Kelkoo, for instance, all the items have a price and this can be used for ranking. The school league tables, on the other hand, present the results of national academic tests in core curriculum subjects, along with contextual information like the percentage of students in the school with special educational needs. This definition of properties is the second step of comparison and leads us to the heuristic:

Things should be compared against shared properties. (H4)

The third step of comparison is a compositional step in which objects and properties are brought together.

It is commonly said that you can't compare apples and oranges. These heuristics do not support that position, since apples and oranges share a common parent, fruit. However, they do limit the comparison to shared properties e.g., vitamin C content. Note that this puts an implicit limit on how distant a common parent can be, since it must be close enough for the objects to share properties. However, further refinement of these heuristics is needed before they could be used in, say, an autonomous agent. As they stand the heuristics are sufficient to help people to formulate searches.

2.1 Example: Is Behemoth Less Fuel Efficient Than Similar Vehicles?

We start our exploration of search tasks by detailing the process of building a query to answer the question stated above. Our goal is to give an insight into the kinds of actions performed during such searches and use them to ground our higher level description of search tasks that follows in the next section.

Our example uses an ontology built in Protégé about vehicles and their fuel efficiency. The searches used the version of SPARQL in Protégé 3.2 beta. We chose to use this partly for convenience (the ontology had been built in an older version of Protégé) but also because SPARQL, being syntactically similar to SQL, can be understood by most computer scientists. First, we present the ontology and then the search.

The question concerns a fictional 4-wheel drive vehicle which we call "Behemoth". Behemoth is manufactured by a fictional company we call Monster Motors. To provide a testbed we constructed a small OWL ontology in Protégé which describes describes individual vehicles, vehicle types (LargeCar, SmallCar, OffroadVehicle etc.), their components (e.g. engines) as well as different types of tests and measurements and the corresponding measurement units.

Sample fuel consumption measurements for the real vehicles in the ontology came from three sources:

- the Green Vehicle Guide produced by the Australian government (http://www.greenvehicleguide.gov.au/)
- The Fuel Consumption Guide 2005 produced by Natural Resources Canada (http://www.tc.gc.ca/programs/environment/fuelpgm/guidsub.htm)

- o and the Excel spreadsheet of fuel consumption data issued by the UK Vehicle Certification Agency in May 2005 (http://www.vcacarfueldata.org.uk/)

These samples of data from different sources introduced some realism into the scenario since, typically for this domain, different agencies use different standards for testing and the values are reported in a variety of units. The UK data are collected according to the specifications of EU Directive 98/69, whereas the Canadian data are collected according to the Federal Test Procedure (FTP) used in Canada and the USA for new vehicle testing, and the Australian data is collected according to an international standard adopted by the United Nations and commonly called Euro2 (it is based on the EU standards). The data are published in a variety of different Imperial and SI units depending on the conventions of the countries concerned. The tough issue for the semantic web arising out of this apparent trivia is that real data quickly gets complicated. Things which look similar, for example two measurements in mpg (miles per gallon) published in Canada and the UK, may not be comparable. Therefore, simple queries are not sufficient to get sensible answers.

2.2 Constructing the Query in SPARQL

To answer our question "Is Behemoth less fuel efficient than similar vehicles?" we constructed a query in the three steps outlined above. In step 1 we define a set of vehicles similar to Behemoth. In step 2 we set the parameters that define "comparable" fuel consumption measurements. In step 3 we compose a query out of the results of the first two steps.

STEP 1 (define objects). To formulate a search for vehicles similar to Behemoth we first examine Behemoth itself, using a search we will call "rel-ent" (short for "relations and entities"). This returns any entities directly linked to the search instance via any relations. Its exploratory role is similar to the reflection interface used in Search on TAP [3]. The search is presented below along with the result of the query. Items highlighted in bold are discussed in the text. The queries and results come directly from Protégé. However, for clarity and brevity we have edited the results to remove Protégé specific Frame IDs.

```
SELECT ?rel ?ent WHERE { :Behemoth ?rel ?ent }
Slot(rdf:type)                  Cls(OffroadVehicle)
Slot(hasComponent)SimpleInstance(MonsterEngineB of [Cls(VehicleEngine)])
Slot(hasManufacturer)           SimpleInstance(MonsterMotors of [Cls(Manufacturer)])
Slot(hasSpecification)SimpleInstance(HighwayFuelConsumptionMeasurement_38 of
                                [Cls(HighwayFuelConsumptionMeasurement)])
Slot(hasSpecification)SimpleInstance(UrbanFuelConsumptionMeasurement_37 of
                                [Cls(UrbanFuelConsumptionMeasurement)])
```

We can apply the heuristic that things with a common parent are similar (H2). Behemoth is an instance of the class **OffroadVehicle** so this could be the default definition of "similar". However, the user may want a broader search. Again we apply a rel-ent search this time to the OffroadVehicle class.

```
SELECT ?rel ?ent  WHERE { :OffroadVehicle ?rel ?ent }
Slot(rdf:type)                  Cls(owl:Class)
Slot(owl:disjointWith)          Cls(LightTruck)
Slot(owl:disjointWith)          Cls(Van)
Slot(owl:disjointWith)          Cls(LargeCar)
Slot(owl:disjointWith)          Cls(MediumCar)
Slot(owl:disjointWith)          Cls(SmallCar)
Slot(owl:disjointWith)          Cls(TwoSeaterCar)
Slot(rdfs:subClassOf)           Cls(VehicleType)
```

One option might be to take the next step up the hierarchy and construct a superclass query for instances at the same level of the hierarchy as Behemoth with the common ancestor **VehicleType** (VehicleType is the parent class for OffroadVehicles). (Note, since SPARQL doesn't implement inheritance, the extra layer of the class hierarchy is represented by the variable ?x).

```
SELECT ?anyVehicle  WHERE { ?anyVehicle rdf:type  ?x . ?x rdfs:subClassOf :VehicleType }
SimpleInstance(MonsterVan of [Cls(Van)])
SimpleInstance(Behemoth of [Cls(OffroadVehicle)])
SimpleInstance(NewBeetleTDI of [Cls(SmallCar)])
SimpleInstance(Durango4x4 of [Cls(OffroadVehicle)])
SimpleInstance(Ecoskate of [Cls(TwoSeaterCar)])
SimpleInstance(X5 of [Cls(OffroadVehicle)])
SimpleInstance(SmartFortwoCDI of [Cls(TwoSeaterCar)])
SimpleInstance(X3 of [Cls(OffroadVehicle)])
SimpleInstance(MonsterLimo of [Cls(LargeCar)])
```

This responds with all the vehicles in the (small) knowledgebase. Some of these, such as the Ecoskate and NewBeetleTDI are not really like Behemoth – we would not expect it to have fuel efficiency similar to small cars. So here the user chooses a subset of vehicle classes consisting of the Van and LargeCar classes.

```
SELECT ?likeBehemoth WHERE {{ ?likeBehemoth rdf:type  :OffroadVehicle}
        UNION{ ?likeBehemoth rdf:type  :LargeCar}  UNION  {?likeBehemoth rdf:type :Van }}
SimpleInstance(X3 of [Cls(OffroadVehicle)])
SimpleInstance(Behemoth of [Cls(OffroadVehicle)]
SimpleInstance(Durango4x4 of [Cls(OffroadVehicle)])
SimpleInstance(X5 of [Cls(OffroadVehicle)])
SimpleInstance(MonsterLimo of [Cls(LargeCar)])
SimpleInstance(MonsterVan of [Cls(Van)])
```

Until now we have broadened the search to include new classes of vehicles that may be similar to Behemoth. This involved looking above it in the class hierarchy. However, according to H3 which states that similar entities share properties, shared properties (parameters) should be decided upon to focus the search. For these the system should look down the hierarchy. To do this we look more closely at the MonsterEngineB component of Behemoth using a further exploratory rel-ent search.

```
SELECT ?rel ?ent WHERE { :MonsterEngineB ?rel ?ent }
Slot(hasManufacturer)           SimpleInstance(MonsterMotors of [Cls(Manufacturer)])
Slot(rdf:type)                  Cls(VehicleEngine)
Slot(hasNumberOfCylinders)      6
Slot(usesFuel)                  SimpleInstance(PetrolFuel of [Cls(Fuel)])
Slot(componentOfVehicle)        SimpleInstance(Behemoth of [Cls(OffroadVehicle)])
Slot(hasEngineCapacity)         3.5
```

Looking at this we notice that **MonsterEngineB** has 6 cylinders. This will certainly impact on its fuel consumption so the user narrows the search down to only include vehicles with engines that have 6 or more cylinders. (Note, the UNION syntax of SPARQL forces a verbose syntax at this point).

```
SELECT ?likeBehemoth
WHERE {{ ?likeBehemoth rdf:type :OffroadVehicle . ?likeBehemoth :hasComponent ?engine.
        ?engine rdf:type :VehicleEngine . ?engine :hasNumberOfCylinders ?NumCylinders .
        FILTER (?NumCylinders >= 6)}
UNION { ?likeBehemoth rdf:type :LargeCar . ?likeBehemoth :hasComponent ?engine.
        ?engine rdf:type :VehicleEngine . ?engine :hasNumberOfCylinders ?NumCylinders .
        FILTER (?NumCylinders >= 6)}
UNION {?likeBehemoth rdf:type :Van . ?likeBehemoth :hasComponent ?engine.
        ?engine rdf:type :VehicleEngine . ?engine :hasNumberOfCylinders ?NumCylinders .
        FILTER (?NumCylinders >= 6)}}
```

SimpleInstance(**X3** of [Cls(OffroadVehicle)])
SimpleInstance(Behemoth of [Cls(OffroadVehicle)])
SimpleInstance(**Durango4x4** of [Cls(OffroadVehicle)])
SimpleInstance(**X5** of [Cls(OffroadVehicle)])

To summarize, using our heuristics H2 and H3 to define what is "similar" to Behemoth, four Vehicles are retrieved from the knowledge base. They are: **X5, X3, Durango4x4** and **Behemoth** itself.

STEP 2 (define properties). To start formulating a search for the fuel consumption aspect of the query we reuse the rel-ent results for Behemoth above. There were two fuel consumption measurements: HighwayFuelConsumptionMeasurement_38 and UrbanFuelConsumptionMeasurement_37. We can do a rel-ent search on one of these to understand their related entities and explore ways to produce a search.

```
SELECT ?rel ?ent WHERE { :HighwayFuelConsumptionMeasurement_38 ?rel ?ent }
```

Slot(**hasValue**)	**9.1**
Slot(rdf:type)	Cls(**HighwayFuelConsumptionMeasurement**)
Slot(usesTestMethod)	SimpleInstance(FuelConsumptionTestMethod_Canadian) of [Cls(FuelConsumptionTestMethod)])
Slot(hasUnit)	SimpleInstance(**UnitSI_IPER100km** of [Cls(UnitSI)])
Slot(dataForVehicle)	SimpleInstance(Behemoth of [Cls(OffroadVehicle)])
Slot(reportedBy)	SimpleInstance(**TransportCanada** of [Cls(TestingAgency)])

First we investigate broadening the search. The SimpleInstance HighwayFuelConsumptionMeasurement_38 is a member of the class HighwayFuelConsumptionMeasurement. We can perform a rel-ent on this to find out more about it. Here we rely on H2 just as in step 1

```
SELECT ?rel ?ent WHERE { :HighwayFuelConsumptionMeasurement ?rel ?ent }
```

Slot(owl:disjointWith)	Cls(CombinedFuelConsumptionMeasurement)
Slot(owl:disjointWith)	Cls(UrbanFuelConsumptionMeasurement)
Slot(rdfs:subClassOf)	Cls(**FuelConsumptionMeasurement**)
Slot(rdf:type)	Cls(owl:Class)

We can see that it is disjoint with two other classes and all three are children of the class FuelConsumptionMeasurement. We can formulate a superclass query to encompass all the SimpleInstances of these.

```
SELECT ?anyFuelCons WHERE { ?anyFuelCons rdf:type ?x .
       ?x rdfs:subClassOf :FuelConsumptionMeasurement }
```

SimpleInstance(HighwayFuelConsumptionMeasurement_22 of [Cls(HighwayFuelConsumptionMeasurement)])
SimpleInstance(UrbanFuelConsumptionMeasurement_61 of [Cls(UrbanFuelConsumptionMeasurement)])
SimpleInstance(UrbanFuelConsumptionMeasurement_16 of [Cls(UrbanFuelConsumptionMeasurement)])
SimpleInstance(HighwayFuelConsumptionMeasurement_38 of [Cls(HighwayFuelConsumptionMeasurement)])
SimpleInstance(CombinedFuelConsumptionMeasurement_27 of [Cls(CombinedFuelConsumptionMeasurement)])
SimpleInstance(CombinedFuelConsumptionMeasurement_30 of [Cls(CombinedFuelConsumptionMeasurement)])
...

In addition, we noted before that different agencies report fuel consumption measurements made to different standards and in different units. We add TransportCanada as an additional term to limit the data to measurements made under one set of conditions and fix the units to the SI standard. We now have a quite complex search for fuel consumption measures.

```
SELECT ?fuelCons ?x WHERE { ?fuelCons rdf:type ?x . ?x rdfs:subClassOf :FuelConsumptionMeasurement .
 ?fuelCons :reportedBy :TransportCanada . ?fuelCons :hasUnit :UnitSI_lPER100km}
```

```
SimpleInstance(UrbanFuelConsumptionMeasurement_61 of [Cls(UrbanFuelConsumptionMeasurement)])
   Cls(UrbanFuelConsumptionMeasurement)
SimpleInstance(UrbanFuelConsumptionMeasurement_16 of [Cls(UrbanFuelConsumptionMeasurement)])
   Cls(UrbanFuelConsumptionMeasurement)
SimpleInstance(HighwayFuelConsumptionMeasurement_24 of [Cls(HighwayFuelConsumptionMeasurement)])
   Cls(HighwayFuelConsumptionMeasurement)
SimpleInstance(UrbanFuelConsumptionMeasurement_23 of [Cls(UrbanFuelConsumptionMeasurement)])
   Cls(UrbanFuelConsumptionMeasurement)
SimpleInstance(HighwayFuelConsumptionMeasurement_17 of [Cls(HighwayFuelConsumptionMeasurement)])
   Cls(HighwayFuelConsumptionMeasurement)
SimpleInstance(HighwayFuelConsumptionMeasurement_2 of [Cls(HighwayFuelConsumptionMeasurement)])
   Cls(HighwayFuelConsumptionMeasurement)
```

STEP 3 (composition). The final step is to merge the two components of the query for fuel consumption values of vehicles similar to that of Behemoth. This can be done via another UNION query that attaches the constraint based search formulated in step 2 to each of the vehicles found in step 1. We added an ordering term at the end to produce the results as a ranking.

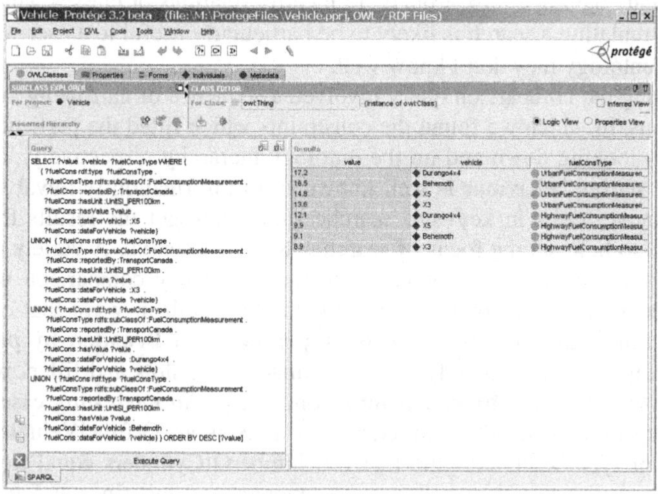

Fig. 1. Screenshot of the final query (left panel) and the search results (right panel) in Protégé

The final result of the search is presented in Figure 1 as a screen shot from Protégé. From this the user might conclude that while Behemoth is not the most fuel efficient vehicle in its class it is the not worst either. The Durango4x4 has worse UrbanFuelConsumption. Both the Durango4x4 and the X5 have worse HighwayFuelConsumption.

You may ask why we subjected you to such a long example. It was to show that formulating a semantic search, with complex parameters, in a scenario where the user does not have a god-like knowledge of the structure of the resources is hard. It can require time spent exploring the resources, and a knowledge of syntax. This is not beyond the capabilities of intelligent users, but we know that, for users, search is a means to an end, not an end in itself. Therefore, they prefer it to be simple.

3 Components for Searching

The search example above got rather complex, but patterns emerged which point towards the kinds of operations a search engine might need to support. We propose that a component based approach could be developed. This does not require any new search language but instead uses existing languages to formulate reusable blocks of query statements. The user supplies simple keyword-like inputs, and can plug the components together to make more complex statements. This might by done in a form filling interface or by visualization. Our method does not subscribe to a particular style of interface but only to the underlying "library" of reusable components. Table 1 summarizes the kinds of search components that we believe are needed.

The exploratory search we called **rel-ent**, which looks at all the entities that are the immediate children of the search item and the relations to them, is an example of the classes of components for *reflection* which can be used to find out more about an object by exploring the graph immediately around it. This process of going to a relevant place and "having a look around" to identify relations or classes which could be useful in formulating a search is likely to be particularly useful to a user who is working with an ontology they don't know well.

Formulating the comparison query involved a sequence of narrowing and broadening operations, in which we found the constraints which fitted the particular information need by looking down and up the ontology hierarchy respectively. This kind of query *focus* setting behaviour is well known from information retrieval where users add and remove terms in keyword searches until they get the results they require. Components to help set the focus of searches will be essential. A variety of these are suggested in Table 1. For example, in the fuel efficiency comparison we explored options of how to search for things similar to Behemoth in ways that could be replaced by components like **Broaden by superclass** and **Broaden by peer classes**. The narrowing operations mainly used combinations of slots and fillers which could be supplied by a **Narrow by constraints** component. An interesting case is where a chain of constraints can be constructed such as X is an OffroadVehicle that has a component of type VehicleEngine that hasNumberOfCylinders equal to 6 or more. This is more challenging than building a component that just finds and applies multiple constraints on one entity.

In formulating the search we talked about things which were similar to Behemoth and fuel consumption measurements which were comparable. This translated into a sequence of *focus* searches. Nonetheless, *similarity* is a distinct concept that we believe needs to be supported by components. For example, one approach is **Class Match**, where similarity is defined as "instances of the same class as a known instance". This exploits the domain knowledge embedded in the ontology. Another possibility might be to use a **Case-based** approach where results are ranked by their similarity to a search instance. This is more flexible than the constraint setting approach because matching items don't necessarily have to match every slot in the query instance. We can also anticipate similarity searches for different kinds of literals. For example, a **String match** to find results like "Durango4X4" for a search for "Durango", or a **Number match** that find numbers that are close to an input given the range of values stored in the knowledge base for instances of that type.

Table 1. Candidate Search Components

Component Type	Example Components
Reflection – local search that looks for things in the vicinity of a node	**Rel-ent** – find everything with a link from a known node **Ent-rel** – Find everything with a link *to* a known node **AquaLog** – look for relations like those specified by a natural language query
Similarity – looks for things that are "like" a certain search.	**Exact match** – finds Literals that exactly match the search term **Class Match** – find things of the same class as an identified instance (siblings) **String match** – find any string that is a close match to a given string **Number match** – finds numbers "close" to a input based on the range of values in the knowledge base **Case-based** – a nearest neighbour search based on a set of property values
Focus – refine a search by narrowing or broadening	**Broaden by superclass** – locate an ancestor class of the search term **Broaden by peer classes** – locate classes at the same level of the hierarchy to add to the search **Broaden by synonyms** – A search which uses linguistic resources **Narrow by subclass** – locate a subclass of the current term **Narrow by constraints** – add property values which must be fulfilled by a search
Assembly – put together search components in a complex search	**Semantic Conjunction** – Semantic AND **Conjunction** – Boolean AND **Disjunction** – Boolean OR
Select – select what data to view	**Select by type** – indicate properties of an object to view **Select by certainty** – set level of confidence required in data to view **Select by provenance** – set sources which are trusted

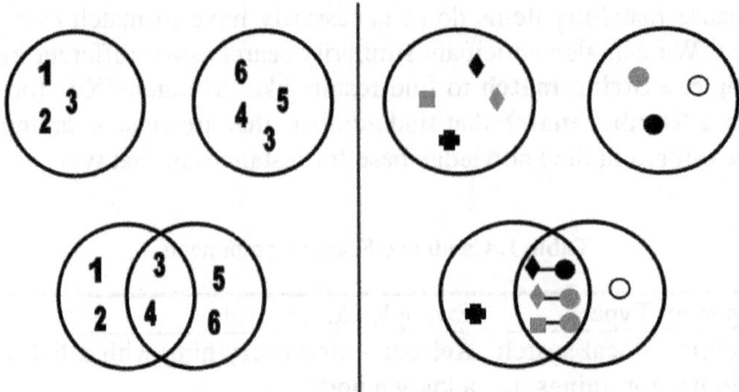

Fig. 3. Conjunction – the results of two searches are combined by finding overlapping elements (*left*). Semantic conjunction – the results of two searches are combined by finding cross-linking semantic relations (*right*).

The last step of the comparison search involved putting two searches together as subcomponents of a more complex search. Components will also be required for this kind of *assembly* operation. Note that in cases such as the one we presented this is more complex than the Boolean operators familiar in IR systems. Figure 2 illustrates the difference. In a Boolean "AND" operation (*left*) the objects in the two sets are of the same type (numbers here though in IR usually documents), the answer comprises the overlap between the two sets. The analog for a semantic search (*right*) needs to combine two initial searches which produce objects of different kinds. The answer is a set of relations between objects from the two sets; in our example the :dataForVehicle relation linked vehicles to fuel consumptions. In this mode, an object can occur more than once in the answer set as part of different relations.

Two other search components that are worth noting at this point are those which *select* the type of data required in the answer and those which *sort* it into an order. In an SQL based syntax, such as SPARQL these appear at the beginning and end of the search statement. However, we observe some areas of common ground that makes them partial mirrors of each other. For example, we might want to **Select by provenance**. Alternatively, we might want to rank the results according to its trustworthiness using **Rank by provenance**. For data which had been annotated automatically, e.g. by information extraction, we might want to have **Select by certainty** and **Rank by certainty** components that exploit stored knowledge about the accuracy of the automatic annotation process. For the user *select* and *sort* have similar outcomes.

To summarize, we have identified the need for search components that can do reflection around a node, similarity search, broadening and narrowing of focus, the combination of components, and selection and ranking of results. Although the process by which we identified these component types came out of a comparison search we believe they are at a level of abstraction that would suit a wide range of searches. The next step is to consider the kind of architecture that would be needed.

4 Blueprint for a Component Based Architecture

We envisage search components having an intermediary role between the user interface and the formal query language, taking as input user search terms and outputting an appropriate formal query. This is a problem solving methods [17] approach which is neutral as to whether the components are realised as, for example, agents, web services, or an API.

The simplest variety of component is one that takes a single input (see Table 2). For example, imagine the first action of our fuel efficiency search. We can imagine that a user interface guides the user to select the reflection component rel-ent. The user selects the :Behemoth object to add to the search (perhaps using a similarity component for text searching in literals). The component inserts :Behemoth into the standard syntactic pattern for rel-ent and sends on a well formed SPARQL query.

Table 2. Examples of input and output for search components with single inputs

Component	Input	Output
Reflection Rel-ent	:Behemoth	SELECT ?rel ?ent WHERE { :Behemoth ?rel ?ent }
Similarity Class Match	:Behemoth	SELECT ?likeThis WHERE {?likeThis rdf:type ?x . :Behemoth rdf:type ?x}

A more complex variety of components take multiple inputs, such as those that take a list of constraints. Here an interface needs to provide some guidance for the user to specify the role of each term in the search, whether it is the thing searched for or a constraint. This might be provided minimally by a simple form which supports the user in selecting appropriate types and relations from the ontology. A straightforward case is a search of a single class constrained by a number of properties that apply directly to it, such as the constraints on fuel consumption measurements in the first row of Table 3. More complex constraints arise when the property is not directly related to the item being sought. In the fuel consumption example, the user selected as constraints for :OffroadVehicles that they should have :VehicleEngine populated and that the engine should have 6 or more cylinders. The number of cylinders is indirectly linked to vehicles via :VehicleEngine.

One of the toughest challenges posed by the design of the component based architecture is how to compose complex searches from simpler components. That is to say, if components like those in Tables 2 and 3 are the bricks how do we build a wall? We have already discussed in general terms how semantic conjunction differs from Boolean conjunction and came to the conclusion that it involves finding the relations between the items output by two searches. In Table 4 below, we explore three approaches reusing elements of the fuel consumption example.

Semantic conjunction II (instance/instance) is the closest to Boolean conjunction. The input is the outputs from STEP 1 and STEP 2 of the original comparison search, i.e. a list of n vehicles and a list of m fuel consumption measurements. The conjunction method seeks links between the items in the two lists, i.e., it looks for fuel

Table 3. Examples of inputs and output for search components with multiple inputs. The nested bracket syntax associates constraints to the type they apply to.

Component	Input	Output
Focus Narrow by constraints on direct properties	(:FuelConsumptionMeasurement (:reportedBy :TransportCanada) (:hasUnit :UnitSI_lPER100km))	SELECT ?fuelCons ?x WHERE { ?fuelCons rdf:type ?x . ?x rdfs:subClassOf :FuelConsumptionMeasurement . ?fuelCons :reportedBy :TransportCanada . ?fuelCons :hasUnit :UnitSI_lPER100km}
Focus Narrow by constraints on indirect properties	(:OffroadVehicle (:hasNumberOfCylinders >=6))	SELECT ?likeThis WHERE {{ ?likeThis rdf:type :OffroadVehicle . ?likeThis :hasComponent ?e . ?e rdf:type :VehicleEngine . ?e :hasNumberOfCylinders ?n . FILTER (?n >= 6)}}

Table 4. Examples of input and output for assembly search components. The square bracket syntax indicates a list of instances resulting from a search.

Component	Input	Output
Assembly Semantic Conjunction II Pairing of instances	[:Behemoth, :X3, etc.] [:UrbanFuelConsumption Measurement_37, :HighwayFuelConsumption Measurement_38, etc.]	SELECT ?rel WHERE { :HighwayFuelConsumption Measurement_38 ?rel :Behemoth . }etc.
Assembly Semantic Conjunction IC Union with instances and constraints	[:Behemoth, :X3, etc.] (:FuelConsumption Measurement (:reportedBy :TransportCanada) (:hasUnit :UnitSI_lPER100km))	SELECT ?value ?vehicle ?fuelConsType WHERE { { ?fuelCons rdf:type ?fuelConsType . ?fuelConsType rdfs:subClassOf :FuelConsumptionMeasurement . ?fuelCons :reportedBy :TransportCanada . ?fuelCons :hasUnit :UnitSI_lPER100km . ?fuelCons :hasValue ?value . ?fuelCons :dataForVehicle :Behemoth .?fuelCons :dataForVehicle ?vehicle} UNION etc. }
Assembly Semantic Conjunction CC Merging two sets of constraints	(:OffroadVehicle (:hasComponent :VehicleEngine)) (:VehicleEngine (:hasNumberOfCylinders >=6)) (:FuelConsumption Measurement (:reportedBy :TransportCanada) (:hasUnit :UnitSI_lPER100km))	SELECT ?value ?vehicle ?fuelConsType WHERE { ?fuelCons rdf:type ?fuelConsType . ?fuelConsType rdfs:subClassOf :FuelConsumptionMeasurement . ?fuelCons :reportedBy :TransportCanada . ?fuelCons :hasUnit :UnitSI_lPER100km . ?fuelCons :hasValue ?value . ?fuelCons :dataForVehicle ?vehicle . ?vehicle rdf:type :OffroadVehicle . ?vehicle :hasComponent ?e . ?e rdf:type :VehicleEngine . ?e :hasNumberOfCylinders ?n . FILTER (?n >= 6) }

consumptions for the individual vehicles. There are a number of problems with this approach. First, it assumes that one to one links between the two lists can be found, which may not always be the case. Second, it is a brute force method that requires the generation of *n times m* sub-searches, which is likely to become costly for all but very short lists. (Note, since multiple links are possible to and from any item in the lists, and links can exist in both directions it is not possible to reduce this number.)

Semantic conjunction IC (instance/constraints) is the kind of search we used in STEP 3 of the fuel consumption example. A list of n instances (vehicles) is merged with a set of constraints (describing the kind of fuel consumption measurements that are comparable) and the n sub-searches are linked using UNION. For this to be done automatically the system would have to perform a set of searches to identify suitable links between the type in the instance list and the types of instance being selected in the constraint search. In the example, two variables were being selected at the end of STEP 2: ?fuelCons, the fuel consumption value itself, and ?x the type of measurement (highway, urban or combined). We made the UNION in STEP 3 using :dataForVehicle to link ?fuelCons to a vehicle. However, there may conceivably be several possible pairings between instances and multiple variables, and several links to choose from for each pair. The system needs to select among them automatically or support the user by offering a list of the available options. Therefore, while this semantic conjunction has the advantage of generating just *n* sub-searches, this is balanced against the fact that it requires reasoning on the ontology to provide support to the user in elucidating the connections and selecting appropriate links.

Semantic conjunction CC (constraints/constraints) is the approach that produces the most succinct search, since it produces a single large search that merges all the constraints from two searches. (Note, in Table 4, only this search statement is presented unabridged.) Obviously, the trade-off for this is that the complexity of the reasoning to find suitable links in the ontology to bind together the two searches is greater since there is now a many-to-many search for possible links to be performed.

5 Summary and Future Work

We have identified the need for query formulation systems for the semantic web which allow users to go beyond simple keyword search without having to learn a formal query language. The contribution of this work is to identify a set of abstract search components at a higher level than the basic elements of query languages. These could underpin a component based interface between storage and query systems that work with query languages, and high level GUI based search facilities.

The first benefit of a component based approach is that we can implement it stepwise, starting with components that take a single input and combining them using semantic conjunction II, before moving on to the more complex components and assembly methods. We are working towards a practical implementation of the approach in a system we call SemSearch [18], which uses a Google like syntax for basic queries and is currently being extended to incorporate search components in an "advanced" mode. A second benefit is that a system based on abstract search components is (almost) domain independent. A third benefit is that the approach is naturally extensible. The current analysis has been limited to one kind of search problem, comparison. If we find, when investigating other complex queries, that new operations are needed we simply add more components. We anticipate that one such extension will tackle search in heterogeneous environments, with multiple ontologies and knowledge bases, i.e. the real semantic web.

Acknowledgements

This work was funded by the X-Media project (www-x-media-project.org) sponsored by the European Commission as part of the Information Society Technologies (IST) programme under EC grant number IST-FP6-026978 and partly funded by the Advanced Knowledge Technologies (AKT) Interdisciplinary Research Collaboration (IRC), sponsored by the UK Engineering and Physical Sciences Research Council under grant number GR/N15764/01. The authors thank Yuangui Lei and Marta Sabou for helpful discussions and comments on the text.

References

1. Berners-Lee T., H.J., Lassila O., *The Semantic Web.* Scientific American, 2001: p. 34-43.
2. Gruber, T.R., *Towards principles for the design of ontologies used for knowledge sharing.*, in *Formal ontology in conceptual analysis and knowledge Representation*, R.P.N. Guarino, Editor. 1993, Kluwer Academic publishers.
3. Guha, R., R. McCool, E. Miller. *Semantic Search.* in *WWW2003, Proc. of the 12th International Conference on World Wide Web.* 2003: ACM Press.
4. Guha, R., R. McCool, *TAP: a Semantic Web Platform.* Computer Networks, 2003. **42**(5): p. 557-577.
5. Lopez, V., M. Pasin, E. Motta. *AquaLog: An Ontology-portable Question Answering System for the Semantic Web.* in *ESWC 2005.* 2005. Creete, Grece.
6. Lopez, V., E. Motta, V. Uren. *PowerAqua: Fishing the Semantic Web.* in *ESWC 2006.* 2006. Montenegro.
7. Haase, P., Broekstra, J., Eberhardt, A., Volz, R. *A comparison of RDF query languages.* in *ISWC 2004.* 2004. Hiroshima, Japan: LNCS 3298.
8. Golfarelli, M., Mandeoreli F., Martoglia, R., Proli, A., Rizzi S., Tiberio, P., *Critical analysis of query languages and ontology-based query rewriting techniques.* June 2005, Web Intelligent Search based on DOMain ontologies (WISDOM) Deliverable D3.R1.
9. Zhang, L., Y. Yu, J. Zhou, C.X. Lin, Y.Yang. *An enhanced model for searching in semantic portals.* in *WWW 2005.* 2005. Chiba Japan.
10. Stojanovic, N. *An Approach for Defining Relevance in the Ontology-based Information Retrieval.* in *Web Intelligence WI 2005.* 2005.
11. Ding, L., Pan, R., Finin, T., Joshi, A., Peng Y., Kolari P. *Finding and ranking knowledge on the semantic web.* in *(Third International Semantic Web Conference) ISWC 2005.* 2005: LNCS 3729.
12. Vallet-Weadon, D., Fernandez-Sanchez, M., Castells-Azpilicueta, P., *The quest for semantic retrieval on the semantic web.* Upgrade, 2005. **VI**(6): p. 19-23.
13. Goble, C.A., R. Stevens, G. Ng, S. Bechhofer, N.W. Paton, P.G. Baker, M. Peim, A. Brass, *Transparent Access to Multiple Bioinformatics Information Sources.* IBM Systems Journal Special issue on deep computing for the life sciences, 2001. **40**(2): p. 532 - 552.

14. Stuckenschmidt, H., F.van Harmelen, A. de Waard, T. Scerri, R. Bhogal, J. van Buel, I. Crowlesmith, C. Fluit, A. Kampman, J. Broekstra, E. van Mulligen, *Exploring large document repositories with RDF technology: the DOPE project.* IEEE Intelligent Systems, 2004. **19**(34-40): p. 22-28.
15. Baker, C.J.O., Su X., Butler, G., Haarslev, V. *Ontoligent interactive query tool.* in *Proceedings of Canadian Semantic Web Working Symposium 2006.* 2006.
16. Hoang, H.H., Tjoa, A.M. *The Virtual Query Language for Information Retrieval in the SemanticLIFE framework.* in *International Workshop on Web Information Systems Modeling (WISM 2006).* 2006. Luxembourg.
17. Motta, E., *Reusable Components for Knowledge Modelling: Principles and Case Studies in Parametric Design.* 1999, Amsterdam: IOS Press.
18. Lei, Y., Uren, V.S., Motta, E.,. *SemSearch: A Search Engine for the Semantic Web.* in *EKAW 2006.* 2006. Podebrady, Czech Republic.

SemSearch: A Search Engine for the Semantic Web

Yuangui Lei, Victoria Uren, and Enrico Motta

Knowledge Media Institute (KMi), The Open University, Milton Keynes
{y.lei, v.s.uren, e.motta}@open.ac.uk

Abstract. Existing semantic search tools have been primarily designed to enhance the performance of traditional search technologies but with little support for ordinary end users who are not necessarily familiar with domain specific semantic data, ontologies, or SQL-like query languages. This paper presents SemSearch, a search engine, which pays special attention to this issue by providing several means to hide the complexity of semantic search from end users and thus make it easy to use and effective.

1 Introduction

Semantic search promises to produce precise answers to user's queries by taking advantage of the availability of explicit semantics of information in the semantic web. For example, when searching for news stories about *phd students*, with traditional searching technologies, we often could only get news entries in which the term "phd students" appears. Those entries which mention the names of students but do not use the term "phd students" directly will be missed out. Such news entries however are often the ones that the user is interested in. In the context of the semantic web, where the meaning of web content is made explicit, the meaning of the keyword (which is a general concept in the example of phd students) can be figured out. Furthermore, the underlying semantic relations of metadata can be exploited to support the retrieval of related information.

A number of tools have been recently developed [4,3,6,1,5], which enhance the performance of traditional search technologies. While these tools do provide comprehensive support for semantic search, they are however not suitable for ordinary end users who are not necessarily familiar with domain specific semantic data, ontologies, or SQL-like query languages. Some tools [4,1] suffer from the problem of "knowledge overhead", which is requiring end users to be equipped with extensive knowledge on the back-end ontologies, data repositories or the specified sophisticated query language *before* they use them. Some lack support for complex queries, e.g., semantic-based keyword search engines [3,6]. Others [5] heavily rely on the natural language processing techniques that they use.

The semantic search engine we present here, SemSearch, pays special attention to the issue of end user support. It provides several means to address the problems suffered by state-of-art tools. A prototype of the search engine has

S. Staab and V. Svatek (Eds.): EKAW 2006, LNAI 4248, pp. 238–245, 2006.

been implemented and applied in the semantic web portal of our lab[1]. An initial evaluation shows promising results.

The rest of the paper is organized as follows. We begin in Section 2 by presenting an overview of SemSearch. We then explain the Google-like query interface in Section 3. Thereafter, we describe the major steps of the semantic search process in sections 4 and 5. Finally, we conclude with a discussion of our contributions and future work in Section 6.

2 An Overview of SemSearch

One major goal in this work is to hide the complexity of semantic search from end users and to make it easy to use and effective for naive users. To achieve this goal, we identified the following key requirements:

- **Low barrier to access for ordinary end users.** Our semantic search engine should overcome the problem of knowledge overhead and ensure that ordinary end users are able to use it without having to know about the vocabulary or structure of the ontology or having to master a special query language.
- **Dealing with complex queries.** In contrast with existing semantic-based keyword search engines which only answer simple queries, our semantic search engine should allow end users to ask relatively complex queries and provide comprehensive means to handle them.
- **Precise and self-explanatory results.** Our semantic search engine should be able to produce precise results that on the one hand satisfy user queries, and on the other hand are self-explanatory. Thus, ordinary end users can understand the results (e.g. what they are and why they are there) without having to consult the back-end semantic data repositories or their underlying ontologies.
- **Quick response.** Our semantic search engine should provide quick response to user queries, thus encouraging ordinary end users to harvest the benefit of the semantic web technology. This requires that we make the mechanism of semantic search as simple as possible.

To meet these requirements, we chose the keyword-based searching route rather than the natural language question answering route, and deliberately avoided linguistic processing which is a relatively expensive process in terms of search. We overcome the limitation of current keyword-based semantic search engines by supporting a Google-like query interface which supports complex queries in terms of multiple keywords. Figure 1 shows a layered architecture of our semantic search engine. It separates end users from the back-end heterogeneous semantic data repositories by several layers.

- **The Google-like User Interface Layer** allows end users to specify queries in terms of keywords. It extends traditional keyword search languages by

[1] `http://semanticweb.kmi.open.ac.uk:8080/pages/semantic_searhing.jsp/`

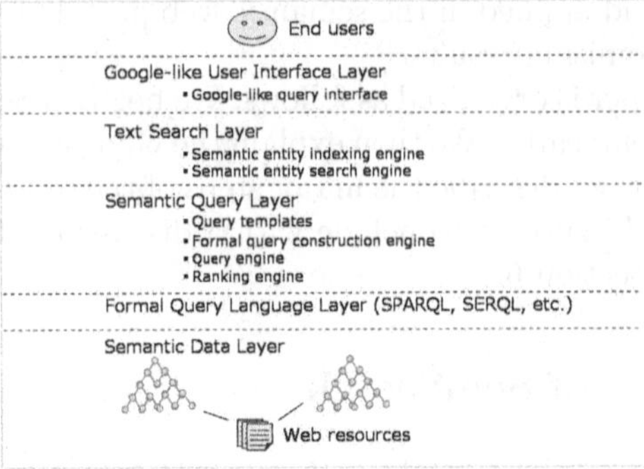

Fig. 1. An overview of the SemSearch architecture

allowing the explicit specification of i) the queried subject and ii) the combination of multiple keywords.

- **The Text Search Layer** interprets user queries by finding out the explicit semantic meanings of the user keywords. Central to this layer are two components: i) a semantic entity index engine, which indexes documents and their associated semantic entities including classes, properties, and individuals; and ii) a semantic entity search engine, which supports the searching of semantic entity matches for the user keywords.
- **The Semantic Query Layer** produces search results for user queries by translating user queries into formal queries. This layer comprises three components, including i) a formal query construction engine, which translates user queries into formal queries, ii) a query engine, which queries the specified meta-data repository using the generated formal queries, and iii) a ranking engine, which ranks the search results according to the degree to which they satisfy the user query.
- **The Formal Query Language Layer** provides a specific formal query language that can be used to retrieve semantic relations from the underlying semantic data layer.
- **The Semantic Data Layer** comprises semantic metadata that are gathered from heterogeneous data sources and are represented in different ontologies.

The search process of SemSearch comprises four major steps:

- **Step1.** Making sense of the user query, which is to find out the semantic meanings of the keywords specified in a user query.
- **Step2.** Translating the user query into formal queries.
- **Step3.** Querying the back-end semantic data repositories using the generated formal queries.
- **Step4.** Ranking the querying results.

Step1 is carried out within the Text Search Layer. The rest of the steps are associated with the Semantic Query Layer.

3 The Google-Like Query Interface

The SemSearch query interface extends traditional keyword search languages by allowing the explicit specification of i) the queried subject which indicates the type of the expected search results, and ii) the combination of keywords. The query interface uses the operator ":" to capture the query subject and the operators "and" and "or" to specify the combination of keywords (apart from the subject keyword). A user query in SemSearch looks like "*subject:keyword1 and/or keyword2 and/or keyword3 ...*".

With this query syntax, the example of "news about phd students" can be easily specified as *news:phd students*, where the term *news* is the query subject and the term *phd students* is a required keyword. More complex queries in which multiple keywords (except the subject keyword) are involved also can be easily specified. For example, when querying for projects in which both Enrico and John participate, the query can be specified as *project:Enrico and John.*

The SemSearch query interface provides a flexible and powerful approach to user query specification. First, it does not require end users to be familiar with any particular ontology, semantic data, or any special query language. Second, it does not confine users to any pre-defined query subjects and values. Further, in contrast with current semantic-based keyword search engines which only accept one keyword as input, this query interface supports the specification of relatively complex queries that specify both multiple keywords and the expected type of results. Finally, the query process is simpler than question answering tools as the search engine does not need to spend time calculating which of the keywords are in a user's query.

4 Interpreting User Queries

As mentioned earlier in Section 2, interpreting user queries is the first step of the search process in SemSearch. The task of this step is to find out the semantic meanings of the keywords specified in user queries so that the search engine knows what the user is looking for and how to satisfy the user query.

From the semantic point of view, one keyword may match i) general concepts (e.g., the keyword "phd students" which matches the concept *phd-student*), ii) semantic relations between concepts, (e.g. the keyword "author" matches the relation *has-author*), or iii) instance entities (e.g., the keyword "Enrico" which matches the instance *Enrico-Motta*, the keyword "chief scientist" which matches the values of the instance *Marc-Eisenstadt* of the property *has-job-title*). The ideal goal of this task is to find out the exact semantic meaning of each keyword. This is however not easy to achieve, as there may be more than one semantic entity which matches a keyword. Thus, we relaxed the goal to that of finding out all the semantic entity matches for each keyword.

For the purpose of finding out semantic entity matches, we used the *labels* of semantic entities as the main search source. The rational for this choice is that, from the user point of view, labels often catch the meaning of semantic entities in an understandable way. In the case of instances, we also used their short literal values as the search source. So that when the user is searching for "chief scientist", the instance that has such a string as a value of its properties can be reached.

In order to produce fast response, the search engine first indexes all the semantic entities contained in the back-end semantic data repositories, including classes, properties, and instances. It then searches the indexed repository to find out matches for keywords. Thus, two components are developed in the search engine, namely the semantic entity index engine and the semantic entity search engine. As it narrows the search sources to labels and short literals of semantic entities, the search engine is able to find out semantic entity matches for each keyword. These matches are the possible semantic meanings of keywords.

Please note that for the sake of getting quick response, we only use text search to find string matches for user keywords at the moment. We avoid using techniques like WordNet [2] based comparison to find matches. This might cost us some good matches, e.g., losing the match *table* if the user is searching for *desk*. But one to one comparison is time consuming and expensive in real-time scenarios. This is indeed a trade-off as well as a research challenge that we need to address in future.

5 Translating User Queries into Formal Queries

In this step, the search engine takes as input the semantic matches of user search terms and outputs appropriate formal queries. To better understand how to construct formal queries from user queries, we classify user queries into two types: i) simple queries which only comprise two keywords, and ii) complex queries where more than two keywords are involved.

Simple user queries. As the types of semantic entity match combinations are fixed in simple user queries, we developed a set of templates to describe how to retrieve relations between two semantic entities. Among all the combinations, there are three most possible types between two keywords. This is because we can make the assumption that the subject keyword matches a class concept. Figure 2 shows the templates for these combinations[2].

Now let us investigate the first combination where both keywords in a query match classes. The search results are expected to be the instances of the class C_s (i.e. the match of the subject keyword) which have explicitly specified relations with the instances of the class C_k (i.e. the match of the other keyword). For example, when querying for news about "phd students", the expected results are the news entries in which phd students are involved. Further, the search results are also expected to be self-explanatory, e.g., to motivate why certain news entries appear and others do not. Thus, along with the retrieving of news instances, the related phd students and the relations between students and news entries

[2] We used the Sesame SeRQL language (http://www.openrdf.org/) as the formal query language in the SemSearch prototype.

Keywords matches	SeRQL query templates
Subject match: class Cs Keyword match class Ck	select {i1},{li1},{p},{lp},{i2},{li2} from {i1} rdf:type {Cs}, [{i1} rdfs:label {li1}], {i2} rdf:type {Ck}, [{i2} rdfs:label {li2}], {i1} p {i2}, [{p} rdfs:label {lp}] union select {i1},{li1},{p},{lp},{i2},{li2} from {i1} rdf:type {Cs}, [{i1} rdfs:label {li1}], {i2} rdf:type {Ck}, [{i2} rdfs:label {li2}], {i2} p {i1}, [{p} rdfs:label {lp}]
Subject match: class Cs Keyword match instance Ik	select {i1},{li1},{p},{lp},{i2},{li2} from {i1} rdf:type {Cs}, [{i1} rdfs:label {li1}], [{i2} rdfs:label {li2}], {i1} p {i2}, [{p} rdfs:label {lp}] where i2=Ik union select {i1},{li1},{p},{lp},{i2},{li2} from {i1} rdf:type {Cs}, [{i1} rdfs:label {li1}], [{i2} rdfs:label {li2}], {i2} p {i1}, [{p} rdfs:label {lp}] where i2=Ik
Subject match: class Cs Keyword match property Pk	select {i1},{li1},{p},{lp},{i2},{li2} from {i1} rdf:type {Cs}, [{i1} rdfs:label {li1}], [{i2} rdfs:label {li2}], {i1} P {i2}, [{p} rdfs:label {lp}] where p=Pk union select {i1},{li1},{p},{lp},{i2},{li2} from {i1} rdf:type {Cs}, [{i1} rdfs:label {li1}], [{i2} rdfs:label {li2}], {i2} p {i1}, [{p} rdfs:label {lp}] where p=Pk

Fig. 2. The SeRQL query templates for two semantic entities

also need to be retrieved. Therefore, the search results of the query *news:phd students* are expected to be triples of *(news, relation, phd-sudent)*.

Please note that there are situations where no class matches could be found for the subject keyword. The focus of user query in such situations varies according to the type of the semantic matches of keywords. We have also developed templates for such queries. Due to the lack of space, please refer to [8] for details.

In the context of simple queries, the task of query formulation is to initiate the template that corresponds to the combinations of the semantic matches of the user keywords. As each keyword may match more than one semantic entity, often more than one query needs to be constructed. More specifically, if the subject keyword matches n_s semantic entities and the other keyword has n_k matches, there are $n_s * n_k$ queries that need to be constructed. This problem becomes more acute when there are many keywords involved in the user query. We will discuss how to reduce the number of formal queries in the following.

Complex user queries. For complex queries (which involve more than two keywords), the search engine needs to combine the semantic matches of each keyword together and construct queries for each of the combinations. A key operational problem is that in real world situations there can be a large number of matches and hence much more combinations.

For keywords k_1, k_2, ..., k_n, suppose that the number of the semantic matches of the keyword k_i is n_i. There will be $n_1 * n_2 * ... * n_n$ (which can be represented as $\prod_{i=1}^{n} n_i$) different combinations when considering all the keywords as required ones. Each combination of the matches corresponds to a RDF-based formal query. Apart from considering all the keywords as required ones, the search engine also needs to investigate the combinations where one or more keywords are left out, in order to produce complete result sets to end users. The total number can become huge when i) there are many keywords involved and ii) some keywords are very generic and thus have many matches.

Rules are therefore needed to reduce the number of matches for each keyword. We used several heuristic rules, including i) the subject keyword always matches class entities when there are more than two keywords involved in the user query, ii) choosing the closest entity matches to the keyword as possible, and iii) choosing the most specific class match among the class matches. These rules can significantly reduce the number of entity matches.

For each combination, a formal query is constructed. In SeRQL, a formal query often comprises three building blocks: the *head* block, which describes what needs to be retrieved, the *body* block, which describes how, and the *condition* block, which expresses conditions. In addition, in order to cover relations of two entities in both directions, the query also comprises a *union* block. Figure 3 shows the construction algorithm. As shown in the figure, the construction of all these blocks depends on the type (i.e. class, property, or instance) of the semantic entity match of each keyword contained in a combination of keywords' matches. Please refer to [8] for details.

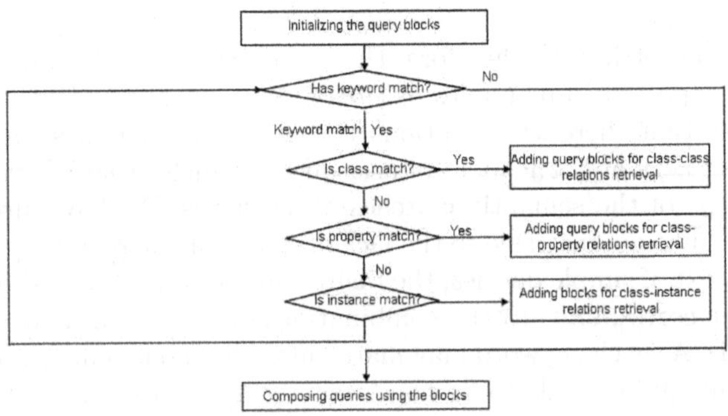

Fig. 3. The algorithm of formal query construction for complex user queries

6 Conclusions and Future Work

The core observation that underlies this paper is that, in the case of semantic search that promises to produce precise answers to user queries, it is important to ensure that it is easy to use and effective for ordinary end users who are not necessarily familiar with domain specific semantic data, ontologies, or SQL-like query languages. Our semantic search engine, SemSearch, provides several means to address this issue. A prototype has been implemented based on the Sesame RDF query engine and Lucene text search engine [3]. The prototype has been applied to the semantic web portal of our lab (KMi) and the 3rd European Semantic Web Conference (ESWC06) [4]. Figure 4 shows a screenshot of the search results of the query example *news:phd students* in the KMi application.

Future work will focus on i) developing comprehensive means to perform semantic matching between keywords and semantic entities and ii) extending the

[3] `http://lucene.apache.org/`

[4] `http://search.eswc06.org/`

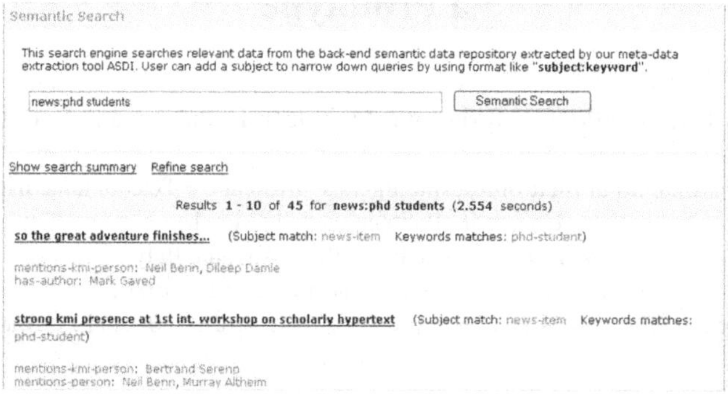

Fig. 4. A screenshot of the search results of the query example *news:phd students*

search engine to a tool that could guide end users to build up complex queries step by step by using the component-based approach presented in [7].

Acknowledgements

We wish to thank Marta Sabou for her valuable comments on this paper. This work was funded by the Advanced Knowledge Technologies Interdisciplinary Research Collaboration (IRC) GR/N15764/01 and the X-Media project (www.x-media-project.org) under EC grant number IST-FP6-026978.

References

1. O. Corby, R. Dieng-Kuntz, and C. Faron-Zucker. Querying the Semantic web with Corese Search Engine. In *Proceedings of 15th ECAI/PAIS, Valencia (ES)*, 2004.
2. C. Fellbaum. *WORDNET: An Electronic Lexical Database.* MIT Press, 1998.
3. R. Guha, R. McCool, and E. Miller. Semantic Search. In *Proceedings of the 12th international conference on World Wide Web*, pages 700–709, 2003.
4. J. Heflin and J. Hendler. Searching the Web with SHOE. In *Proceedings of the AAAI Workshop on AI for Web Search*, pages 35 – 40. AAAI Press, 2000.
5. V. Lopez, M. Pasin, and E. Motta. AquaLog: An Ontology-portable Question Answering System for the Semantic Web. In *Proceedings of European Semantic Web Conference (ESWC 2005)*, 2005.
6. C. Rocha, D. Schwabe, and M. de Aragao. A Hybrid Approach for Searching in the Semantic Web. In *Proceedings of the 13th International World Wide Web Conference*, 2004.
7. V. Uren and E. Motta. Semantic search components: a blueprint for effective query language interfaces. In *The International Conference on Knowledge Engineering and Knowledge Management (EKAW 2006)*, October 2006.
8. Y.Lei, V. Uren, and E.Motta. SemSearch: A Search Engine for the Semantic Web. Technical Report kmi-06-11, Knowledge Media Institute, the Open University, http://kmi.open.ac.uk/publications/pdf/semsearch_paper.pdf, 2006.

Rich Personal Semantic Web Clients: Scenario and a Prototype

G. Tummarello, C. Morbidoni, M. Nucci, F. Piazza, and P. Puliti

Dipartimento di Elettronica, Intelligenza Artificiale e Telecomunicazioni
Università Politecnica delle Marche,
Via Brecce Bianche – 60131 Ancona, Italy
{g.tummarello, c.morbidoni, upf,
p.puliti}@deit.univpm.it, mik.nucci@gmail.com

Abstract. In this paper we introduce a novel kind scenario where users use Rich Personal Semantic Web Clients to cooperatively create knowledge within "Semantic Web Communities". Such communities are formed around P2P channels which work by exchanging patches of RDF information among clients. Once sufficient information has been collected locally at each client, rich and fast browsing of such "Semantic Web" becomes possible without generating external traffic or computational load. A prototype of such client, DBin, is presented and issues such as user interfaces and social aggregation model are discussed. We will focus in particular on the "Brainlet" paradigm, which enables community leaders to create and deliver domain specific user interfaces. The Brainlet creation process does not require programming skills, so that Semantic Web communities can be started up by domain experts rather than programmers.

1 Introduction

In this paper we introduce a novel kind scenario where users use Rich Personal Semantic Web Clients to cooperatively create knowledge within "Semantic Web Communities". The idea is to enable users to create and experience the Semantic Web (SW) in their local repositories and have these exchange annotations using semantic P2P "topic" channels which exchange patches of RDF information. Such an application model can in a sense be though of as a file-sharing for metadata with on top "community configurable" user interfaces (*Brainlets*, as we will discuss later). Similar to a file-sharing, the client connects directly to other peers; instead of files, however, it downloads and shares RDF metadata about resources which the group has defined "of interest". This creates a flow of RDF information which ultimately allows the participants to build rich personal SW databases therefore supporting high speed local browsing, searching, personalized filtering and processing of information. In implementing this idea in our prototype DBin [1], a number of issues came out, relating independent yet interconnected aspects. At a user interface level, once data has been collected, the real issue becomes how to enable the user to interact with it in a natural way, e.g. in a way much more attractive and meaningful than a list of

S. Staab and V. Svatek (Eds.): EKAW 2006, LNAI 4248, pp. 246–255, 2006.

"properties" and "resources". While this "visualization problem" seems a separately treatable problem, we claim that in this scenario it is not. We propose, to leverage the existence of "groups" by providing a way for a "group leader" to suggest "interaction profiles" with the data that is exchanged within that channel. Upon joining a group, the user is then suggested to download what we call a *Brainlet*, that is a package of configuration and a priori knowledge which provide editing and browsing facilities to best interact with the information shared in the group. The main motivation behind Brainlets is enabling domain experts, rather than programmers, to create rich SW environments and communities.

A Novel Scenario

The scenario considered in this paper is new under many aspects. Many of the P2P approaches based on SW technologies proposed so far (e.g. [2], [3], [4], [5]), use metadata and ontologies to build a semantically structured definition of resources, the main purpose being optimizing the retrieval of actual files. An example of user query is "Retrieve all publications about SW by author X", which needs a certain a priori knowledge of the domain to be formulated.

Differently, a typical use case of DBin is that of a user, perhaps new to SW, who is interested in learning (more) about the ongoing research on SW. By simply joining a 'SW topic group', the user can receive new and unexpected information (e.g. papers, the conferences or author's names). In this case users are not exclusively interested in "hits" locating remote resources, but rather into learning as much as possible about the domain so that more uses of this information become possible (e.g. Personalized browsing, joining with local information etc).

2 The RDFGrowth P2P Engine: Basic Concepts

In this section we give an high level overview of RDFGrowth, the P2P algorithm which is the main metadata exchanging layer in DBin. The following discussion is intended to highlight the basic concepts used in RDFGrowth (and relevant to understand the overall philosophy of DBin), rather than explaining in detail how it works. For a detailed discussion see [6].

Related Works and RDFGrowth Requirements

Previous P2P Semantic Web applications, such as [2] and [5], have explored interactions among groups of trusted and committed peers. In such systems peers rely on each other to forward query requests and collecting and returning results. In contrast, we consider the real world scenario of peers where cooperation is relatively frail. By this we mean that peers are certainly expected to provide some external service, but commitment should be minimal and in a "best effort" fashion. The RDFGrowth algorithm has been designed to address this requirement of scalability, minimum commitment among peers and minimum external burden: peers are not required to perform any complex or time consuming operation, as such as query routing, replication, collecting and merging.

RDFN: The Only Query Allowed

As a complex graph query might simply hog any machine, the only RDF query allowed during metadata exchanges, is a simple and basic one, which not only is fast to execute but also can be cached very effectively, we call it RDFN. Intuitively requesting the RDFN of a URI *a* from a peer *p*, means asking *p* to give out all the information directly associated to *a* that *p* owns. As shown in Figure 1, this surrounding information of a resource can be break down into small pieces, named MSGs, which, in absence of Bnodes, are simply all the statements having the resource as subject or object.

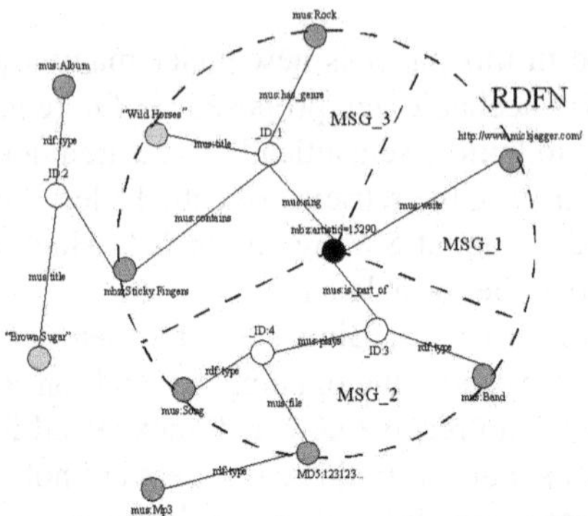

Fig. 1. The RDFN of the resource painted in black is delimited by the dotted circle. White nodes represent blank nodes. The RDFN is composed by several slices, each one is an MSG, basically a closure on blank nodes starting from a given triple, and represents the minimum unit of knowledge that is exchanged.

MSGs

An MSG is a subgraph with a well defined structure and is actually the minimum amount of information that can be exchanged in the system. As shown in Figure 1, MSGs can be intuitively defined as sub-graph which partition the whole graph and which intersect only on grounded nodes (URIs or literals). See [6] for a complete discussion on the RDFN and MSG definitions and theory. Its theoretical properties allows to exchange information in a fine granularity, incremental fashion, along with its context. We will see later, in fact, how authorship information can be efficiently attached at MSG level, allowing personalized trust policies and information revocation.

GUED (Group URIs Exposing Definition)

Users connects to a RDFGrowth network by selecting a topic group and joining it. The client then receive an operator (GUED), which, once applied on a RDF graph, retrieves all the resources which are of interest within the group. A GUED can be implemented as a set of queries. As an example, for a Michael Jackson group, a possible GUED might be "select all the URIs identifying his songs, albums, concerts and interviews". Once received the GUED operator, the peer executes it once on his DB and the resulting set of URIs are "published" in the p2p network, as an advertisement that they are in fact of interest and will be willing to answer requests from other peers about the "RDF Neighbours".

RDFN Hashes and Exchange Strategy
The algorithm cycles over the set of 'on topic' URIs (selected by the GUED) and for each of them searches for peers who have different surrounding informations (RDFN) than the local ones. This process is performed by looking into a Distributed Hash Table in which hashes of RDFNs (say simple MD5) are exposed by each peer. Once an hash is detected which is different from the one exposed by the local peer, an exchange is initiated. During the exchange peers synchronize their knowledge about the resource. In addition to simple hashes more advanced heuristics can be applied to identify new information present in the network and choose the peer from which it is more profitable to request information.

Discovering New Resources of Interest
RDFGrowth allows peers not only to learn more about the resources they already know (i.e. they do have in their local graph), but also to discover new resources of interest within a group. This is addressed by having each peer publishing an additional node (*GUED node*), which RDFN is exchanged by default among group participants. The RDFN of the GUED node, at each peer, is composed by all the resources which are the result of the GUED operator applied on the local graph. This is detailed and better explained in [6].

Considerations
A key point in this approach to metadata sharing is that the algorithm grows a local triple store at every peer, this not only enables fast browsing and complex query execution (performed using local computational power on the local DB, no external commitment), but also makes it possible for metadata to naturally cross the borders across communities. As an example, suppose that in a "movie community" someone posts a picture of an actor and in a "rap music" community the same actor has been mentioned as performer. Then a user participating at same time to both communities would, by the logic of the RDFGrowth algorithm, make so that the picture is also "posted" in the movie group.

A "growth only" scenario, as the one addressed here, matches the monotonic nature of the RDF semantics. To obtain more information can't "hurt" since, by definition, previously inferred statements will still hold when new data becomes available. It is of course possible, in the real world applications, to rely on "context" information to apply non monotonic rules on the local database, without consequences on the shared knowledge. Local filtering policies based on digital signatures (section 4) are an example of such context information which support several fundamental higher level non monotonic behaviours of the overall system.

3 Dealing with the Actual Data

Relaying on RDFGrowth, DBin users only exchanges pieces of RDF graphs describing the resources of interest., which might be real world concepts (such as a person) or digital content (e.g. mp3 files, pictures, documents) actually retrievable on the Internet. In many cases the user would like to be able to reach the actual data. In DBin this facilities are provided by the URIBridge module ,which relay on a publishing service allowing, at metadata creation time, to upload the files one is annotating, and, at metadata fruition time, to download the files that the metadata describe. During the upload phase a resolvable URL is given to the digital data and is used to create metadata about the data itself. Then this URI will be used by other peers, after having imported the annotations, to obtain the data itself (e.g. over standard HTTP protocol).

4 Identities and Authorship of Annotations

Provenance of information in our system, as it is based on replication of metadata among peers, does not means 'who gave me the information', but 'who was to first insert a peace of metadata into the system', that is the author of the annotation. This said, we need a methodology for 'marking' every peace of metadata added to the system with verifiable statements about the authorship.

The MSG definition and properties highlighted in the previous section, when combined with a canonicalized serialization as suggested in [7], enable signing MSGs themselves in a efficient way. This methodology, described in detail in [8], also assures that the context (in this case the authorship) will remain within the metadata when they will be exchanged over the network, as well as enables multiple signature to be attached to the same MSG, also at different times. Each user in DBin is provided with a user identifier (a URI) and a couple of public and private keys (the public one being made available to the other users by means of the URIBridge described in section 3). Every time a user adds an annotation to the system, the annotation itself will contain the user's identifier as well as the URL of the public key, and will be signed using the user's private key. In this way clients are able to retrieve the public key and to identify the author of an annotation, without caring about the which peer actually gave them the metadata itself.

Once the authorship of a MSG can be verified, a variety of filtering rules can be applied at will. These, in our system, are always non-destructive; information that doesn't match certain trust criteria can be hidden away but does not get deleted. Is it straightforward, for example, to implement a local 'black list' policy, allowing users to add authors to that list and to filter the local knowledge in order to hide all the information signed by the same user's identity.

5 User Interface: "Brainlets"

There has been a lot of work recently on Semantic Web visualization and a number of user interface have been proposed [9], [10], [11], [12], [13]. While pro and cons can be argued for each specific approach, it is clear that user interface issues are complex ones with no clear single solution. In designing the architecture of a RPSWC, rather than a single answer to this issue, we thought about a general set of "application oriented" generic GUI tools by which 'power users' can build applications specifically targeted to the domain of interest. We call these *domain specific applications*

“Brainlets”. They are implemented as plug-ins and can be though of as “configuration packages” preparing the client to operate on a specific domain (e.g. Wine lovers, Italian Opera fans etc..). Given that Brainlets include customized user interface, the user might perceive Brainlets as full “domain applications” which are run by the RPSWC.

The main components included in a Brainlet are:

- The ontologies to be used for annotations in the domain (e.g. The beer ontology);
- A general GUI layout: which components to visualize and how they interact;
- Templates for domain specific “annotations”, e.g. a “Movie Brainlet” might have a “review” template that users fill;
- Templates for readily available, “precooked” domain queries, which are structurally complex domain queries with a few free parameters, e.g. “give me the name of the cinema in city X where the best movie of genre Y is being shown tonight”;
- A suggested trust model and information filtering rules for the domain. e.g. public keys of well known “founding members” or authorities, preset “browsing levels”;
- A set of script to guide the user in choosing URIs for domain concepts; *g)* A basic RDF knowledge package, conforming to the information shared in a specific group.

Most importantly, Brainlets can be created as much as possible with no programming skills. In DBin implementation, basic Brainlets can be configured by editing XML files and more advanced ones can however be made including custom Eclipse plug-ins as needed. Most of the previously mentioned features have been implemented as shown in Figure 2, a screen shot of “Beer2Beer”, an example of XML based Brainlet.

5.1 Configuring a Brainlet

To create a Brainlet, one copies from a given empty template which configures an eclipse plug-in to append a new "Brainlet" to the list of those known by DBin. This is done by means of an Eclipse RCP [14] extension point, which enables to install a plug-in with specified APIs and properties. Then, each Brainlet has its own XML configuration file, which, in addition to purely layout configuration (e.g. the positioning of the GUI blocks) allow to define the Brainlet's core properties and facilities. The basic properties are the Brainlet name, version and URI, which usually indicates the web site from which to download the package. An overview of the other possible configurations follows.

Ontologies and Default RDF Knowledge

Probably the most important step in creating a new Brainlet is the choice of appropriate ontologies to represent the domain of interest. Once they have been identified, the corresponding OWL files are usually included and shipped in the Brainlet itself although they could be placed on the Web. Each of them will be declared in the XML file, specifying the location of the OWL file, a unique name for the ontology and it's base namespace. In the same way basic knowledge of the domain can be included.

Navigation of Resources

The way concepts and instances are presented and browsed is crucial to the usability of the interface and the effectiveness in finding relevant information. Graph based visualizers are notably problematic when dealing with a relevant number of resources. For this reason, the solution that the main DBin Navigator provides is based on flexible and dynamic tree structures. Such approach can be seen to scale very well with respect to the number of resources, e.g. in Brainlets such as the SW Research one. The peculiarity of the approach is that every Brainlet creator can decide which is the 'relation' between each tree item and its children by the use of semantic web queries (in DBin these are expressed using the SeRQL syntax [15]). There can be multiple topic branches configured in the Navigator, specifying different kinds of relation between parent and child items. This enables the user to explore the resources of the domain under different points of view. The right side of Figure 2 shows the Navigator view configured to show two tree branches, one (beers by type) gives an ontology driven hierarchical view on the domain, the other (beers by brewery) is a custom classification of the objects of domain, taking in consideration, in this case, the brewery which produces a beer.

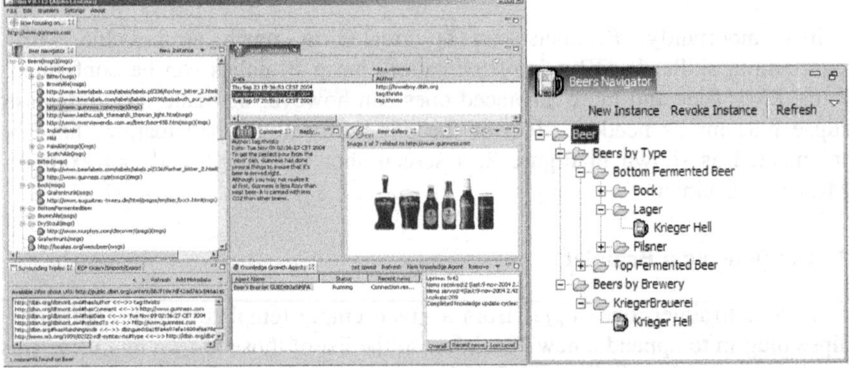

Fig. 2. (Left) a screen shot of the Beer2Beer Brainlet running. The principal "views" are: an ontology (and instances) browsing Navigator, the Knowledge Agents view, showing statistics about the currently running knowledge agents, and a set of "Annotation" views. Among these a comment view, a picture gallery and an "annotation listing" view. (Right).

Selection Flows

At user interface level, a Brainlet is composed by a set of 'view parts', as defined in the Eclipse platform terminology, Figure 2. Usually, each part takes a resource as a main "focus" and shows a particular aspect of the knowledge 'related' to the resource (e.g. it's properties, images associated, etc...). Selection flows among these parts are also scripted at this point; it is possible to establish the precise cause effect chain by which selecting an icon on a view will cause other views to change. This is done specifying, for each view part, which other one will be notified when a resource has been selected.

"Precooked Queries"
Within a specific domain there are often some queries that are frequently used to fulfill relevant use cases. Continuing our "Beer" example, such a query could be "find beers [stronger|lighter] than X degrees". The "Precooked queries" facility gives the Brainlet creators the ability to provide such "fill in the blanks" queries to end users.

URI Wizards
It is very important to avoid that users choose different URIs to indicate the very concept. This could be the case when inserting new concepts in an offline session or when the user doesnt properly search in the existing DB for the existence of a concept. For this purpose we introduce the concept of URI Wizard. URI Wizards define procedures which guide the user in assigning an identifier to a newly created instance. Different procedures can be associated to different type of resources present in the domain. For example an intuitive procedure to choose an identifier for a particular beer (e.g Peroni), might be that of visiting an authoritative web site (e.g. RateBeer.com), searching it for 'Peroni', and using the URL of the resulting web page to identify the concept. This is a very simple methodology for choosing URI but we believe it to be very powerful and somehow sound, as it leverages the work of existing and established web communities.

Custom Domain Dependent Annotation Templates
Brainlets use the ontologies to assist the users in creating simple annotations (e.g suggesting which properties can be associated to a resource based on its type). A Brainlet creator can however also chose to create "complex annotation types" using a specially defined OWL ontology. An example of such complex annotations is the "Beer Comparison" annotations, which directly compare beers stating which one is better or worse and why. Upon selecting "Add advanced annotation" in DBin the system determines which advanced annotations can be applied to the specified resource and provides a wizard.

5.2 Ontology Issue and Social Model

Brainlets are therefore preloaded by power users with domain specific user interaction facilities, as well as with domain ontologies suggested by the Brainlet creator. This seems to induce an interesting social model, mostly based on consensus upon Brainlets choice, which can help some of the well known issues in distributed metadata environments, a central one being the ontology mismatch problem. Brainlets, by providing an aggregation medium for ontologies, users, data representation structures, are therefore good catalyst of the overall semantic interoperability process. As users gather around popular Brainlets for their topic of choice, the respective suggested ontologies and data representation practice will form an increasingly important reality. If someone decided to create a new Brainlet or Semantic Web application in general which could target the same user group as the said popular Brainlet, there would be an evident incentive in using compatible data structures and ontologies.

6 Conclusions

In this short paper we introduced a novel SW scenario where information is created, exchanged and browsed by Rich Personal Semantic Web Clients. In doing so we illustrated DBin, our prototype meant to demonstrate the usefulness and scalability of such model.

While such model does not allow the user to immediately perform queries or browsing, we believe that this is a familiar paradigm for Internet users as it is not so much different from popular P2P file sharing applications. In the same way as many users have gotten used to wait to obtain data by running a classic P2P file sharing, DBin users will "peacefully" discover new information about topics in which they express interest in. Content and annotations produced by the user, on the other hand, can reach precisely those who had expressed interest in them and naturally cross the boundary of the P2P group they were posted originally to. Given RDFGrowth design, in fact, relevant annotations are intrinsically and automatically bridged by the peers that visit multiple groups or return at later times. We believe that the most important aspect in our system is the holistic integration of different components under a single "scenario philosophy", in other words, the ability for such application to enable real Internet users, for the first time, to "take a look" from the top of the SW tower. To enable this, we propose pragmatic solutions suggested by the scenario itself, which of course can hardly be thought as satisfying in to all possible user needs, however we believe that they might be "good enough" for a large number of use cases and user interest groups.

The prototype we discussed here, DBin, is programmed in Java and based on the Eclipse Rich Client platform. As such, DBin is naturally multi-platform, features an OS native look and feel and is highly extensible trough the well known Eclipse plug-ins and extension points technology. Both the framework and modules presented here are open source under the GPL license.

References

[1] "The DBin project" http://www.dbin.org

[2] Wolfgang Nejdl, Boris Wolf , "EDUTELLA: A P2P Networking Infrastructure Based on RDF" 2002 WWW2002, Honolulu

[3] Min Cai, Martin Frank , "RDFPeers: A Scalable Distributed RDF Repository based on A Structured Peer-to-Peer Network" 2004 13th International World Wide Web Conference WWW2004, New York

[4] Wolfgang Nejdl, Wolf Siberski, Martin Wolpers, Alexander L"ser, Ingo Bruckhorst , "SuperPeer Based Routing and Clustering Strategies for RDF Based Peer-To-Peer Networks", 12th International World Wide Web Conference, 2003, Budapest

[5] Paul Alexandru Chirita, Stratos Idreos, Manolis Koubarakis, and Wolfgang Nejdl , "Publish/Subscribe for RDF-based P2P Networks" ESWS, 2004, Heraklian, Greece

[6] Giovanni Tummarello, Christian Morbidoni, Joackin Petersson, Paolo Puliti, Francesco Piazza, "RDFGrowth, a P2P annotation exchange algorithm for scalable Semantic Web applications", First P2PKM Workshop, 2004, Boston

[7] Jeremy Carroll, "Signing RDF Graphs" 2nd International Semantic Web Conference, 2003, Sanibel Island, Florida, USA
[8] G. Tummarello, C. Morbidoni, P. Puliti, F. Piazza, "Signing individual fragments of an RDF graph", 14th International World Wide Web Conference, 2005, Chiba, Japan
[9] R. Albertoni, A. Bertone, M. De Martino, "Semantic Web and Information Visualization", Proceedings of the First Italian Workshop on Semantic Web Applications and Perspectives, 2004, Ancona , Italy
[10] "RDF Gravity - RDF Graph Visualization Tool" Technical Report: HPL-2004-57
[11] E Pietriga, "Isaviz: a visual environment for browsing and authoring rdf models ", 11th International World Wide Web Conference, 2002, Honolulu, Hawaii, USA
[12] "RDFX" Technical Report: HPL-2004-57
[13] Welkin, a graph-based RDF visualizer, 2004, http://simile.mit.edu/welkin/
[14] "Eclipse Rich Client Platform", http://www.eclipse.org/rcp/
[15] Jeen Broekstra, Arjohn Kampman, "SeRQL: An RDF Query and Transformation Language" 3rd International Semantic Web Conference, 2004, Hiroshima, Japan

I^2DEE: An Integrated and Interactive Data Exploration Environment Used for Ontology Design

Fabien Jalabert, Sylvie Ranwez, Vincent Derozier, and Michel Crampes

LGI2P Research Center, EMA/Site EERIE, Parc scientifique G. Besse,
F – 30 035 Nîmes cedex 1, France
firstname.lastname@ema.fr

Abstract. Many communities need to organize and structure data to improve their utilization and sharing. Much research has been focused on this problem. Many solutions are based on a Terminological and Ontological Resource (TOR) which represents the domain knowledge for a given application. However TORs are often designed without taking into account heterogeneous data from specific resources. For example, in the biomedical domain, these sources may be medical reports, bibliographical resources or biological data extracted from GOA, Gene Ontology or KEGG. This paper presents an integrated visual environment for knowledge engineering. It integrates heterogeneous data from domain databases. Relevant concepts and relations are thus extracted from data resources, using several analysis and treatment processes. The resulting ontology embryo is visualized through a user friendly adaptive interface displaying a knowledge map. The experiments and evaluations dealt with in this paper concern biological data.

1 Introduction

Exploring, using and sharing the data of a given community require precise organization. Such a dataset can represent the knowledge of the domain under consideration: human and social sciences, biology, economics or a virtual enterprise... However, such data may be very extensive and heterogeneous. Terminological and Ontological Resources (TORs) are common solutions for organizing and structuring information. TORs are intended to describe and formalize domain knowledge using concepts and relationships.

Major efforts on the part of the Knowledge Engineering community have provided tools and methods for TOR design. Information extraction research tries to elect candidate concepts or extract semantic relations from textual corpora. Experts in the domain then refine and organize concepts and relations to produce a reliable ontology. Obviously, corpora setting choices are crucial and must be as appropriate as possible to the application objective of the project. Choices are often limited to textual data. However, the knowledge of a whole domain is often broader than the content of bibliographical resources. Heterogeneity is probably the main curb that has discouraged efforts to integrate multiple domain databases. Life science analysis tools often use ontologies for information retrieval, expression data analysis or epidemiology, for

S. Staab and V. Svatek (Eds.): EKAW 2006, LNAI 4248, pp. 256 – 271, 2006.

example. Oddly, ontology engineering is never based on domain databases that contain useful information: biological items (genes, chemicals, etc.) are linked with concepts (annotations, etc.) or between each others (implied by biological reality).

With this aim, we designed and implemented an integrated and interactive data exploration environment called I^{2}DEE. It integrates heterogeneous data and produces a map that is adjusted to application and context. A domain expert then browses this map to carry out his task. Multiple applications can be based on the I^{2}DEE knowledge map. We implemented two experiments concerning gene expression analysis and knowledge engineering. This paper describes the latter, in the life science domain, which explains our subsequent choices. We designed a workflow that integrates multiple databases into a data warehouse. A small part of this warehouse is then extracted on user demand, depending on contextual needs. During the whole process, textual data are complemented by experimental and biological data. The user handles a graphic user interface that displays the map.

The paper is organized as follows. The next section exposes the issues concerned and the state of the art. It details several approaches and fixes our own. Section 0 presents our approach concerning data integration. Section 0 describes the workflow that enables concepts and relations to be extracted from multiple databases. Section 0 presents the visual results and discusses the uses and utility of I^{2}DEE. Limits and prospects are then discussed before the Conclusion.

2 Research Problematic and State of the Art

TOR design requires the expert to have both domain expertise and a real understanding of the intended use of the resulting TOR. Computer automation is mainly involved in carrying out two steps: the first is term extraction and clustering in order to elect candidate concepts. The second is the extraction of semantic relationships ("is a", "part of", etc.) from corpora to organize the structure and formalize previous concepts. *A priori* corpus composing and *a posteriori* evaluation, consistency checking and deployment do not cause cognitive overload or interaction lock. These steps are therefore not discussed in this paper and the current section presents the state of the art of the tools and methods available to assist the expert in term selection and organization.

2.1 Concept Extraction

The first related works concerned thesaurus design for information retrieval. The methods mainly rely on distributional corpora analysis and measures [39]. [38] presents recent state of art concerning such methods applied to ontology learning. The best known measures and weightings are frequency and TF.IDF (*Term Frequency x Inverse Document Frequency*) [43].

Previous weightings enable terms to be ordered, but experts need deeper organization of those terms to select the relevant ones. Association measures and clustering algorithms are therefore generally applied. A common hypothesis is that the recurring association of two words is not the result of chance. Co-occurrence based methods (or mutual information) [23] provide a similarity measure that is helpful for term contextualization and clustering. More specific methods search for contiguous sequential patterns [28]. For two term methods, relations are called collocations [22][34], whereas they are referred to as n-grams [44] in a predictive approach.

Such straightforward statistical approaches match corpora reality, but do not take semantics into consideration. [36] describe the state of the art of a linguistic approach for improving the semantics of knowledge extraction. Z.H. Harris suggests applying distributional methods to syntactic items [32]. Several natural language processing tools used in knowledge engineering are based on such an approach: *LEXTER* [20] (a project replaced by Syntex+Upery), *ZELLIG* [31], *NOMINO* [37], *ACABIT* [27] and *FASTR* [35].

Various works provide interactive software for visualizing lexical networks. HyperLex [46] is based on using co-occurrences to disambiguate usage context. [42] helps to find *contexonyms* (substitutable words in a machine translation approach). [30] studies in-depth graph topology using another measure called *proxemy*.

[40],[24] make an inventory of many TOR editors and IDEs. The main features can be grouped together in 4 main classes:

- following formalisms or methodologies;
- providing logical engines for inference or consistency checks, for example;
- providing distributed architecture to allow collaborative work;
- displaying data in a user friendly interactive interface

To conclude, ontology learning methods are based on two resources: existing ontologies are sometimes reused, merged, enriched or restructured, and computer aided methods rely on information extraction from corpora. The corpus is composed continuously using domain literature. We have not found any TOR design environment that allows integration of domain knowledge from heterogeneous resources (i.e. including non textual resources and semantic or linguistic relations). Section 0 presents a proposed solution for such data integration.

In this approach, visualization features are crucial. Vast quantities of heterogeneous data are imported, so the usual tree approach, developing graphical components based only on "is-a" relations, may not be sufficient for user's needs.

2.2 Context

Our goal is clearly defined: assisting a domain expert (biologist) by providing a TOR IDE with enhanced integration and interactive features. Interactions are associated to a knowledge map. So, questions concerning the nature and visualization of data cannot be bypassed.

The questions regarding **nature** include: Which data is relevant in ontology design? How to integrate such heterogeneous data? How to generalize this process?

Concerning the **visualization** problematic, the user is rapidly overloaded with information. So, how to filter data? How to let him/her add new resources which minimum effort? Which features help him/her to manage vast quantities of information with the lowest possible cognitive and learning load (zoom, pan, overview, optical and semantic lenses, etc.)? How to lay out and efficiently browse a map?

This paper provides proposals to these questions that have been implemented in a biological context. We are involved in two projects that confirm the interest of the knowledge map. The first is gene expression analysis and the second is ontology design for information retrieval and scientific monitoring. The following results only detail the latter application. The biological context concerns *Plasmodium falciparum*, the parasite responsible for *malaria*.

3 Approach to Integration

3.1 Data Heterogeneity

Biology uses huge amounts of data that can be divided into four classes: **bibliographical resources, conceptual resources, biological databases** and **experimental data**. At present, many ontology design tools use only bibliographic and conceptual resources. We believe that there is useful biological knowledge in domain databases that are not included in ontologies and scientific articles. We also consider that experimental data are crucial for adjusting content to the user's needs.

Bibliographical resources: The most widespread is PubMed [15], which is used by the whole biomedical community and provides XML descriptions of over 14 million articles; abstracts are available for more than a half of them. OMIM [12] focuses on biological knowledge about genes and human genetic disorders. BioMed Central [2] and PubMed Central [16] provide full access to articles. Such bibliographical resources contain a biological knowledge often hidden in huge amount of texts. This property has motivated a good deal of research that has already produced various results [45]. In our process we focus on PubMed.

Conceptual resources: The increasing amount of biological data gives rise to new problems of data access. Biologists need tools providing unified access in a custom research framework. There are numerous formal ontologies in life science. The best known are: Gene Ontology (GO, [6]) used to annotate genes and proteins, and MeSH [11] to index documents in PubMed. UMLS [17] is a conceptual warehouse containing more than a hundred ontologies (in multiple languages). Such a resource is crucial to enabling semantic interoperability and ontology mapping and reuse. I²DEE integrates UMLS (including Go and MeSH) and GoDataBase [1], which provides links with chemicals and genes, an *ultrametric* distance (length of shortest path), bibliographical links and synonymic relations.

Biological databases: represent the shared knowledge of life sciences. These resources are responsible for the main heterogeneity problematic. There are fairly general resources: UniProt [18] and GeneBank [5] concern proteins and genes, KEGG [9] metabolic pathways and GOA [7] provides annotations. All these resources describe multiple organisms. There exist more specific resources: PDB [13] provides structural protein information (for example protein folding, helix, sheets, secondary structure, etc.), EntrezGene [4] normalizes and centralizes gene names and accession numbers for cross-referencing, and PlasmoDB [14] concerns only *Plasmodium falciparum*. Our environment integrates EntrezGene, KEGG and PlasmoDB. Annotations are links between a gene or protein and a concept. Another relation may mean a protein is a gene product. However other information is more difficult to represent: secondary or 3-dimensional structures, sequences and n-ary chemical reactions.

Experimental Data: such data are the prime input in the building of a relevant corpus. But their heterogeneity is a difficult problem of interest to the whole life science community. The research of the MAGE team [10] is an example of gene expression data sharing effort.

In this experiment, the starting point was a list of the *Plasmodium falciparum* genes on a DNA microarray.

3.2 Common Extensible Schema

Most research works integrate data using a consensual schema. The aim is to obtain a mainspring domain model preserving the best expressivity of integrated resource schemas. Adding resources requires considerable engineering. For example: GUS [8] (used by PlasmoDB) contains over 300 tables.

We adopted a contrasting approach by using a simple schema, a graph. This causes a lack of expressivity with respect to advanced requests. But extensibility is much higher: most knowledge can be translated to graph model with little additional engineering. A graph is also a well studied structure providing many algorithms for analyzing, drawing, etc. The graph is typed and valued.

4 Description of the Environment

I²DEE covers the whole data processing chain: from corpus extraction and database integration to domain knowledge visualization. Fig. 1 presents an overview of the architecture. I²DEE has a separate server side in charge of data integration and a client side that provides a set of user-friendly specific applications. The integration process, detailed in 0, builds a graph structured data warehouse. The user inputs keywords or documents in a client application. APIs support the implementation of graphical clients, data access and submap extraction (Section 0).

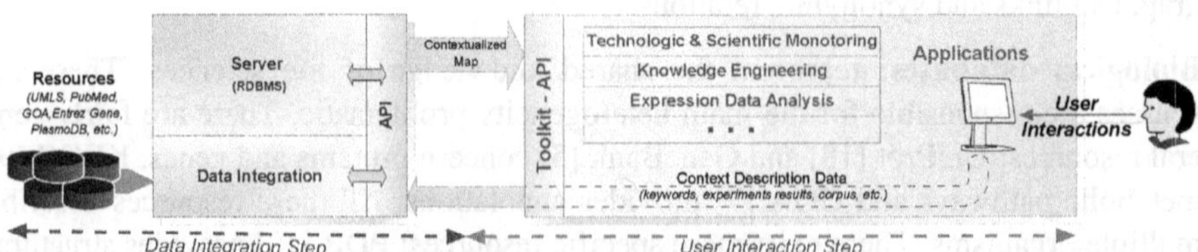

Fig. 1. Overview of the architecture of I²DEE

4.1 Integration Step: Building the Warehouse

The integration process (Fig. 2) is divided into two steps. Firstly, the integration process integrates multiple databases in a graph modelled data warehouse. Optional filtering reduces time consumption of huge resources like PubMed. Integrated textual data are then parsed to produce and index of occurring concepts or biological elements (chemicals, genes, etc.) with documents, definitions, etc. Finally, a distributional analysis enriches the warehouse providing frequency, co-occurrences relations. The second step consists in extraction from the warehouse of a user's needs-adjusted submap on client application demand. All these process are detailed below.

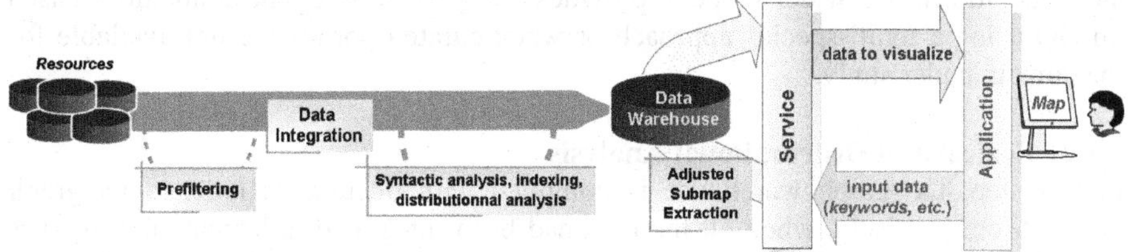

Fig. 2. Integration process

4.1.1 Integrated Databases

Data was integrated sequentially in an order determined by functional dependencies. UMLS was integrated first because its concepts are referred to in most of the databases. PubMed was next because it uses UMLS concepts but is also referred to by many resources. Other resources were then integrated: GODatabase, Gene, GOA, KEGG and PlasmoDB. Persistence in I²DEE is provided by a MySQL server. The rest of this section describes each of the resource integration processes implemented.

UMLS - MetamorphoSys is a tool that helps to set up the installation of UMLS. It builds files that are optimized for RDBMS (Relational Data Base Management System) upload (it currently supports MySQL & Oracle SQL specifications). UMLS consists of four base layers. We only integrate extreme layers: the lowest contains occurrences (or *atoms*) of words in ontologies, and the highest is at the level of concept mediation. We also integrated the semantic relations.

At the end of this step, there were one million concepts and about four to five millions atoms. UMLS required about 20Go of hard-disk space.

PubMed is provided in compressed XML format. We used the BioText [3] library to convert data into a relational schema. In order to save time and space, we filtered PubMed, retaining only documents containing user-defined keywords ("*microarray*", "*gene expression*", "*plasmodium*", "*malaria*", etc...).

This filter retains about one hundredth of the initial document set (≈ 50 Go). This represents 120000 documents and associated information: authors, keywords, chemicals, genes, and journals.

GoDatabase is available in a flat file directly loadable into an RDBMS. The ontology is already available in UMLS, so only updating for new concepts was required. In addition, this database contains a pre-computed utrametric distance (shortest path between concepts in Go's DAG). Finally, it provides definitions, cross-references and synonymic relations.

Entrez Gene is available in XML format. We used a specific organism subset concerning *Plasmodium falciparum.* We extracted information from the database to manage aliasing (different names and accession numbers for the same gene), bibliographical references (PubMed documents for a gene) and miscellaneous comments.

PlasmoDB provides the most recent and curated genomic information concerning *Plasmodium falciparum.* We used mainly the annotations.

GOA is redundant with GO and PlasmoDB provides more updated lists of genes and annotations. In a wider scope, it provides a way to request gene annotations based on GO using a multi-species approach or when curated portals are not available for the domain under study.

4.1.2 Lexical and Distributional Analysis

In this step, the graph warehouse is compiled with documents indexed by graph nodes. More precisely, when all the data had been integrated, a lexical analysis was used to produce an index of occurrences of concepts in the textual data (cf. 0: documents, surveys, definitions, etc.). The concepts we refer to are provided by UMLS, frequent string tokens extracted from corpora and biological name entities (gene, protein, chemicals etc.), The freeware programs we tried were not reliable enough due to a specific feature of biomedical corpora: named entities (genes, chemicals, etc.) contain parentheses, dashes, dots, commas, digits, etc. We implemented our own parser, which breaks down the document by searching for the longest segments. This tool uses a dictionary of lemmas and the list of concepts and *string* provided by UMLS. Spelling and some other variations (inflexion, comma, etc.) are taken into account. The algorithm is based on a lemma tree backtracking search. The analysis of around 120,000 summaries takes only few minutes. We have not yet quantified the tool's precision and recall, but the first tests gave satisfactory results.

At this stage we had an ordered list of knowledge elements for each textual resource. Finally we carried out a distributional analysis to give frequencies, co-occurrences and collocations.

4.1.3 Sub-map Extraction

The resulting data was still too voluminous. UMLS produced more than one million nodes and PubMed several hundred more. The more specific biological databases are smaller resources. The user would not be able to visualize and analyze all this information. An automatic process was used to extract a small contextualized map on user demand. This step is mainly driven by the intended usage of the map and user input data (documents, gene lists, keywords, etc).

The initial input in our experiment was a 500 microarray spotted gene list (called core nodes). All nodes two genes at most from the core nodes were then added. We did not take co-occurrence relations into account, nor the ultrametric distance, which leads to excessive connectivity. The resulting subgraph consisted of 5,000,000 nodes because UMLS contains semantic types that link concepts to several millions of nodes.

A weighting algorithm was used to reduce this subgraph by means of a link analysis inspired approach [19],[41]: core nodes were given the value 1, directly linked nodes 0.5 and other nodes 0. From the core outwards, each vertex propagates its weight to its neighborhood. Let n_i be a vertex and n_j one of its neighbors.

$$rank(n_j) \leftarrow rank(n_j) + \frac{rank(n_i)}{degree(n_i)} \quad (1)$$

This method rapidly limits the extension of the graph using a threshold. We fixed the number of nodes between 5,000 and 15,000. This value represents a multiplicative factor of 10 with respect to the initial number of core genes. This choice is consistent because genes are usually linked to about 6 concepts and documents.

When relevant nodes had been selected using the threshold, we navigated bottom-up through the hierarchical relations ("is a", "part of", etc.) and added all ancestors to the subgraph. Finally we added the previously ignored relations (co-occurrences, *ultrametric* distance, etc.) The sub-map used in the following section consists of 6,000 nodes including around 2,000 concepts.

4.2 Interaction Step: Adaptable User-Friendly Interface

The first section introduced our goal of providing a knowledge map. This map is specific to an expert domain, the application and the task involved. A user-friendly interface is required to allow the user to explore this domain knowledge warehouse. I^{2}DEE adjusts the map according to context (c.f. 0). Customization is carried out on two levels: content and visualization. The expert is not able to browse the huge amount of data integrated by I^{2}DEE , so it is necessary to define which data are useful for a given application. For example, the user may not be interested in visualizing genes and clusters. The graphic client needs to adapt the view to the domain and task, by selecting which data should be displayed, and which should be masked. But the expert's task can be split into subtasks such as selecting terms, structuring "is-a" or "part-of" relationships, etc. Each of these subtasks must have its own visualization and must take into account the data heterogeneity. The warehouse merges several graphs having different topologies. Therefore we need a generic algorithm that efficiently lays out any topologies. It should enable the user to switch easily between multiple domain views according to application contexts. So we chose a dynamic method [29] based on a physical model: force directed layout. The principle is to arrange the graph vertices over a horizontal plane and link them by forces (generally called springs): The layout self-adjusts automatically. Forces are repulsive, attractive or both. The semantics extracted from the domain databases were applied to such forces. A short distance between two vertices reflects indirect relations between these vertices. Moreover, by changing display properties (visibility of an element, mobility of a node, activation of an edge), multiple views can be assigned to the semantics. As an example, in the following we will reorganize the graph around the "part-of" and the "is-a" relation.

We implemented I^{2}DEE using Prefuse [33], a Java visualization toolkit to which we added new features. The GUI enables thousands of nodes to be displayed. The frame rate only becomes poor with tens of thousands of edges (CeleronM 1.4 GHz). The software architecture enables a filtering step to facilitate multiscale visualization. The rendering is accelerated using double buffering. Many common features are implemented: overview, zoom, pan, selection, high definition screenshots, etc.

We altered the model to add dynamic type management and display properties (visibility, mobility, force activation, etc.), and removed the inertia in force integrator, etc. The next section presents the results of multiple views.

5 Visual Results

5.1 Intended Usage

The following results illustrate the aims of I^{2}DEE with regard to prospects for ontology design. The current application does not yet include common features such as forms to edit concept properties, import and export features, etc. Several existing tools should be able to provide such functionalities rapidly, and we are considering several alternatives: adding I^{2}DEE as a Protégé plug-in or using APIs (Protégé or Jena for example).

Increasing amounts of data and the use of such a data warehouse leads to new difficulties. I^{2}DEE was designed to help manipulate huge amounts of data. Ontology reuse should increase design speed and resource interoperability. Increasing quantities of data should improve design quality, include in-corpus domain knowledge (not only bibliographical domain description) and contextualize resources. The environment helps the domain expert and knowledge engineer: (1) to note that several model choices are available and (2) to identify the solution chosen by the most similar terminology or ontology. These steps may help the user to understand and could warn him about possible ambiguity. Finally (3), if the user chooses the global alternative of one resource, the environment allows global reuse with simple interaction.

5.2 Commented Screenshots

NOTE – *The screenshots presented take into consideration the fact that this paper will be printed. The hard copy constraint does not enable the viewing of animations or colors, or zooming to view details. We shall soon make available some video captures of the environment.*

The first screenshots in Fig. 3 display about 2,000 concepts. No gene or document is drawn. There are about 6,000 edges divided into 3 classes: co-occurrences relations, biological annotations and semantic relationships ("is-a", "part-of", etc.). The three screenshots in Fig. 3 show the distribution of these classes of relations for the whole graph.

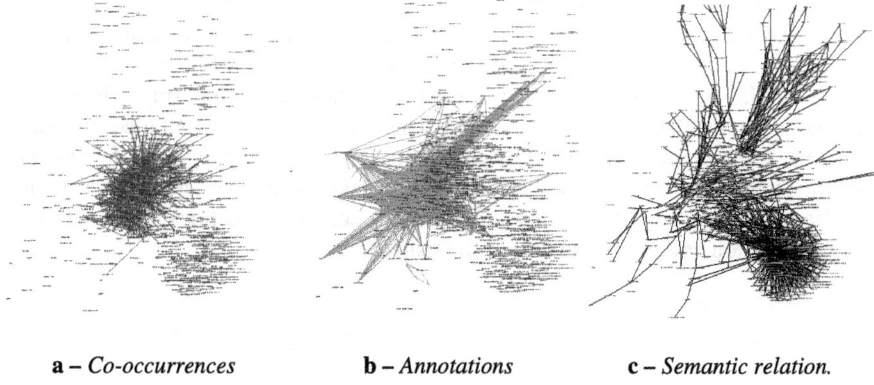

a – *Co-occurrences* **b** – *Annotations* **c** – *Semantic relation.*

Fig. 3. Three main relations in the global knowledge map

The co-occurrences shown in Fig. 3-a produce an entanglement situated in the centre of the graph. This is characteristic of a social or lexical network: in spite of a low average degree of connectivity, it is generally hard to visualize [21]. The annotations in Fig. 3-b are also situated in a delimited part of plane in the centre of the graph. This reflects the use of terms in the experimental domain. Finally, the semantic relations in Fig. 3-c extend to the outskirts of the graph, with a hub bottom right. The topology of the remaining relations produces a lattice-like topology caused by multiple hierarchies (often hierarchical "is-a" or "part-of" relationships from differing ontologies and points of view).

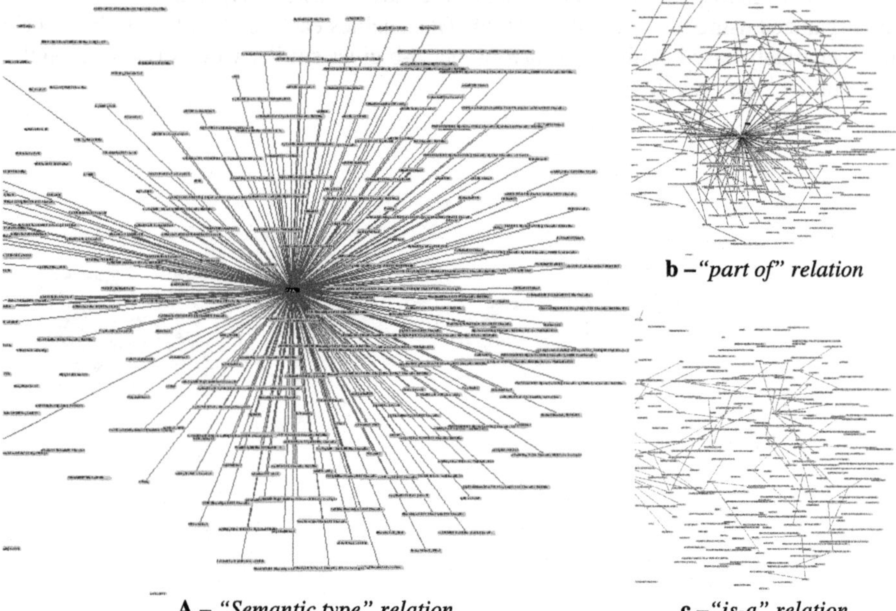

b – *"part of" relation*

A – *"Semantic type" relation* **c** – *"is-a" relation*

Fig. 4. Full screen captures of the hub laid out using three combinations of relations. Relations are drawn separately.

The hub (detailed in Fig. 4) is structured by three relationships: the semantic type provided by UMLS (Fig. 4-a) gives a star layout whose centre is the "cell component" concept (the zoom feature gives good readability). The "part-of" relation (Fig. 4-b) gives a similar topology: a flattened tree whose centre is "cytoplasm". The depth of this tree is higher than semantic star type. This may imply more detailed knowledge modeling. Entanglement is caused by competitive forces from the "part of" and "is-a" relations, which are transversal. This experiment testifies that simultaneous activation of different forces associated to complementary semantic relations may disturb the user's perception and understanding of the map.

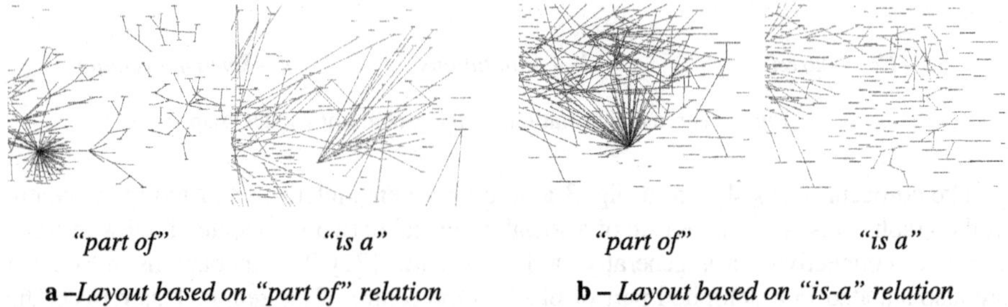

Fig. 5. Graphs of semantic relations using two different force-based layouts. The first uses "part of", the second "is-a".

One solution is to enable the user to selecting alternately which relationship should be used to organize the map, depending of the current task. In Fig. 5-a, the screenshots are organized using the "part of" relation. This enables each relation type to be visualized separately based on the same layout. Fig. 5-b gives similar views organized on the basis of the "is a" relation.

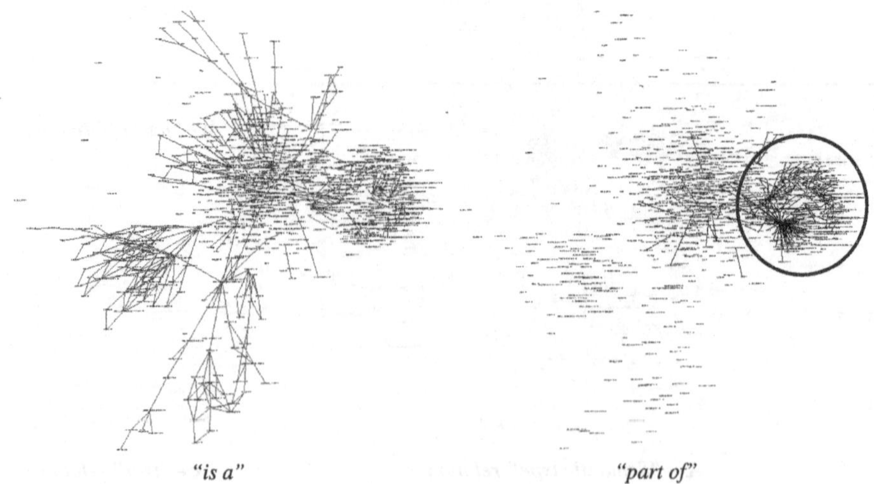

Fig. 6. Distribution of "is-a" and "part-of" relations in global map view

The results of this experiment are unambiguous: alternate organization of the view using one relation is essential in producing an understandable map (planar in this example).

The screenshots in Fig. 6 show the global distribution of the "is-a" and "part of" relations in the map. The multi-hierarchies on the peripheries of the map are a result of the "is a" relation, which is not surprising since it is the most frequent relation used in ontologies. Detailed analysis of the terms indicated that general terms are found in the center of branches and specialty concepts towards the outside. The "part of" relation is limited to the hub region (as shown by the circle in the right-hand view of Fig. 6).

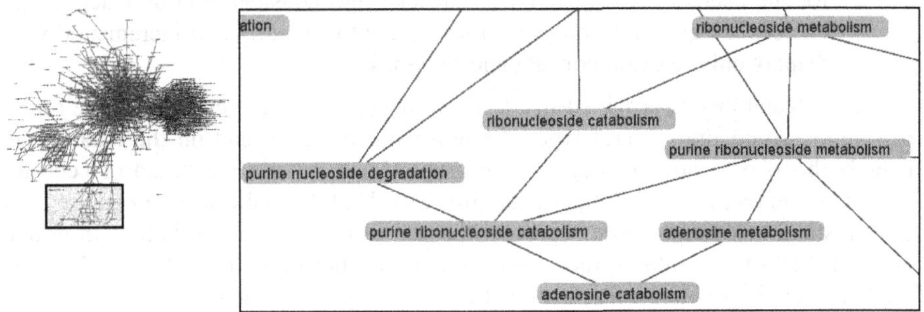

Fig. 7. Zoom of the end of an "is-a" DAG branch

Fig. 7 details the content of an "is a' branch in the graph, whose topology is a directed acyclic graph (DAG). Such a structure can result from two phenomena. The most obvious one is that original resource that describes this region in UMLS is based on a DAG structure like GO. The second one is that two hierarchies partially cover the same concepts from different points of view. In Fig. 7, for example, *adenosine catabolism* is more precise than *purine ribonucleoside catabolism* and *adenosine*, which are more precise than *purine ribonucleoside metabolism.* Such a view can help the user to decide which modeling solution is best suited to his/her application. The expert can delete relations that do not respect tree structure or modify the model by creating two new subtrees (c.f. Fig. 8) and model the adenosine metabolism as a composite concept.

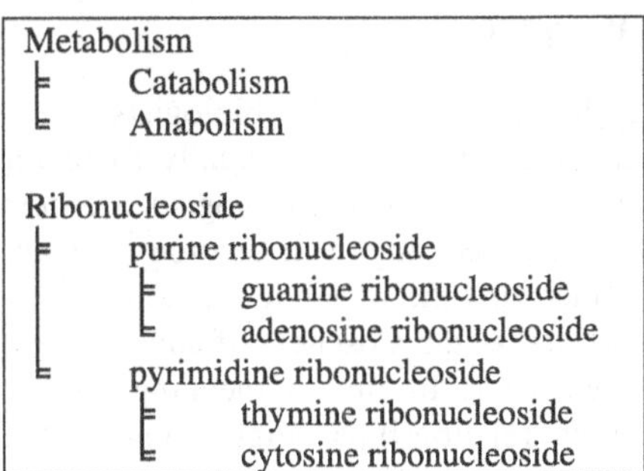

Fig. 8. The concept adenosine ribonucleoside can be considered as a concept made up of two primitive concepts each belonging to a different hierarchy

5.3 Adaptability

The above results show the importance of integrating heterogeneous data in a common view and allowing the user to customize this view depending of the current task. In an ontological computer aided design application, such features cause two problems:

- The user must continuously choose the best view for a given task, so he or she must have a good understanding of I²DEE's behavior, and each view switch costs time and cognitive load.
- Even after several filtering steps, the quantity of information is still too great for the user. Adapting methods that take into consideration user actions and choices are crucial in order to filter data automatically and incrementally and display only relevant concept and relations.

Such adaptability is provided in I²DEE by special weighting criteria. These criteria can be classified into several types. **Structural** criteria depend on the location and neighborhood of a node or edge in the graph. Such criteria are based or centrality measures, degree, ranking (Page Rank, Hits, etc.) [19]. **Distribution** criteria are based on statistical calculations that represent the use of concepts and relations in domain corpora. Measures could include frequency, co-occurrences, TF.IDF, the Harrissian method, etc. **Relevance** criteria rank the similarity of elements with the expected result representation (input corpora). For example, semantic vector approaches [43] enable documents from the domain corpus to be compared with concepts. Finally, **reliability and confidence** criteria estimate the helpfulness of a resource by counting the proportion of its elements that are validated or eliminated. Such criteria include whether an ontology appears more appropriate to a given domain and provides better modeling, for example, or perhaps another ontology may have been generated using a poorly supervised method.

Learning is based on interactions. It is easy to rank deleted items with low criteria values, and to consider other items that have been edited and maintained to be useful. But what about the many other items that user does not edit? The goal of adaptability is not to constrain the user to treat every item. So we put forward the following hypothesis: the more a user edits and deletes items, the more he or she has evaluated the neighborhood and wishes to retain the elements in it. We suggest benefiting from the network structure by using structural ranking propagation calculations.

5.4 Uses: Limits and Prospects

The system is currently being evaluated by biologists, revealing that they are not literate in knowledge engineering. They continually focus on biological knowledge and not on conceptual modeling. Although biologists are domain experts, they have difficulty understanding and processing such ontology design tasks. They search for the biological relations underlying the semantic relations.

They tend quickly to prioritize the closeness of concepts over the relations that link them. Moreover, the user needs to find a meaning and semantics in direct co-occurrence relations. Indirect relationships, neighboring small cliques, definitions, etc. need to be analyzed. More information about context is required in order to explain such edges.

Generally, user feedback was positive. Co-occurrence relations reflect biological reality. One user commented that the training data were not really suitable for evaluating our environment because of the state of scientific knowledge among the community about such organisms. He explained that the display was closer to a bacterium than a eukaryote. But this is a consistent result because *Plasmodium falciparum* is a simple parasite.

At present content adaptability is based on preexisting methods and visualization adaptability is controlled by hand by the user. Our system does not include machine learning yet. Future works will consider user interactions as feedback so that the system can dynamically filter data and select the associated visualization.

Our information visualization team is designing an experimental visualization environment called MolAge. This force-based tool converts multidimensional data into complete graphs and allows multidimensional data to be gathered and visualized. Until now the amount of data to be laid out has exceeded the capacity of our MolAge environment [25]. However recent upgrades allow us to consider migration to this environment and thus to benefit from its advanced features: semantic spectra, building scenarios, etc. [26]. In particular, it is easy and fast to test new features and lens, distortions, and to parameterize them.

6 Conclusion

The integrated and interactive data exploration environment (I²DEE) presented in this paper has been applied in the context of the design and definition of ontologies. Two major contributions have been identified. The first one concerns the integration of experimental data from domain databases, in our case biology. By this way the environment improves the adaptation to a specific context and fits user needs in their various tasks: bibliographical search, data analyses, etc. The second contribution concerns the interactive manipulation of the heterogeneous data that have been integrated. A dynamic knowledge map is presented to users, who can interact with it in order to emphasize some parts of the map, to generate deeper requests to a database or analyze some neighborhoods, for example.

The first evaluation process carried out with biologists confirmed the relevance of our approach. Some limits have been identified and highlighted some prospects for our work. Some of them concern computer performances. We are working on improvements that may overcome these limits. Others involve user interaction difficulties: the user needs to understand I²DEE's behavior and features. A new version with additional functionalities is under development that will better satisfy biologists" needs and therefore become a software support for their current tasks.

References

Web References

[1] Amigo – Gene Ontology Software and Databases, http://www.godatabase.org
[2] BioMed Central, http://www.biomedcentral.com/
[3] BioText, http://biotext.berkeley.edu/

[4] Entrez Gene, http://www.ncbi.nlm.nih.gov/entrez/query.fcgi?db=gene
[5] Genebank, http://www.ncbi.nlm.nih.gov/Genbank/
[6] GO – the Gene Ontology, http://www.geneontology.org/
[7] GOA – Gene Ontology Annotation, http://www.ebi.ac.uk/GOA/index.html
[8] GUS, The Genomics Unified Schema, http://www.gusdb.org/
[9] KEGG: Kyoto Encyclopedia of Genes and Genomes http://www.genome.jp/kegg/
[10] MAGE, MicroArray and Gene Expression, http://www.mged.org/Workgroups/MAGE/mage.html
[11] MeSH, Medical Subject Headings, http://www.nlm.nih.gov/mesh/meshhome.html
[12] OMIM, Online Mendelian Inheritance in Man, http://www.ncbi.nlm.nih.gov/entrez/query.fcgi?db=OMIM
[13] Pdb, the rcsb Protein DataBank, http://www.rcsb.org/pdb/
[14] PlasmoDB, The Plasmodium Genome Resource, http://plasmodb.org/
[15] PubMed – http://www.pubmed.gov
[16] PubMed Central, http://www.pubmedcentral.nih.gov/
[17] Umls, Unified Medical Language System, http://www.nlm.nih.gov/research/umls/
[18] Uniprot, The Universal Protein Resource, http://www.expasy.uniprot.org/

Bibliographical References

[19] Borodin, A., Roberts, G. O., Rosenthal, J. S., et Tsaparas, P. Link analysis ranking: algorithms, theory, and experiments. ACM Tranactions. On Internet Technology (TOIT), vol. 5:1, pp. 231-297, 2005.
[20] Bourigault, D., Lexter, a Natural Language tool for terminology extraction, 7th EURALEX International Congress, pp. 771-779, Göteborg, 1996.
[21] Boutin, F., Hascoët, M., Multi-Level Exploration of Citation Graphs, ECDL'04 – European Conference of Digital Library, n. 3232, pp 366– 377, 2004.
[22] Choueka Y. *Looking for needles in a haystack*, Conference on User-Oriented Context Based Text and Image Handling (RIAO 88). Cambridge, MA. 1988.
[23] Church K.W. et Hanks P. Word Association Norms, Mutual Information and Lexicography. Proceedings of the 27th Annual Meeting of the Association for Computational Linguistics, pp. 76-83, Vancouver, 1989.
[24] Corcho O., Fernández-López M. et Gómez-Pérez A.. Methodologies, tools and languages for building ontologies: where is their meeting point ? Data Knowledge Engineering, vol. 46:1, pp. 41-64 : Elsevier Science Publishers B. V., 2003.
[25] Crampes M., Ranwez S., Velickovski F., Mooney C and Mille N. An Integrated Visual Approach for Music Indexing and Dynamic Playlist Composition, MMCN2006, 13th Annual Multimedia Computing and Networking, San Jose, California, January 18-19, 2006.
[26] Crampes M., Ranwez S., Villerd J., Velickovski F., Mooney C, Emery A and Mille N. Concept Maps for Designing Adaptive Knowledge Maps, *Information Visualization Journal*, Palgrave, September 2006
[27] Daille, B., Conceptual structuring through term variations, in F. Bond, A. Korhonen, D. MacCarthy and A. Villacicencio (eds.), proc. ACL 2003, Workshop on Multiword Expressions : Analysis, Acquisition and Treatments, pp.9-16, 2003.
[28] Dias G., Guilloré S. and Lopes J.G.P. Extracting Textual Associations in Part-of-Speech Tagged Corpora. Fifth EAMT Workshop "Harvesting existing resources" Ljubljana, Slovenia, May 11 - 12, 2000.
[29] Eades, P. A heuristic for graph drawing. Congressus Numerantium 42, pp. 149-160, 1984.
[30] Gaume, B., Duvignau, K., Gasquet, O., and Gineste M.-D., Forms of meaning, meaning of forms, Journal of Experimental and Theoritical Artificial Intelligence, 14(1), 61–74.
[31] Habert, B., Naulleau, E., Nazarenko, A., Symbolic word clustering for medium-size corpora, proc. 16th COLING, Copenhagen, vol. 490(5), 1996.
[32] Harris Z. Mathematical Structures of Language, NY, John Wiley & Sons, 1968.

[33] Heer J. Prefuse: a software framework for interactive information visualization Masters of Sc., Computer Science Division, Univ. of California, Berkeley, 2004.

[34] Hindle D. et Rooth M. Structural ambiguity and lexical relations, Computational Linguistics, Special issue on using large corpora, Vol. 19:1, pp. 103-120, 1993.

[35] Jacquemin C. FASTR : A unification grammar and a parser for terminology extraction from large corpora. Journées IA'94, pp. 155-164, Paris, 1994.

[36] Jacquemin, C. and Bourigault, D., Term Extraction and Automatic Indexing, In R. Mitkiv, ed., Handbook of Computational Linguistics, pp. 599-615. Oxford University Press, 2003.

[37] Lauriston, A., Automatic recognition of complex terms : Problems and the TERMINO solution, Terminology vol. 1(1), pp. 147, 1994.

[38] Malaisé V. Méthodologie linguistique et terminologique pour l'exploitation d'outils d'extraction terminologique et la constitution d'ontologies différentielles à partir de corpus textuels, Thèse de doctorat, Université Technologique de Compiègnes, October 2005.

[39] Manning, C. and Schütze, H. Foundations of Statistical Natural Language Processing, MIT Press. Cambridge, MA: May 1999.

[40] Mizoguchi R. Ontology Engineering Environments, Handbook on Ontologies, pp. 175-298, S. Staab et R. Studer, 2004.

[41] Page L., Brin S., Motwani R. et Winograd T. The PageRank Citation Ranking: Bringing Order to the Web, Stanford Digital Library Technologies Project, 1998.

[42] Ploux, S., Ji, H., A model for matching semantic maps between languages (French/English, English/French) Computational Linguistics, vol. 29:2, pp. 155-178, 2003.

[43] Salton G. et McGill M.J. Introduction to Modern Information Retrieval, McGraw Hill, 1983

[44] Suen C. Y. N-Gram Statistics for Natural Language Understanding and Text Processing, IEEE Trans. on Pattern Analysis and Machine Intelligence, vol. PAMI-1:2, pp.164-172, 1979.

[45] Swanson D.R. Fish oil, Raynaud's syndrome, and undiscovered public knowledge, *Perspectives in Biology and Medicine*, vol 30:1, pp. 7-18, 1986.

[46] Véronis, J. Hyperlex : lexical cartography for information retrieval. *Computer, Speech and Language,* vol. 18 (3), pp. 223-252, 2004.

Evaluating a Thesaurus Browser for an Audio-visual Archive

Véronique Malaisé[1], Lora Aroyo[2], Hennie Brugman[3], Luit Gazendam[4], Annemieke de Jong[5], Christian Negru[2], and Guus Schreiber[1]

[1] Vrije Universiteit Amsterdam, The Netherlands
schreiber@cs.vu.nl, vmalaise@few.vu.nl
[2] Technische Universiteit Eindhoven, The Netherlands
l.m.aroyo@tue.nl, c.m.negru@student.tue.nl
[3] Max Planck Institute for Psycholinguistics, Nijmegen, The Netherlands
Hennie.Brugman@mpi.nl
[4] Telematica Instituut, Enschedé, The Netherlands
Luit.Gazendam@telin.nl
[5] Dutch Institute for Sound & Vision, Hilversum, The Netherlands
adjong@beeldengeluid.nl

Abstract. In this article we report on a user study aimed at evaluating and improving a thesaurus browser. The browser is intended to be used by documentalists of a large public audio-visual archive for finding appropriate indexing terms for TV programs. The subjects involved in the study were documentalists of the Dutch National Audiovisual Archives and of broadcasting corporations. The study provides insight into the value of various thesaurus browsing and searching techniques.

1 Introduction, Objectives and Approach

In this paper we report on a user study with a thesaurus developed for cataloguers of a audio-visual broadcast archive. This work is part of the CHOICE project[1] which aims to support annotation and search of the broadcast archive of the Dutch Institute for Sound & Vision. As part of this project we built a thesaurus browser for the GTAA[2] thesaurus. The thesaurus browser is a general SKOS/RDF browser [7]. We converted the original database representation of the thesaurus to SKOS (for conversion principles and representation details see [9]).

The purpose of the browser is to support cataloguers both of Sound & Vision and of the broadcast corporations in finding the appropriate indexing terms. Indexing is still mainly a manual process. Sound & Vision is in the process of moving to a completely digital archiving process and as a consequence heavier demands are put on the cataloguers. In fact, the browser is considered a simple baseline tool. The project also works on semi-automatic techniques for extracting

[1] http://www.nwo.nl/catch/choice/
[2] Dutch abbreviation for "Common Thesaurus Audio-visual Archives".

S. Staab and V. Svatek (Eds.): EKAW 2006, LNAI 4248, pp. 272–286, 2006.

indexing terms from context documents (TV guides, articles). Initial results of the semi-automatic support can be found in another paper [3]. This paper only discusses the browser.

The objective of the evaluation study was to improve the efficiency of the thesaurus browser in finding terms. We were particularly interested in how the browser aligns with cataloging practice. The subjects were people who are cataloguing audio-visual programs as part of their daily job. The study consisted of two parts. First we had a number of evaluation sessions with an initial version of the browser (Secs. 2-3). Based on the results of this first evaluation, the browser was adapted and evaluated in a second study (Secs. 4-5). In Sec. 6 we reflect on the outcomes and discuss related work.

From a general knowledge-engineering perspective, this paper focuses on questions related to user access to large knowledge structures, such as thesauri. Large knowledge structures typically incorporate many different viewpoints that one can take on the concepts involved [2]. As knowledge engineers we are used to organize concepts into large subtype hierarchies, but this may not always be the most appropriate way for accessing these concepts, given the user and his task context. Finding concepts in large concept structures for semantic-annotation purposes is becoming an increasingly important knowledge-access task [4]. This paper gives a detailed insight into knowledge-access problems in the domain of annotation of audio-visual archives.

The CHOICE project is part of the Dutch CATCH (Continuous Access To Cultural Heritage) Programme, funded by NWO (Dutch Science Foundation). A special characteristic of CATCH is that the teams of researchers are working part-time in the heritage institution. At the moment 10 of such projects are underway.

2 Thesaurus Browser

Cataloguers at Sound & Vision index TV programs by assigning to these a set of controlled terms, selected from the GTAA thesaurus. Currently, they only have access to these terms in the form of alphabetically sorted flat lists. Although the GTAA has internal structure this is not exploited by the current generation of software tools. Therefore, as a first step to improve the cataloging process, a thesaurus browser was designed and implemented.

2.1 Requirements

We identified the following requirements:

- Because the GTAA Browser will be used by both incidental and regular users and because these users are located both inside and outside of Sound & Vision, a *web application* was preferred.
- The thesaurus content is regularly updated, for example person' names and locations are regularly added. There is one authoritative resource for the GTAA, which is a relational database system maintained at Sound & Vision. The browser should therefore directly interact with this database.

- The browser should be able to display and exploit all structures that are present in the thesaurus in appropriate and intuitive ways. The same is true for structures and information that we add to the thesaurus. It should provide at least the existing searching and browsing functionalities, *i.e.* direct access to terms according to the facet to which they belong (this notion of facet is detailed in the following section) and an alphabetical search facility.
- For interoperability with other CATCH projects the thesaurus should be accessible through open web standards.

2.2 Browser – Version 1 Implementation

Fig. 1 shows the architecture of the GTAA Browser. The browser is implemented as a web application which can retrieve thesaurus data from an extensible set of data sources. One of those is Sound & Vision's primary source of the GTAA, a relational database. Using this source, radio and television professionals will always have the latest modifications of the GTAA available. To accommodate the needs of researchers in CHOICE and CATCH the browser can also use an RDF/OWL representation of the thesaurus as its data source. This RDF/OWL store can be updated on request using a separate web application.

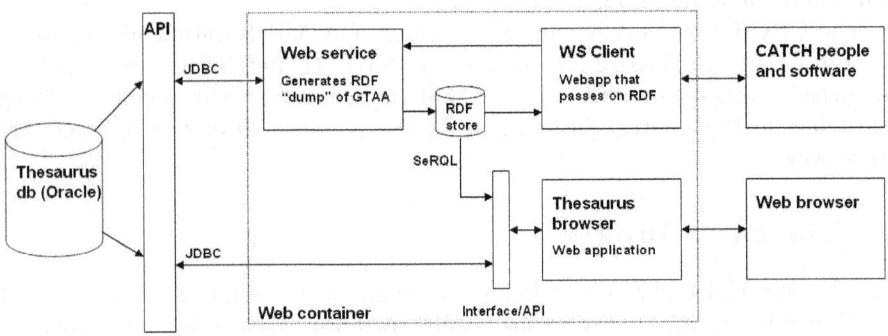

Fig. 1. Architecture of the browser

A screen shot of version 1 of the GTAA browser is shown in Fig. 2. The interface is divided into three main parts:

- the upper part, with 6 tabs (number 1 on the figure) representing the different dimensions ("facets") of the GTAA;
- the middle part, where different information about the Terms are displayed (number 2 on the figure);
- the bottom part, consisting of an alphabetical search engine (number 3 on the figure).

Each of these three parts is discussed in more detail in the following paragraphs.

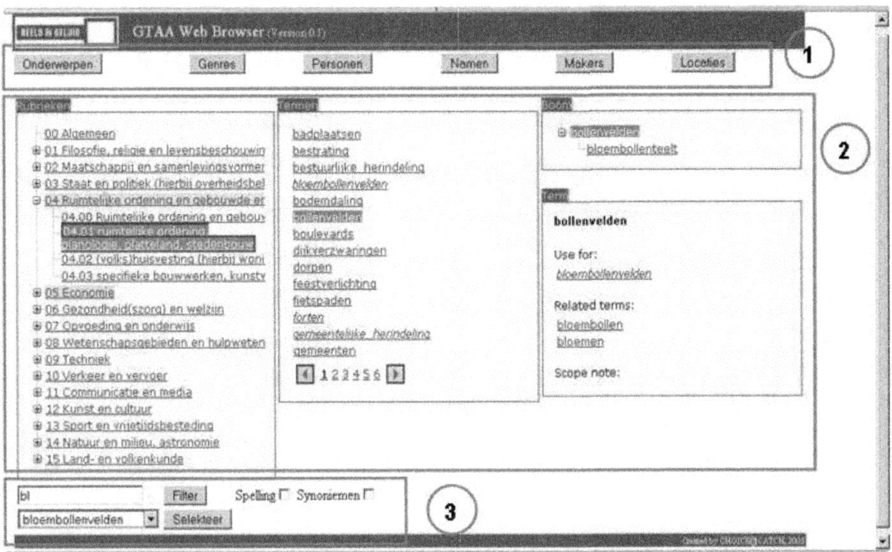

Fig. 2. First interface of the browser

GTAA Facets. The six tabs represent the different facets of the thesaurus: six disjoint groups of Terms, divided into top level categories. These facets are (between parentheses the Dutch term): Subjects (*Onderwerpen*), Genres (*Genres*), People (*Personen*), Names (*Namen*) , Makers (*Makers*) and Locations (*Locaties*). The facets correspond to different fields in the indexing scheme of Sound & Vision for TV programs. They are given by the thesaurus structure and cannot be personalised by the user. The browser gives direct access to terms belonging to any of these facets by clicking on the corresponding tab. Fig. 2 shows the Subjects facet. The Subjects and the Genres facets are organized according to the ISO 2788 relationships: **BroaderTerm/NarrowerTerm**, **RelatedTerm**, and **Use/UseFor**. The **BroaderTerm/NarrowerTerm** is a hierarchical relationship that represents a description of subsets of documents (the **NarrowerTerm** should be used to describe a subset of the documents that can be described by the correponding **BroaderTerm**). **BroaderTerm/NarrowerTerm** can represent a subclass relationship, as well as a part-of relationship, or some application specific relationship. **RelatedTerm** links two Terms that are closely related in a specific domain, like a Ship and a Sailor for example. Some Terms are also associated with **ScopeNotes**, textual comments about the use of the given Term. Terms from the Subjects facet are also grouped into Categories. These are an alternative way of grouping Terms, beside the **BroaderTerm/NarrowerTerm** hierarchy, by generic domain: Philosophy, Economy, etc. Terms from the four other facets are alphabetical flat lists, sometimes associated with **ScopeNotes**. As the Subjects facet is the most structured one, we detail its display in the middle part of the browser window (number 2 of Fig. 2) in the following subsection.

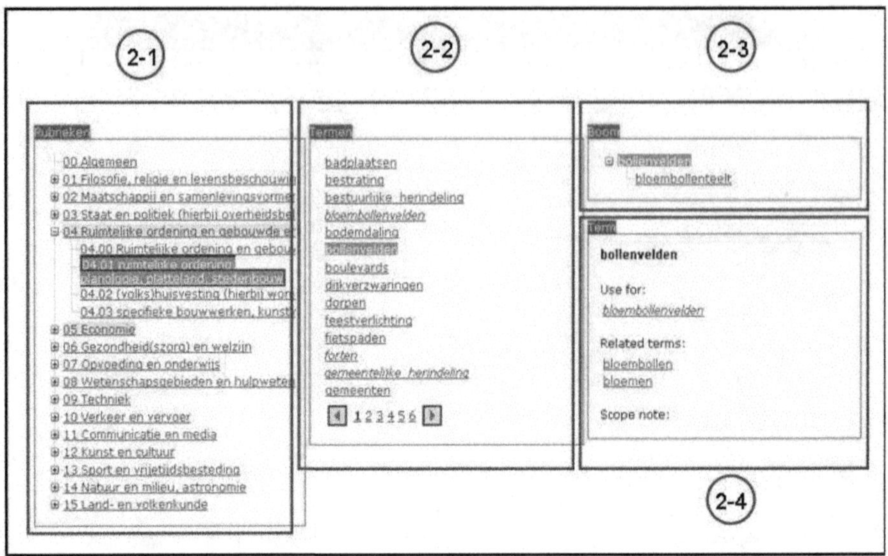

Fig. 3. Middle panel of the GTAA browser

Browsing Relationships Between Terms. A close-up of the middle panel of the Web Browser is shown in Fig. 3, where we can see that it is divided into four parts.

The left part (panel 2-1) displays the different Categories and Sub-Categories (*Rubrieken* and *Sub-Rubrieken* in Dutch) into which the Subjects Terms are categorized[3]. Clicking on a Category or Sub-Category displays in panel 2-2 the list of the Terms which belong to it[4]. The sample screen shot displays the terms from the sub-category *Urbanism and Organization of Public Space* highlighted in blue. Preferred terms are displayed in normal font and non-preferred in italics. Clicking on a term in this panel selects it, while the Category(ies) to which it belongs to are highlighted in orange in panel 2-1. Panels 2-3 and 2-4 are also instantiated or updated when a term is selected. They display the relevant **BroaderTerm/NarrowerTerm** tree (2-3) and other available information about the term such as **Related Terms** (2-4). Terms displayed in panels are clickable, enabling the user to navigate through neighbors of the selected term.

Alphabetical Search. In version 1, the search functionality was only valid in the facet that was active: if the user submits a query in the Subjects facet, the alphabetical search is limited to this facet. When the user types the first letters of a term, a refinement button (labeled *Filter*) gives the list of the preferred and non-preferred terms of the facet that begin with the same characters.

[3] A term can be categorized in up to three different (Sub-)Categories.

[4] If the Category contains more than 14 Terms, the first 14 Terms are displayed in alphabetical order, and other ones can be reached by clicking the different page number at the bottom of this panel.

3 User Study: Part I

3.1 Setup

Formative evaluation of the GTAA thesaurus browser in two parts was performed to determine whether it supports the cataloguers internal and external to Sound & Vision in their tasks of annotating audiovisual material, in particular in terms of navigation, browsing and searching. With the analysis of the study results we aim at answering questions about:

- the usefulness of browsing a hierarchical structure of terms versus alphabetical lists for finding out relevant terms;
- the intuitiveness of the search and navigation facilities;
- the effectiveness of the presentation of the controlled vocabulary, of the cross-links between the terms, of the categories and of the different dimensions of the GTAA thesaurus (namely the facets).

Subjects. The first user study concerned in total nine cataloguers: five thesaurus experts from Sound & Vision, two domain experts from NOS and two domain experts from EO[5]. Most of them (7 out of 9) are using annotation software daily.

Procedure. The experimental session lasted around 60 minutes per subject supervised by an examiner and video-recorded. To make sure the testing conditions are similar to all users we started with a brief (about 5 minutes) introduction of the experiment and the browser. Next, each of the subjects spent time for a "directed play-around" to get acquainted with browser's functionality, reading a list of guidelines[6] and reporting on problems. Subsequently, they watched an audio-visual document with a duration of 2 minutes and we asked to provide indexing terms for that document using the browser. They could use three strategies to find these terms:

- Use the Categories hierarchy to display lists of terms (henceforth *Browsing search* or *Browsing functionality*), in the Subject facet;
- Type in some letters in the alphabetical search box and check for a matching term by clicking on the *Filter* button (henceforth *Filter search*);
- Type in a whole term in the alphabetical search box and check for a matching term in the thesaurus (henceforth *Alphabetical search*).

From this first step on, the different relationships of the Subject facet could also be used to navigate in the thesaurus' content, as well as the alphabetical lists in the other facets. No complex query composition functionality was provided to search for a term.

At places, where problems occurred the examiner initiated a dialog with the user in order to clarify the problem and to gather additional information on

[5] NOS and EO are Dutch broadcasting organizations.

[6] The guidelines can be found at `http://www.cs.vu.nl/~guus/public/choice-guidelines.pdf`. These are the adapted guidelines user for the second study.

it. Finally, each of them filled one usability questionnaire with five clusters of questions (overall interface, search facilities, term browsing, subject facets and additional functionality) and one personalia questionnaire focusing on sex, age and proficiency. All subjects were allowed to also use pre-selected on-line reference material on the topic of the audiovisual document during the annotation session.

Metrics. We evaluated the efficiency, satisfaction, learnability and effectiveness of the GTAA thesaurus browser by using the following metrics:

Number of problems during play-around: is used to calculate the overall learnability of the browser by counting the problems occurred over the number of steps and the overall time spent during the play-around;

Total time spent during play-around (in minutes): idem for number of problems;

Number of problems during annotation: is used to calculate the overall effectiveness by counting the number of problems over the steps and the overall time spent during annotation;

Number of times alphabetical search was used during annotation: gives an estimate of the efficiency of the alphabetical search in the two user studies.

Number of times hierarchy search was used during annotation: idem for alphabetical search;

Number of times filter search was used during annotation: idem for alphabetical search;

Number of steps during annotation: is used in the calculation of the efficiency of the browser for the annotation tasks;

Number of resulting indexing terms during annotation: is used to calculate the success factor in terms of overlapping with the terms indicated in the gold standard;

Number of steps per index term during annotation: is used as a measure of efficiency;

Total time spent on search tasks during annotation (in minutes): is used in the calculation of search efficiency of the browser in both user studies;

Total time spent during annotation (in minutes): is used in the calculation of the efficiency and effectiveness of the browser in both user studies.

We mark something as a *problem* when the user indicates that there is an obstacle to perform a task. For example, the user searches for "Afghanistan", types the term in the search field (in the "Genres" facet), and it brings no results back, because the user didn't select the facet "Locations". Software bugs were also identified during the user studies, but were not counted as problems for the calculation of the effectiveness of the browser, nor in the total time spent with the browser.

A *step during annotation* is defined as a set of meaningfully connected atomic actions to perform an annotation task. For example, when the user is searching for "Afghanistan" he may first try to use the hierarchy in the Subject facet by error, then go to the Location tab, then type in some letters and get results from the filter list. This would result in three steps.

The *gold standard* was defined by thesaurus experts from Sound & Vision. It contained twelve indexing terms from the GTAA thesaurus, which they considered as appropriate to annotate the audiovisual document used in both user studies. We counted the total number of GTAA indexing terms that each subject used for the annotation and the total number of the ones which match the gold standard. We only considered exact matches in this evaluation, but an option for future studies could be to use a similarity function, for example based on the hierarchical structure of the thesaurus, to compare selected terms to the gold standard.

Questionnaire. In order to assess the usability of the GTAA browser the participants were asked to fill out a questionnaire[7] (50 questions on a 7-point scale, 8 open questions). User satisfaction is expressed as a normalized value in the range [1,7], where 1 is highly satisfied and 7 is highly not satisfied. In order to identify trends in the user groups and discriminate different levels of expertise the participants we asked to also fill in a questionnaire about their personal characteristics with respect to gender, age, computer and annotation proficiency (10 questions).

3.2 Results

Table 1 shows the results of the study for the defined metrics. We can observe the following:

- Both during play-around and annotation a significant number of problems were encountered (on average $3.69 + 2.89 = 6.56$). On analysis these problems were mainly concerned with relatively trivial issues. For example, case-sensitive search and lack of auto-completion proved problematic. Another cause of problems was the lack of synchronization when updating parts of the screen (categories, term lists, etc.). Before the second user test the browser was accordingly adapted.
- A less trivial cause of problems was the confusion about combined use of the "filter" and "select" buttons for alphabetical search. For example, consider the following scenario:

```
SEARCH GOAL: "peace troops"
1. choose facet "Subjects"
2. enter query "peace" and click Filter button
3. select from drop-down list "peace troops" click
   Select button to activate search on "peace troops"
```

  From the videos we observed that such scenarios were quite common. Participants would typically get stuck in step 3. It turned out that it was unclear to them where the drop-down box was and also that an additional "select" click was required. To remedy this, we improved the guidelines. Also, the organization on the screen was not logical (jump from bottom to top). This is improved in the adapted browser.

[7] The questionnaire can be found at `http://www.cs.vu.nl/~guus/public/choice-quest.pdf` (in Dutch).

Table 1. Results for the first part of the user study. Time measurements are in min.

Stage/Metric	Subjects									
	S1	S2	S3	S4	S5	S6	S7	S8	S9	**Average**
During play-around										
#problems	3	4	5	4	3	2	3	4	5	3.67
total time spent	11	19	22	19	20	14	15	20	18	18
During annotation										
#problems	3	4	4	2	3	2	3	2	3	2.89
#alphabetical search used	8	9	7	6	7	4	7	9	6	7.00
#hierarchy search used	1	2	0	1	0	5	1	1	1	1.33
#filter search used	2	2	2	2	1	1	1	1	1	1.44
#steps	47	30	22	29	31	28	35	37	40	33.22
#resulting index terms	9	10	8	4	9	6	8	5	7	7.33
#steps per index term	5.22	3.00	2.75	7.25	3.44	4.67	4.38	7.40	5.71	4.87
total time spent on search	29	24	18	21	20	12	18	10	13	18
total time spent	38	33	29	30	31	20	25	19	22	27

- From the results it is clear that most of the subjects were mainly using alphabetical search. The explanation they gave was that they already knew the term they were looking and therefore hierarchical search is not appropriate. From the hierarchy search they mainly used the use-for and related-term relationships. The filter-search was also used infrequently; this appeared mainly to be caused by the problem reported before. The added value was in fact unclear to them.
- Subjects were performing a large number of total steps (on average 33.22) to find indexing terms. Analysis of the videos showed that the main reasons for this were (i) inefficiency of the screen layout, (ii) insufficient feedback on the action performed, and (iii) the filter-search problem mentioned earlier.
- On average the resulting number of indexing terms was 7.33, i.e. roughly 60% of the gold standard. We think this is adequate.
- On average 4.87 steps were needed to find an index term. The minimum number of steps needed to find a term would be 3 (see scenario above). This means there is definitely room for efficiency improvement.

Table 3 further on in this paper shows aggregated results of the questionnaire on user satisfaction. We discuss the results in Sec. 5 in relation to those of the second study.

4 Thesaurus Browser – Adapted Version

In accordance with the results of this first user study, we adapted the browser (Fig. 4). The next paragraphs describe the most important modifications that were made.

Alphabetical Search (Number 1 on Figure 4). Alphabetical search turned out to be important for users, so we made some small technical improvements, such as

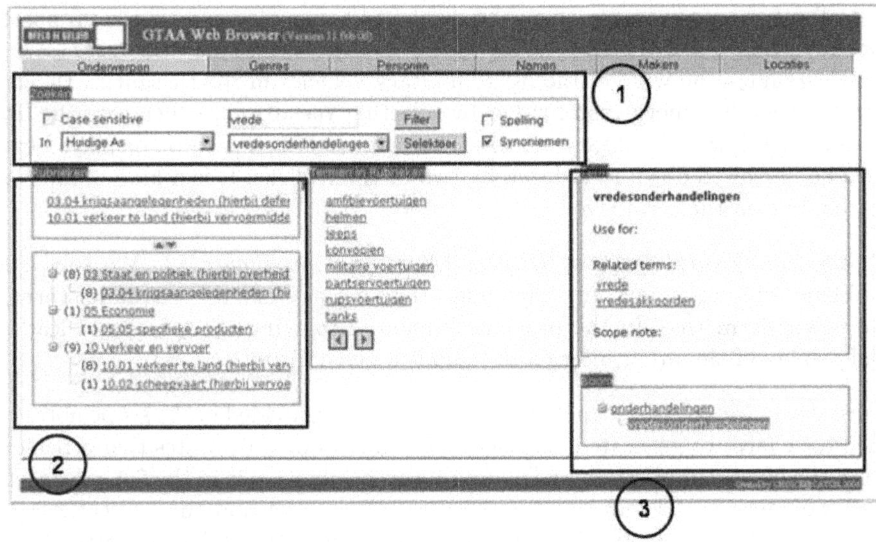

Fig. 4. Adapted interface of the Web Browser

a default behavior of case-insensitive search and the possibility to search within (i) the active facet, (ii) a given facet or (iii) any facet. As an additional facility in cases where the characters typed in do not match a thesaurus Term, the browser displays also:

- A list of spelling suggestions
- Terms that match the input through an intermediate list of synonym terms.

The spelling suggestion tool was adapted from a generic module and the synonym list has been computed using the online versions of the Van Dale and the Muiswerk dictionaries[8].

Selection of Multiple Categories (Number 2 on Figure 4). One of the reasons why the browsing search was not preferred as a first step to search for a term is that the Categories are too broad: they contain too many terms to make the display of the whole list interresting for finding out a term. But we took advantage of the fact that most Subject terms are part of more than one Category to offer the user an additionnal filtering functionality. Categories and sub-categories are now displayed in association with the number of Terms belonging to them. When the user selects a category, its Terms are still displayed in the middle part, but panel 1 on Fig. 4 is also updated with the list of *other* categories these Terms can belong to, and the number of overlapping terms. For example, if a user selects the Category `Military Issues`, the terms related to `Military Issues` are displayed,

[8] Respectively at the URL `http://www.vandale.nl/opzoeken/woordenboek/` and `http://www.muiswerk.nl/WRDNBOEK/INHOUD.HTM`.

and all other categories in which the displayed terms also appear are proposed for narrowing down the number of terms. If the user selects also `Traffic and Transportation`, he will get the list of military vehicles in the thesaurus. He can narrow down his query even further by selecting `Vessels`, in which case the list is narrowed down to military vessels. The number of terms to be displayed can thus be narrowed down to a dozen by two or three clicks. It is a kind of faceted search, but on the term level[9].

BroaderTerm/NarrowerTerm Display (Number 3 on Figure 4). We solved a problem of ergonomy in changing the diplay of the **BroaderTerm/ NarrowerTerm** tree. In the previous version, displaying the tree could lead a bad display of the other information about a given Term.

Cross-Facet Links. We extracted some information provided in the scope notes of the People facet to generate cross-facet links: if a scope note states that a person has a specific occupation, say King, and if this occupation is in the Subjects facet, then we generate a browsable link between the person and the subject `Kings`. This helps the user to browse directly (potentially) other relevant parts of the GTAA than the current facet.

5 User Study Part II

5.1 Setup

The second user study targeted evaluation of the adapted version of the GTAA browser according to the same measures and experimental goals as in the first study. In total seven subjects, six from Sound & Vision and one from NOS, followed the same experimental design and procedure (with an improved explanation form). None of the subjects participated in the first study.

Results. Table 2 shows the results for the second user study. We observed the following:

- There is a decrease in the number of problems (2.14 vs. 3.67). Thus, there is a clear indication of a higher level of effectiveness.
- The time used for play-around is longer (25 min. vs. 18 min.). This is logical because the guidelines were more elaborate and the complexity of the search increased. So, a longer learning curve is needed.
- The total time spent during annotation decreased (16 min. vs. 27 min.)m as well as the total number of steps per session (25.57 vs. 33.22) and the number of steps per index term (3.74 vs. 4.87). This indicates an increase in the efficiency of the search. As the minimum number of steps per index term is 3 (see Sec. 3), the result in the second study is actually approaching maximum efficiency.

[9] As opposed to the document level, for which facets would be the broadcasting date, the genre, etc. on top of the different controlled terms used as metadata.

Table 2. Results for the second part of the user study. Time measurements are in min.

Stage/Metric	Subjects							
	S10	S11	S12	S13	S14	S15	S16	**Average**
During play-around								
#problems	1	3	3	4	3	0	1	2.14
total time spent	29	24	26	16	26	33	22	25
During annotation								
#problems	1	2	2	1	3	2	3	2.00
#alphabetical search used	7	9	9	12	6	9	5	8.14
#hierarchy search used	4	1	0	2	1	1	2	1.57
#filter search used	2	2	0	0	5	0	0	1.29
#steps	26	25	28	28	37	18	10	24.57
#resulting index terms	6	7	6	7	5	9	6	6.57
#steps per index term	4.33	3.57	4.67	4.00	7.40	2.00	1.67	3.74
total time spent on search	12	9	19	14	10	10	15	13
total time spent	15	12	22	19	13	14	18	16

- The average time used for search was 13 min. This is close to 80% of the total annotation time. In comparison: in the first study it was 67%.
- The use of alphabetical search increased slightly (8.14 vs. 7.00), while at the same annotation time went down. This means we achieved at least partially the goal of making alphabetical search more effective (see previous section).
- The hierarchy search increased marginally (1.57 vs. 1.33); the filter search marginally decreased (1.29 vs. 1.44). The number of times these functionalities were used prevents any generalization. Our hypothesis is that due to the improved alphabetical search there was no real need for the other search types. In this context it is worthwhile to point out that the subjects were used to alphabetical search already, and had little to no experience with other search types. The Categories were not displayed in their previous annotation tool, and thus these groups of terms were not yet used in a real-life annotation task. They were not yet adapted to fit this task, contrary to the thesaurus content, which is updated on a daily basis. The Categories proved to be too broad to enhance a browsing type of search.

Table 3 shows the aggregated results of the user-satisfaction questionnaire. We observe here a marginal increase in the satisfaction of the users with respect to the general browser functionality, the subject-facet functionality and the search functionality, as well as a marginal decrease in the satisfaction for the browser functionality. The differences in the aggregated values of the first and second studies are too small to be able to make any generalization. However, some of the values on individual questions support the hypothesis that the satisfaction of the users increased with the adapted browser, while the number of steps required to perform the task decreased.

While the users in the first study were doubting the usefulness of the browsers hierarchical structure (3.11), the participants in the second study show strong

Table 3. Results of the questionnaire about user satisfaction in both studies. Results were aggregated per question group (left column).

Question group	Average score 1 = lowest, 7 = highest	
	User study 1	User study 2
General browser functionality	4.79	5.26
Subject-facet functionality	4.64	5.10
Search functionality	4.82	4.87
Browse functionality	5.02	4.57

consensus that the thesaurus structure in the adapted browser helped them discover related terms (5.29) and the relationships between them (5.17). Most of the users in the first study preferred to use the alphabetical search above the hierarchical one in the "Subject"-facet (6.44), where in the second study we can see a clear change in a positive direction (5.00) although still preferring the alphabetical search to the hierarchical. The level of complexity in the hierarchical search was appreciated more by the users of the adapted browser in the second study (5.43 vs 4.48), as well as using hierarchical structure in combination with the search (4.71 vs 4.13). Many of the users both in the first and in the second test were not happy that it took too long to find the appropriate main category in the hierarchy (2.82 vs 2.86). This comment is mainly concerning the broadness of these groupings. Further, there were no significant improvements in the hierarchy presentation in the browser, thus no major changes were expected, as shown from the previous values.

6 Discussion and Related Work

This study shows some insights of the use of knowledge structures like thesauri in application settings. The cataloguers were used to quite basic tools for finding index terms and were dazzled by the complexity of the browser interface. They are used to alphabetical search and therefore we gained most performance value by optimizing this part of the search, as can be seen in he second user study. For searching a hierarchical representation is apparently not of much value. However, for disambiguating terms, showing the respective places in the hierarchy could be a quick means for selecting the right concept. We could also notice a difference of strategies between the subjects from Sound and Vision (experts of the thesaurus content) and from broadcasting corporations. The later were more eager to strat searching a term by browsing. Thus, such a browsing facility could be helpful to the general public for searching the public Website of Sound and Vision.

Despite the learning curves (see the times needed for the play-around sessions), the cataloguers were in general positive about the use of such a tool in their daily work. This is apparent from the questionnaire, but also from the fact that, based on the results of this study, Sound & Vision is seriously considering of incorporating the thesaurus browser in their archiving process.

Other studies evaluate thesaurus browsers by user studies, but they usually focus on the task the thesaurus helps achieving, and not on the thesaurus usability and functionalities themselves. Several authors [8,6,1] have considered the selection of a term as a particular part of their evaluation, but they evaluate it against the recall or precision of documents retrieved. Blocks [1] explicitly stresses the fact that, as their interface enables query expansion on the basis of the **NarrowerTerm** relationship in the thesaurus, the tendency of users to search for the most specific query term is a waste of time: the set of terms that they choose for formulating the query would be taken into account with a query involving their common hypernym, by which the users started browsing the thesaurus in the first place. Our purpose is the opposite: making sure that the browser proposes relevant functionalities for different search strategies in order to retrieve the *most specific and relevant term* for indexing a document. The perspective of evaluating a tool dedicated to helping the selection of a keyword for *indexing* has not been taken into account very often, and this indexing task has specific requirements.

As mentioned in the introduction, the thesaurus browser in just a small piece in the larger puzzle of supporting semantic annotation. We see it as a baseline tool for cataloguers, who may always have the need to do some manual work on annotation. The majority of the research is aimed at providing automatic tools for generating candidate indexing terms [3]. In the digital archiving process of the future we expect the emphasis to lie on semi-automatic annotation, with the role of the cataloguer shifting to the person who performs quality control on suggested indexing terms and/or selecting the most appropriate ones from the terms suggested. Also this process would benefit from a usable thesaurus browser. The fact that the tool is based on the RDF/OWL specification makes it a good candidate for reuse with other RDF/OWL-based thesauri. This is in fact a realistic extension. Many institutions still rely on their in-house thesaurus, but would benefit from larger a wider scope of thesauri [5]. For example, geographical data in GTAA are likely to be incomplete and it might be a better approach to use geo-spatial data from other sources, such as the Getty Thesaurus of Geographical Names[10].

Acknowledgments

The authors are grateful to the 16 participants in the experiments from Sound & Vision, NOS and EO. Johan Oomen provided useful comments. This research is supported by the CHOICE, which is part of the DUTCH CATCH Programme funded by the Dutch National Research Foundation NWO. The evaluation of the GTAA browser was performed as a usability case study at LaQuSo Lab, Eindhoven University of Technology.

[10] `http://www.getty.edu/research/conducting_research/vocabularies/tgn/`

References

1. Dorothee Blocks. *A qualitative analysis of thesaurus integration for end-user searching.* PhD thesis, University of Glamorgan, Hypermedia Research Unit, School of Computing, UK, 2004.
2. P. Borst, J. M. Akkermans, and J. Top. Engineering ontologies. *Int. J. Human-Computer Studies*, 46:365–406, 1997.
3. L. Gazendam, V. Malaisé, G. Schreiber, and H. Brugman. Deriving semantic annotations of an audiovisual program from contextual texts. In *Semantic Web Annotation of Multimedia (SWAMM'06) workshop, held in conjunction with WWW'06, Edinburgh, UK*, 2006.
4. S. Handschuh and S. Staab. Annotation of the shallow and the deep web. In S. Handschuh and S. Staab, editors, *Annotation for the Semantic Web*, volume 96 of *Frontiers in Artificial Intelligence and Applications*, pages 25–45. IOS Press, Amsterdam, 2003.
5. L. Hollink, A. Th. Schreiber, J. Wielemaker, and B. J. Wielinga. Semantic annotation of image collections. In S. Handschuh, M. Koivunen, R. Dieng, and S. Staab, editors, *Knowledge Capture 2003 – Proceedings Knowledge Markup and Semantic Annotation Workshop*, pages 41–48, 2003.
6. Eric H. Johnson and Pauline A. Cochrane. A hypertextual interface for a searcher's thesaurus. In *Proc. Second Annual Conference on the Theory and Practice of Digital Libraries (Digital Libraries 95), Austin, Texas, USA, June*, pages 77–86, 1995.
7. A. Miles and D. Brickley. SKOS core guide. Technical report, W3C Working Draft, 2 November 2005. http://www.w3.org/TR/2005/WD-swbp-skos-core-guide-20051102.
8. Heiner Stuckenschmidt, Anita de Waard, Ravinder Bhogal, Christiaan Fluit, Arjohn Kampman, Jan van Buel, Erik van Mulligen, Jeen Broekstra, Ian Crowlesmith, Frank van Harmelen, and Tony Scerri. A topic-based browser for large online resources. In E. Motta and N. Shadbolt, editors, *Proc. 14th Int. Conference on Knowledge Engineering and Knowledge Management (EKAW'04), Northamptonshire, UK, 5-8 October.* Springer-Verlag, 2004.
9. M. van Assem, V. Malaisé, A. Miles, and G. Schreiber. A method to convert thesauri to SKOS. In *Proc. Third European Semantic Web Conference (ESWC'06), Budvar, Montenegro*, June 2006. Accepted for publication. http://www.cs.vu.nl/~mark/papers/Assem06b.pdf.

Frequent Pattern Discovery from OWL DLP Knowledge Bases

Joanna Józefowska, Agnieszka Ławrynowicz, and Tomasz Łukaszewski

Institute of Computing Science, Poznan University of Technology,
ul. Piotrowo 3a, 60-965 Poznan, Poland
{jjozefowska, alawrynowicz, tlukaszewski}@cs.put.poznan.pl

Abstract. The Semantic Web technology should enable publishing of numerous resources of scientific and other, highly formalized data on the Web. The application of mining these huge, networked Web repositories seems interesting and challenging. In this paper we present and discuss an inductive reasoning procedure for mining frequent patterns from the knowledge bases represented in OWL DLP. OWL DLP, also known as Description Logic Programs, lies at the intersection of the expressivity of OWL DL and Logic Programming. Our method is based on a special trie data structure inspired by similar, efficient structures used in classical and relational data mining settings. Conjunctive queries to OWL DLP knowledge bases are the language of frequent patterns.

1 Introduction

World Wide Web is a huge network of information resources. The Semantic Web [2] is the World Wide Web enriched by machine-readable meta-data. With Semantic Web technologies, semantically rich and formalized information networks can be created, queried and searched. Across these huge, interconnected datasets, hypotheses can be generated and verified (for example from the life science domain) thus leading to a derivation of new knowledge from the existing data. It would be very beneficial for the Semantic Web users if new and interesting knowledge could be discovered and further shared in a way similar to the data exchange today. Discovery of new and potentially interesting knowledge from huge data sets is the domain of interest of *data mining.* The task of data mining is to search for *patterns* in *data.* Most of the methods of data mining proposed so far operate on a single table with data. This representation requires the preprocessing and aggregation of data into a single table and can cause the loss of meaning or the loss of information. The alternative are the methods operating on original, non-preprocessed data sets which exploit implicit semantics, hidden in the structure of data. The semantic information can be also included explicitly in the data mining process in the form of rules and relationships existing in a given domain (so called *background knowledge*). *Relational data mining* [6] (RDM) approaches that mine patterns from relational data bases belong to the later group of methods. These methods are a part of a larger group of approaches called *inductive logic programming*, ILP [15], where data is represented

S. Staab and V. Svatek (Eds.): EKAW 2006, LNAI 4248, pp. 287–302, 2006.

in logic-based languages like Datalog. The Semantic Web knowledge bases are also represented in languages built on logic-based formalisms such as *description logics*, (DL). Our goal is to provide methods for mining data sets expressed in the languages from the ontological layer of the Semantic Web, which can be referred as to *Semantic Web Mining.* In this paper we investigate the task of frequent pattern discovery in knowledge bases represented in OWL DLP, the subset of *Web Ontology Language* that lies at the intersection of the expressivity of OWL DL and Logic Programming. These patterns represent frequently occurring, in some dataset, characteristics of some concept. The concept can be for example the client of some bank and the characteristics can be his or her age, place of living, credit cards owned, loans granted. Finding frequent characteristics may help for example in targeting the bank services. Using expressive languages may help, in turn, to represent various (possibly complex) relationships existing in a given domain of which the concept of our interest is a part. The rest of the paper is organized as follows. In Section 2 we present the related work, in Section 3 we present the data mining setting, in Section 4 we present the inductive reasoning procedure, in Section 5 the experimental results are presented and Section 6 concludes the paper.

2 Related Work

The work related to ours can be divided into two groups: relational data mining and data mining from more expressive representations. The problem of discovery of frequent relational patterns was introduced by [4]. An ILP method called WARMR was proposed to solve this problem. WARMR adapts the levelwise method, originally used in APRIORI algorithm operating on item sets. Instead of item sets WARMR uses the notion of atom sets as first order logic, function-free, conjunctive formulas. Atom sets are also referred to as queries that have almost all of the variables existentially quantified (so-called undistinguished variables) and the free variables (distinguished ones) bound by a *key* predicate. The role of the key predicate is to indicate what is counted during the calculation of the support of a given query. The support of a query is defined in terms of the number of distinguished variables bindings for which the key predicate can be proved. The search space of possible patterns, quite simple for item sets, can be very huge in case of relational patterns. Also the subset relation that is used as a generality measure in case of item sets is no longer valid for atom sets. Instead of the subset relation WARMR uses, widely used in ILP methods, an approximation of logical implication called θ-subsumption. WARMR searches the space of patterns one level at a time starting from the most general patterns and iterating between the candidate generation and the candidate evaluation phases. In the pattern generation phase WARMR performs a lot of tests for equivalence under θ-subsumption in order to prune infrequent and redundant queries.

Although proved to be useful, an early version of WARMR is inefficient, thus WARMR has been further optimized in many different ways [3]. In [16] and [17] another relational data mining method named FARMER was introduced. FARMER uses the first order logic notation, but it does not depend on a time consuming test for equivalence. The special data structure called *trie*, inspired by some implementation of APRIORI, is used instead. FARMER is equivalent to WARMR under some restrictions and achieves better performance.

Relational data mining methods have some drawbacks. Firstly, θ-subsumption is not fully semantic measure as it is not equal to the logical implication. Using Horn rules as a representation language limits the methods for example in modeling hierarchical structures. Description logic, in turn, was developed to be able to represent rich structural knowledge. Unfortunately, it does not allow any interaction of variables in arbitrary ways, which is the property of the Horn clausal logic. Thus, the combination of the expressive power of DL and Horn clausal logic as a representation language in data mining seems to be highly desirable. To the best of our knowledge, there is only one approach, named SPADA [11], that is developed to use such an expressive representation for frequent pattern mining. SPADA uses hybrid $\mathcal{AL}$-log [5] language for the association rule discovery in multiple levels of description granularity. The current version of SPADA admits, however, only very basic part of the language of the $\mathcal{DL}$ component. Also, either the patterns that can be found contain concepts only from the same level of taxonomy or some concepts are replicated in some, lower levels of taxonomy.

Recently a new combination of DL and function-free Horn rules, so-called $\mathcal{DL}$-*safe rules* [13], has been presented. It allows using a very expressive DL, while still preserving the *decidability* property of such combination. Recent tests [14] show also that KAON2[1] reasoner implementing this approach outperforms other reasoners in the case of a high number of instances in the knowledge base which is exactly the case in our task. In [9] we have discussed the potential of using this combination for frequent pattern discovery in knowledge bases represented in DL and containing Horn rules. As a proof-of-concept, we have presented an approach taking into account OWL DLP knowledge bases, that was inspired by an early version of WARMR and not optimised. The pattern mining in this approach took considerable amout of time, because the candidate pattern generation mechanism barely benefited from what was found in the previous levels. In [10] we have presented the method based on a special trie structure, similar to that used in APRIORI and FARMER, where we obtained considerable speedup as compared to our early, naive approach. In both cases OWL DLP language was taken into consideration, but in the latter case the language was further significantly restricted. In this paper we present a procedure for frequent pattern discovery from OWL DLP knowledge bases, which at the same time uses an efficient trie structure and does not restrict the language like in the case of the method presented in [10]. It also applies fully semantic generality measure.

[1] http://kaon2.semanticweb.org

3 Frequent Patterns in OWL DLP Knowledge Bases

3.1 Pattern Discovery Task

The general formulation of the frequent pattern discovery problem was specified by [12]. It was further extended to deal with more expressive language in the case of RDM methods in [4]. With respect to these formulations of the frequent pattern discovery problem we define our task as:

Definition 1. *Given*

- *a knowledge base in OWL DLP* $\mathcal{KB}$,
- *a set of patterns in the language* $\mathcal{L}$ *of queries* Q *that all contain a reference concept* $\hat{C}$,
- *a minimum support treshold minsup specified by the user*

and assuming that queries with support s are frequent in $\mathcal{KB}$ *given* $\hat{C}$ *if* $s \geq minsup$, *the task of frequent pattern discovery is to find the set* $\mathcal{F}$ *of frequent queries.*

The $\hat{C}$ parameter determines what is counted. The atom of the query built from the reference concept contains the only one distinguished variable that can appear in the query (*key* variable).

Definition 2. *A support of the query* Q *with respect to the knowledge base* $\mathcal{KB}$ *is defined as the ratio between the number of instances of the* $\hat{C}$ *concept that satisfy the query* Q *and the total number of instances of the* $\hat{C}$ *concept (the trivial query for the total number of the instances is denoted* Q_{ref}*):*

$$support(\hat{C}, Q, KB) = \frac{|answerset(\hat{C}, Q, KB)|}{|answerset(\hat{C}, Q_{ref}, KB)|} \tag{1}$$

Example 1. As an illustrative example within this paper we consider the ontology describing bank services and clients. Its TBox is presented below:

$NoProblemAccount \sqsubseteq Account$
$NoProblemAccount \sqsubseteq \forall hasLoan.OKLoan$
$Man \sqsubseteq Client$
$Woman \sqsubseteq Client$
$FinishedLoan \sqsubseteq Loan$
$OKLoan \sqsubseteq Loan$
$ProblemLoan \sqsubseteq Loan$
$OKFinishedLoan \sqsubseteq FinishedLoan \sqcap OKLoan$
$\top \sqsubseteq \forall isOwnerOf^{-}.Client$
$\top \sqsubseteq \forall isOwnerOf.(Account \sqcup CreditCard)$
$\top \sqsubseteq \forall hasLoan^{-}.Account$
$\top \sqsubseteq \forall hasLoan.Loan$
$\top \sqsubseteq \leq 1 hasLoan$

Moreover *Account*, *Client*, *CreditCard* and *Loan* are disjoint with each other, *Man* and *Woman* are disjoint, and *OKLoan* is disjoint with *ProblemLoan*. In the ABox we have the following assertions:

Man(Marek).	*Account(a1).*	*isOwnerOf(Marek, a1).*
Man(Adam).	*Account(a2).*	*isOwnerOf(Marek, c1).*
Woman(Anna).	*Account(a3).*	*isOwnerOf(Anna, a2).*
Woman(Maria).	*CreditCard(c1).*	*isOwnerOf(Anna, c2).*
	CreditCard(c2).	*isOwnerOf(Maria, a3).*

Let's assume that our reference concept is *Client*. Then the query Q_{ref} has the form *q(key):-Client(key)* and has 4 items in its answerset. Let's assume further that we would like to calculate the support of the example query Q of the form *q(key):-Client(key), isOwnerOf(key, x), Account(x), isOwnerOf(key, y), CreditCard(y)*. The query Q has two items in its answerset that are the clients having at least one account and at least one credit card. The support of the query Q is then calculated as:

$$support(\hat{C}, Q, KB) = \tfrac{2}{4} = 0.5$$

3.2 The Data Mining Setting

The data mining task is defined in terms of patterns that we look for, the data in which we mine patterns (extensional *background knowledge* or instances) and possibly intensional *background knowledge* in the form of general rules describing the given domain. Additionally some *declarative bias* can be specified to restrict the search space of patterns. We assume pattern mining in knowledge bases $\mathcal{KB}$ represented in OWL DLP, which contain the terminological (TBox) and the assertional (ABox) parts consistent with each other. The intensional background knowledge in our approach is represented in a TBox. An ABox contains instances (extensional background knowledge). Our goal is to find frequent patterns in the form of conjunctive queries over $\mathcal{KB}$.

In the RDM methods, the declarative bias is defined in the form of mode declarations used to control the variable naming and modes (input/output) and the order in which atoms are added to the trie. In our approach we can also specify the list of atoms from which queries are to be built. However, without the loss of generality we can assume that queries are built from all of the atoms within the given ontology. It is not necessary to specify variable modes, which can be determined on the basis of the information from the TBox.

We have chosen the OWL DLP language as a starting point for our investigation on data mining from the Semantic Web, to start from simple while still powerful enough language. OWL DLP is the Horn fragment of OWL DL i.e. we can say that OWL DL statement is in DLP if it can be written, semantically equivalently, as a set of Horn clauses in the first-order logic. We direct the reader to [7] for more details about the bidirectional translation of premises and inferences from/to the OWL DLP to/from Logic Programs. As a point of reference we took the practical definition from [8] that an OWL DL statement is in

OWL DLP if and only if some given transformation algorithm can rewrite it as a semantically equivalent Horn clause in the first-order logic. We conform to the definition of the OWL DLP language presented in that paper. This definition was used in the reference implementation of the query answering method based on the $\mathcal{DL}$-safe rules approach, KAON2 [13], that combines a DL ($\mathcal{KB}$-DL) and a Horn rules (P) component. In a $\mathcal{DL}$-safe rule each variable occurs in a non-DL atom in the rule body, what makes the rule applicable only to the explicitely introduced individuals. This property is suitable for our purpose as we are interested in finding frequent characteristics of some concepts on the basis of the number of instances in the ABox. The semantics of the combined knowledge base ($\mathcal{KB}$-DL, P) in the $\mathcal{DL}$-safe rules approach is given by the translation into the first-order logic as $\pi(\mathcal{KB}\text{-DL}) \cup P$. The main inference in ($\mathcal{KB}$-DL, P) is the query answering, i.e. deciding whether $\pi(\mathcal{KB}\text{-DL}) \cup P \models \alpha$ for a ground atom α. For the details of the transformation π we refer the reader to the paper [13].

More specifically the frequent patterns that we look for have the form of the conjunctive $\mathcal{DL}$-safe queries whose answer set contains individuals of the $\hat{C}$ concept. In our work we adapt the definition of the conjunctive query from [13] to our restricted subsets of the languages of the $\mathcal{KB}$.

Definition 3. *Let $\mathcal{KB}$ be an OWL DLP with $\mathcal{DL}$-safe rules knowledge base, and let $x_1, \ldots, x_n$ and $y_1, \ldots, y_m$ be the sets of distinguished and non-distinguished variables, denoted as $\boldsymbol{x}$ and $\boldsymbol{y}$, respectively. A conjunctive query over $\mathcal{KB}$, written as $Q(\boldsymbol{x}, \boldsymbol{y})$, is a conjunction of $\mathcal{DL}$-atoms of the form $A(s)$ or $R(s, t)$ for R an atomic role, and s and t distinguished or non-distinguished variables. The basic inferences are:*
Query answering. *An answer of a query $Q(\boldsymbol{x}, \boldsymbol{y})$ w.r.t. $\mathcal{KB}$ is an assignment θ of individuals to distinguished variables, such that $\pi(\mathcal{KB}) \models \exists y : Q(\boldsymbol{x}\theta, \boldsymbol{y})$,*
Query containment. *A query $Q_2(\boldsymbol{x}, \boldsymbol{y_1})$ is contained in a query $Q_1(\boldsymbol{x}, \boldsymbol{y_2})$ w.r.t. $\mathcal{KB}$ if $\pi(\mathcal{KB}) \models \forall \boldsymbol{x} : [\exists \boldsymbol{y_2} : Q_2(\boldsymbol{x}, \boldsymbol{y_2}) \rightarrow \exists \boldsymbol{y_1} : Q_1(\boldsymbol{x}, \boldsymbol{y_1})]$.*

For the sake of clarity we use the following notation for the queries:

$$q(key) : -C(key), \alpha_1, ..., \alpha_n$$

where q(*key*) denotes that *key* is the only one distinguished query variable and α_1,...,α_n represent DL-atoms of the query. With regard to our definition of the frequent pattern discovery we look for the patterns containing the $\hat{C}$ concept. We call them $\mathcal{K}$-queries.

Definition 4. *Given the reference concept $\hat{C}$, the $\mathcal{K}$-query is the conjunctive query that contains, among other atoms, the atom of the form $\hat{C}$(key) in the body and where the variable* **key** *is the distinguished variable.*

A trivial pattern is the query of the form: q(*key*):-$\hat{C}$(*key*). We assume all the queries to be $\mathcal{DL}$-safe and to have the linked-ness property. For the *Client* being the $\hat{C}$ concept the following example $\mathcal{K}$-query can be imagined: *q(key):-Client(key), isOwnerOf(key, x), Account(x), hasLoan(x,y), Loan(y).*

The generality notion that we use in our approach is based on the *query containment.*

Definition 5. *Given two $\mathcal{K}$-queries Q_1 and Q_2 to the knowledge base $\mathcal{KB}$ we say that Q_1 is at least as general as Q_2 under query containment, $Q_1 \succeq Q_2$, iff Q_2 is contained in the query Q_1.*

According to the definition of the query support we can say that the query containment is monotonic w.r.t. support in the case of queries with the same sets of distinguished variables. As the evaluation of a candidate pattern Q is based on the computation of the pattern support w.r.t. the knowledge base $\mathcal{KB}$, it, in turn, boils down in our approach to the query answering where the queries have the form of $\mathcal{K}$-queries.

4 Algorithm

Our algorithm is based on the idea of the levelwise search known from the APRIORI algorithm [1]. An important property of the APRIORI-like algorithms is that for every pair of patterns *p1* and *p2*:

$$p1 \succeq p2 \Rightarrow support(p1) \geq support(p2)$$

It can be thus apriori determined that more specific patterns subsumed by an infrequent pattern are also infrequent. The space of patterns is searched one level at a time starting from the most general patterns. The pattern space forms a lattice spanned by a specialization relation $\preceq$ between patterns, where *p1* $\succeq$ *p2* denotes that pattern *p1* is more general than pattern *p2*. The lattice structure based on the specialization relation guides the search for patterns and thanks to that it is not necessary to search the whole, very huge space of patterns.

Also WARMR and FARMER approaches are based on this levelwise method of the pattern discovery. FARMER is moreover based on a special *trie* data structure that was introduced in a variation of APRIORI. In our approach we propose to adapt the trie data structure to work for our language of patterns. In the trie data structure, nodes correspond to the atoms of the query. Every path from the root to a node corresponds to a query (see Figure 2). Evaluation of the generated patterns is done during trie expansion. New nodes are added to the trie, only if the resulting queries are frequent. Thus only leaves that correspond to frequent queries are expanded. Following the classification introduced in [16] we distinguish three ways in which atoms can be added as leaves to the trie, as described in Definition 6.

Definition 6 (Refinement rules). *Atoms are added to the trie as:*

1. ***dependent atoms*** *(which use at least one variable of the last atom in the query). Atoms with the following predicates can be considered as dependent:*
   (a) for a node with concept predicate:
      - *top-level concepts*
      - *top-level properties*
      - *direct subconcepts of the given concept*

   (b) for a node with property predicate:

- *top-level concepts*
- *top-level properties*
- *direct subproperties of the given property*

2. ***right brothers** of a given node;*
3. ***a copy** of a given node.*

Top-level concepts are obtained by firstly classifying the concept taxonomy and then retrieving the concepts that do not have any super concept in the classified taxonomy. The top-level properties are the properties that do not have any superproperty. New nodes are added to the trie with accordance to the presented division into three classes. For each predicate, when it is added in some atom to the trie for the first time, the list of *admissible predicates* is computed. Admissible predicates are the predicates that can be used in the dependent atoms of the atom built from the given predicate. Also, the way in which the predicates can be used in the dependent atoms is determined (which variables can be shared with the parent node). This information is then stored in a hash structure. When the atom with the given predicate is expanded for the next time, the list of admissible predicates is retrieved from the hash structure. From all the potential admissible predicates (listed in Definition 6) that can be used in the dependent atoms only those are chosen that when added will not be inconsistent with the TBox. Each dependent atom is supposed to have at least one variable in common with its parent. Before adding any predicate to the list of admissible predicates, it is checked if the intersections of descriptions (from two predicates) that are going to describe these shared variables in a query are satisfiable. The computed dependent atoms are added as children of a given node.

In the next step the right brothers of a given node are added also as its children. Right brother copying mechanism takes care that all possible subsets are generated. The trie data structure allows to keep the children in order. Every subset is generated only once, that is only one permutation out of a set of dependent atoms is considered. If necessary, the variable names of the right brothers are changed when they are being copied. The variables that are being changed are so called *output variables* (not existing in preceding atoms in the trie). To maintain a proper variable naming we keep track of which of the given atom variables are the output variables (and are going to be changed) and which are going to stay the same when, for example, new binary node is being added as a child to the binary parent.

Similar test, as in the case of computing the list of admissible predicates, is performed while adding any new node to the trie. With every node in the trie the information is associated about the descriptions of all variables occuring in the path from the root to the given node. These descriptions are built as an intersection of all descriptions from the path (concepts, domains and ranges of properties) describing the given variable. While adding a new atom to the trie the test is performed for each variable occuring in the given atom that occurs already in the path from the root of the trie. The test consist in checking if the intersection of the descriptions of this variable from the new atom and from the path is satisfiable (*checkDescsIntersectionSatisfiable* function).

Also some other rules are introduced in order to avoid generation of redundant literals. Top-level concepts and top-level properties are added in dependent atoms only to the nodes representing concepts and properties at the highest possible level. It allows to avoid generating atoms that anyhow would be copied in the next step as the right brothers. Also we do not add the atoms that duplicate functional and inverse functional properties in the query. Because of the lack of the unique names assumption it would result in generating semantically equivalent and therefore redundant queries. When adding a new atom we check its grandparent, parent and brothers with regard to the role functionality (*checkPropertyConstraints* function). We do not create also the copy of the atom (by the 3rd refinement rule) that represents the functional or the inverse functional property.

The ideas presented above are summarized in the trie expansion algorithm presented below. Atoms in the algorithm have the form $P(\boldsymbol{x}, \boldsymbol{y})$, where P denotes a predicate name and $\boldsymbol{x}$ and $\boldsymbol{y}$ distinguished and undistinguished variables.

Algorithm 1. ***Trie expansion***

```
classify taxonomy;
computeAdmissiblePredicates(Cref);
leafList ← Cref(key);
while leafList not empty do
    for all A(x_a, y_a) ∈ leafList do
        if admissible predicates of A not computed then
            computeAdmissiblePredicates(A);
        endif
        for all D ∈ admissible predicates of A do
            build dependent atom D(x_d, y_d) of A(x_a, y_a)
            if checkPropertyConstraints() and checkDescsIntersectionSatisfiable() then
                if D(x_d, y_d) is frequent then
                    addChild(A(x_a, y_a), D(x_d, y_d));
                    /* add D(x_d, y_d) as child of A(x_a, y_a) */
                endif
            endif
        endfor
        for all B(x_b, y_b) ∈ right brothers of A(x_a, y_a) do
            create B'(x_b, y_b') which is a copy of node B(x_b, y_b);
            if checkPropertyConstraints() and checkDescsIntersectionSatisfiable() then
                if a copy B'(x_b, y_b') of B(x_b, y_b) is frequent then
                    addChild(A(x_a, y_a), B'(x_b, y_b'));
                endif
            endif
        endfor
        create A'(x_a, y_a') which is a copy of node A(x_a, y_a);
            if checkPropertyConstraints() then
```

```
            if a copy A'(x_a, y_a') of A(x_a, y_a) is frequent then
                addChild(A(x_a, y_a), A'(x_a, y_a'));
            endif
        endif
    endfor
    update leafList;
endwhile
```

4.1 Illustrative Example

As an illustration of our method let's consider the example below:

Example 2. (Following Example 1). Let's assume that we have the TBox from Example 1 and the ABox which is bigger than in previous example, but for the sake of clarity we will not discuss it within this example. Then our method works as follows. First we classify a taxonomy and as an effect we obtain the classification presented in Figure 1.

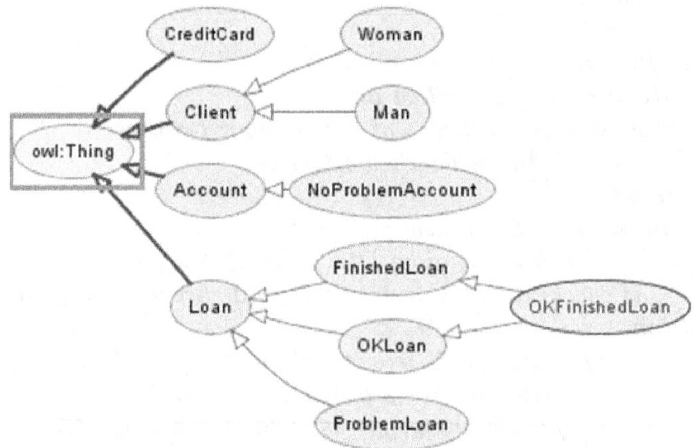

Fig. 1. Classified taxonomy (displayed with Protege OWL Viz)

The top-level concepts in the example are: *CreditCard*, *Client*, *Account*, *Loan*. For the predicate *Client* admissible predicates are: $isOwnerOf$ (an atom built from this predicate can have only the first variable in common with the atom with *Client* predicate), Man and $Woman$. The part of the trie generated when asking about *Client* as a reference concept is presented in Figure 2. The numbers on edges refer to three ways in which the atoms can be added to the trie. Also some of the lists of variable descriptions associated with nodes are shown in this Figure. As it was explained earlier in this Section, every path from the trie top to any of its leaves represents a pattern. The trie in Figure 2 is built

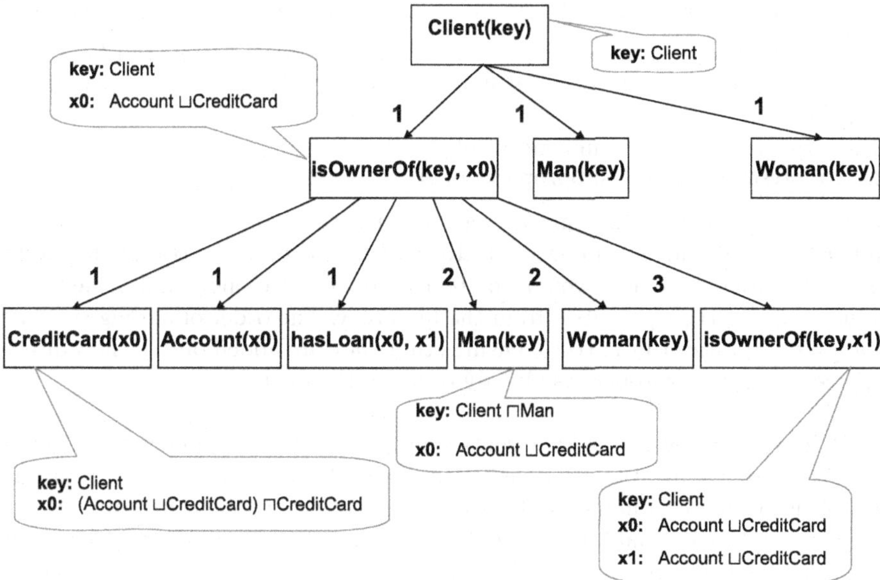

Fig. 2. A part of a trie generated when asking about *Client* as a reference concept

up to the level 3, that is up to the patterns that have the length of 3 atoms. The example pattern at this level is: $q(key)\ :\ -Client(key), isOwnerOf(key, x0)$, $CreditCard(x0)$. The discovered patterns represent the frequently occuring in the data base characteristics of some concepts. The example pattern represents the clients that have some credit card.

4.2 Completeness

Our algorithm generates every valid, frequent, closed pattern where closed patterns are defined as follows.

Definition 7 (Closed query). *A $\mathcal{K}$-query is called closed if it is not possible to add literals to this query without affecting the semantics.*

Lemma 1. *Given is a query Q which occurs in the trie T generated by our Algorithm, and an atom $A \notin Q$ which is a valid refinement of Q. Then a query $Q' = (Q_1, A, Q_2)$ exists in the trie T, for some subdivision of Q into Q_1 and Q_2, such that $Q = (Q_1, Q_2)$.*

Proof. As A is a valid refinement of Q, there is a prefix (Q_p, A_p) of Q such that the atom A is either a dependent atom of A_p or a copy of A_p. The dependent atom is added by the 1st refinement rule of the algorithm, the copy is generated by the 3rd refinement rule of the algorithm. Let us now consider relations between A_p and A:

(I) A is a dependent atom of A_p. There are the following "dependency" relations:

1. A represents a top level concept or a top level property and can be added as a dependent atom of A_p, if it is not causing infrequent or unsatisfiable query;
2. A represents a direct subconcept of A_p;
3. A represents a direct subproperty of A_p;

Subconcepts/subproperties that are not direct descendants of a given concept/property are not added as dependent atoms at this level to the trie. If they were added the resulting query would not be closed, because one could always add to such a query their parent(s) from the hierarchy. The order of adding subconcepts/subproperties to the trie T ensures that they are added only if their direct superconcepts/superproperties already occur in the query.

(II) If A is a copy of A_p, A represents a property. If this property is not functional (or inverse functional) then the copy of A_p is created and the output variable is given a new name by the 3rd refinement rule of the algorithm. Otherwise the copy of A_p would not be created, because the query in which the atom with functional (inverse functional) property occurs cannot be closed. To such a query one can always add any number of copies of such atom without affecting the semantics. Any number of the output variables in these atoms will denote the same individual.

Let us now consider the place of injection of the atom A into the query Q in order to obtain the query Q' (2nd refinement rule of the algorithm).

If A_p is the last atom of Q, A is added at the end, after A_p and the query Q' exist in the trie T. If A_p is not the last atom and has a different successor A_{p+1} then order of A and A_{p+1} in the list of children of A_p in the trie T is one of the following:

1. A occurs before A_{p+1} (Ap, A, A_{p+1}) when A_{p+1} is a right-hand brother of A in the trie T.
2. A occurs after A_{p+1}, $(Ap, A_{p+1}, ..., A)$ when A is a child of A_p and a right brother of A_{p+1} in the trie T. In order to determine the exact injection place of A, we recursively apply our arguments, taking into account A_{p+1} and A.

Theorem 1 (Completeness). *For every closed, frequent $\mathcal{K}$-query Q_1 in the pattern space, there is at least one semantically equivalent closed $\mathcal{K}$-query Q_2 in the trie T.*

Proof (Sketch). We assume that queries are generated according to the refinement rules from Definition 6 up to the user specified length. For the query Q_1 of the length 1 it is obvious that there will be a corresponding query Q_2 of the form $q(x) : -Cref(x)$ in the root of the trie. If the reference concept $Cref$ is not a top level concept we can always add its ancestors from the concept hierarchy to the query Q_2 to make this query closed. For the query Q_1 of another length this can be shown by induction on the length of the query: an equivalent query for $Q_1/last(Q_1)$ exists in the trie T. When atom $last(Q_1)$ is a valid refinement of the equivalent query, one can apply Lemma 1.

5 Experimental Results

The experimental evaluation of the method can be performed in several ways. Firstly it can be tested whether using domain knowledge in the form of the ontology can increase the efficiency of the frequent pattern mining with regards to the setting where no knowledge is available and all the possible patterns have to be generated. The efficiency can be measured objectively in terms of the number of candidate patterns evaluated and the time needed for the pattern generation. It can be tested also whether using the ontology can reduce the number of the generated patterns that are semantically redundant. Secondly, it may be potentially evaluated, although it is not easy to measure, how the ontology can help with the interpretation of the discovered patterns.

The goal of the preliminary experiment presented in this paper was to estimate whether using the ontology can increase the efficiency of the data mining. In order to test our methods we have used the financial dataset from the PKDD'99 Discovery Challenge to create our ontologies on the basis of this data. The ontologies are published online to serve as a benchmark under the SEMINTEC project page [2]. The experiments were performed on the machine with 1500MHz processor and 504MB of RAM. Below the results are presented of a simple experiment performed on the ontology part containing only the gold credit card holders, when asked for *CreditCard* as a reference concept (*minsup*=0.2) and up to the 5th level (that is up to the queries of the length of 5 atoms). The numbers in the Figure refer to the number of patterns generated at each level (that is at each pattern length). There is the number of candidates that were generated and then tested with the ABox with regards to their support. Then there is the number of the patterns that had the support higher than 0.2. Also the ratio is computed between the patterns discovered and the candidates generated. The lower the number of the candidates with regards to the number of the patterns the better is the perfomance of the method, because there is less queries needed to be posed to the data base. Also, as our method generates every closed pattern, the lower the number of patterns, the better is the efficiency of the method, because it generates less patterns that are semantically redundant.

The results where computed in three settings: the original method, the method where we do not check property functionality and thus we create copies of functional properties and the method where there is no ontology available at all and every possible pattern is created and tested. The third setting serves for the estimation whether we can gain in the performance thanks to using the ontology during the pattern mining. The second setting was performed to see how big is the influence on the method performance of generating the copies of the functional properties. In the first two settings the processing time at the first level is higher than at the second level because it includes also the setup time. On the Figure we can see that when the ontology is used, the frequent pattern mining process is significantly faster than in the naive approach. There is lower number of patterns generated at each level (although it cannot be directly

[2] SEMINTEC project, http://www.cs.put.poznan.pl/alawrynowicz/semintec.htm

	The original method				No functionality check				Naive approach			
Level	Cnd	Pt	Pt/Cnd	Time	Cnd	Pt	Pt/Cnd	Time	Cnd	Pt	Pt/Cnd	Time
1	4	2	50,00%	4s	4	2	50,00%	5s	50	2	4,00%	22s
2	6	5	83,33%	2s	6	5	83,33%	3s	155	11	7,10%	57s
3	28	25	89,29%	11s	31	28	90,32%	12s	418	98	23,44%	148s
4	140	139	99,29%	65s	184	181	98,37%	99s	1731	953	55,05%	1182s
5	786	773	98,35%	511s	//////	//////	//////	//////	//////	//////	//////	//////
Total	964	944	97,93%									

Cnd - Number of candidates; ////// - experiment interrupted due to the high computation time
Pt - Number of patterns

Fig. 3. Experimental results on gold credit card holders dataset (*CreditCard* as a reference concept

compared, because the naive approach generates also the patterns that are not closed). Shorter processing times of our method are not only achieved because of the effect of not generating the copies of functional properties, which can be deduced from the second setting where these copies were generated.

The patterns generated in this experiment are, however, not very long and further investigation is needed on the algorithm performance (especially to estimate when the pruning of infrequent atoms from the dependent atoms lists takes bigger effect). Our method has the problem with the convergence. It is caused by the application of the 3rd refinement rule (generating the copies of atoms). It should be noted, however, that without the application of the 3rd refinement rule we cannot obtain every possible, closed pattern. The method that applies this third way of adding the nodes to the trie generates significantly more patterns that one would obtain only considering single copies of properties. It is caused by the fact that without the Unique Name Assumption, queries q(x):-Client(x), isOwnerOf(x,y) and q(x):-Client(x),isOwnerOf(x,y_1), isOwnerOf(x,y_2) can return the same result (as it can be deduced that y_1 is equivalent y_2). In the future we are going to work on how to deal with this problem.

The experimental results presented here are the preliminary ones. We have not yet optimized our implementation and the times presented here are mostly for the illustration of the problem. In the next step of our research we will focus on further intensive experimental evaluation of the feasibility of this kind of approach. Therefore in the future we are going to have more experimental results, on different sizes and complexities of ontologies, concerning especially the potential benefits of guiding the search of patterns by the ontology instead of merely evaluating all combinations.

6 Conclusion and Future Work

In this paper we have presented a method for pattern discovery from the ontological layer of the Semantic Web. Ontologies that represent the domain knowledge can be used for driving the search process into more promising areas in the space of patterns. Ontologies not only can be taken as input but they can also help in the in-depth interpretation of the discovered patterns. Newly discovered knowledge can be used, in turn, for the input ontologies evolution. Frequent patterns can be further processed into association rules or used for conceptual clustering where each query describes a cluster of the instances of the reference concept and where the clusters can be formed into hierarchy on the basis of the query containment relation. Further processing of the discovered patterns is the potential subject of our future work.

Our method mines frequent patterns in OWL DLP knowledge bases. As it has been mentioned there exists only one other approach, system SPADA, that aims at frequent pattern discovery using hybrid language that combines description logic and the Horn clausal logic. In SPADA, the Horn rule component is unrestricted, but description logic component is quite restricted. In our approach the Horn rule component is restricted, but we in turn focus on the description logic component. In the future we are going to consider also more expressive languages within the $\mathcal{DL}$-safe rules approach.

We have shown that our method generates every valid closed pattern. The main drawback of our current algorithm is that it generates semantically redundant patterns, especially in the case where no restriction on adding the copies of atoms is imposed. In [16] similar problem was described of receiving semantically equivalent patterns as a result of adding the leaf nodes in the form of copies of nodes. The next step can be the investigation of different settings to deal with this problem (possibly under Unique Name Assumption). Our approach is currently under intensive experimental investigation, focused primarily on the potential benefits of guiding the search for patterns by the ontology when compared to the naive approach where every possible pattern is generated. In a short time we plan to have investigated different sizes and complexities of the terminological parts as well as of the assertional parts of the knowledge bases.

Acknowledgments. Work partially supported by Polish Ministry of Scientific Research and Information Technology (under grant number KBN 3T11F 025 28).

We would like also to thank Boris Motik for the support concerning KAON2.

References

1. Agrawal, R. Mannila, H., Srikant, R., Toivonen, H. and Verkamo, A. I. (1996) Fast discovery of association rules. Advances in Knowledge Discovery and Data Mining. AAAI Press, Menlo Park, CA, pp. 307 328
2. Berners-Lee T., Hendler J., and Lassila O. (2001) The Semantic Web. Scientific American, 284(5):34- 43
3. H. Blockeel, L. Dehaspe, B. Demoen, G. Janssens, J. Ramon, and H. Vandecasteele (2002), Improving the efficiency of Inductive Logic Programming through the use of query packs, Journal of Artificial Intelligence Research 16, 135-166.
4. Dehaspe, L., Toivonen, H. (1999) Discovery of frequent Datalog patterns. Data Mining and Knowledge Discovery, 3(1): 7-36

5. Donini, F., Lenzerini, M., Nardi, D., Schaerf, A. (1998) AL-log: Integrating datalog and description logics, Journal of Intelligent Information Systems, 10:3, 227-252
6. Dzeroski S., Lavrac N., (Eds.) (2001) Relational data mining. Springer
7. Grosof B. N., Horrocks I., Volz R., Decker S. (2003) Description Logic Programs: Combining Logic Programs with Description Logic. In Proc. of the Twelfth Int'l World Wide Web Conf. (WWW 2003), 4857. ACM
8. Hitzler P., Studer R., Sure Y. (2005) Description Logic Programs: A Practical Choice For the Modelling of Ontologies. In Proc. of the 1st Workshop on Formal Ontologies meet Meet Industry, FOMI'05, Verona, Italy
9. Józefowska J., Ławrynowicz A., Łukaszewski T. (2005) Towards discovery of frequent patterns in description logics with rules, Proc. of the International Conference on Rules and Rule Markup Languages for the Semantic Web (RuleML-2005), Galway, Ireland, LNCS, Springer-Verlag, 84-97
10. Józefowska J., Ławrynowicz A., Łukaszewski T. Faster frequent pattern mining from the Semantic Web, Intelligent Information Processing and Web Mining Conference, IIS:IIPWM'06, Advances in Soft Computing, Springer Verlag 2006, 121-130
11. Lisi F.A., Malerba D. (2004) Inducing Multi-Level Association Rules from Multiple Relation, Machine Learning Journal, 55, 175-210
12. Mannila, H., Toivonen, H. (1997) Levelwise search and borders of theories in knowledge discovery. Data Mining and Knowledge Discovery 1(3): 241 - 258
13. Motik B., Sattler U., Studer R. (2004) Query Answering for OWL-DL with Rules. Proc. of the 3rd International Semantic Web Conference (ISWC 2004), Hiroshima, Japan, pp. 549-563
14. Motik B., Sattler U. Practical DL Reasoning over Large ABoxes with KAON2. Submitted for publication
15. Nienhuys-Cheng, S., de Wolf, R. (1997) Foundations of inductive logic programming, vol. 1228 of LNAI. Springer
16. Nijssen, S., Kok, J.N. (2001) Faster Association Rules for Multiple Relations. Proceedings of the IJCAI'01, 891-897
17. Nijssen, S., Kok, J.N. (2003) Efficient frequent query discovery in FARMER. In Proceedings of the PKDD 2003, volume 2431 of Lecture Notes in Artificial Intelligence, Springer-Verlag, 350-362

Engineering and Learning of Adaptation Knowledge in Case-Based Reasoning

Amélie Cordier, Béatrice Fuchs, and Alain Mille

LIRIS UMR 5205
CNRS/INSA de Lyon/Université Claude Bernard Lyon 1/
Université Lumière Lyon 2/Ecole Centrale de Lyon
Bâtiment Nautibus (710),
43, Boulevard du 11 Novembre 1918 - 69622 VILLEURBANNE CEDEX
{acordier, bfuchs, amille}@liris.cnrs.fr
http://liris.cnrs.fr/

Abstract. Case-based reasoning (CBR) uses various knowledge containers for problem solving: cases, domain, similarity, and adaptation knowledge. These various knowledge containers are characterised from the engineering and learning points of view. We focus on adaptation and similarity knowledge containers that are of first importance, difficult to acquire and to model at the design stage. These difficulties motivate the use of a learning process for refining these knowledge containers. We argue that in an adaptation guided retrieval approach, similarity and adaptation knowledge containers must be mixed. We rely on a formalisation of adaptation for highlighting several knowledge units to be learnt, i.e. dependencies and influences between problem and solution descriptors. Finally, we propose a learning scenario called "active approach" where the user plays a central role for achieving the learning steps.

1 Introduction

Case-based reasoning (CBR) is a reasoning paradigm which consists in solving new problems by adapting the solutions of previously solved problems. The CBR cycle is constituted of five steps: elaborate, retrieve, reuse, revise and retain. Each step is of particular importance in the resolution of the problem and involves specific knowledge.

In CBR, problem-solving experiences constitute basic knowledge units: the cases. During a reasoning cycle, cases are stored in a case-base which may possibly be reorganised. The storage of a solved case is considered as the most traditional approach to CBR learning. Stored cases can be used in later reasoning cycles and gradually improve the system's abilities.

Case-based reasoning is particularly well suited to situations in which domain theory is weak or not easy to formalise. CBR systems have long been considered as interesting alternatives to knowledge-based systems, since, in theory, they require a smaller knowledge engineering effort to become usable in real world domains. It has even been argued that CBR was a solution to the bottleneck of

S. Staab and V. Svatek (Eds.): EKAW 2006, LNAI 4248, pp. 303–317, 2006.

knowledge acquisition since it is easier to collect a number of cases than to build a knowledge base.

However, CBR does not avoid completely the need for a knowledge base and one has to face the knowledge acquisition problem. In fact, CBR systems also rely on other types of knowledge containers to reason on cases: domain ontologies, similarity measures and adaptation knowledge.

Similarity knowledge is used to remember the relevant cases and adaptation knowledge is used to adapt the solutions of stored cases. Experience shows, however, that similarity and adaptation knowledge available are difficult to turn into models, being vague or incomplete, and furthermore, they may evolve. It is therefore advisable to propose tools enabling to acquire and/or learn this knowledge. This would allow us to refine and improve knowledge as the system is being used.

This raises the issue of the management of the knowledge base of a CBR system from its design to its implementation and maintenance. In this paper we propose to view CBR from a knowledge management perspective. First, we consider the problem of knowledge management during the design and use of CBR systems, then we analyse the reasoning cycle, highlighting the various types of knowledge involved in each step. In particular, we will show that it is very difficult to formalise similarity and adaptation knowledge as they evolve with time. After discussing the close link between these two kinds of knowledge units, we show how the different learning approaches can make use of such a link. We present the model of adaptation by substitution on which we base ourselves and we put forward several scenarios for learning adaptation knowledge. We will emphasise the main role the user has to play in this process.

2 CBR Knowledge: A Typology

Case-based reasoning systems are knowledge-based systems (KBS) which, if we follow Richter's proposition [18], make use of four distinct knowledge sources: domain description vocabulary, cases, similarity knowledge and knowledge of solution transformation which we call adaptation knowledge.

2.1 Knowledge Management in CBR Systems

We can distinguish several phases in the life cycle of a CBR system: design, production and maintenance.

During the system's design and realisation phase, the designers define –in agreement with domain experts– problem solving methods to be used. An important engineering effort must be made to build the system's knowledge bases, define an initial base of solved cases, describe domain knowledge and formalise similarity and adaptation knowledge. The system can also be used with known cases to instantiate the case-base with examples and provide a starting point for reasoning. The issue of the knowledge representation formalism is also addressed at that time. The main actors of that phase are of course the experts, who are true vectors of domain knowledge, as well as the designers who facilitate the passage from the knowledge level to the symbol level [17].

During the production phase, the system is used to solve –or help solving– new problems. The reasoning cycle carrying out this task is examined in the following section. Problems may be posed to the system by users or system experts. Interactions between the users and system take place at the beginning and the end of the cycle, but also during the production phase, as we shall see later on. As soon as the system is used, a maintenance procedure must ensure the evolution of the initial knowledge base. At the end of each problem solving step, the newly solved case is stored in the case-base to be re-used later on. As a result, there is a gradual increase in the size of the case-base and this highlights the need to organise and maintain it throughout the life of the system. To deal with this issue, several works propose indexing or classification techniques to facilitate the retrieval of stored cases. Other approaches are based on strategies of retention and forgetting [19] to retain only the more relevant cases and avoid overloading the case-base. Among all these various approaches, some occur during the retain phase whereas others are done outside the production phase. Finally, let us note that maintenance operations can be done by the system itself or by the expert user. The system can also ask the expert for assistance.

2.2 Reasoning Cycle

As we mentioned earlier, CBR solves new problems by remembering and adapting already solved problems. The CBR cycle is composed of five steps:

- *Elaborate.* This step is not included in the classic CBR cycle introduced in [1]. Even if it was implicitly done in several systems, it was firstly explicitly mentioned in [8]. During this step, the information necessary to the resolution of a problem are collected and structured to form a new case: the target case. The system solicits the user or its outside environment (databases, information systems) to obtain the information needed to continue its reasoning.
- *Retrieve.* The retrieval step consists in searching the case-base for one or several solved cases deemed to be similar to the target case. The selection of a similar case is based on a similarity measure. Some systems use several stored cases and combine them to solve a problem, but most of the time, only one case is used to continue the process. It is called the source case. The selection of the source case can be done either by the system or by the user.
- *Reuse.* This step enables the system to solve the target case by adapting the selected source case solution which is first copied, then possibly adapted to satisfy the requirements of a given problem. The adaptation rests on adaptation knowledge which can be of different forms according to the various systems.
- *Revise.* The solution proposed by the system may not suit the user, or, once it has been applied, might be unable to solve the given problem. The user has therefore the opportunity to modify, amend or even refuse the proposed

solution. The revise step allows one to identify the possible causes of failures and to propose further adaptations to obtain a satisfactory solution: the revised case. This step is the basis of the learning process, leading to the improvement of existing adaptation knowledge and giving rise to new adaptation knowledge.

– *Retain.* Traditionally, the retain step is considered as the step during which the case-base is enriched by the revised target case. This retention implies an update of indexes used to retrieve the cases and sometimes a maintenance process is needed to reorganise the case-base. But the retention step is also a means to learn other types of knowledge. Indeed, it is during this step that additional knowledge can be acquired in various ways.

A concise but complete overview of the work in each of theses steps can be found in [16].

2.3 Knowledge Acquisition and Learning

The study of the reasoning cycle in CBR has highlighted the diversity of knowledge involved in this process. Table 1 proposes a synthesis. For each knowledge unit, the following are defined: the various forms of knowledge, the steps during which this specific knowledge can be acquired and the methods used for its acquisition and learning.

One notes that, except for domain knowledge, it is rare to find in the system knowledge that can be formalised *a priori.* In fact, even if it is possible to represent similarity or adaptation knowledge in the initial knowledge base, this knowledge remains vague or uncertain and must be improved during the system use.

2.4 About Similarity and Adaptation Knowledge

The relation between similarity and adaptation knowledge needs to be studied. Adaptation is one of the most difficult step of CBR and therefore any effort to facilitate it is useful.

In [20], Smyth introduces the concept of adaptation-guided retrieval. He argues that the sources cases most similar to the target case are not always the easiest to adapt, in particular when the similarity rests on surface features. Retrieval must therefore search not only for similar cases, but especially easily adaptable cases.

In the same light, Leake [13] suggests that a good retrieval of a case reduces the adaptation effort. In fact, the traditional semantic similarity measures may lead to bad results since they occasionally retrieve source cases which are certainly very like the target case, but are difficult or even impossible to adapt. This remark shows the limitations of similarity measures with regard to the whole reasoning process. Leake therefore proposes to include in the similarity measure a notion of adaptation cost to make it more pertinent. Hence, in this approach, the evaluation of the similarity between the target case and the various source cases takes place in two steps: first, a classic similarity measure is evaluated by

Table 1. CBR knowledge typology

Knowledge type	Form of Knowledge	Acquisition Step	Acquisition/Learning Approaches
Case	Problem part and solution part (descriptor sets), Reasoning traces (steps from problem to solution)	Design: use of known cases to train the system Retain: storage of cases solved during the reasoning cycle	Classification Indexing
Domain knowledge	Concepts: properties and relations with other concepts, Rules, Dependencies	Initial acquisition relatively easy if domain theory is weak	Description and modelling by the expert
Similarity knowledge	Predefined numeric measures, Empirical measures based on descriptors comparison, More complex measures taking into account adaptability, Weights, Similarity paths, Etc.	Initial acquisition not easy, no design methodology, Retrieval: acquisition of new knowledge and improvement of existing knowledge	Modelisation by the expert, Introspective learning, Automatic symbolic learning (data mining, neural networks ...) Etc.
Adaptation knowledge	Adaptation rules, Adaptation operators, Adaptation cases		

comparing the cases, then, the most similar retrieved cases are ranked according to their adaptability.

Lieber on the other hand, proposes an adaptation approach making use of similarity paths. Behind this notion lies the idea of a decomposition of adaptation into simpler adaptation sub-tasks. To expose similarities between two complex problems, it is often necessary to use domain knowledge. The approach proposed in [14] aims to decrease the difficulty of adaptation by increasing the similarity between the problems, which involves decomposing a complex problem into several simpler sub-problems. Intermediary problems are linked together by relations. Each relation corresponds to a specific adaptation enabling the passage from one problem to another. A similarity path is therefore composed of a linear sequence of intermediary problems linked together by relations. The first step of adaptation which involves the building of the similarity path can take place during the retrieval step. All that remains to do during the second adaptation phase is to calculate the elementary adaptations corresponding to each step of the similarity path. In [15], the authors demonstrate how, in a concrete case (the treatment of breast cancer), the notion of similarity paths may appear as a tool to assist in the acquisition and creation of models of adaptation knowledge.

These three examples highlight clearly the dual relation existing between similarity knowledge and adaptation knowledge. More generally, it is not advisable to consider the different stages of CBR separately and independently from one another, but rather as contributing to a common objective. The elaboration stage, for example, aims to improve retrieval by establishing suitable descriptors. In the same way, the retrieval step tends to facilitate adaptation by using an adaptability criteria to select a source case. A case's adaptability must therefore be taken into account in the retrieval step. This is why learning adaptation knowledge if of particular importance. In the following part, we consider the strategies for knowledge learning.

3 Learning Adaptation Knowledge

3.1 Learning Strategies

Adaptation is studied according to three main directions: unifying approaches which propose general adaptation models; catalogues of adaptation strategies applicable to several domains; and methods for acquiring adaptation knowledge which, in a particular domain, try to highlight the general principles to explain the adaptation process. A distinction is made between different approaches of acquisition of adaptation knowledge: knowledge light approaches (according to [21]) consist in re-using knowledge available in the system to infer new knowledge while other approaches try to acquire new knowledge by using the interface between the system and its environment. The former approaches take place outside the problem solving phase, whereas the latter take place during the solving process and therefore present numerous possibilities of interactions with the user.

The approach presented in [7] can be classified in the first category: it consists in determining pairs of cases and using differences between their attributes to improve adaptation rules. The adaptation rules thus created are then refined and generalised. Each rule has associated measures of confidence calculated according to its degree of generalisation.

On the same line of thought, [15] propose an approach of knowledge learning based on a particular search technique called *frequent pattern extraction*. The main idea is to use the differences between cases taken in pairs. Indeed, these differences can be interpreted as the result of an adaptation effort. It is then possible to deduce some adaptation knowledge.

Among the approaches of the second category, we may note that of [12]. According to Leake, knowledge learning takes on several forms. At first, Fox and Leake proposed an approach using introspective reasoning to give systems the possibility of learning new knowledge enabling them to improve their overall efficiency. In [3], the authors apply introspective reasoning to improve indexing of cases. They extend this approach to the other stages of CBR and in particular, to the adaptation stage. In the DIAL system, the proposed reasoning focuses mainly on case adaptation and the learning of various types of knowledge is more or less linked to this stage. [11] considers case adaptation as a process combining a group of abstract transformations with memory search strategies. A trace of the actions taking place during an adaptation phase is stored and constitutes an adaptation case. Thus, when a new case is encounter, it can be adapted either from scratch or based on the use of adaptation cases and introspective reasoning [10]. Adaptation knowledge is acquired via a CBR cycle within the main CBR cycle. This approach of learning of adaptation knowledge enables an ongoing refining of adaptation strategies by adapting adaptation cases [9]. Leake also proposes to evolve similarity knowledge as adaptation knowledge is being learnt. The idea is to use knowledge contained in adaptation cases to predict adaptation costs. The proposed method is called RCR (Re-application Costs and Relevance). It enables us to assess the difficulty of adapting a problem and brings therefore further detail to the similarity measure [13].

One of the drawback of the approaches that aim to use knowledge already available in the system to infer new adaptation knowledge is their limitation to the vocabulary of the case-base. They do not allow one to infer knowledge that is not explainable using the existing knowledge of the application. Furthermore, they only give the user a minor role which consist in validating the inferred knowledge. On the contrary, approaches which allow the learning of knowledge during the reasoning process provide the possibility of adding new knowledge to the system and the opportunity for the user to play an actual role in the process. We stick to the second approach and our wish is to place the user at the centre of the learning process so that he can simultaneously play an active role in the solution of the problem and in the learning of adaptation knowledge.

3.2 Learning to Improve Adaptation

In this work, we base ourselves on a formalisation of adaptation by substitution. The framework of our study was set out in [4]. Adaptation knowledge is modelled as a set of dependencies. The dependencies we use are similar to those used in analogical reasoning [5], [6].

After presenting the notions and notations used, we identify the sources as well as the knowledge units targeted by the learning process (learning targets) and we propose some learning strategies. We illustrate the various strategies in the domain of the assessment of the price of a second-hand motor vehicle. In this problem, cases are vehicles characterised by some features as well as by their selling price on the used car marketplace. The aim is then to calculate, given a certain number of dependencies, the estimated selling price of a new vehicle according to the set of known descriptors.

In our approach, we make a difference between acquisition and learning. We speak of learning in reference to machine learning, that is to say when the system is able to learn on his own, using knowledge already available. We use acquisition when knowledge comes from outside the systems. Thus acquisition approaches often involve a user which interacts with the system.

An Adaptation Model. The adaptation model proposed in [4] is briefly described below. Our hypothesis is that a case is composed of a problem part and a solution part. It is possible to represent a case using a set of descriptors. A descriptor consists in a name and a value. We note:

- d as descriptors of problem parts and D as descriptors of solution parts,
- $\{d_i^s\}_{i=1..n}$ as descriptors of a source problem and $\{D_j^s\}_{j=1..N}$ as descriptors of its solution,
- $\{d_i^t\}_{i=1..n}$ as descriptors of a target problem and $\{D_j^t\}_{j=1..N}$ as descriptors of its solution calculated by adaptation.

In two given cases, the retrieval step estimates the differences between the pairs of problem descriptors (Δd_i). The adaptation is based on a group of relationships between the problem and its solution called *dependencies* which indicates that some problem descriptors have an influence upon some solution descriptors. Thereby, adaptation knowledge is mainly constituted of dependencies.

A dependency is a triple $(d_i, D_j, \mathcal{I}(D_j/d_i))$ indicating the variation of the solution descriptor D_j in relation to the problem descriptor d_i. $\mathcal{I}(D_j/d_i)$ is called influence function and indicates how to calculate the variation of D_j knowing the variation of d_i. Adaptation combines these influence functions $\mathcal{I}(D_j/d_i)$ with the differences Δd_i between problem descriptors to estimate the variations ΔD_j. These variations are applied to source solutions descriptors D_j^s in order to obtain target solution descriptors D_j^t.

Dependencies are therefore essential as they contain, through influences, adaptation knowledge. Dependencies are domain knowledge which must be assessed at the beginning of the system's design to enable its reasoning. But this knowledge remains empirical and uncertain, it must therefore be refined through the use of the system. This remark is justified by the very existence of a revision step in the CBR cycle. Indeed, if adaptation knowledge was complete, the system would be able to guarantee that the adaptation result is correct.

In the adaptation model presented here, dependencies also explicit the close relationships between similarity and adaptation knowledge. They link problem and solution descriptors thus highlighting the role they play in the evaluation of similarity.

Learning Targets. Using the formalisation of adaptation presented before, we have identified three main adaptation knowledge learning targets: influence functions, dependencies and classes of problems.

Influence Functions. Influence functions allow one to calculate the variation of a solution descriptor according to the variation of a problem descriptor. They can be of various types and of variable complexities but, most of the time, they can be assimilated to numeric functions. These functions, even if they are assessed during the system's design, can be refined throughout the problem resolution experiences. For example, it is possible to adjust function applicability thresholds or to modify some parameters to make functions more and more precise.

Dependencies. During the resolution of a new problem, an adaptation failure can points out an unknown dependency. Indeed, it is likely that an experience shows that a problem descriptor ignored until now has an influence, under specific conditions, on a solution descriptor. In such a situation, a new dependency must be elaborated and associated with a suitable set of dependencies. It is also possible that several dependencies put in relation a unique problem descriptor with a unique solution descriptor but using different influence functions. In this case, another problem descriptor should be available. This descriptor will be used to select the dependency and, as a result, the influence to use. It is the responsibility of the elaboration step of identifying these descriptors.

Classes of Problems. A class of problems correspond to a group of problems that can be solved using similar adaptation knowledge. Concretely, a class of problems is composed of a set of dependencies necessary to solve a particular kind of problem. Thus, discovering a new class of problems is equivalent to identify a new category of problems unknown until now and consequently impossible to adapt. Identifying a new class of problems is also a way to acquire adaptation knowledge.

Knowledge Acquisition and Learning Methods. An adaptation failure in a CBR system reflects a lack of adaptation knowledge. It's during the revise step that this failure is observed: the modifications made by the user on the solution or the inability of the system to find a suitable solution to the problem are good indicators of this situation. The revise step is thus, most of the time, the starting point of the acquisition and learning process. In the following, we describe some methods combining acquisition and learning techniques applicable in the CBR field.

Exploiting the Revise Step. The adaptation process, using the influence functions, estimates differences between solution descriptors. We note these differences: $\Delta_{adapted}D_j$. Applied to source solution descriptors, these differences allow one to estimate the values of the target solution descriptors (D_j^t). These differences represent the modifications made by the system.

Other differences are produced by the user during case revision. They are noted as $\Delta_{revised}D_j$. They allow one to quantify the difference between one target solution descriptor D_j^t before and after the user's revision. In consequence, these differences represent the adjustment made by the user. We note D_j^{tr} as target solution descriptor j after the revise step.

In this model $\oplus$ (resp. $\ominus$) is an abstract operator which should be defined according to the types of the descriptors. For simplicity sake, we will assimilate this operator to the numeric operator $+$ (resp. $-$) in our example. Thus, we have:

- $D^t_j = D^s_j \oplus \Delta_{adapted} D_j$, and
- $\Delta_{revised} D_j = D^{tr}_j \ominus D^t_j$

These notations are used in the figure 1 which presents relationships between the various descriptors considering in particular the retrieve and the reuse steps. D^{tr}_j are produced by the user: as soon as the system knows them, it is able to evaluate $\Delta_{revised} D_j$.

The differences $\Delta_{revised} D_j$ bring to light problems on the influence functions used to infer the values of the descriptors. Observing such differences can lead to the trigger of a learning process. Indeed, if a solution has been revised by the user before its storage, it is possible to exploit the differences represented by $\Delta_{adapted} D_j$ and $\Delta_{revised} D_j$ during a learning process.

An influence function is characterised by its parameters as well as by thresholds indicating domains on which the function can be applied. Studying $\Delta_{revised} D_j$ and $\Delta_{adapted} D_j$ can allow one to refine both of these elements.

Retrieve Process on the Solutions. Another possibility to acquire adaptation knowledge, inspired by [9], consists in doing a *retrieve step* on the revised source solutions stored in the case-base and to classify the retrieved cases according to their similarity with the revise target solution. If the better case, from the solution point of view, does not match with the source case used to solve the target problem, then we can suppose that one or more dependencies used during the retrieve step were incorrect or incomplete and have to be adjusted.

We believe that various methods can allow the acquisition and learning of adaptation knowledge in this specific situation. Several ideas can be explored: applying an introspective reasoning to do a comparison of descriptors in order to deduce modifications to be made on influence functions; setting a cooperative environment to allow the user to specify on his own how dependencies have to be corrected; etc.

Replaying the Reasoning Cycle with the User. If the revise step does not allow one to obtain a satisfactory solution to the current problem, it may then be useful to implicate the user in the reasoning cycle. The system and the user will then try to solve the problem together. In order to do this the system will provide an *assistance* to the user. This assistance can consist of a presentation of the knowledge used and of an explanation of the system's reasoning process. Allowing the user to specify or complete the knowledge used to solve the problem will certainly lead to a more satisfactory solution.

We also believe that it is possible to acquire and/or learn adaptation knowledge by exploiting a trace of the user's actions. This knowledge can certainly be represented as adaptation cases. Such interactive approaches enable one to discover new classes of problems and even to guide the classification of a given problem into a suitable class of problems.

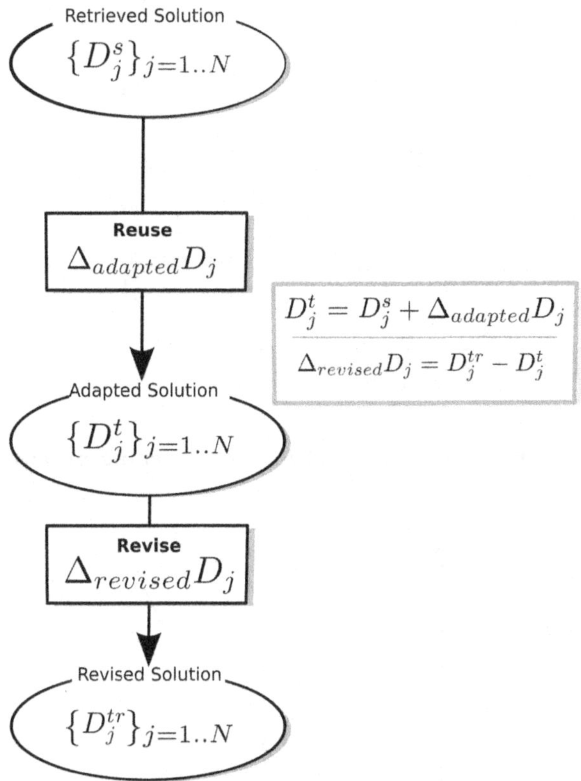

Fig. 1. Relationships between solution descriptors. This figure presents relationships and differences between solution descriptors during reuse and revise steps of the CBR cycle.

Acquisition and Learning Processes: A Scenario. As a synthesis, figure 2 presents various possible learning situations as well as applicable methods in each situation. We want to insist on the fact that is advisable to allow a cooperation between the system and the user at any time and not only after a reasoning failure.

Finally, it is possible to draw a link with data mining approaches that can advantageously complete the approaches introduced before. For example, [15] use data mining techniques to help the discovery of new possible dependencies. In this work, the authors also use theses techniques to check the applicability of an influence function to some known cases.

Illustration Through an Example. This example comes from a well known domain: the used cars selling marketplace. The problem is to estimate the price of a car knowing some of its characteristics and having experience in the form of cases stored in a case-base. A case is a car description composed of various descriptors. One of these descriptors is the price of the car: the price is known

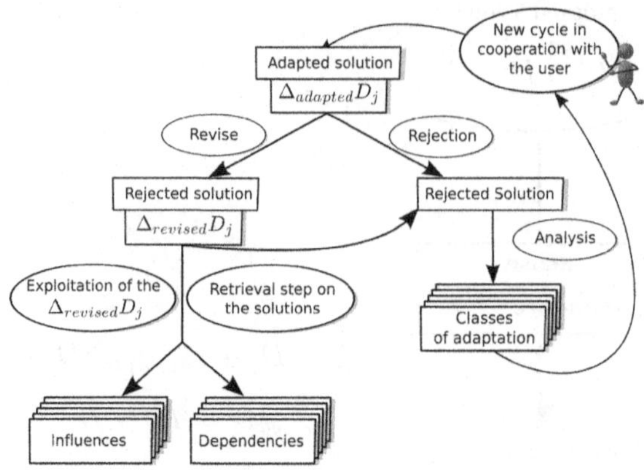

Fig. 2. Knowledge acquisition and learning process

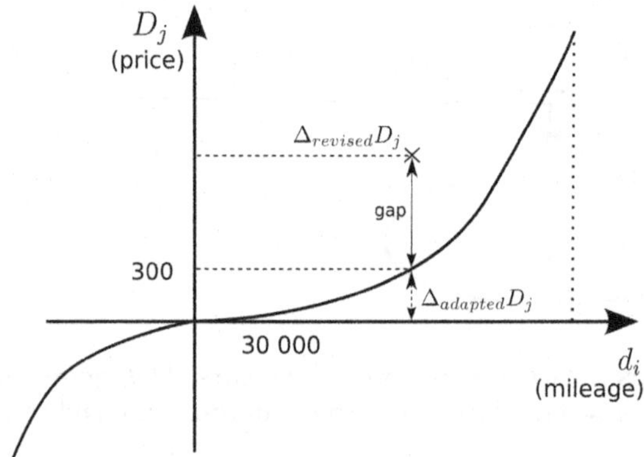

Fig. 3. Graphical representation of a part of an influence function. We can see that the function is only defined for a particular range of Δd_i values (mileage values). This means that the case is not adaptable in this domain. This figure also represents the difference $\Delta_{adapted}D_j$ and $\Delta_{revised}D_j$ to illustrate the possibility of an adaptation knowledge learning.

if the case is solved. In this section we briefly illustrate the concepts introduced before on this problem.

We assume that a car is described by several descriptors: mileage, age, power, colour, type of car (private car or collector car), price, etc.

We first consider the influence functions. A linear influence function allows one to compute a price variation of a car considering a variation of its mileage in comparison with a reference car: this is a simple problem. A simple numeric function indicates that a price variation of one mile induce a variation of .01 euro. Thus a difference of 30 000 miles between two cars will implies a difference of 300 euros between their respective prices. It is possible to learn adaptation knowledge by refining some of the function parameters: for example, the value of the coefficient can be adjusted. The thresholds of the function can also be modified: for example, we can learn that if the car is less than 300 miles, the influence function is not applicable anymore.

The figure 3 presents an influence function in the domain of the simplified example we use: evaluating the price of a used car. In this domain, adjusting a dependency can be done by modifying an influence function or by discovering a new dependency: for example, the fact that the power has implications in the evaluation of a car price.

Let's suppose that we have learnt a new dependency: the price of a car depends not only on its mileage but also on its age. We now need to use two dependencies to solve the problem. This is an extremely simple example of the dependencies we can learn.

In this domain, we can consider that the methods used to estimate the price of a private car and those used to estimate the price of a collector car are not the same. These two problems correspond to two different classes of problems.

4 Conclusion

In this paper we have drawn up an overview of the different kind of knowledge involved in CBR allowing to characterise its reasoning process from the knowledge point of view. We have shown in what extent CBR in general and the learning of adaptation knowledge more precisely could take benefit of a unification of the similarity and adaptation knowledge. Then, based on an adaptation model using the dependency concept, we have identified knowledge units to be learnt and suggested several learning scenarios which have been illustrated through an simple example. Currently, an implementation of these ideas is being achieved using the JColibri tool [2], a framework for prototyping of CBR systems. There are several perspectives to this work. At this time, research is ongoing for setting an experimentation protocol. It aims at validating learnt knowledge and quantifying the global enhancement of the system's competence obtained by the learning scenario. This experimentation can serve as a basis for a comparative study with other approaches based on machine learning techniques applied to CBR. During our first experiment, we have limited the study to simple dependencies, i.e. where a single problem descriptor has an influence on a single solution descriptor. Next, we will have to take into account the most general case where a single solution descriptor is influenced by several problem descriptors. Furthermore, we have also limited the study to the case where dependencies are numerical functions. We have to study the generalisation of this approach to complex cases, i.e. when some descriptors are symbolic.

Acknowledgements

The authors would like to thank the referees whose remarks and comments were very helpful to improve this paper.

References

1. Aamodt, A. and Plaza, E.: Case-based reasoning: Foundational issues, methodological variations, and system approaches. AICOM **7**, pp. 39-59.
2. Bello-Tomas, J.J., Gonzalez Calero, P. and Diaz-Agudo, B.: JColibri: An Object-Oriented Framework for Building CBR Systems. European Conference on Case-Based Reasoning 2004, (2004).
3. Fox, S. and Leake, D.B.: Using Introspective Reasoning to Guide Index Refinement in Case-Based Reasoning. Sixteenth Annual Conference of the Cognitive Science Society, Atlanta, GA, (1994), pp. 324-329.
4. Fuchs, B., Lieber, J., Mille, A. and Napoli, A.: Towards a unified theory of adaptation in Case-Based Reasoning. Proceedings of the third International Conference on Case-based Reasoning, ICCBR-99, Lecture notes in Artificial Intelligence, Germany: Springer Verlag, (1999).
5. Gentner, D. and Forbus, K.: MAC/FAC: A model of similarity-based retrieval. Thirteenth Annual Conference of the Cognitive Science Society, Hillsdale, NJ: Lawrence Erlbaum, (1991), pp. 504-509.
6. Gick, M. L. and Holyoak, K.J.: Analogical problem solving. Cognitive Psychology, **12**, (1980), pp. 306-355.
7. Hanney, K. and Keane, M.T.: Learning Adaptation Rules from a Case-Base. Proceedings of the Third European Workshop on Advances in Case-Based Reasoning, Lecture Notes In Computer Science, (1996).
8. Herbeaux, O. and Mille, A.: ACCELERE: a case-based design assistant for closed cell rubber industry. Knowledge-Based Systems, **12**, (1999), pp. 231-238.
9. Leake, D.B.: Learning Adapatation Strategies by Introspective Reasoning about Memory Search. AAAI-93 Workshop on Case-Based Reasoning, AAAI Press, Menlo Park, CA, (1993), pp. 57-63.
10. Leake, D.B.: Becoming an Expert Case-Based Reasoner : Learning to Adapt Prior Cases. Eighth Annual Florida Artificial Intelligence Research Symposium, (1995), pp. 112-116.
11. Leake, D.B., Kinley, A. and Wilson, D.: Acquiring Case Adaptation Knowledge : A Hybrid Approach. Proceedings of the Thirteenth National Conference on Artificial Intelligence, AAAI Press, Menlo Park, CA, (1996).
12. Leake, D.B., Kinley, A. and Wilson, D.: Multistrategy Learning to Apply Cases for Case-Based Reasoning. Third International Workshop on Multistrategy Learning, AAAI Press, Menlo Park, CA, (1996), pp. 155-164.
13. Leake, D.B., Kinley, A. and Wilson, D.: Case-Based Similarity Assessment: Estimating Adaptability from Experience. Fourteenth National Conference on Artificial Intelligence, AAAI Press, Menlo Park, CA, (1997), pp. 674-679.
14. Lieber, J.: Reformulations and Adaptation Decomposition. International Conference on Case-Based Reasoning - ICCBR'99, LSA, University of Kaiserslautern, Munich, Germany, (1999).
15. Lieber, J., d'Aquin, M., Bey, P., Napoli, A., Rios, M. and Sauvagnac, C.: Acquisition of Adaptation Knowledge for Breast Cancer Treatment Decision Support.9th Conference on Artificial Intelligence in Medicine in Europe2003 - AIME 2003, Protaras, Chypre, (2003).
16. Lopez de Mantaras et al.: Retrieval, reuse, revision and retention in case-based reasoning. The Knowledge Engineering Review, (2005).
17. Newell, A.: The Knowledge Level. AI, **19**(2), (1982), pp. 87-127.

18. Richter, M.M.: Classification and Learning of Similarity Measures. Studies in Classification, Data Analysis and Knowledge Organisation, Springer, (1992).
19. Smyth, B. and Keane, M.T.: Remembering To Forget : A Competence-Preserving Case Deletion Policy for Case-Based Reasoning Systems. IJCAI, (1995), pp. 377-383.
20. Smyth, B. and Keane, M.T.: Adaptation-Guided Retrieval: Questioning the Similarity Assumption in Reasoning. Artificial Intelligence, **102**(2), (1998), pp. 249-293.
21. Wilke, W., Vollrath, I., Althoff, K. D. and Bergmann, R.: A Framework for Learning Adaptation Knowledge Based on Knowledge Light Approaches. Adaptation in Case-Based Reasoning: A Workshop at ECAI 1996, Budapest, (1996).

A Methodological View on Knowledge-Intensive Subgroup Discovery

Martin Atzmueller and Frank Puppe

Department of Computer Science
University of Würzburg, 97074 Würzburg, Germany
Phone: +49 931 888-6739; Fax: +49 931 888-6732
{atzmueller, puppe}@informatik.uni-wuerzburg.de

Abstract. Background knowledge is a natural resource for knowledge-intensive methods: Its exploitation can often improve the quality of their results significantly. In this paper we present a methodological view on knowledge-intensive subgroup discovery: We introduce different classes and specific types of useful background knowledge, discuss their benefit and costs, and describe their application in the subgroup discovery setting.

1 Introduction

Knowledge-intensive learning methods (e.g., [1]) use background knowledge for a simple reason: Utilizing background knowledge can often significantly improve both the quality of their results and the efficiency of the search process. In this paper, we describe how to exploit background knowledge for subgroup discovery, a method that has first been formalized by Klösgen [2] and Wrobel [3]: Subgroup discovery is a powerful and broadly applicable technique aiming at discovering interesting subgroups concerning a certain target property of interest, e.g., in the subgroup of smokers with a positive family history the risk of coronary heart disease (target property) is significantly higher than in the general population.

Background knowledge can help to improve subgroup discovery in several ways, e.g., it can increase the representational expressiveness and also focus the subgroup discovery algorithm on the relevant patterns. Then, similar to a constrained query to a web search engine, the user is not flooded with too many (uninteresting) results. Furthermore, for increasing the efficiency of the search method the search space can often be constrained. However, knowledge acquisition is often challenging and costly, known as the 'knowledge acquisition bottleneck': Then, an important idea is to ease knowledge acquisition by reusing existing domain knowledge, i.e., knowledge that is already known to the user, or that is contained in existing ontologies or knowledge bases. Therefore, we propose to apply as much background knowledge as possible, with potentially reduced costs by knowledge reuse.

The rest of the paper is organized as follows: We first briefly introduce subgroup discovery in Section 2. After that, we propose several types of background knowledge in Section 3, discuss their benefit and costs, and describe how they can be applied for subgroup discovery in Section 4. Finally, we conclude the paper with a discussion and summary in Section 5, and point out interesting directions for future work.

S. Staab and V. Svatek (Eds.): EKAW 2006, LNAI 4248, pp. 318–325, 2006.

2 Subgroup Discovery

The main application areas of subgroup discovery [2,3] are exploration and descriptive induction, to obtain an overview of the relations between a target variable and a set of explaining variables. A subgroup discovery setting includes a target variable (concept of interest), a subgroup description language, a specific quality function, and a search strategy for which, e.g., a beam search technique [3] is often applied:

Let Ω_A be the set of all attributes. For each attribute $a \in \Omega_A$ a range $dom(a)$ of values is defined; we assume $\mathcal{V}_A$ to be the (universal) set of attribute values of the form $(a = v)$, $a \in \Omega_A, v \in dom(a)$. A single-relational propositional subgroup description $sd = \{e_1, e_2, \ldots, e_n\}$ is defined by the conjunction of a set of selection expressions (selectors) $e_i = (a_i, V_i)$, i.e., selections on domains of attributes, $a_i \in \Omega_A, V_i \subseteq dom(a_i)$. We define Ω_{sd} as the set of all possible subgroup descriptions. The interestingness of a subgroup can be flexibly formalized by a (user-defined) quality function $q : \Omega_{sd} \to R$ (e.g., [2]) that is used in order to evaluate a subgroup description $sd \in \Omega_{sd}$. Typical quality criteria include the difference in the distribution of the target variable concerning the subgroup and the general population, and the subgroup size. Usually the (post-processed) k best subgroups and/or the subgroups with a quality above a minimum threshold are presented to the user as the result of the subgroup discovery method.

3 Types and Classes of Background Knowledge

The proposed classes of background knowledge include constraints, ontological knowledge and abstraction knowledge which we describe below: Constraints specify conditions that the mined patterns need to satisfy, e.g., quality and language constraints. Ontological knowledge describes general properties of the objects contained in the domain ontology and can be used to infer additional constraints. Abstraction knowledge is given by 'virtual' rule-based attributes. Figure 1 shows the knowledge hierarchy, from the three knowledge classes to the specific types, and the objects they apply to.

Constraint knowledge can be applied, e.g., for filtering patterns by their quality, and for restricting the search space. We distinguish the following types:

- **Language constraints** can, e.g., restrict the maximal number of conjuncts of a subgroup description. The description language itself can range from purely conjunctive languages to languages allowing internal disjunctions and negation.
- **Quality constraints** relate, e.g., to a minimum quality value, a minimum support, or a statistical significance threshold, that the subgroup patterns need to satisfy.
- **Value exclusion constraints** and **attribute exclusion constraints** are applied for filtering the domains of attributes and the attribute space, respectively.
- **Value aggregation constraints** can be specified in order to form abstracted disjunctions of attribute values, e.g., intervals for ordinal values. For example, consider the attribute *age* with the values '< 40', '$40 - 50$', '$50 - 70$', '> 70': Then, we can derive the aggregated values '≤ 50' and '> 50'. In general, aggregated values are not restricted to intervals, but can cover any combination of values.
- **Attribute combination constraints** are applied for filtering/excluding certain combinations of attributes, e.g., if these are already known to the domain specialist.

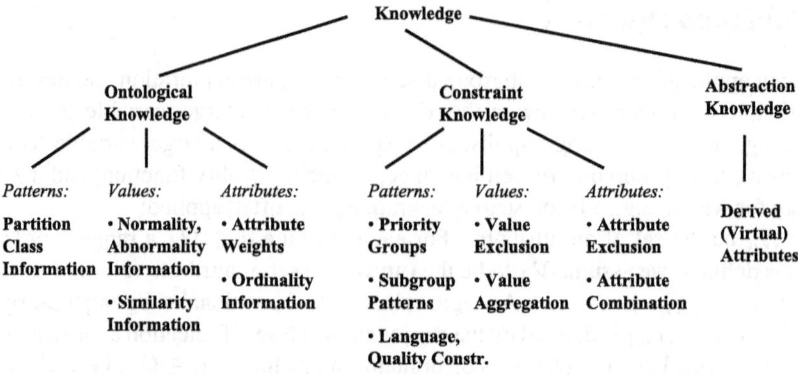

Fig. 1. Hierarchy of (abstract) knowledge classes and specific types

- **Priority groups** are partially disjunctive sets of attributes with an assigned priority. The subgroup discovery method starts with the attribute set with the highest priority. If the currently considered subgroups cannot be improved any further, then it iteratively takes the next (prioritized) set of attributes into account.
- **Subgroup pattern constraints** given by selected subgroup patterns can be used, e.g., to avoid the rediscovery of already known subgroups, for comparison to a (new) set of subgroups, and for deriving new attributes as discussed in Section 4.

Ontological knowledge is commonly used for the development of knowledge systems. The knowledge can either be defined by the user, or can partially be learned semi-automatically (e.g., [4]). It consists of the following types:

- **Attribute weights** denote the relative importance of attributes, and are a common extension for knowledge-based systems, e.g., for case-based reasoning systems [4].
- **Abnormality/Normality information** is usually easy to obtain for diagnostic domains, e.g., in the medical domain the set of 'normal' attribute values contains the expected values, and the set of 'abnormal' values contains the unexpected/pathological ones; often the unexpected values are more interesting for analysis. Each attribute value is attached with a label specifying a normal or an abnormal state. Normality information only requires a binary label. Abnormality information defines several categories, e.g., consider the value range {normal, marginal, high, very high} of the attribute *temperature*. The values *normal* and *marginal* denote normal states of the attribute while the values *high* and *very high* describe abnormal states.
- **Similarity information** between attributes values is often applied in case-based reasoning: It specifies the relative similarity between the individual attribute values. For example, for a nominal attribute *color* with the value range *white*, *gray*, *black* we can state that the value *white* is more similar to *gray* than it is to *black*.
- **Ordinality information** specifies if the value domain of a nominal attribute can be ordered, e.g., the qualitative ones *age* and *liver size* are ordinal while *color* is not.
- **Partition class information** provides semantically distinct groups of attributes. These partially disjoint subsets usually correspond to certain problem areas of the application domain, e.g., in the medical domain of sonography such partitions are representing different organ systems like *liver*, *pancreas*, *stomach*, and *kidney*.

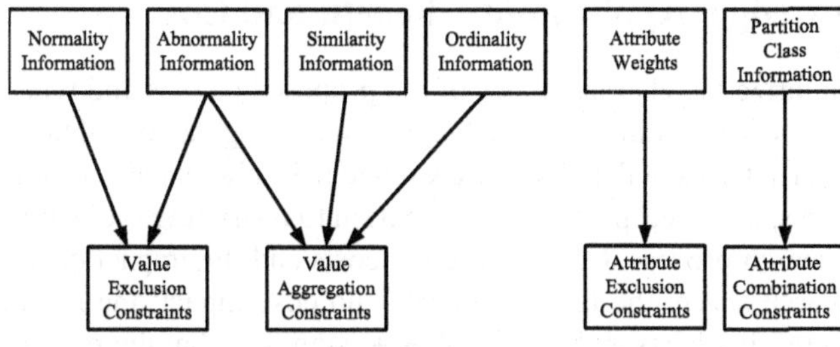

Fig. 2. Deriving constraints using ontological knowledge

Figure 2 shows how ontological knowledge can be used in order to derive further 'basic' constraints. Below, we summarize how new constraints can be inferred using ontological knowledge.

- We can construct attribute exclusion constraints using attribute weights to filter the set of relevant attributes by a weight threshold or by subsets of the weight space.
- Using abnormality/normality knowledge we can specify global value exclusion constraints for a set of abnormal values, or for the normal values.
- Using similarity or abnormality/normality information we can filter and model the value ranges of attributes: If the similarity between two attribute values is very high, then they can potentially be analyzed as an *aggregated value*. Similarly, global abnormality groups can be defined by sets of abnormality degrees specifying which values to combine. For example, in the medical domain attribute values such as *probable* and *possible* (with different abnormality degrees) can often be aggregated.
- Ordinality information can be easily used to construct aggregated values, which are often more meaningful for the domain specialist: We can consider all adjacent combinations of attribute values, or all ascending/descending combinations starting with the minimum or maximum value, respectively. Whenever abnormality information is available, we can partition the value range by the given *normal* value and only start with the most extreme value. An example is discussed in Section 4.1.
- Partition class information can be used to infer attribute combination constraints in order to prevent the combination of individual attributes that are contained in separate partition classes. Alternatively, inverse constraints can also be derived, e.g., to specifically investigate inter-organ relations in the medical domain.

Abstraction knowledge is given by derived (rule-based) attributes. These abstractions often correspond to certain known dependencies between attributes, e.g., in the medical domain, we can infer the *body mass index*, given the attributes *height* and *weight*. For deriving a value v_a of a nominal attribute a, a rule of the form $r_{v_a} = cond(r_{v_a}) \rightarrow v_a$ is used, where the rule condition $cond(r_{v_a})$ contains conjunctions and/or disjunctions of (negated) attribute values $v_i \in \mathcal{V}_A$. The derived attributes serve three main purposes:

- They focus the subgroup discovery method on the relevant analysis objects.
- They decrease multi-correlations between attributes that are not interesting.
- Derived attributes can reduce missing values for a given concept, since they can be constructed such that a defined value is more often computed if the respective concept would have a missing value otherwise.

Due to the limited space we refer to [5] for a detailed discussion. Abstraction knowledge is probably the most costly class of background knowledge: If the abstractions are not based on discovery results, then they have to be formalized manually by the expert.

4 Background Knowledge: Applicability, Benefit and Cost

In the table below we summarize the characteristics of the proposed classes and types of background knowledge (CK = constraint knowledge, OK = ontological knowledge, AK = abstraction knowledge) in terms of the 'derivable knowledge' (if applicable), their syntactical and cognitive costs, and their potential contribution to restricting the search space and/or focusing the search process. Considering the costs and the impact of the knowledge types on the search space, the label - indicates no cost/impact; the labels +, ++, and +++ indicate increasing costs and impact. A +(+) signifies, that the respective element has low costs if it can be derived/learned, and moderate costs otherwise. Similarly ++(+) indicates this for moderate and high costs.

In our experience, the most important types of knowledge with an especially good cost/benefit ratio are *quality constraints*, *attribute exclusion constraints*, *normality information*, *ordinality information*, and especially *derived attributs* (indicated in bold type). In the next section, we provide examples for applying most of these knowledge types. After that, we summarize how we can exploit background knowledge for subgroup discovery.

Knowledge		*Derivable*	*Costs*		Search	
Class	*Type*	*Knowledge*	*Syn.*	*Cog.*	*Restr.*	*Foc.*
CK	Language C.	–	–	+	++	+
CK	**Quality Constr.**	–	–	++	++	++
CK	Value Exclusion Constr.	–	(+)	+	+	+
CK	Val. Aggregation Constr.	–	(+)	+(+)	++	+
CK	**Attr. Exclusion Constr.**	–	(+)	+(+)	++	++
CK	Attr. Combination Constr.	–	(+)	+(+)	++	++
CK	Priority Group Constr.	–	+	++	–	+
CK	Subgroup Pattern Constr.	Deriv. Attr.	+(+)	+(+)	–	++
OK	**Normality Information**	Val. Excl.	+	+	++	++
OK	Abnormality Information	Val. Excl.	++	++	++	++
		Val. Aggr.			+	++
OK	Similarity Information	Val. Aggr.	+(+)	+(+)	++	++
OK	**Ordinality Information**	Val. Aggr.	+	+	+++	++
OK	Attribute Weights	Attr. Excl.	(+)	+(+)	++	++
OK	Partition Class Inform.	Attr. Comb.	+	+	++	++
AK	***Derived Attributes***	Deriv. Attr.	+++	+++	–	+++

4.1 Background Knowledge – Examples

Let A be a nominal attribute with the range $dom(A) = \{a_1, a_2, a_3, a_n, a_5, a_6, a_7\}$ of attribute values, e.g., A could correspond to the (discretized) attribute *body weight* with values like *massive underweight*, *strong underweight*, *underweight*, *normal weight*, *overweight*, *strong overweight*, and *massive overweight*. Ordinality information can be easily applied in order to derive a restricted set of aggregated values denoting different weight groups. If we want to exclude all combinations not being neighbors (excluding irrelevant combinations like (a_1, a_3)), we obtain only 77 combinations of all adjacent attribute values, in contrast to considering all possible 127 attribute value combinations:

$$(a_1, a_2), (a_1, a_2, a_3), \ldots, (a_1, \ldots, a_7), (a_2, a_3), (a_2, \ldots, a_7), \ldots (a_6, a_7)\,.$$

In the medical domain we often know that a certain attribute value denotes the *normal* value (in our example 'normal weight' = a_4). This value is often not interesting for the analyst who might focus on the 'abnormal' value combinations. Combining normality and ordinality information, we then only need to consider 10 combinations:

$$(a_1), (a_1, a_2), (a_1, a_2, a_3), (a_2, a_3), (a_3), (a_7), (a_7, a_6), (a_7, a_6, a_5), (a_6, a_5), (a_5)\,.$$

If we are interested only in combinations including the most extreme value (typical in medicine), we can further reduce the number of 'meaningful' combinations to 6:

$$(a_1), (a_1, a_2), (a_1, a_2, a_3), (a_7), (a_7, a_6), (a_7, a_6, a_5)\,.$$

The savings of such a reduction of value combinations, which can be derived using ordinality, normality information and interestingness assumptions, are huge: If there are 10 attributes like A with seven values each, then the size of the search space considering all possible selector combinations is reduced from $128^{10} = 10^{21}$ to $7^{10} = 3 \cdot 10^8$.

Concerning abstraction knowledge, let us consider an additional attribute B denoting the *body height* with the (ordinal) value range $dom(B) = \{b_1, b_2, b_3, b_n, b_5, b_6, b_7\}$.

In the following, we assume that both A and B are quantitative nominal attributes. Then, we can derive the attribute *body mass index (BMI)* given the body weight (attribute A) and the body height (attribute B). The matrix shows the combinations of the respective attribute values: The derived attribute values corresponding to a high body mass index are given by the entries $1, 2, 3, 4$ in ascending order, while a '0' denotes the 'normal' case.

	a_1	a_2	a_3	a_4	a_5	a_6	a_7
b_1	0	0	1	2	3	4	4
b_2		0	0	1	2	3	4
b_3			0	0	1	2	3
b_4				0	0	1	2
b_5					0	0	1
b_6						0	0
b_7							0

It is easy to see that in this example the 'meaningful' combinations of the respective attribute values are always on the diagonal, or form triangular matrices, e.g., considering the entries '3' and '4' of the matrix. In our example, these combinations correspond to relatively small people with a large body weight: In principle, the distribution of the individual values can be arbitrary. Then, the distributions of the combined attribute values can also be of arbitrary shape. By constructing selection expressions containing internal disjunctions we can only select quadrangular sub-matrices and would thus include larger groups that can 'confound' the 'new values', i.e., the original value combinations, since the quadrangular sub-matrices might contain at least one potentially misleading value combination. In contrast, using derived attributes we can carve out arbitrary parts of the matrix, e.g., the triangular sub-matrices shown in the example. Then, a derived attribute capturing the specific value combinations is more expressive and meaningful for the user, and can focus the analysis significantly.

4.2 Applying Background Knowledge for Subgroup Discovery

In the following, we describe knowledge elements considering their effect(s) for the subgroup discovery task, i.e., restricting the search space, focusing the search process, post-processing the results, and increasing the representational expressiveness.

Restricting the Search Space and Focusing Search. Most of the knowledge classes described in Section 3 can be directly integrated in the subgroup discovery step:

- Language constraints and quality constraints are applied as filters in order to restrict the search space and to focus the search process, e.g., by providing concise/simple description languages and by pruning uninteresting hypotheses below minimal quality and interestingness thresholds.
- Constraint knowledge (and ontological knowledge that is used to derive constraint knowledge) such as value exclusion constraints, value aggregation constraints and attribute exclusion constraints helps to focus the search process. While attribute exclusion and value exclusion constraints restrict the search space just by construction, value aggregation constraints do not necessarily restrict the search process since new values are introduced. However, value aggregation constraints can

provide significant quality improvements with low costs, if the aggregated values are more meaningful for the user. Additionally, if only the generated new values are taken into account, e.g., for ordinal value groups, then the search space remains the same or is even restricted. Furthermore, attribute combination constraints that inhibit the examination of specified sets of attributes can prune large (uninteresting) areas of the search space. Priority groups are utilized to focus the search process by construction: The attributes of the different priority groups are taken into the search space subsequently according to the requirements of the user.

- Subgroup pattern constraints contained in the background knowledge can be included into the process by considering them as starting points for the search process. Furthermore, derived attributes can be incrementally defined using (discovered) subgroup patterns during the discovery step. Additionally, by comparison to already known subgroup patterns we can inhibit the rediscovery of subgroups.
- Abstraction knowledge can be applied for increasing the representational expressiveness as discussed below, and for focusing the search process on the relevant objects. If only these are considered, then the search space can also be restricted.

Post-processing the Discovered Subgroups. The most important type of background knowledge for post-processing is given by specific known subgroup patterns itself: For example, in the medical domain often a lot of the existing relations are already known and can be formalized as subgroup patterns. By comparison with the discovered knowledge, (unexpected) patterns that conform to, deviate, or contradict the given domain knowledge can be identified. In addition to specific subgroup patterns we can also apply partition class information in order to mark subgroups that conform to the partition classes, or to identify subgroups that contain attributes included in different partition classes. This depends on the requirements of the user, e.g., in the medical domain different organ systems can be considered.

Increasing the Expressiveness of Subgroup Patterns. For increasing the representational expressiveness, (derived) attributes and subsets of the value range of an attribute can be utilized to infer new attributes and values, respectively, that are more meaningful for the user: The power of derived attributes lies in their ability of abstracting (known) associations of attributes into new attributes. These correspond to new concepts that are usually more meaningful, reasonable, and ultimately more important for the user. Thus, the search process can be focused significantly. Furthermore, the power of the statistical evaluations is increased significantly if missing values are minimized: Since abstraction knowledge can be used to infer missing values in their respective context, derived attributes can help to improve the missing value problem significantly.

Furthermore, aggregated values forming a disjunctive selection expression can be more meaningful and reasonable for the user, e.g., considering different aggregated age groups in the medical domain. We can apply abnormality or similarity information in order to derive value aggregation constraints. Then, these new values can be directly utilized in the search process. Additionally, the description language itself plays an important role, since it is used to define the subgroups. As a simple and concise description language often conjunctive languages without internal disjunctions are applied.

5 Conclusion

In this paper we presented a methodological view on exploiting background knowledge for subgroup discovery. We described several classes of background knowledge, and discussed the benefit, cost, and application of the particular types of knowledge.

In contrast to existing approaches utilizing background knowledge, including Inductive Logic Programming (ILP) (e.g., [6]), constraint-based data mining (e.g., [7]), and association rule learning techniques (e.g., [8]), we propose to integrate several new types of additional background knowledge: It can be used to easily infer new background knowledge on the fly, e.g., constraints, and can be refined incrementally according to the requirements of the discovery task. Furthermore, we propose special abstraction knowledge that can be applied dynamically. Compared to common preprocessing methods, the background knowledge concerning aggregations of attributes or attribute values is applied dynamically on the data. The original data set is not changed by the knowledge-intensive approach; instead, either the discovery method is 'configured' applying the knowledge, or 'virtual' attributes/attribute values are introduced.

We already successfully applied parts of the presented approach in different case studies in the medical domain [5,9]: For these, the application of background knowledge was essential, since a naive approach resulted in (too) many subgroups that were not regarded as interesting or were already known to the domain specialists.

In the future, we want to examine methods that enable the automatic construction of abstraction knowledge. An 'intelligent' adaptation and fine-tuning of aggregations of attribute values is another interesting issue to consider.

References

1. Richardson, M., Domingos, P.: Learning with Knowledge from Multiple Experts. In: Proc. 20th Intl. Conference on Machine Learning (ICML-2003), AAAI Press (2003) 624–631
2. Klösgen, W.: Explora: A Multipattern and Multistrategy Discovery Assistant. In: Advances in Knowledge Discovery and Data Mining. AAAI Press (1996) 249–271
3. Wrobel, S.: An Algorithm for Multi-Relational Discovery of Subgroups. In Komorowski, J., Zytkow, J., eds.: Proc. 1st European Symposium on Principles of Data Mining and Knowledge Discovery (PKDD-97), Berlin, Springer (1997) 78–87
4. Baumeister, J., Atzmueller, M., Puppe, F.: Inductive Learning for Case-Based Diagnosis with Multiple Faults. In: Advances in Case-Based Reasoning. Volume 2416 of LNAI., Berlin, Springer (2002) 28–42 Proc. 6th European Conference on Case-Based Reasoning.
5. Atzmueller, M., Puppe, F., Buscher, H.P.: Exploiting Background Knowledge for Knowledge-Intensive Subgroup Discovery. In: Proc. 19th Intl. Joint Conference on Artificial Intelligence (IJCAI-05), Edinburgh, Scotland (2005) 647–652
6. Zelezny, F., Lavrac, N., Dzeroski, S.: Using Constraints in Relational Subgroup Discovery. In: Intl. Conference on Methodology and Statistics, University of Ljubljana (2003) 78–81
7. Boulicaut, J.F., Jeudy, B.: Constraint-based data mining. In: The Data Mining and Knowledge Discovery Handbook. Springer (2005)
8. Liu, B., Hsu, W.: Post-Analysis of Learned Rules. In: Proc. 13th National Conference on Artificial Intelligence (AAAI-96), Menlo Park, CA, AAAI Press (1996) 828–834
9. Atzmueller, M., Baumeister, J., Hemsing, A., Richter, E.J., Puppe, F.: Subgroup Mining for Interactive Knowledge Refinement. In: Proc. 10th Conference on Artificial Intelligence in Medicine (AIME 05). LNAI 3581, Berlin, Springer (2005) 453–462

Iterative Bayesian Network Implementation by Using Annotated Association Rules

Clément Fauré[1,2], Sylvie Delprat[1], Jean-François Boulicaut[2], and Alain Mille[3]

[1] EADS CCR, Learning Systems Department, Centreda 1, F-31700 Blagnac
{clement.faure, sylvie.delprat}@eads.net
[2] LIRIS UMR 5205, INSA Lyon, Bâtiment Blaise Pascal, F-69621 Villeurbanne
[3] LIRIS UMR 5205, Université Lyon 1, Nautibus, F-69622 Villeurbanne
{amille, jboulica}@liris.cnrs.fr

Abstract. This paper concerns the iterative implementation of a knowledge model in a data mining context. Our approach relies on coupling a Bayesian network design with an association rule discovery technique. First, discovered association rule relevancy isenhanced by exploiting the expert knowledge encoded within a Bayesian network, i.e., avoiding to provide trivial rules w.r.t. known dependencies. Moreover, the Bayesian network can be updated thanks to an expert-driven annotation process on computed association rules. Our approach is experimentally validated on the Asia benchmark dataset.

1 Introduction

One major goal of the knowledge discovery from databases (KDD) community is to support the discovery of valuable patterns within the data. Considering 0/1 data analysis, the association rule mining technique is quite popular and we assume the reader is familiar with it [1]. It has been studied extensively both from the computational point of view and the objective interestingness perspective (i.e., using measures like frequency and confidence). Indeed, many algorithms have been designed for computing frequent and valid association rules. When the computation is tractable, it gives a huge number of rules which include many irrelevant ones: this is known to be a bottleneck for association rule based KDD processes. Application-independent redundancy has been addressed seriously by means of the closed sets and related approaches (see, e.g., [2]). Our approach to this problem is to use a well-specified subset of frequent and valid association rules called the frequent δ-strong rules, i.e., frequent rules with at most δ exceptions and a minimal left-hand-side property thanks to its δ-freeness[3,4]. A second issue concerns application-dependant redundancy. Apart from rather simple template-based strategies, few authors have been considering how to remove rules which do not provide valuable information given an explicitly encoded model for available knowledge [5]. In this paper, we assume that novelty is indeed a key property to enhance subjective interestingness. In [6], the authors use a Bayesian Network (BN) to filter truly interesting frequent sets, i.e., sets

S. Staab and V. Svatek (Eds.): EKAW 2006, LNAI 4248, pp. 326–333, 2006.

whose frequencies are somehow surprising given the expected distribution captured by the BN. In [7], we have extended this approach to support relevant association rule mining when we assume that (a) a BN captures expert knowledge about domain dependencies, and (b) we compute only our sub-collections of non redundant frequent and valid association rules (i.e., the δ-strong rules). The intuition is that encoded dependencies can help us to filter out the patterns that reflect these dependencies. Doing so, we support the presentation of more interesting rules. In this paper, we address the obvious dynamics of knowledge discovery processes by considering that the knowledge model has to be iteratively updated. Our idea is that the initial model can be updated thanks to an expert-driven annotation of the extracted rules. Doing so, our methodology iteratively improves both the model for expert domain knowledge and the relevancy of the extracted patterns. A preliminary experimental validation on the well-known "Asia" dataset is given.

2 Modelling and Using Expert Knowledge

Our proposal relies on five steps and the paper concerns Steps 2 to 4:

1. Modelling an initial BN which specifies *a priori* expert domain knowledge.
2. Computing concise collections of frequent association rules with high confidence (i.e., the maximal number of exception is small w.r.t. the used frequency threshold).
3. Supporting rule post-processing (i.e., filtering) by using the knowledge model.
4. Supporting expert-driven annotation of the most interesting rules.
5. Updating the BN structure and parameters given the collected annotations.

2.1 Association Rule Post Processing Using a Bayesian Network

Modelling and exploiting knowledge to support the discovery of relevant association rules have been already studied. For instance, [8] considers the exploitation of expert knowledge elicited by expert rules. This has been formalized later into a belief system [9]. However, this kind of approach has a major limitation. Indeed, a rule is said to be interesting if it differs from the rules according to what is currently defined in the belief system, but not by looking at what could be inferred from these rules. Jaroszewicz et al. [6,10] have tackled this issue by modelling Bayesian networks for which "inference" is nicely integrated within the model. They describe the use of a BN to compute the added-value of frequent itemsets [1]. For each frequent itemset, the difference between its frequency value within the data and its expected frequency value inferred from the BN is computed. The more interesting patterns are the ones with the higher absolute difference value between these two measures. These itemsets can also be submitted to the expert to suggest updates of the structure and the parameters of the BN.

We have a similar approach but we exploit further the complementarities between Bayesian networks and association rules, namely dependency links between variables (directed edges of the graph, association relationship expressed

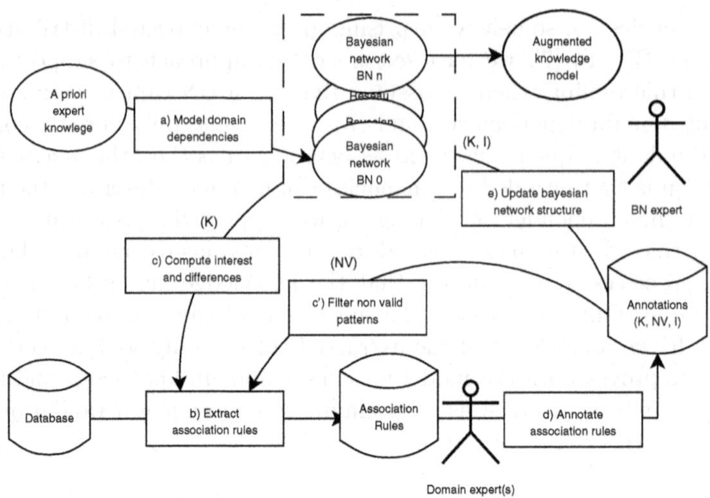

Fig. 1. A detailed view on our data mining process

by a rule) and frequencies for specific events (conditional probabilities defined in a BN, frequency of an association rule). We address "separately" these two relationships. First, we define an interestingness measure on association rule w.r.t. a BN. Then we propose an algorithm for computing relations of independence in the association rules w.r.t. the structure of the BN.

Due to the lack of space, we do not provide the needed definitions for the classical concepts related to 0/1 datasets and association rules on one hand (see, e.g., [1,4]) and Bayesian networks on the other hand (see, e.g., [11]).

Interestingness Measure of an Association Rule Given a Bayesian Network. Let us assume that DB is a Boolean database (i.e. a database where each record is a set of Boolean values), and $H = \{A_1, \ldots, A_n\}$ is the set of n Boolean attributes. An itemset I is just a subset from H. An association rule R is a pattern $X \Rightarrow Y$, where X and Y are itemsets such that $Y \neq \emptyset$ and $X \cap Y = \emptyset$. The frequency of an itemset I in DB is the number of records from DB where the conjunction of all attributes from I is true. Most of the objective interestingness of association rules are based on the frequency of their set components. For instance, the confidence of $X \Rightarrow Y$ is the frequency of $X \cup Y$ divided by the frequency of X, i.e., the conditional probability to observe a true value for the attributes in Y when the attributes from X are true. A Bayesian network BN is a directed acyclic graph (DAG) defined by a set of nodes corresponding to the attributes in H and by $E \subset H \times H$ its set of edges. Each node is associated with a conditional probability distribution $P_{A_i|\Pi_{A_i}}$, where $\Pi_{A_i} = \{A_j | (V_{A_j}, V_{A_i}) \in E\}$ are the parents of node A_i. One of the most important properties of Bayesian networks is that they uniquely define the joint probability distribution over H. Thus, given a database DB and a Bayesian network BN, it is possible to compute the expected confidence of an association rule $R = X \Rightarrow Y$ By extending

[6], we have defined in [7] a metric *Int* to evaluate the interest of a given association rule w.r.t. the encoded knowledge in a Bayesian network. Basically, it measures the difference between the confidence of the rule estimated on the data and the one inferred from the Bayesian network. Discussing this further is out of the scope of this paper.

Computation of the Structural Differences Between an Association Rule and a Bayesian Network. So far, we know how to compute collections of association rules, we have a formalism to express some expert knowledge, and finally a metric using such an encoded knowledge when ranking association rule interestingness. What is missing is a way to exploit the information of conditional independence implicitly captured by the network BN. Therefore, our goal is to highlight which parts of an association rule really contribute —according to BN— to the observation of the whole rule, and which parts are not.

Let us first introduce the D-separation property which has been formally defined by J. Pearl [11]. D-separation is a property of two sets of nodes X and Y w.r.t. another set of nodes Z. Informally, X and Y are said to be D-separated by Z if no information can flow between them when Z is observed.

We want to apply this notion —which is a pure graphical property— on association rules w.r.t. the BN structure. For any association rule $R = X \Rightarrow Y$, we will compute the D-separation test $< X_i \,|\, X \backslash X_i \,|\, Y_j >$, where $X_i \in X$ and $Y_j \in Y$. We end up with a matrix that sums up the results of all the D-separations tests. If an item of the rule (X_i or Y_i) has a "true" value for all its D-separation tests, then it will be highlighted as being in the *D-separated part* of the rule. It means that thanks to the rule, an informative association has been found in the data which is not modelled in the current BN structure.

2.2 Post-processing and Annotation of Association Rules

Let us assume that BN reflects most of the domain dependencies. This network might have been defined either from scratch by an expert or through a mixed approach involving expert but also machine learning. Notice however that the initial BN does not have to be "complete". For instance, it can capture only obvious dependencies, including known taxonomies over the attributes. As we go through the KDD processes, it can be updated to capture more and more domain knowledge, thus supporting the presentation of more and more valuable association rules. At each iteration, the expert might annotate the rules by labeling which parts represent what kind of information. This annotation can be used to improve the knowledge model BN.

Once our δ-strong rules have been extracted (using the solver described in [4]), we compute their interest (as defined in [7]) as well as their "topological" differences w.r.t. the current instance for BN. These measures are used to filter uninteresting rules (interest compared with a user-defined threshold ϵ). It divides the rules in two classes. A first class contains the rules that do not provide further information w.r.t. BN (interest below ϵ). The expert who is inspecting the rules can decide to ignore them. The second class represents the rules that we call ϵ-interesting. They express that some dependencies observed on the data are not described properly by BN. The goal is to remove the rules that are ϵ-interesting but either (a) already known by the domain expert or (b) containing non valid patterns. The idea is to refine the knowledge model by integrating step by step dependencies that were not identified at previous iterations. Understanding what information is contained by a given association rule is however a difficult task. This is why we want to highlight rule-like subpatterns of an association rule that represent a notion of D-separation between items on the left-hand side (LHS) and items on the right-hand side (RHS) given BN structure and the observation of all the LHS items. We can further divide the association among the ϵ-interesting rules in three different types:

K The rule contains a pattern *already known* by the expert but that is not modelled in the current BN. It means that the structure and the parameters of the network have to be updated to integrate the causality related to this pattern. Doing so, such a pattern will not be presented as ϵ-interesting in the next iteration.

NV The rule contains a pattern which appears to be *not valid* given the expert knowledge. This might be due to statistical coincidences (false positive).

I The rule holds a pattern that is potentially *interesting*. It has been "surprising" for the expert, and a deeper analysis has confirmed its relevancy.

In a real world data mining process, the number of association rules that fit in the categories (K) and (NV) can be huge. Moreover, a relation of association may contain mixed kinds of patterns, which might lead to tedious analysis tasks. We propose to ask the domain expert for annotations on the most interesting extracted association rules. He/she has to perform annotation following a precise method[1], that will enables her/him to:

- specify whether an association rule contains one or more known patterns (K), non valid patterns (NV) or a potentially interesting one (I).
- define without ambiguity the "shape" of these patterns through the definition of a list of patterns which can only have one item in the right-hand side of the rule.
- be generic concerning the description of the detected patterns (providing only the name of the attribute or an attribute-value pair).
- define, when needed, a conjunction of attributes or items in the left-hand side of the pattern.
- associate a verbal-probability to patterns labeled as "already known" by following the idea of probability-ladder presented in [12].

These annotations can then be exploited to update the structure and the parameters of BN.

3 Experimental Validation

Let us consider an initial BN that already captures nicely a particular domain knowledge for the Asia dataset (i.e., a well-known benchmark within the

[1] This method is not detailed here due to space limitations.

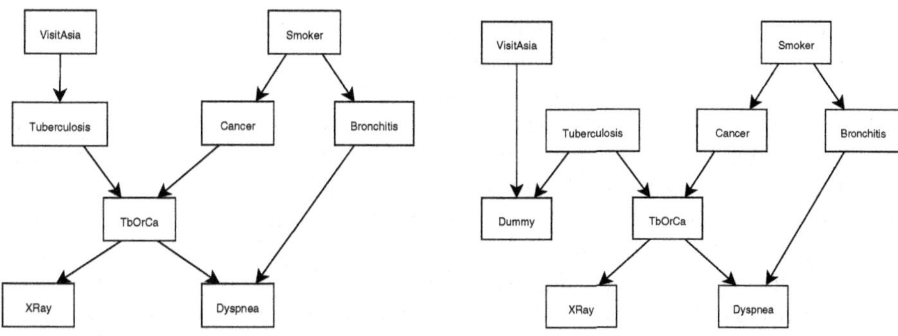

Fig. 2. Original Asia network (left) and modified one (right)

Bayesian network community). From this network, we produced a dataset of 10,000 records. As we look for association rules, we focus on the *presence* of events. The initial BN structure is then modified so that the "VisitAsia" node is no longer directly connected to the "Tuberculosis" node. Our goal is to apply our methodology and see whether we can recover the right "Asia" network structure. Both networks are given in Figure 2.

Let us now follow the method described in Figure 1 step by step.

(a) The modified "Asia" BN serves as a basis for our experiments.

(b) From the generated dataset, we extract a concise collection of association rules (minimum absolute support value of 100, i.e., 0.01% of the database and maximal number of exceptions $\delta = 10$, i.e., a guarantee that the minimal confidence is 0.9). A total of 16 association rules are extracted immediately.

Table 1. Association rules extracted from the Asia dataset. Underlined items do not belong to the *D-separated part* of the rule.

Association rule	Interest	D-separated part
Tuberculosis ⇒ XRay Dyspnea TbOrCa	0,04	
VisitAsia ⇒ XRay Dyspnea	0,46	VisitAsia ⇒ Xray Dyspnea
Smoking Dyspnea Bronchitis TbOrCa ⇒ XRay	0,03	Smoking Dyspnea Bronchitis ⇒
Dyspnea Bronchitis TbOrCa ⇒ XRay	0,02	Dyspnea Bronchitis ⇒
Smoking Bronchitis TbOrCa ⇒ XRay	0,02	Smoking Bronchitis ⇒
Bronchitis TbOrCa ⇒ XRay	0,02	Bronchitis ⇒
Smoking Dyspnea TbOrCa ⇒ XRay	0,02	Smoking Dyspnea ⇒
Smoking TbOrCa ⇒ XRay	0,02	Smoking ⇒
Dyspnea TbOrCa ⇒ XRay	0,02	Dyspnea ⇒
TbOrCa ⇒ XRay	0,02	
Smoking Dyspnea Cancer ⇒ XRay TbOrCa	0,02	
Dyspnea Cancer ⇒ XRay TbOrCa	0,02	
Dyspnea Bronchitis Cancer ⇒ Smoking XRay TbOrCa	0,00	
Smoking Cancer ⇒ XRay TbOrCa	0,02	Smoking ⇒
Cancer ⇒ XRay TbOrCa	0,02	
Bronchitis Cancer ⇒ Smoking XRay TbOrCa	0,01	

(c) Interest measure and D-separations are computed on these rules w.r.t. the modified "Asia" *BN*. **(c')** Filtering out non valid patterns is optional and depends on the identification of such patterns. Obtained results are shown in Table 1. By looking at these results, let us recall that association rule mining captures only patterns over true values, i.e., presence of particular events. For example, the third rule should be read as "when we observe that a person is a smoker, a presence of dyspnea and bronchitis diagnosis and special node TbOrCa is activated, then it is often associated with abnormal x-ray result". The underlined part of the rules denotes what we call the *core dependencies* of the rule w.r.t. *BN* structure. The last column shows a pattern of the association rule which contains missing information within the current network. Looking at these results, only one association rule has a relatively high interest value. This association rule states that "when we observe that a person has visited Asia then it is associated with abnormal x-ray results and a presence of dyspnea". Clearly, this rule brings an information which is not modelled as a dependence in our modified *BN* structure while it was represented in the original one. It is thus possible to find rules that exhibit a difference between the available knowledge model and the data. We can however wonder whether such discovered associations are truly interesting. Furthermore, if this is the case, what are the modifications to be made to the model to reflect these observations in the data? This is of course where an expert judgment is crucially needed.

(d) An expert can now perform annotations. For our running example, assume that he/she has to put down that the rule which contains the "VisitAsia" relation belongs to the interesting category.

(e) Finally, this annotation is forwarded to the expert who is in charge of *BN* revision. By looking at the interesting pattern, it leads to a structural modification that provides the initial *BN* structure. We consider that the association rule actually found is sufficient for an expert to suggest the "right" revision. Notice that if we compute the rules on the same dataset but using the initial Asia network, we observe that the "VisitAsia" association rule no longer holds a D-separated pattern.

On the same datasets, we also applied the approach when the rules are extracted with APRIORI [1] (i.e., computing all the frequent and valid rules instead of the non redundant sub-collection of our δ-strong rules). Doing so, 115 association rules were generated. Among all these rules, we found three different variants of the mentioned relation between "VisitAsia" and "abnormal x-ray", including "Dyspnea" as well. Clearly, working on such redundant collections is harder: the expert will have to go through all the rules to find out patterns describing an association that involves "VisitAsia".

4 Conclusion

Looking for relevant patterns in 0/1 data, we have been considering application-dependant redundancy. Our approach concerns association rule filtering when expert knowledge about attribute dependencies is encoded within a Bayesian network and when a rule appears to be expected given this model. This paper has focused on the possible revision of such a knowledge model by using discoveries derived from the inspection and the annotation of selected association rules. The idea is that such a KDD process somehow converges towards actionable patterns: discovering new and valid statements in the data suggest refinement on the knowledge model which better captures important dependencies and thus enables to iterate on a more focused pattern discovery phase.

References

1. Agrawal, R., Mannila, H., Srikant, R., Toivonen, H., Verkamo, A.I.: Fast discovery of association rules. Advances in Knowledge Discovery and Data Mining, AAAI Press (1996) 307–328.
2. Bastide, Y., Pasquier, N., Taouil, R., Stumme, G., Lakhal, L.: Mining minimal non-redundant association rules using frequent closed itemsets. In: Proceedings CL 2000. Volume 1861 of LNCS., London, UK, Springer-Verlag (2000) 972–986.
3. Boulicaut, J.F., Bykowski, A., Rigotti, C.: Approximation of frequency queries by means of free-sets. In: Proceedings PKDD 2000. Volume 1910 of LNCS., Lyon, F, Springer-Verlag (2000) 75–85.
4. Boulicaut, J.F., Bykowski, A., Rigotti, C.: Free-sets: a condensed representation of boolean data for the approximation of frequency queries. Data Mining and Knowledge Discovery **7**(1) (2003) 5–22.
5. Liu, B., Hsu, W., Mun, L.F., Lee, H.: Finding interesting patterns using user expectations. IEEE Transactions on Knowledge and Data Engineering **11**(6) (1999) 817–832.
6. Jaroszewicz, S., Simovici, D.A.: Interestingness of frequent itemsets using bayesian networks as background knowledge. Proceedings ACM SIGKDD 2004, New York, USA, ACM Press (2004) 178–186.
7. Fauré, C., Delprat, S., Mille, A., Boulicaut, J.F.: Utilisation des réseaux bayésiens dans le cadre de l'extraction de rg̀les d'association. Proceedings EGC 2006, Lille, F, Cepadues (2006) 569–580 In French.
8. Padmanabhan, B., Tuzhilin, A.: A belief-driven method for discovering unexpected patterns. Proceedings KDD 1998, New York, USA, AAAI Press (1998) 94–100.
9. Padmanabhan, B., Tuzhilin, A.: Small is beautiful: discovering the minimal set of unexpected patterns. Proceedings ACM SIGKDD 2000, Boston, USA, ACM Press (2000) 54–63.
10. Jaroszewicz, S., Scheffer, T.: Fast discovery of unexpected patterns in data, relative to a bayesian network. Proceedings ACM SIGKDD 2005, Chicago, USA, ACM Press (2005) 118–127.
11. Pearl, J.: Probabilistic reasoning in intelligent systems: networks of plausible inference. Morgan Kaufmann (1988).
12. Druzdzel, M.J., Diez, F.: Criteria for combining knowledge from different sources in probabilistic networks (2000).

Multilayered Semantic Social Network Modeling by Ontology-Based User Profiles Clustering: Application to Collaborative Filtering

Iván Cantador and Pablo Castells

Escuela Politécnica Superior, Universidad Autónoma de Madrid
Campus de Cantoblanco, 28049 Madrid, Spain
{ivan.cantador, pablo.castells}@uam.es

Abstract. We propose a multilayered semantic social network model that offers different views of common interests underlying a community of people. The applicability of the proposed model to a collaborative filtering system is empirically studied. Starting from a number of ontology-based user profiles and taking into account their common preferences, we automatically cluster the domain concept space. With the obtained semantic clusters, similarities among individuals are identified at multiple semantic preference layers, and emergent, layered social networks are defined, suitable to be used in collaborative environments and content recommenders.

1 Introduction

The swift development, spread, and convergence of information and communication technologies and support infrastructures in the last decade, which is reaching all aspects of businesses and homes in our everyday lives, is giving rise to new and unforeseen ways of inter-personal connection, communication, and collaboration. Virtual communities, computer-supported social networks [1,8,10,11], and collective interaction applications are indeed starting to proliferate in increasingly sophisticated ways, opening new research opportunities on social group analysis, modeling, and exploitation. In this paper we propose a novel approach towards building emerging social networks by analyzing the individual motivations and preferences of users, broken into potentially different areas of personal interest.

The issue of finding hidden links between users based on the similarity of their preferences or historic behavior is not a new idea. In fact, this is the essence of the well-known collaborative recommender systems [2,9,13], where items are recommended to a certain user concerning those of her interests shared with other users or according to opinions, comparatives and ratings of items given by similar users. However, in typical approaches, the comparison between users and items is done globally, in such a way that partial, but strong and useful similarities may be missed. For instance, two people may have a highly coincident taste in cinema, but a very divergent one in sports. The opinions of these people on movies could be highly valuable for each other, but risk to be ignored by many collaborative recommender systems, because global similarity between the users might be low.

S. Staab and V. Svatek (Eds.): EKAW 2006, LNAI 4248, pp. 334–349, 2006.

Here we propose a multi-layered approach to social networking. Like in previous approaches, our method builds and compares profiles of user interests for semantic topics and specific concepts, in order to find similarities among users. But in contrast to prior work, we divide the user profiles into clusters of cohesive interests, and based on this, several layers of social networks are found. This provides a richer model of interpersonal links, which better represents the way people find common interests in real life.

Our approach is based on an ontological representation of the domain of discourse where user interests are defined. The ontological space takes the shape of a semantic network of interrelated domain concepts and the user profiles are initially described as weighted lists measuring the user interests for those concepts. Taking advantage of the relations between concepts, and the (weighted) preferences of users for the concepts, our system clusters the semantic space based on the correlation of concepts appearing in the preferences of individual users. After this, user profiles are partitioned by projecting the concept clusters into the set of preferences of each user. Then, users can be compared on the basis of the resulting subsets of interests, in such a way that several, rather than just one, (weighted) links can be found between two users.

Multilayered social networks are potentially useful for many purposes. For instance, users may share preferences, items, knowledge, and benefit from each other's experience in focused or specialized conceptual areas, even if they have very different profiles as a whole. Such semantic subareas need not be defined manually, as they emerge automatically with our proposed method. Users may be recommended items or direct contacts with other users for different aspects of day-to-day life.

In recommendation environments there is an underlying need to distinguish different layers within the interests and preferences of the users. Depending on the current context, only a specific subset of the segments (layers) of a user profile should be considered in order to establish her similarities with other people when a recommendation has to be performed. We believe models of social networks partitioned at different common semantic layers could be very useful in the recommender processes offering more accurate and context-sensitive results. Thus, as an applicative development of our automatic semantic clustering and social network building methods, we present and empirically study in this paper several collaborative filtering models that retrieve information items according to a number of real user profiles and within different contexts.

In addition to these possibilities, our two-way space clustering, which finds clusters of users based on the clusters of concepts found in a first pass, offers a reinforced partition of the user space that could be exploited to build group profiles for sets of related users. These group profiles might enable an efficient strategy for collaborative recommendation in real-time, by using the merged profiles as representatives of classes of users.

The rest of the paper has the following structure. Section 2 describes the semantics representation framework upon which our social network models are built. The proposed clustering techniques to build the multi-level relations between users are presented in Section 3. The exploitation of the derived networks to enhance collaborative filtering is described in Section 4. Section 5 describes a simple example where the techniques are tested. An early experiment with real subjects and user profiles is presented in Section 6, and conclusions are given in Section 7.

2 Ontology-Based User Profiles and Preference Spreading

In contrast to other approaches in personalized content retrieval, our approach makes use of explicit user profiles (as opposed to e.g. sets of preferred documents). Working within an ontology-based personalization framework [16], user preferences are represented as vectors $u_i = (u_{i,1}, u_{i,2}, ..., u_{i,N})$ where the weight $u_{i,j} \in [0,1]$ measures the intensity of the interest of user i for concept c_j (a class or an instance) in the domain ontology, N being the total number of concepts in the ontology. Similarly, the objects d_k in the retrieval space are assumed to be described (annotated) by vectors $(d_{k,1}, d_{ik2}, ..., d_{k,N})$ of concept weights, in the same vector-space as user preferences. Based on this common logical representation, measures of user interest for content items can be computed by comparing preference and annotation vectors, and these measures can be used to prioritize, filter and rank contents (a collection, a catalog, a search result) in a personal way.

The ontology-based representation is richer and less ambiguous than a keyword-based or item-based model. It provides an adequate grounding for the representation of coarse to fine-grained user interests (e.g. interest for items such as a sports team, an actor, a stock value), and can be a key enabler to deal with the subtleties of user preferences. An ontology provides further formal, computer-processable meaning on the concepts (who is coaching a team, an actor's filmography, financial data on a stock), and makes it available for the personalization system to take advantage of. Furthermore, ontology standards, such as RDF and OWL, support inference mechanisms that can be used to enhance personalization, so that, for instance, a user interested in *animals* (superclass of *cat*) is also recommended items about *cats*. Inversely, a user interested in *lizards* and *snakes* can be inferred to be interested in *reptiles*. Also, a user keen of *Czech Republic* can be assumed to like *Prague*, through the *locatedIn* transitive relation. These characteristics will be exploited in our personalized retrieval model.

In real scenarios, user profiles tend to be very scattered, especially in those applications where user profiles have to be manually defined. Users are usually not willing to spend time describing their detailed preferences to the system, even less to assign weights to them, especially if they do not have a clear understanding of the effects and results of this input. On the other hand, applications where an automatic preference learning algorithm is applied tend to recognize the main characteristics of user preferences, thus yielding profiles that may entail a lack of expressivity. To overcome this problem, we propose a semantic preference spreading mechanism, which expands the initial set of preferences stored in user profiles through explicit semantic relations with other concepts in the ontology (see picture 1 in Figure 1). Our approach is based on the Constrained Spreading Activation (CSA) strategy [4,5]. The expansion is self-controlled by applying a decay factor to the intensity of preference each time a relation is traversed.

Thus, the system outputs ranked lists of content items taking into account not only the preferences of the current user, but also a semantic spreading mechanism through the user profile and the domain ontology. In fact, previous experiments were done without the semantic spreading process and very poor results were obtained. The profiles were very simple and the matching between the preferences of different users was low. This observation shows a better performance when using ontology-based profiles, instead of classical keyword-based preferences representations.

We have conducted several experiments showing that the performance of the personalization system is considerably poorer when the spreading mechanism is not enabled. Typically, the basic user profiles without expansion are too simple. They provide a good representative sample of user preferences, but do not reflect the real extent of user interests, which results in low overlaps between the preferences of different users. Therefore, the extension is not only important for the performance of individual personalization, but is essential for the clustering strategy described in the following sections.

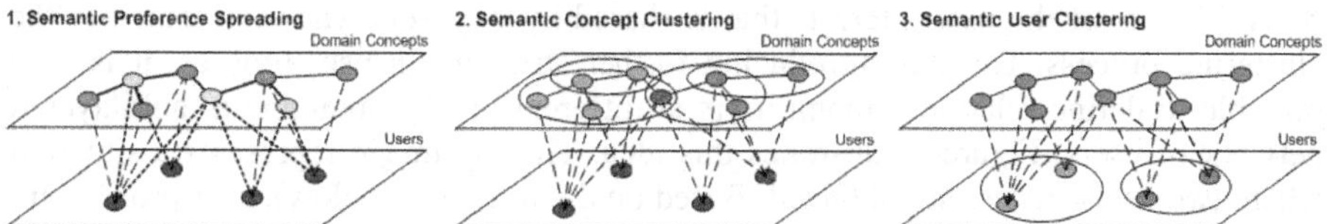

Fig. 1. Overall sequence of our proposed approach, comprising three steps: 1) semantic user preferences are spread, extending the initial sets of individual interests, 2) semantic domain concepts are clustered into concept groups, based on the vector space of user preferences, and 3) users are clustered in order to identify the closest class to each user

3 Multilayered Semantic Social Networks

In social communities, it is commonly accepted that people who are known to share a specific interest are likely to have additional connected interests [8]. For instance, people who share interests in traveling might be also keen on topics related in photography, gastronomy or languages. In fact, this assumption is the basis of most recommender system technologies [3,7,12,14]. We assume this hypothesis here as well, in order to cluster the concept space in groups of preferences shared by several users.

We propose here to exploit the links between users and concepts to extract relations among users and derive semantic social networks according to common interests. Analyzing the structure of the domain ontology and taking into account the semantic preference weights of the user profiles we shall cluster the domain concept space generating groups of interests shared by certain users. Thus, those users who share interests of a specific concept cluster will be connected in the network, and their preference weights will measure the degree of membership to each cluster. Specifically, a vector $c_j = (c_{j,1}, c_{j,2}, ..., c_{j,M})$ is assigned to each concept vector c_j present in the preferences of at least one user, where $c_{j,i} = u_{i,j}$ is the weight of concept c_j, in the semantic profile of user i. Based on these vectors a classic hierarchical clustering strategy [6,15] is applied. The clusters obtained (picture 2 in Figure 1) represent the groups of preferences (topics of interests) in the concept-user vector space shared by a significant number of users. Once the concept clusters are created, each user is assigned to a specific cluster. The similarity between a user's preferences $u_i = (u_{i,1}, u_{i,2}, ..., u_{i,N})$ and a cluster C_r is computed by:

$$sim(u_i, C_r) = \frac{\sum_{c_j \in C_r} u_{i,j}}{|C_r|} \quad (1)$$

where c_j represents the concept that corresponds to the $u_{i,j}$ component of the user preference vector, and $|C_r|$ is the number of concepts included in the cluster. The clusters with highest similarities are then assigned to the users, thus creating groups of users with shared interests (picture 3 in Figure 1).

The concept and user clusters are then used to find emergent, focused semantic social networks. The preference weights of user profiles, the degrees of membership of the users to each cluster and the similarity measures between clusters are used to find relations between two distinct types of social items: individuals and groups of individuals.

On the other hand, using the concept clusters user profiles are partitioned into semantic segments. Each of these segments corresponds to a concept cluster and represents a subset of the user interests that is shared by the users who contributed to the clustering process. By thus introducing further structure in user profiles, it is now possible to define relations among users at different levels, obtaining a multilayered network of users. Figure 2 illustrates this idea. The top image represents a situation where two user clusters are obtained. Based on them (images below), user profiles are partitioned in two semantic layers. On each layer, weighted relations among users are derived, building up different social networks.

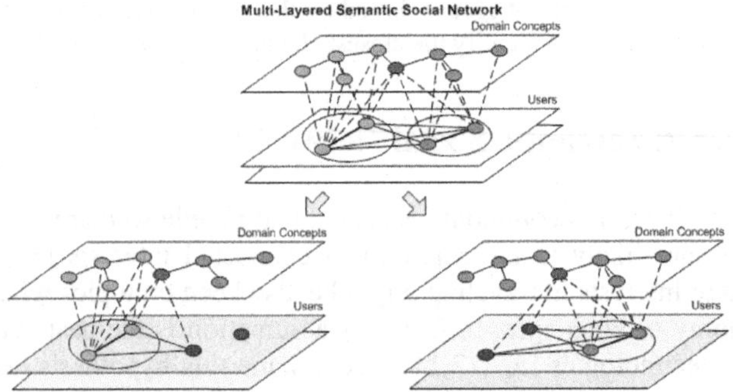

Fig. 2. Multilayered semantic social network built from the clusters of concepts and users

The resulting networks have many potential applications. For one, they can be exploited to the benefit of collaborative filtering and recommendation, not only because they establish similarities between users, but also because they provide powerful means to focus on different semantic contexts for different information needs. The design of two information retrieval models in this direction is explored in next section.

4 Multilayered Models for Collaborative Filtering

Collaborative filtering applications adapt to groups of people who interact with the system, in a way that single users benefit from the experience of other users with which they have certain traits or interests in common. User groups may be quite heterogeneous, and it might be very difficult to define the mechanisms for which the system adapts itself to the groups of users, in such a way that each individual enjoys or even benefits from the results. Furthermore, once the user association rules are defined, an efficient search for neighbors among a large user population of potential neighbors has to be addressed. This is the great bottleneck in conventional user-based collaborative filtering algorithms [12]. Item-based algorithms [3,7,14] attempt to avoid these difficulties by exploring the relations among items, rather than the relations among users. However, the item neighborhood is fairly static and do not allow to easily apply personalized recommendations or inference mechanisms to discover potential hidden user interests.

We believe that exploiting the relations of the underlying social network which emerges from the users' interests, and combining them with semantic item preference information can have an important benefit in collaborative filtering and recommendation. Using our semantic multilayered social network proposal explained in previous sections, we present here two recommender models that generate ranked lists of items in different scenarios taking into account the links between users in the generated social networks. The first model (that we shall label as UP) is based on the semantic profile of the user to whom the ranked list is delivered. This model represents the situation where the interests of a user are compared to other interests in a social network. The second model (labeled NUP) outputs ranked lists disregarding the user profile. This can be applied in situations where a new user does not have a profile yet, or when the general preferences in a user's profile are too generic for a specific context, and do not help to guide the user towards a very particular, context-specific need. Additionally, we consider two versions for each model: a) one that generates a unique ranked list based on the similarities between the items and all the existing semantic clusters, and, b) one that provides a ranking for each semantic cluster. Thus, we consider four retrieval strategies, UP (profile-based), UP-r (profile-based, considering a specific cluster C_r), NUP (no profile), and NUP-r (no profile, considering a specific cluster C_r).

The four strategies are formalized next. In the following, for a user profile u_i, an information object vector d_k, and a cluster C_r, we denote by u_i^r and d_k^r the projection of the corresponding concept vectors onto cluster C_r, i.e. the j-th component of u_i^r and d_k^r is $u_{i,j}$ and $d_{k,j}$ respectively, if $c_j \in C_r$, and 0 otherwise.

Model UP. The semantic profile of a user u_i is used by the system to return a unique ranked list. The preference score of an item d_k is computed as a weighted sum of the indirect preference values based on similarities with other users in each cluster, where the sum is weighted by the similarities with the clusters, as follows:

$$pref\left(d_k,u_i\right)=\sum_r nsim\left(d_k,C_r\right)\sum_l nsim_r\left(u_i,u_l\right)\cdot sim_r\left(d_k,u_l\right) \quad (2)$$

where:

$$sim\left(d_k,C_r\right)=\frac{\sum_{c_j\in C_r} d_{k,j}}{\left\|d_k\right\|\sqrt{\left|C_r\right|}},\quad nsim\left(d_k,C_r\right)=\frac{sim\left(d_k,C_r\right)}{\sum_l sim\left(d_k,C_l\right)}$$

are the single and normalized similarities between the item d_k and the cluster C_r,

$$sim_r\left(u_i,u_l\right)=\cos\left(u_i^r,u_l^r\right)=\frac{u_i^r\cdot u_l^r}{\| u_i^r \|\cdot\| u_l^r \|},\quad nsim_r\left(u_i,u_l\right)=\frac{sim_r\left(u_i,u_l\right)}{\sum_t sim_r\left(u_i,u_t\right)}$$

are the single and normalized similarities at layer r between user profiles u_i and u_l, and

$$sim_r\left(d_k,u_i\right)=\cos\left(d_k^r,u_i^r\right)=\frac{d_k^r\cdot u_i^r}{\left\|d_k^r\right\|\cdot\left\|u_i^r\right\|}$$

is the similarity at layer r between item d_k and user u_i.

The idea behind this first model is to compare the current user interests with those of the others users, and, taking into account the similarities among them, weight all their complacencies about the different items. The comparisons are done for each concept cluster measuring the similarities between the items and the clusters. We thus attempt to recommend an item in a double way. First, according to the item characteristics, and second, according to the connections among user interests, in both cases at different semantic layers.

Model UP-r. The preferences of the user are used by the system to return one ranked list per cluster, obtained from the similarities between users and items at each cluster layer. The ranking that corresponds to the cluster for which the user has the highest membership value is selected. The expression is analogous to equation (2), but does not include the term that connects the item with each cluster C_r.

$$pref_r(d_k,u_i)=\sum_l nsim_r(u_i,u_l)\cdot sim_r(d_k,u_l) \quad (3)$$

where r maximizes $sim(u_i,C_r)$.

Analogously to the previous model, this one makes use of the relations among the user interests, and the user satisfactions with the items. The difference here is that recommendations are done separately for each layer. If the current semantic cluster is well identified for a certain item, we expect to achieve better precision/recall results than those obtained with the overall model.

Model NUP. The semantic profile of the user is ignored. The ranking of an item d_k is determined by its similarity with the clusters, and the similarity of the item and the profiles of the users within each cluster. Since the user does not have connections to other users, the influence of each profile is averaged by the number of users M.

$$pref(d_k,u_i)=\frac{1}{M}\sum_r nsim(d_k,C_r)\sum_l sim_r(d_k,u_l) \quad (4)$$

Designed for situations in which the current user profile has not yet been defined, this model uniformly gathers all the user complacencies about the items at different semantic layers. Although it would provide worse precision/recall results than the models UP and UP-r, this one might be fairly suitable as a first approach to recommendations previous to manual or automatic user profile constructions.

Model NUP-r. The preferences of the user are ignored, and one ranked list per cluster is delivered. As in the UP-r model, the ranking that corresponds to the cluster the user is most close to is selected. The expression is analogous to equation (4), but does not include the term that connects the item with each cluster C_r.

$$pref_r(d_k,u_i)=\frac{1}{M}\sum_l sim_r(d_k,u_l) \quad (5)$$

This last model is the most simple of all the proposals. It only measures the users' complacencies with the items at the layers that best fit them, representing thus a kind of item-based collaborative filtering system.

5 An Example

For testing the proposed strategies and models a simple experiment has been set up. A set of 20 user profiles are considered. Each profile is manually defined considering 6 possible topics: *animals, beach, construction, family, motor* and *vegetation.* The degree of interest of the users for each topic is shown in Table 1, ranging over *high, medium,* and *low* interest, corresponding to preference weights close to 1, 0.5, and 0.

Table 1. Degrees of interest of users for each topic, and expected user clusters to be obtained

	Motor	*Construction*	*Family*	*Animals*	*Beach*	*Vegetation*	**Expected Cluster**
User1	High	High	Low	Low	Low	Low	1
User2	High	High	Low	Medium	Low	Low	1
User3	High	Medium	Low	Low	Medium	Low	1
User4	High	Medium	Low	Medium	Low	Low	1
User5	Medium	High	Medium	Low	Low	Low	1
User6	Medium	Medium	Low	Low	Low	Low	1
User7	Low	Low	High	High	Low	Medium	2
User8	Low	Medium	High	High	Low	Low	2
User9	Low	Low	High	Medium	Medium	Low	2
User10	Low	Low	High	Medium	Low	Medium	2
User11	Low	Low	Medium	High	Low	Low	2
User12	Low	Low	Medium	Medium	Low	Low	2
User13	Low	Low	Low	Low	High	High	3
User14	Medium	Low	Low	Low	High	High	3
User15	Low	Low	Medium	Low	High	Medium	3
User16	Low	Medium	Low	Low	High	Medium	3
User17	Low	Low	Low	Medium	Medium	High	3
User18	Low	Low	Low	Low	Medium	Medium	3
User19	Low	High	Low	Low	Medium	Low	1
User20	Low	Medium	High	Low	Low	Low	2

As it can be seen from the table, the six first users (1 to 6) have *medium* or *high* degrees of interests in *motor* and *construction.* For them it is expected to obtain a common cluster, named cluster 1 in the table. The next six users (7 to 12) share again two topics in their preferences. They like concepts associated with *family* and *animals.* For them a new cluster is expected, named cluster 2. The same situation happens with the next six users (13 to 18); their common topics are *beach* and *vegetation,* an expected cluster named cluster 3. Finally, the last two users have noisy profiles, in the sense that they do not have preferences easily assigned to one of the previous clusters. However, it is comprehensible that User19 should be assigned to cluster 1 because of her high interests in *construction* and User20 should be assigned to cluster 2 due to her high interests in *family.*

Table 2 shows the correspondence of concepts to topics. Note that user profiles do not necessarily include all the concepts of a topic. As mentioned before, in real world applications it is unrealistic to assume profiles are complete, since they typically include only a subset of all the actual user preferences.

Table 2. Initial concepts for each of the six considered topics

Topic	Concepts
Motor	Vehicle, Motorcycle, Bicycle, Helicopter, Boat
Construction	Construction, Fortress, Road, Street
Family	Family, Wife, Husband, Daughter , Son, Mother, Father, Sister, Brother
Animals	Animal, Dog, Cat, Bird, Dove, Eagle, Fish, Horse, Rabbit, Reptile, Snake, Turtle
Beach	Water , Sand, Sky
Vegetation	Vegetation, Tree (instance of Vegetation), Plant (instance of Vegetation), Flower (instance of Vegetation)

We have tested our method with this set of 20 user profiles, as explained next. First, new concepts are added to the profiles by the CSA strategy mentioned in Section 2, enhancing the concept and user clustering that follows. The applied clustering strategy is a hierarchical procedure based on the Euclidean distance to measure the similarities between concepts, and the average linkage method to measure the similarities between clusters. During the execution, *N–1* (with *N* the total number of concepts) clustering levels were obtained, and a stop criterion to choose an appropriate number of clusters would be needed. In our case the number of expected clusters is three so the stop criterion was not necessary. Table 3 summarizes the assignment of users to clusters, showing their corresponding similarities values. It can be shown that the obtained results completely coincide with the expected values presented in Table 1. All the users are assigned to their corresponding clusters. Furthermore, the users' similarities values reflect their degrees of belonging to each cluster.

Table 3. User clusters and associated similarity values between users and clusters. The maximum and minimum similarity values are shown in bold and italics respectively.

Cluster	Users						
1	*User1* **0.522**	*User2* **0.562**	*User3* 0.402	*User4* 0.468	*User5* 0.356	*User6* 0.218	*User19* *0.194*
2	*User7* **0.430**	*User8* **0.389**	*User9* 0.374	*User10* 0.257	*User11* 0.367	*User12* *0.169*	*User20* 0.212
3	*User13* **0.776**	*User14* **0.714**	*User15* 0.463	*User16* 0.437	*User17* 0.527	*User18* *0.217*	

Once the concept clusters have been automatically identified and each user has been assigned to a certain cluster, we apply the information retrieval models presented in the previous section. A set of 24 pictures was considered as the retrieval space. Each picture was annotated with (weighted) semantic metadata describing what the image depicts using a domain ontology. Observing the weighted annotations, an expert rated the relevance of the pictures for the 20 users of the example, assigning scores between 1 (totally irrelevant) and 5 (very relevant) to each picture, for each user. We show in Table 4 the final concepts obtained and grouped in the semantic Constrained Spreading Activation and concept clustering phases. Although most of the final concepts do not appear in the initial user profiles, they are very important in further steps because they help in the construction of the clusters. Our plans for future work include studying in depth the influence of the CSA in realistic empirical experiments.

Table 4. Concepts assigned to the obtained user clusters classified by semantic topic

Cluster	Concepts
1	**MOTOR**: Vehicle, Racing-Car, Tractor, Ambulance, Motorcycle, Bicycle, Helicopter, Boat, Sailing-Boat, Water-Motor, Canoe, Surf, Windsurf, Lift, Chair-Lift, Toboggan, Cable-Car, Sleigh, Snow-Cat **CONSTRUCTION**: Construction, Fortress, Garage, Road, Speedway, Racing-Circuit, Short-Oval, Street, Wind-Tunnel, Pier, Lighthouse, Beach-Hut, Mountain-Hut, Mountain-Shelter, Mountain-Villa
2	**FAMILY**: Family, Wife, Husband, Daughter , Son, Mother-In-Law, Father-In-Law, Nephew, Parent, 'Fred' (instance of Parent), Grandmother, Grandfather, Mother, Father, Sister, 'Christina' (instance of Sister), Brother, 'Peter' (instance of Brother), Cousin , Widow **ANIMALS**: Animal, Vertebrates, Invertebrates, Terrestrial, Mammals, Dog, 'Tobby' (instance of Dog), Cat, Bird, Parrot, Pigeon, Dove, Parrot, Eagle, Butterfly, Fish, Horse, Rabbit, Reptile, Snake, Turtle, Tortoise, Crab
3	**BEACH**: Water, Sand, Sky **VEGETATION**: Vegetation, 'Tree' (instance of Vegetation), 'Plant' (instance of Vegetation), 'Flower' (instance of Vegetation)

The four different models are finally evaluated by computing their average precision/recall curves for the users of each of the three existing clusters. Figure 3 shows the results. Two conclusions can be inferred from the results: a) the version of the models that returns ranked lists according to specific clusters (UP-r and NUP-r) outperforms the one that generates a unique list, and, b) the models that make use of the relations among users in the social networks (UP and UP-r) result in significant improvements with respect to those that do not take into account similarities between user profiles.

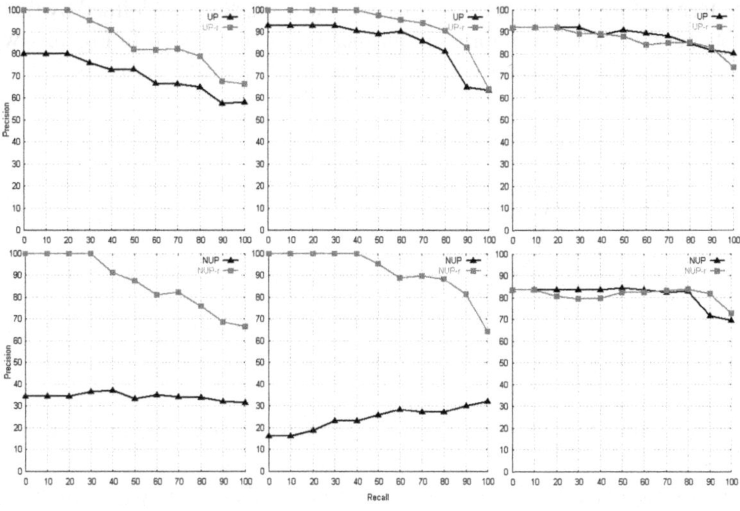

Fig. 3. Average precision vs. recall curves for users assigned to cluster 1 (left), cluster 2 (center) and cluster 3 (right). The graphics on top show the performance of the UP and UP-r models. The ones below correspond to the NUP and NUP-r models.

6 Early Experiments

We have performed an experiment with real subjects in order to evaluate the effectiveness of our proposed recommendation models. Following the ideas exposed in the simple example of the previous section, the experiment was setup as follows.

The set of 24 pictures used in the example was again considered as the retrieval space. As mentioned before, each picture was annotated with semantic metadata describing what the image depicts, using a domain ontology including six certain topics: *animals*, *beach*, *construction*, *family*, *motor* and *vegetation*. A weight in [0,1] was assigned to each annotation, reflecting the relative importance of the concept in the picture. 20 graduate students of our department participated in the experiment. They were asked to independently define their weighted preferences about a list of concepts related to the above topics and existing in the pictures semantic annotations. No restriction was imposed on the number of topics and concepts to be selected by each of the students. Indeed, the generated user profiles showed very different characteristics, observable not only in their joint interests, but also in their complexity. Some students defined their profiles very thoroughly, while others only annotated a few concepts of interest. This fact was obviously very appropriate for the experiment done. In a real scenario where an automatic preference learning algorithm will have to be used, the obtained user profiles would include noisy and incomplete components that will hinder the clustering and recommendation mechanisms.

Once the 20 user profiles were created, we run our method. After the execution of the semantic preference spreading procedure, the domain concept space was clustered according to similar user interests. In this phase, because our strategy is based on a hierarchical clustering method, various clustering levels (representable by the corresponding dendrogram) were found, expressing different compromises between complexity, described in terms of number of concept clusters, and compactness, defined by the number of concepts per cluster or the minimum distance between clusters. In Figure 4 we graph the minimum inter-cluster distance against the number of concept clusters.

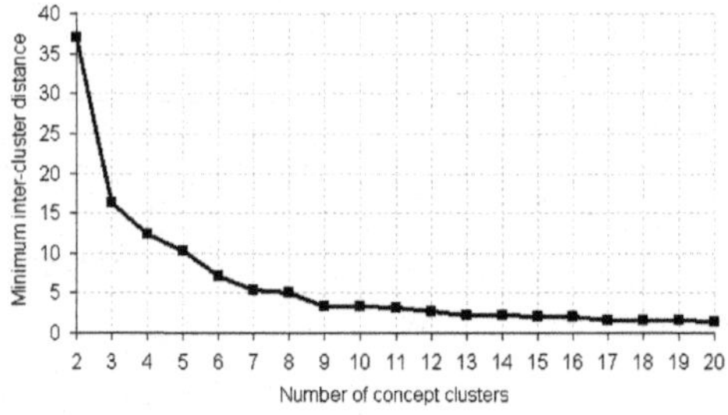

Fig. 4. Minimum inter-cluster distance at different concept clustering levels

A stop criterion has then to be applied in order to determine what number of clusters should be chosen. In this case, we shall use a rule based on the *elbow criterion*, which says you should be choose a number of clusters so that adding another cluster does not add sufficient information. We are interested in a clustering level with a relative small number of clusters and which does not vary excessively the inter-cluster distance with respect to previous levels. Therefore, attending to the figure, we will focus on clustering levels with $R = 4, 5, 6$ clusters, corresponding to the angle (elbow) in the graph. Table 5 shows the users that most contributed to the definition of the different concept cluster, and their corresponding similarities values.

Table 5. User clusters and associated similarity values between users and clusters obtained at concept clustering levels $R = 4, 5, 6$

R	Cluster	Users								
4	1	*User01* 0.388	*User02* 0.370	*User05* 0.457	*User06* 0.689	*User19* 0.393				
	2									
	3	*User03* 0.521	*User04* 0.646	*User07* 0.618	*User09* 0.209	*User12* 0.536	*User15* 0.697	*User16* 0.730	*User18* 0.461	
	4	*User08* 0.900	*User10* 0.089	*User11* 0.810	*User13* 0.591	*User14* 0.833	*User17* 0.630	*User20* 0.777		
5	1	*User03* 0.818	*User07* 0.635							
	2									
	3	*User04* 0.646	*User09* 0.209	*User12* 0.536	*User16* 0.730	*User18* 0.461				
	4	*User01* 0.395	*User02* 0.554	*User05* 0.554	*User06* 0.720	*User15* 0.712	*User19* 0.399			
	5	*User08* 0.900	*User10* 0.089	*User11* 0.810	*User13* 0.591	*User14* 0.833	*User17* 0.630	*User20* 0.777		
6	1	*User6* 0.818								
	2									
	3	*User18* 0.481								
	4	*User02* 0.554	*User05* 0.554	*User06* 0.720	*User19* 0.399					
	5	*User08* 0.900	*User13* 0.591	*User11* 0.810	*User17* 0.630	*User20* 0.777				
	6	*User01* 0.786	*User04* 0.800	*User07* 0.771	*User09* 0.600	*User10* 0.214	*User12* 0.671	*User14* 0.857	*User15* 0.829	*User16* 0.814

It has to be noted that not all the concept clusters have assigned user profiles. However, there are semantic relations between users within a certain concept cluster, independently of being associated to other clusters or the number of users assigned to the cluster. For instance, at clustering level $R = 4$, we obtained the weighted semantic relations plotted in Figure 5. Representing the semantic social networks of the users, the diagrams of the figure describe the similarity terms $sim_r(u_i, u_l)$, $i, l \in \{1, 20\}$ (see equations 2 and 3). The color of each cell depicts the similarity values between two given users: the dark and light gray cells indicate respectively similarity values greater and lower than 0.5, while the white ones mean no existent relation. Note that a relation between two certain users with a high weight does not necessary implicate a high interest of both for the concepts on the current cluster. What it means is that they interests agree at this layer. They could really like it or they might hate its topics.

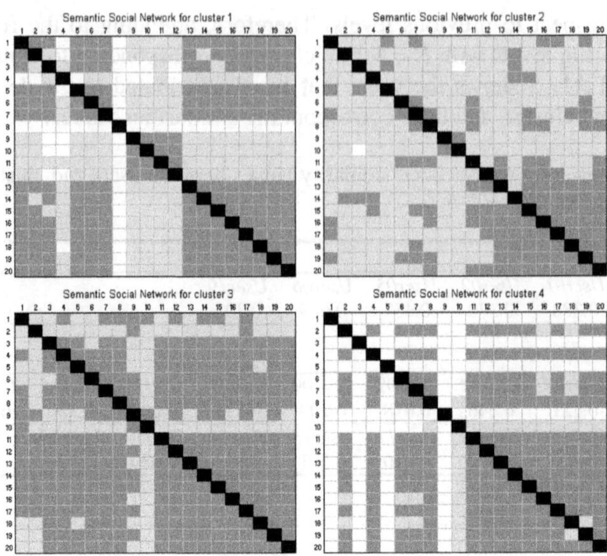

Fig. 5. Symmetric user similarity matrices at layers 1, 2, 3 and 4 between user profiles u_i and u_l ($i, l \in \{1, 20\}$) obtained at clustering level R=4. Dark and light gray cells represent respectively similarity values greater and lower than 0.5. White cells mean no relation between users.

Table 6 shows the concept clusters obtained at clustering level $R = 4$. We have underlined those general concepts that initially did not appear in the profiles and were in the upper levels of the domain ontology. Inferred from our preference spreading strategy, these concepts do not necessary define the specific semantics of the clusters, but help to build the latter during the clustering processes.

Table 6. Concept clusters obtained at clustering level R=4

Cluster	Concepts
1	**ANIMALS**: Rabbit **CONSTRUCTION**: <u>Construction</u>, Speedway, Racing-Circuit, Short-Oval, Garage, Lighthouse, Pier, Beach-Hut, Mountain-Shelter, Mountain-Villa, Mountain-Hut, **MOTOR**: <u>Vehicle</u>, Ambulance, Racing-Car, Tractor, Canoe, Surf, Windsurf, Water-Motor, Sleigh, Snow-Cat, Lift, Chair-Lift, Toboggan, Cable-Car
2	**ANIMALS**: <u>Organism</u>, <u>Agentive-Physical-Object</u>, Reptile, Snake, Tortoise, Sheep, Dove, Fish, Mountain-Goat, Reindeer **CONSTRUCTION**: <u>Non-Agentive-Physical-Object</u>, <u>Geological-Object</u>, <u>Ground</u>, <u>Artifact</u>, Fortress, Road, Street **FAMILY**: <u>Civil-Status</u>, Wife, Husband **MOTOR**: <u>Conveyance</u>, Bicycle, Motorcycle, Helicopter, Boat, Sailing-Boat
3	**ANIMALS**: <u>Animal</u>, <u>Vertebrates</u>, <u>Invertebrates</u>, <u>Terrestrial</u>, <u>Mammals</u>, Dog, 'Tobby' (instance of Dog), Cat, Horse, Bird, Eagle, Parrot, Pigeon, Butterfly, Crab **BEACH**: Water, Sand, Sky **VEGETATION**: <u>Vegetation</u>, 'Tree' (instance of Vegetation), 'Plant' (instance of Vegetation), 'Flower' (instance of Vegetation)
4	**FAMILY**: <u>Family</u>, Grandmother, Grandfather, Parent, Mother, Father, Sister, Brother, Daughter, Son, Mother-In-Law, Father-In-Law, Cousin, Nephew, Widow, 'Fred' (instance of Parent), 'Christina' (instance of Sister), 'Peter' (instance of Brother)

Some conclusions can be drawn from this experiment. Cluster 1 contains the majority of the most specific concepts related to *construction* and *motor*, showing a significative correlation between these two topics of interest. Checking the profiles of the users associated to the cluster, we observed they overall have medium-high weights on the concepts of these topics. Cluster 2 is the one with more different topics and general concepts. In fact, it is the cluster that does not have assigned users in Table 6 and does have the most weakness relations between users in Figure 5. It is also notorious that the concepts 'wife' and 'husband' appear in this cluster. This is due to these concepts were not be annotated in the profiles by the subjects, who were students, not married at the moment. Cluster 3 is the one that gathers all the concepts about *beach* and *vegetation*. The subjects who liked vegetation items also seemed to be interested in beach items. It also has many of the concepts belonging to the topic of *animals*, but in contrast to cluster 2, the annotations were for more common and domestic animals. Finally, cluster 4 collects the majority of the *family* concepts. It can be observed from the user profiles that a number of subjects only defined their preferences in this topic.

Finally, as we did in the example of section 5, we evaluate the proposed retrieval models computing their average precision/recall curves for the users of each of the existing clusters. In this case we calculate the curves at different clustering levels (R = 4, 5, 6), and we only consider the models UP and UP-r because they make use of the relations among users in the social networks, and offer significant improvements with respect to those that do not take into consideration similarities between user profiles. Figure 6 exposes the results.

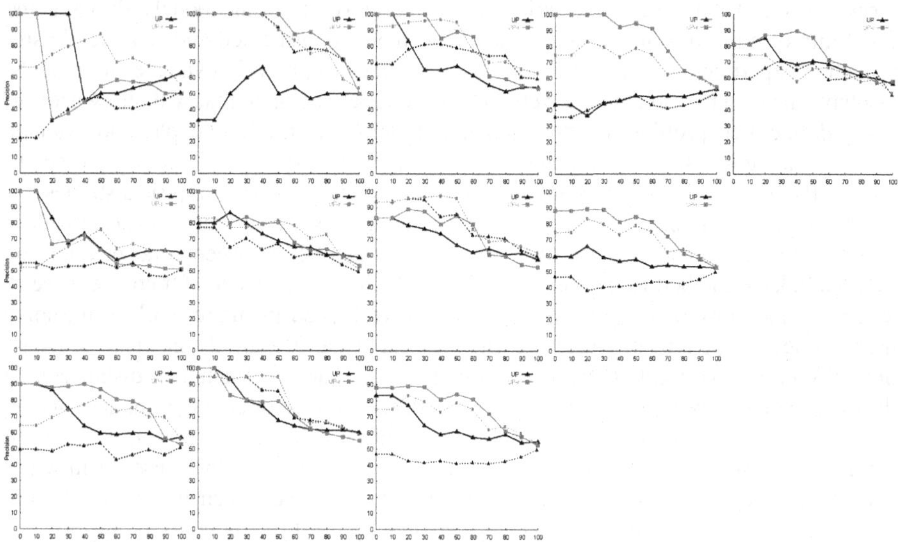

Fig. 6. Average precision vs. recall curves for users assigned to the user clusters obtained with the UP (black lines) and UP-r (gray lines) models at levels R=6 (graphics on the top), R=5 (graphics in the middle), and R=4 (graphics on the bottom) concept clusters. For both models, the dotted lines represent the results achieved without semantic preference spreading.

Again, the version UP-r, which returns ranked lists according to specific clusters, outperforms the version UP, which generates a unique list assembling the contributions of the users in all the clusters. Obviously, the more clusters we have, the better performance is achieved. The clusters tend to have assigned fewer users and seem more similar to the individual profiles. However, it can be seen that very good results are obtained with only three clusters. Additionally, for both models, we have plotted with dotted lines the curves achieved without spreading the user semantic preferences. Although more statistically significative experiments have to be done in order to make founded conclusions, it can be pointed out that our clustering strategy performs better when it is combined with the CSA algorithm, especially in the UP-r model. This fact let give us preliminary evidences of the importance of spreading the user profiles before the clustering processes.

7 Conclusions and Further Work

In this work, we have presented an approach to the automatic identification of social networks according to ontology-based user profiles. Taking into account the semantic preferences of several users we cluster the ontology concept space, obtaining common topics of interest. With these topics, preferences are partitioned into different layers.

The degree of membership of the obtained subprofiles to the clusters, and the similarities among them, are used to define social links that can be exploited by collaborative filtering systems. Early experiments with real subjects have been done applying the emergent social networks to a variety of collaborative filtering models showing the feasibility of our clustering strategy. However, more sophisticated and statistically significative experiments need to be performed in order to properly evaluate the models. We have planned to implement a web-based recommender agent that will allow users to easily define their profiles, see their semantic relations with other people, and evaluate the existing items and recommendations given by the system. Thus, we expect to enlarge the repositories of items and user profiles, and improve our empirical studies.

Our implementation of the applied clustering strategy was a hierarchical procedure based on the Euclidean distance to measure the similarities between concepts, and the average linkage method to measure the similarities between clusters. Of course, several aspects of the clustering algorithm have to be investigated in future work using noisy user profiles: 1) the type of clustering (hierarchical or partitional), 2) the distance measure between two concepts (Manhattan, Euclidean or Squared Euclidean distances), 3) the distance measure between two clusters (single, complete or average linkage), 4) the stop criterion that determines what number of clusters should be chosen, and, 5) the similarity measure between given clusters and user profiles; we have used a measure considering the relative size of the clusters, but we have not taken into account what proportion of the user preferences is being satisfied by the different concept clusters.

We are also aware of the need to test our approach in combination with automatic user preference learning techniques in order to investigate its robustness to imprecise user interests, and the impact of the accuracy of the ontology-based profiles on the correct performance of the clustering processes. An adequate acquisition of the concepts of interest and their further classification and annotation in the ontology-based profiles will be crucial to the correct performance of the clustering processes.

Acknowledgements

The research leading to this document has received funding from the European Community's Sixth Framework Programme (FP6-027685 – MESH), and the Spanish Ministry of Science and Education (TIN2005-06885). However, it reflects only the authors' views, and the European Community is not liable for any use that may be made of the information contained therein.

References

1. Alani, H., O'Hara, K., Shadbolt, N.: *ONTOCOPI: Methods and Tools for Identifying Communities of Practice*. Intelligent Information Processing 2002, pp. 225-236, 2002.
2. Ardissono, L., Goy, A., Petrone, G., Segnan, M., Torasso, P.: *INTRIGUE: personalized recommendation of tourist attractions for desktop and handset devices*. Applied Artificial Intelligence, Special Issue on Artificial Intelligence for Cultural Heritage and Digital Libraries 17(8-9), pp. 687-714. Taylor and Francis, 2003.
3. Balabanovic, M., Shoham, Y.: *Content-Based Collaborative Recommendation*. Communications ACM, pp. 66-72, 1997.
4. Cohen, P. R. and Kjeldsen, R.: *Information Retrieval by Constrained Spreading Activation in Semantic Networks*. Information Processing and Management 23(2), pp. 255-268, 1987.
5. Crestani, F., Lee, P. L.: *Searching the web by constrained spreading activation*. Information Processing & Management 36(4), pp. 585-605, 2000.
6. Duda, R.O., Hart, P., Stork, D.G.: *Pattern Classification*. John Wiley. 2001.
7. Linden, G., Smith, B., York, J.: *Amazon.com Recommendations: Item-to-Item Collaborative Filtering*. IEEE Internet Computing, 7(1):76-80, 2003.
8. Liu, H., Maes, P., Davenport, G.: *Unraveling the Taste Fabric of Social Networks*. International Journal on Semantic Web and Information Systems 2 (1), pp. 42-71, 2006.
9. McCarthy, J., Anagnost, T.: *MusicFX: An arbiter of group preferences for computer supported collaborative workouts*. ACM International Conference on Computer Supported Cooperative Work (CSCW 1998). Seattle, Washington, pp. 363-372, 1998.
10. Mika, P.: *Ontologies Are Us: A Unified Model of Social Networks and Semantics*. Proceedings of the 4th International Semantic Web Conference (ISWC 2005), pp. 522-536, 2005.
11. Mika, P.: *Flink: Semantic Web technology for the extraction and analysis of social networks*. Web Semantics: Science, Services and Agents on the WWW 3(2-3), pp. 211-223, 2005.
12. Montaner, M., López, B., Lluís de la Rosa, J.: *Taxonomy of Recommender Agents on the Internet*. Artificial Intelligence Review 19, pp. 285-330, 2003.
13. O'Conner, M., Cosley, D., Konstan, J. A., Riedl, J.: *PolyLens: A recommender system for groups of users*. 7th European Conference on Computer Supported Cooperative Work (ECSCW 2001). Bonn, Germany, pp. 199-218, 2001.
14. Sarwar, B.M., et al.: *Item-Based Collaborative Filtering Recommendation Algorithms*. 10th International World Wide Web Conference, ACM Press, pp. 285-295, 2001.
15. Ungar, L., Foster, D.: *Clustering Methods for Collaborative Filtering*. Proceedings of the Workshop on Recommendation Systems at the 15th National Conference on Artificial Intelligence, AAAI Press, 1998.
16. Vallet, D., Mylonas, P., Corella, M. A., Fuentes, J. M., Castells, P., Avrithis, Y.: *A Semantically-Enhanced Personalization Framework for Knowledge-Driven Media Services*. IADIS WWW/Internet Conference (ICWI 2005). Lisbon, Portugal, 2005.

Towards Knowledge Management Based on Harnessing Collective Intelligence on the Web

Koji Zettsu[1] and Yasushi Kiyoki[1,2]

[1] National Institute of Information and Communications Technology,
4-2-1 Nukui-Kitamachi, Koganei, Tokyo 184-8795 Japan
zettsu@nict.go.jp

[2] Faculty of Information Environment, Keio University,
5322 Endo, Fujisawa, Kanagawa 252-8520, Japan
kiyoki@mdbl.sfc.keio.ac.jp

Abstract. The Web has acquired immense value as an active, evolving repository of knowledge. It is now entering a new era, which has been called "Web 2.0". One of the essential elements of Web 2.0 is harnessing the collective intelligence of Web users. Large groups of people are remarkably intelligent, and are often smarter than the smartest people in them. Knowledge as collective intelligence is socially constructed from the common understandings of people. It works as a filter for selecting highly regarded information with collective annotation based on bottom-up consensus and the unifying force of Web-supported social networks. The rising interest in harnessing the collective intelligence of Web users entails changes in managing the knowledge of individual users. In this paper, we introduce a concept of knowledge management based on harnessing the collective intelligence of Web users, and explore the technical issues involved in implementing it.

1 Introduction

The Web is entering a new era, which has been called "Web 2.0". One of the essential elements of Web 2.0 is harnessing collective intelligence[1]. In the Web 2.0 era, the Web is evolving from a collection of hyperlinked documents into a conversational "mess" of overlapping communities, where discussion and chat emerge and, as a result, friendships become more entrenched. From this perspective, retrieving Web pages relevant to a given query is no longer the ultimate goal. Instead, this goal is being replaced by the desire to discover communities of knowledge and acquire collective intelligence. Below are motivating examples:

- More and more people try to see "what's getting a lot of attention now" by monitoring blogs. The world of Web 2.0 is a world in which the former audience decides what is important, not a few people in a back room. The collective attention of the blogosphere selects for value.
- For most casual users, information requirements are not specific initially and are usually subject to change during their search. When users conduct searches by trial-and-error, they learn what information is available on the

S. Staab and V. Svatek (Eds.): EKAW 2006, LNAI 4248, pp. 350–357, 2006.

Web from the search results for ad hoc queries. Based on the knowledge discovered from these search results, such as major topics or representative Web communities, people may discover more specific information sources and more specific queries that help them narrow down their searches.
- Web content authors, or bloggers, take a great interest in who is interested in their content. They try to establish communication with those people, and as a result, a community of interest is formed beyond organizational/cultural boundaries.

Individual users have a constant need to capture, codify, locate, and distribute everyday knowledge. Increasing interest in harnessing the collective intelligence of Web users requires changes to the way the knowledge of individual users is managed. In this paper, we introduce a concept of knowledge management based on harnessing the collective intelligence of Web users, and explore the technical issues involved in implementing it.

2 Basic Concepts

2.1 Knowledge as the Collective Intelligence of Web Users

The Web provides a platform for establishing networks made up of communities of people (or organizations or other social entities) connected by social relationships, such as friendship, collaboration, or information exchange based on common interests. These Web-supported social networks can be regarded as virtual communities. From a sociological perspective, knowledge is considered to be socially constructed. Social processes influence the processes of generating and applying knowledge. As a consequence, knowledge cannot be described as objective truth, but as what a social system considers to be true. In this sense, the collective intelligence of Web users can be viewed as a common (or shared) understanding between people, which is the type of knowledge that people tend to take for granted. For example, a folksonomy, like del.icio.us and Flickr, is a form of user-generated classification that emerges through bottom-up consensus. Similarly, Wikipedia is based on collective authorship and understanding.

Users pursuing their own selfish interests build collective value as an automatic byproduct. The collective intelligence of Web users can be viewed as "the wisdom of crowds" [2], which describes a deceptively simple idea that has profound implications: large groups of people are remarkably intelligent, and are often smarter than the smartest people in them. Even if most of the people within a group are not especially well-informed or rational, the group can still reach a collectively wise decision. Our basic idea is to exploit the collective intelligence of Web users, or "the wisdom of crowds", as the basis of knowledge.

2.2 Knowledge Management at the Personal Level

In today's competitive knowledge-based society, knowledge work may be characterized by stronger communication needs, weakly structured and less predictable processes, the assignment of multiple roles to one person rather than a single job position per person, and the increasing importance of teamwork in the form of project teams, networks, and communities in addition to work groups and departments. The boundaries of organizations are more blurred and knowledge workers may engage in a large number of communication, coordination, and cooperation processes and practices that cross these boundaries. In addition, the increased mobility of knowledge workers requires multiple, virtual workspaces that can be personalized according to the needs and practices of their users.

In response to these quite recent changes in the conditions of knowledge work, knowledge management is shifting from the organizational to the personal level. To practice knowledge management at the personal level, individual users constantly need to: (1) quickly locate the right information, (2) receive only relevant information and the context in a timely manner, (3) switch between learning and practicing as the knowledge obtained from the Web becomes less structured and predictable, and (4) maintain communications and build trust among peers to understand the competencies, interests, and needs of peers (i.e., users must be both collectors and sharers of knowledge).

Personal knowledge management is "a collection of processes that an individual needs to carry out in order to gather, classify, store, search and retrieve knowledge in his/her daily activities" [3]. Activities are not confined to business/work-related tasks but also include personal interests, hobbies, home, family, and leisure activities. Personal knowledge management can be viewed as "a conceptual framework to organize and integrate information that we, as individuals, feel is important, so that it becomes part of our personal knowledge base" [4]. Personal knowledge management thus provides a strategy for transforming what might be random pieces of information into something that can be systematically applied and that expands our personal knowledge.

3 Challenges to Implementation

Figure 1 illustrates a generic framework for developing the collective intelligence of Web users. The Web is viewed as a field for individual propagation of personal knowledge. Users pursue their own selfish interests on the Web. Knowledge discovery and Web mining technologies are required to extract the personal knowledge distributed over the Web. This personal knowledge is collected into knowledge bases. Various communities aggregate their personal knowledge and organize their own collective intelligence. Collective intelligence varies from community to community because it is valid for the people committing to the development of the community's policy or consensus.

Knowledge management can be viewed as a life cycle of knowledge tasks. Below we present a typical life cycle and discuss the challenges in implementing knowledge management based on harnessing the collective intelligence.

Knowledge Identification. In knowledge management at the personal level, individuals are responsible for identifying knowledge sources according to

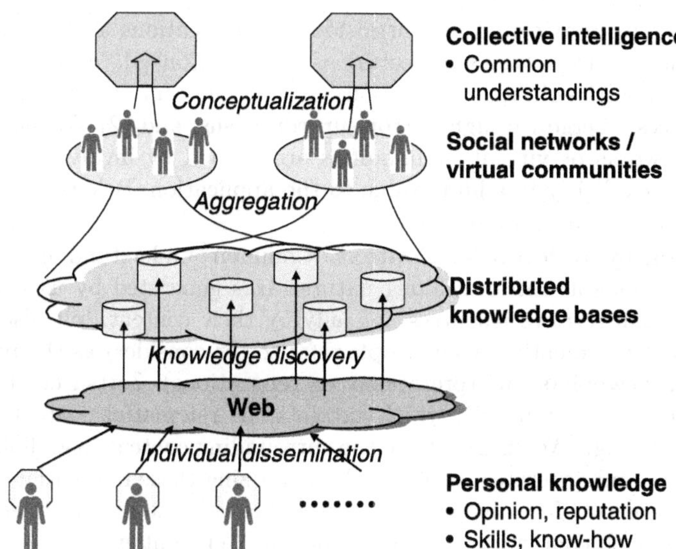

Fig. 1. Generic framework for developing collective intelligence of Web users

their own interests and competencies. However, Web search engines require an exact match of search terms to locate a piece of information, while a user's information needs may not be specific initially and usually change during a search. This suggests the need for a type of Web search engine that allows users to clarify their information needs progressively by examining what kinds of information are available on the Web in their domain of interest. Narrowing the domain of interest and the domain of the search could be carried out simultaneously.

Knowledge Acquisition and Creation. In the Web 2.0 era, the Web is evolving from a collection of hyperlinked documents into a conversational mess. The unit of knowledge acquisition is shifting from Web pages to semantically coherent units of Web content representing, for example, personal opinions, explanations, or interpretations of a specific subject. For example, a unit may consist of a sequence of blog entries (and the comments/trackbacks to them). Knowledge creation identifies these opinions, explanations, or interpretations as knowledge elements.

Knowledge Organization. Each person has his/her individual views on the world and the things he/she has to deal with every day. However, there is a common basis of understanding that we use to communicate with each other. This common understanding relies on an idea of how the world is organized, which is often called a "conceptualization" of the world. A conceptualization provides a context in which knowledge elements can be uniformly organized based on a specific common understanding. A conceptualization is never universally valid, but rather is valid for a limited number of persons committing to that conceptualization.

Knowledge Application. The central idea of applications that harness collective intelligence is "the architecture of participation" [1]. More specifically, the characteristics of these applications are that: (1) common understandings of resources emerge through bottom-up consensus, and (2) Web-supported social networks or virtual communities are formed by involving users implicitly or explicitly in adding value to the application. Below, examples of application scenarios are discussed.

Searching by Referential Context. Common understandings of Web content enable retrieval along natural axes generated by user activity. Users can retrieve resources not only by their content, but also by the context representing what people refer to (or consider) as the resources (e.g., viewpoints, interpretations, or reputations). Zettsu et al.[5] proposed "aspect mining", which extracts the referential context of Web content (e.g., Web pages) from the surrounding content (e.g., link source pages), and generates keywords characterizing these referential contexts as "aspects". Intuitively, an aspect indicates how people refer to the target Web content, or viewpoints on the Web content.

Community-oriented Search. Harnessing collective intelligence works as a kind of filter in bringing "the wisdom of crowds" into play. The collective attention of Web-supported social networks or virtual communities produces well-selected information. In a community-oriented search, a user first finds communities related to his/her domain of interest, and retrieves information that is highly regarded by those communities. This is a natural extension of the way we might ask about people in our daily lives. The collective intelligence of the social networks of people, or communities, play a key role in searching for "trustworthy" information.

Knowledge Evolution. One of the key lessons of Web 2.0 is that "users select for value". Thus, a mechanism of natural selection based on reuse rates is a good candidate for continuous refinement of collective intelligence. The mechanism would retain knowledge with a high reuse rate, but discard knowledge with a low reuse rate. As a result, highly reused knowledge would survive. Natural selection mechanisms have a high affinity with collective intelligence. However, it is also important to retain knowledge that may be reused rarely but is very important in a specific situation. Trouble shooting is a good example. It may therefore be necessary to introduce a notion of context-dependence in evaluating the importance of knowledge.

4 Technical Issues

4.1 Integration of Horizontal and Vertical Searches

The term "horizontal search" refers to broad searches that cover the entire Web. For example, Web search engines like Google retrieve all the Web pages that contain the search terms. The strength of horizontal searching is its broad coverage of Web content (i.e., it is exhaustive). A "vertical search" is a narrower search focused on specific topics or categories. Examples are real estate, travel, or shopping searches.

Knowledge-intensive activities at the personal level require capturing, filtering, and combining knowledge from various sources in keeping with the labile interests of users. A horizontal search of the entire accessible Web is a starting point for finding almost everything relevant to a user's interest. It facilitates the discovery of general knowledge about the domain of interest, which helps identify more specific sources and more specific queries to narrow down the search. Vertical searching is a great way of supplementing a horizontal search. It facilitates searching for actionable knowledge that is directly related to the user's activities or decision making (e.g., making a hotel reservation).

We propose a fundamental framework for integrating horizontal and vertical searches. A user issues vague queries to existing Web search engines (1. horizontal search). The system collects Web pages in the search results and classifies or clusters the Web pages to discover major topics relevant to the user's queries (2. mining search results). For each topic, the system identifies specialized database and routes the query after appropriate modification (3. vertical search). Finally, the system aggregates the results of the vertical search, and presents the search results (4. presentation of results) with explanations describing (a) how the queries were interpreted by the system (e.g., topics) according to the horizontal search results, and (b) what kinds of vertical searches were conducted (i.e., query modification and routing). The proposed framework uses metadata for specialized DBs for query modification and routing, which facilitates adding specialized DBs as plug-ins.

4.2 Just-in-Time Knowledge Discovery

The Web is a shifting universe and Web content is always changing. In particular, blogs are updated every minute, reflecting real-world events almost in real time. In this sense, the Web is a "live" medium. Therefore, to exploit the collective intelligence of Web users, it is important to capture knowledge every time that knowledge is requested. Traditional knowledge discovery and data mining, which are targeted at static databases, need to be able to handle the sheer volume of information arriving from various sources, even though the arrival of a piece of information is difficult to predict. The rising interest in stream data mining is aimed at discovering knowledge from information streams. However, it is still limited to discovering sequential patterns in information streams, which is far from the concept of knowledge as collective intelligence. The ultimate solution is to apply online and incremental algorithms to conventional knowledge discovery and data mining techniques. From the perspective of collective intelligence, online/incremental classification and clustering of information streams, similar to RSS feeds, are the most important issues.

As the collective attention of the blogosphere selects for value, monitoring what is currently receiving a lot of attention in the blogosphere is important in acquiring the "groupthink" of Web users. Especially, extracting opinions or reputations from blogs is an emerging issue. Opinion mining [6,7] processes a set of search results for a given item, generating a list of product attributes (quality, features, etc.) and aggregating opinions about each of them (poor, mixed, good). While most of the current approaches focus on sentiment classification, i.e., classifying opinion texts or sentences as positive or negative, they need to be enhanced to identify diverse opinions more specifically by classifying/clustering opinions or generating summaries of opinions.

4.3 Global Infrastructure for Knowledge Sharing

Organizing the collective intelligence of Web users requires handling and analyzing multi-site and multi-owner knowledge repositories. Our challenge is to create a global infrastructure for sharing heterogeneous knowledge repositories across community boundaries.

The "knowledge grid" has recently emerged as an integrated infrastructure for coordinating knowledge sharing in distributed environments[8]. The knowledge grid uses the basic functions of a grid and defines a set of additional layers to implement the functions of distributed knowledge discovery. The knowledge grid enables collaboration between knowledge providers who must mine data stored in different information sources, and knowledge users who must use a knowledge management system operating on several knowledge bases. Our intention is to implement a mechanism for aggregating knowledge on top of the knowledge grid in order to organize collective intelligence based on conceptualizations.

4.4 Aggregating Knowledge According to Conceptualizations

Conventional approach for organizing common understandings focuses on constructing shared ontologies based on bottom-up consensus[9]. Instead, we propose an approach which is aimed at aggregating knowledge dynamically for a given domain of interest. In the context of multi-database systems, Kiyoki et al.[10] proposed a model for achieving semantic interoperability between data items in heterogeneous databases. Their "mathematical model of meaning" is used to find different data items with equivalent or similar meaning, or to recognize the different meanings of an item. The mathematical model of meaning consists of: (1) defining a normed semantic space, (2) constructing a class of projections which represents a phase of meaning, and (3) constructing a mechanism to select a subspace of the normed space according to the context. Intuitively, in this model, a semantic space consisting of orthogonal concepts is constructed and all data items are mapped on to the semantic space. Then, a subspace is selected according to the "context", which is also represented by a set of orthogonal concepts, and data items are projected on to the subspace. Finally, the similarity between the data items in the subspace is evaluated. The main feature of this model is that the specific meaning of a data item can be recognized disambiguously and dynamically according to the context.

The idea of a mathematical model of meaning could be exploited to aggregate knowledge according to a specific conceptualization. Here, every item of knowledge is mapped to a semantic space, and conceptualizations are defined as subspaces of the semantic space. Because the subspace represents the "context" of conceptualization, projecting knowledge on to the subspace would result in aggregation of knowledge according to the context. The context-dependent relevance between various items of knowledge would be evaluated in terms of the similarity between all the items of knowledge in the subspace.

5 Conclusions

We introduced the concept of knowledge management based on harnessing collective intelligence on the Web. The Web can be viewed as a field for individual propagation of personal intelligence with users pursuing their own selfish interests. A community aggregates personal intelligence based on its own conceptualization and forms common understandings as collective intelligence. We discussed the resulting impacts on the knowledge life cycle and challenges that must be overcome to create a new paradigm of knowledge management. In addition, we discussed technical issues in implementing knowledge management based on harnessing collective intelligence. These range from Web information searches, knowledge discovery and data mining, to a global infrastructure for knowledge sharing, and aggregation of knowledge based on conceptualization in exploiting collective intelligence.

References

1. O'Reilly, T.: What is web 2.0. In: http://www.oreillynet.com/pub/a/oreilly/tim/news/2005/09/30/what-is-web-20.html. (2005)
2. Surowiecki, J.: The Wisdom Of Crowds. Anchor Books (2005)
3. Tsui, E.: Technologies for personal and peer-to-peer knowledge management. In: http://www.csc.com/aboutus/lef/mds67_off/uploads/P2P_KM.pdf. (2002)
4. Frand, J.L., Hixon, C.: Personal knowledge management: Who, what, why, when, where, how. In: http://www.anderson.ucla.edu/faculty/jason.frand/researcher/speeches/PKM.htm. (1999)
5. Zettsu, K., Tanaka, K.: Referential context mining: Discovering viewpoints from the web. In: Proceedings of the The 2005 IEEE/WIC/ACM International Conference on Web Intelligence (WI'05), Compiegne, France (2005) 321–325
6. Liu, B., Hu, M., Cheng, J.: Opinion observer: analyzing and comparing opinions on the web. In: Proceedings of the 14th International World Wide Web Conference. (2005) 342–351
7. Morinaga, S., Yamanishi, K., Tateishi, K., Fukushima, T.: Mining product reputations on the web. In: Proceedings of the 8th ACM SIGKDD International Conference on Knowledge Discovery and Data Mining. (2002) 341–349
8. Cannataro, M., Talia, D.: The knowlege grid: Designing, building, and implementing an architecture for distributed knowledge discovery. Communications of the ACM **46**(1) (2003)
9. Stuckenschmidt, H., van Harmelen, F.: Information Sharing on the Semantic Web. Springer-Verlag (2005)
10. Kiyoki, Y., Kitagawa, T., Hayama, T.: A metadatabase system for semantic image search by a mathematical model of meaning. ACM SIGMOD Record **23**(4) (1994) 34–41

A Formal Approach to Qualitative Reasoning on Topological Properties of Networks

Andrea Rodríguez[1,3] and Claudio Gutierrez[2,3]

[1] Department of Computer Science, Universidad de Concepción
andrea@udec.cl

[2] Department of Computer Science, Universidad de Chile
cgutierr@dcc.uchile.cl

[3] Center for Web Research, Universidad de Chile

Abstract. Qualitative reasoning uses a limited set of relevant distinctions of the domain to allow a flexible way of representing and reasoning about it. This work presents a conceptual framework for qualitative reasoning about information networks from a spatial-topological point of view. We consider the properties of connectivity and some topological invariants to describe the structural characteristics of and the topological relationships between networks. The paper presents a data model for networks which generalizes the notion of graph, founded in algebraic and topological considerations. Such conceptual tool can be useful in different domains, from social to technological networks.

1 Introduction

Topological properties are related to the concept of *connectivity*, upon which different relations may be defined; for example, *overlapping, inside, disjoint* and *meet.* An important extension beyond the power of traditional query languages for graph and networks is the incorporation of topological relationships into the primitves of query languages. These facts have already been recognized in the spatial domain, where topological relations have played an important role for spatial reasoning [9,1] and query languages [13].

A formal approach to this subject is beneficial for several reasons. The formalism serves as a tool to identify and derive systematically relationships while avoiding redundant and contradicting relations and notions, and helps proving the completeness of the set of relationships. The formal method can be applied to determine the relation between any two networks and to reason formally about them. Algorithms to determine relationships can be specified exactly, and mathematically sound models will help to define formally the relationships. The formalism can extend definitions on networks to more general concepts on networks.

Topological and spatial reasoning is a well established subject dealing with the development of formal models for defining and reasoning about topological characteristics of spatial objects and topological relations [10]. When trying to extend these techniques to sets of overlapping networks the following important issues arise:

S. Staab and V. Svatek (Eds.): EKAW 2006, LNAI 4248, pp. 358–365, 2006.

- The standard notion of graph does not suffice to represent faitfully the information. Note that an edge could be part of a network which does not have both of its end-nodes (e.g. the sub-network of Latin American routes consisting of Chilean cities and LanChile's routes: a flight going out of the country is an edge which has only one node in the sub-network).
- Graphs do not behave like sets of point nor as "point-less objects." Hence from a topological point of view, the approach should be a mixture of point-set topology and point-less topology
- The classic set of operations on graphs must be enriched to be able to express in a flexible manner spatio-topological relations among networks.
- Standard spatial notions cannot be taken as on-the-shelf technology for networks.

This work presents a formal framework for topological reasoning on relationships among network properties, particularly focusing on connectivity aspects. It discusses the level of abstraction needed, that is, what are the "good" objects in this domain, and what are the "good" operations to act over these objects. It presents several operations on them and studies their properties. In addition, it introduces the main approaches used in spatial reasoning for defining topological relations between networks. Such definitions can be applied to broad application domains, such as social networks, technological networks, and conceptual or metadata networks. In particular we:

Related Work. To the best of our knowledge the subject of this paper has not been addressed formally. There is related work on spatial reasoning which is useful in our context, and that we describe below.

In the spatial domain, qualitative reasoning of topological relations has obtained particular attention from the research community, since it allows automatic reasoning based on a cognitively plausible representation of spatial concepts [10]. Most of the work on topological qualitative reasoning define ontologies of spatial entities, where some fundamental concepts are contact, parthood and boundary [4,1,9]. Stell and Worboys [14] present a theory of parthood and boundary that can be connected to different formalisms for topological relations. This formalism represents set of regions as a bi-Heyting algebra [7] and expresses certain important constructors on the regions purely in terms of the operations presented in the algebra. One of the examples they give is the algebra of graphs. We follow some of these ideas when looking for the right data structure for networks and operations over it, but consider a more general notion of graph.

Two well known ontologies for topological spatial relations are the Region Connected Calculus (RCC) [1] and the point-set topological model [9,8]. RCC is a logic-based formalization of topological relations that uses a basic connectivity relation between closed regions. The point-set topological model defines topological relations based on the set intersection of the interior, boundary and exterior of spatial objects. Such formalism uses relation algebra [6] to create an inference mechanism given by the composition of topological relations [11]. Although both models result in the same set of topological relations between spatial regions, they differ in their reasoning capabilities. While reasoning with relation algebras has computational advantages, axiomatic theories are richer in their expressive power.

2 The (abstract) Model

In this section we introduce a general framework to model networks and present the algebraic properties of different categories of objects and their operations. We will use the basic graph terminology as in Diestel's Book [12].

Definition 1 (Semigraph). *Let $U = (V_U, E_U)$ be a graph.*

1. *A* semigraph *over U is a pair (V, E), where $V \subseteq V_U$ and $E \subseteq E_U$.*
2. *A* net *is a semigraph (V, E) such that for each $uv \in E$ it holds that either $u \in V$ or $v \in V$.*

Note that a *graph* (in the classical sense) is a semigraph such that $E \subseteq V \times V$. In what follows, there will be always a *universe* graph $U = (V_U, E_U)$ which will be the "space" on which the objects we deal with live in.

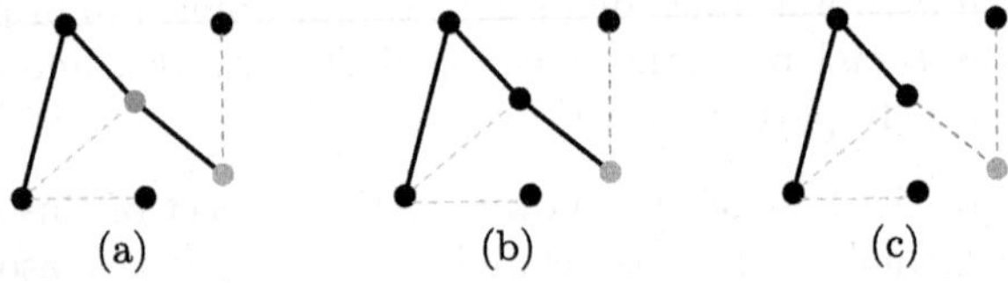

Fig. 1. Basic notions: (a) semigraph, (b) net, and (c) graph. Dark nodes and edges belong to the semigraph, net or graph, respectively.

Notations. Let $V \subseteq V_U$ be a set of nodes, let $E \subseteq E_U$ be a set of edges, and let G be an arbitrary semigraph. We will denote by V_G its set of nodes and by E_G its set of edges.

Use uv to denote the undirected edge $\{u, v\}$. A node v and an edge e are *incident* if $e = vw$ for some w. $\text{inc}(V)$ is the set of edges $\{uv \in E_U : u \in V \vee v \in V\}$. Similarly, $\text{inc}(E)$, is the set of nodes $\{v \in V_U : uv \in E\}$ $sg(V)$ will denote the semigraph $(V, \text{inc}(V))$. Similarly, $sg(E)$ will denote the semigraph $(\text{inc}(E), E)$, and $sg(G)$ will denote the semigraph $(V_G \cup \text{inc}(E), E_G \cup \text{inc}(V))$.

Definition 2 (Basic operations on semigraphs). *Let $G_1 = (V_1, E_1)$ and $G_2 = (V_2, E_2)$ be semigraphs.*

1. *The* union *of G_1 and G_2 (denoted $G_1 \cup G_2$) is the semigraph $(V_1 \cup V_2, E_1 \cup E_2)$.*
2. *The* intersection *of G_1 and G_2 (denoted $G_1 \cap G_2$) is the semigraph $(V_1 \cap V_2, E_1 \cap E_2)$.*
3. *The* difference *of G_1 and G_2 (denoted $G_1 - G_2$) is the semigraph $(V_1 - V_2, E_1 - E_2)$. In particular, the* complement *of G_2, denoted G_2^c, is the semigraph $U - G_2$.*

Using the fact that the product of two Boolean algebras with the operations defined pairwise is again a Boolean algebra we get:

Proposition 1. *The set of* semigraphs *with the operations of union, intersection and complement, together with* 0 *defined as* $(\emptyset, \emptyset)$ *and* $1 = (U, U \times U)$ *is a Boolean algebra.*

The Algebraic Structure of Networks. One can enrich the Boolean Algebra structure of semigraphs described above by defining closure operators over semigraphs, and hence, a structure of Topological space (Kuratowski space).

A closure operator (*cl*) must satisfy some properties for each element of the domain. Two basic properties are $\mathrm{cl}(\emptyset) = \emptyset$ and $G \subseteq \mathrm{cl}(G)$. In addition, by property $\mathrm{cl}(G \cup H) = \mathrm{cl}(G) \cup \mathrm{cl}(H)$, one needs to specify only cl over single nodes and single edges. From the idempotence property ($\mathrm{cl}(\mathrm{cl}(G)) = \mathrm{cl}(G)$) it follows that $\mathrm{cl}(v)$ should add no nodes (or do trivial things like adding nodes independent of v, e.g. the whole universe, all isolated nodes, etc.) Similarly for $\mathrm{cl}(e)$ for an edge e. In fact, the only two natural choices for closure are: (1) $\mathrm{cl}_E(G) = sg(E(G))$, and (2) $\mathrm{cl}_V(G) = sg(V(G))$. But the topologies they generate are not essentially different:

Lemma 1. *Let* T_E *and* T_V *the topologies induced by the closure operators* cl_E *and* cl_V *respectively. Then* G *is open in* T_E *if and only if* G *is closed in* T_2*.*

Heyting Algebras Via Closure Operators. Every topology provides a complete Heyting algebra in the form of its open set lattice. The Heyting algebra is defined as follows: objects are open sets; operations are set-theoretical union and intersection; and the element $A \Rightarrow B$ is the interior of the union of $A^c \cup B$, where A^c denotes the complement of the open set A.

For the operator cl_V the open sets are standard full subgraphs of U (complements of the closed sets in the topology T_V). Here the border (given by the topology) of G is the set of edges in the complement of G which are incident to G. The operator cl_E is the dual of the previous one.

The Heyting Algebra of Nets. Note that the objects defined in the Heyting algebras induced by the open sets of the topological spaces defined above were essentially graphs (or complements of graphs).

It is possible to extend the set of objects to be considered to semigraphs without loose edges (what we have called *nets*) and still having a structure of Heyting algebra by slightly modifying the operations of join and meet. Nets are operationally generated as follows: (1) choose a set of nodes V and (2) choose a set of edges incident to V. The induced operations (in order to be closed in this new universe) are the standard union and the meet $G_1 \wedge G_2$ defined as $(G_1 \cap G_2) \cap sg(V(G_1 \cap G_2))$ (observe that the standard intersection of semigraphs could leave isolated edges).

Proposition 2. *Let* $R(U)$ *be the set of nets over* U*. If we define* $0 = \emptyset$ *(the empty semigraph),* $G_1 \vee G_2$ *as the union,* $G_1 \wedge G_2$ *as defined above, and* $G_1 \Rightarrow G_2$ *as* $sg(V_1^c) \cup G_2$*, then* $(R(U), \vee, \wedge, \Rightarrow, 0)$ *is a Heyting algebra.*

Note that this is not a bi-Heyting algebra because the existence of nets R such that there are edges $uv \notin R$ with $u, v \in R$. Example: let $R = U - \{uv\}$. Then there is no unique minimal solution for $U \leq R \cup X$, because, for example, $X_1 = (\{u\}, uv)$ and $X_2 = (\{v\}, uv)$ are minimal solutions.

Interestingly, the problem described in the previous paragraph is the only barrier to have a bi-Heyting algebra.

Proposition 3. *Let $R^*(U)$ the set of full nets over U (i.e. nets such that the complement has no isolated edges, that is, it is again a net). If we define the same operations as in Proposition 2 and $1 = U$ and $G_1 \setminus G_2$ as $(sg(E_2^c) \cup G_2^c) \wedge G_1$, then $((U), \vee, \wedge, \Rightarrow, \setminus, 1, 0)$ is a bi-Heyting algebra.*

3 Possible Approaches to Define Connectivity in Networks

We examined the structure and operations over networks. In this section we will study the notion of when two objects (semigraphs) in this universe are "connected" or have "relationships".

3.1 A Pure Topological Approach

Although pure topological notions are oriented to capture the concept of *continuity*, several notions from topology can be borrowed to speak of spatial notions [8,9]. We start from these notions, but will be interested in the notions of *connectivity* or *relationship*, and thus some concepts will naturally not be applicable in our context.

Following the approach of Egenhofer [8] we will build the framework on the notions of *boundary* and *interior*. Due to the particularities of our domain, we will add a third notion, that of *frontier*.

Definition 3 (Interior, Frontier, Boundary, Closure). *Let U be the universal graph, and H a semigraph in U.*

1. *The* boundary *of a semigraph H (in U), denoted $\partial(H)$, is the set of edges which are incident to H and its complement, i.e., the set of edges uv of U such that $u \in H$ and $v \notin H$. (Note that edges $uv \notin H$ with $u \in H$ and $v \in H$ are not in the boundary).*
   In particular, we define $\delta(H) = \partial(H) \cap H$ as the real boundary.
2. *The* frontier *of a semigraph H (in U), denoted $\mathrm{fr}(H)$, is the set of nodes of H adjacent to nodes not in H. (Or equivalently: the set of nodes of H incident to $\partial(H)$.)*
   In particular, we define $\mathrm{fr}'(H)$, the real *frontier, as the subset of the nodes of $\mathrm{fr}(H)$ incident to edges not in H.*
3. *The* interior *of a semigraph H (in U), denoted $\mathrm{int}(H)$, is the semigraph consisting of all nodes and edges of H not incident with elements not in H.*
4. *The* closure *of a semigraph H (in U), denoted $\mathrm{cl}(H)$, is the semigraph $H \cup \partial(H)$.*

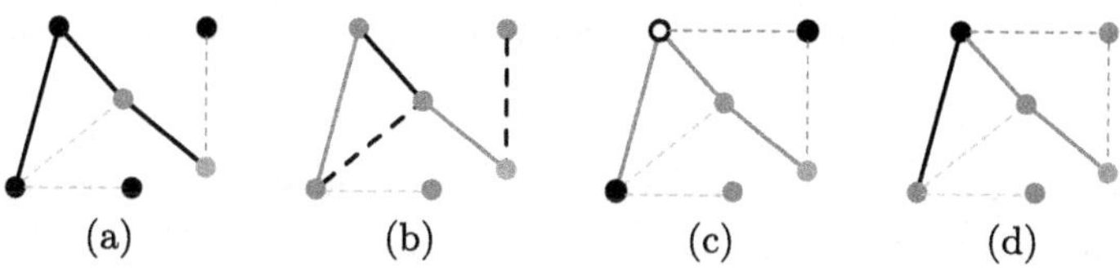

Fig. 2. Basic topological notions. Dark nodes and edges constitute the semigraph. (a) reference semigraph; (b) boundary (continuous dark line is the real boundary); (c) frontier (filled dark nodes form the real frontier); and (d) interior.

Proposition 4 (The boundary ∂)

1. *$\partial(H)$ has no interior.*
2. *$\partial(H) = \mathrm{cl}(H) \cap \mathrm{cl}(G - H)$, i.e. the boundary of H is the intersection of the closure of H and its complement.*
3. *$\partial(H) = \partial(G - H)$, i.e. the boundary of H equals the boundary of its complement.*
4. *$\partial(H) = \emptyset$ iff $H = \emptyset$ or $H = G$.*

Based on these definitions, one can derive topological relations between networks by considering the intersections between their topological invariants (i.e., interior, boundary and frontier), that is, the intersections between the components of networks that do not change under topological transformations (e.g. translation, scaling, and rotation).

Given any two connected nets H_1 and H_2 in U, let $int(H_1)$ and $int(H_2)$ be their interiors, and $D(H_1)$ and $D(H_2)$ be the union of their respective real frontiers with real boundary. Table 1 presents the eight matrices that derive the 10 possible 4-intersection matrices between nets.

3.2 The Region Connected Calculus RCC

RCC is a formalism for spatial reasoning that takes regions of space instead of points of classical geometry as primitives. For this, a primitive notion of connectivity is introduced by means of a binary predicate $C(x, y)$, whose semantics is that of "x is connected to y.""

In the context of networks, the basic primitive is naturally defined as follows:

Definition 4. *$C(x, y)$ is true iff there is a path from x to y in $x \cup y$ (where path is the standard notion in graph theory [12])*

Note that if $x \cap y \neq \emptyset$ then $C(x, y)$, but the notion defined allow $C(x, y)$ to be true even though $x \cap y = \emptyset$.

The RCC definitions (we will use the RCC-8 framework) are axiomatized in standard first-order logic using quantifiers over variables ranging over the objects of the domain (regions in the spatial case) (see Table 2). The axioms for semigraphs concides roughly with the naive intuition in the spatial domain.

Table 1. The basic 2x2 matrices upon which all possible 4-intersections matrices are derivable. Dark nodes and edges belong to one or both nets.

Matrices	Examples	Matrices	Examples
$\begin{array}{l\|cc} & int(H_2) & D(H_2) \\ \hline int(H_1) & 0 & 0 \\ D(H_1) & 0 & 0 \end{array}$	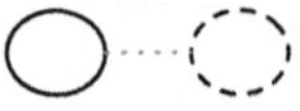	$\begin{array}{l\|cc} & int(H_2) & D(H_2) \\ \hline int(H_1) & 0 & 0 \\ D(H_2) & 0 & 1 \end{array}$	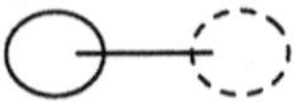
$\begin{array}{l\|cc} & int(H_2) & D(H_2) \\ \hline int(H_1) & 1 & 0 \\ D(H_1) & 0 & 0 \end{array}$		$\begin{array}{l\|cc} & int(H_2) & D(H_2) \\ \hline int(H_1) & 1 & 0 \\ D(H_1) & 0 & 1 \end{array}$	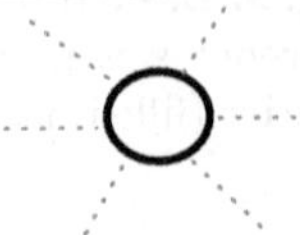
$\begin{array}{l\|cc} & int(H_2) & D(H_2) \\ \hline int(H_1) & 1 & 0 \\ D(H_1) & 1 & 0 \end{array}$		$\begin{array}{l\|cc} & int(H_2) & D(H_2) \\ \hline int(H_1) & 1 & 0 \\ D(H_1) & 1 & 1 \end{array}$	
$\begin{array}{l\|cc} & int(H_2) & D(H_2) \\ \hline int(H_1) & 1 & 1 \\ D(H_1) & 1 & 0 \end{array}$	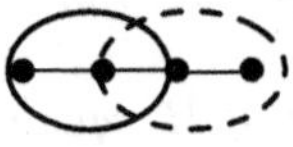	$\begin{array}{l\|cc} & int(H_2) & D(H_2) \\ \hline int(H_1) & 1 & 1 \\ D(H_1) & 1 & 1 \end{array}$	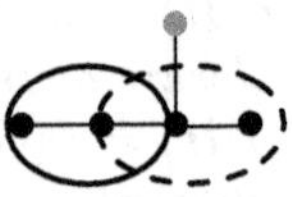

Table 2. RCC-8 definitions depending on the range of the quantification of the variables involved: over semigraphs and over nets. $\text{inc}(x, y)$ means x is incident to y.

Relation	Interpretation	Quantif. over semigraphs
$DC(x, y)$	x is disconnected from y	No path between x and y in $x \cup y$
$P(x, y)$	x is a part of y	$x \subseteq y$
$PP(x, y)$	x is a proper part of y	$x \subset y$
$EQ(x, y)$	x is equivalent with y	$x = y$
$O(x, y)$	x overlaps y	$x \cap y \neq \emptyset$
$DR(x, y)$	x is discrete from y	$x \cap y = \emptyset$
$PO(x, y)$	x partially overlaps y	$x \cap y \neq \emptyset \wedge x \not\subseteq y \wedge y \not\subseteq x$
$EC(x, y)$	x is externally connected to y	$x \cap y = \emptyset \wedge \text{inc}(x, y)$
$TPP(x, y)$	x is a tangential proper part of y	$x \subset y \wedge \text{inc}(x, y^c)$
$NTTP(x, y)$	x is a nontangential proper part of y	$x \subset y \wedge \neg\, \text{inc}(x, y^c)$

The problems are subleties centered on non-existent edges between two nodes of the domain. In this framework it is more evident the insufficiency of graphs as basic data structure for qualitative reasoning. In such case, $C(x, y)$ must be defined as intersection of nodes and the definitions would colapse into standard set theoretical notions among nodes.

4 Conclusions

This work presents a formal framework for qualitative reasoning about topological properties of networks. It studies the structure of sets of overlapping networks from a spatio-topological point of view, defines a data structure and operations associated with networks, and states and proves main properties of them.

For future work, we plan to select a standard set of operations that serves as basic for a query language design and that can relate the abstract model to the approaches for defining the connectivity in networks.

Acknowledgements. This work has been funded by Nucleus Millenium Center for Web Research, Grant P04-067-F, Mideplan, Chile.

References

1. D. A. Randell, Z. Cui, A. G. Cohn, *A Spatial logic based on regions and connection*, Proc. 3rd. Int. Conf. on Knowledge Representation and Reasoning, Morgan Kaufmann, San Mateo, pp. 165-176.
2. A. G. Cohn, B. Bennett, J. Gooday, N. M. Gotts, *Qualitative Spatial Representation and Reasoning with the Region Connection Calculus*, Geoinformatica, 1, 1-44 (1997)
3. J. de Kleer, J. Brown, *A Qualitative Physics Based on Confluences.* Artificial Intelligence 24, 7-83, (1984)
4. B. Smith, *Mereotopology - A Theory of parts and boundaries*, Data and Knowledge Engineering, 20, 287-303 (1996)
5. J. Sharma, D. Fleweling, M. Egenhofer, *A Qualitative Spatial Reasoner*, International Symposum on Spatial Data Handing, pp. 665-681, September 1994.
6. A. Tarski, *On The Calculus of Relations*, Journal of Symbolic Logic, 6(3), 73-89 (1941)
7. S. Vickers, *Topology via Logic*, Cambridge University Press, 1989.
8. M. J. Egenhofer, *A Formal Definition of Binary Topological Relationships*, Lecture Notes in Computer Science, Vol. 367, pp. 457-472, June 1989.
9. M. J. Egenhofer, R. Franzosa *Point-Set Topological Spatial Relations*, International Journal of Geographic Information Science, 5(2), 161-174 (1991)
10. Loiviero Stock *Spatial and Temporal Reasoning*, Kluwer Academic Publishers, 1997.
11. M. J. Egenhofer *Deriving the Composition of Binary Topological Relations*, Journal of Visual Languages and Computing, 5, 133-149 (1994)
12. R. Diestel, *Graph Theory*, Springer, New York, 1997.
13. E. Clementini, J. Sharma, M. Egenhofer, *Modeling Topological Spatial Relations: Strategies for Query Processing*, International Journal of Computer and Graphics, 18 (6),815-822 (1994)
14. J. G. Stell, M. F. Worboys, *The Algebraic Structure of Sets of Regions*, Lecture Notes in Computer Science, Vol. 1329, pp. 163-174, Octuber 1997.

Towards a Knowledge Ecosystem

Piercarlo Slavazza, Roberto Fonti, Massimo Ferraro, Christian Biasuzzi, and Luca Gilardoni

Quinary SpA - Via Pietrasanta 14 – 20141 Milan – Italy
{slp, for, fem, bic, gil}@quinary.com

Abstract. People who belong to an organization own common knowledge that, with time, grows, evolves and is transferred from one person to another. As it happens in an ecosystem, each individual has his own work environment and personal goals, but also interacts with others, using common knowledge and contributing to its improvement.

According to this vision, we have created a knowledge management environment equipped with a set of tools to better support cooperation by working along two main directions: the first one relies on establishing a community driven central repository enhanced with Semantic Web technologies, which allows information to be organized according to its semantic structure by exploiting classification, information extraction, and semantic filtering techniques. The second direction relies on enriching users' everyday work environment – including emails, web browsers, RSS aggregators, and desktops – by providing tools that exploit contextual information, directing more relevant information where it is needed and adding value to the information as it is generated and shared.

The system we describe in this paper on the one hand opens up corporate knowledge even to individuals who are normally unwilling to use a traditional KM system and, on the other hand, makes access much easier to those users who are already willing to share, leading to a healthier knowledge ecosystem which grows through seamless cross fertilization.

1 Introduction

An ecosystem is a set of living creatures considered together with their physical environment. Creatures live and behave on their own and the limited space they share forces the development of complex, mutual, interactions and 'social' behaviours: the ecosystem is healthy when the inhabitants live and evolve with mutual benefit.

The ecosystem metaphor could be applied to an organization producing knowledge. People working in such an environment, "knowledge workers" as they are normally known [1], usually belong to different subgroups, are involved in different projects, have different personal goals, interests and ambitions. Such a system succeed when it evolves at a steady pace; that is to say when individuals collaborate together in order to produce new knowledge, each benefiting from and building on the things other people have built before. The system, in the opposite, fails when at a given time the needed knowledge is not easily accessible – because is not shared as it

S. Staab and V. Svatek (Eds.): EKAW 2006, LNAI 4248, pp. 366–380, 2006.

is hidden in the local employees' hard drives – it is lost because of rapid turnovers in the staff or finally it is duplicated because of loose interaction between employees and poor sharing support.

Traditional KM systems generally help organizations by maintaining common repositories where information (often unstructured) is collected and shared. A major problem however is that they offer very weak and often cumbersome means for connecting together documents, metadata, users and the context around information, making hard to add on one side and to reuse on the other. Moreover they often miss what we could call an effective "desktop presence", that is a tight integration with the desktop tools the user is familiar with: the browser, the email client, the RSS aggregator, etc. We believe that a successful KM system should be proactive in its support to the user, pushing relevant information where it is needed and capturing context around information directly from final user tools, on one side reducing the burden of learning a new tool and of switching to it, and on the other exploiting information that can be gathered through the interaction.

K@, the knowledge management system we present in this paper, addresses this problems by firstly relying on Semantic Web technologies that act as a glue where documents, metadata and users can be "reified" in unique resources, suitable to be organized according to several means – such as ontologies, taxonomies and community filters. Furthermore, it features tools that support the ecosystem by working in the user environment. The tools feed users with knowledge from the shared repository without the need to ask for it: they receive annotated emails in their inbox that the system has processed and enriched with contextual knowledge (see later on: Semantic Email); they can search both the Intranet and the Internet from the standard Google page and are notified about related material already in the shared repository while browsing the Internet (see section 4). The system collects as much information as possible from the context when users decide to share some information: they can forward an email with attachments to the shared repository; they can use a bookmarklet to post URLs; they can drag and drop documents from the desktop to a shared folder.

Each of these tools is targeted at a particular environment but, altogether, they are part of the knowledge ecosystem and contribute to a simple and effective knowledge flow between individuals, with the net result that the whole community is continuously involved in the knowledge life cycle thus supporting the steady growth of the ecosystem.

K@: An Evolutionary Knowledge Sharing Environment

K@ is a web based collaborative platform for knowledge management, developed by Quinary since 2002, supporting users in managing a document base and the processes around it. With K@ users can access and share a common repository of documents while the system keeps track of people interaction. Documents, including both physical documents residing inside the organisation, external URLs, notes and Wiki pages, may be organized according to one or more taxonomies, supporting multiple inheritance (DAGs): the environment provides a basic framework for sharing information by matching the way an organization is structuring its processes. The core system supports browsing and searching using free text queries and provides a number of tools to track user behaviour (who added a document or a node in a taxonomy, who added classification links between nodes and taxonomies, who visited nodes or read documents) to facilitate sharing and keeping track of workgroup activities. K@ exist both as a generic environment for knowledge sharing and as a part of a vertical solution tailored for the legal domain called LKMS/Mnemosyne ([5],[6]).

K@ has been designed since the beginning with the aim of supporting a better way to maintain a richer knowledge structure. In 2004 we added a semantic layer, being able to support the association between documents and semantic annotations with respect to a formal ontology, according to Semantic Web standards, and we are currently enhancing the system with the features described in this paper.

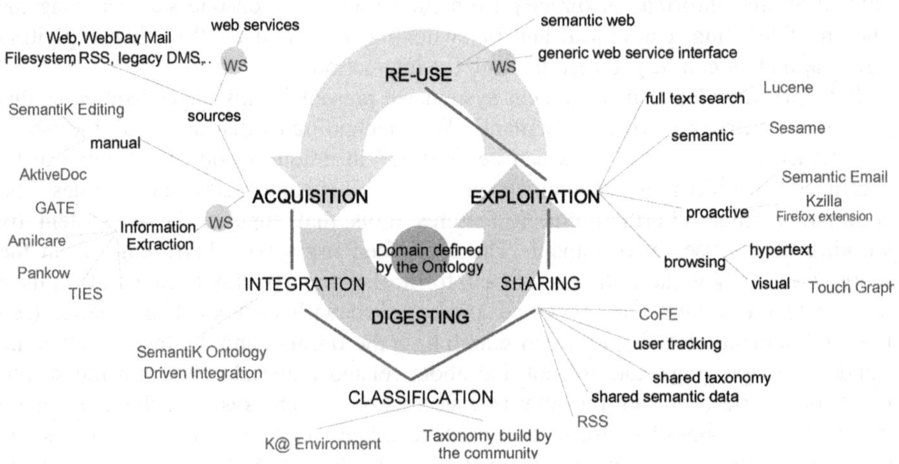

Fig. 1. The knowledge flow: acquisition, sharing and reuse

K@ covers all the aspects of the knowledge flow with the primary goal of enhancing knowledge reuse.

The first step, acquisition, can be fulfilled both by users and by autonomous agents: it concerns insertion of documents from different sources and their annotation, possibly aided by information extraction systems (some of them are listed in Fig. 1). We will talk about knowledge acquisition tools in section 2.

The second step, described in the lower part of the Figure, aims at digesting the collected information, transforming it from unstructured data to an organized network of shared resources. The composition of ontology, taxonomy and user tracking is the formula used for reaching this goal. It will be the subject of section 3.

Finally, K@ features tools for exploiting knowledge, not only through browsing and searching, but also in a proactive way, where meaningful information are pushed to the users in their work environment. These tools best help in figuring out the knowledge ecosystem and are the topic of section 4.

2 Contextual Knowledge Acquisition

Traditional KM systems are focused on handling common repositories of documents and on integrating with simple workshare tools aiming at managing processes from a procedural point of view, such as workflows. Just providing means to copy documents from a large number of sources to a shared repository is far from being a perfect knowledge acquisition solution. Knowledge codified in documents text is only half of the whole and definitely the easier to acquire. Most relevant information is given by the context in which documents and other material have been collected. Moreover, when dealing with enterprise knowledge management you have to focus on two aspects: the first is "internal knowledge", created by individuals who are part of the organization; the second is "external knowledge", that enters the organization in the form of emails, web URLs, etc.. Retaining both is equally important: when users produce contents or deal with external material, K@ tools are directly available in the usual working environment to facilitate acquisition and sharing by exploiting contextual information.

The most general tool to add information to the system enables users to insert into the shared repository documents along with a set of metadata. A wide number of documents types are handled, not only texts but also semi-structured documents (such as spreadsheets or html pages), and multimedia content as well[1]. This can be done through a web based interface, where the inserting user has full control on metadata that can be added, through a webDAV based one, or through custom interfaces built upon K@ web services. When using the generic form based web interface all contextual information must be either derived from document content through IE techniques or has to be provided directly by the user.

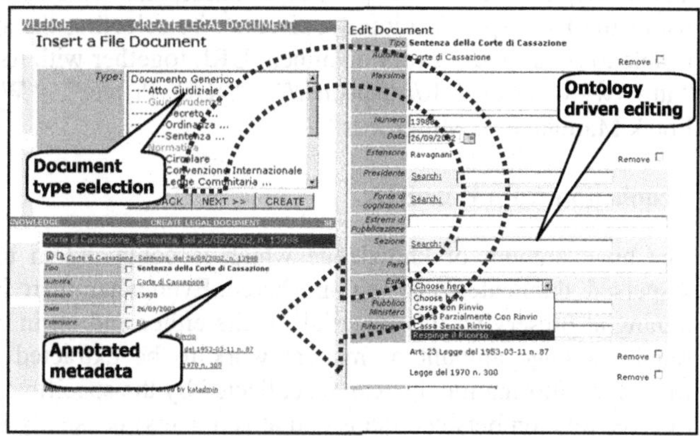

This data entry system allows for defining a set of domain dependent metadata (annotations): the forms are dynamically created based upon the kind of document (such as, for example, a technical report rather than a conference paper or a legal document), and meta-data values are "reified" and shared among other annotations (see next section for more details).

A great attention has been paid to guarantee a smooth user experience. While the annotation process is driven by ontologies to guarantee soundness and consistency, ontology management complexity is hidden to the end user through conventional form wizards. Ontology support is also exploited to guide user input, minimizing the need to specify implicit information and driving possible text analysis functionalities, as described in [5].

---

[1] Automatic techniques for extracting knowledge from documents other than textual ones are envisaged and will be studied within the X-Media project (http://www.x-media-project.org/).

Built upon these core features, a number of specialised mechanisms have been developed to exploit information that may be derived from the context given by usage of normal working tools.

Acquisition While Browsing

A huge amount of information is currently available either on the web or intranets. The best way to gather such information is obviously by collecting URLs during Internet browsing and by exploiting contextual information to enrich collected data. The browser itself can provide part of the information – the URL itself as well as page metadata, while part can be extracted from the browsing process – e.g. where a URL is mentioned. Simple tools working in the browser enable a smooth collection of this context.

The first technique is based on bookmarklet, a JavaScript technique portable on all browsers that allows exploiting information on the URL being browsed. We used the technique to read metadata information in the web page, if present in standard META tag (language, description and keyword) and to use it, together with URL and title, to pre-fill the web-based form mentioned above. The URL information is also used there to show related material easing classification.

A second technique relies on a Firefox extension (Linky: http://linky.mozdev.org/) that adds a contextual menu to handle links in a web page (*href* and *src*): it lets you open or download a set of links selected in a web page. We have modified Linky to post selected URLs to K@ via web services: K-Linky, as we named the extension, is able to handle some basic HTML structures such as lists, in such a way that also titles and descriptions are extracted. For example, the W3C RDF homepage contains the list of the RDF specification documents[2]: by selecting the surrounding text, K-Linky is able to send to K@ every document URL together with its title and description, e.g. "http://www.w3.org/TR/rdf-primer/", "RDF Primer", "W3C Recommendation – Frank Manola, Eric Miller, eds.".

Acquisition from E-mail

The huge amount of knowledge which is contained in mail archives is currently dispersed, duplicated, and seldom shared. Even when there is an organization strategy aiming at preserving this material[3], mails either end up in unmanageable archives or require a huge amount of manual work to be extracted and saved appropriately. Moreover information that can be collected by the specific context (senders, receivers, threads, relation between mails and attachments) is usually lost or hardly recoverable. Our approach here simply relies on enabling users to add K@ among the mail recipients – or to forward relevant mail to K@.

Meta information is extracted from emails: sender and recipients information is used in order to find out which people are involved in the email (using matching techniques described in details in the following sections). Attachments are treated as first class objects, they are inserted in K@ and the relation with the originating email

---

[2] http://www.w3.org/RDF/#specs

[3] This is becoming frequent but mostly to cope with regulatory constraints such as those coming from Sarbannes-Oaxley or security constraints to filter illegal mails, hence targeting very specific aspects and not coping at all with sharing issues.

is kept through metadata. Moreover, it is tracked if the message is a reply to another message previously acquired in K@. Mail content can be analysed by applying Information Extraction, as for any other document.

Acquisition from Syndicated Content

K@ can work as a shared RSS aggregator: a number of feeds can be monitored and news imported in the repository together with the associated metadata (source, author, title, description and link) and classified in a given node.

Once in K@, the news will be shared among the whole community (or possibly the one interested in the related topic), which will be able to further enrich their metadata through a more domain-oriented perspective (via the tools described in the following sections).

This way K@ allows a given community not only to be always up-to-date with regard to some syndicated content, but also to relate the most relevant one to its corporate context.

Even if RSS feeds have reached a very extensive use, there could still be a large number of Web sources of interest which doesn't yet provide them; in most cases, the HTML tags convey semantic information (such as in table tags or very often in CSS classes), hence the relevant information can be efficiently extracted from web pages by means of web scraping techniques, possibly xpath based (as proven as well by the Microformats [9] effort). Hence, K@ – by integrating the Curiosity xpath based web scraper [3] – supports acquisition of knowledge both through generic web scraping, and from Microformats scraping, possibly benefiting of their existing semantic structure by means of the Knowledge Integration layer mentioned later.

3 Knowledge Digesting

The K@ system aims at supporting a knowledge ecosystem where users and an open set of service-based autonomous agents interact in order to create a net of relations between documents, their parts and metadata derived from content, and the context inferred from user communities. We refer to this process as the "knowledge digesting" process.

As stated in section 1, such task is envisaged as a process where there is a shared repository, but it doesn't exist the figure of a "knowledge administrator", which would drive and somehow coordinate the process of making sense. We think that such a role cannot easily face both the speed the knowledge practices of the community change, and the way each singular user can perceive the organization of the shared knowledge.

The fitness of this strongly collaborative perspective has been confirmed by the current trends about social environments, as also proven by online collaborative services such as del.cio.us or wikipedia.

Hence, in the K@ environment, the community has a total control over the knowledge management process; as it happens in an ecosystem cycle, users (including automated agents, like e.g. information extraction agents) feed the others with knowledge produced in annotating documents, in categorizing information, in organizing it accordingly to their needs and even in revising or correcting others' annotations.

Anatomy: The Knowledge Structure

K@ aims at being adaptable to every domain an organization is interested in; hence, given such a domain, K@ can be deployed with a custom set of metadata that can properly and deeply describe it, and used for annotating material. In the legal domain, we could have metadata speaking of laws, judges, courts, etc.; in the computer science domain, we could have metadata about technologies, publications, conferences, authors, etc.

In K@, metadata are described by means of formal ontologies, and they are managed using Semantic Web technologies, as described in more detail in [5]. By using ontologies, metadata can be defined as string values (e.g. a document title) or as resources uniquely identified and re-usable in other annotations (e.g. a document author). Furthermore, this ontological methodology also allows for inter-linking metadata resources – in order to eventually produce graphs of resources. A great effort has been spent in putting in place functionalities aimed at preserving uniqueness of metadata (through a knowledge integration layer) and at making search of existing resources effective (through an ontology-driven search engine): this way, each user can contribute at expanding this net of relations which involves documents and ontological resources, by re-using annotations made by other users, and revising or enriching them.

This knowledge framework allows users exactly to act as in an ecosystem where each action (in the form of knowledge production and/or transformation) is taken on the basis of other existing knowledge, during a process that eventually leads to an effective community perspective.

Users can be greatly aided in the annotation task by autonomous agents. K@ provides a Service Oriented Architecture through which agents can offer their services. Such agents can do for example Information Extraction (and Relation Extraction) from documents. Moreover, we may also have agents able at finding out new links between resources, by querying for instance external services starting from possibly incomplete knowledge[4].

In general, for each annotation added to K@, its provenance is tracked, that is, the user or the agent who stated it, and its support, in terms of external references or evidence from the original text as determined by IE agents[5]. So, it is always possible to weight the knowledge present in K@ by looking at its "authoring/annotation context": the nature of the agent that stated the assertion (is it a human? an autonomous software agent?), its trust (is she a domain expert?) and the trust of the motivating source (is it a reliable or anyway popular source – in K@ or Internet?).

A different point of view in trying to derive semantics from data is provided by statistical text analysis. K@ integrates a module responsible for extracting keywords from documents by computing most relevant terms on the basis of the classical information retrieval formula *tfidf* [14]. Similarly, for every node keywords are

[4] As examples of such services, we can cite the integration of the Google-based ontology population service Pankow [2], and the development of a service harvesting legal information from the Italian NormeInRete public database (http://www.normeinrete.it).

[5] Currently the system provides just basic support to provenance facilities (e.g. limited in granularity), while research of full-fledged solutions is part of the objectives of the X-Media project.

calculated by aggregating terms of all documents contained. Such keywords could provide a brief description of node contents, as in the following example:

```
Node: Machine Learning (144 documents), top terms : learning,
semantic, ontology, extraction, knowledge, uima, information, web,
text, machine, corpus, data, classification, mining, proceedings
```

Digesting: Imposing the Community Perspective

The information anatomy definition and extraction (as defined in the previous section) constitute a fundamental tool for defining the knowledge structure because, starting from documents, they identify resources (as metadata) and ontological links between them. Anyway, the generated network could be too wide or sparse in order to satisfy the knowledge needs for a particular user at a particular time, and further filters could be useful. Digesting such knowledge and superimposing a community perspective is an important process because it allows for defining context of interests, permitting on one side to focus and on the other to bring to the user new unknown information – even as a serendipity effect.

Defining, discovering and highlighting relations should be therefore intended as the step that follows the definition of the knowledge anatomy in the process of structuring raw knowledge. In K@, users are given a number of tools – described in the next paragraphs – for grouping documents and possibly resources following a variety of rationales, by taking into account the knowledge anatomy but also the community links.

Taxonomies

In K@ taxonomy nodes are mainly used for (multi)classification purposes: users can file documents under whatever nodes they want, and they can also revise classification made by others or add more classification links.

Taxonomy nodes and classification links aren't given a fixed semantics – such as *is-a* or *part-of* relations: in the case of documents classified in a node, it is just implied an unqualified correlation between the documents with respect to the "topic" represented by the node. In case of nodes hierarchy it is implied an unqualified relation of subordination/inclusion between their topics.

As time passes, market trends and techonology push will likely modify the topics "topography" in the community feelings: hence, in order to promptly cope with such a steady evolution, the hierarchy in the K@ taxonomy can be easily revised by each user by means of proper tools – such as a "clipboard" for moving around documents and nodes.

Virtual Nodes

In organizing the knowledge by means of taxonomies, users are guided by a number of rationales which cannot often be easily formalized. That's why, as explained in the previous section, K@ allows for that great degree of freedom in taxonomy handling and encourages collaboration very strongly. In fact, the digesting process usually follows a path of abstractions which eventually produces mental structures whose semantics can be only loosely captured by formal tools.

K@ features a number of Knowledge Retrieval tools (see section 4 for more details) embracing full text search and filters acting on taxonomy nodes, ontological resources and knowledge agents.

These tools altogether allow the user to define a range of search criteria so wide that they can be used in order to formally define even complex classes of documents and resources (as, for example, the class of popular authors writing articles published by O'Reilly that contain the word "Java" and that are classified in the node "SOA"); so, K@ allows for saving searches as Virtual Nodes, that means associating a search criteria with a taxonomy node in such a way that links are automatically computed between that node and all the documents satisfying the criteria. Virtual Nodes add a layer of knowledge abstraction because they may act over knowledge, which had been already consumed by the community, by (partially) defining its anatomy and taxonomy relations.

Collaborative Filtering

In K@ all kind of user activities are tracked: documents and metadata editing, browsing between documents, taxonomy and ontological resources, taxonomy editing and searches. This intensive user profiling allows for pursuing the identification of communities, which may be exploited for both off line social analysis, driving to better understanding of the organisation, and to enhance the proactivity of the system. The interaction graph of K@ users may be exported for analysis with system such as UCInet [17], in order to perform, for example, subgroup identification analysis.

Moreover, tracking data are used to augment the proactivity of the system and to support focused browsing and searching in a number of ways, ranging from simple hooks to similar queries when searching, to suggestions for further possible relevant information when browsing. About this latter matter we are currently experimenting Collaborative Filtering (by means of the CoFE engine [7]); however, unlike traditional recommendation systems, we do not exploit explicit ratings, but rather we infer them from the tracked user behaviour – by weighting, for example, how many times the user has viewed a document or a taxonomy node. This would, once again, minimize the burden imposed on the users by exploiting knowledge seamlessly gathered by the community interactions

4 Knowledge Exploitation and Reuse

As discussed in previous section, knowledge within the system may be exploited to explore content along four different dimensions:

- Taxonomies: representing the community perspective;
- Ontology: exploiting relations defined in the domain ontology;
- Users: exploring users interactions with the system (e.g. the last documents inserted/viewed, etc.);
- Keywords: derived from statistical text analysis as described in section 3.

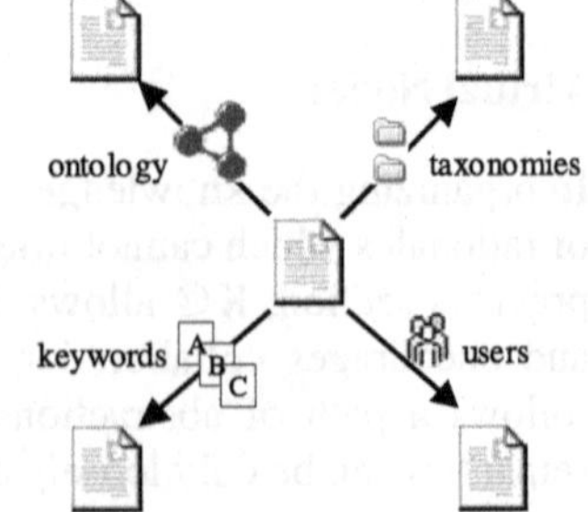

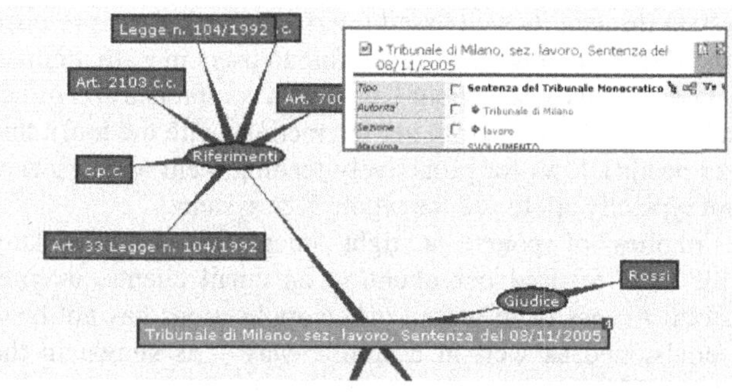

Fig. 2. Metadata resources visual browsing

Exploitation may take place in different ways depending on the tools used. Accessing the sharing environment through a web browser (or through mobile devices via WML pages and WAP) is the most flexible and powerful way to use K@ and explore content. We paid particular attention to usability issues – both in terms of the clicks needed to perform the most common tasks, browsing, searching and editing in particular, and in terms of tailoring presentations depending on user's habits. Taxonomies and ontologies, for example, may be explored using either folder and files metaphors or advanced visual tools such as the one presented in Fig. 2.

K@ provides a full text search engine, based on Apache Lucene, extended to support indexing of the most common document formats. Search results can be progressively refined by filtering on keywords, nodes, semantic properties and users interaction.

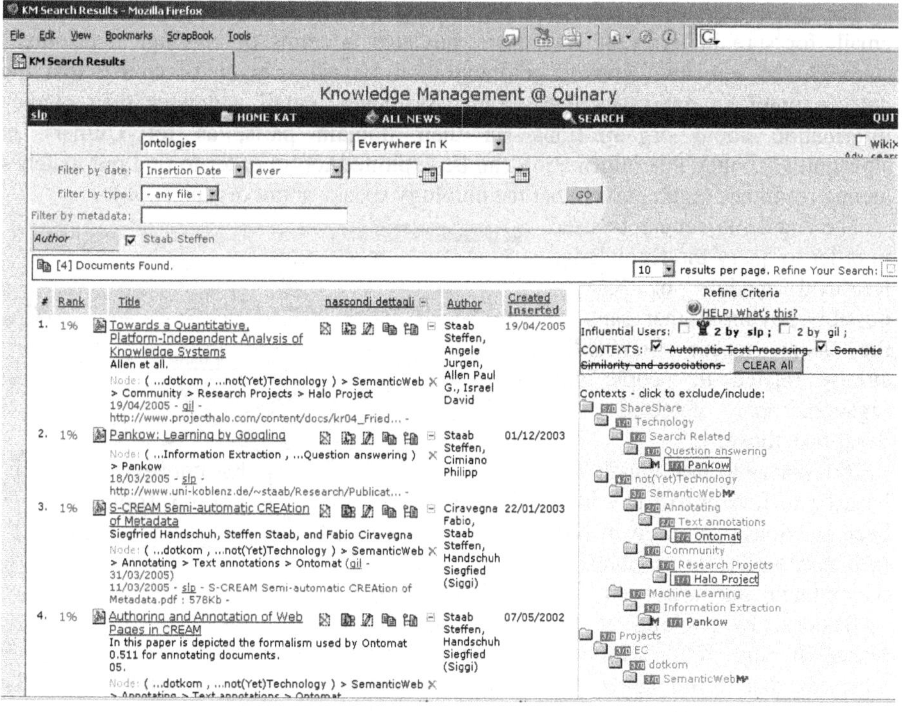

Besides accessing the system through its web based interface, the desktop presence is a key feature in making the acquired knowledge accessible to users in a streamlined way. In fact, desktop tools observing user behaviour can have a comprehension of her working context at a particular time (inferred from her interactions with the tool); this immediate awareness of user needs allows for proactively feeding them with relevant knowledge, even to users not typically apt to use the whole K@ system.

The desktop presence implies of course a tight integration with desktop applications; up to now, we have focused our attention on email clients, internet browsers and RSS aggregators. Access from within office applications has not been yet attempted but can be envisioned as well in a similar way – as shown in the OntoOffice tool from Ontoprise [10].

Semantic Email

In section "Acquisition from e-mail" we showed how emails can be acquired in K@; nonetheless, we think the user should be supported as well when she accesses the corporate mailbox by using her own email client, by adding to the email semantics coming from K@ knowledge base.

Emails are poorly semantically annotated, as only a few data are present therein in a structured form: just the email addresses of the sender and the recipients, the email subject, possibly references to past emails. So, the aim is trying to find out the anatomy of this information and consequently discover the knowledge, which could be relevant in the email context – with respect to the user profile as well.

The email addresses can be used for finding out which people are involved in the email: for sure in terms of K@ users, but also in terms of ontological resources (through the semantic Knowledge Integration Layer) – given of course that the domain ontology envisages these roles. Moreover, email addresses may convey information about organizations (in their domain parts, as for Quinary in slp@quinary.com): this information can be exploited too in order to find out matches among resources (again, given that the ontology speaks about organization).

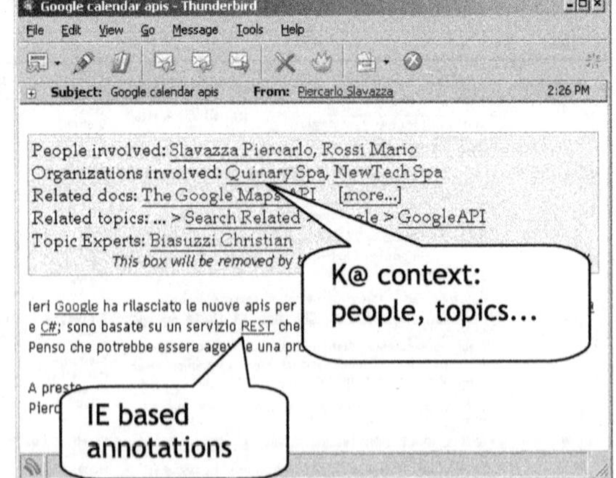

The email subject can be used in order to query the Knowledge Retrieval module of K@ – possibly giving higher rank to the most recent knowledge strictly related to people and organizations detected as described above.

References to past emails can be used to find out if they have been previously inserted in K@ (see section 0), or if some of their attachments have been.

Besides, by looking at the places in the K@ taxonomy where the discovered related documents have been classified, it is possible to infer the topics the email could be about, and consequently the K@ users who are expert of those topics and could therefore assist the user in handling the email and the process it may belong to.

Finally, the Information Extraction agents can be (depending on the domain) applied as well to the email content and possibly to the email subject, contributing to further enriching the email K@ context.

All the gathered knowledge – made of documents, taxonomy nodes, resources and K@ users, together with their relations – is related to the user profile, as it has been inferred from her past interaction with the K@ environment, and is filtered on the basis of the topics the user is interested in and of the people the user is likely to trust.

In K@, this process of email context deduction, is made at the mail server level by means of a mail server proxy: the user emails are fetched from her corporate mailbox, their context is derived as described above, and the most relevant knowledge (likely just a few but significant cues) is prepended in the email body to its original content – see figure above. Then, the user could access a more detailed perspective by means of hyperlinks in the mail body; moreover, if some knowledge has been produced by Information Extraction agents, hyperlinks could have been inserted in the original mail content itself.

Browser Semantic Enhancement: Kzilla

In most cases, it's a matter of fact that a user in search of knowledge opens her Internet browser and tries some searches in Google; and actually that process often works well, but it always misses the community perspective on the results produced. Such perspective would help the user in improving her insight and understanding about the relevance of the Google search results, in particular with respect to the judgment and the needs of the corporate community she belongs to.

We developed an extension for the Firefox browser[6], Kzilla, which observes the user interaction with Google, and enrich the search results page in two ways: firstly by highlighting results already in K@ with a flag put aside the result (informing the user that the document has been judged important by the community and signalling her that other related and relevant data has been already digested by some other people) and secondly by attaching to the Google page the results obtained by querying K@ with the same Google criteria (see Fig. 3); the K@ results could greatly augment the value of the search outcome, because K@ – as explained in section 0 – could not only contain Internet documents, but also corporate documents.

Kzilla assists users also while browsing the Internet in general. In fact, for every loaded page, it checks its presence in K@ and again notify the user; in addition, it features a sidebar where the results of a K@ search using as keywords the page title, are shown together with a list of K@ documents belonging to the same Internet domain of the current page.

With similar purpose, we have integrated Magpie [4], a browser add-on that uses an ontology infrastructure to semantically mark-up web documents on-the-fly – deriving automatically references for concepts from our ontology: the tool supports the user in making sense of browsed pages on the web against internal knowledge, highlighting references to annotated material.

---

[6] We decided to focus our work on Firefox for a number of reasons: it is lightweight, open-source, cross platform and easily extensible. Besides, it is rapidly gaining popularity among users.

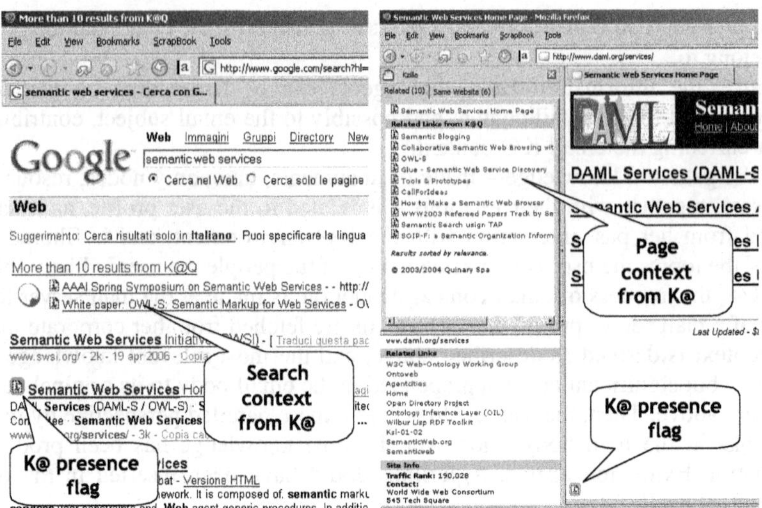

Fig. 3. Kzilla enriched context in Google search and in page browsing

Syndication

K@ establish its notification system on a number of flexible and powerful RSS feeds, allowing users to stay in touch with news about a specific domain of interest using their favourite RSS aggregator. Feeds can be defined on a taxonomy node or a combination of nodes.

Besides, an RSS feed is also provided for each virtual node. RSS feeds can also provide information about extracted keywords. This feature is particularly useful for being alerted of emerging trends on a particular subject with minimum involvement.

5 Related Work

Several KM tools aim at giving users a unified access to their own corpora of knowledge, for organization, navigation, and search; in the Semantic Desktop area, among the most prominent, we can cite Haystack [12] and Gnowsis [13]: both of them allow for integrating emails, bookmarks, files (possibly with their metadata), RDF repositories. These tools can provide access both through a web application and through desktop clients. Both however features a custom rich client interface not easily acceptable by end users.

Piggybank [8] is a Firefox extension which allows for accessing the structured information possibly associated (through custom web scraping or RDF annotations) to the web pages visited by the user; moreover, it allows for pushing this knowledge both in a private repository and in a shared one, where data can be further edited and tags assigned. While it pushes the collaborative and distributed aspect, it currently focuses only on web material.

There are a number of wikis which have been enhanced with semantic annotation capabilities: among the most prominent, Semantic Mediawiki [15] and Platypus [16].

Ontoprise has delivered several tools based on Semantic Web technologies targeting knowledge retrieval, recommender systems and knowledge integration: SemanticMiner, SemanticGuide and SemanticIntegrator [11].

Our semantic email model shares some insights with Zoë [18], an email server featuring email searching and browsing through a web application, where each email is presented together with its overall context (attachments, contributors, organizations…), which is in turn browsable through hyperlinks.

Altogether, the cited tools shares with K@ the aim of organizing knowledge by leveraging enriched contexts in (possibly) collaborative environments, by providing both desktop and web utilities, and by (possibly) relying on Semantic Web technologies for knowledge representation and integration. However, we think that none of them succeeds in fully satisfying all the knowledge needs of a user: in fact, individually, they miss the desktop or, on the contrary, the community, and they lack support for true multimodal interaction with the system.

6 Conclusions and Future Work

In this paper we presented a KM system provided with tools able to organize knowledge in a rich and structured way and to be proactive in supporting the user during her everyday work. We have shown how, using mainly Semantic Web technologies, these tools can connect documents, metadata and users, creating a community driven repository structured along several directions: taxonomies, ontologies, communities, keywords. We have described tools able to act in the user environment, providing her with appropriate and important data, helping her to share knowledge, capturing the context around the information.

As in a knowledge ecosystem, users are able to pursue their own goals, while at the same time exploiting and helping to produce the common knowledge. This knowledge is analyzed, organized and shared to be used in an effective way, making the ecosystem healthy.

Most of these tools are already in the industrial stage, and are included in a commercial solution deployed. Some other tools, namely the ones related to semantic-email browsing, collaborative filtering and virtual nodes machinery, are currently in the research and development pipeline, with experimental installations only.

Future work will bring us to complete and evaluate the solutions developed so far and to possibly experiment new Semantic Web and KM techniques, e.g. by supporting the ontology lifecycle and moving to larger scale semantic annotations, supporting different media.

Acknowledgements

Part of the R&D activities behind the work reported has been carried out within the IST-Dot.Kom project (http://www.dot-kom.org), sponsored by the European Commission as part of the framework V, (grant IST-2001-34038), and currently it is partly funded by the X-Media project (http://www.x-media-project.org/) sponsored by the European Commission as part of the Information Society Technologies (IST) programme under EC grant number IST-FP6-026978. Many of the improvements to the user interface have been possible through experience gained with our customers, and, notably, with Toffoletto and Soci (http://www.toffoletto.it/).

References

1. Drucker, P. (1988) The Coming of the New Organization. Harvard Business Review,
2. Cimiano, P., S. Staab. Learning by Googling. SIGKDD Explorations 6 (2): 24-34. December 2004.
3. Curiosity: an xpath based web scraper and push platform. http://www.go-curiosity.com/
4. Dzbor M., J.B. Domingue, E. Motta. Magpie – towards a semantic web browser. Proceeding of the 2nd Intl. Semantic Web Conf., October 2003, Florida US
5. Gilardoni L., C. Biasuzzi, M. Ferraro, R. Fonti, P. Slavazza. LKMS – A Legal Knowledge Management System Exploiting Semantic Web Technologies. Proc. of the 4th International Semantic Web Conference, Galway, Ireland, November 6-10, 2005 (ISWC 2005)
6. Mnemosyne : Legal Knowledge Management System. http://mnemosyne.quinary.com/EN-en/index.html
7. Herlocker, J., J. Konstan, A. Borchers, J. Riedl. An Algorithmic Framework for Performing Collaborative Filtering. Proceedings of the 1999 Conference on Research and Development in Information Retrieval. Aug. 1999
8. Huynh D., S. Mazzocchi, D. Karger. Piggy Bank: Experience the Semantic Web Inside Your Web Browser, LNCS, Volume 3729, Oct 2005, Pages 413 – 430
9. Microformats data formats: http://microformats.org/
10. Ontoprise GmbH. OntoOffice Tutorial. http://www.ontoprise.de/documents/tutorial_ ontooffice.pdf, 2003.
11. Ontoprise products suite: http://www.ontoprise.de/content/e1171/index_eng.html
12. Quan D., D. Huynh, and D. R. Karger. Haystack: A Platform for Authoring End User Semantic Web Applications, ISWC 2003
13. Sauermann L., S. Schwarz. Introducing the Gnowsis Semantic Desktop. In Poster track at the International Semantic Web Conference ISWC 2004
14. Sebastiani F. Machine learning in automated text categorization, ACM Computing Surveys, 34(1), 147, (2002).
15. Semantic Mediawiki. http://meta.wikimedia.org/wiki/Semantic_MediaWiki
16. Tazzoli, R., et al.: Towards a Semantic Wiki Wiki Web. ISWC 2004
17. UCINET, Social Network Analysis Software: http://www.analytictech.com/ucinet.htm
18. Zoë: Intertwingling Your Email. http://zoe.nu/

A Tool for Management and Reuse of Software Design Knowledge

Paulo Gomes and André Leitão

AILab, Centro de Informática e Sistemas da Universidade de Coimbra
pgomes@dei.uc.pt, aleitao@student.dei.uc.pt

Abstract. As software systems become bigger and more complex, researchers try to find ways to increase development productivity and efficiency. Knowledge generated during the software development process can be a valuable asset for a software company. But in order to take advantage of this knowledge, the company must store it for reuse. This can be achieved through the use of knowledge management tools integrated in CASE tools. This paper provides an overview of a system integrated in a CASE tool that manages and reuses software design knowledge. We describe how knowledge is stored and reused based on a Case-Based Reasoning approach. This tool aids the software designer in new ways: searching the design repository, suggesting designs, learning new knowledge from the user interaction, and other capabilities. We show the innovative aspects of our system.

1 Introduction

Knowledge generated in the software development process is in general not stored and consequently can not be reused later in other projects. The reuse of software development knowledge can improve productivity and the quality of software systems [1-5]. Another advantage of storing and reusing this kind of knowledge is that it minimizes the loss of know-how when a member of the development team leaves the company. Storage, management and reuse of software development knowledge enables also the sharing of know-how among development teams and across different projects.

Software development has several phases [6]: analysis, design, implementation, testing and integration. From these phases, we focus in the design phase, during which the structure and behavior of the system is specified. Design is a complex an ill-defined task [7], making it hard to model and automate the process. Software engineers reuse knowledge generated during the design phase in other projects that they are working on. We are interested in studying the management of design knowledge in a software development company, involving several software designers.

Most of the decisions concerning software design are made using the designers' experience. The more experience a designer has, the better s/he can perform its job. Reasoning based on experience is a basic mechanism for designers, enabling them to reuse previous design solutions in well known problems or even in new projects. In

S. Staab and V. Svatek (Eds.): EKAW 2006, LNAI 4248, pp. 381 – 388, 2006.

artificial intelligence there is a sub area called Case-Based Reasoning (CBR, see [8, 9]) that uses experiences, in the form of cases, to perform reasoning. Case-Based Reasoning (CBR) can be viewed as a methodology for developing knowledge-based systems that uses experience for reasoning about problems [10]. The main idea of CBR is to reuse past experiences to solve new situations or problems. A *case* is a central concept in CBR, and it represents a chunk of experience in a format that can be reused by a CBR system. Usually a case comprises three main parts: problem, solution, and outcome [9]. Another important part of the CBR methodology is the *case library*. It stores all the cases organized using indexing schemes. Due to the high number of cases that the library can have, most of the CBR systems use indexing structures that enable fast retrieval of relevant cases from memory. At an abstract level CBR can be described by a reasoning cycle [8] that starts with the problem description, which is then transformed into a target case (or query case). Using the target case, the first phase in the CBR cycle is to retrieve from the case library the cases that are relevant for the target case. The reuse phase (also designated as adaptation phase) adapts the retrieved case to the target case, yielding a solved case (or new case). The next step for a CBR system is to revise the new case, returning a tested and repaired case. Finally, the retain phase learns the solved case by storing it in the case library. We think that CBR is a suited methodology for building a design system that can act like an intelligent design assistant.

We developed a computational system – REBUILDER UML – that can perform three tasks: store, manage and reuse of software design knowledge. To achieve these goals, we propose a system based on CBR. This reasoning framework is flexible enough to comply with different knowledge types and reasoning mechanisms, enabling the software designer to use whatever design assistant s/he wants to use. We also integrated an ontology, which enables several semantic operations like indexing software objects and computing semantic distances between software objects.

The next section describes our approach and the architecture of our system. Section 0 presents the knowledge base structure and content. Sections 0 and 0 describe how the knowledge is managed and reused. Finally section 0 concludes and presents future directions.

2 REBUILDER UML

REBUILDER UML is a descendant from REBUILDER I [11-14], which was developed with two main goals: create a corporative memory of software designs, and provide the software designer with a design environment capable of promoting software design reuse. This is achieved in our approach with CBR as the main reasoning process, and with cases as the main knowledge building blocks. REBUILDER I comprises four different modules: Knowledge Base (KB), UML Editor, Knowledge Base Manager and CBR engine (see Fig. 1). REBUILDER UML addresses the limitations of REBUILDER I, especially the ontology performance. REBUILDER I has two main limitations duc to the use of WordNet. Performance issues, for instance, finding the semantic distance between two concepts can take several seconds, which is unacceptable for the system usage. The second limitation is the shallowness of WordNet that is not adequate for specific domains like computing and software engineering.

Specific concepts used in most of the software systems being modeled, do not exist in WordNet. Another aspect of REBUILDER I that was modified in REBUILDER UML is the application philosophy, instead of having a client server architecture, REBUILDER UML is a plug in for a CASE tool, which can easily be used within a development team, or by a single software engineer. This change has made the system more flexible regarding situation usability.

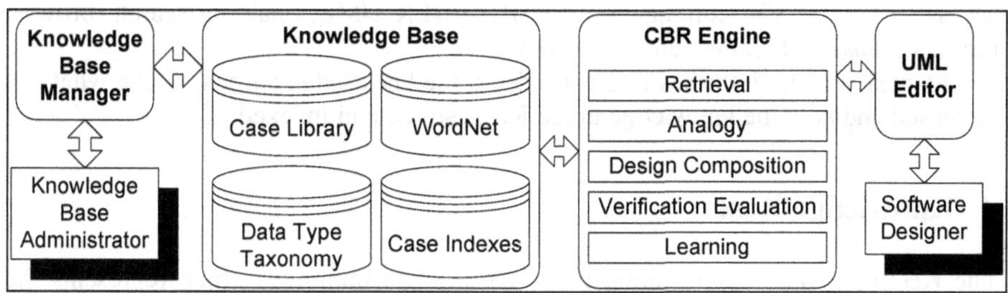

Fig. 1. REBUILDER I architecture

REBUILDER UML is implemented as a plug in for Enterprise Architect (EA www.sparxsystems.com.au), a commercial CASE tool for UML modeling, and it comprises three main modules (see Fig. 2): the knowledge base (KB), the CBR engine, and the KB manager. The KB is the repository of knowledge that is going to be reused by the CBR engine. The main goal of the system is to reuse UML class diagrams, which are stored as cases in the case library and reused by the CBR engine. The knowledge base manager enables all the knowledge stored in the system to be maintained.

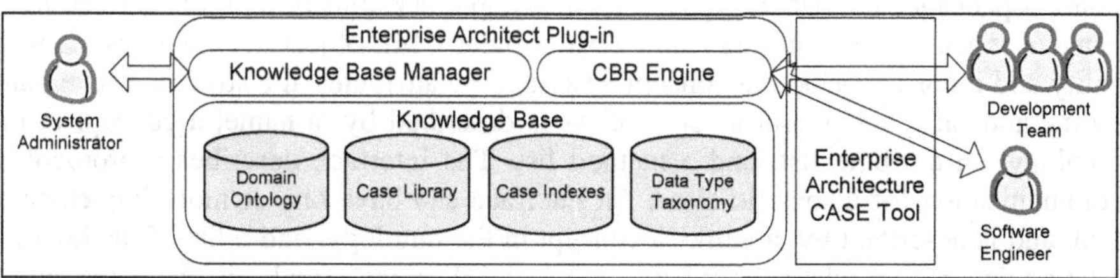

Fig. 2. The architecture of REBUILDER UML, based as a plug-in for Enterprise Architect

There are two types of users in REBUILDER UML, software engineers and the system administrator. A software engineer uses the CASE tool to model a software system in development, and s/he can use REBUILDER UML actions to reuse old diagrams. These diagrams can origin from previous systems, or by the development team in which the software engineer is integrated. The other user type is the system administrator, which has the aim of keeping the KB fine tuned and updated. Since each software engineer has a copy of the central KB, the system administrator is responsible for making new releases of the KB and installing it in the systems of the development team (or teams). Thus, the role of the administrator is very important for REBUILDER UML to be used properly by several users, enabling the sharing of knowledge among them. Despite this, the system can also be used in a stand alone fashion, acting as an intelligent knowledge repository for a single user. In this setup, the user is at the same time playing both roles, reusing knowledge and maintaining it.

The integration with EA is made by a plug in, enabling REBUILDER UML to have access to the data model of EA, and also to its model repository. Visually the user interacts with REBUILDER UML through the main menu of EA. The user has access to the specific commands of REBUILDER UML, enabling search, browse, retrieval, reuse and maintenance operations.

The next section describes in greater detail the knowledge base, showing what can be reused and how the knowledge in the KB is stored and indexed.

3 Knowledge Base

The KB comprises four different parts: the domain ontology, which represents the concepts, relations between concepts, attributes and axioms of the domain being modeled; the case library that stores all the UML class diagrams, called cases; the case indexes, which are associations between class diagram objects and ontology concepts; and the data type taxonomy, which is a simple taxonomy of programming data types used for semantic comparison.

A case in REBUILDER UML represents a specific UML class diagram (see Fig. 3 for an example of a class diagram). Conceptually a case comprises: a name used to identify the case within the case library; the main package, which is an object that comprises all the objects that describe the main class diagram; and the file name where the case is stored. Cases are stored using XML/XMI since it is a widely used format for data exchange.

UML class diagram objects considered are: packages, classes, interfaces and relations. A package is an UML object used to group other objects, and it is defined by: a name, a concept in the ontology, and a list of other UML objects. A class describes an entity and it corresponds to a concept described by attributes at a structural level, and by methods at a behavioral level. A class is described by: a name, a concept in the ontology, an attribute list, and a method list. The interface describes a protocol of communication for a specific class. An interface can have one or more implementation, and is described by: a name, a concept in the ontology, and a list of methods. A relation describes a relationship between two UML objects, and it is characterized by several attributes, which are: a name, the source object, the destination object, the relation type (association, generalization, dependency, or realization), cardinality, and aggregation. An attribute refers to a class and is characterized by a name that identifies the attribute within the class it belongs; the attribute's scope in relation to the external objects: public, private, or protected; the attribute's data type; and the attribute's default value. A method describes a request or message that can be submitted to a class, and is described by: a name that identifies the method within the class to which it belongs; the method's scope in relation to the external objects: public, private, or protected; the list of the input parameters; and the list of output parameters. A parameter can be a reference or a value that is used or generated by a class method, and is described by: a name identifying the parameter within the method to which it belongs, and the parameter's data type.

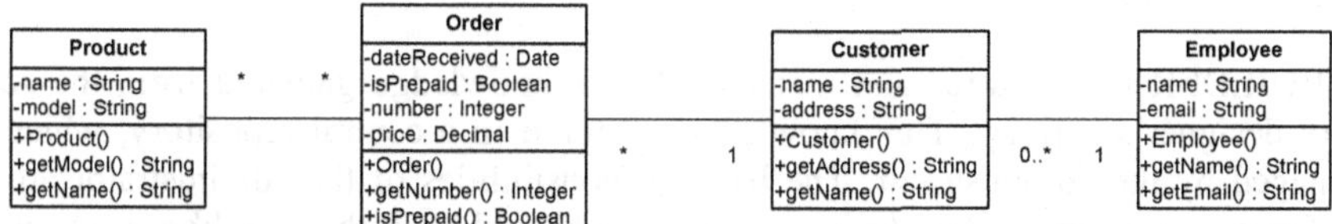

Fig. 3. An example of an UML class diagram

The domain ontology defines concepts, which are represented by a set of words. Words that can be used to represent the same concept are called synonyms. A word associated with more than one concept is called a polysemous word. For instance, the word mouse has two meanings, it can denote a rat, or it can express a computer mouse. Besides the list of words, a concept has a list of semantic relations with other concepts in the ontology. These relations are categorized in four main types: *is-a*, *part-of*, *substance-of* and *member-of*, but the administrator can specify other types of relations. An example of part of an ontology is presented in Fig. 4.

The ontology is used for computing the semantic distance between two concepts. Another purpose of the ontology is to index cases, and for this task, REBUILDER UML associates a concept to each diagram object. This link is then used as an index to the ontology structure, which can be used as a semantic network for case or object retrieval. Considering the diagram of Fig. 3 as *Case1*, Fig. 4 represents part of the case indexing, with objects *Product*, *Customer* and *Employee* indexed in the ontology.

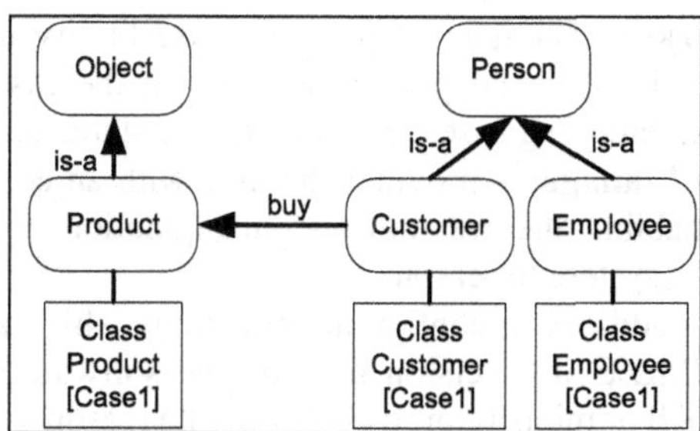

Fig. 4. An example of case indexing considering the diagram of Fig. 3 as *Case1*

As cases can be large, they are stored in files, which make case access slower then if they were in main memory. To solve this problem we use the case indexes. These provide a way to access the relevant case parts for retrieval without having to read all the case files from disk. Each object in a case is used as an index. REBUILDER UML uses the concept associated to each object to index the case in the ontology. This way, the system can retrieve a complete case, using the case package, or it can retrieve only a subset of case objects, using the objects' indexes. This allows the user with the possibility to retrieve not only packages, but also classes and interfaces.

4 Knowledge Management

REBUILDER UML stores and manages design knowledge gathered from the software designer's activity. This knowledge is stored in a central repository, which is managed by the administrator. The basic responsibilities of the administrator are to configure the system and to decide which cases should be in the case library. Another task that s/he has to perform is to revise new diagrams submitted by the software designers.

Deciding the contents of the case library is not an easy task, especially if the case base has a large number of cases. In this situation the KB manager provides a tool which enables the administrator to retrieve the most similar cases to the one being evaluated. If the new case is different enough, then it is added to the case library, otherwise the administrator stores the new case in a list of obsolete cases.

When a diagram is submitted by a software designer as a candidate to a new case to be added to the case library, the administrator has to check some items in the diagram. First the diagram must have concepts associated to the classes, interfaces and packages. This is essential for the diagram to be transformed into a case, and to be indexed and reused by the system. Diagram consistency and coherence must also be checked.

The KB Manager module is used by the administrator to manage the KB, keeping it consistent and updated. This module comprises all the functionalities of the UML editor, and it adds case base management functions to REBUILDER UML. These are used by the KB administrator to update and modify the KB. The available functions are:

- **KB Operations** – create, open or close a KB;
- **Case Library Manager** – opens the case library manager, which comprises functions to manipulate the cases in the case library, like adding new cases, removing cases, or changing the status of a case;
- **Ontology Manager** – provides the user with an editor to modify the ontology, enabling the creation and manipulation of concepts, which are used by the system to reason;
- **Settings** – adds extra configuration settings which are not present in the normal UML Editor version used by the software designers. It also enables the KB administrator to configure the reasoning mechanisms.

5 Knowledge Reuse

Reuse of UML class diagrams can be done in two ways: retrieval of objects and retrieval of cases. The retrieval mechanism searches the ontology structure looking for similar objects/cases and then ranks and presents them to the designer.

Retrieval comprises two phases: retrieval of a set of relevant objects/cases from the case library, and assessment of the similarity between the target problem and the retrieved objects/cases. The retrieval phase is based on the ontology structure, which is used as an indexing structure. The retrieval algorithm uses the classifications of the target problem object as the initial search probe in the ontology. This algorithm is flexible enough to retrieve three different types of UML objects: packages, classes and interfaces, depending on the type of object selected as target problem. The retrieval algorithm starts in the concepts associated with the query objects and then starts to expand to neighbor concepts until it finds enough objects or cases.

The second step of retrieval is ranking the retrieved objects by similarity with the target object. Since there are three types of target objects (packages, classes and interfaces) we have developed a specific similarity metric for each type of objects.

- **Package Similarity Metric:** this metric is based on four different aspects: the similarity between packages' concepts, similarity between packages' dependencies (Dependencies are a type of UML relations that can exist between packages, expressing a package's dependency on another package), similarity between packages' class diagrams, and similarity between the sub-packages (a recursive call to this metric). Basically this metric assesses structure similarity and semantic similarity of packages and it's objects.
- **Class Similarity Metric:** the class similarity metric is based on three items: concept similarity of classes being compared, inter-class similarity comprising the assessment of relation similarity between classes, and intra-class similarity which evaluates the similarity between classes' attributes and methods.
- **Interface Similarity Metric:** the interface similarity metric is the same as the class similarity, except in the intra-class similarity, which is based only in method similarity, since interfaces do not have attributes.

The retrieved objects/cases can then be copied and reused in the current diagram. Even that the software engineer does not use all of the retrieved objects/cases, s/he can explore the design space using the retrieved knowledge. This enables a more efficient way of designing systems and increases productivity, enabling novice engineers to get a first solution, from which they can iteratively build a better solution.

6 Conclusions and Future Work

This paper presents a CASE tool capable of reusing and sharing knowledge about software development. This tool has evolved from a previous one, based on lessons learned. REBUILDER UML has some major differences with its predecessor, namely: the ontology is now specific and domain oriented, making it easier to manage, maintain and with better performance; the application architecture is more flexible, allowing the system to be used in a wide range of scenarios (single system to a company usage level); integration with a commercial UML editor, making it more suitable for usage in software development companies. Other systems that reuse diagrams do not address the multi-user issue, and do not focus on knowledge management aspect, which brings new problems and aspects into focus.

There are some limitations that are being addressed, like ontology development. We are working in a tool for extracting ontologies semi automatically, so that it can be used to help the system administrator to develop the ontology. Another issue, also dealing with the ontology is the integration of tools to help the ontology management.

Future work includes the development of new reasoning modules, more specifically modules that make the system-user interaction easier.

References

1. Coulange, B., *Software Reuse*. 1997, London: Springer-Verlag.
2. Gamma, E., et al., *Design Patterns: Elements of Reusable Object-Oriented Software*. 1995, Reading: Addison-Wesley. 395.
3. Jacobson, I., M. Griss, and P. Jonsson, *Software Reuse: Architecture Process and Organization for Business Success*. 1997, New York: ACM Press. 497.
4. Meyer, B., *Reusability: The Case for Object-Oriented Design*. IEEE Software, 1987. **4**(2, March 1987): p. 50-64.
5. Prieto-Diaz, R., *Status Report: Software Reusability*. IEEE Software, 1993(May).
6. Boehm, B., *A Spiral Model of Software Development and Enhancement*. 1988: IEEE Press.
7. Tong, C. and D. Sriram, *Artificial Intelligence in Engineering Design*. Vol. I. 1992: Academic Press.
8. Aamodt, A. and E. Plaza, *Case-Based Reasoning: Foundational Issues, Methodological Variations, and System Approaches*. AI Communications, 1994. **7**(1): p. 39-59.
9. Kolodner, J., *Case-Based Reasoning*. 1993: Morgan Kaufman.
10. Althoff, K.-D., *Case-based reasoning*, in *Handbook on Software Engineering and Knowledge Engineering*, S.K. Chang, Editor. 2001, World Scientific. p. 549-588.
11. Gomes, P., *A Case-Based Approach to Software Design*, in *Department of Informatics Engineering*. 2004, University of Coimbra: Coimbra.
12. Gomes, P., et al. *REBUILDER: A CBR Approach to Knowledge Management in Software Design*. in *Sixth International Workshop on Learning Software Organizations (LSO'04)*. 2004. Banff, Alberta, Canada.
13. Gomes, P., et al. *Case Retrieval of Software Designs using WordNet*. in *European Conference on Artificial Intelligence (ECAI'02)*. 2002. Lyon, France: IOS Press, Amsterdam.
14. Seco, N., P. Gomes, and F.C. Pereira. *Using CBR for Semantic Analysis of Software Specifications*. in *7th European Conference on Case-Based Reasoning (ECCBR 2004)*. 2004. Madrid, Spain.
15. Seco, N., P. Gomes, and F.C. Pereira. *Modelling Software Specifications with Case Based Reasoning*. in *The First International Workshop on Natural Language Understanding and Cognitive Science (NLUCS'04)*. 2004. Porto, Portugal.

The ODESeW Platform as a Tool for Managing EU Projects: The Knowledge Web Case Study

Asunción Gómez-Pérez[1], Angel López-Cima[1], M. Carmen Suárez-Figueroa[1], and Oscar Corcho[2]

[1] OEG - Facultad de Informática. Universidad Politécnica de Madrid (UPM) Campus de Montegancedo, s/n. 28660 Boadilla del Monte. Madrid. Spain
{asun, alopez, mcsuarez}@fi.upm.es

[2] University of Manchester. School of Computer Science. Oxford Road, Manchester, United Kingdom
Oscar.Corcho@manchester.ac.uk

Abstract. ODESeW allows developing ontology-based Web portals. It provides functionalities to edit and browse information, taking into account access privileges, and to update automatically changes carried out on the underlying ontologies. In this paper, we describe the ontologies used in a specific deployment of the ODESeW platform, oriented to the management of EU R&D projects. We also present the functions offered in this specific deployment, giving as an example the EU Knowledge Web Network of Excellence portal.

1 Introduction

One important aspect of project management is the generation of reports on the current state of the project, so that the project progress can be monitored by project members or by outsiders. The quality of the project documentation thus generated has an important influence on the level of detail of the monitoring that can be performed, on decision-making, and on other project management activities.

Let us focus on the specific setting of the R&D projects funded by the European Commission (EC). These projects are run by a consortium of several academic and industrial partners from different EU countries. Progress reports are not only issued to monitor the project evolution inside the consortium, but also to inform the EC project officer of that evolution. Project reporting requires input from every partner in the consortium. These inputs are submitted to the project coordinator, who is responsible for the generation and submission of the consolidated information. Normally, the project coordinator has to put in a huge effort to harvest these partial reports from each partner, to generate the consolidated documents and to maintain consistency among different versions of the partial reports, the project description and the original plan. This task is even harder if we consider that there are no specialized tools to help building reports, tracking changes and ensuring consistency.

In this paper we show how we have improved the EU R&D project management by using an ontology-based project portal that provides, among other functionalities, a set of project management functions. These functions are based on knowledge of

S. Staab and V. Svatek (Eds.): EKAW 2006, LNAI 4248, pp. 389–396, 2006.

project management and reporting that has been formalized by a set of ontologies, and that has been used for the construction of several EU project portals. For our descriptions we will focus on the FP6 Network of Excellence (NoE) Knowledge Web[1], which is the one posing more challenges and constraints given the amount of institutions, workpackages and deliverables.

To build such a project portal we have used the Semantic Web application development framework ODESeW [4]. This framework can be easily extended with new knowledge (new ontologies about the project management); besides, it eases the development of new advanced functionalities on top of the portal, since the semantics of the portal content is exposed explicitly. Finally, such a framework facilitates the reusability of knowledge and functionalities among applications, as explained in [4].

The paper is organized as follows: section 2 provides a brief description of the ODESeW framework; section 3 describes how periodic progress reports are structured in EU projects so that we can get a better idea of the amount of work involved in their generation; section 4 presents the ontologies used within the project portal. Section 5 gives a brief description of the functionalities provided by the portal. Finally, section 6 provides a conclusion and outlines a vision of the work to be done in the future.

2 The Development Framework ODESeW

ODESeW (Semantic Web Portal based on WebODE) was first described in [2] as a tool that could be used for the automatic generation of Web portals in which all the information was indexed by means of ontologies. This system was built on top of the WebODE ontology engineering workbench [1], thus inheriting many of its features.

The portals generated with ODESeW could be used as the Intranets and Extranets of the projects, taking into account that different users will have different read and write permissions in the portal. Besides, ODESeW provided functions such as a search engine, content implementation in different languages (RDF, RDFS and OWL) and administrator functionalities for user management, read/write permission management, and a selection of ontologies to be used in the portal.

In this version of ODESeW, it switches from being a tool for building ontology-based portals into a more complete framework for building Semantic Web applications. This new version offers developers a set of services and tools that can be used in a Semantic Web application and gives, by default, navigation and visualization models that allow visualizing, editing and navigating the content in the portal. Such models can be modified and extended easily, permitting developers to create specific visualization and navigation models. The technical details are provided in [4].

3 Project Management and Periodic Progress Reports

As commented in the introduction, collaborative projects usually require the creation of periodic project progress reports that project coordinators can use to monitor the project and that, in the case of the EU R&D projects, must be sent to the European

[1] http://knowledgeweb.semanticweb.org/

Commission (EC) at regular intervals during the project execution. EC reports can be divided in the following sections:

```
1.  Activity Report
    1.1. Report on Workpackage (WP) activities
    1.2. Published executive summary
    1.3. Update plan for using and disseminating knowledge
    1.4. Information about: publications, invited talks, workshop and
         conference organized, etc
2.  Management Report
    2.1. Financial statement
    2.2. Summary financial report consolidating the costs of contractors
    2.3. Audits certificates
    2.4. Brief description of the work performed by each contractor dur-
         ing the period
    2.5. Budgeted cost and actual costs
    2.6. Budgeted person-month and actual person-month
    2.7. Summary explanation of the impact of major deviations from cost
         budget and from person-month budget.
3.  Distribution of EC funding to partners.
4.  Interim Reports
```

The task of preparing a progress report normally consists of the following steps (which are executed by the project coordinator):

- Request progress reports from each of the partners involved in the consortium.
- Receive the partial progress reports and compile all that information in a single document, removing duplicates, detecting inconsistencies, etc. This step is performed iteratively until all the information is provided.
- Prepare a final summary, stressing the most important aspects of the results.

To help in these tasks, collaborative editing tools are used. However, much manual work must still be done, mainly on the project coordinator side, to make a good quality document for the EC. That is, a document containing all the information that is relevant inside the report period, with no duplicates, etc. It is important that the information there included be presented in a good homogeneous format.

4 A Set of Ontologies for EU R&D Project Management

In this section we describe the domain model used in the Semantic Web application that we have created for EU R&D project management. This domain model consists of a set of interlinked ontologies, namely, several *project description ontologies*, a *user role ontology* and a *management ontology*. We will give some details about the process followed to build such ontologies.

4.1 The Ontology Building Process

These ontologies have been developed following the METHONTOLOGY methodology [3]. One of the first tasks proposed by this methodology is that of searching for other ontologies in the same or in similar domains in order to reuse them (or part of them), so that we can avoid developing them form scratch.

For developing the *project description ontologies*, we used Oyster[2] [5] which permits searching for ontologies in similar domains. After analyzing the results provided by Oyster, the most appropriate ontologies were: the ontology used in the *OntoWeb* project[3] (Semantic Web Research Community Ontology[4]) and the ontologies used in the *Esperonto* project.

Once we identified which parts of the ontologies could be reused, we extended them following the steps proposed by the conceptualization phase of METHONTOLOGY. Thus, to extend the reused ontologies, we acquired the domain knowledge from the Knowledge Web Technical Annex. Besides, comments from project partners were considered in the refinement of these ontologies.

For the development of the *user role* and *management ontologies*, we did not reuse any ontology, we built them from scratch following the same methodology.

4.2 Project Description Ontologies

To describe a collaborative project we have used five ontologies, which can be easily reused for describing other similar projects. These ontologies are the following :

- The **Documentation Ontology**, which models knowledge of documentation used in the project. The main concept of this ontology is *Documentation,* a concept organized according to the type of document within a taxonomy.
- The **Event Ontology**, which models knowledge of events that are related to the project. The main concept of this ontology is *Event.*
- The **Organization Ontology,** which models knowledge of organizations involved in the project. The main concept in this ontology is *Organization*, a concept split into three subclasses. The most important information about organizations involved in a project is related to the organization itself and its location.
- The **Person Ontology,** which models knowledge of persons who work in the project. This ontology is focused on general-purpose personal information. The main concept of this ontology is *Person.* We have divided this concept into four different types: university staff, company staff, project officer, and student.
- The **Project Ontology,** which models the Technical Annex of a project, including information about WPs, tasks, projects, areas, etc. This ontology is not organized in a taxonomy; it only includes several concepts and the relationships between them.

4.3 The User Role Ontology

This ontology models the knowledge needed for managing different user profiles within the project. In the case of Knowledge Web, the roles that each user plays in the project are represented by each concept of the ontology.

ODESeW manages the *user role ontology* internally and independently of the application domain; this, however, does not mean that it cannot be extended for specific domains. Figure 1 shows the user roles that participate in the generation of progress reports and the extension needed for managing a NoE like Knowledge Web.

[2] http://oyster.ontoware.org/
[3] http://www.ontoweb.org/
[4] http://ontobroker.semanticweb.org/ontos/swrc.html

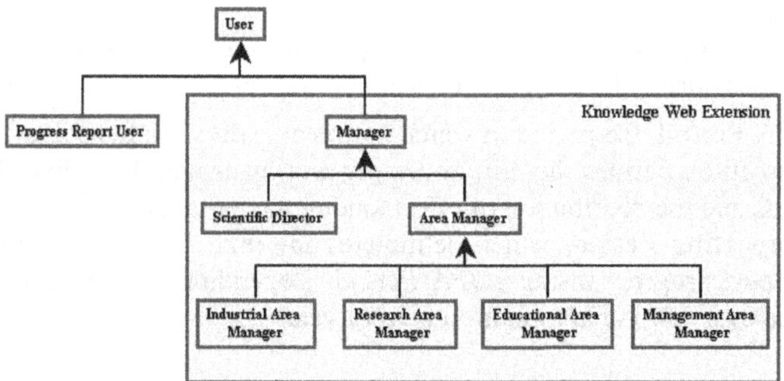

Fig. 1. The taxonomy of the *user role ontology*

4.4 The Management Ontology

This ontology contains the knowledge needed to manage collaborative projects. It identifies the most relevant concepts and properties used to collect information from partners and to generate the consolidated report. We can identify three main concepts:

- **Period**, which specifies different types of periods such as a *Reporting Period* or a *Joint Process Activity (JPA) Period*, that is, different periods identified in a project where the description of the work can be reviewed and changed.
- **Effort**, which represents the effort expended or to be expended in a project period, either in a task or a WP or by organization.
- **Report**, which represents a partial or complete report generated by a partner or by several partners. Partial reports are used to compile a complete report, which is then sent to the coordinator partner.

In the case of Knowledge Web, this ontology has been extended (as shown in Figure 2) with other partial reports, such as the *Project Overview Report* and different *Area Reports*, all required to create the complete report.

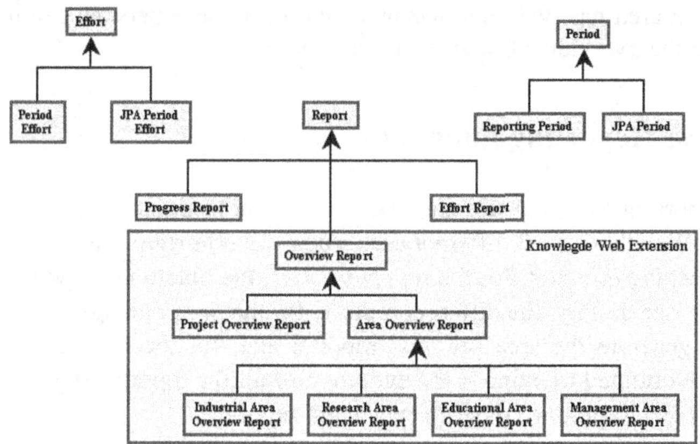

Fig. 2. The taxonomies of the *management ontology*

4.4.1 Periods

The *Period* concept modeled in the *management ontology* represents different kinds of time frames during the project. The main periods are:

- **The JPA Period**, the period in which a project is divided. In each of these periods, the consortium defines the milestones per workpackage, the deliverables to report to the EC and the distribution of effort among the partners.
- **The Reporting Period**, which delimitates the time frame where the consortium must report progress inside a *JPA Period*. Depending on the project, this period could be every two or six months or every year.

4.4.2 Efforts

Two kinds of efforts can be found in the *management ontology*:

- **JPA Period Effort**, which represents the effort devoted by the consortium in each *JPA Period* on each WP.
- **Periodic Effort**, which is the effort expended by each partner on a specific WP in a *Reporting Period.*

4.4.3 Report

The management reports generated on each *Periodic Report* and supported by the current version for the reporting period are:

- **The Effort Report**, which represents the total effort put in during a *Reporting Period* by the whole consortium.
- **The Progress Report**, which represents the progress in a WP during a *Reporting Period.* In most of the projects, the data required in a progress report are: an overview, a description of the work carried out and the current status of each deliverable, the delays according to the definition of the project on each JPA, and the meetings held during the active period. Only the WP leader can include information in this report.
- **The Area reports**, which present an overview of all the work carried out during a *Reporting Period* in an Area. In Knowledge Web there are four areas (Industrial, Research, Educational and Management) and each of them is supported by a set of WPs. Each area has two area managers and only these persons can include information in the overview of their managed areas.

5 Progress Reporting Functions

Progress reporting functions are classified according to the user types. In the case of Knowledge Web there are 3 different user types: *the reporting user*, *the area manager* and *the managing director*. For the *reporting user*, the functions provided are oriented to guide the user through the different reports; for the *area manager*, the functions are oriented to generate the area progress reports; and, for the *managing director*, the functions are oriented to monitor the evolution of all the reports, to generate the complete reports and to produce other management reports.

5.1 Functions for Reporting Users

When a reporting user logs into the system and enters the reporting section, the portal shows all the tasks to be done. These tasks are: WP progress reports, for each WP that the user's organization is leader of; and Effort report for the organization to which the user belongs.

The decision on which WPs and which effort reports are to be included is made on the basis of the user profile, which is obtained automatically by the portal. The portal also shows a time line with the schedules of the period reporting: WP and effort report stage, quality assessment, report updating, quality assurance and submission.

5.2 Functions for Area Managers

In a large project, WPs can be organized in different areas. Each area has a person that is responsible for it, known as the area leader. In the activity report, area managers can include an overview of the general progress.

5.3 Functions for the Managing Director

The managing director belongs to the project coordinator organization and is in charge of monitoring the progress of all reports produced by individual partners.

When a user logs into the system and accesses the reporting system, the portal shows the effort reports of all the project partners together with the progress reports of all the WPs. Besides, there is a link to a view for monitoring the current status of all reports, which shows a table that relates partners and WPs and also displays the current status of each progress and effort reported by the partner, using color coding.

The activity report is one of the documents that must be delivered by the project coordinator to the European Commission. This document compiles all the WP progress reports into one document. The document produced is presented in HTML and MS Word formats and it includes the front page, the table of contents, the header and footer of each page, and the font style selected by the project template. This document is a draft version which the managing director can modify with specific information that only the project coordinator is allowed to include.

6 Conclusion and Future Work

The current version of the EU R&D project management portal covers section 1.1, some points of 1.4 and the section 2.6 of the management reports of an EC project (see Section 3). Such sections are the most collaboration-intensive parts of the generation process and the information to be used there is public to the consortium.

The use of these project management functions have reduced drastically the effort applied to producing management documentation for the EU R&D project. These reports required collaboration from different partners in the project, which made the process time and effort consuming. This system reduces the amount of e-mails sent by the different project partners to the project coordinator, including the partial documents that have to be consolidated in a common version. It also reduces the number of errors that result from using intermediate versions of the documents and ensures that the results reported are consistent with the project description.

This tool also helps the project coordinator, represented by the managing director, to monitor the status of the current period report, detecting in this way any delay or major deviation with respect to the original workplan.

But the most important issue is that the progress report can be easily personalized for different projects just by changing or updating the existing ontologies, that is, including more fields in the report and different types of users in the report. The proof that this system works and can be reused is that we have used it (with the corresponding adaptations) in the context of several EU R&D projects.

In the short term we plan to give full support for the generation of activity reports. We also plan to include more management documents, such as financial reports. Besides, we plan to support no only HTML and MS Word formats, as it has been done till now, but also other commonly used formats like LaTeX or the XML format that is being proposed by the EC as a common format for these reports.

Acknowledgements

This paper has been supported by the EU IST NoE Knowledge Web.

References

1. Arpírez, JC.; Corcho, O.; Fernández-López, M.; Gómez-Pérez, A. WebODE in a nutshell. AI Magazine 24(3):37-48. Fall 2003
2. Corcho, O.; Gómez-Pérez, A.; López-Cima, A.; López-García, V.; Suárez-Figueroa, M.C. 2003. "ODESeW. Automatic Generation of Knowledge Portals for Intranets and Extranets". International Semantic Web Conference 2003 (ISWC03). Lecture Notes in Computer Science (2870). PP: 802-817.
3. Fernández-López, M.; Gómez-Pérez, A.; Pazos-Sierra, A.; Pazos-Sierra, J. "Building a Chemical Ontology Using METHONTOLOGY and the Ontology Design Environment". IEEE Intelligent Systems & their applications. January/February 1999. PP: 37-46.
4. López-Cima A.; Corcho O.; Gómez-Pérez A. 2006. A platform for the development of Semantic Web portals. In: Proceedings of the 6th International Conference on Web Engineering (ICWE2006). Stanford, July 2006.
5. Palma, R.; Haase, P. 2005. "Oyster - Sharing and Re-using Ontologies in a Peer-to-Peer Community". International Semantic Web Conference 2005: 1059-1062.

Posters and Demos

Lylia Abrouk, New approach for document automatic annotation

Riccardo Albertoni, Monica De Martino, Semantic Similarity of Ontology Instances tailored on the Application Context

Georg Buscher, Joachim Baumeister, Frank Puppe, Dietmar Seipel, Semi-Distributed Development of Agent-Based Consultation Systems

Sylvain Dehors, Catherine Faron-Zucker, Rose Dieng-Kuntz, QBLS:Semantic Web Technology for E-learning in Practice

Gyorgy Frivolt, Maria Bielikova, Growing World Wide Social Network by Bridging Social Portals Using FOAF

David Hyland-Wood, David Carrington, Simon Kaplan, A Semantic Web Approach to Software Maintenance

Afraz Jaffri, Hugh Glaser, Ian Millard, Benedicto Rodriguez, Using a Semantic Wiki to Interact with a Knowledge-Based Infrastructure

Lobna Karoui, Ontological Concepts Evaluation Based on Context

Tomáš Kliegr, Clickstream analysis - the semantic approach

Cristian Pérez de Laborda, Matthäus Zloch, Stefan Conrad, RDQuery - Querying Relational Databases on-the-fly with RDF-QL

Yaozhong Liang, Harith Alani, Nigel Shadbolt, Ontologies Change and Queries Break: Towards a Solution

Helena Lindgren, Introducing a Formalisation of an Activity-Theoretical Model of the Clinical Investigation of Dement

Angel Lopez-Cima, Asun Gomez-Perez, M. Carmen Suarez, Oscar Corcho, Managing R&D European Projects with ODESeW

David Manzano-Macho, Asun Gomez-Perez, Daniel Borrajo, HOLA: A Hybrid Ontology Learning Architecture

Christian Morbidoni, Giovanni Tummarello, Michele Nucci, Francesco Piazza,

Paolo Puliti, DBin – enabling SW P2P communities

Miklos Nagy, Maria Vargas-Vera, Similarity Mapping with Uncertainty for Knowledge Management of Heterogeneous Scientific Databases

Jan Nemrava, Refining search queries using WordNet glosses

Giang Nguyen, Michal Laclavik, Babik Marian, Gatial Emil, Ciglan Marek, Zoltan Balogh, Oravec Viktor, Ladislav Hluchy, Knowledge acquisition, organization and maintenance for heterogeneous information resources

Sodel Vazquez Reyes, William Black, Toward a Knowledge Base for Answering Causal Questions

Chantal Reynaud, Brigitte Safar, Hassen Kefi, Structural Techniques for Alignment of Structurally Dissymetric Taxonomies

Zdenek Zdrahal, Paul Mulholland, Trevor Collins, Exploring Paths Across Stories

Author Index

Vol. 4029: L. Rutkowski, R. Tadeusiewicz, L.A. Zadeh, J.M. Zurada (Eds.), Artificial Intelligence and Soft Computing – ICAISC 2006. XXI, 1235 pages. 2006.

Vol. 4027: H.L. Larsen, G. Pasi, D. Ortiz-Arroyo, T. Andreasen, H. Christiansen (Eds.), Flexible Query Answering Systems. XVIII, 714 pages. 2006.

Vol. 4021: E. André, L. Dybkjær, W. Minker, H. Neumann, M. Weber (Eds.), Perception and Interactive Technologies. XI, 217 pages. 2006.

Vol. 4020: A. Bredenfeld, A. Jacoff, I. Noda, Y. Takahashi (Eds.), RoboCup 2005: Robot Soccer World Cup IX. XVII, 727 pages. 2006.

Vol. 4013: L. Lamontagne, M. Marchand (Eds.), Advances in Artificial Intelligence. XIII, 564 pages. 2006.

Vol. 4012: T. Washio, A. Sakurai, K. Nakajima, H. Takeda, S. Tojo, M. Yokoo (Eds.), New Frontiers in Artificial Intelligence. XIII, 484 pages. 2006.

Vol. 4008: J.C. Augusto, C.D. Nugent (Eds.), Designing Smart Homes. XI, 183 pages. 2006.

Vol. 4005: G. Lugosi, H.U. Simon (Eds.), Learning Theory. XI, 656 pages. 2006.

Vol. 3978: B. Hnich, M. Carlsson, F. Fages, F. Rossi (Eds.), Recent Advances in Constraints. VIII, 179 pages. 2006.

Vol. 3963: O. Dikenelli, M.-P. Gleizes, A. Ricci (Eds.), Engineering Societies in the Agents World VI. XII, 303 pages. 2006.

Vol. 3960: R. Vieira, P. Quaresma, M.d.G.V. Nunes, N.J. Mamede, C. Oliveira, M.C. Dias (Eds.), Computational Processing of the Portuguese Language. XII, 274 pages. 2006.

Vol. 3955: G. Antoniou, G. Potamias, C. Spyropoulos, D. Plexousakis (Eds.), Advances in Artificial Intelligence. XVII, 611 pages. 2006.

Vol. 3949: F. A. Savacı (Ed.), Artificial Intelligence and Neural Networks. IX, 227 pages. 2006.

Vol. 3946: T.R. Roth-Berghofer, S. Schulz, D.B. Leake (Eds.), Modeling and Retrieval of Context. XI, 149 pages. 2006.

Vol. 3944: J. Quiñonero-Candela, I. Dagan, B. Magnini, F. d'Alché-Buc (Eds.), Machine Learning Challenges. XIII, 462 pages. 2006.

Vol. 3930: D.S. Yeung, Z.-Q. Liu, X.-Z. Wang, H. Yan (Eds.), Advances in Machine Learning and Cybernetics. XXI, 1110 pages. 2006.

Vol. 3918: W.K. Ng, M. Kitsuregawa, J. Li, K. Chang (Eds.), Advances in Knowledge Discovery and Data Mining. XXIV, 879 pages. 2006.

Vol. 3913: O. Boissier, J. Padget, V. Dignum, G. Lindemann, E. Matson, S. Ossowski, J.S. Sichman, J. Vázquez-Salceda (Eds.), Coordination, Organizations, Institutions, and Norms in Multi-Agent Systems. XII, 259 pages. 2006.

Vol. 3910: S.A. Brueckner, G.D.M. Serugendo, D. Hales, F. Zambonelli (Eds.), Engineering Self-Organising Systems. XII, 245 pages. 2006.

Vol. 3904: M. Baldoni, U. Endriss, A. Omicini, P. Torroni (Eds.), Declarative Agent Languages and Technologies III. XII, 245 pages. 2006.

Vol. 3900: F. Toni, P. Torroni (Eds.), Computational Logic in Multi-Agent Systems. XVII, 427 pages. 2006.

Vol. 3899: S. Frintrop, VOCUS: A Visual Attention System for Object Detection and Goal-Directed Search. XIV, 216 pages. 2006.

Vol. 3898: K. Tuyls, P.J. 't Hoen, K. Verbeeck, S. Sen (Eds.), Learning and Adaption in Multi-Agent Systems. X, 217 pages. 2006.

Vol. 3891: J.S. Sichman, L. Antunes (Eds.), Multi-Agent-Based Simulation VI. X, 191 pages. 2006.

Vol. 3890: S.G. Thompson, R. Ghanea-Hercock (Eds.), Defence Applications of Multi-Agent Systems. XII, 141 pages. 2006.

Vol. 3885: V. Torra, Y. Narukawa, A. Valls, J. Domingo-Ferrer (Eds.), Modeling Decisions for Artificial Intelligence. XII, 374 pages. 2006.

Vol. 3881: S. Gibet, N. Courty, J.-F. Kamp (Eds.), Gesture in Human-Computer Interaction and Simulation. XIII, 344 pages. 2006.

Vol. 3874: R. Missaoui, J. Schmidt (Eds.), Formal Concept Analysis. X, 309 pages. 2006.

Vol. 3873: L. Maicher, J. Park (Eds.), Charting the Topic Maps Research and Applications Landscape. VIII, 281 pages. 2006.

Vol. 3864: Y. Cai, J. Abascal (Eds.), Ambient Intelligence in Everyday Life. XII, 323 pages. 2006.

Vol. 3863: M. Kohlhase (Ed.), Mathematical Knowledge Management. XI, 405 pages. 2006.

Vol. 3862: R.H. Bordini, M. Dastani, J. Dix, A.E.F. Seghrouchni (Eds.), Programming Multi-Agent Systems. XIV, 267 pages. 2006.

Vol. 3849: I. Bloch, A. Petrosino, A.G.B. Tettamanzi (Eds.), Fuzzy Logic and Applications. XIV, 438 pages. 2006.

Vol. 3848: J.-F. Boulicaut, L. De Raedt, H. Mannila (Eds.), Constraint-Based Mining and Inductive Databases. X, 401 pages. 2006.

Vol. 3847: K.P. Jantke, A. Lunzer, N. Spyratos, Y. Tanaka (Eds.), Federation over the Web. X, 215 pages. 2006.

Vol. 3835: G. Sutcliffe, A. Voronkov (Eds.), Logic for Programming, Artificial Intelligence, and Reasoning. XIV, 744 pages. 2005.

Vol. 3830: D. Weyns, H. V.D. Parunak, F. Michel (Eds.), Environments for Multi-Agent Systems II. VIII, 291 pages. 2006.

Vol. 3817: M. Faundez-Zanuy, L. Janer, A. Esposito, A. Satue-Villar, J. Roure, V. Espinosa-Duro (Eds.), Nonlinear Analyses and Algorithms for Speech Processing. XII, 380 pages. 2006.

Vol. 3814: M. Maybury, O. Stock, W. Wahlster (Eds.), Intelligent Technologies for Interactive Entertainment. XV, 342 pages. 2005.

Vol. 3809: S. Zhang, R. Jarvis (Eds.), AI 2005: Advances in Artificial Intelligence. XXVII, 1344 pages. 2005.

Vol. 3808: C. Bento, A. Cardoso, G. Dias (Eds.), Progress in Artificial Intelligence. XVIII, 704 pages. 2005.

Lecture Notes in Artificial Intelligence (LNAI)

Vol. 4248: S. Staab, V. Svátek (Eds.), Managing Knowledge in a World of Networks. XIV, 400 pages. 2006.

Vol. 4223: L. Wang, L. Jiao, G. Shi, X. Li, J. Liu (Eds.), Fuzzy Systems and Knowledge Discovery. XXVIII, 1335 pages. 2006.

Vol. 4213: J. Fürnkranz, T. Scheffer, M. Spiliopoulou (Eds.), Knowledge Discovery in Databases: PKDD 2006. XXII, 660 pages. 2006.

Vol. 4212: J. Fürnkranz, T. Scheffer, M. Spiliopoulou (Eds.), Machine Learning: ECML 2006. XXIII, 851 pages. 2006.

Vol. 4211: P. Vogt, Y. Sugita, E. Tuci, C. Nehaniv (Eds.), Symbol Grounding and Beyond. VIII, 237 pages. 2006.

Vol. 4203: F. Esposito, Z.W. Ras, D. Malerba, G. Semeraro (Eds.), Foundations of Intelligent Systems. XVIII, 767 pages. 2006.

Vol. 4201: Y. Sakakibara, S. Kobayashi, K. Sato, T. Nishino, E. Tomita (Eds.), Grammatical Inference: Algorithms and Applications. XII, 359 pages. 2006.

Vol. 4196: K. Fischer, I.J. Timm, E. André, N. Zhong (Eds.), Multiagent System Technologies. X, 185 pages. 2006.

Vol. 4188: P. Sojka, I. Kopeček, K. Pala (Eds.), Text, Speech and Dialogue. XIV, 721 pages. 2006.

Vol. 4183: J. Euzenat, J. Domingue (Eds.), Artificial Intelligence: Methodology, Systems, and Applications. XIII, 291 pages. 2006.

Vol. 4180: M. Kohlhase, OMDoc – An Open Markup Format for Mathematical Documents [version 1.2]. XIX, 428 pages. 2006.

Vol. 4177: R. Marín, E. Onaindía, A. Bugarín, J. Santos (Eds.), Current Topics in Aritficial Intelligence. XIII, 621 pages. 2006.

Vol. 4160: M. Fisher, W.v.d. Hoek, B. Konev, A. Lisitsa (Eds.), Logics in Artificial Intelligence. XII, 516 pages. 2006.

Vol. 4155: O. Stock, M. Schaerf (Eds.), Reasoning, Action and Interaction in AI Theories and Systems. XVIII, 343 pages. 2006.

Vol. 4149: M. Klusch, M. Rovatsos, T.R. Payne (Eds.), Cooperative Information Agents X. XII, 477 pages. 2006.

Vol. 4139: T. Salakoski, F. Ginter, S. Pyysalo, T. Pahikkala, Advances in Natural Language Processing. XVI, 771 pages. 2006.

Vol. 4133: J. Gratch, M. Young, R. Aylett, D. Ballin, P. Olivier (Eds.), Intelligent Virtual Agents. XIV, 472 pages. 2006.

Vol. 4130: U. Furbach, N. Shankar (Eds.), Automated Reasoning. XV, 680 pages. 2006.

Vol. 4120: J. Calmet, T. Ida, D. Wang (Eds.), Artificial Intelligence and Symbolic Computation. XIII, 269 pages. 2006.

Vol. 4114: D.-S. Huang, K. Li, G.W. Irwin (Eds.), Computational Intelligence, Part II. XXVII, 1337 pages. 2006.

Vol. 4108: J.M. Borwein, W.M. Farmer (Eds.), Mathematical Knowledge Management. VIII, 295 pages. 2006.

Vol. 4106: T.R. Roth-Berghofer, M.H. Göker, H. A. Güvenir (Eds.), Advances in Case-Based Reasoning. XIV, 566 pages. 2006.

Vol. 4099: Q. Yang, G. Webb (Eds.), PRICAI 2006: Trends in Artificial Intelligence. XXVIII, 1263 pages. 2006.

Vol. 4095: S. Nolfi, G. Baldassarre, R. Calabretta, J.C. T. Hallam, D. Marocco, J.-A. Meyer, O. Miglino, D. Parisi (Eds.), From Animals to Animats 9. XV, 869 pages. 2006.

Vol. 4093: X. Li, O.R. Zaïane, Z. Li (Eds.), Advanced Data Mining and Applications. XXI, 1110 pages. 2006.

Vol. 4092: J. Lang, F. Lin, J. Wang (Eds.), Knowledge Science, Engineering and Management. XV, 664 pages. 2006.

Vol. 4088: Z.-Z. Shi, R. Sadananda (Eds.), Agent Computing and Multi-Agent Systems. XVII, 827 pages. 2006.

Vol. 4087: F. Schwenker, S. Marinai (Eds.), Artificial Neural Networks in Pattern Recognition. IX, 299 pages. 2006.

Vol. 4068: H. Schärfe, P. Hitzler, P. Øhrstrøm (Eds.), Conceptual Structures: Inspiration and Application. XI, 455 pages. 2006.

Vol. 4065: P. Perner (Ed.), Advances in Data Mining. XI, 592 pages. 2006.

Vol. 4062: G. Wang, J.F. Peters, A. Skowron, Y. Yao (Eds.), Rough Sets and Knowledge Technology. XX, 810 pages. 2006.

Vol. 4049: S. Parsons, N. Maudet, P. Moraitis, I. Rahwan (Eds.), Argumentation in Multi-Agent Systems. XIV, 313 pages. 2006.

Vol. 4048: L. Goble, J.-J.C.. Meyer (Eds.), Deontic Logic and Artificial Normative Systems. X, 273 pages. 2006.

Vol. 4045: D. Barker-Plummer, R. Cox, N. Swoboda (Eds.), Diagrammatic Representation and Inference. XII, 301 pages. 2006.

Vol. 4031: M. Ali, R. Dapoigny (Eds.), Advances in Applied Artificial Intelligence. XXIII, 1353 pages. 2006.